Contemporary Industrial Organization

A Quantitative Approach

Lynne Pepall

Dan Richards

George Norman

WILEY

John Wiley & Sons, Inc.

Vice President and Publisher:	George Hoffman
Acquisitions Editor:	Lacey Vitetta
Senior Editorial Assistant:	Emily McGee
Assistant Marketing Manager:	Diane Mars
Project Editor:	Jennifer Manias
Senior Production Manager:	Janis Soo
Assistant Production Editor:	Annabelle Ang-Bok
Designer:	Seng Ping Ngieng

This book was set in 10/12 Times Roman by Laserwords and printed and bound by the Hamilton Printing Company. The cover was printed by the Hamilton Printing Company.

This book is printed on acid-free paper.

Founded in 1807, John Wiley & Sons, Inc. has been a valued source of knowledge and understanding for more than 200 years, helping people around the world meet their needs and fulfill their aspirations. Our company is built on a foundation of principles that include responsibility to the communities we serve and where we live and work. In 2008, we launched a Corporate Citizenship Initiative, a global effort to address the environmental, social, economic, and ethical challenges we face in our business. Among the issues we are addressing are carbon impact, paper specifications and procurement, ethical conduct within our business and among our vendors, and community and charitable support. For more information, please visit our website:www.wiley.com/go/citizenship.

Library of Congress Cataloging-in-Publication Data

Pepall, Lynne, 1952-
    Contemporary industrial organization : a quantitative approach / Lynne Pepall, Daniel J. Richards, George Norman.
        p. cm.
    Includes bibliographical references and index.
    ISBN 978-0-470-59180-2 (hardback)
  1. Industrial organization (Economic theory)-Mathematical models. 2. Industrial organization.
I. Richards, Daniel Jay. II. Norman, George, 1946- III. Title.
    HD2326.P4667 2010
338.6-dc22

                                                        2010037959

Printed in the United States of America
10 9 8 7 6 5 4 3 2 1

Brief Contents

Contents

About the Authors

Lynne Pepall is Professor of Economics and Dean of the Graduate School of Arts and Sciences at Tufts University. Professor Pepall received her undergraduate degree in mathematics and economics from Trinity College, University of Toronto, and her PhD in economics from Cambridge University in England. She has written numerous papers in industrial organization, appearing in *The Journal of Industrial Economics, International Journal of Industrial Organization*, *Journal of Economics and Management Strategy*, *Economic Journal*, *Canadian Journal of Economics*, *Economica*, and the *American Journal of Agricultural Economics*. She has taught industrial organization and microeconomics at both the graduate and undergraduate levels at Tufts University since 1987. Professor Pepall lives in Newton, Massachusetts, with her two sons, a dog, three rabbits and her husband, a co-author of this book. She thanks Dan, Ben, and Will for their support, patience, and affection throughout this project.

Dan Richards is Professor of Economics at Tufts University. Professor Richards received his A.B. in economics and history from Oberlin College and his PhD in economics at Yale University. Professor Richards has written numerous articles in both macroeconomics and industrial organization, appearing in the *American Economic Review*, *Quarterly Journal of Economics*, *Journal of Industrial Economics*, *Economica*, *the B. E. Journals in Economic Analysis and Policy (Contributions and Topics)*, *Canadian Journal of Economics*, the *Journal of Money*, *Credit, and Banking*, and the *American Journal of Agricultural Economics*. He came to Tufts in 1985 and has taught at both the graduate and undergraduate levels. He served as Director of the Graduate Program in Economics from 1989 through 1998, and has also served as a consultant to the Federal Trade Commission. From 1996 to 2005 he taught in the Sloan Fellows Program at MIT's Sloan School of Management. Professor Richards lives in Newton, Massachusetts, with his two sons, a dog, three rabbits, and his wife, a co-author of this book. He thanks all of his co-habitants for their inspiration and support but especially the ones named Lynne, Ben, and Will.

George Norman holds the William and Joyce Cummings Family Chair of Entrepreneurship and Business Economics at Tufts University. He came to Tufts in 1995 from Edinburgh University, where he had served as head of the department of economics. Prior to that, Professor Norman was the Tyler Professor of Economics at the University of Leicester (England). Professor Norman attended the University of Dundee (Scotland) where he was awarded the MA in economics with first class honors. He received his PhD in economics from Cambridge University. His more than 70 published articles have appeared in such professional journals as the *American Economic Review*, *Review of Economic Studies*, *Quarterly Journal of Economics*, *Journal of Industrial Economics*, and *International Journal of Industrial Organization*. He is currently an Associate Editor for two journals, the *Bulletin of Economic Research* and *Regional Science and Urban Economics*. He is also on the editorial board of the *BE Journals in Economic Analysis and*

Policy. In addition to this book, Professor Norman has written and edited, either alone or in collaboration with others, 17 other books. Professor Norman has taught courses in industrial organization and microeconomic theory at both the graduate and undergraduate levels. He has also taught introductory economics, corporate strategy, international economics, and entrepreneurship. Professor Norman lives in Newbury, Massachusetts, with his wife Margaret who, while *not* a co-author, has provided invaluable support and assistance in his work on this book.

Preface

We are happy to offer a more consistently mathematical version of our textbook, ***Industrial Organization: Contemporary Theory and Empirical Applications,*** now in its fourth edition (IO/4e). In that text, we have always had to face the difficult task of balancing the tension between making modern industrial analysis accessible to a wide spectrum of students while also presenting the formal abstract modeling that truly gives the analysis its power. The more overtly mathematical quality of this new version avoids this conflict. At the same time we want to reassure users of the IO/4e on two fronts. First, those whose students found even that text mathematically challenging should know that we are hard at work writing a version that is more broadly accessible. Second, in both the the new text here and the one under way, we have kept the organization virtually identical to that of IO/4e. This is, we plan to offer an alternative, less mathematical exposition of this same material. Those moving from IO/4e to either of these new texts will not face a change in organization.

The change from IO/4e begins in Chapters 2 and 3. There we provide a basic yet thorough review of the notions of consumer and producer surplus, welfare loss, and scale and scope economies, all in a formal mathematical fashion. This includes the rigorous derivation of the cost function starting with a Cobb-Douglas production relation. In the latter case, we continue to show how key parameter estimates are related to the elasticity of substitution and the conditional factor demand equations. As in IO/4e, we then present an empirical application of this material using Christiansen and Greene's (1976) well-known translog model.

Chapter 4 follows with a formal discussion of the measurement of market structure and power. This includes a derivation of the Lerner Index and Hall's (1988) growth theory modification that permits direct empirical estimation of this index. We follow this with a presentation of the many attempts to estimate the aggregate welfare loss from monopoly power, beginning with Harberger (1954).

Chapters 5 and 6 address pricing and product design strategies. The first of these focuses on the standard price discrimination topics of personalized pricing, menu pricing, and group pricing—here again, presented with formal derivations. The second examines horizontal and vertical differentiation as well as bundling and tying. It also includes Stavins' (2001) empirical analysis of airline price discrimination.

Chapters 7 and 8 introduce the reader to the basic models of oligopoly. Chapter 7 presents the single-period version of both the Cournot and Bertrand models. The latter case includes Hotelling's (1929) analysis of price competition with spatially (horizontally) differentiated products. We also discuss the difference between strategic substitutes (Cournot) and strategic complements (Bertrand) that characterize these two models. The chapter concludes with a review of the empirical investigation of price competition in the southern California retail gasoline market presented by Hastings (2004).

Chapter 8 follows with an analysis of dynamic games. It begins with the familiar Stackelberg analysis, then moves on to consider an alternative game of sequential quality choice in a vertically differentiated market. This sets the scene for a discussion of first- and second-mover advantage and, more fundamentally, the notions of credibility and subgame perfection.

Chapters 9, 10, and 11 address, in order, the three major areas of antitrust litigation. Chapter 9 addresses the issues of predation and entry deterrence. This includes a discussion of predatory pricing and also other techniques, such as long-term contracts, that may be employed to drive rivals from the market. Here we emphasize the critical need for the predator to be able to commit to its strategy for the predation to be successful, as in Dixit's (1980) capacity expansion model. Such commitment may, of course, be easier in the context of imperfect and asymmetric information—as in Milgrom and Roberts (1982). All of these issues and models are addressed here. The chapter ends with a presentation of the Ellison and Ellison (2010) study of possible predation in the pharmaceutical industry.

Chapter 10 is an extended examination of collusion and antitrust policy. It begins with an exploration of the ways in which multiple equilibria and indefinite repetition can permit firms to reach and sustain a cooperative equilibrium. It continues by providing evidence on the impact of cartels, including a detailed presentation of Kwoka's (1997) study of the Washington, DC real estate cartel. This is followed by analysis of optimal antitrust policy toward cartels, including the recent use of leniency policies that offer immunity to the first cartel member to cooperate with authorities. We also describe recent experimental evidence on leniency programs provided by Hinloopen and Soetevent (2006). Chapter 11 examines the impact of horizontal mergers. It begins with the "merger paradox" and possible theoretical modifications that make mergers profitable, such as cost savings or analyzing the mergers as a sequential process. We then present the basic elements of computerized merger simulation.

Chapters 12 and 13 address the topic of vertical relations between (and within) firms. The first of these two chapters analyzes the potential procompetitive and anticompetitive effects of vertical mergers. Specific topics include double marginalization, price discrimination, and foreclosure. It concludes with a presentation of the empirical analysis of vertical integration in the ready-mix concrete industry by Hortaçsu and Syverson (2007). Chapter 13 follows with an examination of vertical restraints, particularly resale price maintenance and exclusive dealing or territorial restrictions. It includes analysis of the role vertical restraints may play in fostering promotion and service efforts and the use of vertical restrictions to suppress competition. It also includes an empirical study, namely, Sass' (2005) investigation of the impact of vertical restrictions in the U.S. beer industry.

Chapter 14 examines the theoretical and empirical issues that surround advertising. We begin with a derivation of the Dorfman-Steiner condition, then turn to the informational content of advertising as originally suggested by Nelson (1970) and later extended by many others. We also examine the incentive of a firm to suppress the informational content of advertising (Andersen and Renault, 2006) and the role of advertising in competition (Grossman and Shapiro, 1984). The chapter ends with a description of Ackerberg's (2001) study of advertising, information, and prestige based on the introduction of Yoplait's low-fat yogurt product line in two Midwest cities.

Chapters 15 and 16 are devoted to the analysis of research and development R&D. Chapter 15 begins by laying out a taxonomy of possible innovations and then examining the replacement and efficiency effects and their role in R&D competition, particularly allowing for the role of uncertainty. We also examine R&D competition when there are spillovers. This allows us to consider the policy question of whether R&D cooperation should be permitted. We then present Keller's (2002) empirical study of technological spillovers across regional markets.

Chapter 16 then follows with an examination of patent policy. It examines optimal patent policy models such as Nordhaus (1969) and continues with Reinganum (1989), Gilbert and Shapiro (1990), Klemperer (1990), and Gallini (1992). This segues naturally to a discussion of patent races, patent thickets, and patent licensing. The chapter concludes with the Hall and Ziedonis (2001) study of the impact of patent law and patent policy in the semiconductor industry.

Network effects are the topic of Chapter 17. Here, we begin with the theoretical model of Rohlfs (1974) and continue with a model of price competition and network externalities in a spatial framework. We then take on issues of compatibility and industry standards, starting with the model of Katz and Shapiro (1985) and continuing with the analysis of Besen and Farrell (1994). A presentation of Gandal's (1994) study of network effects in the early spreadsheet market concludes this chapter.

Finally, in Chapter 18, we return to the idea of strategic commitment. Here, we review the nature of strategic substitutes and complements and the advantages (and disadvantages) that an agent gains from being able to commit irrevocably to a specific strategy. This, of course, forces us to confront the classic issues raised by Fudenberg and Tirole (1984) regarding "fat cat," "puppy dog," and "lean and hungry look" strategies. Exploring the role of strategic commitment also allows us to introduce a new topic—namely, strategic trade analysis—in which national commitments can be so crucial.

One result of all of these changes is that this new book is a little shorter than IO/4e. In our view, this is a reflection of the fact that it is also tighter. We have made every effort to write a consistently rigorous but accessible text in which topics are organized in a manner that motivates and facilitates progression from one chapter to the next. It should serve as a relatively complete, but concise, introduction to modern industrial economics.

As always, we owe substantial debts to many faculty and students who have contributed ideas, suggested coverage, and corrections. While we cannot possibly name all those who so contributed, we do want to acknowledge those individuals whose help was especially important. This includes: David Audtretsch, Giacomo Calzolari, Phoebe Chan, Jim Dana, Glen Ellison, Sara Fisher-Ellison, Paolo Garella, Sebastian Gay, Christos Genakos, Justine Hastings, Jun Ishii, John Kwoka, Corinne Langinier, Quihong Liu, George Lobell, Jill McCluskey, Michael Noel, Jennifer Offenberg, Jennifer Reinganum, James Roberts, Michael Salinger, Phillip Schmitt-Dengler, Jay Shimshack, Dean Showalter, Joanna Stavins, Tom Vukina, and Madeline Zavodny.

Part I
Microeconomic Foundations

These first four chapters review the basic microeconomic building blocks of industrial economics. Chapter 1 describes the basic analytic framework, especially the critical feature of strategic interaction that we use to investigate firm behavior and market outcomes in settings of less-than-perfect competition. In Chapter 2, we review the basic microeconomics of the two polar textbook cases of perfect competition and pure monopoly. These two cases help introduce the notions of consumer surplus, producer surplus, and overall efficiency that are necessary for an economic evaluation of market outcomes. Chapter 3 presents the fundamentals of cost analysis. Specifically, it describes how one may derive a cost function from the underlying production technology. This permits us to give precision to measures of scale economies—both for single-product and multiproduct firms. These and other measures are, of course, important determinants of the equilibrium market structure. Finally, in Chapter 4 we turn to a direct discussion of market structure and market power. We emphasize the distinction between these two concepts. We also make clear the measurement problems that afflict any measure of market power as well as the endogeneity of structural indices in particular.

At the end of this section, students should have a solid grasp of microeconomic fundamentals, particularly as they apply to issues of imperfect competition. This includes welfare analysis, the measurement of deadweight loss, and price-cost distortions. It also includes an understanding of the nexus from production technology to cost functions, and to equilibrium market structure. Students will also recognize the importance of strategic interaction for determining the outcome in specific market settings. However, the analytics of such interaction are deferred to Part III. In addition, students will understand that these concepts have empirical content as we present both the classic Christensen and Greene (1976) analysis of railway cost functions and the series of empirical papers on the welfare cost of monopoly that followed Harberger's (1954) original study.

1

Industrial Organization and Imperfect Competition: What, How, and Why

In 2002, the U.S. Justice Department launched an investigation of a possible price-fixing conspiracy among makers of dynamic random access memory (dram) chips. By 2005, five firms had been found guilty. In that same year, Procter and Gamble acquired Gillette in one of the largest-ever mergers of two consumer products firms. The following year 2006 witnessed a price war in computer chips between Intel and AMD that ran through 2007. Near the end of 2009, Microsoft reached an agreement with the European antitrust authorities about offering its customers choice over web browsers that ended a decade of legal conflict that cost the firm roughly €1.67 billion.

Students often feel that there is a considerable gap between stories like these and the economics they study in the classroom. It is not unusual to hear the complaint that economics is "too abstract" or "too mathematical" to be relevant to these events. This is unfortunate, because stories like these are common and fill the daily business press. If economics is not relevant to such cases, we should probably worry about the discipline.

This book is, in part, an effort to show that economics can illuminate the everyday events of the business world like those just described. At a deeper level, our goal is to develop a way of thinking about such phenomena—a mental framework that enables students to form hypotheses about the market forces underlying such events and to consider how to test those hypotheses against empirical evidence. This inevitably requires some mathematics. Yet we do not view this as a limitation. To the contrary, our view is that it is precisely because the real world is complicated that any careful thinking about it benefits from the discipline of formal mathematical modeling in which one can see how each assumption influences the outcome. We believe that our book demonstrates the usefulness of an economics approach to understanding business stories like the ones above. But it is this ability to think like an economist—to build an analytical model that yields testable predictions—that is our larger aim. The analytical framework that we present for this purpose rests firmly on the contemporary analysis of strategic interaction. It is particularly applicable to the economic topics and policy issues that fall under the heading of *industrial organization*.

1.1 WHAT IS INDUSTRIAL ORGANIZATION?

Broadly speaking, industrial organization is the study of how the production of goods and services is organized. In economics, it is common to assume that production takes place in perfectly competitive markets—that somewhat utopian vision of markets populated by numerous small firms and characterized by economic efficiency. Yet, as illustrated above, popular business stories remind us on a daily basis that many markets do not fit this description. Some, like the market for operating systems, are dominated by one very large firm. Others, such as the computer chip market or the soft-drink market, may be populated by two major companies. Still others, such as the automobile industry, have more than two, but still just a handful of key producers. In all these cases, the perfectly competitive model does not apply. For these imperfectly competitive markets, the question then becomes, what model does work? How does the market outcome change when production is concentrated in one firm, or two, or perhaps a few more? Industrial organization is the study of these issues. Put somewhat differently, it is the study of imperfect competition.

To understand what happens in imperfectly competitive markets requires explicit consideration of the market environment. How many firms are there? Does each have roughly similar costs, or does one have a noticeable cost advantage (or disadvantage)? Is entry by new firms easy? What decision variables do managers have? Do they set prices? Or is production so complicated that they must first plan their production schedule and then sell the output at whatever price clears the market? What ability do they have to influence the provision of complementary services such as showrooms or shop displays?

Real-world firms have to confront these questions all the time. The job of the industrial organization economist is to analyze the behavior of these firms and to derive some predictions from that analysis to help us understand market outcomes. In turn, to be truly useful, those predictions should be amenable to testing using modern econometric analysis.

1.2   HOW WE ANALYZE IMPERFECT COMPETITION

One reason that analyzing imperfect competition is difficult is the interdependence that characterizes the firms' decisions in their markets. When Southwest Airlines considered opening service to New England in the 1990s, it had to recognize that this would have a nontrivial effect on the other airlines already serving this market. They might react by cutting fares, or by changing their flight times, or perhaps by cutting back on Boston service so as to avoid a glut on the market. Similarly, when Pepsi thinks about putting in a high bid to become the National Football League's official soft drink, it has to wonder how Coke will respond. Will it bid even higher? If it does, should Pepsi raise its bid still further? Or what if Coke decides to respond to the advertising advantage that Pepsi gains by launching a price war in the soft-drink market?

Imperfect competition is played out against a background of interdependence, or what economists call a setting of *strategic interaction*. This means that determining a firm's optimal behavior is also difficult. Because the firms are likely to be aware of the interdependency of their actions, each firm will wish to take into account its rivals' responses to its action. Yet that response will also depend on how the rivals think the first firm will react to their reaction and so on. A firm in this situation needs to "put itself in its rival's shoes" to see how the rival will respond to different actions that the firm could take. The firm must do this in order to figure out what its best course of action is.

To understand the logic of strategic interaction, we use game theory. Game theory provides us with the necessary framework for an analysis of settings in which the participants or players recognize that what they do affects other players and, in turn, what other players do affects them. It is for this reason that much of the recent work in industrial organization uses game theory to understand market outcomes under imperfect competition.

While not all of the analysis in this book relies on game theory, a good bit of our discussion is aimed at developing and applying the logic of game theory to market settings.

Game theory permits us to analyze strategic interaction in both a clear and logically consistent manner. For this reason, it has become an indispensable tool in industrial organization. It is equally important, however, to recognize that game theory and, more generally, the understanding of strategic interaction serves a broader goal of understanding what industrial organization is about. This perhaps is best expressed by reference to a quote

Reality Checkpoint
Show Time!

Perhaps no example of strategic interaction is more common than the annual or even seasonal game television networks play in scheduling their programming. The objective is to get the highest "average audience" rating as calculated by the A. C. Nielsen Company and defined as the percentage of homes with a television that is tuned to a program during an average minute of prime-time viewing. This value determines the advertising fees that a network can charge and, hence, is crucial to the network's profit. Indeed, scheduling strategy is understood throughout the broadcast entry as a crucial element in network success, and a variety of well-known tactics have emerged over the years. These include: (1) *quick openers* —starting the evening with one's strongest shows to set up the rest of the viewing night; (2) *infant protection*—the avoidance of scheduling promising new shows to compete with strong rival programming and/or using an existing strong network show to serve as a lead-in for the new one; (3) *counterprogramming*—scheduling, say, a police show in a slot where the major competition is a comedy; and (4) *bridging*—scheduling shows an hour long or longer so that competing shows of an hour's length begin in the middle of the scheduled program.

For example, the longtime ratings champ on network television has been Fox's *American Idol*, which typically runs on both Tuesday and Wednesday evenings from January to May. Indeed, *Idol* is so popular that it could lose half of its audience and still be rated in the top 10. It also serves as a strong lead-in for an already popular Fox show, *House*.

Part of the response of other networks has been to reschedule their best shows to avoid being crushed. In 2007, ABC moved its hit series *Lost* from a 9:00 pm start on Wednesdays to a 10:00 pm start after *Idol* finishes. ABC also decided to reschedule its popular reality show *Dancing with the Stars* so that it runs on Monday and Tuesday evenings and does not start until May, when *Idol* goes off the air. NBC similarly moved its shows *Earl* and *The Office* from Tuesday nights to Thursday nights to escape the *Idol* juggernaut.

Industry executives openly admit that the anticipation of the arrival of *Idol* in January makes it particularly difficult for new shows that premier in September. The slots the networks have most available for a new show are precisely those vacated by the existing shows, namely, the ones that compete directly with *Idol*. This means that any new show that starts on Tuesday or Wednesday nights in September has to fear that it is living on borrowed time unless it can quickly establish a loyal following. Even then, its best hope is that it will be moved in January away from the *Idol*-dominated times. Otherwise, the new show is likely to suffer the same fate as all but a few *Idol* contestants: "I don't mean to be rude, but . . ."

See B. Carter, "For Fox Rivals, 'American Idol' Remains a Schoolyard Bully." *New York Times* (20 February 2007), p. C1.

from John Maynard Keynes who wrote insightfully that "the theory of economics does not furnish a body of settled conclusions immediately applicable to policy. It is a method rather than a doctrine, an apparatus of the mind, a technique of thinking which helps its possessor to draw correct conclusions."[1] The same can be said of modern industrial organization. It is a technique of thinking. To be precise, it is a means of thinking strategically and applying the insights of such analysis to model imperfect competition.

Of course, no model is a complete description of reality. A complete model detailing each and every aspect of the actual marketplace would be far too lengthy and unwieldy to be of much use. Instead, any market model is like a road map. It is a deliberate simplification of a very complicated terrain, omitting some features and thereby emphasizing others. The aim of the model is to capture and make transparent the essential features of the interaction among firms. In this light, to say that the real world is more complicated than the model is no criticism. If the modeling achieves its aim of making clear the underlying structure and the principles governing the market outcome, then its abbreviated portrait of the real world is its strength. This is why mathematics is so important. Mathematical modeling allows one to identify the simplifying assumption clearly and therefore to see the extent to which that assumption is driving the results. If the assumption is later deemed to be implausible, it can then be easily changed, and the formal model can be worked through again to its new logical conclusion.

Typically, however, rather than test the assumptions themselves, it is simpler to test the predictions of the model against actual data and observational evidence. Armed with ever-increasingly sophisticated statistical techniques, such testing has also become an essential part of the field of modern industrial organization. Throughout this book, you will find numerous examples of such testing.

The combination of theory and evidence provides a useful guide to the likely outcome of strategic interaction in a variety of settings. In each such case studied, the basic interpretation of the model and associated data is that "this is how to think about what happens in an imperfectly competitive market when..." This is how one does industrial organization.

1.3   WHY: ANTITRUST POLICY AND INDUSTRIAL ORGANIZATION THEORY

The text of the principal U.S. antitrust statutes is given in the Appendix to this chapter. Suffice to say at this point that such legislation came early to the United States with the passage of the first major antitrust law—the Sherman Act—in 1890. This predates much of the formal modeling of imperfect competition—and certainly its dissemination. However, economists had had an intuitive grasp of the potential problems of monopoly power as far back as Adam Smith. In his classic work, *The Wealth of Nations* (1776), Smith had written on both collusion among ostensibly rival firms and on the raw exercise of monopoly power:

> People of the same trade seldom meet together, even for merriment or diversion, but the conversation ends in a conspiracy against the public, or in some contrivance to raise prices.

> The monopolists, by keeping the market constantly understocked, by never fully supplying the effectual demand, sell their commodities much above the natural prices...

[1]   Keynes (1929).

By the late 19th century, many Americans had become convinced that a few large firms and trusts, such as Standard Oil and American Tobacco, had exploited their market power in just the ways Smith had forecast. A consensus emerged—one that has endured throughout the history of antitrust legislation—that some form of legal framework was needed to maintain competition in the marketplace. Moreover, while few people had any understanding of formal economics, there was a reasonably wide familiarity with the sentiments of Adam Smith.

Thus it was that popular sentiment, reinforced by shrewd Smithian insight, led to the enactment of the first U.S. antitrust law, the 1890 Sherman Act. It is somewhat remarkable just how directly the concerns of Adam Smith are reflected in the two primary sections of the Sherman Act. Section 1 prohibits contracts, combinations, and conspiracies "in restraint of trade." Section 2 makes illegal any attempt to monopolize a market. The view that government institutions were necessary to achieve these aims was also later reflected in the Clayton and Federal Trade Commission Acts.

Antitrust policy, in the beginning, focused primarily on prosecuting and preventing collusive agreements to raise prices under the authority of Section 1. Early cases such as the *Trans-Missouri Freight Association* and the *Addyston Pipe* cases of 1897 and 1898, respectively, established this tradition. That preventing collusive behavior remains a central aim of antitrust policy to this day,[2] is evidenced by the successful prosecution of the DRAM manufacturers mentioned at the start of this chapter.

Unlike the Section 1 statute, the enforcement of Section 2 on monopolization has been more limited. Despite wide public perception that many of the giant firms emerging from the Industrial Revolution had abused and exploited their monopoly power, it was 12 years before one of these, the Standard Oil Company of New Jersey, was prosecuted under Section 2.[3] That case eventually led to the famous Supreme Court ruling in 1911 that Standard Oil had illegally monopolized the petroleum refining industry. Similar findings against other trusts, including most notably the Tobacco Trust,[4] followed quickly. Yet unlike the price-fixing cases, these monopolization decisions were less clear about what actions were illegal. In particular, the court established a "rule of reason" framework for monopolization cases that permitted the courts to examine not only whether monopolization of an industry had occurred but, if so, what the market context was surrounding the formation of that monopoly and the business practices used to achieve it. Only if this additional inquiry found an explicit intent to monopolize or an obvious exploitation of monopoly power was there a true violation.

Practically speaking, the rule-of-reason approach meant that there was a lot of ambiguity in exactly what actions were illegal. This had two important results. First, those who feared that such a legal framework might weaken antitrust enforcement were motivated to pursue additional reforms so that Section 2 of the Sherman Act would not become a "paper-toothed tiger."[5] This effort led in 1914 to the passage of the Clayton Act meant to stop monopolization in its incipiency by limiting the use of a number of business practices such as rebates, tying, and exclusive contracts that were employed by Standard Oil in establishing its dominance. Section 7, which was later amended in the 1950s, was passed

---

[2]   *United States v. Trans-Missouri Freight Association*, 166 U.S. 290 (1897) and *United States v. Addyston Pipe & Steel Co.*, 85 F. 271 (6 Cir. 1898).

[3]   *Standard Oil Co. of New Jersey v. United States*, 221 U.S. 1 (1911). See also Posner (1971).

[4]   *United States v. American Tobacco Co.*, U.S. 221 U.S. 106 (1911).

[5]   Berki (1966), p. ix.

to prevent anticompetitive mergers. It also led to passage of the Federal Trade Commission Act in 1914 to establish an administrative agency, the Federal Trade Commission (FTC), endowed with powers of investigation and adjudication to handle Clayton Act violations. As later amended, the FTC act also outlawed "unfair methods of competition" and "unfair and deceptive acts or practices." Creation of the FTC gave antitrust policy an additional arm of law enforcement beyond that provided by the Justice Department (DOJ).

The second major result stemming from adoption of a rule-of-reason approach was the origin of academic interest in antitrust that emerged later with the *U.S. Steel* case of 1920. In that case, the Court made clear that in its view "the law does not make mere size an offense or the existence of unexerted power an offense—it does not compel competition nor require all that is possible."[6] As a result, the Court found U.S. Steel—a firm that, through a series of mergers, had grown to control over 70 percent of U.S. steel-making capacity—innocent of any antitrust violations.

In light of this decision, many analysts concluded that without a good economic road map by which to understand imperfect competition, the making of antitrust policy was a difficult proposition at best. It was the subsequent effort to provide that road map that initiated the field that we now call industrial organization.

Economists such as Edward Chamberlin (1933) and Edward Mason (1939), both at Harvard, led the way. In their view, the microeconomics of the time offered little guidance either to policy makers or to the legal system as to what evidence might be useful in determining the likely outcome a market would produce. The Supreme Court's dismissal of the government charges of monopolization in the U.S. Steel case was based on an argument that no exploitation of monopoly power or intent to monopolize had been shown. Only U.S. Steel's large market share had been documented, and "*the law does not make mere size an offense*" (emphasis added). Unless there was good reason to believe that a large market share offered strong evidence of monopolization, or until there was a coherent argument that identified other observable characteristics implying illegal behavior, the court's decision had a fair bit of justification.

More generally, economists at that time realized that any informed legal judgment would require some practical way to determine from observable evidence whether the industry in question was closer to perfect competition or to monopoly. Accordingly, they viewed the highest priority of industrial economics to be the determination of whether (and if so, how) one could infer illegal behavior from either firm size or other structural features. It was to provide this policy guide that the field of industrial organization began to emerge. The very name of the field—industrial organization—dates from this time.

Early work, therefore, focused on a set of key questions: How is the production of the industry organized? How is the market structured? How many firms are there, and how large are they relative to each other? Are there clear barriers to entry? It was recognized from the outset, however, that answering these questions would not be enough to provide the legal framework needed by legislators and courts to determine whether or not the antitrust laws had been violated. Achieving this goal required not only that an industry's structural features be revealed but that clear links between structure and market outcomes also be identified. That is, industrial economists needed to obtain data on prices, profits, and market structure, and then use these data to identify statistical relationships between various market structures on the one hand and industrial performance on the other.

---

[6]   *United States v. United States Steel Corporation*, 251 U.S. 417 (1920).

This was the agenda explicitly announced by Edward Mason in 1939 when he wrote, "The problem, as I see it, is to reduce the voluminous data concerning industrial organization to some sort of order through a classification of market structures. Differences in market structure are ultimately explicable in terms of technological factors. The economic problem, however, is to explain, through an examination of the structure of markets and the organization of firms, differences in competitive practices including price, production and investment policies."[7] In sum, the early industrial organization economists viewed their goal as one of establishing links between market structure and the conduct of firms in the market. In turn, that conduct would determine the likely outcome or performance of the market in terms of economic efficiency or general social welfare. For this reason, this early approach is typically referred to as the Structure-Conduct-Performance (SCP) approach. Presumably, if the outcome for a particular industry given its structure was sufficiently bad, legal action was justified either to alter the conduct that structure would otherwise generate or, if necessary, to change the structure itself.

The basic principle behind the SCP paradigm was that perfect competition and monopoly are usefully viewed as opposite ends of a spectrum of market structures along which all markets lie. One natural measure of market structure is the degree of concentration, or the percentage of market output produced by the largest firms in an industry. Accordingly, the practice of industrial economics at that time became first one of accurately describing the structure of different markets; and second, deriving empirical relations between structures and outcomes in terms of price–cost margins, innovative efforts, and other performance measures. Research focused on statistically examining the broad hypotheses on market structure and performance implied by the SCP paradigm. As noted, structure was often measured by the degree of concentration or the percentage of total market output accounted for by the few largest firms. Finding a road map for policy was interpreted to mean providing numerical answers to questions, such as how much a bit more concentration or a bit higher entry barriers would raise price above cost.

In pursuit of the SCP quest, the 1930s, 1940s and 1950s witnessed numerous studies attempting to document and to measure the link between industrial performance—say, profitability—and an industry's structural features, such as concentration. In some respects, this goal was met. For example, by looking at a cross section of industries, each with a different structure and a different overall profitability, scholars found some positive correlation between the industry's profit rate and the extent to which production was concentrated in the hands of just a few firms. Further studies found a similar positive link between advertising and profitability. The first of these results gave support to the view that an industry with more than one, but still just a few, large firms was indeed somewhat close to the monopoly pole. The second finding was interpreted as evidence that firms used advertising to build customer loyalty and, thus, to deter other firms from entering the market. In turn, this permitted the incumbent firms to enjoy monopoly power and profit.

1.3.1   The "New" Sherman Act and the Dominance of Structure-Based Analysis

The early findings of SCP scholars increasingly seemed to suggest that perhaps a firm's "mere size" could imply a legal offense if it is sufficiently large. The real question then

[7]   Mason (1939), p. 61–74.

became whether or not these developments would influence antitrust law. This question was answered in the affirmative with the 1945 Alcoa decision.[8]

While there was no doubt that Alcoa was the largest aluminum producer in North America, there was considerable debate over its market share. Ultimately, the Court defined Alcoa's relevant market to be primary aluminum ingot production and found that Alcoa supplied 90 percent of the market. It then found that Alcoa had illegally abused the market power that went with this size.

The Alcoa decision was a major policy validation of the SCP approach; others soon followed. In 1946, the Supreme Court found the big three tobacco companies (American Tobacco, Ligget & Myers, and R. J. Reynolds), who controlled 75 percent of domestic cigarette production, guilty of monopolization.[9] A number of similar cases continued over the next 20 years, culminating with such well-known ones as the 1962 *Brown Shoe* case and the 1964 case against the Grinnell Corporation. All of these cases gave increasing weight to market structure as an indictment of proposed or past actions.[10] The (in)famous price discrimination case of *Utah Pie* (1967) may also be read as an indictment of any outcome in which a few large firms come to dominate the market.[11] In that case, the Court viewed the pricing strategies of the bigger nationwide companies to be evidence of predatory intent against a smaller firm primarily because the shares of the larger firms grew over a four-year period. In short, the period from 1945 into the late 1960s reflects the growing dominance of the SCP framework as the major intellectual influence on antitrust policy.[12]

This "New" Sherman Act policy found its intellectual support in the cross-industry analyses of the SCP approach. Because our understanding of the potential pitfalls of empirical research has grown tremendously, as has our ability to do much more sophisticated empirical analysis that avoids those pitfalls, it is probably fair to say that these early studies are no longer highly regarded by economists. There are, in fact, many problems with these early findings, some of which we will discuss more fully below. At the time of their writing, however, the early SCP studies were quite influential. Moreover, their influence ranged beyond the United States. Particularly after the Second World War, the influential role of the United States served to spread the U.S. antitrust approach. This was true for both Japan and West Germany. In each country, the sustained presence of U.S. forces was accompanied by strong decartelization measures. Explicit legislation aimed at preserving competition found support in other countries as well.[13] Britain passed its Monopolies Act in 1948. In 1957, the initial Common Market agreement (the Treaty of Rome), which established the European Community for Steel and Coal, included in both its Articles 65 and 66 explicit prohibitions against agreements aimed at restricting the "normal operation of competition" and even outlawed "unauthorized concentrations" of market power.[14] These policy initiatives reflected a similar, and probably earlier, spread of the SCP approach to industrial economists around the world.[15]

---

[8]   *United States v. Aluminum Co. of America (ALCOA)*, 148 F.2d 416 (2 Cir. 1945).

[9]   *American Tobacco Company v. United States*, 328 U.S. 781 (1946).

[10] *Brown Shoe Co. v. United States*, 370 U.S. 294 (1962) and *United States v. Grinnell Corp.*, 236 F.Supp. 244 (D.R.I. 1964).

[11] *Utah Pie Co. v. Continental Baking Co., et al.*, 386 U.S. 685 (1967).

[12] For an excellent survey of antitrust history, see Mueller (1996).

[13] See Please (1954).

[14] See Resch (2005).

[15] See for example Stern (1955).

However, there was at least one key difference between American antitrust policy and that of its international associates. Outside the United States, there was a general suspicion that unfettered competition was not necessarily the ideal to which antitrust policy ought to aspire. Instead, there was some presumption that state regulation and even state ownership were useful tools for curbing the abuse of market power. In this context, it is worthwhile noting that the United States is a much larger country than say, Canada, or Japan and the United Kingdom. Hence, its markets tend to be bigger as well. As a result, if the minimum size necessary for efficient operation is the same in all countries, firms that achieve that size will have much larger market share in nations outside the United States. In turn, this offers more potential for market abuse, and Europeans may have been particularly sensitive to this concern. Faced with a choice between large, efficient firms that may abuse their power or small, inefficient ones that cannot, the third option of large firms directed by the state on behalf of the public may have seemed a good alternative.

1.3.2   The Tide Changes: The Chicago School and Beyond

Matters began to change in the 1970s. In part, this reflected a growing awareness among academic scholars that the SCP paradigm had important failings. One of these was that the vast array of empirical findings that the SCP researchers had amassed was actually subject to different interpretations. For example, consider the frequent finding that firms with large market shares tend to earn greater profit. This could be taken as a verification of the basic SCP view that the larger a firm's market share, the greater its monopoly power and the higher its profit. However, a more benign interpretation of this evidence is also possible. It could be that the most efficient or the lowest-cost firm gains the largest share of the market, so that both large size and healthy profit are simply reflections of a firm's superior technology or talent.[16]

Other problems also became important. While accounting profit is easily obtained, measuring the truly relevant economic profit is far more difficult. Additional measurement issues such as defining the relevant market and distinguishing between short-run and long-run outcomes can also be difficult to resolve.

Yet while the SCP approach had many problems they all stem from just two key failures. One was a failure to recognize that structure is itself endogenous. The other was a failure to recognize the role of strategic interaction. The first point implies that regressions in which some measure of market structure is taken as an exogenous right-hand-side variable are likely to be misspecified and therefore yield biased or inconsistent results. The second means that even when structure can be taken as given, the market outcome cannot be determined without fully working out the nature of the rivalry between the constituent firms. In some cases, even a market with just two firms may yield outcomes that are quite close to the perfectly competitive equilibrium.[17]

---

[16]   As shown later, this is a standard result in a Cournot model in which costs differ across firms. Specifically, if P is market price, η is the market demand elasticity at that price, and c_i and s_i are the ith firm's unit cost and market share, respectively, then it must be the case that: $\frac{P-c_i}{P} = \frac{s_i}{\eta}$. Lower-cost firms will have larger market shares, larger profit margins, and larger total profit.

[17]   Something of an exception in this regard was the work of Joseph Bain (1956), a former student of Edward Mason, who made many important contributions to the field. In particular, Bain recognized that beyond the market structure as measured by the size distribution of firms, the degree to which entry was easy or difficult would be a critical influence on the market outcome. This point was later developed and emphasized by Baumol, Panzar, and Willig (1982).

For all these reasons, the cross-industry scholarship that provided the foundation for the aggressive antitrust policy of the 1950s and 1960s began to fall sharply into disfavor. Moreover, the weaknesses in the SCP paradigm was accompanied by a discomfort that many felt concerning the more aggressive antitrust enforcements mentioned above. In the *Brown Shoe* case, for example, the Court disallowed the merger of two firms (Brown and Kinney), even though they only controlled about 5 percent of the national market (though a greater percent of individual local markets). Similarly, the *Utah Pie* case seemed to be a decision that did more to protect a specific competitor (Utah Pie) than to protect competitive forces.

The rising concern over flaws in both the SCP approach and the public policy it had fostered made possible a countermovement led by lawyers and economists from the Chicago School such as Richard Posner, Robert Bork, and Sam Peltzman. These and other scholars began to point out that many of the practices that the courts had been viewing as harmful to competition and economic welfare could, when viewed through the lens of corporate strategy, be seen as actually improving economic efficiency and bringing benefits to consumers. This work initially focused on vertical relationships either between a firm and its suppliers or between a firm and its distributors. Many such vertical contracts include restrictions such as those that grant franchisees exclusive territories, or that require distributors to sell at some minimum price. Chicago School economists argued that there were good economic reasons for these practices and that these restrictions actually brought benefits to consumers. Gradually, these arguments became successful, and many practices that had been previously found to be *per se* or outright illegal the court now began to review for their "reasonability" on a case-by-case method.[18]

Soon the Chicago School influence on vertical relationships spread to more of antitrust policy. In 1974, the U.S. Supreme Court rejected the government's efforts to block a large merger in a case involving the General Dynamics Corporation.[19] Many mergers that would previously have been prevented soon followed, justified both on grounds of cost savings and the potential for new entrants to constrain any attempt by the newly merged firm to exercise monopoly power. The government also lost several key cases accusing large firms, such as Kodak and IBM, of monopolization in violation of the Sherman Act. In addition, the precedent of the *Utah Pie* case was firmly rejected during these subsequent years. It became increasingly clear—most notably in a case involving a complaint by Zenith Corporation charging that seven Japanese television manufacturers had attempted to drive out competitors—that in the courts' view, efforts to eliminate rivals by pricing below cost rarely made sense.[20]

The Chicago School's contributions are difficult to underestimate, and its legal influence is felt to this day. These scholars were right to point out the need to examine the logic and reasonability of a firm's conduct. However, they were hampered by the fact that, as of that time, no language or framework in which to view such strategic behavior on a consistent basis had been developed. Yet such a framework was emerging. Building on the work of Von Neumann and Morgenstern (1944) and Nash (1951), Nobel Prize laureates Richard Selten, John Harsanyi, Michael Spence, and Thomas Schelling all made a number of crucial contributions that permitted game theory to become the analytic framework examining strategic interaction. The past three decades have witnessed the rapid spread

---

[18]   See *Continental T.V. Inc. v. GTE Sylvania, Inc.*, 433 U.S. 36 (1977), *State Oil v. Khan, et al*, 522 U.S. 3 (1997) and, most recently, *Leegin Creative Leather Products, Inc. v. PSKS, Inc.*, 551 U.S. 877 (2007).

[19]   *United States v. General Dynamics Corp.* 415 U.S. 486 (1974).

[20]   *Matsuhita Electric Industrial Co. v. Zenith Radio Corp.*, 475 U.S. 574 (1986).

of game theory to analyze virtually every aspect of imperfect competition. As a result, the field of industrial organization has again been transformed and now reflects, at least in part, what some call a Post-Chicago view and what others simply refer to as the "new IO."[21]

We have already noted that there is much to be said for pursuing a game-theoretic understanding of the strategic interaction of firms. What is important to note at this point is that as game-theoretic analysis spread through modern industrial organization, its insights have, to some extent, led to a diminishment of the Chicago School's impact. However, it would be wrong to identify the advent of game-theory models and the new Post-Chicago approach as a total rejection of the Chicago School's work. For example, the Merger Guidelines adopted jointly by the Federal Trade Commission and the Justice Department have deep roots in the Cournot-Nash game-theoretic model that we describe more fully in Chapter 12. While these guidelines are far from permissive, they still allow for many more mergers than would ever have legally occurred in the "New Sherman Act" years of the 1950s and 1960s.

These developments have been accompanied by similar ones elsewhere. In 1997, the European Union adopted the Treaty of Amsterdam that amended the earlier Common Market treaties in keeping with its goal of full economic integration. Articles 81 and 82 of the treaty replaced articles 65 and 66 of the earlier Treaty of Rome and the European Commission Director-General for Competition implemented language that was perhaps even more similar to that of the United States. This reflected the widespread recognition that adoption of a common antitrust policy for all union members became a real necessity as European firms increasingly operated across European borders. Like its U.S. counterpart, European antitrust policy has incorporated much of the post-SCP learning. This has perhaps been particularly true for the courts that have questioned a number of early Commission decisions.

However, important distinctions do remain between the U.S. and European approaches with respect to specific cases, with Europe typically pursuing stricter and more aggressive enforcement. Thus, in 2001, the European Commission blocked GE's acquisition of Honeywell International, even though the United States had already approved that merger earlier. Somewhat similarly, Microsoft was ordered by the European Commission in 2003 to offer a version of its *Windows* operating system that did not automatically include Microsoft's *Media Player* media software, as well as to provide the technical information to others that would allow them to develop programs fully compatible with the *Windows* platform. When *Microsoft* did not comply satisfactorily with these orders, the Commission levied substantial fines totaling hundreds of millions of dollars. While the United States had earlier found Microsoft guilty of antitrust violations, nothing in the final settlement of that case seemed nearly as harsh. These decisions and others perhaps reflect the historically greater mistrust Europeans have of unregulated large corporations that we mentioned earlier. They also show that debate about both the appropriate underlying economic analysis and the appropriate public policy remains lively and important.

In sum, concerns over antitrust policy have been a major motivation for industrial economists since the modern inception of that policy in the late 19th century, through the emergence of the SCP approach in the mid-20th century, and continuing to the present post-Chicago paradigm that is so prominent at the start of the 21st century. Throughout this time, competition has been regarded as a cornerstone of a free market economy both

---

[21] Schmalensee (1988) provides a survey of the then "new IO" that is still relevant. Kovacic and Shapiro (2000) survey the influence of game theory on modern antitrust policy. Kwoka and White (2004) offer a discussion of recent antitrust cases.

in the United States and elsewhere. We want to know how firms compete when they have market power, what implication that competition has, and what the role of public policy might be in helping imperfectly competitive markets achieve outcomes closer to the competitive ideal. The reason we study industrial organization is to understand market competition in all its dimensions and to develop appropriate public policy when the imperfections in that competition yield unsatisfactory outcomes.

Summary

Industrial organization is the study of imperfect competition. Industrial economists are interested in markets that one actually encounters in the real world. However, these real-world markets come in many shapes and flavors. For example, some are comprised of a few large firms; others have one large firm and many smaller ones. In some, the products are greatly differentiated, while in others they are nearly identical. Some firms compete largely by trying to keep prices as low as possible. In other markets, advertising and other forms of nonprice competition are the dominant tactics. This range of possibilities has meant that over time, industrial economics has become a field rich with practical insights regarding real business behavior and public policy. This book is all about these developments.

Firms in imperfectly competitive industries need to make strategic decisions—that is, decisions that will have identifiable impacts on other participants in the market, be they rival firms, suppliers, or distributors. As a result, making any such choice must inevitably involve some consideration of how these other players in the game will react. Examples of such strategic choice variables include price, product design, decisions to expand capacity, and whether or not to invest heavily in research and development of a new product. This book presents the modern analysis of market situations involving such strategic interaction—an analysis that is rooted in noncooperative game theory. We use this analysis to examine such issues as why there are so many varieties of cereals, or how firms maintain a price-fixing agreement, or how advertising and product innovation affect the nature of competition. We also describe how the predictions of these models have been tested.

Our interest is in more than just determining the profit-maximizing strategies that firms in a particular market context should adopt. As economists, we are interested in the market outcomes that result when firms adopt such strategies, and whether those outcomes are close to those of the competitive ideal. If not, we then need to ask whether (and how) public policy can improve market allocations. Our hope is to convey the value of economic research and the gains from learning "to think like an economist." More generally, we hope to demonstrate the vitality and relevance of industrial organization, both in theory and in practice.

Problems

1. List three markets that you think are imperfectly competitive. Explain your reasoning.

2. Explain why a perfectly competitive market does not reflect a setting of strategic interaction.

3. The Appendix to this chapter lists the current major antitrust laws of the United States. Review Sections 2 and 7 of the Clayton Act. What potential threats to competition do these sections address?

4. Suppose that sophisticated statistical research provides clear evidence that, all else being equal, worker productivity increases as industrial concentration increases. How would you interpret this finding?

5. Why do you think that the U.S. courts have consistently disallowed any form of price-fixing agreements among different firms, but been more tolerant of market dominance by one firm?

References

Bain, Joseph. 1956. *Barriers to New Competition*. Cambridge: Harvard University Press.

Baumol, W. J., J. C. Panzar, and R. D. Willig. 1982. *Contestable Markets and the Theory of Market Structure*. New York: Harcourt Brace Jovanovich.

Berki, S. (Ed). 1996. *Antitrust Policy: Economics and Law*. Boston: D.C. Heath and Company.

Chamberlin, E. H. 1933. *The Theory of Monopolistic Competition*. Cambridge: Harvard University Press.

Kaysen, Carl, and Donald Turner. 1959. *Antitrust Policy*. Cambridge: Harvard University Press.

Keynes, J. M. 1929. *Introduction, to D. H. Robertson, Money*. New York: Harcourt Brace and Company.

Kovacic, W. E., and C. Shapiro. 2000. "Antitrust Policy: A Century of Legal and Economic Thinking." *Journal of Economic Perspectives*, 14: 43–60.

Kwoka, J. E., and L. J. White. 2004. *The Antitrust Revolution: Economics, Competition, and Policy*. 4th Edition. Oxford: Oxford University Press.

Mason, E. S. 1939. "Price and Production Policies of Large Scale Enterprise." *American Economic Review*, 29: 61–74.

Mueller, Dennis C. 1996. "Lessons from the United States's Antitrust History." *International Journal of Industrial Organization*, 14: 415–445.

Nash, J. 1951. "Noncooperative Games." *Annals of Mathematics*, 54: 286–295.

Please, A. 1954. "Some Aspects of European Monopoly Legislation". *Journal of Industrial Economics*, 3 (December): 34–46.

Posner, R. 1971. "A Statistical Study of Antitrust Enforcement." *Journal of Law and Economics*, 13 (October).

Resch, A. 2005. *Phases of Competition Policy in Europe*. Institute of European Studies, Working Paper 050401. Berkeley: University of California.

Schelling, T. 1959. *The Strategy of Conflict*. New York: Oxford University Press.

Schmalensee, R. 1988. "Industrial Economics: An Overview." *Economic Journal*, 98: 643–681.

Stern, E. H. 1955. "Industrial Production and Profits in the United Kingdom and the United States." *Economic Journal*, 3 (August), 1955.

Von Neumann, J., and O. Morgenstern. 1944. *Theory of Games and Economic Behavior*. Princeton: Princeton University Press.

Appendix

Excerpts from Key Antitrust Statutes

The United States:

THE SHERMAN ACT

Sec. 1. Every contract, combination in the form of trust or otherwise, or conspiracy, in restraint of trade or commerce among the several States, or with foreign nations, is declared to be illegal. Every person who shall make any contract or engage in any combination or conspiracy hereby declared to be illegal shall be deemed guilty of a felony, and, on conviction thereof, shall be punished by fine not exceeding $10,000,000,000 if a corporation, or, if any other person, $350,000, or by imprisonment not exceeding three years, or by both said punishments, in the discretion of the court.

Sec. 2. Every person who shall monopolize, or attempt to monopolize, or combine or conspire with any other person or persons, to monopolize any part of the trade or commerce among the several States, or with foreign nations, shall be deemed guilty of a felony, and, on conviction thereof, shall be punished by fine not exceeding $10,000,000,000 if a corporation, or, if any other person, $350,000, or by imprisonment not exceeding three years, or by both said punishments, in the discretion of the court.

THE CLAYTON ACT, INCLUDING KEY AMENDMENTS OF THE ROBINSON-PATMAN ACT AND CELLER-KEFAUVER ACT

Sec. 2

(a)   Price; selection of customers

It shall be unlawful for any person engaged in commerce, in the course of such commerce, either directly or indirectly, to discriminate in price between different purchasers of commodities of like grade and quality, where either or any of the purchases involved in such discrimination are in commerce, where such commodities are sold for use, consumption, or resale within the United States or any Territory thereof or the District of Columbia or any insular possession or other place under the jurisdiction of the United States, and where the effect of such discrimination may be substantially to lessen competition or tend to create a monopoly in any line of commerce, or to injure, destroy, or prevent competition with any person who either grants or knowingly receives the benefit of such discrimination, or with customers of either of them: Provided, That nothing herein contained shall prevent differentials which make only due allowance for differences in the cost of manufacture, sale, or delivery resulting from the differing methods or quantities in which such commodities are to such purchasers sold or delivered: Provided, however, That the Federal Trade Commission may, after due investigation and hearing to all interested parties, fix and establish quantity limits, and revise the same as it finds necessary, as to particular commodities or classes of commodities, where it finds that available purchasers in greater quantities are so few as to render differentials on account thereof unjustly discriminatory or promotive of monopoly in any line of commerce; and the foregoing shall then not be construed to permit differentials based on differences in quantities greater than those so fixed and established: And provided further, That nothing herein contained shall prevent persons engaged in selling goods, wares, or merchandise in commerce from selecting their own customers in bona fide transactions and not in restraint of trade: And provided further, That nothing herein contained shall prevent price changes from time to time where in response to changing conditions affecting the market for or the marketability of the goods concerned, such as but not limited to actual or imminent deterioration of perishable goods, obsolescence of seasonal goods, distress sales under court process, or sales in good faith in discontinuance of business in the goods concerned.

(b)   Burden of rebutting prima-facie case of discrimination

Upon proof being made, at any hearing on a complaint under this section, that there has been discrimination in price or services or facilities furnished, the burden of rebutting the prima-facie case thus made by showing justification shall be upon the person charged with a violation of this section, and unless justification shall be affirmatively shown, the Commission is authorized to issue an order terminating the discrimination: Provided, however, That nothing herein contained shall prevent a seller rebutting the prima-facie case thus made by showing that his lower price or the furnishing of services or facilities to any purchaser or purchasers was made in good faith to meet an equally low price of a competitor, or the services or facilities furnished by a competitor.

(c) Payment or acceptance of commission, brokerage, or other compensation

It shall be unlawful for any person engaged in commerce, in the course of such commerce, to pay or grant, or to receive or accept, anything of value as a commission, brokerage, or other compensation, or any allowance or discount in lieu thereof, except for services rendered in connection with the sale or purchase of goods, wares, or merchandise, either to the other party to an agent, representative, or other intermediary therein where such intermediary is acting in fact for or in behalf, or is subject to the direct or indirect control, of any party to such transaction other than the person by whom such compensation is so granted or paid.

(d) Payment for services or facilities for processing or sale

It shall be unlawful for any person engaged in commerce to pay or contract for the payment of anything of value to or for the benefit of a customer of such person in the course of such commerce as compensation or in consideration for any services or facilities furnished by or through such customer in connection with the processing, handling, sale, or offering for sale of any products or commodities manufactured, sold, or offered for sale by such person, unless such payment or consideration is available on proportionally equal terms to all other customers competing in the distribution of such products or commodities.

(e) Furnishing services or facilities for processing, handling, etc.

It shall be unlawful for any person to discriminate in favor of one purchaser against another purchaser or purchasers of a commodity bought for resale, with or without processing, by contracting to furnish or furnishing, or by contributing to the furnishing of, any services or facilities connected with the processing, handling, sale, or offering for sale of such commodity so purchased upon terms not accorded to all purchasers on proportionally equal terms.

(f) Knowingly inducing or receiving discriminatory price

It shall be unlawful for any person engaged in commerce, in the course of such commerce, to be a party to, or assist in, any transaction of sale, or contract to sell, which discriminates to his knowledge against competitors of the purchaser, in that, any discount, rebate, allowance, or advertising service charge is granted to the purchaser over and above any discount, rebate, allowance, or advertising service charge available at the time of such transaction to said competitors in respect of a sale of goods of like grade, quality, and quantity; to sell, or contract to sell, goods in any part of the United States at prices lower than those exacted by said person elsewhere in the United States for the purpose of destroying competition, or eliminating a competitor in such part of the United States; or, to sell, or contract to sell, goods at unreasonably low prices for the purpose of destroying competition or eliminating a competitor.

Sec. 3

Sale, etc., on agreement not to use goods of competitor

It shall be unlawful for any person engaged in commerce, in the course of such commerce, to lease or make a sale or contract for sale of goods, wares, merchandise, machinery, supplies, or other commodities, whether patented or unpatented, for use, consumption, or resale within the United States or any Territory thereof or the District of Columbia or any insular possession or other place under the jurisdiction of the United States, or fix a price charged therefore, or discount from, or rebate upon, such price, on the condition, agreement, or understanding that the lessee or purchaser thereof shall not use or deal in the goods, wares, merchandise, machinery, supplies, or other commodity of a competitor or competitors of the lessor seller, where the effect of such lease, sale, or contract for sale or such condition, agreement, or understanding may be to substantially lessen competition or tend to create a monopoly in any line of commerce.

Sec. 7

No person engaged in commerce or in any activity affecting commerce shall acquire, directly or indirectly, the whole or any part of the stock or other share capital and no person subject to the jurisdiction of the Federal Trade Commission shall acquire the whole or any part of the assets of another person engaged also in commerce or in any activity affecting commerce, where in any line of commerce or in any activity affecting commerce in any section of the country, the effect of such acquisition may be substantially to lessen competition, or to tend to create a monopoly.

EUROPEAN UNION ANTITRUST ARTICLES

The European Union's antitrust policy is embedded in Articles 81 through 89 of Title VI of the Treaty Establishing the European Community. The first two of these parallel the two main sections of the Sherman Act. Article 81 prohibits collusive agreements and coordinated actions among firms. Article 82 outlaws the abuse of a dominant market position. The remaining articles address broad issues of implementation (Article 83), the division of power between states and the European Commission (Articles 84 and 85, in part as membership in the Union is finalized), the application of the antitrust laws to public service providers (Article 87), and the antitrust treatment of state aid. All nine articles appear below.

RULES ON COMPETITION

SECTION 1

RULES APPLYING TO UNDERTAKINGS

Article 81

1. The following shall be prohibited as incompatible with the common market: all agreements between undertakings, decisions by associations of undertakings, and concerted practices that may affect trade between Member States and which have as their object

or effect the prevention, restriction, or distortion of competition within the common market, and in particular those which:

   a. directly or indirectly fix purchase or selling prices or any other trading conditions;
   b. limit or control production, markets, technical development, or investment;
   c. share markets or sources of supply;
   d. apply dissimilar conditions to equivalent transactions with other trading parties, thereby placing them at a competitive disadvantage;
   e. make the conclusion of contracts subject to acceptance by the other parties of supplementary obligations which, by their nature or according to commercial usage, have no connection with the subject of such contracts.

2. Any agreements or decisions prohibited pursuant to this article shall be automatically void.

3. The provisions of paragraph 1 may, however, be declared inapplicable in the case of:

   – any agreement or category of agreements between undertakings,
   – any decision or category of decisions by associations of undertakings,
   – any concerted practice or category of concerted practices,

which contributes to improving the production or distribution of goods or to promoting technical or economic progress, while allowing consumers a fair share of the resulting benefit, and which does not:

   a. impose on the undertakings concerned restrictions which are not indispensable to the attainment of these objectives;
   b. afford such undertakings the possibility of eliminating competition in respect of a substantial part of the products in question.

Article 82

Any abuse by one or more undertakings of a dominant position within the common market or in a substantial part of it shall be prohibited as incompatible with the common market insofar as it may affect trade between Member States.

  Such abuse may, in particular, consist of:

(a) directly or indirectly imposing unfair purchase or selling prices or other unfair trading conditions;
(b) limiting production, markets, or technical development to the prejudice of consumers;
(c) applying dissimilar conditions to equivalent transactions with other trading parties, thereby placing them at a competitive disadvantage;
(d) making the conclusion of contracts subject to acceptance by the other parties of supplementary obligations which, by their nature or according to commercial usage, have no connection with the subject of such contracts.

Article 83

1. The appropriate regulations or directives to give effect to the principles set out in Articles 81 and 82 shall be laid down by the Council, acting by a qualified majority on a proposal from the Commission and after consulting the European Parliament.
2. The regulations or directives referred to in paragraph 1 shall be designed in particular:

a.   to ensure compliance with the prohibitions laid down in Article 81(1) and in Article 82 by making provision for fines and periodic penalty payments;
b.   to lay down detailed rules for the application of Article 81(3), taking into account the need to ensure effective supervision on the one hand, and to simplify administration to the greatest possible extent on the other;
c.   to define, if need be, in the various branches of the economy, the scope of the provisions of Articles 81 and 82;
d.   to define the respective functions of the Commission and of the Court of Justice in applying the provisions laid down in this paragraph;
e.   to determine the relationship between national laws and the provisions contained in this section or adopted pursuant to this article.

Article 84

Until the entry into force of the provisions adopted in pursuance of Article 83, the authorities in Member States shall rule on the admissibility of agreements, decisions, and concerted practices and on abuse of a dominant position in the common market in accordance with the law of their country and with the provisions of Article 81, in particular paragraph 3, and of Article 82.

Article 85

1.   Without prejudice to Article 84, the Commission shall ensure the application of the principles laid down in Articles 81 and 82. On application by a Member State or on its own initiative, and in cooperation with the competent authorities in the Member States, which shall give it their assistance, the Commission shall investigate cases of suspected infringement of these principles. If it finds that there has been an infringement, it shall propose appropriate measures to bring it to an end.
2.   If the infringement is not brought to an end, the Commission shall record such infringement of the principles in a reasoned decision. The Commission may publish its decision and authorize Member States to take the measures, the conditions and details of which it shall determine, needed to remedy the situation.

Article 86

1.   In the case of public undertakings and undertakings to which Member States grant special or exclusive rights, Member States shall neither enact nor maintain in force any measure contrary to the rules contained in this Treaty, in particular to those rules provided for in Article 12 and Articles 81 to 89.
2.   Undertakings entrusted with the operation of services of general economic interest or having the character of a revenue-producing monopoly shall be subject to the rules contained in this Treaty, in particular to the rules on competition, insofar as the application of such rules does not obstruct the performance, in law or in fact, of the particular tasks assigned to them. The development of trade must not be affected to such an extent as would be contrary to the interests of the Community.
3.   The Commission shall ensure the application of the provisions of this Article and shall, where necessary, address appropriate directives or decisions to Member States.

SECTION 2

AIDS GRANTED BY STATES

Article 87

1. Save as otherwise provided in this Treaty, any aid granted by a Member State or through State resources in any form whatsoever which distorts or threatens to distort competition by favouring certain undertakings or the production of certain goods shall, insofar as it affects trade between Member States, be incompatible with the common market.

2. The following shall be compatible with the common market:

    a. aid having a social character, granted to individual consumers, provided that such aid is granted without discrimination related to the origin of the products concerned;

    b. aid to make good the damage caused by natural disasters or exceptional occurrences;

    c. aid granted to the economy of certain areas of the Federal Republic of Germany affected by the division of Germany, insofar as such aid is required in order to compensate for the economic disadvantages caused by that division.

3. The following may be considered to be compatible with the common market:

    a. aid to promote the economic development of areas where the standard of living is abnormally low or where there is serious underemployment;

    b. aid to promote the execution of an important project of common European interest or to remedy a serious disturbance in the economy of a Member State;

    c. aid to facilitate the development of certain economic activities or of certain economic areas, where such aid does not adversely affect trading conditions to an extent contrary to the common interest;

    d. aid to promote culture and heritage conservation where such aid does not affect trading conditions and competition in the Community to an extent that is contrary to the common interest;

    e. such other categories of aid as may be specified by decision of the Council acting by a qualified majority on a proposal from the Commission.

Article 88

1. The Commission shall, in cooperation with Member States, keep under constant review all systems of aid existing in those States. It shall propose to the latter any appropriate measures required by the progressive development or by the functioning of the common market.

2. If, after giving notice to the parties concerned to submit their comments, the Commission finds that aid granted by a State or through State resources is not compatible with the common market having regard to Article 87, or that such aid is being misused, it shall decide that the State concerned shall abolish or alter such aid within a period of time to be determined by the Commission.

If the State concerned does not comply with this decision within the prescribed time, the Commission or any other interested State may, in derogation from the provisions of Articles 226 and 227, refer the matter to the Court of Justice direct.

On application by a Member State, the Council may, acting unanimously, decide that aid which that State is granting or intends to grant shall be considered to be compatible with the common market, in derogation from the provisions of Article 87 or from the regulations provided for in Article 89, if such a decision is justified by exceptional circumstances. If, as regards the aid in question, the Commission has already initiated the procedure provided for in the first subparagraph of this paragraph, the fact that the State concerned has made its application to the Council shall have the effect of suspending that procedure until the Council has made its attitude known.

If, however, the Council has not made its attitude known within three months of the said application being made, the Commission shall give its decision on the case.

3.   The Commission shall be informed, in sufficient time to enable it to submit its comments, of any plans to grant or alter aid. If it considers that any such plan is not compatible with the common market having regard to Article 87, it shall without delay initiate the procedure provided for in paragraph 2. The Member State concerned shall not put its proposed measures into effect until this procedure has resulted in a final decision.

Article 89

The Council, acting by a qualified majority on a proposal from the Commission and after consulting the European Parliament, may make any appropriate regulations for the application of Articles 87 and 88 and may in particular determine the conditions in which Article 88(3) shall apply and the categories of aid exempted from this procedure.

2

Basic Microeconomics

The starting point for all analysis of imperfect competition is the standard model of a monopoly firm that sells units of a single product at the same uniform price to many consumers. However, to understand the impact that this extreme departure from a competitive environment has, it is necessary to have the polar opposite case of perfect competition available as a reference. We therefore begin our analysis with the standard textbook analysis of perfect competition and pure monopoly. We then note that even within the standard assumption of uniform pricing, this analysis is more complicated than it may appear to be. In subsequent chapters, we shall explore such complications further as we also relax the assumption of a uniform or common price paid by all consumers.

2.1 COMPETITION VERSUS MONOPOLY: THE POLES OF MARKET PERFORMANCE

We assume a market demand curve describing the aggregate quantity Q that consumers willingly purchase as a function of the market price, P. We describe this relation as

$$Q = Q^D(P) \tag{2.1}$$

and assume that it is continuous and twice differentiable. We further assume that it is downward sloping, that is, $Q' < 0$. In many settings, it is convenient to work with the so-called inverse demand function described by

$$P = Q^{D-1}(Q) = P(Q) \tag{2.2}$$

where $P(Q)$ is continuously downward sloping.

Let the number of firms in the market be n, and let the output of a single firm be denoted as q_i, where i is an integer satisfying $1 \leq i \leq n$, and denotes a firm's identity. For the case of $n = 1$, i.e., for the monopoly case, it is clear that $q_i = Q$, and the two variables may be used interchangeably. For all values of n, we have that

$$Q = \sum_{i=1}^{n} q_i \tag{2.3}$$

In the present case of perfect competition, we assume that n is sufficiently large that $\frac{\partial Q}{\partial q_i} \approx 0$ for all i. In other words, the production choice of any one firm is assumed to have effectively zero impact on the total output, Q, on the market. In turn, by equation (2.2), this means that no single firm's production decision alters the market price. Each firm in a perfectly competitive market takes the market price P as unchanging, regardless of that firm's individual output level.

Every firm, whether it is a monopoly or has rivals, is assumed to pursue profit-maximization as its goal. Firm profit π_i is defined as total revenue less total costs. Revenue is simply price times output $P(Q)q_i$. Total cost C is a function of the firm's output as described by the function

$$C = C(q_i) \tag{2.4}$$

which is again assumed to be continuous, and to have a first derivative $C'(q_i) \geq 0$. The firm's profit maximization problem may now be expressed as follows:

$$\operatorname*{Max}_{q_i} \pi_i = P(Q)q_i - C(q_i) = \pi(q_i) \tag{2.5}$$

For a perfectly competitive firm, the fact that $\frac{\partial Q}{\partial q_i} \approx 0$, means that the necessary first-order condition for profit-maximization is

$$P = C' \tag{2.6}$$

where we have suppressed the functional notation for convenience. The profit-maximizing competitive firm produces where the market price, which is taken as given, is equal to the firm's marginal cost.

In contrast, the monopolist operates in a setting in which $\frac{\partial Q}{\partial q_i} \approx 1$, as its output and the market output are the same. Hence, the necessary first-order condition for the profit-maximizing monopolist (again suppressing functional notation) is

$$P + QP' = C' \tag{2.7}$$

The left-hand side of equation (2.7) is the general expression of marginal revenue MR for any firm. To see this, we recall that revenue is simply the product of quantity and price, or $R = QP(Q)$. Since marginal revenue MR is defined as the derivative of revenue with respect to quantity, the identification of the left-hand side of equation (2.7) as marginal revenue follows immediately.

The right-hand side of (2.7) is marginal cost. Thus, this equation is the usual requirement for profit maximization that $MR = MC$. As already noted, the difference between the competitive and monopoly firm is that the second term in the marginal revenue expression QP' is negative for the monopoly firm as an increase in the monopolist's output lowers the market price but has zero effect on price for the competitive firm. Put differently, marginal revenue is equal to price for the competitive firm, but less than price for the monopolist. Hence, under competition, the market price is equal to the marginal cost at each and every firm. Under monopoly, the market price exceeds the marginal cost of the monopoly firm.

An alternative and useful way to make the preceding point is as follows. Define the point elasticity of firm demand ε as follows:

$$\varepsilon = -\frac{\partial q_i}{\partial P}\frac{P}{q_i} = -\frac{1}{\left(\dfrac{\partial P}{\partial q_i}\right)}\frac{P}{q_i} = -\frac{1}{\left(\dfrac{\partial P}{\partial Q}\right)\left(\dfrac{\partial Q}{\partial q_i}\right)}\frac{P}{q_i} \tag{2.8}$$

Then the firm's profit-maximizing condition may be rewritten as

$$P\left(1 - \frac{1}{\varepsilon}\right) = C' \Rightarrow P = \left(\frac{\varepsilon}{\varepsilon - 1}\right)C' \tag{2.9}$$

It is evident from (2.8) that the demand elasticity facing the competitive firm is infinite, since $\partial Q/\partial q_i = 0$. Any attempt to sell at a price other than the market price will generate massive changes in its demand. Hence, by (2.9), the competitive firm price is equal to marginal cost. However, the demand elasticity facing the monopolist firm is the same as the elasticity of market demand at that price, since $\partial Q/\partial q_i = 1$. It is easy to demonstrate as well that the monopolist must always select a point where that elasticity exceeds 1. If that elasticity were less than 1, it would imply that a reduction in output would not only reduce costs as $C' > 0$, but also raise revenue as $\partial P/P > \partial Q/Q$. In such a setting, the monopolist would definitely want to reduce Q, thereby lowering cost, raising revenue, and, hence, increasing its profit. Thus, in equilibrium, the monopoly production cannot imply a price at which $\varepsilon < 1$. As equation (2.8) suggests, however, a fall in Q and the associated rise in P will tend to move the market to a point where demand is more elastic. In the context of equation (2.9), then, the equilibrium requirement that the monopolist produce an output at which the price elasticity of demand exceeds one again means that, unlike the competitive outcome, the monopoly outcome yields a price above marginal cost.

In order to contrast the competitive and monopoly market outcomes more completely, we need to determine the equilibrium quantity as well as the price that will prevail in each case. For the competitive case, this requires that we derive the industry supply curve. The profit-maximizing condition that price equals marginal cost for the competitive firm, in fact, implies that supply curve. At any given price P, we find the profit-maximizing output level for each firm as indicated by equation (2.6). The total industry output Q at that price will be the sum of all the individual firm outputs. Repeating this process for each and every price then generates the supply relation between total output and price, $Q(P)$. In other words, the competitive supply curve is just the horizontal summation of all the individual firm marginal cost curves. Formally, we have

$$C_i'(q_i) = P \Rightarrow q_i = C_i'^{-1}(P) \tag{2.10}$$

and

$$Q^S = \sum_{i=1}^{n} q_i = \sum_{i=1}^{n} C_i'^{-1}(P) = F(P) \Rightarrow P = F^{-1}(Q) = f(Q) \tag{2.11}$$

The monopolist, of course, has no supply curve. The exercise of calling out a price and finding out how much production that price will elicit is meaningless in the case of a monopolist whose production decisions determine the price. However, the monopolist does have a cost schedule. In this respect, there is no reason to assume that the monopolist is either more or less efficient than the n competitive firms. Indeed, we may think of the monopolist as a firm that merges together the n independent firms. In this case, the marginal cost schedule of the monopolist is the same as the horizontal summation of all the individual marginal cost curves. That is, the monopolist marginal cost curve is identical with the supply curve of the competitive industry.

Figures 2.1(a) and 2.1(b) illustrate the two cases. The competitive equilibrium is described in Figure 2.1(a). Here, the intersection of the competitive supply $f(Q)$ and the market demand $P(Q)$ curves determine the equilibrium price and quantity outcomes, P^C and Q^C. At this output level, each and every one of the numerous competitive firms is maximizing profit and so, producing at an output q_i at which its marginal cost is equal to P^C.

The monopoly case is illustrated in Figure 2.1(b). The monopolist produces where marginal revenue equals marginal cost. The latter is again measured as the horizontal summation of all the individual marginal cost curves and so, as noted above, is equivalent to the competitive supply curve. However, as also shown earlier, the monopoly firm's marginal revenue is always less than the price. Therefore, the point at which marginal revenue and marginal cost are equal must occur at an output Q^M less than Q^C. In turn, this implies a monopoly price $P^M > P^C$.

Recall that the demand curve reflects the amount that consumers would willingly purchase an each alternative price. In other words, market demand reflects the expenditures consumers would voluntary make to purchase a given quantity, Q. The total value of those expenditures—the total value that consumers place on any given quantity—is, then, the area under the demand curve up to that point. Likewise, production also reflects voluntary actions. At any given production level, the area under the marginal cost curve reflects the minimal total cost of producing that output and, hence, the absolute minimum producers would have to receive to bring that level of production to the market willingly.

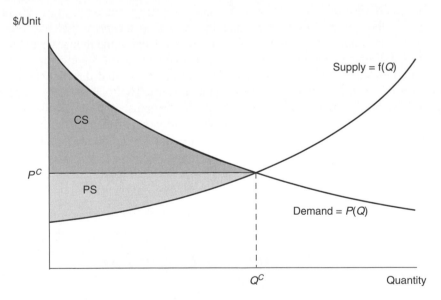

Figure 2.1(a)   Competitive market equilibrium
In the competitive equilibrium, the price P^C equals the marginal cost which, in turn, is equalized across firms. The associated equilibrium output Q^C maximizes the total surplus equal to the sum of consumer surplus CS and producer surplus PS.

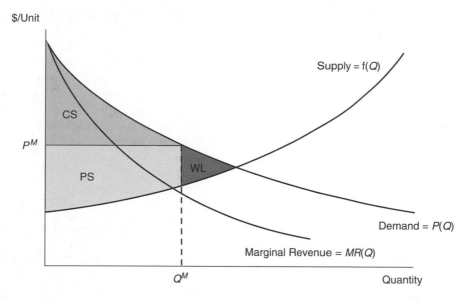

Figure 2.1(b) Monopolized market equilibrium

The monopolist produces Q_M units, which is less than the competitive industry produces Q_C. As a result, the equilibrium monopoly price P^M exceeds the competitive price P^C and is therefore also above marginal cost. The inefficiency of the outcome is captured by the welfare or deadweight lost WL.

If the area below the demand curve reflects total value and the area below the marginal cost curve reflects the total cost, then the area between the two reflects net value, or what is commonly referred to as the *net total social surplus*. In each equilibrium, this total surplus is divided into two parts. The first part is consumer surplus CS, the portion of the total surplus that flows to consumers. This is the area below the demand curve—but above the equilibrium price measured over the equilibrium volume of output. Again, the area below the demand curve up to any level of output measures the total expenditure consumers would have willingly made for that many units, while the product of the equilibrium price and quantity, $P^C Q^C$ in Figure 2.1(a) and $P^M Q^M$ in Figure 2.1(b), is the actual expenditure made. Accordingly, the difference between the two is a measure of the surplus enjoyed by consumers. Formally, we have

$$CS(Q) = \int_0^Q P(Q)\, dQ - P(Q)Q \qquad (2.12)$$

Similarly, in each figure, the remaining surplus is producer surplus PS, reflecting that part of the total surplus that accrues to firms. Again, assuming that all sales occur at the same price, the producer surplus is defined as the total revenue $P(Q)Q$ less the area below the cost curve. Here, the formal definition is

$$PS(Q) = P(Q)Q - \int_0^Q f(Q)\, dQ \qquad (2.13)$$

The maximum total surplus is achieved at the intersection of the demand and competitive supply (aggregate marginal cost) curves. To produce beyond this amount would add more in costs than it does in consumer value, and so reduce the total surplus. Indeed, such transactions would not occur voluntarily. Either consumers or producers would have to

---

Reality Checkpoint

Hung Up On Monopoly

It is not always easy to find examples of the classic monopoly behavior described in economics textbooks. However, Tyco International's control of the plastic hanger market in the late 1990s may have come pretty close. Retail firms such as J. C. Penney and K-Mart use only plastic hangers to display their clothing goods. Starting in about 1994, Tyco used mergers and acquisitions of rival firms to gain control of 70 to 80 percent of the market for plastic hangers. In a number of geographic regions, Tyco became the only plastic hanger firm available. In 1996, Tyco acquired a Michigan-based hanger firm, Batts, that was one of the largest suppliers to the Midwest region. Immediately thereafter, Tyco raised prices by 10 percent to all its customers. Some clients grumbled, but most accepted the higher prices. Others, though, such as K-Mart and VF (makers of Lee and Wrangler jeans), informed

Tyco that they had an alternative hanger supplier, namely, a company called WAF. For a brief moment, Tyco appeared to have backed off raising the price. Yet the firm's underlying strategy soon became clear. In the fall of 1999, Tyco bought the WAF Corporation. Within a few months, it not only raised prices to all its customers again, but this time, it also added in a new delivery charge. Tyco also pursued an aggressive repurchase program so as to corner the market on used hangers. If it did not control the supply of this alternative to new hangers, Tyco would have faced increasing difficulty in charging a high price.

See M. Maremont, "Lion's Share: For Plastic Hangers You Almost Need To Go To Tyco International," *Wall Street Journal* (15 February 2000), p. A1.

---

be compelled (or subsidized) into making these additional exchanges. Likewise, to produce less than the amount Q^C forfeits some surplus that could have been earned, either by consumers or producers (or both).

The inefficiency of the monopoly outcome is now apparent. Because the monopoly firm sets a price above marginal cost, the equilibrium output level is reduced below the competitive level Q^C to the lower amount Q^M. As just noted, this results in a reduction of the total surplus by the amount *WL*. This reduction or welfare loss is often called the *deadweight loss of monopoly*. It reflects the cost of resource misallocation, as resources that could have generated additional value as indicated by the demand curve now flow to other industries, where they are presumed to earn their opportunity cost as indicated by f(Q). Formally, the value of this welfare loss is

$$WL = \int_{Q^M}^{Q^C} \left[P(Q) - f(Q) \right] dQ \qquad (2.14)$$

2.2 INTERTEMPORAL CONSIDERATIONS AND CONSTRAINTS ON MONOPOLY POWER

So far, our analysis has ignored time considerations, in that we have ignored the fact that firms operate for more than one period. In particular, our assumption that firms seek to maximize the difference between the current period's revenue and costs, or current profit, is strictly valid only if time is comprised of disjointed periods, such that actions today have no consequences for outcomes later. While some actions may be of this nature, this will not generally be the case. Indeed, there will be a number of settings in which we wish to investigate a firm's decision to incur a cost today in return for additional profit at a later time. Hence, we must have some way of comparing profits and costs at different points in time if we are to provide a useful analysis of the strategic interaction among firms over a number of periods.

In order to understand how firms make decisions in which the costs and benefits are experienced not just in one period but, instead, over time, we borrow some insights from financial markets in which the transactions trading current for future income are explicit. An investor who purchases a share of Microsoft stock or who buys a government bond is giving up funds that could be used to purchase goods now. However, that share of stock or bond gives the investor a claim to income—dividends or interest plus any capital gains—received at a future date. Prices in these markets are thus explicitly intertemporal values. Hence, we can use the techniques of those markets to evaluate similar trades of current versus future profit.

The key technique that we borrow from financial markets is the notion of present value or discounting. To understand the concept of discounting, imagine that one deposits $1,000 in a bank that pays 3 percent interest per year. Then in one year, the $1,000 will have grown to $1,030 principal plus interest. The same would be true, of course, if one instead bought 100 share of XYZ Corporation for $10, collected 30 cents per share in dividends one year later, and then sold the shares off again at a price of $10 per share. In each of these cases, $1,000 today is exchanged for $1,030 one year later. In other words, the price of a claim to $1,030 paid a year from now is $1,000 today. If instead the interest rate paid on deposits had been 5 percent, or had the stock paid 50 cents per share in dividends, the $1,000 paid today would buy $1,050 a year from now. In general, if we denote the interest rate as r, then we have that $1,000 today exchanges for $(1+r)$ times $1,000 in one year. More generally, an initial amount Y trades for $(1+r)Y$ paid in 12 months.

Notice that in each of the transactions just described, the promised (with certainty) receipt of $1,050 in the future is worth less than $1,050 today. To be precise, it is worth $1,050/(1+r)$ today. More generally, the value of a piece of paper (e.g., a loan contract or share of stock) promising its owner a payment of Z in one period is just $Z/(1+r)$. The term $1/(1+r)$ is typically referred to as the *discount factor* and is often presented just as R. In other words, $R = 1/(1+r)$. Because Z dollars of income received one period from now is valued less than Z dollars now, we say the future amount is discounted. This has nothing to do with inflation and any possible cheapening of the currency over time. It simply reflects the fact that individuals prefer to have their consumption now and have to be paid a premium—an interest rate return—in order to be persuaded to wait.

It is easy to extend our analysis to the case of two periods. If, as in our original example, one deposits $1,000 loan at 3 percent interest for two years, then after 12 months one will have accumulated $1,030. If this is then reinvested for a second year, again at 3 percent interest, then after another 12 months one will have $1,030(1.03) = $1,060.90$. Hence, the price for a claim of $1,060.90 to be received in two years' time is can be alternatively expressed as $1,060.90/(1.03)^2 = $1,000$. More generally, an investment of Y today will yield $Y(1+r)^2$ or YR^{-2} in two years. By extension, a loan of Y dollars for t years will yield an amount of $Y(1+r)^t$ or YR^{-t} when it matures t years from now. By inversion, the value Y today (or what we will now refer to as the present value PV) of Z dollars not received until t periods into the future is $R^t Z$.

The only remaining question is how to value a claim that provides different amounts at different dates in the future. For example, consider an investment that will, after completion in one year, generate Z_1 in net revenue; Z_2 in net revenue two years from now; Z_3 three years from now, and so on. The present value of Z_1 in one period is RZ_1. Similarly, the present value of the Z_2 to be received in two periods is $R^2 Z_2$. Continuing in this manner then reveals that the present value PV of this entire stream of payments received at different dates extending T periods into the future is

$$PV = RZ_1 + R^2 Z_2 + R^3 Z_3 + \cdots + R^T Z^T = \sum_{t=1}^{T} R^t Z_t \qquad (2.15)$$

In all of the foregoing, time has been treated as a discrete variable in which units occur in noninfinitesimal amounts ($t = 1, 2, \ldots T$) and the compounding happens just once per period. We may prefer in some instances to treat time as a continuous variable in which compounding happens continuously. To see how this changes matters, we start by supposing that although the interest rate quoted per period is still r, it is compounded m times per period. This means that within a single period, there are m subperiods. Over each such subperiod, the interest earned is r/m and this compounds m times per period. Over t full periods then, there will be mt subperiods and also mt compoundings. We therefore have that, starting with Y dollars, the future value Z in t periods will be

$$Z = Y \left(1 + \frac{r}{m}\right)^{mt} \qquad (2.16)$$

We may approach continuous compounding by letting m grow very large. In that case, we may write:

$$Z = Y e^{rt} \qquad (2.17)$$

making use of the fact that: $\lim_{t \to \infty} \left(1 + \frac{r}{m}\right)^m = e^r$. It follows that the value today of Z dollars received t periods in the future when time is treated continuously is $Y = Z e^{-rt}$. The continuous analogy to equation (2.15) is then

$$PV = \int_0^T e^{-rt} Z(t)\, dt \qquad (2.18)$$

An important special case of both equations (2.15) and (2.18) arises when the payment received in each period Z_t or $Z(t)$ is the same and equal to $\bar{Z}$ and the terminal period T approaches infinity. In that case, both equations simplify to the same expression, namely:[1]

$$PV = \frac{\bar{Z}}{r} \qquad (2.19)$$

---

[1]   Note that the summation in (2.15) starts with period $t = 1$, while the lower limit of the integral in (2.18) is $t = 0$. There is no conflict. As time becomes continuous, the interval between compoundings grows shorter and shorter, and the limit approaches 0, so that interval 1 is arbitrarily close in time to the starting time.

Thus, if the interest rate r were 3 percent, a promise to pay a constant \$30 forever starting one year from now would have a present value of $PV = \$30/0.03 = \$1,000$. Note that for all present value formulas, an increase in the interest rate r implies a decrease in the present value of any given future income stream.

2.2.1 Time and the Evolution of Industry Structure

Considerations of time allow us to introduce some potential constraints on the exercise of monopoly power and, consequently, on the amount of welfare loss that accompanies such power. One such mechanism reflects the dynamics of industrial structure. In our textbook analysis above, we simply assumed that the market had either a competitive or monopoly structure. We did not ask how that structure was achieved or whether it is stable. In this sense, the analysis is short-run in character. This is not to say that it is inaccurate. The welfare loss associated with monopoly pricing is real, but there may be some question as to whether it will be long-lasting. Whether or not this is the case depends in part on whether the economic profit or surplus that the monopoly firm earns will attract entry and competition over time.

A sensible requirement for a long-run equilibrium is that there is no incentive for the industry structure to change. In other words, there should be no incentive for any firm to exit or enter the industry. There are many ways to impose this condition. A common one, however, is to assume that no firm could raise its profit either by entering or exiting.[2] In the case of entry by a new firm, this condition implies that total revenue Pq_i after entry is less than total cost $C(q_i)$ or, equivalently, that firms enter so long as the post-entry price covers their average cost.

We will return to a more complete discussion of average (and marginal) cost again in Chapter 3, when we discuss the production technology and its implications for the firm's costs more completely. For now, we simply note that imposing the long-run equilibrium competition that price is less than average cost for any new entrant provides a way to determine the equilibrium structure of the industry. To the extent that that structure has more than one firm in it—that is, to the extent that the market permits entry by rivals over time—the ability of a firm that is currently a monopoly to sustain its position is reduced. Indeed, the threat of such entry may induce an incumbent monopolist to reduce price now even before entry. This in fact is the fundamental idea behind the idea of contestable markets.[3]

At the same time, it is well to recognize that a firm with monopoly power may be able to take actions that induce the exit of rivals over time and that push the evolution of market structure toward the monopoly pole. In short, market structure at any point in time may not be an accurate gauge of the intensity of competition in that industry. We also note that, because both entry and entry deterrence typically require that a cost be incurred today in return for higher profits in the future, analysis of these issues inevitably involves comparison of profits at different points of time and the use of the discounting techniques just discussed.

---

[2]   A nearly equivalent statement of equilibrium structure is that each firm within the industry earns non-negative profits (and so have no incentive to leave), while any firm not in the industry would earn nonpositive profit if it entered (and so has no incentive to do so).

[3]   See, for example, Baumol, Panzar, and Willig (1982).

Reality Checkpoint

Piracy on the High (Air)waves: Discounting, Monopoly Power, and Public Policy

In the United States, direct satellite television is largely provided by two services, Direct TV and Dish Network. Subscribers to these services pay between $20 and $80 per month, depending on the package of TV programs they wish to view. In return, they get a satellite dish, receiver, and decoder that permits them to view the programming in as many as four rooms in their house. In recent years, the number of satellite TV subscribers has grown rapidly to something on the order of 20 million. Yet even with this growth, satellite TV still has only about a third of the subscribers that its competitor, cable TV.

However, there is one category of subscribers in which satellite TV does outperform cable. This is the category of illegal, nonpaying subscribers. The satellite TV firms have some idea as to how many dishes have been sold and installed over the years. Their estimate leaves them with about 1 to 3 million more dishes in place than actually subscribed to satellite services. The firms reckon that at least half of these represent users who obtain the service illegally by tapping into the satellite transmission.

To engage in such theft, the would-be airwaves pirate needs the basic hardware equipment—the dish and receiver—and also a smart card that tells the receiver what programs to decode. Anyone can buy such a smart card —new or used—on eBay.com and other sites. This is where the pirates enter the picture. A number of firms buy the smart card, then use hackers to break the code and write a script that tells the receiver to unscramble everything. Some illicit firms then simply sell the cards. Others sell the script that reprograms the card.

Of course, the satellite firms are aware of all this. They therefore periodically send out an Electronic Counter Measure (ECM) signal that puts out a new code and/or corrupts unauthorized cards. However, the best satellite pirates have become quite good at detecting when an ECM is coming and quickly write new scripts that restore the cards' operating ability.

How much are these illegal services worth? Consumers who subscribe to Direct TV or the Dish Network might expect to pay something like $65 per month for the complete package that includes all the channels of these networks. This typically includes the hardware, which is "rented" for free. Assume that the typical consumer has a current residence and therefore satellite TV horizon of five years. Then with an annual interest rate of 4 percent (compounded monthly), this implies a present value of about $3,565 for complete and legitimate satellite service over this time span. Illegal users pay about $225 to acquire their own hardware. They also pay about $25 to subscribe to the hacker services that provide them with updated scripts to keep their cards working. This works to a present value of just under $1,600, implying a savings of $1,965. However, illegal users do take some risks. Recently, the satellite firms have cracked down on the pirate companies and, in the process, obtained the lists of their customers. Those customers face very large potential fines. Typically, the satellite firms offer those caught the option of paying $5,000 to avoid further legal charges. Yet even with all their best efforts, the satellite firms reckon that the typical illicit consumer has at most a one-in-three chance of being caught and paying that fine. Thus, the expected value of the fine is $5,000/3 = $1,667. If it takes two years on average to catch the thief, then the present value of the fine—again, assuming a 4 percent annual interest rate—is $1,540. Hence, an educated guess of the total expected cost to the illicit satellite user in present value terms is $1,600 + $1,667 = $3,267. Including the risk of getting caught has reduced the savings to $298, a small but perhaps nontrivial amount. Even in a black market, consumers earn some surplus.

Source: D. Lieberman "Millions of Pirates Are Plundering Satellite TV," *USA Today* (2 December 2004), p. C1.

2.2.2   Durable Goods and the Coase Conjecture

A second way in which attention to time considerations may reveal a constraint on monopoly power arises in connection with durable goods. Unlike, say, food, many goods such as household appliances and automobiles last a number of years. In turn, this means that a monopolist has to think carefully about the price she sets and the volume that she sells today. That supply will still be around to influence market outcomes one or two periods later. Nobel laureate Ronald Coase argued nearly 40 years ago (Coase (1972)) that this durability might greatly reduce, if not eliminate, the ability of the monopolist to set prices above the efficient level, even in the current period.

Consider the following example. The time frame has two discrete periods. A monopolist has two units of a durable good that will provide services to an owner in each of the two periods with no loss due to depreciation. There are two such potential consumers. One values the services of the good at \$50 per period; the other values these services at \$30 per period. Thus, for the high-value consumer the present value of services from the good is $50 + R\$50 = (1 + R)\$50$, while for the low-value consumer it is $(1 + R)\$30$. Because the monopolist has the two units already, marginal production cost is 0. In turn, this implies that the maximum total surplus available in this market is $(1 + R)\$80$. Any outcome that yields this surplus is efficient, but any outcome that yields a total surplus less than $(1 + R)\$80$ is inefficient.

Of course, the monopolist seeks to maximize his own surplus, not the total surplus. In doing so, he will recognize the following constraints. First, any first period price below $(1 + R)\$30$ will result in both consumers purchasing the good then, and the market process will effectively end; that is, there will be no more sales in period 2. The monopolist has nothing left to sell in the second period, and both consumers continue to enjoy the services of the good then because it is durable. Second, any price above $(1 + R)\$30$ will result in the sale of either one unit in the first period, if the price is still less than $(1 + R)\$50$, or no units if it is higher. In the first case, the monopolist will enter the second period with one unit left, which she can then sell to the low-value consumer for \$30. In the second case, she will face the choice between selling both units at a price of \$30, or one unit at a price of \$50. Clearly, the best option in this case is to sell both at \$30 for a total second-period profit of \$60.

An important implication of the foregoing analysis is that any and all second-period sales must take place at a price of \$30. There is simply no way that the monopolist can make a first-period commitment to any second-period price above this amount. Given this, we can now consider the strategy of making one first-period sale to the high-value consumer at a price of $(1 + R)\$50$ from the viewpoint of that consumer. The difficulty with this strategy is then immediately apparent. Confronted with a first-period price of $(1 + R)\$50$, the high-value consumer can either buy then—and earn 0 surplus—or defer her purchase to the second-period, knowing that the price will then be \$30 and that she will therefore earn a surplus of $R\$20$ in present-value terms. She will obviously choose the latter. It follows that the monopolist cannot hope to make a first-period sale at $(1 + R)\$50$. The fact that this implies a second-period price of \$30 makes this impossible.

What about a price below $(1 + R)\$50$ but above $(1 + R)\$30$? Consider the first-period price, $(1 + R)\$(30 + \varepsilon)$, where ε is a small positive constant. Such a price gives the high-value consumer a surplus of $(1 + R)\$(20 - \varepsilon)$. If she instead waits and purchases the good next period at \$30, she earns a surplus with present value $R\$20$. Thus, in order for the monopolist to sell to this consumer in the first period, requires that she offers a price such that

$$(1 + R)\$(20 - \varepsilon) > R\$20 \rightarrow \varepsilon \le \frac{\$20}{1 + R} \tag{2.20}$$

In other words, the maximum price that the monopolist can set in the first period if she wishes to sell just one unit is $(1 + R)\$\left(30 + \frac{\$20}{1+R}\right) = (1 + R)\$30 + \$20$.

In light of the above, we can now greatly simplify the monopolist's problem. She can either sell two units in the first-period sales at a price of $(1 + R)\$30$; or one unit in the first period at a price of $(1 + R)\$30 + \$20$ and a second unit in the following period at a price of $\$30$; or no units in the first period but both units in the second period at a price of $\$30$. The corresponding profits are shown in Table 2.1 below.

A little algebra will confirm that the first-row option in Table 2.1 gives the greatest profit in present-value terms. That is, the monopolist will maximize profit by setting a first-period price of $(1 + R)\$30$ and selling both units immediately, one to each consumer. The monopolist will then earn a surplus of $2(1 + R)\$30$. The high-value consumer will earn a surplus of $(1 + R)\$20$, while the low-value consumer will earn 0 surplus. The total surplus will thus be $2(1 + R)\$30 + (1 + R)\$20 = (1 + R)\$80$, the maximum amount possible. In other words, the durable feature of the good has constrained the monopolist to set efficient prices—prices that maximize the surplus. This is Coase's conjecture. It is the supposition that durability constrains monopoly pricing so as to eliminate any deadweight loss.

However, just as the efficacy of entry as a discipline on monopoly behavior can be weakened, so too can the impact of durability. Consider, then, how the above example would have been altered had the low-value consumer only valued the services of the durable good at $\$20$ per period or $(1 + R)\$20$ in total. In this case, it is now no longer the case that any and all second-period sales must take place at the maximum price of the low-value consumer, which is now $\$20$. If the monopolist sells no units in the first-period and enters the second-period with two units to sell, she will prefer to sell just one unit to the high-value consumer at $\$50$ rather than both units at $\$20$ apiece. It follows that the high-value consumer can no longer bargain so aggressively in the first period. She will prefer any price of $(1 + R)\$(50 - \varepsilon)$ in the first period that gives her a surplus of $(1 + R)\$\varepsilon$ to a price of $\$50$ in the second-period that gives her a surplus of 0. Thus, by making ε arbitrarily small, the monopolist can induce the high-value consumer to buy in the first period and then sell at a price of $\$20$ to the low-value consumer in the second period. Neither consumer will enjoy any surplus, while the monopolist will earn a profit of $(1 + R)\$50 + R\$20$. As can be easily verified, the maximum surplus available in this case is $(1 + R)\$70$, which is $\$20$ greater than the surplus actually realized. Here, durability has not eliminated the deadweight loss of monopoly.

Table 2.1   Price options and corresponding profit for the durable goods monopolist

First-Period Price	Second-Period Price	Present Value of Profits
$(1 + R)\$30$	NA	$2(1 + R)\$30$
$(1 + R)\$30 + \$20$	$\$30$	$(1 + R)\$30 + \$20 + R\$30$
$>(1 + R)\$50$	$\$30$	$2R\$30$

The difference in the two cases reflects the distribution of consumer valuations. In both cases, this distribution is discrete. However, the jump from one valuation to the next is more substantial in the second case. Heuristically, valuations are less continuous in that setting. This points to a generalization regarding the Coase conjecture: the more continuous the consumer valuations, the more durability constrains monopoly pricing of durable goods to be efficient. Indeed, as the distribution becomes perfectly continuous, the monopolist may be forced to set competitive prices. In general, durability will, like potential entry, impose some limits on the exploitation of monopoly power and the extent of the associated welfare loss.[4]

2.2.3   The Nonsurplus Approach to Economic Efficiency[5]

Let us return to the second example in the discussion of the Coase conjecture above in which the Coase conjecture fails. Recall that the efficient first-period price is $(1 + R)$20$ resulting in a total surplus of $(1 + R)$70$, but that the monopolist instead sets an initial price of $(1 + R)$50$ and a subsequent second-period price of $20, resulting in a deadweight loss of $20. We may ask now how matters might be different had there been 50 high-value consumers and 50 low-value ones, again assuming that the monopolist has just two units.

The first thing to note is that the total surplus now available on the market is $2(1 + R)$50$. At a first-period price of $(1 + R)$50$, two units will be sold to 2 of the 50 high-value consumers, and all of this surplus will go to the monopolist. In fact, no other price is possible. None would buy at a higher price; but at any lower price the high-value consumers would actively compete with higher bids until again the price rose to $(1 + R)$50$. Here is another case in which profit maximization by the monopolist is consistent with efficient resource allocation.

Why does this happen here? Why is it that now, despite the sizeable differences in consumer valuations between the two groups, monopoly pricing involves no deadweight loss? The answer lies in considering more deeply just what that deadweight loss of monopoly signifies. The deadweight loss of monopoly is really just the additional surplus that the monopolist could generate if she increased her output to the efficient level. The problem for the monopolist in the conventional setting (e.g., Figure 2.1(b)), is that she cannot appropriate the full value of this marginal surplus for herself. As she sells the additional output and moves down the demand curve, she sells units at a lower price. Even if she captures all the surplus on the marginal units, her net gain is less than this, because she now earns less on inframarginal units.

It is the inability of the monopolist to appropriate all the surplus generated by her production that lies at the heart of the welfare loss of monopoly. When there are 50 high-value consumers, however, and the monopolist only has two units to sell, this problem no longer exists. The monopolist can sell the efficient amount without lowering the price to any inframarginal consumer. Within the feasible range of sales, the monopolist generates $(1 + R)$50$ of surplus for each unit sold and acquires all this surplus for herself.

---

[4]   Stokey (1981) offers a formal derivation of the Coase Conjecture. See also Thepot (1998).

[5]   This section and the previous one make extensive use of the nonsurplus approach developed in Makowski and Ostroy (1995). It has had an important influence on our understanding of market participation. It also plays a central role in the business strategies advocated by Brandenburger and Nalebuff (1996).

When there are 50 high-value consumers, the monopolist's output potential is small relative to the total market. At the margin, her decision to increase or decrease sales by one unit and sell it at $(1 + R)\$50$, leaves the surplus of all other market participants unaffected. The marginal consumer earns a surplus of 0 in either case. Note that this is similar to the perfectly competitive case. There, too, each firm is sufficiently small relative to the market that it has no effect on the surplus earned by all other participants. The profit of a single competitive firm at the margin is 0, and this is precisely the same as that firm's contribution to the surplus or welfare created by market trading. The same can be true for a monopolist if it is small relative to the overall market.

The understanding that the crucial factor giving rise to inefficient outcomes is that there are market participants at the margin able to alter the surplus of other participants is known as the *nonsurplus approach to economic analysis*. For our purposes, it makes the important point that it is not the number of sellers, but rather their size relative to the market that gives rise to a welfare loss. In other words, it is not the fact that the monopolist is the only seller; it is the fact that she is large relative to the market that leads to inefficient outcomes.[6]

Summary

We have formally presented the basic microeconomic analysis of markets characterized by either perfect competition or perfect monopoly. In both cases, the goal of any firm is assumed to be to maximize profit. The necessary condition for single-period profit maximization is that the firm produces where marginal revenue equals marginal cost. Because firms in competitive markets take market price as given, price equals marginal revenue for the competitive firm. As a result, the competitive market equilibrium is one in which price is set equal to marginal cost. In turn, this implies that the competitive market equilibrium is efficient in that it maximizes the sum of producer and consumer surplus.

The pure monopoly case does not generally yield an efficient outcome. The monopoly firm understands that it can affect the market price, and this implies that marginal revenue will be less than the price for a monopoly firm. As a result, the monopolist tends to restrict output below the competitive level and set price above marginal cost. In turn, this leads to a deadweight welfare loss. Too few resources are employed in the production of the monopolized commodity, and the total surplus is not maximized. The lost surplus is typically called the *deadweight* or *welfare loss of monopoly*.

There are, however, some constraints that may reduce the ability of the monopolist to set inefficient prices. When entry is possible over time, or when the good in question is durable, or simply when the monopoly firm's feasible production is small relative to the total market demand, the welfare loss associated with monopoly power is weakened. In some cases, it may be eliminated entirely. While it is critically important to understand the welfare loss that monopoly power often brings, it is also important to recognize that there are some natural constraints on such power.

Pure competition and pure monopoly are useful concepts. Whether they are realistic equilibrium outcomes for actual markets is another question. The answer largely depends on underlying production and cost relationships. These will help determine the number of firms that can profitably compete in a market, the ease of entry, and other features that influence the intensity of market competition. We address these issues in the next chapter.

---

[6]   The nonsurplus approach is developed in Makowski and Ostroy (1995). It has had an important influence on our understanding of market participation. It also plays a central role in the business strategies advocated by Brandenburger and Nalebuff (1996).

Problems

1. Suppose that the annual demand for prescription antidepressants such as Prozac, Paxil, and Zoloft is, in inverse form, given by P = 1000 − 0.025Q. Suppose that the competitive supply curve is given by: P = 150 + 0.033Q.
    a. Calculate the equilibrium price and annual quantity of antidepressants.
    b. Calculate (i) producer surplus and (ii) consumer surplus in this competitive equilibrium.

2. Let the market demand for widgets be described by Q = 1000 − 50P. Suppose further that widgets can be produced at a constant average and marginal cost of $10 per unit.
    a. Calculate the market output and price under perfect competition and under monopoly.
    b. Define the point elasticity of demand ε_D at a particular price and quantity combination as the (negative) ratio of price to quantity times the slope of the demand curve. That is, $\varepsilon_D = -\frac{P}{Q}\frac{dQ}{dP}$. What is the elasticity of demand in the competitive equilibrium? What is the elasticity of demand in the monopoly equilibrium?
    c. Denote marginal cost as MC. Show that in the monopoly equilibrium, the following condition is satisfied: $\frac{P-MC}{P} = -\frac{1}{\varepsilon_D}$.

3. Let inverse demand be given by $P = A - Q$, where total industry output is equal to the individual output q of each of n firms. Let each firm have a cost function given by $C(q) = 0.5bq^2 + F$, where $b > 0$ and $F > 0$.
    a. Derive the profit maximizing output choice for each firm taking n as given.
    b. Derive the equilibrium price taking n as given and assuming each firm maximizes profit.
    c. Now let n be endogenous and solve for the equilibrium value of n.
    d. Solve for the long-run equilibrium values of n, P, and q for the specific case of: $A = \$100$; $b = 1$; and $F = \$50$.

4. Tyco International controlled the plastic clothes hanger market in the 1990s. Suppose that the inverse demand for hangers is given by: $P = 3 - Q/16,000$. Suppose further that the marginal cost of producing hangers is constant at $1.
    a. What is the equilibrium price and quantity of hangers if the market is competitive?
    b. What is the equilibrium price and quantity of hangers if the market is monopolized?
    c. What is the deadweight or welfare loss of monopoly in this market?

References

Baumol, W. J., J. C. Panzar, and R. D. Willig. 1982. *Contestable Markets and the Theory of Market Structure*. New York: Harcourt Brace Jovanovich.
Brandenburger, A., and B. Nalebuff. 1996. *Co-opetition*. Cambridge: Harvard University Press.
Coase, R. 1972. "Durability and Monopoly." *Journal of Law and Economics*, 15 (1972): 143–149.
Makowski, L., and J. Ostroy. 1995. "Appropriation and Efficiency: A Revision of the First Theorem of Welfare Economics." *American Economic Review*, 85 (September): 808–827.
Stokey, N., 1981. "Rational Expectations and Durable Goods Pricing." *Bell Journal of Economics*, 12 (Fall): 112–128.
Thepot, J. 1998. "A Direct Proof of the Coase Conjecture." *Journal of Mathematical Economics*, 29 (Spring): 57–66.

3

Technology and Cost Relationships

Four firms—General Mills, Kellogg, General Foods (Post), and Quaker Oats—currently account for about 80 percent of sales in the U.S. ready-to-eat breakfast cereal industry. By contrast, the largest four manufacturers of games and toys account for 35 to 45 percent of these products—less if video games are included. While there may be many reasons for this difference, one cannot help but suspect that cereal and toy manufacturers use different technological processes and that, in turn, these differences in the underlying production technology are part of the explanation. In the previous chapter, we described how the welfare cost of monopoly reflected a divergence between the price paid by consumers for a good or service and the true resource cost incurred in producing that good or service at the margin. Yet, we left unexamined how that cost is determined by the underlying production technology. We also did not examine the implications this may have for market structure. We address both of these issues here.[1]

3.1   PRODUCTION TECHNOLOGY AND COST FUNCTIONS FOR SINGLE-PRODUCT FIRMS

We regard the firm's technology to be a production relationship that describes how a given quantity of inputs is transformed into the firm's output. In this sense, we adopt a traditional neoclassical approach in which a firm is mainly envisioned as a production unit with profit maximization as its goal. In turn, this implies minimizing the cost of producing any given level of output. In employing this framework, we do not wish to suggest that alternative approaches such as those focusing on either agency theory (Jensen and Meckling 1976), transactions costs (Williamson 1981), or ownership relations (Grossman and Hart 1986) are not useful. All of these approaches include valuable insights into the question first raised explicitly by Coase (1937) regarding the nature of the firm.[2] Our choice simply reflects the fact that despite its limitations, the neoclassical approach remains insightful for our purposes. At the same time, the reader will do well to keep in mind that the

---

[1]   Panzar (1989) presents a more extended review of this topic.
[2]   See also Milgrom and Roberts (1992) and Bolton and Scharfstein (1998).

firms we model here are treated as simple, profit-maximizing production units and not as complex, organic organizations.

Consider a firm producing the quantity q of a single product according to the production function

$$q = f(x_1, x_2, \ldots, x_k) \tag{3.1}$$

This function specifies the quantity q that the firm produces from using k different inputs at levels x_1 for the first input, x_2 for the second input, and so on through the kth input, of which x_k is used. The technology is reflected in the precise form of the function, $f()$. For example, a commonly used production function is the Cobb-Douglas relation in which there are just two inputs, capital x_1, and labor x_2, written as follows:

$$q = x_1^\alpha x_2^\beta \tag{3.2}$$

where α and β are both positive.

The firm chooses output q and associated inputs $x_1, x_2, \ldots, x_k$ to maximize profits. This implies that for any specific output q, the firm will wish to choose the level of each input $x_1, x_2, \ldots, x_k$, so as to minimize the total cost of producing that output given the prices $w_1, w_2, \ldots, w_k$ of the k inputs, the nature of the production relation linking inputs to the output level q. Any fixed cost F unrelated to production will be part of the total cost the firm incurs, but will not affect the firm's variable input decision. These are chosen to solve the problem:

$$\underset{x_i}{\text{Minimize}} \ \text{Total Cost} = \sum_{i=1}^{k} w_i x_i + F \tag{3.3}$$

subject to the constraint $f(x_1, x_2, \ldots, x_k) = q$.

To illustrate, we again turn to the Cobb-Douglas example of equation (3.2). Denote by w_1 the rental cost of the capital input and by w_2 the wage cost of the labor input. The firm's problem then becomes

$$\text{Minimize: } rx_1 + wx_2 + F; \text{ subject to } q = x_1^\alpha x_2^\beta. \tag{3.4}$$

The associated Lagrangian function is

$$L = w_1 x_1 + w_2 x_2 + \lambda(q - x_1^\alpha x_2^\beta) + F \tag{3.5}$$

and the necessary first order conditions are

(a) $\dfrac{\partial L}{\partial x_1} = w_1 - \lambda \alpha x_1^{\alpha-1} x_2^\beta = 0 \Rightarrow w_1 x_1 = \lambda \alpha q$

(b) $\dfrac{\partial L}{\partial x_2} = w_2 - \lambda \beta x_1^\alpha x_2^{\beta-1} = 0 \Rightarrow w_1 x_2 = \lambda \beta q$

(c) $\dfrac{\partial L}{\partial \lambda} = q - x_1^\alpha x_2^{\beta-1} = 0$ $\hfill (3.6)$

From (3.6a) and (3.6b), we have

$$w_1 x_1 + w_2 x_2 = \lambda(\alpha + \beta)q \tag{3.7}$$

which gives an expression for total costs. However, these same two equations also imply that

(a) $\left(\dfrac{w_1 x_1}{\alpha}\right)^{\alpha} = \lambda^{\alpha} q^{\alpha}$

(b) $\left(\dfrac{w_2 x_2}{\beta}\right)^{\beta} = \lambda^{\beta} q^{\beta}$ $\tag{3.8}$

which together imply that

$$\lambda = \left(\frac{w_1}{\alpha}\right)^{\frac{\alpha}{\alpha+\beta}} \left(\frac{w_2}{\beta}\right)^{\frac{\beta}{\alpha+\beta}} q^{\frac{1}{\alpha+\beta} - 1} \tag{3.9}$$

Substituting the expression for λ from (3.9) into (3.7) then yields

$$\text{Total Cost} = C(w_1, w_2, q) = w_1 x_1 + w_2 x_2 + F$$

$$= \left(\frac{w_1}{\alpha}\right)^{\frac{\alpha}{\alpha+\beta}} \left(\frac{w_2}{\beta}\right)^{\frac{\beta}{\alpha+\beta}} (\alpha + \beta) q^{\frac{1}{\alpha+\beta}} + F \tag{3.10}$$

Equation (3.10) is the Cobb-Douglas cost function allowing for any fixed cost F. It is a specific example of all cost functions in that it expresses total production cost as a function of total output q, given the input prices and the production parameters. At this juncture, one feature of the cost function in equation (3.10) deserves mention. This is that, for any positive values of α and β, the exponents on the input prices sum to unity. Formally, we say that costs are homogeneous of degree 1 in input prices. This is a feature we expect to characterize all cost functions. Since the choice of inputs depends on relative prices, a general increase that raises all input prices by the same proportionate amount but leaves relative prices unchanged will not alter the least-cost combination of inputs needed to produce a given output q. Hence, the only effect of such a rise in prices will be to raise the cost of producing q by the same proportionate amount.

Solving (3.10) for different levels of output q, we obtain the minimum cost of each possible production level per unit of time. This relationship between costs and output is what is described by the cost function for the firm. For the remainder of this section, we take the input prices w_1 and w_2 as given, and therefore suppress their representation in the analysis. Hence, we write the cost function simply as $C(q)$. From this function, we derive two key cost concepts: average or unit cost and marginal cost.

Average cost: The firm's average cost is simply a measure of the expenditure per unit of production and is given by total cost divided by total output. This cost measure does depend on output; hence, its algebraic representation is $AC(q)$. Formally, $AC(q) = C(q)/q$. We may also decompose average cost into its fixed and variable components. Average fixed cost is simply total fixed cost per unit of output or F/q. Average variable cost $AVC(q)$ is, similarly, just the total variable cost per unit of output, $[C(q)-F]/q$. Thus, in the Cobb-Douglas case of (3.10), we have

$$(a)\ AC(q) = \frac{(w_1 x_1 + w_2 x_2) + F}{q} = \left(\frac{w_1}{\alpha}\right)^{\frac{\alpha}{\alpha+\beta}} \left(\frac{w_2}{\beta}\right)^{\frac{\beta}{\alpha+\beta}} (\alpha+\beta)q^{\frac{1}{\alpha+\beta}-1} + \frac{F}{q}$$

$$(b)\ AVC(q) = \frac{(w_1 x_1 + w_2 x_2)}{q} = \left(\frac{w_1}{\alpha}\right)^{\frac{\alpha}{\alpha+\beta}} \left(\frac{w_2}{\beta}\right)^{\frac{\beta}{\alpha+\beta}} (\alpha+\beta)q^{\frac{1}{\alpha+\beta}-1}$$

$$(c)\ AFC(q) = \frac{F}{q} \tag{3.11}$$

Marginal cost: The firm's marginal cost $MC(q)$ is defined as change in total cost resulting from a small change in output—that is, a change at the margin. This is equivalent to saying that marginal cost is the derivative of the cost function with respect to q. Hence, $MC(q) = dC(q)/dq$. Again, referring to our specific Cobb-Douglas case of (3.10), we have:

$$MC(q) = \frac{dC(q)}{dq} = \left(\frac{w_1}{\alpha}\right)^{\frac{\alpha}{\alpha+\beta}} \left(\frac{w_2}{\beta}\right)^{\frac{\beta}{\alpha+\beta}} q^{\frac{1}{\alpha+\beta}-1} \tag{3.12}$$

An important relationship between average cost and marginal cost is revealed by differentiating the average cost function with respect to q. In general, we have

$$\frac{dAC(q)}{dq} = \frac{d[C(q)/q]}{dq} = \frac{qC'(q) - C(q)}{q^2} = \frac{q[MC(q) - AC(q)]}{q^2} \tag{3.13}$$

From this it follows that average cost will be falling when marginal cost is less than average cost and rising when marginal cost exceeds average cost. It then also follows that average cost and marginal cost must be equal at the minimum average cost. You are encouraged to prove this to yourself using the specific Cobb-Douglas cost function presented here. An illustrative conventional case is shown in Figure 3.1.

We now add a third key cost concept—*sunk cost*. Like fixed cost, sunk cost is a cost that is unrelated to output. However, unlike fixed costs, which are incurred every period, sunk cost is a cost that is incurred just once—typically as a prerequisite for entry. For example, a doctor will need to make a one-time expense to acquire a license to operate. Similarly, a firm may need to do some initial market and product research or install highly specialized equipment before it enters a market. The cost of the license, the research expenditures, and the expenditures on specialized assets are likely to be unrelated to subsequent output, so in this sense they are fixed. More importantly, should the doctor or firm subsequently decide to close down, only part if any of these specialized expenditures will likely be recoverable. It is difficult to sell the license to another doctor. Similarly, the research expenditures are unrecoverable on exit. It will not be possible to sell the specialized assets later for anything like their initial acquisition costs. Consideration of sunk costs typically introduces a temporal dimension to the firm's decision. At the moment just prior to the expenditure, these costs are still a choice. However, looking back at a later date after the costs have been incurred, they are sunk in that they are unrecoverable at that time.

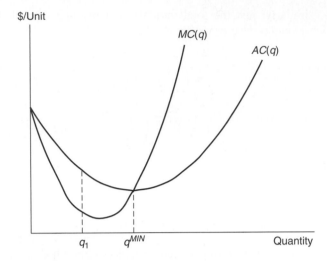

Figure 3.1   Average and marginal cost
Marginal cost below average cost implies that average cost is falling. Marginal cost above average cost implies that average cost is rising. Marginal cost equals average cost when average cost is minimized.

3.1.1   Cost Variables and Output Decisions

As discussed in Chapter 2, profit maximization in a single period of time requires that the firm produce where marginal revenue equals marginal cost. Thus, with one important caveat, marginal cost is the relevant cost concept to determine how much the firm should produce. That caveat is that marginal cost is important for determining how much to produce *given* that the firm is going to produce any output at all.

Consider for example the average cost function of equation (3.11a) and the associated marginal cost function of equation (3.12). Inspection of the latter reveals that if $\alpha + \beta < 1$, marginal cost rises continuously with q. It is also apparent that in this case, we may write

$$AC(q) = (\alpha + \beta)MC(q) + F/q \tag{3.14}$$

For low values of q, the second term on the right-hand side of (3.14) will dominate, and $AC(q)$ will be greater than marginal cost. Hence, equation (3.14) implies that average cost will be falling in this range of production. Suppose then that demand is sufficiently weak that equating marginal cost to marginal revenue may result in price below average cost as in Figure 3.2. This implies a loss on every unit that the firm sells, and is not sustainable in the long run. The firm will eventually shut down in this case and produce no output as soon as it is possible to terminate the fixed cost payment.[3] Such a shutdown will happen even sooner though if price is below average *variable* cost. If the optimal output (q^* in Figure 3.2) yields a price below average variable cost, the firm will shut down immediately, as continuing to operate increases the loss beyond what it would be at a 0 production level, where only the fixed cost would remain.

---

[3]   This raises the question of what is ultimately meant by fixed cost. We describe the cost F as fixed in the sense that it is a given amount that must be paid while the firm is in existence, but that is unrelated to the output level. We will make use of cost relations that include F in many of the models of this text.

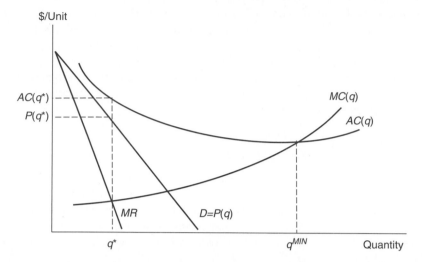

Figure 3.2   Weak demand may mean that producing where MR = MC implies a price below average cost

Consideration of price and average cost also allows us to identify the role played by sunk cost in the firm's decision making. Again, profit per unit in any period is simply price less average cost, $P-AC(q)$. Total profit in any period is just the profit per unit times the number of units, $[P-AC(q)]q$. Before entering an industry, a firm must expect at least to break even. If entry incurs a sunk cost such as a licensing fee or research expense, then the firm will have to believe that it will earn enough profit in subsequent periods to cover that initial sunk cost. Otherwise, it will not enter the market. Let the sunk entry cost be denoted by K. Then, treating time as a continuous variable, the discounting techniques of Chapter 2 require that

$$\int_0^T [P - AC(q)]q(t)e^{-rt}\, dt - K \geq 0 \tag{3.15}$$

for entry to occur. That is, the discounted present value of the expected future profits must be at least as great as the sunk cost of entry. Note though, that once it has entered, the sunk cost is no longer relevant. Once the entry decision has been made and the sunk cost incurred, the best that the firm can do is to follow the prescription above: produce where marginal revenue equals marginal cost so long as (in the short run) price is greater than average variable cost; otherwise shut down. In the long run: produce where marginal revenue equals marginal cost so long as price is greater than average cost; otherwise exit. Sunk entry costs affect the entry decision—not the decision on how much to produce after entry has occurred nor the decision to exit.

3.1.2   Scale Economies, Sunk Costs, and Market Structure

As we noted in our discussion of equation (3.13) above, average cost will fall as output increases when it exceeds marginal cost, but rise when it is less than marginal cost. When average cost declines with output, scale economies exist. The firm's cost per unit declines as it produces more. When average cost rises with output, there are scale diseconomies. Hence, returning to the case illustrated in Figure 3.1, we find that there are scale economies up to production level q^{MIN}, but scale diseconomies beyond that point.

As Figure 3.1 illustrates, the relation between $AC(q)$ and $MC(q)$ suggests a measure of the degree of scale economies or diseconomies. Let us denote such a measure as S. Then a natural way to calculate S is

$$S = AC(q)/MC(q) = \frac{C(q)/q}{dC(q)/dq} = \frac{1}{\eta} \tag{3.16}$$

By this measure, $S > 1$ implies the presence of scale economies, and $S < 1$ implies the presence of scale diseconomies. Note that this is equivalent to defining S as the inverse of the elasticity η of costs with respect to output, where $\eta = \partial \ln C(w_1, w_2, q)/\partial \ln q$. We define the *minimum efficient scale of operations* as the lowest level of output at which economies of scale are exhausted or, in other words, at which $S = 1$. In Figure 3.1, minimum efficient scale is q^{MIN}.

It is easy to see that the presence of fixed costs will tend to give rise to scale economies, since average fixed cost—a component of average total cost—definitely declines as output increases. This is commonly known as "spreading the overhead." The provision of freight rail service between Omaha and Lincoln, Nebraska, for example, requires 60 miles of track and payment of the (implicit) associated rental cost, regardless of the number of trains per day a freight railroad runs on that track. Hence, that portion of average total cost will fall as the railroad operator carries more tons per day.

Yet, a close look at the average cost function for the Cobb-Douglas case of equation (3.11a) will reveal that had $\alpha + \beta > 1$, scale economies would have been present even if there were no fixed costs. Similarly, even with positive fixed costs, the range for which scale economies do exist when $\alpha + \beta < 1$ will be very small if the sum of these two parameters is also small. In short, the nature of the production technology can give rise to important scale effects—economies or diseconomies.

If scale economies are global then the market is a natural monopoly. The term "natural" here is meant to reflect the implication that monopoly is an (almost) inevitable outcome for this market because it is cheaper in such cases for a single firm to supply the entire market than for two or more firms to do so. For example, the least expensive way to produce the quantity q_1 in Figure 3.1 is to have one firm produce the entire amount. If instead, two firms divide this production equally, so that each produces an output $q_i = q_1/2$, each of these two firms will have higher average cost than would the single firm producing q^E.

When scale economies are large relative to the market, only a few firms will be active in the market. In fact, efficiency may require that all the production be done in one firm, even if the scale economies are not global but simply quite large. In general, large scale economies will tend to result in concentrated markets.

Sunk entry costs also play a role in influencing market structure and one that is conceptually similar to the role of scale economies. As noted above however, consideration of sunk costs typically requires explicit consideration of the timing of decisions. In the case of sunk entry costs, the decision to enter (and thereby sink the costs) can only be made with a view to the profits made at a later date after the firm has entered the market.

To take a fairly simple example, imagine a market with an iso-elastic market demand curve with an elasticity everywhere of $\varepsilon = 1$. Imagine further that each firm has a Cobb-Douglas production function as described above in which $\alpha + \beta = 1$, and that there are

Reality Checkpoint
Hotel Phone Costs May Be Fixed

Business travelers stopping at the Hampton Inn in Salt Lake City often find themselves powering down their cell phones and just relying on their room phone, even though this is far more expensive. At some hotels, the cost of using the in-room phone can run as high $2 per minute or even more for domestic calls and 10 or more times that amount for international calls. This compares with a near 0 charge for cell phone calls. So, why does anyone use a hotel room phone?

The main answer is that cell phones do not always work. Reception can be poor, and getting cell phone service simply may not be possible. For many travelers, the need to be in phone contact with others is such that they are willing to pay the high prices of hotel room phones. In turn, those high prices are necessary in part because of the fixed costs the hotels incur whether the phone is use a lot, a little, or not at all. These costs include a fixed rental fee for each line, the expense of employing operators, and the cost of maintaining equipment, all of which is incurred regardless of the intensity with which room phones are used. The hotels charge a hefty fee, well above marginal cost, to earn those fixed costs back.

Unfortunately for the hotels, the advent of cell phones has sharply cut into their room phone revenue. In fact, operating profits per room phone per year in the United States fell from $644 in 2000 to $152 in 2004. This loss in revenue and profit

may have led some hotels to go to rather unusual lengths to beat the cell phone competition. In 2003, the Scottish newspaper, the *Daily Record*, reported evidence that a local firm, Electron Electrical Engineering Services, was selling cell phone jamming devices to hotels and bed-and-breakfast establishments for between $135 and $200 apiece. These devices have the ability to block cell phone reception without the cell phone customer realizing it. All the customer will see is a message that "service is unavailable" in the location from which they are calling. Loreen Haim-Cayzer, the director of marketing and sales for Netline Communications Technologies in Tel Aviv, also acknowledged that her company had sold hundreds of cellphone jammers to hotels around the world, though none in the United States as far as she knew.

Of course, savvy phone users have another option. They can carry a phone card for use whenever their cell phone cannot get a signal. Those who do not, however, will have to rely on the in-room phone . . . and pay the associated fees. These customers may perhaps be forgiven, then, if they suspect that it is more than the costs of such phones that's fixed.

Source: C. Elliot, "Mystery of the Cell Phone that Doesn't Work at the Hotel." *New York Times* (7 September 2004), p. C8; and C. Page, "Mobile Phones Jam Scam." *The Daily Record* (26 August 2003), p. 1.

no fixed costs. It is then readily apparent from equations (3.11) and (3.12) that average cost and marginal cost are identical ($S = 1$) and constant. Denote this constant unit cost as c.

If there are n firms in the market, total output Q is n times the output of each firm q_i, i.e., $Q = nq_i$. Total expenditure E in the market is then $PQ = Pnq_i$. The iso-elasticity of the demand curve implies that this total expenditure is constant. Hence, we may write:

$$q_i = E/nP \qquad (3.17)$$

Now the absolute gap between price and marginal cost is $P - c$. Unfortunately, this is not in itself a terribly useful measure, because it is very dependent on scale. For computer chips, P and c might be $400 and $350, respectively, while for automobiles they might be $24,000 and $21,000, respectively. The automobile margin of $3,000 is far larger than the chip margin of $50, but this just reflects the fact that an automobile is a much bigger ticket item per unit. To purge this scale effect, we need to use a proportional rather than an absolute measure of the price-marginal cost disparity. In this regard, a commonly used proportional measure is the so-called Lerner Index given by $(P - c)/P$. In both the chip and auto examples, this index is equal to 0.125 in each case indicating the same proportional price-cost distortion in each case.

As discussed in Chapter 2, we expect that $P = c$ in perfectly competitive industries, but that P rises above c with monopoly power. For convenience, let us here assume an explicit relationship that captures this effect of increased competition on the difference between P and c. Specifically, let us make the plausible supposition that the Lerner Index just defined declines systematically as more firms compete in the market, as described by the following relation:

$$(P - c)/P = An^{-\sigma} \tag{3.18}$$

where A and σ are both arbitrary positive constants.

Each firm's profit π_i in any given period market period is: $(P - c)q_i$. Combining equations (3.17) and (3.18) reveals that this per period profit may be expressed as:

$$\pi_i = (P - c)q_i = EAn^{-(1+\sigma)} \tag{3.19}$$

Again treating time as a continuous variable and using the discounting techniques of Chapter 2, we then have that over the infinite horizon of the representative firm, the present value $PV(\pi_i)$ of this profit stream is

$$PV(\pi_i) = \int_0^\infty [EAn^{-(1+\sigma)}]e^{-rt} \, dt = \frac{EAn^{-(1+\sigma)}}{r} \tag{3.20}$$

Let K be the sunk cost associated with participating in the market. We assume that firms will enter the market until they no longer earn sufficient profit to cover this sunk cost. Hence, it must be the case that firms will enter until the right-hand-side of equation (3.20) just equals the sunk expense K. Imposing this equality and solving for the equilibrium number of firms n^e, we have

$$n^e = \left[\frac{EA}{rK}\right]^{\frac{1}{1+\sigma}} \tag{3.21}$$

Given the other parameters, higher sunk cost means fewer firms and greater concentration. Yet market size is important, too. Holding sunk cost constant, an industry will be less concentrated as its size measured by total sales rises. Of course, for a given minimum efficient scale concentration will also decline as market size grows. Thus, there is some generality to the notion that larger markets will be less concentrated.

A natural test of the foregoing intuitive relation between market structure and size might be found by looking at local markets. Some direct evidence of precisely this sort has been provided by Bresnahan and Reiss (1991). They gathered data on a number of professions and services from over 200 towns scattered across the western United States. They find that a town of about 800 or 900 will support just one doctor. As the town grows to a population of roughly 3,500, a second doctor will typically enter. It takes a town of over 9,000 people to generate an industry of five doctors. The same positive relationship between market size and the number of firms is also found in other professions. For tire dealers, for example, Bresnahan and Reiss find that a town of only 500 people is needed to support one tire dealer and that five tire dealers can operate when the town reaches a population of 6,000. The smaller market requirements needed to support a given number of tire dealers instead of doctors probably reflects, among other things, the fact that doctors have higher fixed and sunk costs than do the tire dealers.

Sutton (1991, 2001) however, provides an important qualification to the idea that concentration will decline with the size of the market—as, for example, implied by equation (4.4). He notes that such a relationship does not appear to hold in a number of industries, particularly in industries that compete heavily using either advertising, such as processed foods, or R&D, such as pharmaceuticals. Sutton argues that these expenditures are not only sunk but also endogenous. They are sunk in that once the expenditures for a promotional campaign or product design have been incurred, they cannot be recovered. They are endogenous in that in these kinds of industries, sunk cost K is not a fixed amount but, in fact, increases as the market size grows.

The logic of the Sutton argument can be seen by focusing on the sunk entry cost term in equation (3.21). Rather than treat this as sunk cost as a given lump sum, it may be more appropriate to let this term increase with the margin of price over marginal cost as well as market size. In turn, this suggestion may be implemented by linking the necessary amount of sunk cost to both the A term (which rises with the price cost margin) and the E term (reflecting market size as measured by total expenditure). For our purposes, a simple linear relation is all that is needed to illustrate the point. Accordingly, let us assume that the sunk-cost parameter K in equation (3.21) is linearly related to these parameters as follows:

$$K = K_0 + \beta(AE) \tag{3.22}$$

If this is the case, then equation (3.21) now becomes:

$$n^e = \left[\frac{1}{r\left(\frac{K_0}{AE} + \beta\right)} \right]^{\frac{1}{1+\sigma}} \tag{3.23}$$

Equation (3.23) says that the equilibrium number of firms in the industry will grow as market size AE grows, but that this process has an asymptotic limit. Specifically, the number of firms will never exceed $(1/r\beta)^{1/(1+\sigma)}$ no matter how large the market gets. For example, suppose that $\sigma = 1, r = 0.1$ and $\beta = 0.25$. If this is the case, then the equilibrium number of firms in the industry will never exceed six, regardless of market size.[4] As the market size grows, so does the price-cost margin and hence the profit margin. Instead of leading to more firms however, this simply leads to more sunk expenditures K. In turn, this limits any new entry in response to market growth.

---

[4] See Baldwin (1995) for some evidence on this point.

3.2   COST RELATIONS FOR MULTIPRODUCT FIRMS

Since scale economies are a description of the behavior of costs as output increases, investigating their existence in any industry requires that we measure the output of the firms in that industry. This is not always so easy. Consider, for instance, the case of a railroad. One possible measure of output is the rail ton-mile, defined as the number of tons transported times the average number of miles each ton travels. However, not all railroads carry the same type of freight. Some carry mainly mining and forestry products, some carry manufactured goods, and some carry agricultural products. In addition, through the first half of this century, many private U.S. railroads carried passengers as well as freight. Elsewhere in the world, this is still the case. Since all of these different kinds of services have different carrying costs, aggregating each railroad's output into a simple measure such as total ton-miles will confuse any cost analysis. Such aggregation does not allow us to identify whether cost differences between railroads are due to differences in scale or to differences in the kinds of service being offered.

The railroad example points to a gap in our analysis of the firm. In particular, it implies the need to extend the analysis to cover firms producing more than one type of good—that is, to investigate costs for multiproduct firms. The world is full of firms that produce multiple products. Microsoft produces both the Windows operating systems and several applications written for that system. Consumer electronics firms like Sony produce TVs, video games, CD players, and so on. Measuring the output of these firms is clearly less than straightforward.

Even when firms produce what might be considered a single basic product, they typically offer several varieties of that good. In the ready-to-eat breakfast cereal industry, the top four firms market over 80 brands of cereal. If we are to use the technological approach to the firm to gain some understanding of industry structure, we clearly need to extend that approach to handle multiproduct companies. In other words, we need to develop an analysis of costs for the multiproduct firm.

3.2.1   Scope and Scale Economies for Multiproduct Firms

The first issue to address is the factors that make it attractive for firms to produce more than one product. In their path breaking work, Baumol, Panzar, and Willig (1982) resolve this issue by introducing the concept of *economies of scope*. Consider a collection of k goods. Scope economies are said to be present whenever it is less costly to produce this set of goods in one firm than it is to produce that set in k separate firms. Let the total cost of producing k goods, $q_1, q_2, \ldots, q_k$ be given by $C(q_1, q_2, \ldots, q_k)$. Scope economies exist if

$$C(q_1, 0) + C(q_2, 0) + \cdots + C(q_1, q_2, \ldots, q_k) \tag{3.24}$$

As a reference, it is convenient to use the case of $k = 2$, in which case equation (3.24) becomes:

$$C(q_1, 0) + C(0, q_2) - C(q_1, q_2) > 0 \tag{3.25}$$

The first two terms in this equation are the total costs of producing product 1, passenger rail services for example, in one firm and product 2, say freight rails services, in another. The third term is the total cost of having these products produced by the same firm.

If this difference is positive, then scope economies exist. If it is negative, there are diseconomies of scope. If it is 0, then there are neither economies nor diseconomies of scope. Baumol, Panzar, and Willig (1982) then introduce a precise index of scope economies S^C which, for the reference two-good case defined by the ratio

$$S^C = \frac{C(q_1, 0) + C(0, q_2) - C(q_1, q_2)}{C(q_1, q_2)} \tag{3.26}$$

Here we make the conventional assumption that S^C has an upper bound of 1, implying, in this two-product case, that production of each good separately cannot cost more than twice what it costs to produce them together.

Economies of scope can arise for a number of reasons. The first of these is that particular outputs share common inputs. This is the source of economies of scope in the railroad example. There, the common factor is the track necessary to offer either passenger or freight rail service. Many other examples can be identified. For instance, a firm's advertising expenditures benefit all of its products to the extent that such advertising is intended to establish the firm's brand name. Similarly, if different products are manufactured with identical components, then the manufacture of a whole range of such products allows the firm to take advantage of economies of scope in the manufacture of the components. For example, assembly line production with human labor tends to be most efficient at very large production volumes for a single product. However, industrial robots are much better at changing tasks quickly. As a result, the integration of modern computer-assisted design/computer-assisted manufacturing (CAD/CAM) technology with robotic inputs allows the plant to achieve the volume necessary for scale economies while spreading that volume over a variety of goods produced in much smaller batches.

Reality Checkpoint
Talk About Scope Economies, Holy Cow!

Economies of scope arise in many situations—including agricultural production. There is ample evidence that firms producing multiple crops are more cost efficient than firms specializing in just one or two crops. For firms that specialize in particular livestock, the gains from adding other livestock or crops seem to be less clear. However, this may be because livestock production itself already embodies many scope economies even when totally specialized.

Consider a cattle ranch. Raising cattle not only produces beef, but also leather. So, it is clearly cheaper for one farm to produce both products rather than for two farms to do each separately. Yet, the scope economies of cattle production do not stop there.

Cattle carcasses are actually used in hundreds of processes. Glycerin and collagen are both cattle byproducts. Other cattle body parts find their way into vaccines, animal feed, lubricants, asphalt, paper coatings, and fabric softeners. Imagine how much additional cost would be incurred if separate cattle stocks were maintained for the production of each of these goods.

Sources: V. Klinkenborg, "The Whole Cow and Nothing but the Whole Cow." *New York Times* (20 January 2004), p. 18; and C. Morrison Paul and R. Nehring, "Product Diversification, Production Systems, and Economic Performance in U.S. Agricultural Production." *Journal of Econometrics* 126 (June 2005): 525–548.

Another source of scope economies is the presence of cost complementarities. Cost complementarities occur when producing more of one good lowers the cost of producing a second good. There are numerous ways in which such interactions can take place. For example, the exploration and drilling of an oil well often yields not just oil, but also natural gas. Hence, engaging in crude oil production will likely lower the cost of gas exploration. Similarly, a firm that manufactures computer software may also find it easy to provide computer consulting services.

Airlines provide an example of complementarities achieved via network effects. The hub-and-spoke system has been the central component of the provision of airline services to different cities. Under this system, airports designated as hubs act as collection points and are served by large aircraft, for which the cost per passenger mile is relatively low. In contrast, the spoke airports are much smaller, and these destination points are often served by relatively less efficient small planes. Providing air services to many different city pair markets in this way permits the airlines to exploit the scale economies of large aircraft by extending its use over a wide variety of products or, in this case, city-pair passenger services.

Having provided a formal analysis of why firms often choose to produce many different goods, the next question is whether we can develop measures of scale economies for the multiproduct firm similar to the single-product measure S of equation (3.16). The answer to that question is, in general, yes. Both Baumol, Panzar, and Willig (1982) and Bailey and Friedlaender (1982) provide measures of scale effects for multiproduct firms that are reasonably robust. They are also intuitive in that they are sensible multiproduct versions of the declining average cost scale measures used for a single-product firm.

To understand the measures of multiproduct scale economies, we begin with the concept of Ray Average Cost (RAC), again working with the case in which a firm has two products. This firm's cost function is $C(q_1, q_2)$. An output ray is defined as a set of (positive) production levels along which the two separate outputs, q_1 and q_2, are produced in constant proportion (e.g., $q_2 = 0.5q_1$) as in Figure 3.3.

More generally, define a composite good in which the individual component goods, q_1 and q_2 are combined in strict proportions. That is, $q_1 = \lambda_1 q$ and $q_2 = \lambda_2 q$, where λ_1 and λ_2 are positive fractions that sum to unity. We therefore only consider product mixes in which $q_1/q_2 = \lambda_1/\lambda_2$. Then, ray average cost RAC is

$$RAC(q) = \frac{C(\lambda_1 q, \lambda_2 q)}{q} \qquad (3.27)$$

By focusing on the behavior of cost along a production ray, we are considering the behavior of costs for a given product mix. It is this restriction that permits us to treat the two goods together as a single composite product. We know that in the true single product case, the scale economy measure reflects the behavior of average cost as output expands. Similarly, for the two-product case, the issue is the behavior of RAC as the composite output expands. This is indicated by the derivative of RAC with respect to q, which is

$$\frac{dRAC(q)}{dq} = \frac{(\lambda_1 MC_1 + \lambda_2 MC_2)q - C(\lambda_1 q, \lambda_2 q)}{q^2} = \frac{q_1 MC_1 + q_2 MC_2 - C(q_1, q_2)}{q^2}$$

$$(3.28)$$

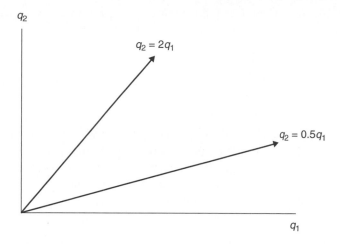

Figure 3.3   Possible production rays for a two-product firm

where MC_i is the marginal cost of producing good i. It follows immediately that the sign of $dRAC(q)/dq$ is determined by the sign of the numerator of this expression. In other words, if $q_1 MC_1 + q_2 MC_2 > C(q_1, q_2)$, then $dRAC(q)/dq > 0$; while if $q_1 MC_1 + q_2 MC_2 < C(q_1, q_2)$, then $dRAC(q)/dq < 0$. We now define the measure of multiproduct scale economies S^M for the case in which M, the number of products, is 2:

$$S^M = S^2 = \frac{C(q_1, q_2)}{q_1 MC_1 + q_2 MC_2} \tag{3.29}$$

The sign of the derivative in (3.28) is fully described by the value of S^M given in (3.29). If $S^M > 1$, this is equivalent to saying that ray average cost decreases with output and so exhibits multiproduct increasing returns to scale. If $S^M < 1$, ray average cost is increasing, and so exhibits multiproduct decreasing returns to scale. If $S^M = 1$, neither scale economies nor diseconomies exist for the multiproduct firm. Note the similarity of this measure with our single-product scale economy index [Equation (3.16)]. In the single-product case, we measured scale economies by the ratio of average to marginal cost. This is more or less what we are doing here, except that average cost is now measured by total cost divided by a weighted average of marginal cost. Moreover, while we have worked out this case for just the two-product firm, it easily generalizes to the case in which there are more than k products so that, in general, we have

$$S^M = \frac{C(q_1, q_2, \ldots, q_k)}{\sum\limits_{i=1}^{k} q_i MC_i} \tag{3.30}$$

The measure S^M just derived pertains to multiproduct scale effects across all products simultaneously. We are also interested, however, in any individual product scale economies. For this purpose, we introduce the concept of average incremental cost for a single product $AIC_i(q)$, where $i = 1, 2$ (in our current case) or $i = 1, 2, \ldots, k$ in general. For our two-good example, $AIC_1(q)$ and $AIC_2(q)$ are defined as

$$
\begin{aligned}
AIC_1(q) &= \frac{C(q_1, q_2) - C(0, q_2)}{q_1} \\
AIC_2(q) &= \frac{C(q_1, q_2) - C(q_1, 0)}{q_2}
\end{aligned}
\tag{3.31}
$$

Average incremental cost for a given product is thus defined as the increase in total cost resulting from producing that product, as opposed to producing none of it, and then dividing that by the level of that good's production to yield a per-unit measure. It must be measured, however, for a given production ray or product mix—hence, the dependency on q indicated. By analogy with our single-product case, a natural measure of product specific scale economies is

$$
S_i = \frac{AIC_i(q)}{MC_i}
\tag{3.32}
$$

As with our earlier case, $S_i > 1$ indicates the presence of scale economies while $S_i < 1$ indicates scale diseconomies.

Consider the multiproduct scale economy measure for the two-product case implied by (3.30). It is

$$
S^M = \frac{C(q_1, q_2)}{\sum\limits_{i-1}^{2} q_i MC_i}
$$

By equation (3.26), we may also write

$$
1 - S^C = \frac{2C(q_1, q_2) - C(0, q_1) - C(q_1, 0)}{C(q_1, q_2)}
\tag{3.33}
$$

In addition, equations (3.31) and (3.32) may be arranged to yield

$$
q_1 MC_1 S_1 = q_1 AIC_1 = C(q_1, q_2) - C(0, q_2);
$$

$$
\text{and}
\tag{3.34}
$$

$$
q_2 MC_2 S_2 = q_2 AIC_2 = C(q_1, q_2) - C(q_1, 0)
$$

Hence, combining (3.33) and (3.34), we may obtain

$$
C[q_1, q_2] = \frac{2C(q_1, q_2) - C(0, q_{21}) - C(q_1, 0)}{1 - S^C} = \frac{q_1 MC_1 S_1 + q_2 MC_2 S_2}{1 - S^C}
\tag{3.35}
$$

Now define

$$
w = \frac{q_1 MC_1}{\sum\limits_{i=1}^{2} q_i MC_i} \quad \text{and} \quad 1 - w = \frac{q_2 MC_2}{\sum\limits_{i=1}^{2} q_i MC_i}
\tag{3.36}
$$

Here, w is roughly the share of total variable costs associated with good 1. In our two-product example, it then follows that $1-w$ is the variable cost share associated with good 2. Substitution of (3.36) into (3.35) and comparison with equation (3.30) then yields

$$S^M = \frac{wS_1 + (1-w)S_2}{1 - S^C} \tag{3.37}$$

Equation (3.37) is a critical result. It shows that a firm can enjoy multiproduct scale economies (i.e., ray average cost can decline with output) even if there are no single-product scale economies—that is, even if S_1 and S_2 are both 1 or even greater than 1 (indicating single product *dis*economies), provided there are sufficiently strong scope economies. By diversifying its output over a mix of products rather than focusing on a single one, the firm exploits the scope effects. In our railroad example, a firm that produces only freight rail service may observe very little scale economies as it carries more tons of freight. However, assuming its track capacity is not exhausted, the inclusion of passenger service permits it to spread the track over more trains and hence a higher (mixed) output level. The general implication of equation (3.37) is then clear. When strong scope economies exist and give rise to multiproduct scale economies, a firm must produce the corresponding set of products if it is to compete effectively.

3.2.2   Different Versions of the Same Core Product

So far, our discussion of multiproduct cost relations has not distinguished between situations in which the two outputs are somewhat related, as is the case with passenger and freight rail service, and those where the two goods are substantially different products, say, cologne and shirts. In the latter case, the two products use quite different production processes, and the presence of scope economies and therefore any multiproduct scale economies seems less compelling. Scope economies are more likely to be found when the goods being produced use similar production techniques or other clear reasons to evidence cost complementarities.

One instance in which we therefore should expect significant scope economies is the joint production of different varieties of the same basic good such as ready-to-eat cereals, canned soups, or varieties of clothing. Nike, for example, produces numerous athletic shoes. Benetton became famous for its wide arrangement of different-colored jerseys. To consider these issues, we need to conceptualize more clearly the meaning of different varieties of the same good. For this purpose, we now introduce a model of product differentiation that will be used extensively in later chapters.

To model differentiated products rigorously requires a formal way of modeling product differentiation. For this purpose, we introduce a market setting that we will use frequently throughout the text. In particular, we imagine that there exists some particular characteristic or index of characteristics that is a critical distinguishing feature between different versions of the good. If we scale the index so that it runs from 0 to 1, we can graph the index as a horizontal line.

We assume a mass M of consumers distributed continuously and uniformly along the index line. For each such consumer, the location or address along the line x_i reflects her most preferred version of the product. That is, x_i represents consumer i's most preferred version of the product, for which she is willing to pay V dollars. For any other address or index value x_j, consumer i is willing to pay only $V - t|x_j - x_i|$, where $t > 0$. Thus, consumer i's willingness to pay for a version of the product diminishes as the difference or distance between that version and her most preferred version grows.

A little thought reveals that the above framework will motivate firms to offer different versions of the basic product if there are any scope economies. A firm producing only one product, type x_i, will find that it can only sell that type to a consumer located some distance from that specific address at a price well below the consumer's maximum V. In contrast, the more varieties of the product the firm offers, the more it offers a set of products that are either exactly or close to most preferred versions of many consumers and, therefore, the more often the firm will be able to sell at a price of V or something close to it.

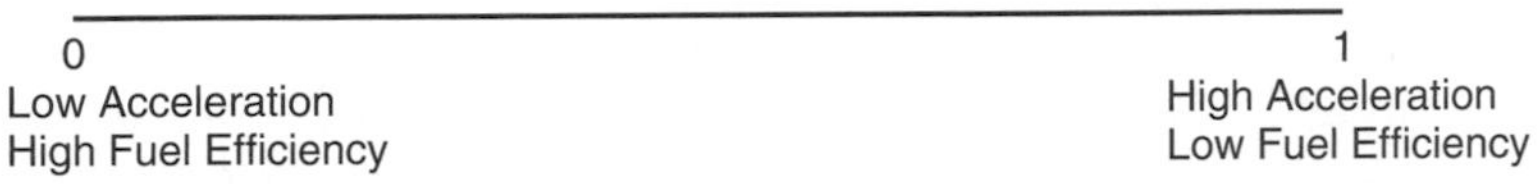

```
0                                                          1
Low Acceleration                                    High Acceleration
High Fuel Efficiency                                Low Fuel Efficiency
```

Figure 3.4   Index of car features

Suppose for example that consumers rate cars based on an index of fuel efficiency and acceleration ability. That is, each consumer's most preferred efficiency and acceleration combination corresponds to an index value running from 0 to 1 as shown in Figure 3.4.

Reality Checkpoint
Flexible Manufacturing at Lands' End

In October 2000, Lands' End started to offer custom-made pants on its website. Customers interested in buying shirts, blouses, chinos, or jeans can simply go to the firm's website and type in measurements such as weight and height, and the characterization of the proportions of their bust, hips, and general body shape. Customers can also choose the fabric, color, and stylistic features such as cuffs, hemming, pocket dimensions, and so forth. A computer program then analyzes the information, calculates the precise design, and sends the information to a manufacturing plant in Mexico. At the plant, a computerized cutting machine creates the pattern, and the item is cut and sewn and shipped to customers two to four weeks later, depending on the volume of orders.

The price in 2007 for a customized pair of traditional-fit men's ringspun denim jeans was $70. This compared to a price of about $40 for a comparable noncustomized pair of jeans at the same website. Shipping was $6 in both cases. Lands' End can charge so much more for the customized jeans because consumers are getting exactly what they want in these products. Indeed, within a year of launching the customized service, the percent of jeans sold at the Lands' End website that were customized rose from 0 to 40. The custom service also helped Lands' End to reduce the amount of unwanted merchandize in its warehouse at the end of each season. In turn, this reduced carrying costs and further raised the profit per item, in part because fewer clothes were sold at clearance.

Source: B. Tedeschi, "E-Commerce Report: A Lands' End Experiment in Selling Custom-Made Pants Is A Success, Leaving Its Rivals to Play Catch-Up." *New York Times* (30 September 2002), p. C3.

Here, zero may be low acceleration ability but high fuel efficiency, while 1 is rapid acceleration but low efficiency. Other combinations of the two features lie between these two extremes. Consumers differ in their most preferred combination of fuel efficiency and acceleration capacity; that is, they differ regarding their most preferred index rating for a car.

If there are any scope economies, a firm will wish to offer cars with somewhat low acceleration abilities but high fuel efficiency and also cars that accelerate fairly quickly but use more fuel. This permits it to sell to different customers while still getting each one to pay V or something close to it. The implication is clear. Firms in this industry will tend to be multiproduct firms in that they offer a variety of cars and not simply hope that "one size fits all." Furthermore, if such scope economies give rise to multiproduct scale economies as just described above, then firms will tend to be large in order to exploit such savings.[5]

3.3   NON-COST DETERMINANTS OF MARKET STRUCTURE

Before turning to some empirical work reflecting how economists estimate actual cost relationships and the extent of any scale or scope economies, we briefly mention two other important determinants of market structure. One is the extent of any network externalities, and the other is government regulation.

For some products, the value to the consumer increases as the number of other consumers also rises. The classic example is a telephone. It is of little use to its owner if she is the only one with a telephone. However, as more and more people get telephones, the value to any one consumer from having a telephone grows. The same is true in some respects for video games, computer software (and hardware), and a host of other products. For example, the more people have *Gears of War*, the more any one player is likely to find playing partners. Such positive feedback, in which the price any one consumer is willing to pay rises as there are more consumers, is referred to as a *network externality*. Such effects are like scale economies on the demand side of the market. Much like production scale economies, they tend to induce higher concentration, because it is advantageous to a firm to have a large network. We return to this topic in Chapter 18.

Government regulation also plays an important role in a number of markets. For example, from 1934 to 1990, the number of taxicabs in Boston operating legally, pursuant to the acquisition of a Certificate of Convenience and Necessity (also known as a medallion), was fixed at 1,525. Similarly, the number of taxicab medallions in New York City was fixed at 11,787 from 1937 to 1997. These examples can be easily multiplied. Government regulation often includes efforts to control the number of firms offering a particular good or service. Hence, public policy also plays a role in determining market structure.

---

[5]   See Panzar (1989) for a good discussion of cost issues in general. See Evans and Heckman (1986) and Roller (1990) for evidence of scope economies in the telephone industry; Cohn, Rhine, and Santos (1989) and DeGroot, McMahon, and Volkwein (1991) for evidence of scope economies in higher education; and Pulley and Braunstein (1992) for evidence of scope economies in finance. See Eaton and Schmitt (1994) for a formal model of flexible manufacturing.

3.4   EMPIRICAL APPLICATION
Cost Function Estimation, Scale and Scope Economies

Since the underlying technology and associated cost implications are central determinants of industrial structure, economists have been interested in getting evidence on cost relationships for a long time. Unfortunately, we rarely have direct evidence on the production technology. Hence, estimating firm cost functions can be a tricky business. However, application of basic microeconomic theory can greatly facilitate the process. Indeed, there is much insight to be gained from considering the firm's cost function.

To see this, consider again our Cobb-Douglas cost function of equation (3.10) and the underlying production technology of equation (3.2). For illustrative purposes, it is convenient to assume away any fixed cost ($F = 0$). In this case, the cost function of (3.10) simplifies to

$$C(w_1, w_2, q) = \left(\frac{w_1}{\alpha}\right)^{\frac{\alpha}{\alpha+\beta}} \left(\frac{w_2}{\beta}\right)^{\frac{\beta}{\alpha+\beta}} (\alpha + \beta)q^{\frac{1}{\alpha+\beta}} \tag{3.38}$$

From the Lagrangian first order conditions (3.6a) and (3.6b), we then can infer that in any cost-minimizing choice of inputs, we must have

$$x_2 = \left(\frac{w_1}{w_2}\right)\left(\frac{\beta}{\alpha}\right)x_1 \tag{3.39}$$

If we substitute this into the production relationship, we then have

$$q = x_1^\alpha \left[\left(\frac{w_1}{w_2}\right)\left(\frac{\beta}{\alpha}\right)x_1\right]^\beta = \left(\frac{\beta w_1}{\alpha w_2}\right)^\beta x_1^{\alpha+\beta} \tag{3.40}$$

Or

$$x_1 = \left(\frac{\alpha w_2}{\beta w_1}\right)^{\frac{\beta}{\alpha+\beta}} q^{\frac{1}{\alpha+\beta}} = x_1(w_1, w_2, q) \tag{3.41}$$

Similarly, by solving instead for x_2 we have

$$x_2 = \left(\frac{\beta w_1}{\alpha w_2}\right)^{\frac{\alpha}{\alpha+\beta}} q^{\frac{1}{\alpha+\beta}} = x_2(w_1, w_2, q) \tag{3.42}$$

Equations (3.41) and (3.42) are the conditional demand functions for the two inputs. In each case, they give the amount of input x_i the firm will optimally hire, conditional upon input prices and the level of output desired. Notice, however, that we could have derived these same expressions had we differentiated the cost function of (3.38) with respect to either of the two associated input prices. That is

$$\frac{\partial C(w_1, w_2, q)}{\partial r} = \left(\frac{\alpha w}{\beta r}\right)^{\frac{\beta}{\alpha+\beta}} q^{\frac{1}{\alpha+\beta}} = x_1(w_1, w_2, q) \tag{3.43a}$$

and

$$\frac{\partial C(w_1, w_2, q)}{\partial w} = \left(\frac{\beta w_1}{\alpha w_2}\right)^{\frac{\alpha}{\alpha+\beta}} q^{\frac{1}{\alpha+\beta}} = x_2(w_1, w_2, q) \tag{3.43b}$$

In other words, differentiation of the cost function with respect to an input price yields the conditional input demand functions associated that price. This is no accident. It is a very general result that extends beyond the simple Cobb-Douglas production relation assumed here, and holds true whether or not there are constant returns to scale.[6]

Note as well that these input demands exhibit a further feature, namely, that they have symmetric cross-price effects. That is

$$\frac{\partial x_1(w_1, w_2, q)}{\partial w_2} = \frac{\partial x_2(w_1, w_2, q)}{\partial w_1} \tag{3.44}$$

Again, this is not unique to our current case, but a feature of all well-behaved cost functions. It says that the impact on the demand for input 1 (say, capital) of a small rise in the price of input 2 (say, labor) is exactly the same as the impact on the demand for factor 2 of a small increase in the price of input 1.

With equation (3.44), we are starting to get at how the firm will substitute one factor for another as their relative price changes. For our two-good example, the formal measure of this substitutability is the elasticity of substitution σ. It is defined as

$$\sigma = \frac{\dfrac{\partial(x_1/x_2)}{(x_1/x_2)}}{\dfrac{\partial(w_1/w_2)}{(w_1/w_2)}} = -\frac{\partial \ln(x_1/x_2)}{\partial \ln(w_1/w_2)} \tag{3.45}$$

In other words, the elasticity of substitution σ measures the proportionate change in the input ratio in response to a proportionate change in the ratio of input prices. Note that since the conditional factor demands can be derived from the cost function, so can the elasticity of substitution.

Equation (3.39) implies that for our Cobb-Douglas case

$$\frac{x_1}{x_2} = \left(\frac{\alpha}{\beta}\right)\left(\frac{w_1}{w_2}\right)^{-1} \tag{3.46}$$

Hence

$$\frac{\partial \ln(x_1/x_2)}{\partial \ln(w_1/w_2)} = -1 \Rightarrow \sigma(r, w) = 1 \tag{3.47}$$

---

[6] This result, often referred to as *Shepherd's Lemma*, is easily derived via the envelope theorem. The intuition, though, is this. Let x_i^* be the optimal amount of input i for a given value of q. Then, the cost of producing q is $w_1 x_1^* + w_2 x_2^*$. A tiny change in, say, $w_1 - \partial w_1$—will basically leave the input combination unchanged (the envelope theorem). Hence, the effect on total cost ∂C will simply be $x_1^* \partial w_1$; that is, $\partial C/\partial w_i = x_i^*(w_1, w_2, q)$.

Thus, the Cobb-Douglas production relation has an elasticity of substitution that is constant and equal to 1, independent of factor prices and the level of production.[7] This invariance is something of a limitation of the Cobb-Douglas framework.

Finally, consider our cost function (3.38) in logarithmic form:

$$\ln C = \ln \left[\left(\frac{\alpha}{\beta} \right)^{\frac{\beta}{\alpha+\beta}} + \left(\frac{\beta}{\alpha} \right)^{\frac{\alpha}{\alpha+\beta}} \right] + \left(\frac{\alpha}{\alpha + \beta} \right) \ln w_1$$

$$+ \left(\frac{\beta}{\alpha + \beta} \right) \ln w_2 + \left(\frac{1}{\alpha + \beta} \right) \ln q \tag{3.48}$$

We know from our discussion of the scale economy measure S described by equation (3.16) that $S = \frac{1}{\partial \ln C / \partial \ln q}$. Hence, our measure of S for the Cobb-Douglas case is $S = \alpha + \beta$. We also know from equation (3.43a) that $\frac{\partial C}{\partial w_1} = x_1$. Further, by definition we have $\frac{\partial \ln C}{\partial \ln w_1} = \frac{\partial C}{\partial w_1} \frac{w_1}{C}$. Putting these results together, and extending the same logic to input 2, we have

$$\frac{\partial \ln C}{\partial \ln w_1} = \frac{w_1 x_1}{C} \tag{3.49a}$$

and

$$\frac{\partial \ln C}{\partial \ln w_2} = \frac{w_2 x_2}{C} \tag{3.49b}$$

Recognizing that $w_1 x_1$ is the total expenditure on input 1, equations (3.49a) and (3.49b) reveal that the derivative of the log of total cost, with respect to the log of an input's price, yields the expenditure on that input as a proportion of total costs. For the earlier Cobb-Douglas case we have:

$$\frac{\partial \ln C}{\partial \ln w_1} = \frac{\alpha}{\alpha + \beta} = \text{expenditure share of } x_1 \tag{3.50a}$$

and

$$\frac{\partial \ln C}{\partial \ln w_2} = \frac{\beta}{\alpha + \beta} = \text{expenditure share of } x_2 \tag{3.50b}$$

In sum, a particular production technology has fairly precise implications for the cost function. Therefore, while we cannot always measure that production relationship itself, we can estimate how costs vary with output and use the parameters of that estimated relationship to make inferences about the underlying technology.

For example, the generic representation of the log of the cost function consistent with our Cobb-Douglas model is

$$\ln C = \text{Constant} + \delta_1 \ln w_1 + \delta_2 \ln w_2 + \delta_3 \ln Q \tag{3.51}$$

---

[7]   Note that this also means that $w_1 x_1 / w_2 x_2$ is constant. As $w_1 x_1$ is the total expense on input 1 and $w_2 x_2$ is the total expense on input 2, this means that the ratio of expenditures for each input is constant, which can only happen if the share of total cost that each input accounted for also stays unchanged.

With observations on input prices and output levels, we may estimate the above equation and then use the estimated coefficients δ_i to recover the underlying production relationships regarding scale economies, input demands, and the elasticity of substitution. Thus, our measure of scale economies derived earlier is $S = 1/\delta_3$. Likewise, our estimates of the conditional input demands are $\delta_1 C/w_1$ for input 1 and $\delta_2 C/w_2$ for input 2. From these we have that $x_1/x_2 = \delta_1 w_2/\delta_2 w_1$, which is easily seen to imply an elasticity of substitution of $\sigma = 1$, exactly as in the Cobb-Douglas case. Note further that if the cost function is to be homogenous of degree 1 in input prices, then $\delta_1 + \delta_2 = 1$. Indeed, if this condition is rejected by the data, it suggests that the model has misspecified the production relation.

Of course, there are many possible production relationships besides the Cobb-Douglas one. Ideally then, one would like to allow for this in any empirical investigation. That is, one would like to specify a general cost function that is consistent with economic theory in general, but that can yield the Cobb-Douglas relation if the data are consistent with that special case. One such flexible specification is the translog cost function. For the basic, two-input case above, this function has the following form:

$$\ln C = \text{Constant} + \delta_1 \ln w_1 + \delta_2 \ln w_2 + 0.5[\delta_{11}(\ln w_1)^2 + \delta_{12}(\ln w_1)(\ln w_2)$$
$$+ \delta_{21}(\ln w_2)(\ln w_1) + \delta_{22}(\ln w_2)^2] + \delta_3 \ln q + \delta_{31}(\ln q)(\ln w_1)$$
$$+ \delta_{32}(\ln q)(\ln w_2) + 0.5\delta_{33}(\ln q)^2 \tag{3.52}$$

Notice that if $\delta_{11}, \delta_{12}, \delta_{21}, \delta_{22}, \delta_{31}, \delta_{32}$, and δ_{33} all equal 0, this specification implies the Cobb-Douglas production. While this particular restriction may not be confirmed by the data, some more general restrictions are implied by economic theory. These include

$$\delta_1 + \delta_2 = 1 \tag{3.53a}$$

$$\delta_{12} = \delta_{21} \tag{3.53b}$$

$$\delta_{11} + \delta_{12} + \delta_{21} + \delta_{22} = 0 \tag{3.53c}$$

$$\delta_{31} + \delta_{32} = 0 \tag{3.53d}$$

The intuition behind these restrictions is reasonably straightforward. Recall that theory implies both that cross-price effects be equal and that an equiproportionate rise in all input prices, holding output constant, should lead to the same proportionate increase in costs C. Equation (3.53b) reflects the first of these requirements and (3.53a) is important for the second. To see this however, we just first understand the logic of (3.53c) and (3.53d).

To understand why equation (3.53c) holds consider input 1. We know that $\frac{\partial \ln C}{\partial \ln w_1} = \frac{\partial C}{\partial w_1}\frac{w_1}{C} = S_1$, given our earlier result that $\partial C/\partial w_1 = x_1$, and defining the share of this input in total cost as $S_1 = w_1 x_1/C$. We may also then write $x_1 = C S_1 w_1^{-1}$. From this we may determine the effect of a change in w_1 on the amount of x_1 employed. This is

$$\frac{\partial x_1}{\partial w_1} = S_1 w_1^{-1}\left(\frac{\partial C}{\partial w_1}\right) + \frac{\partial S_1}{\partial w_1}C w_1^{-1} - S_1 C w_1^{-2} = S_1\frac{x_1}{w_1} + \delta_{11}\frac{C}{w_1} - S_1\frac{C}{w_1^2} \tag{3.54}$$

Defining the own-price elasticity of the demand for input 1 as $\varepsilon_1 = \frac{\partial x_1}{\partial w_1}\frac{w_1}{x_1}$, we then have

$$\varepsilon_1 = S_1 + \frac{\delta_{11}}{S_1} - 1 \tag{3.55}$$

Similarly, if we define the cross-price elasticity of the demand for x_1 as $\varepsilon_{12} = \frac{\partial x_1}{\partial w_2}\frac{w_2}{x_1}$, then given that $x_1 = CS_1 w_1^{-1}$, we have

$$\varepsilon_{12} = \frac{\partial C}{\partial w_2}\frac{w_2}{x_1}S_1 w_1^{-1} + C w_1^{-1}\frac{\partial S_1}{\partial w_2}\frac{w_2}{x_1} = \frac{w_2 x_2}{C} + \frac{\delta_{12}}{w_2}\frac{Cw}{w_1 x_1} = S_2 + \frac{\delta_{12}}{S_1} \tag{3.56}$$

Of course, holding q constant, a change in the relative price of input 1 must affect the demand for that input totally through the substitution effect. Hence, the own-price elasticity and all cross-price elasticities must sum to 0. Since our two-input case also requires that $S_1 + S_2 = 1$, comparison of equations (3.55) and (3.56) reveals that this means $\delta_{11} = -\delta_{12}$. Extending this same logic to input 2 then implies the restriction in (3.53c).

As for restriction (3.53d), in light of the above, it is clear that whether or not this restriction holds the effect on total cost of an equiproportionate rise in all input prices will depend on the level of q. As a result, it would not be possible for costs to be linearly homogenous in input prices for all output levels. Hence, restriction (3.53d) must hold. In turn, restriction (3.53a) then preserves the linear homogeneity feature.

It is straightforward to generalize the translog function to the case of many inputs as well as to the case of multiple outputs. Letting $\bar{w}$ be the vector of input prices, the single output translog cost function with k inputs is simply

$$C(\bar{w}, q) = \alpha_0 + \alpha_1 \ln q + \sum_{i=1}^{k} \beta_i (\ln w_i) + 0.5\delta_1 (\ln q)^2$$

$$+ 0.5 \sum_{i=1}^{k}\sum_{j=1}^{k} \delta_{ij}(\ln w_i)(\ln w_j) + \sum_{i=1}^{k}\rho_i(\ln q)(\ln w_i) \tag{3.57}$$

For m outputs and k inputs, the translog cost function is[8]

$$C(\bar{w}, q) = \alpha_0 + \alpha_1 \ln q + \sum_{i=1}^{k} \beta_i (\ln w_i) + 0.5\sum_{i=1}^{m}\sum_{j=1}^{m}\delta_{ij}(\ln q_i)(\ln q_j)$$

$$+ 0.5 \sum_{i=1}^{k}\sum_{j=1}^{k} \delta_{ij}(\ln w_i)(\ln w_j) + \sum_{i=1}^{m}\sum_{j=1}^{k}\rho_{ij}(\ln q_i)(\ln w_j) \tag{3.58}$$

One of the earliest papers estimating a translog cost function is also one of the most illustrative. Christensen and Greene (1976) applied the translog approach to the electric

---

[8]   For estimation purposes, this assumes that all firms in the data produce some of each of the m goods. Otherwise, the $\ln q_i$ will not be defined for all observations. See Caves, Christensen, and Tretheway (1980) for a simple transformation to deal with this potential problem.

power-generating industry, adding fuel as a basic input along with labor and capital. Denoting the price of fuel as F, their model is

$$
\begin{aligned}
C(\overline{w}, q) = {} & \alpha_0 + \alpha_1 \ln q + 0.5\alpha_2 (\ln q)^2 + \beta_K (\ln w_K) + \beta_L (\ln w_L) + \beta_F (\ln w_F) \\
& + 0.5[\delta_{KK} (\ln w_K)^2 + \delta_{KL} (\ln w_K)(\ln w_L) + \delta_{KF} (\ln w_K)(\ln w_F) \\
& + \delta_{LL} (\ln w_L)^2 + \delta_{LK} (\ln w_L)(\ln w_K) + \delta_{LF} (\ln w_K)(\ln w_F) + \delta_{FF} (\ln w_F)^2 \\
& + \delta_{FL} (\ln w_F)(\ln w_L) + \delta_{FK} (\ln w_F)(\ln w_K)] + \rho_K (\ln q)(\ln w_K) \\
& + \rho_L (\ln q)(\ln w_L) + \rho_F (\ln q)(\ln w_F)
\end{aligned} \tag{3.59}
$$

Imposing the requirements that: $\delta_{KL} = \delta_{LK}$; $\delta_{KF} = \delta_{FK}$; and $\delta_{LF} = \delta_{FL}$ leaves 15 coefficients to be estimated. Beyond this symmetry, our analysis above implies the following additional restrictions:

$$
\begin{aligned}
& \beta_K + \beta_L + \beta_F = 1 \\
& \delta_{KK} + \delta_{KL} + \delta_{KF} = 0; \; \delta_{LL} + \delta_{KL} + \delta_{LF} = 0; \; \text{and} \delta_{FF} + \delta_{KF} + \delta_{LF} = 0 \\
& \rho_K + \rho_L + \rho_F = 0
\end{aligned} \tag{3.60}
$$

Table 3.1 below shows one set of coefficient estimates based on 1970 data.

It is easy to see that the coefficient estimates are structured such that they satisfy the restrictions implied by theory. Again, one particular point of interest that can be derived from these estimates is the extent of any scale economies in electric power generation. For the model at hand, our scale economy measure S is given by

$$
S = \alpha_1 + \alpha_2 \ln q + \rho_K \ln w_K + \rho_L \ln w_L + \rho_F \ln w_F.
$$

Table 3.1   Christensen and Greene (1976) cost function estimates and scale economies in electric power generation

Parameter	Estimate	t-statistic
α_0	7.14	32.45
α_1	0.587	20.87
α_2	0.049	12.94
β_K	0.208	2.95
β_L	−0.151	−1.85
β_F	0.943	14.64
δ_{KK}	0.118	6.17
δ_{KL}	−0.011	−0.75
δ_{KF}	−0.107	−7.48
δ_{LL}	0.081	5.00
δ_{LF}	−0.070	−6.30
δ_{FF}	0.178	10.79
ρ_K	−0.008	−1.23
ρ_L	−0.016	−8.25
ρ_F	0.021	6.64

Using the observed level of output and factor prices, and taking the average scale economies across all firms, the Christensen and Greene results indicate an average value for S in 1970 of about 1.12, implying some (but not huge) unexploited scale economies across the industry. Indeed, they find that nearly half the production observed occurs at a sufficiently large volume (20 trillion kilowatt-hours annually or higher) that virtually all scale economies have been exhausted. This reflects a major increase from the 1950s, due to the growth in electric consumption over this time period.

Summary

This chapter has focused on technology and key cost concepts and their implications on industrial structure. Scale economies tend to increase market concentration. Economies of scope have a similar effect of concentrating the production of different products within a single firm. Scope economies also typically give rise to important multiproduct scale economies. This is particularly the case when the various products are not truly different goods, but rather different versions of the same good. In such product-differentiated markets, the presence of scope and scale economies will again imply a more concentrated structure.

Market size is another important influence on market structure. Because a large market has room for a number of firms (even if each firm is of considerable size), larger markets tend to be less concentrated than small ones. However, increasing market size does not lead to less concentration in markets in which sunk costs also increase with size. These are typically markets in which advertising or research and development costs play a major role.

Finally, both the presence of network effects and government regulation also influence market structure. Network effects such that a good's value to any one user increases as more consumers in total buy the good are like scale economies on the demand side of the market. The greater such network effects, the more firms will need to be large to internalize the externality, and the more concentrated the market will be. Government regulation over entry (and exit) has a direct and obvious impact on industrial structure.

As noted in Chapter 1, there is not necessarily a clear link between market structure and market performance in terms of the efficiency of the market outcome. We explore the implications of alternative market structures and other indications of market power in the next chapter.

Problems

1. Let r be the price of capital and w be the price of labor, and consider the following cost function:

$$C(r, w, q) = \left(\frac{10r}{3}\right)^{1/3} \left(\frac{5w}{3}\right)^{23} q^{1.11} + F$$

   Derive an expression for average cost. Determine the output level at which any scale economies are exhausted.

2. An urban rapid-transit line runs crowded trains (200 passengers per car) at rush hours, but nearly empty trains (10 passengers per car) at off-peak hours. A management consultant argues that the cost of running a car for one trip on this line is about $50 regardless of the number of passengers. Hence, the consultant concludes that the cost per passenger is about 25 cents at rush hour, but rises to $5 in off-peak hours. From this she reasons that the firm had better discourage the off-peak business. Is the consultant a good economist? Why or why not?

3. Taking input prices as given (so to suppress their representation), consider the following cost functions:

$$C(q_1, q_2) = F + cq_1 + cq_2 - \mu q_1 q_2; \ F > 0; \ c > 0; \ \mu > 0$$

$$C(q_1, 0) = F_1 + cq_1; \ F_1 > 0$$

$$C(0, q_2) = F_2 + cq_2; \ F_2 > 0$$

Assume that $F_1 + F_2 < F$. Derive conditions under which the production will exhibit economies of scope.

4. If the production technology is of the Leontief-type, we have $q = \min(K/a, L/b)$ where K is capital input, L is labor input; and a and b are positive constants. If r is the price of capital and w is the price of labor, derive the cost function for a firm with this production technology. To what extent does this cost function exhibit either scale economies or diseconomies?

5. Using the values in Table 3.1,
    a. determine the own-price elasticity of the demand for fuel
    b. determine the cross-price elasticity of the demand for fuel in response to a rise in the price of:
        i.   the capital input
        ii. the labor input

References

Baldwin, John R. 1995. *The Dynamics of Industrial Competition: A North American Perspective.* Cambridge: Cambridge University Press.

Baumol, W. J., J. C. Panzar, and R. D. Willig. 1982. *Contestable Markets and the Theory of Industry Structure.* New York: Harcourt, Brace, Jovanovich.

Bolton, P. and A. Scharfstein. 1998. "Corporate Finance, the Theory of the Firm, and Organizations." *Journal of Economic Perspectives,* 12 (Autumn): 95–114.

Bresnahan, T., and P. Reiss. 1991. "Entry and Competition in Concentrated Markets." *Journal of Political Economy,* 99 (October): 977–1009.

Caves, D., L. Christensen, and M. W. Tretheway. 1980. "Flexible Cost Functions for Multiproduct Firms." *Review of Economics and Statistics,* 62 (August): 477–481.

Christensen, L., and W. Greene. 1976. "Economies of Scale in U.S. Electric Power Generation." *Journal of Political Economy,* 84 (August): 655–676.

Coase, R. H. 1937. "The Nature of the Firm." *Economica,* 4 (March): 386–405.

Cohn, E., S. L. Rhine, and M. C. Santos. 1989. "Institutions of Higher Education as Multi-Product Firms: Economies of Scale and Scope." *Review of Economics and Statistics,* 71 (May): 284–290.

De Groot, H., W. McMahon, and J. F. Volkwein. 1991. "The Cost Structure of American Research Universities." *Review of Economics and Statistics,* 73 (August): 424–431.

Eaton, B. C., and N. Schmitt. 1994. "Flexible Manufacturing and Market Structure." *American Economic Review,* 84 (September): 875–888.

Evans, D, and J. Heckman. 1986. "A Test for Subadditivity of the Cost Function with Application to the Bell System." *American Economic Review,* 74 (September): 615–623.

Grossman, S. and O. Hart, O. 1986. "The Costs and Benefits of Ownership: A Theory of Vertical and Lateral Integration." *Journal of Political Economy,* 94 (August): 691–719.

Jensen, M. C. and W. H. Meckling. 1976. "Theory of the Firm: Managerial Behavior, Agency Costs, and Ownership Structure." *Journal of Financial Economics,* 3 (October): 305–360.

Milgrom, P., and J. Roberts. 1992. *Economics, Organization, and Management*. Upper Saddle River, NJ: Prentice Hall.

Panzar, J. C. 1989. "Technological Determinants of Firm and Industry Structure." In R. Schmalensee and R. Willig (Eds.), *Handbook of Industrial Organization*. Vol. 1. Amsterdam: North-Holland, 3–60.

Pulley, L. B., and Y. M. Braunstein. 1992. "A Composite Cost Function for Multiproduct Firms with an Application to Economies of Scope in Banking." *Review of Economics and Statistics,* 74 (May): 221–230.

Roller, L. 1990. "Proper Quadratic Cost Functions with Application to the Bell System." *Review of Economics and Statistics,* 72 (May): 202–210.

Sutton, John. 1991. *Sunk Costs and Market Structure*. Cambridge, MA: The MIT Press.

———. 2001. *Technology and Market Structure*. Cambridge, MA: The MIT Press.

Williamson, O. E. 1981. "The Economics of Organization: The Transaction Cost Approach." *American Journal of Sociology,* 87 (November): 548–577.

4

Market Structure and Market Power

In Chapter 2, we described the two poles of market outcomes. One is that of perfect competition in which countless small firms competing with each other for consumer dollars, inevitably leading to prices that are close to costs and maximal efficiency. The other is the monopoly outcome, which can result in prices well above cost and a welfare or efficiency loss as the monopolist's gain in profit comes at an even greater expense of consumer surplus. It is natural in this context to ask about the intermediate cases when there are neither many firms nor just one determining the market outcome.

It would be convenient, of course, if there were some monotonic relationship between the efficiency loss and a measure of industrial structure. Analysis and policy would be far easier if we could be sure that as we move from one firm to two, two to three, three to four, and so on ever closer to the competitive ideal, the welfare loss shrank more and more, asymptotically approaching zero. Indeed, identifying this link was the motivating goal of the Structure-Conduct-Performance paradigm. Yet as suggested in Chapter 1, such a mapping is elusive. To begin with, measuring a market's structure is more difficult than one might imagine. While it is easy to measure the number of firms, it is less easy to interpret that number when the firms are of radically different sizes. There is, for example, a difference between an industry comprising three identical firms of equal size and another comprising one firm that serves three-fourths of the industry alongside two that each have a one-eighth market share. Furthermore, as we have already seen, there are situations in which monopolies can yield efficient outcomes. We shall later show that this is also true for markets with a few or just two firm depending on the nature of competition between firms and the pricing tactics employed.

Perhaps most important of all, the industrial structure is itself endogenous. We saw this in the previous chapter in our discussion of Sutton's (1991) work on endogenous sunk cost. The observed number and size of firms may be more the result of the nature and intensity of interfirm competition than the cause.

Yet despite these caveats, it is useful to consider the measurement of market structure and market power. From the perspective of merger policy, for example, industrial structure can at least serve as an initial point of inquiry, if not as a determinative influence. That is, while we cannot know for sure if a two-firm merger in a five-firm industry will reduce social welfare, we can be pretty sure that such a merger in a 100-firm market will be benign. Thus, it makes sense to use market structure as a screening mechanism for possible antitrust challenges. In addition, and as intimated by the point just made, considering measures of market structure and power directs us to focus on the efficiency concerns that are the precise objective of policy. We briefly address both these issues in this chapter.

4.1   MEASURING MARKET STRUCTURE

One way to think about an industry's structure is to construct a concentration curve that plots the cumulative market share accounted for by industry firms, starting with the largest and working on down to the smallest. Figure 4.1 displays concentration curves for each of three representative industries, A, B, and C. Here, the firms' ranked sizes are measured along the horizontal axis, and the cumulative market share is measured on the vertical axis. Industry A has 10 firms, each with a 10 percent market share. Industry B has 21 firms, the largest of which has a 55 percent market share, while each of the remaining 20 firms each has a 2.25 percent share. Finally, in industry C, there are three firms each with a market share of 25 percent and 5 firms each with a market share of five percent.

A concentration curve is a useful illustrative device.[1] However, often we need to summarize industrial structure with just a single parameter or index. A n-firm concentration ratio CR_n is one such index. CR_n is defined as the cumulative market share of the largest n firms. Thus, CR_4 is the percent of industry sales accounted for by the largest four firms, while CR_8 is the share accounted for by the largest eight. For the three hypothetical industries described above, CR_4 is 40, 61.75, and 80 percent, for A, B, and C, respectively, while CR_8 is 80, 70.75, and 100 percent, respectively.

A n-firm concentration ratio then corresponds to a particular point on the industry's concentration curve. It follows that the principal drawback to such a measure is that it

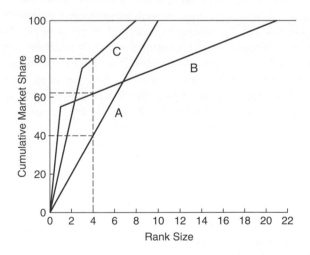

Figure 4.1   Some possible concentration curves

---

[1]   Those familiar with the GINI Coefficient typically used to measure income inequality will recognize the concentration curve as the industrial structure analog of the Lorenz Curve from which the GINI Coefficient is derived. For further details, see C. Damguard, "The Lorenz Curve" at: www. mathworld.wolfram.com/LorenzCurve.html.

Reality Checkpoint
Concentrating on Concentration

Just as we can measure the fraction of an industry's output accounted for by its largest firms, so we can measure the fraction of the economy's entire output (GDP) accounted for by its largest corporations. However, while it may make some sense to speak of a concentration index based on just the top four firms (or top eight firms) when speaking of a single industry, such a small number of firms would account for much too little of GDP to think seriously about. So, in the case of aggregate economic activity, we consider concentration ratios such as CR_{50} or CR_{200}. Such measures can be constructed using data from the Census Bureau's Census of Manufactures. Economist Lawrence White (2002) made such calculations for the United States for various years up to the end of the 20th century. Some of his results are shown below.

These data suggest that, at least since the 1950s, aggregate concentration in manufacturing has shown no increasing or decreasing trend. It is approximately the same in 1997 as it was in 1958, whether one looks at the top 50, 100, or 200 largest firms. White shows that somewhat similar results are obtained if one looks at all nonfinancial corporations, or

Aggregate Concentration for Manufacturing (Value Added Basis); Selected Years, 1947–97

Year	CR_{50}	CR_{100}	CR_{200}
1947	17%	23%	30%
1958	23	30	38
1967	25	33	42
1977	24	33	44
1987	25	33	43
1992	24	32	42
1997	24	32	40

focuses on shares of employment or profit. This, of course, does not mean that firms are not getting bigger. If each firm grows at the same rate as the economy, each of us will find ourselves employed in larger and larger organizations over time, even though concentration is stable. White shows that this too has been happening, and that the size of the average firm has, correspondingly, grown.

Source: L. White, "Trends in Aggregate Concentration in the United States." *Journal of Economic Perspectives* (Fall 2002), p. 137–160.

omits the other information in the curve. For the hypothetical industries described above for example, Industry A appears more concentrated than does industry B using the CR_8 measure, but less concentrated when evaluated with the CR_4 index.

An alternative to CR_n that attempts to reflect more of the information in the concentration curve is the Herfindahl-Hirschman Index or more simply H. For an industry with n firms, this is defined as follows:

$$H = \sum_{i=1}^{n} s_i^2 \tag{4.1}$$

where s_i is the market share of the ith firm. If we measure market shares in percentage terms, then the perfectly competitive market would have an H of 0, while a fully monopolized market would have an H of 10,000. Applying this measure to each of our three hypothetical industries yields an H of 1,000 for Industry A; 3,126.25 for Industry B;

and 2,000 for Industry C, respectively.[2] Thus, H reflects the combined influence of both unequal firm sizes and the concentration of activity in a few large firms. Consequently, while H is a single number, it does provide more information about the concentration curve than does a simple concentration ratio.[3]

In the United States, the Census Bureau is the custodian of the market definitions; and for this purpose, it employs the North American Industry Classification System (NAICS). The Bureau first categorizes the output of business units in the United States into broad sectors of the economy, such as manufacturing, primary metals, agriculture, and forestry products, each of which receives a numeric code. These sectors are then subdivided further, and each is given a two-digit code. The manufacturing sector, for example, is covered by codes 31–33. These are each disaggregated further into the three-digit, four-digit, five-digit, and six-digit levels. Each additional digit represents a further subdivision of the initial classification. Given the nature of the data collection process, the basis of all subdivisions is the similarity of production processes. The classification system permits the construction of concentration data. Before compiling these data, however, the Bureau must determine how to categorize production plants that produce more than one product. Its basic procedure is to assign a plant on the basis of that plant's primary product as measured by sales. Once all the establishments are so assigned, total sales are computed for each market. Market shares and concentration indices are then calculated. These data are published regularly by the Census Bureau. Table 4.1 shows both CR_4 and H for a sample of 25 manufacturing industries.

4.1.1   Measurement Problems: What Is a Market?

Table 4.1 shows the two measures of industrial concentration just discussed, CR_4 and H, for 25 industries. Despite the caveats in our prior discussion, the truth is that the correlation between the two measures for the data shown here is 0.94, implying that each gives roughly the same description of an industry's structure. Although this is somewhat reassuring, there is a larger issue. Whether or not CR_4 and H measures tell the same story, the crucial question is whether or not either tells the right story. In turn, the answer to this question depends in part on whether or not the four-digit industry classification codes conform to a sensibly defined market.

Consider, for example, the automobile industry. As measured here, it focuses on passenger cars. But is this really the relevant market? Or are specialized vehicles such as motorcycles, vans, and pickup trucks also part of the picture? Or think of the beverage industry. Does Pepsi compete only against other carbonated beverages, or should beverages such as fruit juices, iced teas, and flavored milk also be viewed as substitute products? Unless we have a clear procedure for answering such questions, any summary measure of market structure such as either CR_4 or H will become an arbitrary statistic capable of being manipulated either upward or downward at the whim of the researcher. An analyst can then make CR_4 or H arbitrarily small or large by defining the market either broadly or narrowly.

---

[2]   Here we follow the convention of measuring the H in percentage points. Obviously, if we treat the s_i's as proportions, H ranges from 0 to 1.

[3]   A quite readable discussion of the advantages and disadvantages of each ratio is available in Sleuwaegen and Dehandschutter (1986) and Sleuwaegen, Dehandschutter, and DeBondt (1989).

Table 4.1   Concentration measures for selected industries

Industry	NAICS Code	CR_4	H
Breakfast Cereals	311230	78.4	2521.3
Creamery Butter	311512	57.5	1046.1
Soft Drink Mfg	312111	51.9	895.7
Textile & Fabric Finishing Mills	313311	19.5	166.7
Women's Footwear	316214	64.2	1556.1
Manufactured Mobile Home	321991	44.6	685.3
Paper Mills	322121	25.8	259.3
Petroleum Refineries	324110	41.2	639.7
Petrochemical Mfg	325110	84.7	2661.6
Pharmaceuticals & Medicine	325410	34.0	506.0
Explosives	325920	54.2	991.3
Cement Mfg	327310	38.7	568.5
Aluminum Sheet/Plate/Foil	331315	70.8	1856.1
Small Arms Manufacturers	332994	43.3	637.0
Lawn Equip & Garden Tractors	333112	61.6	1117.8
Electronic Computers	334111	75.5	2662.4
Telephone Apparatus	334210	55.6	1398.5
Semiconductors/Related Devices	334413	56.5	1417.1
Electric lamp bulbs & parts	335110	88.5	2757.6
Household Refrigerators	335222	84.5	1998.5
Storage Battery	335911	61.8	1252.8
Automobiles	336111	75.5	1910.9
Heavy Duty Truck	336120	69.5	1512.5
Aircraft	336411	80.7	2560.7
Dolls & stuffed toys	339931	42.8	622.2

Source: "Concentration Ratios in Manufacturing," Bureau of the Census, 2002 Census of Manufacturing. http://www.census.gov/epcd/www/concentration.html

Generally speaking, we would like to include production establishments in the same market if the products that they produce are closely substitutable in consumption. Typically, economists measure substitutability in consumption by the cross-price elasticity of demand η_{ij}. This is defined as the percentage change in demand for good i that occurs when there is a 1 percent change in the price of another good j. The mathematical definition of this elasticity is

$$\eta_{ij} = \frac{\partial q_i}{\partial p_j} \frac{p_j}{q_i} \qquad (4.2)$$

If this measure is large and positive, then goods i and j would be considered to be reasonably close substitutes.[4] Of course, employing this standard means giving a working

---

[4] However, the presence of a high monopoly price may inflate the cross-elasticity measure, a point originally emphasized by Stocking and Mueller (1955). That is, at the high price set by a monopolist, the cross-price elasticity may be large and indicate that other goods are substitutes, when this would not be the finding had the monopolized industry been pricing competitively.

definition of what is meant by *large* and *positive*. One standard in this regard is the one used by the antitrust authorities in evaluating mergers.

When two firms in an industry merge, there is the possibility that the resultant firm will be sufficiently large that it can exert market power. It is therefore critical that the authorities have a way of measuring the market so that they can examine whether an announced merger is likely to have this effect. For this purpose, the authorities adopt the following approach laid out in the Merger Guidelines of the United States, jointly issued by the Department of Justice and the Federal Trade Commission. They start with a narrow product definition and assume, for simulation purposes, that narrow market is monopolized. They then test whether that hypothetical monopolist could profitably impose a small (say, 5 percent) "but significant and non-transitory price increase" (SSNIP). If the answer is yes, because good substitutes do not exist, then the narrow definition is considered appropriate. If the answer is no, because such a price increase would lead enough consumers to switch to other goods that it would not be profitable, then the market is broadened to include the next closest substitute and the experiment is repeated.

The SSNIP standard makes intuitive sense is and is the benchmark market definition used in all U.S. antitrust cases. Unfortunately, though, the SSNIP approach is not as helpful for the general purposes of the industrial census that motivate the NAICS approach and that underlie the data in Table 4.1. Instead, this census tends to group establishments more on the basis of similarity in production techniques than on the basis of substitutability in consumption. For example, wood, ceramic tile, and linoleum are all used as flooring materials and therefore may be viewed as substitutes in consumption. Yet, each is actually listed under a different three-digit NAICS code.

Other problems with the NAICS classifications arise in connection with geographic considerations. The geographic boundaries of a market are just as vital to market definition as are the product boundaries. For example, virtually all newspapers operate in local markets, where typically we find one or two other competitors at most. The fact that, taken as a nationwide industry, newspapers have a CR_4 ratio of 31.4 percent may therefore understate the true extent of monopoly power over local newsprint.[5] A similar problem arises in considering foreign trade and imports.

Finally, two other issues arise in connection with structural measures such as H and CR_4 regardless of how accurately the market's boundaries have been defined. The first of these is that any structural measure has trouble reflecting the vertical relationships in which firms are embedded. In general, the delivery of a final good or service to a customer only comes after many previous steps including the acquisition of the raw materials; their transformation into a semifinished product; and the refinement of the semifinished product into a final consumer product. Retailing is thus just the last step as the product flows "downstream" to the consumer. However, the relation between each step may vary a good bit across firms. An upstream producer of the raw product may be fully integrated through all subsequent steps, right down to the retail market, as is the case with those oil firms that own their own gasoline service stations. Alternatively, the downstream retailer may be independent of upstream suppliers and simply buy finished goods in a spot

---

[5] This issue becomes even more complicated for an industry where large, national firms operate in many local markets. For example, the *New York Times* owns a controlling interest in the *Boston Globe* as well as in other newspapers. The Gannet group controls the newspapers in more than two dozen markets. The banking industry outside the United States reveals a similar pattern of national ownership of local branches.

market or have a formal contract to be supplied by some upstream producer. The point is that the existence and variability of such relationships can cause difficulty in interpreting any market structure measure at one stage of production. For instance, there are many bottling companies, so conventional measures of market concentration in the bottled, tin and soft drink industry are rather low. In turn, this suggests a fairly competitive market. However, the reality is that most bottling companies do not compete with each other, but are instead tied through strict agreements (and often through ownership) to one of the two largest national upstream firms—Coca-Cola or Pepsi, which may suggest less rigorous competition.[6]

The second issue regarding both H and CR_4 is that both are attempts to describe the market configuration at a point in time. Neither therefore considers the possibilities of how that structure may evolve over time. In particular, each leaves out any explicit consideration of entry and exit. Even though an industry may be highly concentrated, the market power of actual firms (as opposed to the hypothetical monopolist of the SSNIP text) may be limited if any attempt to raise prices above cost would be met quickly with entry by new rivals.

4.1.2   The Endogeneity of Market Structure

Consideration of entry issues returns us to the point made earlier that the most difficult problem in interpreting measures such as CR_4 and H is that these structural features are themselves endogenous. For example, consider the cost function in equation (4.3) below:

$$C(q) = c + F \tag{4.3}$$

Here, marginal cost is c and average cost is $c + F/q$. Let us again suppose, as we did in Chapter 3, that demand is isoelastic with an elasticity of 1, so that total expenditure E is fixed. If the number of firms is n and P is the industry price, we then have that

$$q_i = E/nP \tag{4.4}$$

Let us also follow the assumption in Chapter 3 that the price-cost margin $(P-c)/P$ declines as more firms enter the industry. Specifically,

$$\frac{P - c}{P} = n^{-\theta} \tag{4.5}$$

Again, the parameter θ may be taken as a measure of the intensity of competition. As θ increases, prices are forced closer to marginal cost for the same number of firms. If we then define the equilibrium number of firms n^e as that number of firms at which each price is equal to average cost and each firm just breaks even, we have

$$n^e = \left(\frac{E}{F}\right)^{\frac{1}{1+\theta}} \tag{4.6}$$

---

[6]   Some authors, for example, Gort (1962) and, more recently, Davies and Morris (1995), have tried to obtain a precise, quantitative measure of the extent of vertical integration.

The equilibrium number of firms declines as θ grows, because this lowers the price-cost margin for any given number of firms n below the value needed to cover the fixed cost. Substitution of equation (4.6) into equation (4.5) then yields

$$\frac{P-c}{P} = \left(\frac{E}{F}\right)^{-\frac{\theta}{1+\theta}} \tag{4.7}$$

Examination of equation (4.7) quickly reveals that the price-cost margin also declines as θ increases. Together, equations (4.6) and (4.7) indicate that as competition intensifies and drives price closer to marginal cost, the market also becomes more concentrated. When price competition is fierce, firms have to produce on a large scale if they are to achieve the low average cost necessary to survive such a competitive environment, and this limits the number of firms that can survive.

Note, though, that if the above analysis is generally accurate, it suggests that interpreting a concentrated structure as an indication of market power and weak price competition is incorrect. In fact, just the opposite would be true. Markets with fierce price competition would be the more concentrated ones precisely because such competition limits the ability of many firms to survive. This is not to say that such an interpretation will always be correct. Indeed, it most certainly will be incorrect in a number of cases. Nevertheless, the point being made should be clear: the interpretation of any structural measure is clouded once one recognizes that structure is endogenous.

In sum, structural measures like CR_4 and H offer a useful starting point for characterizing a market setting in one summary statistic. Yet, the limitations in these measures are such that they can never be the final word. Market definitions are tricky, especially when the vertical connections between firms are recognized and when entry (and exit) are serious possibilities. More generally, structure is an endogenous variable that may be a result rather than a cause of the intensity of competition. But while it is good to recognize such limitations, it is equally important to recognize that some measures of industrial structure are probably better than none at all. To the extent that one has any theory of the equilibrium structure (e.g., Sutton 1991), that theory is only testable if one has a structural measure.

4.2   MEASURING MARKET POWER—THE LERNER INDEX AGAIN

In both the previous chapter and this one, we have now made frequent reference to the price-cost margin as measured by the Lerner Index (LI), given by $\frac{P-MC}{P}$. Unlike the structural measures, CR_4 and H, the Lerner Index has the advantage that it measures precisely what we are interested in, namely, the distortion between price and marginal cost. As we know from Chapter 2, it is this distortion that leads to the welfare losses associated with monopoly power. So, it would be useful to measure this index directly. However, doing so requires that we have a deeper understanding of what the LI is measuring.

Consider a firm facing a demand curve $P(Q)$ and producing output according to a constant-returns-to-scale production $Q = Q(K, L)$, where k is the capital input and n is the labor input. Assume that the rental price of capital r and the wage rate w are both given. The firm's profit π is then

$$\pi = P(Q)Q - rK - wL = P[Q(K, L)]Q - rK - wL \tag{4.8}$$

The first order conditions necessary for profit maximization are

$$\frac{\partial \pi}{\partial K} = P_Q Q_K Q + P Q_K - r = 0 \tag{4.9a}$$

$$\frac{\partial \pi}{\partial L} = P_Q Q_L Q + P Q_L - w = 0 \tag{4.9b}$$

where P_Q is the slope of the demand curve and Q_K and Q_L are the marginal products of capital and labor, respectively. Recognizing that $P_Q Q + P = \left(1 - \frac{1}{\varepsilon}\right)$, where ε is the elasticity of demand (defined so that it is strictly positive), we may rewrite the first-order conditions as

$$Q_K = \frac{r}{P\left(1 - \frac{1}{\varepsilon}\right)} \tag{4.10a}$$

$$Q_L = \frac{w}{P\left(1 - \frac{1}{\varepsilon}\right)} \tag{4.10b}$$

The firm's total cost is $C(Q) = rK + wL$. Now consider the marginal cost MC of producing one more unit of output. In that case, we have

$$\frac{dC}{dQ} = r\frac{\partial K}{\partial Q} + w\frac{\partial L}{\partial Q} = r\frac{1}{Q_K} + w\frac{1}{Q_L} = MC \tag{4.11}$$

Whether the extra output is produced solely by hiring new capital or new labor, or the optimal combination of the two, substitution of either equation (4.10a) or (4.10b) into (4.11) then yields:

$$MC = P\left(1 - \frac{1}{\varepsilon}\right) \Rightarrow \frac{P - MC}{P} = \frac{1}{\varepsilon} \tag{4.12}$$

That is, the Lerner Index follows directly from the basics of profit maximization and is equal to the reciprocal of the firm's price elasticity of demand. Recall that for a competitive firm, the price elasticity of its demand is infinite, so that the Lerner Index is 0 in that case. However, as the firm increasingly produces a distinct product for which substitutes are increasingly hard to find (i.e., as the elasticity of its demand falls), the firm will optimally raise price higher and higher above marginal cost.

Because it directly reflects the discrepancy between price and marginal cost, the Lerner Index captures much that we are interested in when it comes to the *exercise* of market power. Yet, while the index may be easily conceptualized, its measurement for the typical industry that lies somewhere between the exceptional cases of pure monopoly and pure competition is fairly tricky. To begin with, in any industry with a diverse set of firms, characterizing the entire market environment with one index measure will require obtaining some average index. If the commodity in question is homogenous, so that all firms must sell at exactly the same price, then we can measure a marketwide Lerner Index as

$$LI = \frac{P - \sum_{i=1}^{N} s_i MC_i}{P} \tag{4.13}$$

Here, as before, s_i is the market share of the ith firm and N is the total number of firms. Note that in this simple case, s_i will be the same whether one measures it in terms either the physical units or dollar value of firm i's production.

However, if the product is not homogenous, the average of the individual firm index values will be

$$LI = \sum_{i=1}^{N} s_i \left(\frac{P_i - MC_i}{P_i} \right) \tag{4.14}$$

In this case, the shares or s_i weights will in general depend on whether one uses an expenditure or unit volume measure. As a result, the industry Lerner Index will also depend on this choice.

If these problems are not daunting enough, an even greater difficulty with a Lerner Index measure is that it requires an estimate of marginal cost, and this can be difficult to obtain. One might think that the more obtainable average variable cost is a good proxy but as the simple cost function $C(q) = F + aq^2$ shows this is not necessarily the case.

If one has time series data, Robert Hall (1988) has shown a way to circumvent the need for directly measuring marginal cost using a production theory approach. Recall that production is: $Q = Q(K, L)$. Then we may write

$$dQ = Q_K \, dK + Q_L \, dL \tag{4.15}$$

Dividing through by Q and multiplying the first right-hand-side term by K/K and the second by L/L yields

$$\frac{dQ}{Q} = \frac{Q_K K}{Q} \frac{dK}{K} + \frac{Q_L L}{Q} \frac{dL}{L} \tag{4.16}$$

Assume constant returns to scale. Then, by Euler's Theorem

$$\frac{Q_K K}{Q} + \frac{Q_L L}{Q} = 1 \Rightarrow \frac{Q_K K}{Q} = 1 - \frac{Q_L L}{Q} \tag{4.17}$$

Hence, we may write

$$\frac{dQ}{Q} = \left(1 - \frac{Q_L L}{Q}\right) \frac{dK}{K} + \frac{Q_L L}{Q} \frac{dL}{L} \Rightarrow \frac{dQ}{Q} - \frac{dK}{K} = \frac{Q_L L}{Q} \left(\frac{dL}{L} - \frac{dK}{K} \right) \tag{4.18}$$

The left-hand side of equation (4.18) is the growth in output per unit of capital. Similarly, the term in brackets on the right-hand side is the growth in labor per unit of capital. Let us denote these as q and n, respectively. Let us also define μ such that $\frac{1}{\mu} = 1 - \frac{1}{\varepsilon}$, where ε is the elasticity of demand. Then, by equation (4.10b), we have

$$q = \frac{wL}{P \left(1 - \frac{1}{\varepsilon}\right) Q} n = \mu \frac{wL}{PQ} = u s_L n \tag{4.19}$$

where s_L is the share of labor in total revenue. Using changes in industry from one period to the next, Hall (1988) can measure q, s_L, and n. Hence, he can estimate μ. Given μ, it is straightforward to estimate the Lerner Index. The only complication is that because Hall (1988) uses time series data, he must account for the normal growth δ that would occur in output even if there were no input growth. So, treating μ and δ as parameters to be estimated and v as a random error term, Hall estimates the relation

$$q = \delta + \mu(s_L n) + v \qquad\qquad\qquad (4.20)$$

The results allow Hall (1988) to derive estimates of LI for 20 broad manufacturing sectors in the United States. More recently, Dobbelaere (2004) has made similar estimates for Belgian industries. Both sets of estimates are shown in Table 4.2. These show considerable range, but it is fair to say that by either measure, price is, on average, at least 25 percent above marginal cost across a wide range of markets.

Estimates such as those shown in Table 4.2 serve the useful purpose of giving a sense of the extent of price distortion in an economy over some time period. However, if one needs to have measure of the Lerner Index for a particular industry for a specific point in time, Hall's technique is less helpful, as it requires a number of time periods for the estimation to have any precision. Moreover, even when the LI can be measured, there remains some ambiguity in its interpretation. Suppose, for example, that each firm in an industry has to incur a one-time sunk cost K_S associated with setting up its establishment. Assume further that each firm's marginal cost is constant. Because each firm needs to earn enough operating profit to cover its sunk cost, the equilibrium price level will need

Table 4.2 Estimated lerner index for selected industries

Hall (1988)		Dobbelaere (2004)	
Industry	*Lerner Index*	*Industry*	*Lerner Index*
Food & Kindred Products	0.811	Ferrous and nonferrous ores	0.277
Tobacco	0.638	Non-metallic mineral products	0.244
Textile Mill Products	−0.214	Chemical products	0.205
Apparel	0.444	Metal products (no mach/transp. equip)	0.156
Lumber and Wood	0.494	Agricultural and industrial machinery	0.227
Furniture and Fixtures	0.731	Office machines, prec. instruments	0.247
Paper and Allied Products	0.930	Electrical goods	0.198
Printing	0.950	Motor vehicles	0.174
Rubber & Plastic	0.337	Other transport equipment	0.471
Leather Products	0.524	Meat preserves	0.065
Stone, Clay, and Glass	0.606	Milk and dairy products	0.000
Primary Metals	0.540	Other food products	0.202
Fabricated Metals	0.394	Beverages	0.294
Machinery	0.300	Textiles and clothing	0.143
Electric Equipment	0.676	Timber, wooden products, & furniture	0.172
Instruments	0.284	Paper and printing products	0.200
Miscellaneous Mfg	0.777	Rubber and plastic products	0.314
Communication	0.972	Other manufacturing products	0.143
Electric, Gas, & Sanitary Svcs	0.921		
Motor Vehicles	0.433		
Average	**0.57**	**Average**	**0.207**

to rise above marginal cost. That is, the Lerner Index will need to be positive. However, the more positive that difference is—the greater the price-cost margin—the greater the number of firms that can cover the one-time sunk cost. As a result, we might observe a high Lerner Index in a setting in which there are numerous small firms. In such a case, the high Lerner Index might erroneously indicate little competition, even though no one firm has any substantial market power.[7]

Conversely, the Lerner Index might underestimate market power in settings in which cost-reducing innovations are important. Suppose, for example, that an industry has an old and not very efficient incumbent firm with high marginal cost, but that a rival with a lower marginal cost could potentially enter if it could earn enough to cover its sunk entry cost. The incumbent firm may then find it optimal to price relatively close to its (high) marginal cost to keep its low-cost rival from entering the market, because this prevents the rival from covering its sunk entry cost. Here, the Lerner Index deceptively indicates a fair bit of competition, because price is low relative to the incumbent's marginal cost. However, the relevant (but unavailable) comparison is the price with the potential rival's more efficient technology and lower marginal cost.[8]

Despite these caveats, the Lerner Index remains an important tool for the analysis of market power. Again, this is because it focuses precisely on the concern associated with such power, namely, the elevation of price above marginal cost. We will employ a measure of *LI* in many settings throughout the rest of this book. To give just one example of how the measure may be used here, consider Ellison's (1994) use of the *LI* to gauge the impact of cartel behavior. For this purpose, he studies railroad prices over time in the late 19th century. He finds that, apart from brief price war periods, the *LI* was about 85 percent of its hypothetical monopoly value. In other words, the collusive behavior of railroads then typically kept prices within 15 percent of the pure monopoly price. This is a large amount of price distortion and, if taken as representative of the success of typical cartels, would suggest that price-fixing arrangements often come very close to duplicating the monopoly outcome.

4.3   EMPIRICAL APPLICATION
Monopoly Power: How Bad Is It?

A recurrent question in antitrust policy is just how costly imperfect competition is for the economy overall. If the losses from monopoly power are not large, then devoting any significant resources to antitrust enforcement to prevent such losses is probably not worthwhile. Such scarce resources would be better used in, say, increasing homeland security or providing relief to hurricane victims. If the economic costs of market power are large, however, then allocating resources to combat the abuse of that power is likely to be warranted. Hence, it would be useful if economists had some sense of just how serious the losses from monopoly power actually are.

The first person to attempt an operational answer to this question was Harberger (1954). He recognized that the deadweight loss or triangle that results from prices above marginal cost is, in principle, a precise measure of this loss. He therefore pursued the following line of attack.

---

[7]   See, for example, Elzinga (1989).
[8]   Hovenkamp (1994), among others, has made this argument.

Harberger (1954) starts with the result from Chapter 2 that the deadweight or welfare loss in any market is the area given by

$$WL = \int_Q^{Q^C} [P(Q) - f(Q)]dQ \qquad (4.21)$$

where Q is the observed output, Q^C is the competitive or efficient output level, $P(Q)$ is the demand curve, and $f(Q)$ is marginal cost curve. As a first approximation, Harberger (1954) assumed a linear case with a constant marginal cost MC. Hence, the welfare loss is a triangle, and equation (4.20) simplifies to

$$WL = \frac{1}{2} (P - MC)(Q^C - Q) \qquad (4.22)$$

It is convenient to express this welfare loss as a proportion of total sales revenue PQ to yield

$$WL' = \frac{WL}{PQ} = \frac{1}{2} \frac{(P - MC)}{P} \frac{(Q^C - Q)}{Q} \qquad (4.23)$$

Remember that the elasticity of demand ε is the proportionate increase in output in response to a given proportionate decrease in price. If the price were to fall from its current P level to the competitive level of $P = MC$, then output would rise to the competitive level of Q^C. That is, it rises to

$$\eta = \frac{(Q^C - Q)/Q}{(P - MC)/P} \Rightarrow \frac{(Q^C - Q)}{Q} = \varepsilon \frac{(P - MC)}{P} \qquad (4.24)$$

Since we also know that the industry Lerner Index is $(P - MC)/P$, we can rewrite equation (4.23) as

$$WL' = \frac{WL}{PQ} = \frac{1}{2} \varepsilon (LI)^2 \qquad (4.25)$$

Recalling that the Lerner Index is given by: $LI = (P - MC)/P = 1/\varepsilon$, we may then solve for the deadweight loss relative to industry sales as

$$WL' = \frac{WL}{PQ} = \frac{1}{2} \frac{1}{\varepsilon} \qquad (4.26)$$

That is, for the perfect monopoly case, the deadweight loss as a fraction of current industry sales is simply one-half the Lerner Index or one over twice the elasticity of demand. As the demand elasticity increases, the welfare loss shrinks because other goods are increasingly viewed as substitutes to the monopolized commodity. Note further the sensitivity of the welfare loss to the elasticity estimate. An estimate that $\varepsilon = 1.5$ produces a welfare loss equal to 33 percent of revenue. An estimate of $\varepsilon = 2$ reduces this amount to 25 percent of revenue. That is, a 0.5 change in the elasticity estimate yields an 8 percent change in the welfare loss.

Using a sample of 73 manufacturing industries, Harberger (1954) took the departure of the five-year average industry rate of return from the five-year average for manufacturing overall as an approximation of LI. Because he worked with industry data, and because none of the industries was a pure monopoly, Harberger (1954) could not assume that his LI estimate is the inverse of elasticity of demand, as was the case in equation (4.26). Instead, he combined his LI estimates with an assumed demand elasticity of $\eta = 1$. The dollar value of these estimated distortions is then given by multiplying WL' by industry sales PQ. When Harberger (1954) added these dollar values up and extrapolated the results across the entire economy, he found a surprisingly small welfare cost of monopoly—on the order of one-tenth of 1 percent of Gross Domestic Product (GDP). Currently, the budget of the Justice Department and the FTC is between one and two-tenths of 1 percent of GDP. Much of this is for activities other than antitrust enforcement; and by any measure, Harberger's estimates are very crude. Nevertheless, they are sufficiently compelling to raise serious question about the cost-effectiveness of antitrust policy.

Harberger's (1954) approach however did not go uncriticized. Bergson (1973) noted that Harberger's procedure essentially used a partial equilibrium framework to obtain a general equilibrium measure. He demonstrated that, in principle, this could mean that Harberger's (1954) estimate considerably understated the actual loss. Cowling and Mueller (1978) used firm-level data for 734 companies in the United States and 103 companies in the United Kingdom. The use of firm-level data means that Cowling and Mueller (1978) could apply equation (4.26) directly. Their estimated monopoly welfare costs range from 4–13 percent of GDP in the United States and from 4–7 percent in the UK. These are considerably larger than Harberger's (1954) estimates.

An important source of variation in Cowling and Mueller's (1978) analysis is how advertising costs are treated in measuring LI. This calls attention to the importance of the marginal cost measure in general in determining welfare losses. This issue has been addressed more recently by Aiginger and Pfaffermayr (1997). They start by recognizing that without the pressure of perfect competition, firms can operate in an industry with different cost efficiencies. Hence, the average industry marginal cost $\overline{MC}$ is very likely not the minimum average cost that would be enforced if perfect competition were the rule. Aiginger and Pfaffermayr (1997) then make use of a result (which we shall derive in Chapter 9) from a standard oligopoly model. This result is that the industry price-cost margin measure using $\overline{MC}$ is equal to the industry Herfindahl Index H (here scaled from 0 to 1) divided by the elasticity of industry demand. That is

$$\frac{P - \overline{MC}}{P} = \frac{H}{\eta} \quad \Rightarrow \quad \eta = H\left(\frac{P}{P - \overline{MC}}\right) \tag{4.27}$$

Substituting this result into equation (4.25), we obtain

$$WL' = \frac{WL}{PQ} = \frac{1}{2}\left(\frac{P - MC}{P}\right)\left(\frac{P - MC}{P - \overline{MC}}\right)H \tag{4.28}$$

Note that the term $\left(\frac{P-MC}{P-\overline{MC}}\right)$ is greater than 1, because MC is the marginal cost that would prevail under competition. Aiginger and Pfaffermayr (1997) measure this competitive MC as the marginal cost of the most efficient firm in the industry, under the assumption that this is the cost efficiency that would be required for competitive firms to survive.

Effectively, their approach permits them to decompose the welfare cost of market power into two parts. One is the traditional welfare loss measure due to prices not equal to *industry* average marginal cost, $P - \overline{MC}$. The other is due to the fact that market power allows the survival of firms with higher than minimum costs, $\overline{MC} - MC$. Using data from 10,000 cement and paper firms in the European Union, Aiginger and Pfaffermayr (1997) find that the total welfare loss of market power in these industries is in the order of 9–11 percent of industry sales. Perhaps not surprisingly, they find that these welfare losses are largely due to the cost inefficiencies that imperfect competition permits. Specifically, they estimate that the traditional welfare loss measure is in the order of 2–3 percent of sales, while the cost inefficiency loss is in the order of 7–7.5 percent. Extrapolating these estimates to the entire economy would yield results that are notably closer to the Cowling and Mueller estimates (1978) than those obtained by Harberger (1954).

In evaluating all of these estimates, it is useful to bear in mind at least two caveats. First, an implicit assumption in all these calculations is that it is feasible to have perfect competition in all industries. Yet, as discussed in the last chapter, this will not be the case if the minimum efficient plant size is large relative to the market. In this sense, the estimates of welfare losses due to monopoly price distortions are too high, as there is no way in which all industries could be freed of such market power. Second, the measures are taken from data in which active antitrust enforcement has been the norm. In this sense, the measures are an understatement of the potential for monopoly-induced welfare losses. Had there been no antitrust enforcement, there would have presumably been more market power abuses, and the associated welfare losses would have been greater.

Summary

This chapter has focused on the measurement of market structure and market power. We are often interested in summarizing in a single number or index measure at least a rough idea of how far an industry departs from the competitive ideal. One issue is whether and how such an estimate can be obtained. Another concerns the interpretation of the measures we actually have.

Concentration indices, such as the CR_4 or H, are explicit measures of a market's structure. Both look at firm shares as a fraction of the industry's total output. The H index is generally preferred by economists since it gives a more complete indication of the size distribution of firms. However, in practice, the two measures move fairly closely together. Both measures are also subject to measurement issues, especially with respect to defining the market properly. However, the biggest weakness in such structural measures is that they themselves respond endogenously to competitive pressure. Far from determining the intensity of competition, then, the structural measure may themselves be the result of such pressure.

An explicit measure of market power is the Lerner Index. Since it is based on a comparison of price and marginal cost, this index directly addresses the extent to which the market outcome deviates from the competitive ideal. However, the need to measure marginal cost accurately (along with other measurement issues) makes the Lerner Index as difficult to employ as the structural indices. Hall (1988) shows that a careful application of theory here can help point the way to estimating the *LI* based on widely observable data. While the statistical issues involved in applying this technique are not trivial, a number of researchers have done so with fairly clear and plausible results. However, the need to have extended time series data can make Hall's (1988) approach less helpful in determining the *LI* for an industry at a specific point in time.

From a policy standpoint, justification of antitrust enforcement requires that the welfare loss of monopoly be sufficient at least to cover the cost of antitrust enforcement. Harberger (1954) was the first to pursue this issue in a formal way. Many others have since followed Harberger in researching this topic. These empirical studies have yielded a wide range of estimates of the aggregate deadweight loss as a percentage of GDP. The lower-bound estimate is that monopoly power imposes only a small inefficiency cost of a few tenths of 1 percent of GDP. However, upper-bound estimates range as high as 14 percent. A crucial parameter in such studies is the elasticity of demand assumed.

Problems

1. Consider the expression in equation (4.26) for the industry Lerner Index, H/ε, where H is the Herfindahl Index and ε is the elasticity of demand. Assume that the industry is comprised of n equal size firms and that the price elasticity of demand is -1, so that expenditures on the product are constant at E. In addition, assume that the cost function for each firm i is $C(q_i) = cq_i + F$, where both c and F are positive. Show that the equilibrium number of firms is: $n = \sqrt{\frac{E}{F}}$.

2. Assume again that the industry LI value is given by H/ε. Assume now, however, that marginal cost c also declines as H increases (i.e., $c = c(H)$, with $c' < 0$). Taking the demand elasticity ε as given, determine the magnitude of $c' = dc/dH$ such that an increase in concentration (rise in H) will not lead to an increase in the price p.

3. Consider a five-firm industry in which all five firms are initially the same size with a market share of 20 percent each. Suppose that as the result of an aggressive and successful advertising campaign, firm 1 raises its market share to 25 percent, while the share of each of the other remaining firms declines to 18.75 percent.
   a. What happens to the CR_4 and the H index as the result of this change?
   b. Which index do you think better captures the change in the competitive environment in this case?

4. The following table gives percentage market share data for three U.S. paper product markets in 1994.

Facial Tissue		Toilet Paper		Paper Towels	
Company	% Share	Company	% Share	Company	% Share
Kimberly-Clark	48	Procter & Gamble	30	Procter & Gamble	37
Procter & Gamble	30	Scott	20	Scott	18
Scott	7	James River	16	James River	12
Georgia Pacific	6	Georgia Pacific	12	Georgia Pacific	11
Other	9	Kimberly-Clark	5	Scott	4
		Other	16	Other	18

   a. Calculate the four-firm concentration ratio for each industry.
   b. Calculate each industry's H Index.
   c. Which industry do you think exhibits the most concentration?

5. James Munopilee runs Munopilee Air, which is the sole provider of passenger air service between Eldorado and Erewhon. It flies two flights per day in either direction, with the typical flight being about 85 percent booked. A new entrant, Upstart Airways, has announced plans to offer additional service in the Eldorado–Erewhon market. However, James has filed a complaint with the local transportation authority arguing that his firm is a natural monopoly and that additional air service will only cause losses for both parties. As evidence, James cites the fact that, even now, his planes are not fully booked. Hence, he argues that the market is not large enough to sustain two efficient-sized air carriers. Evaluate the argument put forth by Munopilee Air. What problems do you see in its logic? What information is needed in order to determine whether or not this market is a natural monopoly?

References

Aiginger and Pfaffermayr. 1997. "Looking at the Cost Side of Monopoly". *Journal of Industrial Economics*, 44 (September): 245–267.

Bergson, A. 1973. "On Monopoly Welfare Losses". *American Economic Review*, 63 (December): 853–870.

Cowling, K. and D. C. Mueller. 1978. "The Social Cost of Monopoly Power." *Economic Journal*, 88 (December): 727–748.

Davies, S. W., and C. Morris. 1995. "A New Index of Vertical Integration: Some Estimates for UK Manufacturing." *International Journal of Industrial Organization*, 13: 151–178.

Dobbelaere, S. 2004. "Estimation of Price-Cost Margins and Union Bargaining Power in Belgian Manufacturing." *International Journal of Industrial Organization*, 22 (December): 1381–1398.

Domowitz, I., R. G. Hubbard, and B. Petersen. 1988. "Market Structure and Cyclical Fluctuations in Manufacturing". *Review of Economics and Statistics*, 70 (February): 55–66.

Ellison, G. 1994. "Theories of Cartel Stability and the Joint Executive Committee." *Rand Journal of Economics*, 25 (Spring): 37–57.

Elzinga, K. 1989. "Unmasking Monopoly Power: Four Types of Economic Evidence" in R. Larner and J. Meehan, Jr. (Eds.), *Economics and Antitrust Policy*. Westport, CT: Greenwood Press.

Gort, M. 1962. *Diversification and Integration in American Industry*. Princeton: Princeton University Press.

Hall, R. 1988. "The Relation Between Price and Marginal Cost in U.S. Industry." *Journal of Political Economy*, 96 (October): 921–947.

Harberger, A. 1954. "Monopoly and Resource Allocation." *American Economic Review*, 45 (May): 77–87.

Hovenkamp, H. J. 1994. *Federal Antitrust Law Policy: The Law of Competition and Its Practice*. St. Paul: West Publishing.

Porter, R. 1983. "A Study of Cartel Stability: The Joint Executive Committee, 1880–1886." *Bell Journal of Economics*, 14 (Autumn): 301–314.

Sleuwaegen, L., and W. V. Dehandschutter. 1986. "The Critical Choice Between the Concentration Ratio and the H-Index in Assessing Industry Performance." *Journal of Industrial Economics*, 35 (December): 193–208.

Sleuwaegen, L., W. V. Dehandschutter, and R. DeBondt. 1989. "The Herfindahl Index and Concentration Ratios Revisited." *Antitrust Bulletin*, 34 (Fall): 625–640.

Stocking, G. and W. Mueller. 1955. "The Cellophane Case and the New Competition." *American Economic Review*, 45 (March): 29–63.

Part II
Price and Nonprice Tactics for Firms with Market Power

The two chapters in this short section present an analysis of the tactics that firms with market power may use to extract surplus from the market. Chapter 5 focuses on price discrimination tactics. These include the familiar tactics of personalized pricing, block pricing, menu pricing, and group pricing. Chapter 6 turns to nonprice techniques including quality choices, versioning, and bundling and tying. Examination of these topics permits a deeper understanding of the welfare aspects of imperfect competition. It also allows us to introduce the important concepts of horizontal and vertical differentiation. Because we make substantial use of the Hotelling (1929) spatial model throughout the remainder of the text, the first of these concepts is particularly crucial.

At the end of this section, students will have a precise and detailed understanding of economic efficiency and the incentives that firms have to pursue efficient outcomes. They will also have an understanding of product differentiation and its implications for product pricing. In each of these cases, the goal is to make to the underlying concept operational by demonstrating how it may be modeled mathematically. We also demonstrate the empirical testing of such concepts by reviewing the empirical work of Stavins (2001).

5

Price Discrimination and Monopoly

An important concern in the debate over U.S. healthcare policy has been the high price of prescription drugs. This concern led to the expansion of Medicare to include coverage for prescription drugs starting in 2006. The same issue has encouraged many Americans to buy their prescription drugs in other countries, most notably Canada. Yet for that to happen legally, additional legislation is required. Existing statutes—enacted during the Clinton Administration—permit such imports only if the Secretary of Health and Human Services certifies that the imported drugs "pose no additional risk" to consumers, and no such certifications have been issued. Legislation to remove the certification requirement passed the U.S. House of Representatives in 2003, but has so far not been able to win passage in the U.S. Senate.

Prescription drug prices are indisputably higher in the United States than in Canada. Graham and Robson (2000) collected detailed 1999 price information for 45 brand name prescription drugs, collectively covering approximately 25 percent of the total prescriptions written in the United States. From this sample they calculated that Canadian retail prices were far less than American prices, with the median discount approximately 46 percent. For one drug in their sample, this discount was 95 percent.

In a related study, Graham and Tabler (2001) analyzed the retail prices charged in 2001 by a randomly selected set of pharmacies for three patented drugs in three Canadian and three neighboring American regions. Table 5.1 provides summary information on brand name drug prices that further confirms that these are generally lower in Canada than in the United States, with normal discounts running in the range of 50 percent. At the same time, however, there is considerable evidence that generic drug prices are much lower in the United States than in Canada. A recent study from the Fraser Institute[1] finds that Canadian seniors pay on average 57 percent less than U.S. seniors for brand name drugs, but 101 percent *more* for generic drugs.

When the same firm charges different customers different prices for the same products, the seller is engaging in *price discrimination*. The drug prices shown in Table 5.1 appear to be an example of such discrimination. The question then becomes, what explains such pricing differentials? What is it that makes it profitable for these firms to set and sustain higher prices in one market or the other?

---

[1] "Seniors and Drug Prices in Canada and the United States." 2008 Edition. Canada: Fraser Institute (August 2008).

Table 5.1   Comparison of prescription drug prices (U.S. dollars)

	Celebrex® 200 mg		Lipitor® 40 mg		Paxil® 20 mg	
	Mean	Standard deviation	Mean	Standard deviation	Mean	Standard deviation
Washington	86.26	5.66	110.01	8.97	82.47	3.86
British Columbia	33.17	2.37	52.83	3.50	40.75	2.54
North Dakota and Minnesota	78.08	5.70	107.75	7.03	78.63	6.08
Manitoba	32.36	1.60	52.43	1.52	39.80	2.00
New York	88.57	7.59	117.69	5.44	85.06	4.39
Ontario	34.82	1.96	55.52	2.09	42.62	2.03

Source: Graham and Tabler (2001), "Prescription Drug Prices in Canada and the United States: Part 3 Retail Price Distribution." Public Policy Sources no. 50, Fraser Institute.

This chapter addresses these questions. Our analysis begins by identifying the conditions under which price discrimination is feasible and profitable. It should be borne in mind, of course, that any increased profit must come from a reduction in consumer surplus, improved market efficiency, or some combination of the two. From a policy perspective, it matters a great deal which of these is the case. Hence, we also explore the welfare implications of price discrimination. Finally, it is worthwhile noting that discriminatory prices can affect market competition. This occurs when the buyers are not final consumers but instead, retailers such as drug stores. If large drug store chains are charged different wholesale prices than are small, independent pharmacies, then retail competition between these two groups will not be conducted on a level playing field.

5.1   THE FEASIBILITY OF PRICE DISCRIMINATION

A firm with market power faces a downward-sloping demand curve, so if the firm charges the same price to each consumer—the standard case of nondiscriminatory pricing—the additional (marginal) revenue it gets from selling one more unit of output is less than the price charged. The reason is straightforward. In order to sell the extra unit, the firm must lower its price. Yet if it charges the same price to all consumers, this means lowering the price not only to the new, incremental customers, but rather to all of them. This limits the monopolist's incentive to serve more consumers. Hence, a uniform pricing monopoly undersupplies its product relative to the efficient outcome.

Of course, the monopolist does not care about social welfare and efficiency. Her goal is profit. Yet, uniform pricing is a constraint here as well. It prevents the firm from charging a higher price to those consumers willing to pay a lot for its product. Thus, relaxing the restriction against price discrimination enables the monopolist to earn more profit. As we shall see, however, price discrimination can also induce the monopolist to sell more output and thereby come closer to the efficient production level.

In trying to escape the uniform pricing constraint, the monopolist must overcome two important obstacles. The first of these is the *identification problem*. The monopolist must somehow determine how different types of consumers vary in their demands for its product (e.g., which consumers have a high willingness to pay and which do not).

This is easier for some firms than for others. For example, tax accountants effectively sell one unit of their services to each client in any given year. Realtors and lawyers similarly gather much information from buyers that can help them determine the customer's true willingness to pay. Sometimes, simple information such as where a consumer lives or shops can provide at least a clue as to the value the consumer attaches to the goods being offered.

In those cases where the market is less personalized and more anonymous, the firm may be able to devise strategies that induce consumers to *self-select* according to their true types. What is needed in this case is that the firm offer a set of "packages" aimed at consumers of different types, priced in such a way that a package designed for one type of consumer is not purchased by a different type of consumer. In other words, the design and pricing of the different packages must satisfy what are called *incentive compatibility constraints.* For example, setting a different price for a single opera ticket as compared to a season's subscription encourages operagoers to self-select into those who are really keen on opera and those who feel that seeing one opera a year is sufficient artistic stimulation.

Even if a monopolist can solve the identification problem, there is a second obstacle to price discrimination. This is the force of *consumer arbitrage.* To discriminate successfully, the monopolist must be able to prevent consumers who are offered a low price from reselling their purchases to other consumers to whom the monopolist wants to charge a high price. If discount airline ticket holders can easily sell their boarding passes, an airline will soon find it difficult to sell anyone else a higher-priced ticket. This is why it is important to the pharmaceutical firms that the American and Canadian markets are kept separate. In the absence of such separation, arbitrage would quickly force the firms to charge the same prices everywhere.

Again, preventing consumer arbitrage is easier for some products than it is for others. Accounting, medical, and legal services are not easily resold. Similarly, a senior citizen cannot easily resell a discounted movie theater ticket to a teenager. By contrast, for products such as flat rolled steel, bicycles, and books, arbitrage may be a fact of life.

In short, firms with market power can enhance their profit if they can price discriminate across different consumers. In turn, this requires that they solve the identification and arbitrage problems. We now consider some of the more popular techniques employed to accomplish this objective. Traditionally, such techniques are classified into three broad types: first-degree, second-degree, and third-degree price discrimination.[2] More recently, these types of pricing schemes have been referred to respectively as *personalized pricing, menu pricing,* and *group pricing.*[3] As it turns out, it makes sense to reserve analysis of the second type—menu pricing—for last. We therefore begin with an analysis of personalized pricing and then move to a discussion of group pricing to set the stage for considering the somewhat more complicated analytics of menu pricing.

5.2   FIRST-DEGREE PRICE DISCRIMINATION

First-degree price discrimination, or personalized pricing, occurs when the monopolist is able to charge each consumer the maximum price that that consumer is willing to pay, for *each* unit that the consumer purchases. This is also referred to as *perfect price discrimination*, for obvious reasons. Referring to the identification problem that we discussed

[2]   The distinction between first-, second-, and third-degree discrimination follows the work of Pigou (1920). A more modern treatment appears in Phlips (1983).
[3]   These terms were first coined by Shapiro and Varian (1999).

in section 5.1, implementation of first-degree price discrimination requires that the firm has an observable signal of the true type and willingness to pay of each of its potential consumers—and, of course, that the firm can prevent arbitrage between consumers of different types.

The requirements necessary for so finely tuned a strategy as personalized pricing may seem impractical, but it is worth exploring this case in detail for two reasons. First, it illustrates some of the complicated policy questions that accompany price discrimination in general. Second, in some cases, something like personalized pricing may in fact be possible. Recall, for instance, the tax accountant example. In that case, the firm clearly has very detailed knowledge of the financial strength (or weakness) of his or her clients. A similar example that may strike nearer home is the process by which private universities in the United States determine the financial aid awarded to individual students. Usually, this is done only after the student and her family have completed a financial aid application that provides substantial information regarding the household's finances.

5.2.1   Personalized Pricing

To keep matters relatively simple, suppose that consumers have unit demands. That is, each consumer of type x will purchase exactly one unit of a monopolist's product, provided the price is no higher than the consumer's reservation price $v(x)$. Otherwise, she purchases no units. Let us assume that there is a continuum of consumers ordered by their reservation prices $v(x)$, with $v(0) = \bar{v}$ and $dv(x)/dx < 0$. That is, x serves as a ranking of the willingness to pay across consumers, with the highest ranking of $\bar{v}$ associated with the first consumer at $x = 0$, and then declining monotonically as x increases. Next, assume that the density of consumers of type x is described by a density function $f(x)$. If the firm supplies all consumer types in the interval $x \in [0, s]^4$, its aggregate sales are $q = \int_0^s f(x)dx$. Assume also that the firm's total cost function is $C(q)$. Indeed, continuing in the spirit of keeping matters simple, let us assume that the distribution of consumers is uniform so that $f(x) = 1$, and therefore that $s = q$. Let us also assume that $C(q) = F + cq$, so that marginal cost is constant at c.

Suppose first that the monopolist chooses to charge the same price p to everyone. In that case, all consumers with reservation prices $v(x) \geq p$ will purchase the product. Define the marginal consumer type as the type s who is just indifferent between buying the good and not buying it (i.e., the consumer for whom $v(s) = p$). We can then write the firm's profit as

$$\pi(s) = \pi(q) = pq - C(q) = v(q)q - cq = p(q)q - cq \tag{5.1}$$

The firm's price choice therefore amounts to a choice of the marginal consumer s and therefore the total amount demanded, or q. Maximizing profit with respect to $s = q$ then leads to the first-order condition

$$v(q) + qv'(q) = p(q) + qp'(q) = c \tag{5.2}$$

It is clear that equation (5.2) is equivalent to equation (2.7), the first-order condition derived in Chapter 2 for maximizing monopoly profit. Since $v'(s) = p'(q) < 0$, it is also

---

4   Given that the firm wishes to supply a consumer with reservation price $v(x_1)$, it will also wish to supply all consumers with reservation prices greater than $v(x_1)$.

clear that this price choice is such that price p exceeds the firm's marginal cost. Hence, this outcome is inefficient.

Now consider personalized pricing. If the monopolist knows each consumer's reservation price $v(x)$ and arbitrage is impossible (as in our accountant example), then the firm can set a personalized price $p(x) = v(x)$ for each consumer. This of course extracts the entire consumer surplus from each consumer it serves. With $f(x) = 1$, and recognizing that $s = q$, the firm's profit is now

$$\pi(s) = \int_0^s v(x)dx - cs = \pi(q) = \int_0^q v(x)dx - cq \tag{5.3}$$

Differentiating with respect to $q = s$, gives the first-order condition

$$\frac{d\pi(q)}{dq} = v(q) - c \Rightarrow v(q) = c \tag{5.4}$$

Again, because $v'(q) < 0$, the output that solves equation (5.4) clearly exceeds that implied by (5.2). Indeed, equation (5.4) says that the firm supplies consumers up to the point where the reservation price of the marginal consumer equals marginal cost. In other words, the monopolist now supplies the efficient level of output.

More generally, with a nonuniform distribution of consumers and permitting the cost function $C(q)$ to have a nonconstant (but rising) marginal cost, we find that profit for the uniform pricing case is

$$\pi(s) = v(s) \int_0^s f(x)\,dx - C\left(\int_0^s f(x)\,dx\right) \tag{5.5}$$

while profit for the personalized-pricing case is

$$\pi(s) = \int_0^s v(x)f(x)\,dx - C\left(\int_0^s f(x)\,dx\right) \tag{5.6}$$

The necessary first-order conditions are, respectively

$$v(s) + q\frac{dv(s)}{ds} \bigg/ f(s) = v(q) + qv'(q) = C'(q) \tag{5.7}$$

for the uniform-pricing case, and

$$\frac{d\pi(s)}{ds} = v(s)f(s) - \frac{dC(q)}{dq}f(s) = 0 \Rightarrow v(s) = C'(q) \tag{5.8}$$

for the personalized pricing case. It is easy to see that equations (5.7) and (5.8) imply equations (5.4) and (5.5) when demand is linear and marginal cost is constant, as in our simple example.

It is equally easy to see that personalized pricing, as illustrated by equation (5.4) or (more generally) by (5.8), not only yields an efficient outcome in which the total surplus is maximized, but also results in all that surplus being claimed by the monopolist. This recalls our discussion of the nonsurplus approach in Chapter 2. When the monopolist can claim the entire surplus that her production generates, the market provides the signal necessary for her to produce an efficient amount. Figure 5.1 illustrates the efficiency of the personalized pricing outcome along with the fact that it results in the monopolist claiming the total surplus. This is a hybrid case of linear demand and a rising marginal cost.

5.2.2   Two-Part Pricing

Perfect price discrimination was easy in the foregoing case because, although consumers were different, each bought only one unit (at most). Therefore, there was no difference between charging a different price to each consumer and a different price per unit. Clearly, though, even when this special situation occurs, the monopolist will have to possess very detailed information to know the reservation price of each consumer. However, this is not the only case in which perfect discrimination is possible.

To see this, consider another case in which there is just one type of consumer, but in which that type now may buy more than one unit per period. Specifically, let there be N identical consumers each with the same downward-sloping demand function $q = d(p)$. It is convenient to write the individual demand function in inverse form $p = d^{-1}(q)$.[5] Each consumer's aggregate willingness to pay for quantity q then is

$$v(q) = \int_0^q d^{-1}(x)\, dx \tag{5.9}$$

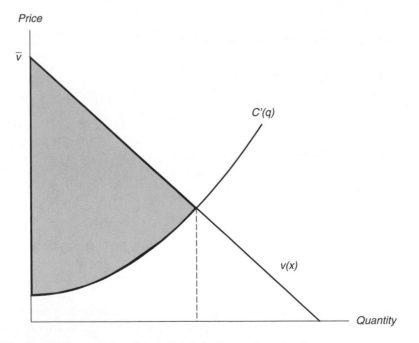

Figure 5.1   Personalized pricing: Price discrimination and monopoly

[5]   In the interests of notational simplicity, we ignore all the exogenous influences on demand such as income and the prices of other goods.

Reality Checkpoint
Call Options

Nonlinear pricing is an increasingly common feature of everyday life. Consider the packages available for cell phone service offered by the four major providers in the United States: AT&T/Cingular, Verizon, Sprint/Nexus, and T-Mobile. Virtually all of these involve some variant of two-part pricing and quantity discount. Family plans, for example, offer two lines for a fixed monthly fee. After that, each minute of calling is free up to a specified maximum. Low-level plans offer something like 700 minutes for free at a monthly fee of, for example, $70, while higher-use plans offer roughly twice as many free monthly minutes for a fee of about $90.

There is also a 3,000-minute plan that usually sells for about $150. Additional phones can be added to a family plan at a fee of $10 per month. There are also single-line plans and even pay-as-you-go plans. The latter are essentially calling card plans that sell, say, 30 minutes or 90 minutes of phone time for $15 or $25, respectively. They are clearly for those who cannot be induced to make more than a few calls, even with a hefty discount.

Sources: L. Magid, "BASICS: Plain Cellphones Can Overachieve, With A Little Help." *The New York Times* (25 January 2007), p. C14; and "The Bottom Line on Calling Plans." *Consumer Reports* (February 2004), p. 11–18.

Suppose that the firm adopts a *two-part pricing* policy $T(q) = A + pq$. In other words, the fee paid by each consumer is broken into two parts. There is a fixed charge A that must be paid simply to have the right to buy the product in any amount. There is also a price p paid for each individual unit consumed. Such multipart pricing schemes are common. Taxi fares and the charges for utilities such as gas, electricity, and water are obvious examples. Cell phone plans typically include a given charge for a set number of minutes plus a penalty paid for every minute over that amount. Likewise, many country and athletic clubs set a flat annual membership fee and then impose additional fees to use the club's facilities or buy the club's goods or services. Ski slopes and theme parks typically charge a fixed admission fee and additional fees (often set to 0) per ride or amusement. Indeed, it was this last example that motivated the seminal analysis of two-part tariffs by Oi (1971).

Returning to our example, if the firm sets a price p per unit, the two-part pricing schedule is *incentive compatible* for each consumer, provided that $A \leq S(q) = v(q) - pq$. In other words, consumers are willing to purchase q units at the unit price p provided that the fixed charge is no greater than the consumer surplus $S(q)$ that this yields. To maximize its profit, it will set the fixed charge at (ε less than) $A = S(q)$. If we again assume a constant marginal cost c, i.e., that $C(Nq) = F + cNq$, the firm's profit is

$$\pi(q) = N[S(q) + pq] - cNq = N[v(q) - pq + pq] - cNq = Nv(q) - cNq \quad (5.10)$$

Note from (5.9) that $dv(q)/dq = d^{-1}(q)$. Hence, maximizing (5.10) gives the first-order condition

$$\frac{d\pi(q)}{dq} = Nd^{-1}(q) - Nc = 0 \Rightarrow p = c \quad (5.11)$$

The firm thus sets the unit price to marginal cost c (or, more generally, $C'(Nq)$). It then uses the fixed charge to extract all of the consumer surplus that the standard consumer earns when purchasing at that price. Note that—as in our personalized pricing case—this again means that the firm produces the efficient amount. The total surplus is therefore maximized; but, again, the monopolist claims it all for herself.

The two-part tariff for the above case is illustrated in Figure 5.2. With linear pricing, the monopolist sets the monopoly price p^m and earns profit from each consumer given by the shaded area M. With the two-part pricing policy, the monopolist sets the unit price $p^c = c$ and imposes a fixed charge $A = M + B + C$. This increases its profit from each consumer by the shaded areas $B + C$.

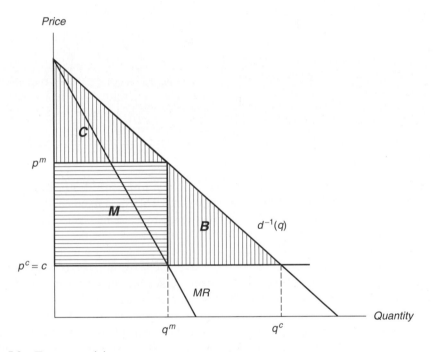

Figure 5.2   Two-part pricing

5.2.3   Block Pricing

In the foregoing two-part tariff example, each consumer was offered the same contract of paying a fixed fee A and then a constant fee of c per unit consumed. Where then is the discrimination?

The answer is that although each consumer is treated identically, the monopolist is now treating each unit bought differently. In particular, the monopolist is recognizing that the consumer's willingness to pay declines with each unit. As Figure 5.2 illustrates, two-part pricing in this case effectively amounts to moving down the demand curve and charging the consumer her maximum willingness to pay for each unit bought.

But what would have happened if consumers had not been identical? In principle, it is simple to extend the two-part pricing schedule to this case, so long as the firm knows each consumer's type i, and the willingness of each type to pay for quantity q is $v_i(q)$. The firm sets the unit price equal to marginal cost and imposes a fixed charge $A_i = S_i(q^c)$ that extracts consumer type i's entire consumer surplus $(v_i(q^c) - p^c q^c)$ at the unit price p^c. Once again, the market outcome is efficient. However, beyond the considerable information required to implement such a scheme, there is also a potentially acute arbitrage problem that must be faced. What is to prevent a consumer (or group of consumers) from agreeing to pay the fixed charge, but then buying in bulk and selling to other consumers who thereby avoid the fixed charge?

In the unit demand case, where each consumer buys at most one unit, this arbitrage problem is easily solved. The firm simply limits each consumer to purchasing no more than one unit per period. Is there a similar rationing system that can be implemented when individual demands are downward sloping? The answer is yes—again, assuming that the firm also has the extensive information required.

The alternative approach is frequently called *block pricing*. In effect, it is a rationing system that ties the quantity bought and total charge to each other. That is, the firm does not permit the consumer to purchase individual units. Instead, it offers q units as a package available at a total price $T(q)$.

To illustrate, let us start with the simple case above, in which consumers do not differ but instead have the identical downward-sloping, inverse demand: $p = d^{-1}(q)$. Then from (5.9), the consumer's maximum willingness to pay for q units is $v(q)$. In this case, the firm can duplicate our two-part tariff case by simply offering each consumer a package $(q, T(q))$ of q units for a total charge $T(q) = v(q)$. Because each consumer is offered a quantity for a total charge that is equal to her willingness to pay for that quantity, such an offer is clearly incentive compatible. The profit from this pricing policy is

$$\pi(q) = Nv(q) - cNq \tag{5.12}$$

which is identical to (5.10) and so gives the same equilibrium. Each consumer is again offered, as a package, the quantity that the consumer would purchase at the competitive price p^c (but at a total charge $T(q^c) = v(q^c)$), which transfers all surplus to the monopolist. Because smaller orders are not permitted, rejection of the firm's offer means buying no units at all.

Now consider what happens if consumers are of different types. If the monopolist knows the demand $q_i = d_i(p_i)$ for each type, and if she can readily identify the type of each consumer, then the packaging tactic is easily extended. She now offers each consumer of type i the bundle $q_i^c = d_i(p^c)$—that is, a package equal in size to the quantity that she would buy if the product were priced competitively. She then sets a price for each package of $T_i(q_i^c) = v_i(q_i^c)$, which just equals the total willingness to pay of consumers of type i and thereby extracts all surplus from them. In other words, block pricing amounts to personalized packaging. For each type, the amount bought is equal to that type's consumption with competitive pricing, so the resulting equilibrium is efficient.

Again, the information requirements for either personalized pricing or personalized packaging are considerable. As we noted at the outset, however, even if the necessary conditions are relatively rare, these practices are worth examining because of the issues they illuminate about price discrimination in general. To the extent that discrimination results in different people paying a different price for the same product, it cannot help but seem inequitable. This is all the more the case when, as here, such discrimination results in the monopolist acquiring the entire surplus. Yet it is worth emphasizing that in all the cases so far, the discriminatory tactic has yielded the efficient outcome, while a uniform pricing strategy in which all consumers are charged the same unit price for each unit bought leads to inefficiency. It is fair to say that analysis of price discrimination in general will often require consideration of both the equity and efficiency issues.

5.3   PRICE DISCRIMINATION WITH LESS INFORMATION

We have emphasized that the personalized-pricing, two-part tariffs, and block-pricing strategies described above require that the firm has substantial information about each of its customers. While this may sometimes be the case it is more likely that the firm's information is not so complete. As a result, the firm will be unable to achieve perfect price discrimination. Yet, this does not eliminate all discriminatory tactics. We now consider alternative techniques of price discrimination. As promised, we first consider third-degree price discrimination and then turn to second-degree discrimination schemes.

5.3.1   Group Pricing or Third-Degree Discrimination

We continue with the assumption that our monopolist sells a single product (as in the first-degree case of section 2) and that the firm can divide its buyers into N groups on the basis of some exogenous, observable characteristic: location, age, sex, and occupation are obvious examples. Each group has a downward-sloping aggregate demand curve $q_i = d_i(p_i)$ for the product, which is known to the monopolist.[6] By assumption, the monopolist can prevent arbitrage *between* groups. However, the information limitations are such that the firm cannot price discriminate *within* a group. This reflects the fact that the groups are typically distinguished by observable characteristics, such as age (e.g., children and/or senior citizens), but that no such distinctive feature permits identification of different types within a particular group. As a result, the firm must adopt a linear pricing policy for each group; however, this still permits it to apply different linear prices to different groups.

There are numerous instances of differential prices by group. The drug price differentials between the United States and Canada mentioned at the start of this chapter are an example of such discrimination based on location. Senior discounts and "kids are free" programs are both examples in which groups are determined by age. An interesting case that is particularly familiar to economists is the fee schedule for membership in the *American Economic Association*, the major professional organization for economists in the United States. Payment of the fee entitles a member to receive professional announcements, newsletters, and three very important professional journals: the *American Economic Review*, the *Journal of Economic Perspectives*, and the *Journal of Economic Literature*, each of which is published quarterly.

The 2009 fee schedule is shown in Table 5.2. As can readily be seen, the aim is to price discriminate on the basis of income. An interesting feature of this scheme is that the Association makes no attempt to check the veracity of the income declared by a prospective member. What they appear to rely upon is that economists will be either honest or even boastful in reporting their incomes. In addition, the Association must hope to avoid the arbitrage problem whereby junior faculty members who pay a low

---

6   We use this notation to indicate that $d_i(p_i)$ is aggregate demand over all consumers in group i.

Table 5.2 Schedule of annual membership fees for the American Economic Association

Regular Members with annual incomes of $66,000 or less	$70
Regular Members with annual incomes above $66,000 but no more than $84,000	$84
Regular Members with annual incomes above $84,000	$98
Student Members (available to registered students—student status must be certified)	$35
Family Member (persons living at the same address as a regular member, additional membership without a subscription to AEA publications)	$14

subscription fee resell to senior faculty members, who pay a high one. Here again, we can only report on casual observation; on this basis, such reselling actually appears to be rare, and the arbitrage problem seems to be effectively nonexistent. Similarly, many academic journals charge a different price to institutions (such as university libraries) than to individuals. A subscription rate to the *Journal of Economics and Management Strategy*, for example, is $45 for an individual, but $115 for an institution.

Airlines are particularly adept at applying third-degree price discrimination. Indeed, it has been suggested that the number of different fares charged to economy-class passengers on a particular flight is approximately equal to the number of passengers! A common feature of this type of price discrimination is that it is implemented by restrictions on the characteristics of the ticket. These include constraints upon the time in advance by which the flight must be booked, whether flights can be changed, the number of days between departure and return, whether the trip involves staying over a Saturday night, and so on. We consider these aspects of airline pricing more fully in Chapter 6.

Other examples of third-degree price discrimination are restaurant "early bird specials" and supermarket discounts to shoppers who clip coupons. Segmenting consumers by date of purchase is also widely practiced. Thus, consumers typically pay more to see a film at a first-run theater when the film is newly released than to see it at a later date at a second-run cinema or, still later, as a rented DVD at home.

Let us now return to our formal example. There are N consumer groups each with its own group demand curve. As before, we also assume a constant marginal cost c. Given that the firm charges price p_i to consumers in group i ($i = 1, \ldots, N$) the firm's profit is

$$\pi = \sum_{i=1}^{N} \pi_i = \sum_{i=1}^{N} p_i d_i(p_i) - C\left(\sum_{i=1}^{N} d_i(p_i)\right) = \sum_{i=1}^{N} p_i d_i(p_i) - F - c\left(\sum_{i=1}^{N} d_i(p_i)\right) \tag{5.13}$$

Maximizing profit with respect to the n prices gives the N first-order conditions

$$\frac{\partial \pi}{\partial p_i} = d_i(p_i) + p_i d_i'(p_i) - cd_i'(p_i) = 0 \quad i = 1, \ldots, N \tag{5.14}$$

These can be rewritten as the familiar inverse-elasticity pricing rule we derived in Chapter 2:

$$p_i\left(1 - \frac{1}{\varepsilon_i}\right) = c \quad \text{or} \quad p_i = \left(\frac{\varepsilon_i}{\varepsilon_i - 1}\right)c \quad i = 1, \ldots, N \tag{5.15}$$

Reality Checkpoint

"Seventeen Tickets for Seven Guitars—Price Discrimination on Broadway"

In New York, about 25,000 people, on average, attend Broadway shows each night. As avid theatergoers know, prices for these tickets have been rising inexorably. The top price for Broadway shows has risen 31 percent since 1998. However, due to various discounts offered through coupons, two-for-one deals, special student prices, and the TKTS booth in Times Square, the actual price paid has gone up by only 24 percent.

Why so much discounting? The value of a seat in a theater, like a seat on an airplane, is highly perishable. Once the show starts or the plane takes off, a seat is worth next to nothing. So, it's better to fill the seat at a low price than not fill it at all.

Stanford economist Phillip Leslie investigated Broadway ticket price discrimination using detailed data for a 1996 Broadway play, "Seven Guitars." Over 140,000 people saw this play, and they bought tickets in 17 price categories. While some of the difference was due to seat quality—opera versus mezzanine versus balcony—a large amount of price differentials remained even after quality adjustments. The average difference of two tickets chosen at random on a given night was about 40 percent of the average price. This is comparable to the price variation in airline tickets.

Leslie used advanced econometric techniques to estimate the values that different income groups put on the various categories of tickets. He found that Broadway producers do a pretty good job, in general, at maximizing revenue. He found the average price set for "Seven Guitars" was about $55, while the value that would maximize profit was a very close $60. His data also indicated that the optimal uniform price would be a little over $50. Again, price discrimination is less about the average price charged and more about varying the price in line with the consumer's willingness to pay. In this connection, Leslie found that optimal price discrimination drew in over 6 percent more patrons than would optimal uniform pricing.

Source: P. Leslie "Price Discrimination in Broadway Theatre." *Rand Journal of Economics*, 35 (Autumn, 2004): 520–541.

where $\varepsilon_i = -d_i'(p_i)p_i/d_i(p_i)$ is the absolute value of the elasticity of demand for consumer group i. An immediate implication of this price equilibrium is that each consumer group is charged a price that is greater than marginal cost.

How do prices vary across groups? It follows from (5.15) that

$$\frac{p_i}{p_j} = \left(\frac{\varepsilon_i}{\varepsilon_i - 1}\right)\left(\frac{\varepsilon_j - 1}{\varepsilon_j}\right) > 1 \quad \text{if} \quad \varepsilon_i < \varepsilon_j \tag{5.16}$$

Equation (5.16) makes clear a central result for group pricing. *The monopolist should charge more to groups with inelastic demand and less to groups with elastic demand.* This result can explain why senior citizens and college students are offered discounts for many products and services, why legal and accounting fees vary with income, why airline travelers willing to travel on standby tickets pay much less than the standard fare, and why prices of similar goods in different countries—as in our opening example—do not reflect differences in the costs of moving goods to those countries. In every case, the group charged the lower price may be presumed to have more elastic demand.

5.3.2   Third-Degree Price Discrimination and Social Welfare

As noted previously, the term "price discrimination" suggests inequity and hence may be considered unjust. In the case of first-degree price discrimination, this sense of injustice may be heightened by the fact that the discrimination transfers the entire surplus to the monopolist. However, in this case, we can take at last some consolation in the fact that the practice yields increased efficiency. The differential pricing that arises under third-degree price discrimination may also seem unjust, even if the monopolist's profit is lower. It is natural, therefore, to ask whether there is any compensation by way of increased efficiency in this case as well.

To answer this question, let us begin by recognizing that, in the absence of group pricing, the monopolist would sell to all customers at a uniform price. In turn, maximizing profit requires that this price be greater than marginal cost, resulting in the familiar dead-weight loss of monopoly. The relevant question, then, is not whether third-degree price discrimination is maximally efficient. It clearly is not, as the price to each group exceeds the firm's marginal cost as shown by equation (5.15). Instead, the relevant question is whether such discrimination worsens or reduces the monopoly distortion under uniform pricing.[7] Unfortunately, the answer to this question is ambiguous.

To understand the source of ambiguity in the welfare effects of group pricing, suppose first that the firm is currently charging the same uniform price to all consumer groups. Presumably, allowing the firm to price discriminate means that prices rise for some groups and fall for others. Consumers in the former group lose from price discrimination, while those in the latter group gain. In addition, the firm gains additional profit from relaxation of the rule that prices be nondiscriminatory.

We can be more specific regarding the welfare effects of third-degree price discrimination by drawing on the work of Schmalensee (1981) and Varian (1985).[8] We start by noting that if demand by consumers in group i at price p is $d_i(p)$, and the maximum price that these consumers are willing to pay is $\overline{p}$, then consumer surplus for this group is $S_i(p) = \int_p^{\overline{p}} d_i(x)dx$, from which it follows that

$$S_i'(p) = dS_i(p)/dp = -d_i(p) \tag{5.17}$$

Now suppose that the firm is constrained to adopt nondiscriminatory pricing. Then, the firm chooses the uniform price p^U given by

$$p^U = \underset{p}{\operatorname{argmax}} \sum_{i=1}^{N} (p - c)d_i(p) \tag{5.18}$$

Demand by group i at the uniform price is $q_i^U = d_i(p^U)$. So, aggregate consumer surplus is $\sum_{i=1}^{N} S_i(p^U)$.

---

[7]   We saw earlier that a monopolist practicing personalized pricing actually chooses the efficient level of output and so leads to no welfare loss. All potential welfare-increasing trades are made.

[8]   Our discussion follows Tirole (1988).

The welfare impact of switching from nondiscriminatory to discriminatory pricing is the change in consumer surplus plus the change in profit:

$$\Delta W = \left(\sum_i \left[S_i(p_i) - S_i\left(p^U\right) \right] \right) + \left(\sum_i (p_i - c)q_i - \sum_i \left(p^U - c\right) q_i^U \right) \quad (5.19)$$

Profit unambiguously rises with price discrimination, since the firm, when allowed to price discriminate, could always choose uniform pricing. By contrast, consumer surplus may rise or fall. Hence, as noted above, the overall welfare impact of price discrimination is ambiguous.

We can, however, use (5.19) to derive upper and lower bounds on this welfare impact. Define $\Delta q_i = q_i - q_i^U$. In other words, Δq_i is the impact of price discrimination on the output that the monopolist supplies to consumers in group i. Now note that the consumer surplus function $S_i(p)$ for each group is convex in the market price. That is:

$$S_i'(p) = -d_i(p) \Rightarrow S_i''(p) = -d_i'(p) > 0 \quad (5.20)$$

An important property of a convex function for our purposes is that, as illustrated in Figure 5.3, it lies everywhere above its tangents. As a result, we may write

$$S_i(p_i) - S_i\left(p^U\right) \geq S_i'\left(p^U\right) \left(p_i - p^U\right) = -d_i\left(p^U\right) \left(p_i - p^U\right) = -q_i^U \left(p_i - p^U\right) \quad (5.21)$$

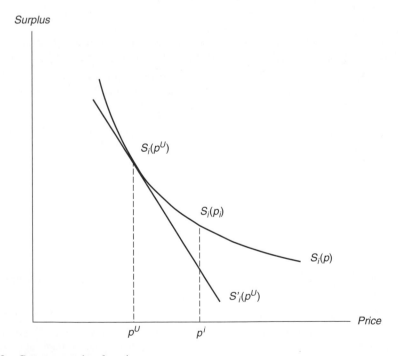

Figure 5.3   Convex surplus function

Substituting into equation (5.19) then gives

$$\Delta W \geq \sum_i -q_i^U \left(p_i - p^U \right) + \sum_i (p_i - c)q_i - \sum_i \left(p^U - c \right) q_i^U$$
$$\Rightarrow \Delta W \geq \sum_i (p_i - c)q_i - \sum_i (p_i - c)q_i^U = \sum_i (p_i - c)\Delta q_i \qquad (5.22)$$

By a similar argument, we have

$$S_i(p_i) - S_i \left(p^U \right) \leq S_i'(p_i) \left(p_i - p^U \right) = -d_i(p_i) \left(p_i - p^U \right) = -q_i \left(p_i - p^U \right) \qquad (5.23)$$

Substitution of this into (5.15) now yields

$$\Delta W \leq \sum_i -q_i \left(p_i - p^U \right) + \sum_i (p_i - c)q_i - \sum_i \left(p^u - c \right) q_i^U$$
$$\Rightarrow \Delta W \leq \sum_i \left(p^u - c \right) q_i - \sum_i \left(p^u - c \right) q_i^U = \left(p^U - c \right) \sum_i \Delta q_i \qquad (5.24)$$

Thus, moving from uniform to group pricing will change welfare by somewhere between $\sum_i (p_i - c)q_i$ and $\left(p^U - c \right) \sum_i \Delta q_i$. It is immediately obvious that the upper bound will be positive only if price discrimination increases total output. That is, a necessary condition for third-degree price discrimination to raise welfare relative to uniform pricing is that it must lead to a rise in the firm's total output.

5.3.3   Group Pricing: An Application with Linear Demand

To better understand our welfare analysis of third-degree discrimination, consider a simple case in which demand for group i is $q_i = a_i - b_i p$, and in which the monopolist has constant marginal cost c. If the monopolist can price discriminate, then price to group i is chosen to maximize $\pi_i = (p_i - c)(a_i - b_i p_i)$. Using equation (5.14), it is straightforward to show that the profit maximizing price and quantity for group i is

$$p_i = (a_i + cb_i)/2b_i; \quad q_i = (a_i - cb_i)/2 \qquad (5.25)$$

It follows that group i will be supplied by the discriminating monopolist if (and only if) $a_i/b_i > c$, where a_i/b_i is the maximum price that consumers in group i are willing to pay for the monopolist's product. We assume that this condition holds for the remainder of the analysis in this section.

Now, assume that the monopolist is not allowed to price discriminate, but continue to assume that all markets are supplied. This means that aggregate demand across all consumer groups is $Q = \sum_i a_i - \left(\sum_i b_i \right) p^U$, and the monopolist chooses the uniform price p^U to solve

$$p^U = \underset{p}{\text{argmax}}(p - c) \left(\sum_i a_i - \left(\sum_i b_i \right) p \right) \qquad (5.26)$$

Again, it is simple to show that the profit-maximizing uniform price is

$$p^U = \left(\sum_i a_i + c \left(\sum_i b_i \right) \right) \bigg/ 2 \left(\sum_i b_i \right) \tag{5.27}$$

The profit-maximizing output supplied to group i is $q_i^U = a_i - b_i p^U$, and total output is

$$Q^U = \sum_i q_i^U = \left(\sum_i a_i - c \left(\sum_i b_i \right) \right) \bigg/ 2 \tag{5.28}$$

Equations (5.25) and (5.28) show that the total output supplied by the monopolist is the same with discriminatory and nondiscriminatory pricing. Given the necessary condition implied by equation (5.24), it then follows immediately that *when demand by each group is linear and all groups are served with and without price discrimination, third-degree price discrimination reduces welfare*.

5.3.4   A Caveat on Welfare and Third-Degree Price Discrimination

There are, however, at least two reasons to be skeptical of such a negative evaluation of group pricing. One of these is that, as we shall see later, when the market is oligopolistic instead of monopolistic, price discrimination can intensify price competition and move the market closer to the competitive ideal. The second and more immediate caveat is that our analysis implicitly assumes that the same markets are served with and without price discrimination. This may very well not be true. One property of price discrimination is that it can make it profitable to serve markets that would not be served with nondiscriminatory prices. If this happens, then the additional welfare from the new markets that third-degree price discrimination introduces may more than offset any loss of welfare in the markets that were previously being served.[9]

Suppose, for instance, that there are two markets—a large regional market in which demand is $q_R = d_R(p)$ and a small village market in which demand is $q_V = d_V(p)$, where we make no particular assumptions regarding the shapes of these demand functions. Assume further that the monopolist is not allowed to price discriminate across the two markets. If both markets are served with no price discrimination, then the uniform price p^U satisfies: $p^U = \underset{p}{\text{argmax}}((p - c)(d_R(p) + d_V(p)))$.

By contrast, if only the large regional market is served, then the firm sets the monopoly price p_R^m for market R. We assume that $p_R^m \neq p^U$. In other words, in order to supply both markets without price discrimination, the firm has to charge other than the monopoly price that would maximize profit in market R by itself and so sacrifice some profit there. Clearly, if market V is "too small," the profit gain from selling in that market will not offset this sacrifice, and the monopolist will instead choose to serve only market R at the monopoly price p_R^m. Suppose, then, that this condition holds—but let us now allow the monopolist to price discriminate. This will, of course, leave the price in market R unaffected at p_R^m, since that is the price that maximizes profit in that location. However, the firm will now also sell in market V at the monopoly price for that market p_V^m. It

---

[9]   Schmalensee (1981) was fully aware of this possibility.

follows that the impact on quantity supplied to market R is $\Delta q_R = 0$, while the change in quantity supplied to market V is $\Delta q_V = q_V^m > 0$. From (5.23), the welfare impact of allowing price discrimination satisfies

$$\Delta W \geq \left(p_R^m - c \right) \Delta q_R + \left(p_V^m - c \right) \Delta q_V = \left(p_V^m - c \right) \Delta q_V > 0 \tag{5.29}$$

We can conclude, then, that *if there are two groups and forbidding price discrimination leads to one of these groups not being supplied, then allowing third-degree price discrimination always increases welfare.*

It is important to note, however, that this conclusion does not generalize to more than two groups, provided that at least two of the groups are supplied in the absence of price discrimination. If there are N groups and uniform pricing leads to only $2 < j < N$ of these groups being supplied, then allowing price discrimination has competing effects. Welfare falls for the j groups if price discrimination does not increase output supplied to these groups (equation (5.24))—this applies, for example, if all demands are linear—while welfare rises for the new groups that are now supplied. Hence, the net effect is ambiguous, theoretically speaking, and totally dependent on the actual parameters of the specific case.

5.4 SECOND-DEGREE PRICE DISCRIMINATION: MENU PRICING

We now turn to the case of second-degree price discrimination, or menu pricing. An essential assumption for both first-degree and third-degree price discrimination is that the monopolist has solved, at least partially, the identification problem. The different types of consumers are identifiable either because of the client-nature of their relationship with the firm, or because they have an easily observable feature such as their age or location. It is, however, entirely possible that while the monopolist knows that there are different types of consumers, the feature that distinguishes the different types is unobservable, being based, for example, on personal tastes or income.

Once we reduce either the seller's ability to identify different customers or to prevent arbitrage among them (or both), complete surplus extraction by means of perfect price discrimination is no longer possible. However, a properly designed variant of the two-part and block-pricing mechanisms discussed earlier can still be used to raise profit above that earned by uniform pricing, though not as much as they did previously. Since the monopolist cannot identify a buyer's type for herself, the trick now is to design these pricing schemes to induce customers to reveal their true types themselves. As we shall see, however, getting consumers to reveal this information comes at some cost—a cost reflected in less surplus extraction. Such a pricing scheme is called second-degree price discrimination or menu pricing.

Rather than continuing with our general approach to consumer demand, we use a (slightly) simplified example. Consumers are assumed to be indexed by a taste parameter θ that is unobservable to the monopolist. Consumers of type θ_i have preferences of the following quasilinear form:

$$U(\theta, q, T) = \begin{cases} V(\theta, q) - T & \text{if they pay } T \text{ and consume } q \text{ units} \\ 0 & \text{if they do not buy the good} \end{cases} \tag{5.30}$$

We assume that $V(\theta, 0) = 0$, $V_q(\theta, q) > 0$, $V_{qq}(\theta, q) < 0$, $V_\theta(\theta, q) > 0$ and $V_q(\theta_2, q) > V_q(\theta_1, q)$ if $\theta_2 > \theta_1$. In other words, $V(\theta, q)$ exhibits positive but decreasing marginal utility, and the marginal utility for a type θ_2 consumer at any quantity q is greater than marginal utility for a type θ_1 consumer if $\theta_2 > \theta_1$.

This utility function is illustrated in (q, T) space in Figure 5.4. The indifference curve $R_\theta(q)$ defines the maximum amount that consumers of type θ are willing to pay for q units of the good or service: $U(\theta, q, R_\theta(q)) = 0$. Note that consumer surplus increases the *lower* the indifference curve the consumer is on, because being on a lower curve means obtaining the same q units for a smaller total expenditure T.

In the remainder of our analysis, we assume that there are two consumer types, with N_1 consumers of type θ_1 and N_2 consumers of type θ_2 and $\theta_1 < \theta_2$. We further assume that the monopolist has constant marginal cost c and knows θ_1, θ_2, N_1, and N_2 but, as noted above, does *not* know the type of each consumer.

Suppose that the monopolist sets a simple linear price p. Then a consumer of type θ maximizes $V(\theta, q) - pq$ giving the first-order condition

$$p = V_q(\theta, q) \tag{5.31}$$

What this tells us is that the derivative of the utility function with respect to q at a given price p per unit yields the consumer's inverse demand function which, from the quasilinear preferences of (5.30), has no income effects. Given our assumptions about $V(\theta, q)$, this implies that we can think of type θ_1 consumers as low-demand and type θ_2 consumers as high-demand.

We now simplify still further by assuming a specific functional form for the utility function:

$$V(\theta_i, q) = \theta_i q - \frac{q^2}{2} \quad \text{for} \quad 0 \le q \le \theta_i \quad \text{and} \quad i = 1, 2 \tag{5.32}$$

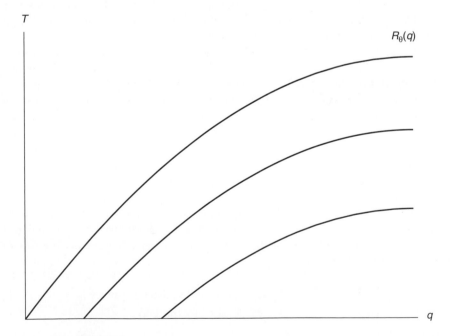

Figure 5.4   Utility function

Hence, $V_q(\theta_i, q) = \theta_i - q$. It follows that the demand function for a type θ_i consumer is the simple linear demand $q = d_i(p) = \theta_i - p$. Clearly, if the seller sets a unit price $p = c$, then demand by a type θ_i consumer is $q_i = \theta_i - c$.

Net consumer surplus for a type θ_i consumer (ignoring any fixed charge) at linear price p is

$$S_i(p) = V(\theta_i, d_i(p)) - pd_i(p) = \frac{(\theta_i - p)^2}{2} \tag{5.33}$$

Thus, at any common price p, type θ_2 consumers enjoy greater consumer surplus than type θ_1 consumers.

Aggregate demand $D(p)$ at price p is the sum of the demand from the N_1 consumers of type θ_1 and the N_2 consumers of type θ_2. Hence

$$D(p) = N_1 d_1(p) + N_2 d_2(p) = N(\theta_m - p) \tag{5.34}$$

where $\theta_m = \lambda\theta_1 + (1 - \lambda)\theta_2$ is the population-weighted mean of θ_1 and θ_2, and $\lambda = N_1/(N_1 + N_2)$ is the proportion of type θ_1 consumers.[10] A uniform pricing monopolist will therefore maximize profit by choosing

$$p = \frac{c + \theta_m}{2} > c \tag{5.35}$$

5.4.1   A Two-Part Tariff

Of course, the price shown in equation (5.35) only maximizes profit under the restriction that the monopolist charges a uniform price to all consumers. We know that relaxing this constraint and permitting some sort of price discrimination will enable the firm to do better. The question then becomes, what sort of discriminatory tactics will work in this setting of limited information where the monopolist cannot tell who is who among consumers?

Note first that the firm cannot adopt the first-degree pricing rule of setting price to marginal cost and then using one fixed charge to extract all consumer surplus from each consumer type. At $p = c$, θ_1-type consumers earn surplus $\frac{(\theta_1 - c)^2}{2}$, while θ_2-type consumers earn the larger surplus $\frac{(\theta_2 - c)^2}{2}$. Any fixed fee $[S_2(c)]$ that captures all the surplus from the θ_2-type consumers excludes the θ_1-types from making any purchases at all, since $S_2(c) > S_1(c)$. Conversely, any fixed fee that extracts all surplus from the θ_1-type consumers will leave some surplus for the θ_2-types.

Pricing at marginal cost while setting two fixed charges—designed to extract all the surplus from each group—will not work either. While θ_1-types can be persuaded to pay a fixed price $S_1(c)$, and then consume $\theta_1 - c$ units, the availability of that option makes it impossible to persuade θ_2-types to pay a fixed price of $S_2(c)$, and then consume $\theta_2 - c$ units. This does not satisfy the incentive-compatibility constraint for type θ_2 consumers. They do better by paying the lower fixed charge $S_1(c)$ and earning positive consumer surplus, even if they are limited to $\theta_1 - c$ units.

In short, the monopolist cannot extract the maximum potential surplus from the market. Doing so requires setting $p = c$, but there is then no way to set fixed or up-front fees that will extract all of the surplus from both groups. Faced with this fact, the monopolist

---

[10]   Note that we assume that the price is low enough that both types of consumers buy the product.

must determine how best to maximize the profit that it can earn, even if that is less than the maximum total surplus the market can potentially generate.

Two possibilities suggest themselves. One is to keep a common fixed fee that is low enough to attract both consumer groups, but give up on the goal of pricing at marginal cost. The other is to continue to price at marginal cost, but think more carefully about the separate buying options that it offers. We consider the first of these—which is really a simple two-part tariff—below.

Suppose that the monopolist sets price $p > c$, but also requires a fixed payment before any units are bought at that price. While it cannot set a fixed fee that captures all the surplus from high-demand consumers (and still attract low-demand ones), it can set a fixed charge that extracts all the consumer surplus of type θ_1 consumers and still sell to type θ_2 consumers. Since this latter step is clearly a necessary part of any profit-maximizing strategy, we know that the fixed fee A must equal $S_1(p)$. In turn, this implies a profit function of

$$\pi(p) = (N_1 + N_2)S_1(p) + (p - c)D(p) = N\left[\frac{(\theta_1 - p)^2}{2} + (p - c)(\theta_m - p)\right] \quad (5.36)$$

Differentiating with respect to p and simplifying gives the first-order condition

$$p^* = c + \theta_m - \theta_1; \ A^* = S_1(p^*) = \frac{1}{2}(2\theta_1 - c - \theta_m)^2 \quad (5.37)$$

Since $\theta_m > \theta_1$, this gives $p^* > c$, and $A^* < S_1(c)$.[11] Because the unit price exceeds marginal cost, the fixed charge must be lower than would be charged to type θ_1 consumers under first-degree price discrimination.

The market outcome at p^* is illustrated in Figure 5.5. Point B shows the consumption and expenditure of θ_1-type consumers (q_1, T_1) and point C shows the consumption and expenditure of θ_2-type consumers (q_2, T_2). Viewed in this way, one can see that an alternative strategy to the simple two-part tariff above would be to return to the block-pricing strategy described in Section 5.2. That is, the firm could offer a package of q_1 units for a price T_1, and a package of q_2 units for a price T_2. Clearly, no θ_1-type consumers would purchase the larger, more expensive package. Furthermore, no θ_2-type consumers would purchase the smaller package, since, as Figure 5.5 shows, these consumers get a smaller surplus from this package than they obtain from the (q_2, T_2) option.

A much more fundamental conclusion can be drawn from this analysis. As just demonstrated, the two packages—(q_1, T_1) and (q_2, T_2)—duplicate the firm's gains from the profit-maximizing two-part tariff. At the same time, the θ_2-type consumers earn more surplus from package (q_2, T_2) than they do from package (q_1, T_1). This means that it is possible to raise the charge for high-demand customers to T_3 such that type θ_2 consumers are just indifferent between the bundle (q_2, T_3) and the bundle (q_2, T_2)—point D in Figure 5.5. Since this means that that these consumers will continue to purchase the q_2 units but now pay more for them, this alternative strategy has to yield more profit than the two-part tariff. Thus, *a common two-part tariff cannot be profit maximizing for the firm*.

---

[11] We assume that the parameters satisfy the further constraint $p^* < \theta_1$ that is necessary for type θ_1 consumers to be willing to purchase the good.

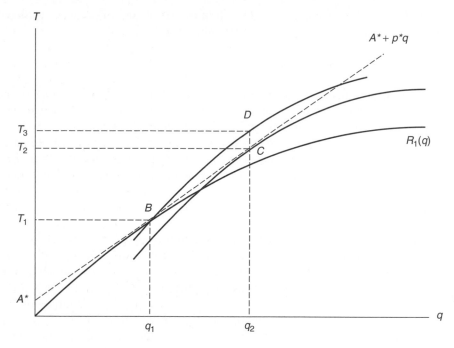

Figure 5.5 Second-degree price discrimination and two-part tariff

5.4.2 Menu Pricing

The idea of offering different (q, T) packages contains the hint of a strategy that the seller can use to increase profit, and it lies at the heart of so-called *menu pricing*. The point is to employ a variation of the block-pricing strategy described earlier by offering buyers a menu of options—in our two-type case, a menu containing two packages (q_1, T_1) and (q_2, T_2). The advantage of this strategy is that it implicitly recognizes that there is no easy way to identify and separate the different types of customers. Instead, the menu must be designed to achieve this purpose—to make consumers *self-select* according to their true types. This imposes a new constraint or cost on the seller and so will not yield as much profit as first-degree price discrimination. However, it will deliver more profit than any alternative pricing strategy.

What is the optimal menu design for our two-type case? We assume the firm offers its consumers two bundles, (q_1, T_1) and (q_2, T_2), with the former designed to be purchased by type θ_1 consumers and the latter by type θ_2 consumers. Given that both types of consumer actually purchase the bundle designed for them, the firm's profit is

$$\pi^b = N[\lambda(T_1 - cq_1) + (1 - \lambda)(T_2 - cq_2)] \tag{5.38}$$

For this to work, the bundles must satisfy the *incentive compatibility constraints* for each consumer type (i.e., neither consumer type must have any incentive to switch to the other bundle).

Consider first the low-demand, type θ_1 consumers. Each such consumer must prefer the bundle (q_1, T_1) to not purchasing,[12] which gives the constraint

$$V(\theta_1, q_1) - T_1 \geq 0 \tag{5.39}$$

Now consider the high-demand type θ_2 consumers. If (5.39) is satisfied, they will certainly purchase from the firm, since they can buy the (q_1, T_1) bundle and get consumer surplus $V(\theta_2, q_1) - T_1$—which, from $\theta_2 > \theta_1$ and (5.39), is certainly positive. If, however, we want these consumers to act true to type and buy the (q_2, T_2) bundle, then the package (q_2, T_2) offered to them must be priced so that it is more attractive than the (q_1, T_1) bundle. That is, any menu of options must satisfy the incentive compatibility constraint

$$V(\theta_2, q_2) - T_2 \geq V(\theta_2, q_1) - T_1 \tag{5.40}$$

In order to maximize profit, the monopolist must set T_1 and T_2 such that (5.39) and (5.40) are exactly satisfied. That is, we must have: $T_1 = V(\theta_1, q_1)$ and $T_2 = V(\theta_2, q_2) - (V(\theta_2, q_1) - T_1)$. Note that this implies that the firm sets (q_1, T_1) to extract all consumer surplus from the low-demand type θ_1 consumers, but sets (θ_2, T_2) so that type θ_2 consumers are left with a positive surplus $V(\theta_2, q_1) - T_1$. This is the cost that the firm incurs as a result of its imperfect information about each consumer's true type. This lack of information means that the firm must "leave some money on the table" if it is to encourage the consumers to act true to type.

Substituting the above values for T_1 and T_2 in (5.38) gives us the profit function

$$\pi^b = N[\lambda(V(\theta_1, q_1) - cq_1) + (1 - \lambda)(V(\theta_2, q_2) - V(\theta_2, q_1) + V(\theta_1, q_1) - cq_2)] \tag{5.41}$$

Differentiating with respect to q_1 and q_2 gives the first-order conditions

$$V_{q_1}(\theta_1, q_1) = c + \frac{1 - \lambda}{\lambda} \left[V_{q_1}(\theta_2, q_1) - V_{q_1}(\theta_1, q_1) \right] \tag{5.42}$$

$$V_{q_2}(\theta_2, q_2) = c \tag{5.43}$$

What do these imply? The left-hand sides of (5.42) and (5.43) are, respectively, the marginal valuations of type θ_1 and type θ_2 consumers. For type θ_2 consumers, this is equal to marginal cost, implying that they are offered the socially optimal quantity. By contrast, the bracketed term on the right-hand side of (5.42) is positive, since type θ_2 consumers place greater value on q_1 units than do type θ_1 consumers. In turn, this implies that for type θ_1 consumers, marginal utility is greater than marginal cost. These consumers are offered less than the socially optimal quantity.

We may confirm the above results directly by returning to our specific utility function of (5.32). Taking into account the incentive compatibility constraints, the firm's profit function, after some simplification, is

$$\pi^b = N \left[\lambda \left(\theta_1 q_1 - \frac{q_1^2}{2} - cq_1 \right) + (1 - \lambda) \left(\theta_2 q_2 - \frac{q_2^2}{2} - \theta_2 q_1 + \theta_1 q_1 - cq_2 \right) \right] \tag{5.44}$$

---

[12] There is the additional constraint that a type θ_1 consumer should prefer the bundle (q_1, T_1) to the bundle (q_2, T_2). We leave it for you to confirm that at the optimum, this constraint is, indeed, satisfied.

We maximize with respect to both q_1 and q_2 to obtain again the first-order conditions

$$\frac{\partial \pi}{\partial q_1} = 0 \quad \Rightarrow \quad q_1^* = \theta_1 - c - \frac{(1 - \lambda)}{\lambda}(\theta_2 - \theta_1) \tag{5.45a}$$

$$\frac{\partial \pi}{\partial q_2} = 0 \quad \Rightarrow \quad q_2^* = \theta_2 - c \tag{5.45b}$$

In sum, menu pricing of the form that we have been discussing exhibits two properties:

1. Low-demand consumers receive no consumer surplus, while high-demand consumers have positive consumer surplus.
2. High-demand consumers purchase a bundle containing the socially optimal quantity, while low-demand consumers purchase a bundle with a suboptimal quantity.

The intuition is simply explained. Because the firm cannot prevent consumer arbitrage (it does not know each consumer's type), T_2 must be set such that type θ_2 consumers receive as much surplus from the (q_2, T_2) bundle as from the (q_1, T_1) bundle. However, by offering a relatively low q_1, the firm reduces the consumer surplus that type θ_2 consumers derive from the (q_1, T_1) bundle. This makes the (q_1, T_1) bundle less attractive to type θ_2 consumers, allowing the firm to increase the charge T_2 for the (q_2, T_2) bundle. Admittedly, reducing q_1 also reduces T_1, but a high-demand consumer loses more utility from a reduction in consumption than does a low-demand consumer.

Menu pricing typically exhibits two other closely related properties, though these cannot be derived easily from our example (you are asked to confirm this property for more specific examples in the end-of-chapter problems). The first of these is that the average price T_2/q_2 is typically less than the average price T_1/q_1. In other words, the second package offers a *quantity discount* in that those who buy the larger package pay a lower unit price.

The closely related feature is that the firm earns greater profit in total from the high-demand consumers. That is, $T_2 - cq_2 > T_1 - cq_1$. To see this first define $\Delta T = T_2 - T_1$ and $\Delta q = q_2 - q_1$. In order for it to be profitable for the monopolist to offer the larger package, we must have that $\Delta T > c\Delta q$. Otherwise, the firm would find it better to offer just the low-demand package. We may then write the profit from the high-demand package as $T_2 - cq_2 = (T_1 + \Delta T) - c(q_1 + \Delta q) = T_1 - cq_1 + \Delta T - c\Delta q$. In other words, the profit from the high-demand package equals the profit from the low-demand package plus the amount $\Delta T - c\Delta q$, which we have just noted has to be positive. The intuition is clear. The firm gives a price break to the high-demand consumers precisely because that group is so responsive to a small discount. It is not worth giving any discount to the low-demand consumers, since even a large cut in the fee would not induce these consumers to purchase more. Yet for high-demand consumers, a price break is warranted because it induces a considerable increase in quantity.

Menu prices with quantity discounts are common. Movie theaters, restaurants, concert halls, sports teams, and supermarkets all make use of them. It is cheaper to buy one huge container of popcorn than many small ones. Wine sold by the bottle is cheaper per unit than wine sold by the glass. A 24-pack of Coca Cola costs less than 24 individual bottles, and it is cheaper per ticket to buy a season's subscription to your favorite football team's home games than to buy tickets to each game individually. In these and many other cases, firms are offering packages of specific amounts with a quantity discount implicit in the prices of the larger packages intended to woo those high-demand consumers.

This raises a further point. Since the incentive compatibility constraint requires that high-demand consumers retain some surplus, would the firm do better by not supplying type θ_1 consumers at all and thereby avoiding this constraint? Admittedly, supplying these consumers is profitable, giving aggregate profit $N_1[V(\theta_1, q_1) - cq_1]$. Yet, as just noted, there is a cost to supplying type θ_1 consumers—namely, $N_2[V(\theta_2, q_1) - V(\theta_1, q_1)]$. Clearly, if the proportion of type θ_2 consumers is "large enough" in some well-defined sense, the firm will prefer to supply only type θ_2 consumers.

In sum, menu pricing enhances the ability of the monopolist to convert consumer surplus into profit, but does not permit the extraction of all surplus. With no costless way to distinguish the different types of consumers, the monopolist must rely on some sort of menu pricing scheme to sort and separate customers. Menu pricing serves this purpose, but must satisfy an incentive compatibility constraint that forces the firm to make a compromise between setting a high charge, which loses sales to low-demand buyers, and a low charge that foregoes the significant surplus that can be earned from the high-demand buyers. This tradeoff remains present as the number of consumer types grows. In general, if consumer willingness to pay can be unambiguously ranked by type, then optimal menu pricing schemes will:

1. Extract the entire consumer surplus of the lowest demand type served, but leave some consumer surplus for all other types;
2. Contain a quantity that is less than the socially optimal quantity for all consumer types other than the highest-demand type; and
3. Exhibit quantity discounting.

Before ending, we note that, contrary to what many consumers may think, the lower price charged for a larger quantity is entirely unrelated to scale economies. In our example the seller has no fixed costs, has constant marginal costs, and thus has no economies of scale. Nevertheless, the firm finds it profitable to offer a quantity discount to high-demand customers in order to exploit opportunities on the demand side of the market, not the supply side.

5.4.3   Menu Pricing and Social Welfare

One way to understand the welfare effects of second-degree price discrimination is to consider a type θ_i consumer. We know from the utility function (5.30) that inverse demand for this consumer is

$$p = V_q(\theta_i, q) \tag{5.46}$$

The total surplus generated by a package (q_i, T_i) sold to a type θ_i consumer and costing c per unit is

$$TS_i = \int_0^{q_i} V_q(\theta_i, q)\, dq - cq \tag{5.47}$$

In other words, the total surplus (consumer surplus plus profit) generated by the package (q_i, T_i) offered to a type θ_i consumer under this pricing policy is the area between the

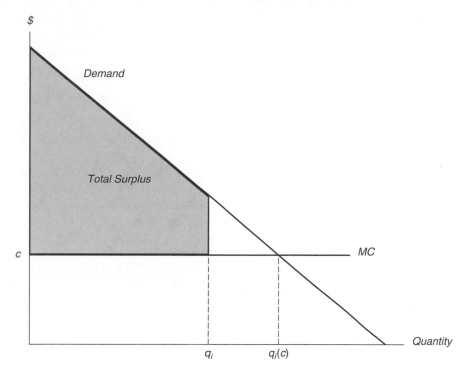

Figure 5.6   Total surplus

inverse demand function and the marginal cost function up to the quantity q_i, as illustrated in Figure 5.6.

Differentiating this total surplus with respect to q yields

$$\frac{dTS_i}{dq} = V_q(\theta_i, q) - c \tag{5.48}$$

which is positive for all q less than the competitive one defined by: $V_q(\theta_i, q) = c$. In other words, the social welfare associated with serving any type θ_i consumer increases as q increases, assuming that the competitive level is never exceeded. For our purposes, this means that menu pricing raises the social welfare associated with serving type θ_i consumers, so long as it increases the quantity that these consumers purchase. As was the case with third-degree price discrimination, this implies that the overall welfare effects of menu pricing are ambiguous. While menu pricing likely increases the units sold to high-demand types and brings them "near to" the socially efficient level, the seller restricts the quantity supplied to lower-demand groups and, in some cases, does not supply these groups at all. Therefore, the net effect on welfare is not clearly a priori.

Once again, however, we can be more precise and describe the impact on social welfare of second-degree price discrimination using basically the same techniques that we used in Section 5.3. Let p^U be the uniform price charged by a the nondiscriminatory monopolist, and let q_i^U be the quantity sold to a type θ_i consumer in the uniform pricing equilibrium. By contrast, let q_i^s be the quantity supplied to a type θ_i consumer with menu pricing and denote by p_i the linear price that the firm would have to set in order to sell this quantity to a type θ_i consumer. Finally, define $\Delta q_i = q_i^s - q_i^U$, the change in quantity sold to type θ_i consumers as the monopolist changes from uniform pricing to menu pricing. By an argument that has much in common with that in Section 5.3, it can be shown that the change in welfare ΔW of second-degree price discrimination is

$$\sum_{i=1}^{N} (p_i - c)\Delta q_i \leq \Delta W \leq \left(p^U - c\right) \sum_{i=1}^{N} \Delta q_i \qquad (5.49)$$

In other words, a necessary condition for second-degree price discrimination to increase welfare is that it increases total output.

We know that this requirement is not met in the case of third-degree price discrimination and linear demands, because then the discriminating monopolist supplies the same total quantity as with uniform pricing. By contrast, second-degree price discrimination in this setting can lead to an increase in the quantity supplied to all markets and so increase social welfare.

To see this, return to our two-good case. Equation (5.49) then becomes

$$(p_1 - c)\Delta q_1 + (p_2 - c)\Delta q_2 \leq \Delta W \leq \left(p^U - c\right)(\Delta q_1 + \Delta q_2) \qquad (5.50)$$

We know, however, that $p_2 = c$. So, the left-hand inequality becomes

$$(p_1 - c)\Delta q_1 \leq \Delta W \qquad (5.51)$$

Hence, a sufficient condition for the switch to menu pricing to increase social welfare is that it increases the quantity sold to a type θ_1 consumer.

Return to our specific example. With second-degree price discrimination, the quantity bought by each type θ_1 consumer is $q_1^s = \theta_1 - c - \frac{(1-\lambda)}{\lambda}(\theta_2 - \theta_1)$. From equation (5.35), the quantity supplied to each type θ_1 consumer with uniform pricing is $q_1^U = \theta_1 - p_m = \theta_1 - \left(\frac{\lambda\theta_1 + (1-\lambda)\theta_2 + c}{2}\right)$. It follows that

$$\Delta q_1 = \frac{\left(2 - 2\lambda + \lambda^2\right)\theta_1 - \left(2 - 3\lambda + \lambda^2\right)\theta_2 - c\lambda}{\lambda} \qquad (5.52)$$

The sign of Δq_1 is determined by the numerator of (5.52). In other words, price discrimination increases the quantity supplied to each type θ_1 consumer if

$$\Delta q_i^n = -2(\theta_2 - \theta_1) + \lambda(3\theta_2 - 2\theta_1 - c) - \lambda^2(\theta_2 - \theta_1) > 0 \qquad (5.53)$$

We know that, by definition, $0 \leq \lambda \leq 1$; and we can see from (5.53) that Δq_1^n is a quadratic in λ. If $\lambda = 0$, we have $\Delta q_1^n = -2(\theta_2 - \theta_1) < 0$; whereas if $\lambda = 1$, we have $\Delta q_1^n = \theta_1 - c > 0$. It follows that there is a value of λ above which $\Delta q_1^n > 0$. In other words, second-degree price discrimination increases welfare, provided that the proportion of low-demand consumers is "great enough."

Summary

We started this chapter with a discussion of prescription drug price differentials that seem not to be related to costs. In a well-functioning market, such differentials can only occur if there is some distinction between the groups in terms of their willingness to pay—and some way to separate the two groups of consumers to prevent arbitrage. We showed that a firm with monopoly power can increase its profits beyond what it would earn from charging each consumer the same uniform price if the firm can figure out a way to separate its consumers into their different types and charge a different price to each type. Our analysis has concentrated on the "traditional" forms of price discrimination: first-degree or personalized pricing, second-degree or menu pricing, and third-degree or group pricing.

In order to implement any kind of price discrimination, the firm has to solve two problems. First, it needs either an observable characteristic by which it can identify the different types of consumer, or it needs some mechanism by which it can encourage consumers of different types to self-select by type. That is, it needs to solve the identification problem. Second, the firm must be able to prevent consumers who pay a low price from selling to consumers offered a high price. It must solve the arbitrage problem.

We have shown how widely observed tactics such as two-part tariffs, menu pricing, and pricing related to age, gender, or time of day serve as means to implement some degree of discriminatory pricing. We have also shown that in many (but not all) such cases, the use of discriminatory techniques can raise social welfare, subject to two qualifications. The first is that in the case of menu and group pricing, the discriminatory practice must somehow raise total output if it is to increase the total surplus. The second is that even when discriminatory pricing raises total surplus, it usually happens that the increased surplus (and more) is transferred to the monopolist.

A further constraint must be satisfied when the monopolist knows that it is supplying consumers of different types, knows the actual types, but has no observable characteristic that allows the firm to tell the specific type of each consumer. The monopolist must then rely on second-degree price discrimination or menu pricing. An important requirement in the application of menu pricing is that the tactic must be incentive compatible with consumers' behavior if it is to have the desired profit-increasing effect. By incentive compatibility, we mean that a pricing mechanism intended to steer customers to particular options must be designed in such a way that other options do not offer the consumer greater surplus; otherwise, the consumer will not make the desired choice. This constraint reduces the monopolist's ability to extract the maximum surplus from the market.

Our analysis has focused on pricing tactics. Instead of prices, however, firms may adjust the design of their products. Indeed, to some extent, menu pricing reflects such a product design in that it amounts to offering different packages—different goods in some sense—in a way calculated to extract as much surplus as possible. We turn to a further consideration of these design issues in the next chapter.

Problems

1. Suppose every consumer has an inverse demand of the form $p = d^{-1}(q)$, so that each consumer's aggregate willingness to pay for quantity q is $v(q) = \int_0^q d^{-1}(x)dx$. Imagine that the firm adopts a linear pricing policy that sets a uniform price per unit p, but requires that all purchases include a minimum amount of units q_{MIN}. What value should the firm choose for q_{MIN}, and what price should it set in order to maximize profit?

2. A monopolist with marginal cost of production of 40 sells to two distinct regions. In Region 1, demand is given by: $Q_1 = 300 - p_1$. In Region 2, it is given by: $Q_2 = 180 - p_2$.
   a. Determine the optimal uniform price and output when discrimination is impossible.
   b. Assume discrimination between the two regions is possible. What price will be set for each country? What quantity will be sold in each?
   c. How does the discriminatory price relate to the elasticity of demand in each country?

3. A local bar owner has a constant unit cost of $2 per drink. He determines that the demand for drinks is different for students than it is for those age 25 and over, with each group comprising about half of his nightly crowd. Specifically, he discovers that the demand for drinks is:
   Age 18–25: $q = 18 - 5p$
   Age 25 and over: $q = 10 - 2p$

    a.   If no discrimination is possible, what is the optimal uniform price assuming it is low enough that both groups buy?

    b.   If the bar owner adopts a two-part pricing policy that is the same for everyone, what will be the cover charge (fixed fee), and what will be the price per drink?

    c.   How would your answer to 3b change if students comprised only 30 percent of the customers?

4.   Return to the specific case used to model menu pricing. That is, assume constant returns to scale for the monopolist, and assume that consumers have utility given by $V(\theta_i, q) = \theta_i q - \frac{q^2}{2}$; for $0 \leq q \leq \theta_i$ and $i = 1, 2$, and $\theta_1 > \theta_2$. Show that the profit-maximizing menu design $[(T_1, q_1),(T_2, q_2)]$ will typically involve a lower per-unit price for the high-demand customers.

5.   Imagine that there are two types of consumers indexed by θ_i with $i = 1, 2$. Let the inverse demand curve for each be: $p = \theta_i(1 - q_i)$, with $\theta_1 > \theta_2$. Let the shares of the total population of N for each type be λ and $1 - \lambda$, for groups 1 and 2, respectively.

    a.   Show that the aggregate demand is $Q(p) = N\left(1 - \frac{p}{\tilde{\theta}}\right)$ where $\tilde{\theta} = \frac{\lambda}{\theta_1} + \frac{1-\lambda}{\theta_2}$, assuming both groups are induced to buy.

    b.   Find the profit-maximizing menu-pricing strategy.

    c.   Find the profit-maximizing uniform-pricing strategy.

    d.   Compare your answers in 5 c and 5d. Which is more efficient?

References

Graham, J. and B. Robson. 2000. "Prescription Drug Prices in Canada and the United States—Part 1: A Comparative Survey." *Public Policy Sources*, 22, Fraser Institute.

—— and T. Tabler, 2001. "Prescription Drug Prices in Canada and the United States—Part 3: Retail Price Discrimination." *Public Policy Sources*, 50, Fraser Institute.

Leslie, P. 2004. "Price Discrimination in Broadway Theatre." *Rand Journal of Economics*, 35 (Autumn): 520–541.

Phlips, L. 1983. *The Economics of Price Discrimination*. Cambridge: Cambridge University Press.

Pigou, A. C., 1920. *The Economics of Welfare*. London: Macmillan Publishing.

Schmalensee, R. 1981. "Output and Welfare Implications of Monopolistic Third-Degree Price Discrimination," *American Economic Review*, 71 (March): 242–247.

Shapiro, C. and H. R. Varian. 1999. *Information Rules*. Boston: Harvard Business School Press.

Shih, J., and C. Mai, and J. Liu. 1988. "A General Analysis of the Output Effect Under Third-Degree Price Discrimination," *Economic Journal*, (March): 149–158.

Varian, H. 1989. "Price Discrimination." In R. Schmalensee and R. Willig (Eds.), *The Handbook of Industrial Organization*, Vol. 1 (Amsterdam: North-Holland, 1989): 597–654.

6

Price Discrimination, Product Variety, Bundling, and Tying

In Chapter 5 we defined price discrimination as occurring whenever a firm sells an identical product to two or more buyers at different prices. Yet what if the products are not identical? The brand name drug example at the beginning of Chapter 5 compares prices of drugs sold in different locations. Are these really the same goods? After all, the firm has incurred costs in transporting the drugs to the different points of sale. Similarly, there is a price differential between the prices of economy class and first-class airline seats on the same flight. But anyone who has been bumped up (or down) knows full well that these airline seats are of very different quality. Toyota offers several hundred varieties of the Toyota Camry with slightly different features. Procter and Gamble offers a wide range of toothpastes in different tastes, colors, and claimed medicinal qualities. Kellogg offers dozens of breakfast cereals that vary in terms of grain, taste, consistency, and color. Books are first released as expensive hardcover editions and only later as cheap paperbacks. Hotels in a ski area are more expensive in winter than in summer.

The common theme of these examples is that they all involve variations of a basic product. This is a phenomenon that we meet every day in buying restaurant meals, refrigerators, haircuts, and many other goods and services. In each of these situations, what we observe is a firm selling different varieties of the same good—distinguished by color, material, or design. As a brief reflection on air fares or the prices of standard versus luxury automobiles will reveal, what we also usually observe is that the different varieties are aimed at different consumer groups and sell at different prices. In other words, many examples of price discrimination arise when the seller offers *differentiated* products.

In considering these as applications of price discrimination, we have to be careful. After all, the cost incurred in producing goods of different types, such as hardback and paperback books or first-class versus coach flights, is different. Phlips (1983) provides perhaps the best definition of price discrimination once we allow for product differentiation:

> Price discrimination should be defined as implying that two varieties of a commodity are sold (by the same seller) to two buyers at different *net* prices, the net price being the price (paid by the buyer) corrected for the cost associated with the product differentiation. (Phlips 1983, p. 6)

Using this definition, it would not be discriminatory to charge $750 extra for a car with antilock brakes if it costs $750 extra to assemble a car with such brakes. By contrast, the difference in price between a coach class fare of $450 and a first-class fare of $8,000 for service between Boston and London could reasonably be seen as almost entirely reflecting price discrimination, because the additional cost of providing first-class service per passenger is well below the $7550 difference in price. Price discrimination across different versions of the same good exists only if the difference in prices is not justified by differences in underlying costs, which is what Phlips means by the *net price*. Perhaps more interesting is the reverse implication of Phlips' definition. Price discrimination also exists when a firm sells two different goods with different costs to different consumers for the same price. Thus, a cement company that charges different prices in different cities is not price discriminating if the difference in prices across cities equals the difference in transport costs, whereas a cement company that charges the same price in every city (uniform delivered pricing) *is* price discriminating.

Introducing product variety into the analysis of price discrimination raises a very important question. Does offering different varieties of a product enhance the monopolist's ability to charge different net prices? Does a firm with market power increase its ability to price discriminate by offering different versions of its product? As we shall see in this chapter, the general answer is *yes*.

We can obtain at least some insight into this issue by recalling the two problems that successful discrimination must overcome—namely, identification and arbitrage. In order to price discriminate, the firm must determine who is who on its demand curve and then be able to prevent resale between separate consumers. By offering different versions or models of its product, the monopolist may be able to solve these two problems. Different consumer types may buy different versions of the product and therefore reveal who they are through their purchase decisions. Moreover, since different customers are purchasing different varieties, the problem of resale is considerably reduced.

6.1   PRICE DISCRIMINATION AND PRODUCT QUALITY

As noted in the introduction, many firms produce a wide range of differentiated products. In some cases these products are of similar quality, but differ in features such as taste and color. They are *horizontally differentiated* and we shall consider how these products might be priced in section 6.2. In other cases, those that we consider in this section, the products are differentiated by quality—first-class versus economy in air travel, Lexus versus Toyota, hardback versus paperback. These products are *vertically differentiated*. When a firm offers different qualities of the same product, it has to decide what qualities should be offered and how products of different qualities should be priced.

6.1.1   A (Relatively) Simple Example

We begin with an example that has much in common with the discussion of second-degree price discrimination in the previous chapter. Suppose that a monopolist can offer two varieties of a product, one of high quality and the other of low quality, where quality is fixed exogenously and observable by potential consumers. Marginal production cost for each variety is constant and equal to c_H for the high-quality and c_L for the low-quality good. The firm knows that its market contains two types of consumers, each of whom will buy either one or no units of the good. There are N_1 type 1 consumers with relatively low reservation prices and N_2 type 2 consumers with relatively high reservation prices for both products. However, there is no observable consumer characteristic that allows the firm to distinguish between these consumer types. It might be, for example, that type 2 consumers have higher incomes than type 1 consumers or have stronger preferences for the product, no matter its quality. Whatever the source of distinction between consumers, the firm cannot observe it.[1]

Let the reservation prices for type 1 (2) consumers be $V_1^H (V_2^H)$ for the high-quality good and $V_1^L (V_2^L)$ for the low-quality good, with $V_i^H > V_i^L (i = 1, 2)$ and $V_1^J < V_2^J (J = H, L)$. Each consumer purchases exactly one unit of this differentiated product, provided the price is less than the relevant reservation price. If this is the case for both products, the consumer purchases the product that offers the greater consumer surplus.

As an example, consider an airline such as Delta Air Lines (DAL) operating direct passenger flights between Boston and Amsterdam. DAL knows that it serves two types of travelers. There are business travelers who are willing to pay relatively high prices for a seat—since they have little option of whether or not to travel—and vacation travelers who are willing to pay relatively low prices. The problem that DAL faces is that it does not know *a priori* the type of a prospective passenger when the passenger logs in to DAL's online booking service.

In analyzing this example, we have to consider several cases. We begin by making Assumption 1: $V_i^H - V_i^L > c_H - c_L (i = 1, 2)$.

For both consumer types, the difference in consumer valuations (reservation prices) of high- and low-quality goods is greater than the difference in their marginal costs. With this assumption, if the firm produces only one good it will produce the high-quality good. In that case, the only question is whether the good should be priced to attract both consumer types or only type 2 consumers.

(a) Case 1: Offer only the high-quality good and sell to both consumer types

The highest price that the firm can set is $p^H = V_1^H$, and the firm's profit is

$$\pi_1 = (N_1 + N_2)(V_1^H - c_H) \tag{6.1}$$

(b) Case 2: Offer only the high-quality good and sell only to type 2 consumers

Now the firm prices the product at $p^H = V_2^H$, and the firm's profit is

$$\pi_2 = N_2(V_2^H - c_H) \tag{6.2}$$

The firm prefers case 2 to case 1, and serves only the higher-paying type 2 consumers when

Condition 1: $N_2(V_2^H - V_1^H) > N_1(V_1^H - c_H)$ $\qquad$ (6.3)

The left-hand side of Condition 1 is the additional revenue the firm derives from type 2 consumers by pricing type 1 consumers out of the market, while the right-hand side is the profit the firm foregoes from type 1 consumers by restricting its sales to only type 2 consumers. If the firm gains from pricing to exclude the type 1 consumers, it must be the

---

[1] For more complete treatment of all possible combinations of relative reservation prices, see Phlips (1983), ch. 14.

case that left-hand side term exceeds that on the right-hand side. There are, of course, many parameter restrictions that will satisfy Condition 1. For example, Condition 1 is more likely to hold if the preference for high quality of type 2 consumers is "very strong" compared to type 1 consumers.

(c) Case 3: Offer both high- and low-quality goods

If the firm offers both qualities, it sets price p^L for the low-quality good and p^H for the high-quality good. Clearly, the firm would rather that type 2 consumers choose to purchase the high-quality product and type 1 consumers choose to purchase the low-quality product. The maximum price that can be set for the low-quality good is, therefore, $p^L = V_1^L$, so that type 1 consumers are just willing to purchase the low-quality good. The price of the high-quality good must satisfy the familiar incentive compatibility constraint that type 2 consumers prefer to purchase the high-quality rather than the low-quality good. Hence, we must have[2]

$$V_2^H - p^H \geq V_2^L - p^L = V_2^L - V_1^L, \text{ which gives } p^H = V_2^H - V_2^L + V_1^L \qquad (6.4)$$

The similarity with our discussion of second-degree price discrimination in the previous chapter should be obvious. Type 1 consumers have their entire consumer surplus extracted, while type 2 consumers enjoy positive consumer surplus $V_2^L - V_1^L$.

Is there price discrimination in this case? The difference in prices is $p^H - p^L = V_2^H - V_2^L$, while the difference in marginal costs is $c_H - c_L$. By Condition 1 above there is, indeed, price discrimination. The difference in the prices of the high-quality and the low-quality good is greater than the difference in their marginal costs.

The final question we consider is under what condition the firm prefers to offer both qualities of product, rather than only one. To answer this question, note that when both products are offered, profit to the firm is

$$\pi_3 = N_1(V_1^L - c_L) + N_2(V_2^H - V_2^L + V_1^L - c_H) \qquad (6.5)$$

Suppose that Condition 1 holds, then the monopolist will offer both products if

$$\text{Condition 2: } N_2(V_2^L - V_1^L) < N_1(V_1^L - c_L) \qquad (6.6)$$

The left-hand side of Condition 2 is the aggregate consumer surplus enjoyed by type 2 consumers when both products are offered—as a result of the firm having to meet the incentive compatibility constraint—while the right-hand side is the profit the firm derives from selling the low-quality good to type 1 consumers. When the foregone surplus (which the firm could capture if it sold the high-quality good to type 2 consumers only) is less than the profit gained from selling the low-quality good to type 1 consumers, then the firm finds it profitable to offer both qualities of the good.

Condition 2 is likely to hold in a variety of cases. For instance, it will hold if the two consumer types do not differ much in their respective valuations of the low-quality good. It will also hold if the low-quality good is "very cheap" to produce relative to a type 1 consumer's valuation of the low-quality good.

---

[2]   You can check that, given our assumptions, at these prices type 1 consumers do not prefer to purchase the high-quality good.

Let us now revisit the case of airline pricing and the very different prices charged to business class and economy air travelers. In order for this to work, the valuation of the business class seats must differ substantially between business travelers and those traveling on holiday. Arbitrage is prevented because the business traveler gets just as much (or slightly more) from paying the business class price and getting the business class seat than she would get from buying a cheaper coach ticket and flying economy class. However, this willingness to pay could change. The recent sharp downturn in economic activity forced many businesses to seek to cut costs in part by requiring employees to fly coach on company activities.[3] Suppose, then, that airlines can no longer use the business class distinction to sort and separate consumers.

If businesses will no longer pay for business class airfare, the business traveler's willingness to pay for air travel will be affected. Nevertheless, they will likely still be willing to pay more for such travel—even if it is a coach seat—than a holiday traveler. Knowing this, the airline would like to exploit this difference and continue to charge business customers a higher price than vacationers, despite the fact that they may both sit in the same part of the plane. However, since it does not know who is who, any attempt to charge a higher price for business travelers will quickly lead to every customer claiming to be on holiday. Of course, the airline could try to identify which passengers really are on holiday, but this would be costly and likely to alienate customers.

If this were the end of our story, it would appear that the airline has no choice but to sell its economy tickets at a single, uniform price. It would then face the usual textbook monopoly dilemma. A high price will earn a large surplus from every customer that buys a ticket, but leads to a smaller, mostly business set of passengers. In contrast, a low price will encourage many more people to fly but, unfortunately, leave the airline with little surplus from any one consumer.

Suppose, however, that business and holiday travelers differ in another respect as well as in their motives for flying. To be specific, suppose that business travelers want to complete their trip and return home to spend time with their families on the weekend, whereas vacationers have no such desire—they are going on holiday with their families. Suppose also that the airline learns through market research that business travelers would pay a premium if they could be guaranteed an open return flight, whereas vacation travelers are more willing to accept "no change" restrictions on their flights. In this case, product differentiation by means of offering two differentiated tickets—one with a requirement that there be at least one Saturday night between outward and return flights and a "no change, no refund" restriction, and the other with no such restrictions—satisfies the conditions of our example. The "no restriction" flight is of higher quality because it is more flexible. It is more expensive to produce, because it requires the airline to have the capacity to offer the flexibility required by the business traveler. Offering such a differentiated airline ticket now achieves the sorting and separation that offering first class did earlier. Business travelers will choose the more expensive unrestricted flight. Holiday travelers who do not mind staying over Saturday night will choose the cheaper, "no change, no refund" ticket.

In short, while the airline cannot extract the entire consumer surplus from the market, it can nevertheless improve its profits greatly by offering two kinds of tickets. This is undoubtedly the reason why the practice just described is so common among airlines and

---

[3]   For evidence that such a rise in the price sensitivity of business consumers of air travel was in fact an important source of declining profit margins in the US airline industry in the early 2000s, see Berry and Jia (2010).

Reality Checkpoint
You Can't Go Before You Come Back

It is not uncommon to find that a coach fare to fly out on Tuesday and return quickly on Thursday costs well over twice the coach fare to fly out on Tuesday and return a week later. So, for travelers wanting to return in two days, an obvious strategy is to buy two round trip tickets—one, say, that departs on Thursday the 10th and returns on Thursday the 17th, and another that departs on Tuesday the 15th and returns on Tuesday the 22nd. The passenger can use the outgoing half of the first ticket on Tuesday the 15th and then fly back on the return flight of the second ticket that flies on the 17th. Unfortunately for such savvy travelers—and for the students and other needy consumers who could use the unused portions of each flight—the airlines are alert to such practices. In particular, when a passenger checks in for a flight, the airline checks to see if the passenger has an unused portion of a return flight. If so, the fee is automatically adjusted to the higher fare. The airlines have a great incentive to make sure that those who are willing to pay a substantial premium to return in two days really do pay it.

Source: "Why It Doesn't Pay to Change Planes or Plans." *London Daily Telegraph* (11 March 2000), p. 27.

other transportation companies (see Reality Checkpoint). Such companies offer different varieties of their product as a means of having their customers self-select into different groups. Automobile and appliance manufacturers utilize a similar strategy—offering different product lines meant to appeal to consumers of different incomes or otherwise different willingness to pay. Stiglitz (1977) labels such mechanisms *screening devices*, because they screen or separate customers along the relevant dimension of willingness to pay.

6.1.2   An Extension: Endogenous Quality

The previous example illustrates some important points, but is based on a number of quite restrictive assumptions. Specifically, we assumed that the different qualities offered by the seller are exogenously given rather than endogenously determined. In this section we consider what happens when the monopolist chooses the qualities of its products as well as their prices. We shall see that the resulting analysis has even more features in common with our analysis of second-degree price discrimination in Chapter 5.[4]

We continue with the assumption that consumers have unit demands—each consumer purchases exactly one unit of the monopolist's product (provided it offers non-negative consumer surplus) and, in choosing between goods of different qualities, purchases the variety that offers the greater consumer surplus. A consumer with taste parameter θ has utility $U = \theta s - P$ if he purchases, where s is an observable index of product quality and P is the price paid. Note that θ is the marginal utility of quality for a type θ consumer. It is to be expected that the price paid will depend upon the product quality, so that $P = P(s)$. The cost of producing a product of quality s is $c(s)$, where c is increasing

---

[4]   Our analysis draws on Mussa and Rosen (1978) and Maskin and Riley (1984). See also Tirole (1988), p. 149–150.

and convex: $c' > 0$; $c'' > 0$. Quality is costly to produce and becomes increasingly costly as quality rises.

We first show that this model is formally equivalent to our model of second-degree price discrimination. To do so let $q = c(s)$ be the unit cost of producing a good of quality s. Then we can write the inverse function $s = V(q) = c^{-1}(q)$. Since c is increasing and convex, V is increasing and concave. Consumer preferences can then be written

$$U = \theta V(q) - P(V(q)) = \theta V(q) - p(q) \tag{6.7}$$

where $p(q) = P(V(q))$. By construction, the firm's costs are linear in q. Comparison with equation (5.30) tells us that these two models are identical at a formal, mathematical level; the only difference between them is what q represents in the two models.

Suppose now that there are two types of consumers, indexed as before by the parameter θ_i with $\theta_1 < \theta_2$. Without loss of generality, we assume $\theta_2 > 1$ as well. While the firm knows the distribution of consumer types, it does not know the actual type of each consumer. Our analysis in Chapter 5 then suggests that type θ_2 consumers are offered the socially efficient quality—such that $\theta_2 = c'(s_2)$—while type θ_1 consumers are offered a product of suboptimal quality, such that $\theta_1 > c'(s_1)$. We now proceed to confirm this intuition.

Assume initially that the firm offers just a single product quality, and that it sets a price for this product that is the same for all consumers, since the firm cannot tell one consumer type from another. One possible strategy is for the firm to price the product to extract all consumer surplus of type θ_1 consumers, so that $P = \theta_1 s$. Profit is $N(\theta_1 s - c(s))$. In this case, the optimal choice of quality satisfies $c'(s) = \theta_1$. Type θ_1 consumers are offered the quality that is socially optimal for them. However, type θ_2 consumers are, at the margin, willing to pay more for a quality increase than it costs. So, for them, the quality is suboptimally low. Alternatively, the firm could choose to serve only type θ_2 consumers. The price can then rise to $P = \theta_2 s$, implying profit is $N_2(\theta_2 s - c(s))$. In this case, the optimal quality choice satisfies $c'(s) = \theta_2$. Type θ_2 consumers are offered the quality that is socially optimal for them, but type θ_1 consumers are priced out of the market. Choosing between these two strategies once again reflects the problem that a firm faces when, although it knows that its customers vary in their preferences, it cannot tell the type of any one customer in particular.

A partial solution may be found by the firm offering two qualities of its product. The firm can cater to both consumer types by offering a low-quality variety s_1 at price P_1 and a high-quality variety s_2 at price P_2. When type θ_1 consumers purchase the low-quality product and type θ_2 the high-quality product, the firm's profit is

$$\pi = N[\lambda(P_1 - c(s_1)) + (1 - \lambda)(P_2 - c(s_2))] \tag{6.8}$$

where N is the total number of consumers, and $\lambda = N_1/(N_1 + N_2)$ is the proportion of type θ_1 consumers.

The firm maximizes profit (6.8) subject to the two usual incentive compatibility constraints. Type θ_1 consumers must enjoy nonnegative surplus from consuming the low quality good:

$$\theta_1 s_1 - P_1 \geq 0 \tag{6.9}$$

The price P_1 must be set such that they prefer to purchase the low-quality variety to not buying at all.

For type θ_2 consumers, the price P_2 must be set such that they prefer to purchase the high-quality variety than the low-quality:

$$\theta_2 s_2 - P_2 \geq \theta_2 s_1 - P_1. \tag{6.10}$$

Comparison with equations (5.39–5.40) of Chapter 5, and recalling that $c(s) = q$ and $s = V(q)$, confirms that we are working with a mathematically equivalent model. Since the firm is assumed to be a profit maximizer, we know from (6.9) and (6.10) that it will set the product variety prices so that $P_1 = \theta_1 s_1$ and $P_2 = \theta_2 s_2 - (\theta_2 - \theta_1)s_1$. The two quality/price offers are designed to extract all consumer surplus from type θ_1 consumers, who have a low valuation of quality, while leaving type θ_2 consumers who have a high valuation of quality with positive consumer surplus $(\theta_2 - \theta_1)s_1$. As before, the firm incurs a cost in the form of surplus that it must forego as a result of its inability to distinguish one type of consumer from another.

Substituting P_1 and P_2 into (6.8) gives the profit function

$$\pi = N[\lambda(\theta_1 s_1 - c(s_1)) + (1 - \lambda)(\theta_2 s_2 - (\theta_2 - \theta_1)s_1 - c(s_2))] \tag{6.11}$$

Differentiating with respect to s_1 and s_2 then gives the necessary first-order conditions for profit maximization:

$$c'(s_1) = \theta_1 - \frac{(1 - \lambda)}{\lambda}(\theta_2 - \theta_1)$$

$$c'(s_2) = \theta_2 \tag{6.12}$$

These are illustrated in Figure 6.1. Our intuition based on the analogy with the menu pricing described in Chapter 5 is confirmed: the quality s_1 of the low-quality variety

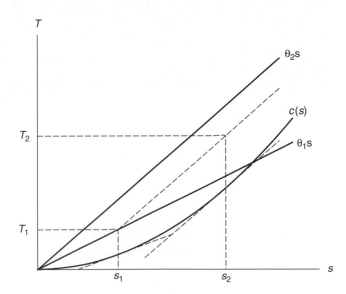

Figure 6.1   Price discrimination and product quality

is socially suboptimal, while that of the high-quality variety is socially optimal. The monopolist uses its ability to match the number of product qualities to the different types of consumers it serves in order to encourage its consumers to *self-select* into their true types. In doing so, it uses a *reduction* in the quality of the *lower-quality* good as a market segmentation device.

As an illustration, consider the specific example in which $c(s) = s^2/2$, so that $c'(s) = s$. Then, substitution reveals that the two product qualities are

$$s_2 = \theta_2; \text{ and } s_1 = \theta_1 - \frac{(1-\lambda)}{\lambda}(\theta_2 - \theta_1) \qquad (6.13)$$

Likewise, if we solve for the product prices, we have

$$P_1 = \frac{\theta_1}{\lambda}(\theta_1 - \theta_2(1-\lambda)); \text{ and } P_2 = \frac{1}{\lambda}((\theta_2 - \theta_1)^2 + \theta_1\theta_2\lambda) \qquad (6.14)$$

The difference in the two prices is $P_2 - P_1 = \theta_2(\theta_2 - \theta_1)/\lambda$, yet the difference in marginal costs is $s_2 - s_1 = (\theta_2 - \theta_1)/\lambda$. With one very special exception ($\theta_2 = 1$), there is price discrimination.[5]

An interesting historical example of market segmentation by reducing the quality of the low-quality product is given by Ekelund, quoting Dupuit (1849) in discussing railroad tariffs:[6]

> It is not because of the few thousand francs which would have to be spent to put a roof over the third-class carriages or to upholster the third-class seats that some company or other has open carriages with wooden benches.... What the company is trying to do is to prevent the passengers who can pay the second-class fare from traveling third-class; it hits the poor, not because it wants to hurt them, but to frighten the rich.... And it is again for the same reason that the companies, having proved almost cruel to third-class passengers and mean to second-class passengers, become lavish in dealing with first-class passengers. Having refused the poor what is necessary, they give the rich what is superfluous. (Ekelund 1970, p. 275)

About the only dispute that we might have with this description is the last sentence. Our analysis shows that "the rich" are offered the quality that is socially optimal *for them*. This might, of course, seem lavish or superfluous in the eyes of normal mortals. Moving forward in time from Dupuit, perhaps this explains why, on international flights, those of us who travel in the back of the plane are treated so much worse than those who travel in the front!

6.1.3   A Further Extension: Damaged Goods

We have shown that a monopolist may differentiate his products "vertically" so that they play a screening role. The quality choices are then endogenous and respond to the preference and cost parameters that characterize the market. The difference in quality between the two versions of the product and the price associated with each are used

---

[5]   Note that the direction of the price discrimination will also depend on whether $\theta_2 > 1$ (higher quality sells at a higher net price) or $\theta_2 < 1$ (higher quality sells at a lower net price).

[6]   The quotation can be found in Phlips (1983), p. 216; and Tirole (1988), p. 150.

to sort and separate customers into different buying groups based on their relative willingness to pay for quality.

A rather curious example of screening is illustrated by Wolfram Research, manufacturers of the *Mathematica*® software package. In making their student version of the software, Wolfram imposes a number of restrictions that do not apply to the full academic or commercial versions. In 2009, Wolfram offered the full version of *Mathematica*® at around $2,495, the academic version at around $1,095, and the student version at around $140.

The motivation for Wolfram's behavior can be understood by our analysis of product differentiation in this chapter. Wolfram realizes that some customers do not need—or at least do not want to pay very much for—the full version of their software. Wolfram markets the low-priced version of *Mathematica*® for these consumers, and then sells the extended version to customers with a high willingness to pay for the improved product. Note that the two products must really differ in some important respect (to consumers at least). If Wolfram did not limit the capabilities of the student version, it would have to worry about arbitrage between the two customer groups, with students buying for their professors!

What about the difference in net prices? How can we be sure that the student version does not cost less? This is where the Wolfram example turns curious. The reason we can be sure that the price differential is not rooted in costs is that the firm makes the student version from the full version. That is, Wolfram starts with a high-quality product—the full version of the software—and then damages it by disabling certain functions. This is referred to by marketing experts as "crimping the product." Whatever it is called, however, it should be clear that it cannot cost less to produce the lower-quality product. Yet, that product sells for a lower price.

Deneckere and McAffee (1996) argue that crimping or deliberately damaging a product to enhance the ability to price discriminate has been a frequent practice of manufacturers throughout history. Among the examples that they cite are IBM's Laser Printer E, an intentionally slower version of the company's higher-priced top-of-the-line laser printer; and simple cooking wine, which is ordinary table wine with so much salt added that it is undrinkable. Some people have even argued that the U.S. Postal Service deliberately reduces the quality of its standard, first-class service so as to raise demand for its two-day priority and overnight mail services.

Each of these examples is a clear case of a difference in net prices. The lower-quality product sells for a lower price, yet—because it starts as a high-quality product and then requires the further cost of crimping—the lower-quality product is actually more expensive to make. Why do firms crimp a high-quality product to produce a low-quality one, instead of simply producing a low-quality one in the first place? The most obvious answer relates to costs of production. Given that a firm with monopoly power such as Wolfram knows that there are consumers of different types willing to buy different varieties of its product, the firm must decide how these consumer types can best be supplied with products "close" to those that they most want at least cost. It may well be cheaper to produce the student version of *Mathematica*® by crimping the full version rather than to set up a separate production line dedicated to manufacturing different versions of the software package.

This example recalls our discussion of scope economies in Chapter 3. Imagine a firm that develops a list of consumers who buy prescription drugs over the Internet. It may start by compiling a list for all drug purchases. The firm may then, however, create separate sublists such as a list of those who buy antibiotics and a list of those who buy drugs for anxiety. Clearly, the sublists are less comprehensive and at least as costly to produce as the comprehensive list. Yet just as clearly, there are some clear scope economies in producing both the comprehensive list and the sublists. Scope economies are likely to be part of the story of why we observe the same firm offering different versions of the product rather than having each version produced separately by different firms.[7]

One interesting question is whether this method of increasing product variety is efficient. Deneckere and McAfee (1996) show that under a number of not particularly restrictive conditions, introducing a low-quality good by damaging a high-quality good is a Pareto improvement, insofar as it increases the welfare of both type 1 and type 2 consumers and increases the profit of the firm.

Suppose that the monopolist is currently producing only a high-quality good and pricing it to sell only to type 2 consumers or those with relatively high valuation of quality. For this to be more profitable than selling the product to both types of consumer, our earlier Condition 1—repeated here—must hold:

$$\text{Condition 1: } N_2\left(V_2^H - V_1^H\right) > N_1\left(V_1^H - c_H\right) \tag{6.15a}$$

Now, suppose that the firm can introduce a low-quality variant by crimping the high-quality variant, the unit cost of the low-quality variant being $c_L > c_H$ as a result of the additional cost associated with crimping. For it to be profitable to introduce this crimped variant, our earlier Condition 2—again repeated here—must hold:

$$\text{Condition 2: } N_2\left(V_2^L - V_1^L\right) < N_1\left(V_1^L - c_L\right) \tag{6.15b}$$

There are many ways in which both conditions can be satisfied, even given that $c_L > c_H$. In the *Mathematica*® case, for example, it is likely that commercial users (type 2) place a much higher valuation on the high-quality variant than do student users (type 1), so Condition 1 is satisfied. At the same time, commercial users are unlikely to place a particularly high valuation on the low-quality variant, so $V_2^L - V_1^L$ is "small" and Condition 2 holds. Given that the two conditions are satisfied, introducing the low-quality variant by crimping the high-quality variant is profitable for the firm. In addition, type 1 consumers are better off in that they are offered a product that they would otherwise not be offered.[8] Type 2 consumers are better off because they are now offered the high-quality product at a lower price (as a result of the incentive compatibility constraint). In other words, introducing a low-quality product by crimping the high-quality product is a Pareto improvement.

6.2   PRICE DISCRIMINATION AND PRODUCT VARIETY

Our discussion in the previous section assumes that the firm offers consumers products that are differentiated by quality, where quality is observable and the ranking of quality is the same for all consumers. Yet, while all consumers prefer high-quality products to low-quality products, their willingness to pay for quality varies. That is, consumers agree on the definition of quality, but they differ in how much they will pay for it. In this section

---

[7]   See, for example, Eaton and Schmitt (1994).

[8]   More formally, they have all but ε of their consumer surplus extracted; but this can be considered an improvement on not having the product at all.

we turn to a different type of product differentiation—namely, horizontal differentiation. In this case consumers have the same willingness to pay for their most preferred product, but they differ in regard to what is the preferred or best product.[9] Different consumers prefer different products even when offered at the same price.

As an example, recall the drug pricing example in Chapter 5, where drugs were differentiated by *location of sale*. Consumers typically view a product for sale in one location to be different from an otherwise identical product for sale in another location. Wisconsin residents prefer a prescription drug such as Lipitor® that is sold at a Wisconsin pharmacy to the same Lipitor® that is being sold in Illinois. A new automobile for sale in one state is not identical to the same new automobile for sale in another state. All else equal, a consumer will likely prefer to purchase their next car from a local dealer rather than from one some distance away.

To illustrate how differentiation by location of sale can lead to price discrimination, consider a company, Boston Sea Foods (BSF), which sells a proprietary brand of clam chowder to consumers distributed over a linear market. All consumers have identical demands for the chowder, $q = d(p)$, and we assume that the density of consumers located a distance r from the firm is $f(r)$. In our analysis it proves convenient to work with demand in inverse form, which we write as $p = d^{-1}(q) = g(q)$.

We assume that BSF has constant marginal production costs c and incurs transport costs tr in transporting one unit of chowder a distance of r miles.[10] In other words, the marginal cost of supplying consumers distance r from the firm is $c + tr$. Finally, we assume that BSF controls delivery of its clam chowder to the different consumer locations—an assumption that is necessary to prevent possible arbitrage between consumers at different distances from BSF.

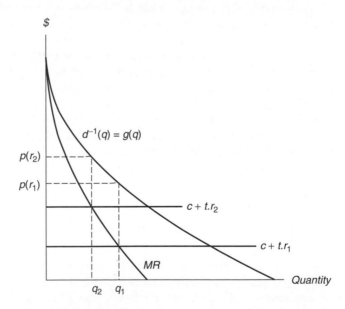

Figure 6.2   Spatial price discrimination

[9]   Our analysis in this section draws on Greenhut, Norman, and Hung (1987), Chapter 6.
[10]   With these assumptions, the shape of the market is not particularly relevant. It could, for example, be a flat surface or a sphere. All we need is that there are $f(r)$ consumers distance r from the firm.

Under these assumptions, the firm maximizes its aggregate profit by choosing the schedule of delivered prices $p(r)$ that maximizes profit at each consumer location. In other words, the firm equates marginal revenue at each consumer location with marginal cost of supplying that location. This is illustrated in Figure 6.2 for two consumer locations r_1 and r_2. Our specific interest is in how the delivered pricing schedule $p(r)$ varies with transport costs tr. Phlips' definition implies that there is no price discrimination if the slope $dp(r)/d(tr) = 1$, that is, if the price rises one-for-one with the cost of production (including transport cost). There is price discrimination, however, if this is not the case.

We begin with a simple identity:

$$\frac{\Delta p(r)}{\Delta(tr)} \equiv \frac{\Delta p(r)}{\Delta q(r)} \frac{\Delta q(r)}{\Delta MR(r)} \frac{\Delta MR(r)}{\Delta MC(r)} \frac{\Delta MC(r)}{\Delta(tr)} \tag{6.16}$$

Of course, profit maximization requires that at each location:

$$MR(r) = MC(r) \tag{6.17}$$

and we have by assumption that

$$MC(r) = c + tr \tag{6.18}$$

It follows that $\Delta MR(r)/\Delta MC(r) = 1$ and $\Delta MC(r)/\Delta(tr) = 1$. Substituting in (6.16) and taking the limit as $\Delta(tr) \to 0$ gives us

$$\frac{dp(r)}{d(tr)} = \frac{dp(r)}{dq(r)} \bigg/ \frac{dMR(r)}{dq(r)} = \frac{dg(q(r))}{dq(r)} \bigg/ \frac{dMR(r)}{dq(r)} \tag{6.19}$$

We can thus conclude: *the slope of the profit-maximizing schedule of delivered prices is given by the ratio of the slope of the inverse demand function to the slope of the marginal revenue function*.

Suppose, for example, that inverse demand is linear and given by $p(r) = g(p(r)) = a - bq(r)$. Hence, marginal revenue $MR(r) = a - 2bq(r)$. Then we have

$$dg(p(r))/dq(r) = -b \text{ and } dMR(r)/dq(r) = -2b \tag{6.20}$$

This implies that $dp(r)/d(tr) = 1/2$. With linear demand, BSF price discriminates in favor of more distant consumers by passing on only 50 percent of transport costs to them.

Returning to our general case, inverse demand is $p(r) = g(q(r))$ and marginal revenue is $MR(r) = d(q(r)) \cdot g(q(r))/dq(r) = g(q(r)) + q(r)g'(q(r))$. The slope of the inverse demand function is $g'(q(r))$ and the slope of the associated marginal revenue function is

$$\frac{dMR(r)}{dq(r)} = 2g'(q(r)) + q(r)g''(q(r)) \tag{6.21}$$

As a result, the slope of the schedule of delivered prices is

$$\frac{dp(r)}{d(tr)} = g'(q(r)) \bigg/ \left[2g'(q(r)) + q(r)g''(q(r)) \right] \tag{6.22}$$

The numerator of (6.21) is negative so long as the inverse demand function is "well behaved." The denominator must also be negative if the second-order condition for profit maximization is to be satisfied. As a result, we know that $dp(r)/d(tr) \geq 0$.

Our interest though is how $dp(r)/d(tr)$ differs from unity. If $dp(r)/d(tr) > 1$, then we can say that BSF discriminates against more distant consumers, that is, the price rises more than proportionately with costs for those further away. If, on the other hand, $dp(r)/d(tr) < 1$, then we know that BSF discriminates against more proximate consumers as the cost to those consumers farther away does not rise commensurately with the transport cost of serving them. From (6.22) it follows that

$$\frac{dp(r)}{d(tr)} \overset{<}{_>} 1 \Leftrightarrow g'(q(r)) + q(r)g''(q(r)) \overset{<}{_>} 0 \tag{6.23}$$

In other words, the direction of price discrimination depends upon the degree of convexity of the demand function.

We can illustrate the foregoing analysis with a particular form of the demand function. Suppose that inverse demand is given by

$$p(r) = a - \frac{b}{x}q(r)^x \quad \text{where } x > -1; x \neq 0 \tag{6.24}$$

It is easy to check that this demand function is convex for $x < 1$ and concave for $x > 1$. Marginal revenue is

$$MR(r) = a - \frac{(1+x)b}{x}q(r)^x \tag{6.25}$$

The slope of the inverse demand function is $dp(r)/dq(r) = -bq(r)^{(x-1)}$, and the slope of the marginal revenue function is $dMR(r)/dq(r) = -(x+1)bq(r)^{(x-1)}$. So from (6.19), we have

$$\frac{dp(r)}{d(tr)} = \frac{1}{1+x} \quad \text{where } x > -1; x \neq 0 \tag{6.26}$$

The firm discriminates in favor of more proximate consumers $(dp(r)/d(tr) > 1)$ if $x < 0$, and in favor of more distant consumers $(dp(r)/d(tr) < 1)$ if $x > 0$. That is, the degree of freight cost absorption incurred by the firm and not passed on to distant consumers increases with the concavity of the inverse demand function.

What do we make of the case when $x = 0$? It turns out that as $x \to 0$, the inverse demand function (6.24) tends to the direct negative exponential demand function

$$q(r) = ae^{-bp(r)} \tag{6.27}$$

We then have the more general result: *the firm discriminates in favor of more proximate consumers when individual demand is more convex than (6.27) and in favor of more distant consumers when individual demand is less convex than (6.27).*

It is instructive to also determine the optimal delivered prices for our example. The profit earned from consumers distance r from the firm is

$$\pi(r) = f(r)\left[aq(r) - \frac{b}{x}q(r)^{1+x} - (c+tr)q(r)\right] \tag{6.28}$$

Maximizing profit with respect to $q(r)$ and simplifying then yields

$$\frac{b}{x}q(r)^x = \frac{a - c - tr}{1 + x} \tag{6.29}$$

Substituting the result in equation (6.29) into (6.24) then gives the optimal delivered prices:

$$p(r) = \frac{ax + c}{1 + x} + \frac{tr}{1 + x} \tag{6.30}$$

This confirms the result in equation (6.26). It is easy to check that $dp(r)/dx < 1$ if $x > 0$, in which case, again, price discrimination favors distant consumers. Likewise, it is easy to see that $dp(r)/dx > 1$ when $-1 < x < 0$, in which case the firm price discriminates in favor of nearby consumers. Equation (6.30) also implies that $dp(r)/dx > 0$ for $x > -1$; $x \neq 0$. The firm finances the additional freight cost of serving distant consumers by increasing its delivered prices at least to some extent.

Prices for the special case $x = 0$ are also telling. As noted, demand is then given by the negative exponential demand function of equation (6.27). It is easy to confirm that the absolute value of the elasticity of demand is then

$$\varepsilon(r) = bp(r) \tag{6.31}$$

Maximizing profit at each consumer location requires that marginal revenue, which is given by $MR(r) = p(r)[1 - 1/\varepsilon(r)]$, equals marginal cost $c + tr$. Substituting from (6.31) and solving for $p(r)$ gives the delivered prices:

$$p(r) = \frac{1}{b} + c + tr \tag{6.32}$$

This implies that when $x = 0$, $dp(r)d(tr) = 1$, and hence there is no price discrimination.

Are there any circumstances that might lead the firm to absorb *all* the transport costs and thus, charge the same uniform delivered price to all consumers no matter where they are located? The answer is yes, but it is a special case. The only situation in which the monopolist will adopt uniform delivered pricing to all consumers is when consumers have perfectly inelastic demands. That is, the monopolist will set a price independent of transport costs only if consumers have a given quantity that they wish to buy regardless of price. The unit demand case that we considered in previous sections, in which consumers purchase exactly one unit of the firm's product (provided the price is less than a reservation price v), but never more than one, is an example of such perfectly inelastic demand. With this type of demand, the profit-maximizing pricing policy for the firm is to set $p(r) = v$ for every consumer, regardless of location. In this way, the firm charges the maximum that each customer is willing to pay.

We motivated this section by claiming that it provides insight into price discrimination when products are horizontally differentiated, that is, when consumers differ in their view about what is a the preferred product, but each consumer is willing to pay the same amount for her preferred product. Clearly, products that are identical other than their location of sale satisfy this criterion when consumers incur costs in buying at more distant locations. The dry cleaner across the street will be seen as different and, more importantly, better than the one 12 blocks away.

We can, however, expand the applicability of our analysis by recalling the analogy first suggested by Hotelling (1929) and discussed briefly in Chapter 3.[11] In this analogy, our geographic line market of Figure 3.4 is replaced by a characteristics line—sweetness, color, style, for example—and a consumer's location or "address" on this line is that consumer's most preferred product characteristic bundle. Consumers then incur psychic or utility costs analogous to transport costs when they have to buy a product that is "far" from their preferred style.[12]

How does this become a model of product differentiation that satisfies the conditions of the analysis we have developed in this section? In the geographic setting, the firm provides transport to each of its consumers r units away. It is as if a dry cleaner offered pickup and delivery. In the more general setting of a product characteristic space, we imagine analogously that the firm starts with a "basic" product, one whose characteristic—such as color if it is a clothing manufacturer or sweetness if it is a soft drink maker—fixes the firm's location or "address." The firm then incurs customization costs in order to modify the characteristics of its product to the most desired characteristic of each consumer—for example, by modifying the sweetness or color or style of the basic product. In other words, the firm offers a range of customized products. This is often referred to as *versioning* in that the firm offers different versions of its basic product to different consumers.

Assume that two further conditions are satisfied. First, the firm is able to identify each consumer's most preferred product characteristics, perhaps by consumer surveys or, in the case of car sales, for example, through direct interaction with the customer. Second, the firm controls the product customization or versioning—equivalent in our spatial example to the firm controlling delivery of the product. All we need then is that the cost of customization is non-decreasing in the "distance" from the firm's basic product to the most desired characteristics of particular consumers and this model is formally equivalent to our spatial model. It follows that we will then again see price discrimination. The difference in the prices of the customized products will not reflect the differences in the costs of customization.

6.3   BUNDLING AND TYING

Our discussion of price discrimination and product differentiation points to the critical role of product design in enabling firms to create or capture more surplus. Grouping ski rides together in fixed amounts and charging a flat fee for them, or putting beer in a case and then selling it at a lower price per unit than when it sells by the bottle can also be viewed as a product design strategy. Viewed in this light, there are two other aspects of product design that the firm can use to increase profit. These are bundling and tying.

6.3.1   Bundling

Assume that there are two goods labeled 1 and 2. Each of these goods is produced with constant marginal (and average) cost denoted by c_1 and c_2, respectively. In other words, we assume that there are no cost advantages of multiproduct production. In particular, there are no scope economies of the type discussed in Chapter 4. Accordingly, the cost of producing a bundle or a package consisting of one unit of each good is $c_B = c_1 + c_2$.

---

[11]   We shall return to this analogy in more detail in later chapters dealing explicitly with product differentiation.

[12]   For this reason, these models are often referred to as address models of product differentiation.

We also assume that a consumer buys exactly one unit of each good per unit of time, provided that the price charged is less than his or her reservation price for that good. The consumer's reservation price or maximum willingness to pay for good 1 is R_1 and for good 2 is R_2. Finally, we assume that the consumer's reservation price for a commodity bundle consisting of one unit of each good is $R_B = R_1 + R_2$. This final assumption—that the reservation price for the bundle is the sum of the reservation prices for the individual goods—is a common one [and one also made by Stigler (1968) in his pathbreaking paper on bundling]. Yet the assumption is, at least in some circumstances, restrictive. If the two goods are complementary goods, such as nuts and bolts, the assumption is almost certainly false. We expect that the willingness to pay for bolts would be quite low in the absence of any nuts and vice versa. For complementary goods, the reservation price for the bundle would likely be higher than the sum of the separate reservation prices for each good consumed separately. Yet while the assumption that $R_B = R_1 + R_2$ is restrictive, it is also useful. It permits us to focus explicitly on the price discrimination motive for bundling.

Suppose that consumers differ in their separate valuations of the two goods—that is, the values of R_1, R_2, and R_B vary across consumers. Some consumers have a high R_1 and a low R_2; for others, just the opposite is true. Some place a high value on both goods. For others, R_1 and R_2 are both quite low. If we draw a quadrant with R_1 on the horizontal axis and R_2 on the vertical axis, as in Figure 6.3, then our assumptions allow us to describe each consumer's reservation prices by a point in the (R_1, R_2) quadrant.

It might be helpful to use a specific example, such as a restaurant menu. We are all familiar with restaurants that offer an à la carte menu from which we can pick individual items and a set menu that contains perhaps an appetizer and an entrée or an entrée and a dessert sold as a bundle. Figure 6.3 illustrates the simplest pricing strategy for the monopolist offering two goods. Sell the two products separately at their monopoly prices, p_1^M and p_2^M. (We leave aside for the moment just how these monopoly prices might be identified.) This could be a restaurant that sells soup at price p_1^M and a sandwich at price p_2^M. Buying both goods costs $p_1^M + p_2^M$. Facing these prices, consumers are partitioned into four groups. Consumers in group A have reservation prices for both goods that are greater than the prices being charged and therefore purchase one unit of each product. Consumers in group B have reservation prices for good 2 that are higher than its price, p_2^M and so buy good 2. However, their reservation prices for good 1 are lower than the price

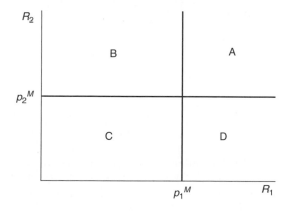

Figure 6.3 Consumers' reservation prices for goods 1 and 2 and simple monopoly pricing
At monopoly prices p_1^M and p_2^M, group A buys both goods; group B buys good 2; group D buys good 1; and group C buys neither good.

p_1^M, and so they do not buy good 1. Similarly, consumers in group D have reservation prices for good 1 that are higher than its price, so they buy good 1. However, they do not buy good 2. Consumers in group C have reservation prices for both goods that are lower than the prices being charged and so do not purchase either product.

Now, suppose that the monopolist adopts a *pure bundling* strategy in which the two goods can be purchased only as a bundle at a fixed price of p_B. In our restaurant setting, this would mean that the only deal on offer is soup plus a sandwich at a fixed price of p_B. The goods cannot be purchased separately at individual prices, p_1 and p_2.

The bundle price is illustrated in Figure 6.4 as a straight line with intercept on each axis of p_B, and so has a slope of -1. Now consumers are partitioned into two groups. Each consumer in group E has reservation prices for the two goods—the sum of which is greater than p_B—and so will buy the package. By contrast, each consumer in group F has reservation prices for the two goods the sum of which is less than p_B, and so will not buy the package.

Figure 6.4 illustrates an interesting feature of the pure bundling strategy. There are consumers who, as a result of the two goods being offered as a bundle, are able to buy one of the goods even though their reservation prices for that good are less than its marginal production cost. This is true in the case of good 1 for all consumers in group E whose reservation price for good 1 is less than c_1, and in the case of good 2 for all consumers in group E whose reservation prices for good 2 are less than c_2.

The third case is that of *mixed bundling*. Here, the monopolist offers to sell the two goods separately at specified prices, respectively, of p_1 and p_2 (which are not necessarily the monopoly prices), and also sells them as a bundle at price p_B (again, not necessarily the pure bundle price). Of course, for this to make sense it must again be the case that $p_B < p_1 + p_2$. Figure 6.5 illustrates such a strategy. The restaurant offers the possibility of buying either soup or a sandwich individually at the stated prices or buying them as a set meal at price p_B.

Once again, we find that consumers are partitioned by this strategy into four groups. The determinants of these groups are, however, slightly different from those considered

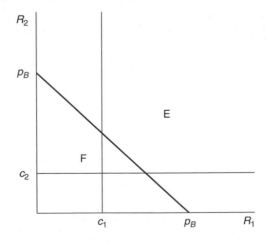

Figure 6.4   Monopoly pricing of a pure bundle of goods 1 and 2
At the bundle price p_B, consumers in group E buy the bundle.

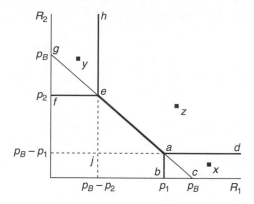

Figure 6.5 Monopoly price under mixed bundling of goods 1 and 2

The firm sets prices p_1 for good 1; p_2 for good 2; and $p_B < p_1 + p_2$ for the bundle.

previously. What we need to do is to determine whether a consumer will buy only one of the two goods, or the bundle, or nothing.

Clearly, anyone who values good 1 at more than p_1 and good 2 at more than p_2—that is, anyone who is willing to buy both goods at the individual prices—will buy the bundle, since its price is less than the sum of the individual prices. Consider now a consumer whose reservation price for good 2 is less than p_2. If this consumer buys anything, she will buy either the bundle or only good 1. Of course, she will make the choice that gives her the greatest consumer surplus. Suppose, then, that her reservation prices are R_1 for good 1 and R_2 for good 2. If she buys the bundle, then she pays p_B and gets consumer surplus of $CS_B = R_1 + R_2 - p_B$. If she buys only good 1, she gets consumer surplus of $CS_1 = R_1 - p_1$.

This type of consumer will buy only good 1 if two conditions are satisfied. First, $CS_1 > CS_B$, which requires that $R_2 < p_B - p_1$. Second, $CS_1 > 0$, which requires that $R_1 > p_1$.

The difference $p_B - p_1$ is easily illustrated in Figure 6.5. Since the line $p_B p_B$ has a slope of -1, the distance ab is equal to the distance bc, which is equal to $p_B - p_1$. So all points below the line jad represent consumers whose reservation prices for good 2 are such that $R_2 < p_B - p_1$; and, of course, all points to the right of ab represent consumers for whom $R_1 > p_1$. So all consumers with reservation prices in the region dab, such as consumer x, buy only good 1.

By exactly the same argument a consumer will buy only good 2 if two conditions are satisfied: first $R_1 < p_B - p_2$ and second $R_2 > p_2$. The difference $p_B - p_2$ is illustrated in Figure 6.5 by the line jeh and all points above fe represent consumers for whom $R_2 > p_2$. Therefore, all consumers with reservation prices in the region feh, such as consumer y, will buy only good 2.

Now consider a consumer for whom $R_2 > p_B - p_1$ and $R_1 > p_B - p_2$. This is a consumer whose reservation price for good 1 is to the right of jeh and for good 2 is above jad. If such a consumer buys anything at all she will buy the bundle, since this gives more consumer surplus than either only good 1 or only good 2. For this consumer to buy the bundle, it is then necessary that $R_1 + R_2 > p_B$, which means that her reservation prices must put her above the line *caeg* in Figure 6.5. In other words, all consumers in the region *daeh*, such as consumer *z*, will buy the bundle.

This leaves only the region *feab*. What will be the choice of these types of consumers? Their reservation prices are less than the individual prices of the two goods, so they will not buy either good individually. In addition, the sums of their reservation prices are less than the bundle price, so they will not buy the bundle. Consumers in *feab* do not buy anything.

When we compare either pure or mixed bundling with simple monopoly pricing, it is clear that mixed bundling always increases the monopolist's sales. What is less clear is whether bundling will increase the monopolist's profits. Mixed bundling is always at least as profitable as pure bundling. After all, the worst that a mixed bundling strategy can do is replicate the pure bundling strategy by setting arbitrarily high individual prices and a bundle price equal to that with pure bundling. However, it is not always the case that some form of bundling is preferable to no bundling at all. A limitation of bundling, as we saw in the pure bundling example, is that it can lead to consumers buying a good when their reservation price for that good is less than the good's marginal cost of production. This is inefficient.

What we should expect is that the profit impact of commodity bundling will depend upon the distribution of consumer preferences for the goods being offered and the costs of making those goods. The fundamental point, made by Adams and Yellen (1976), is that the gains from bundling arise from the differences in consumer valuations.

Reality Checkpoint
All Bundled Up in the Vatican

These are hard times for traditional travel agents. Direct ticketing by airlines and the proliferation of discount Internet sites that permit customers to shop comparatively for the cheapest travel and lodging accommodations have taken their toll. But now the agents are fighting back with a new tool called "insider travel."

Many popular sites make it either difficult or impossible for tourists to get what they really want. Those who visit the Sistine Chapel will often stand in hours-long lines to get a glimpse of Michelangelo's masterpiece. Similarly, Queen Nefertari's tomb in Egypt can only be seen if one gets permission from the country's Supreme Council of Antiquities. Travel agents are increasingly doing the legwork to offer tourists these special features as part of a package. Select Italy will arrange a special, after-hours tour for tourists to see the Sistine Chapel artwork face-to-face. Los Angeles-based Destinations & Adventures International will likewise obtain the necessary permission to view the fabulous wall paintings in the tomb of the ancient Queen Nefertari for an appropriate fee.

That fee can, of course, be intimidating. It can cost a fixed charge of $4,000 for a small group to take advantage of these opportunities, and the fee rises if the group exceeds ten. However, by agreeing to stay at a hotel recommended by the agent or to use other agent-suggested services, tourists can often reduce these fees by anywhere from $400 to $1000. In return, travelers get a personalized trip that can be truly memorable and for which they are willing to pay a lot. One of the larger tour operators, Abercrombie & Kent, claims that packaging a customized event with travel and lodging now makes up half of its business and earns some of the heftiest margins.

Source: C. Jackson, "VIP Travel on the Cheap." *Wall Street Journal* (17 May 2006), p. D1.

Some people may value an appetizer relatively highly (soup on a cold day), others may value dessert relatively higher (Baked Alaska, unavailable at home), but all may wish to pay roughly the same amount for a complete dinner. The à la carte menu is designed to capture consumer surplus from those gastronomes with extremely high valuations of particular dishes, while the complete dinner is designed to retain those with lower variance (p. 488).

6.3.2   Required Tie-In Sales

Tie-in sale arrangements differ from bundling in that they tie together the purchase of two or more products without prescribing the amount that must be bought. Typically, they work when consumption of a service requires the use of two products (e.g., cameras and film or printers and print cartridges). Tying the sale of the two products together is typically a way to extend a quantity discount to consumers whose buying is more price sensitive.

Consider a service that requires two inputs. One of these is a fixed input such as a camera, printer, or copying machine. The other is a variable input such as film, print cartridges, or paper. The fixed input is required for any volume of consumption. In addition, one unit of the variable input is required for every unit of the service. The fixed input is produced by a monopoly supplier, but the variable input is initially produced and sold in a competitive market. The cost of producing the fixed input is c_F, while each unit of the variable input is produced at cost c. Without loss of generality, we simplify by normalizing c_F and c to 0.

Demand for the product comes from two groups of consumers. However, a producer has no way to distinguish one consumer type from another. There are n_1 consumers in group 1, and each has a total willingness to pay for q units of the service, given by

$$V^1(q) = Aq - \frac{q^2}{2} \tag{6.33}$$

Similarly, there are n_2 consumers in group 2 and each has a total willingness to pay for q units of the service, given by

$$V^2(q) = \alpha Aq - \frac{q^2}{2}; \quad \alpha > 1 \tag{6.34}$$

As noted, consumers need to buy exactly one unit of the fixed input for any positive consumption level, but need to buy one unit of the variable input for every unit of the service consumed. Thus, if F is the price of the fixed input and P is the price of the variable input, a consumer's total expenditure is $F + Pq$, where q is the number of units consumed. Each consumer from group 1 chooses a quantity q that will maximize her net surplus— conditional on that surplus being positive. Thus, each group 1 consumer chooses q as the solution to the following problem:

$$\max_{q} V^1(q) - F - Pq \tag{6.35}$$

As can be easily verified, this implies that at price P per unit for the variable input, total demand q_1 from group 1 consumers will be

$$q_1 = \begin{cases} n_1(A - P) & \text{if } (A - P)^2/2 \geq F \\ 0 & \text{otherwise} \end{cases} \tag{6.36}$$

Likewise, the total demand from group 2 consumers, q_2 will be

$$q_2 = \begin{array}{ll} n_2(\alpha A - P) & \text{if } (\alpha A - P)^2/2 \geq F \\ 0 & \text{otherwise} \end{array} \qquad (6.37)$$

Because the variable input is produced at zero cost in a competitive market, $P = 0$. As a result, group 1 consumers will realize a surplus from purchasing the variable input of $A^2/2$, while group 2 consumers will realize a surplus of $\alpha^2 A^2/2$. If the monopolist wants to sell the fixed input to both groups, the lower of these two values is the maximum price it can charge. Thus, the monopolist chooses $F = A^2/2$. As a result, it earns profit π of

$$\pi = n_1\left(\frac{A^2}{2}\right) + n_2\left(\frac{A^2}{2}\right) = n\frac{A^2}{2} \qquad (6.38)$$

Now, assume that the monopolist is able to write a contract that requires any user of the fixed input to purchase units of the variable input also made by the monopolist. Alternatively, the monopolist might be able to design the printer or camera (or whatever the fixed input is) so that it only works with cartridges or film that it makes. In either case, this effectively ends competition in the variable input market. As a result, the monopolist is free to set whatever price P for the variable input that it prefers. Obviously, it will choose the value P that maximizes its total profit. Note, however, that in setting P the monopolist must also take into account the impact that its choice of P has on the price F that it can set for the fixed input. A moment's reflection will indicate that this looks like our analysis of two-part pricing, with the price of the fixed input being the fixed charge and the price of the variable input the variable charge. From our analysis above, with a price P for the variable input, the price of the fixed input is $(A - P)^2/2$ given, of course, that the firm wishes to sell to both types of consumer. As a result, the monopolist sets P to solve the following problem:

$$\underset{P}{\text{Max }} \pi = n_1\frac{(A - P)^2}{2} + n_1 P(A - P) + n_2\frac{(A - P)^2}{2} + n_2 P(\alpha A - P) \qquad (6.39)$$

Solving the foregoing equation yields the profit-maximizing choice of P:

$$P^* = \frac{n_2(\alpha - 1)A}{(n_1 + n_2)} \qquad (6.40)$$

If $\alpha = 1$, so that there is no difference between the two groups, the monopolist's best choice for the variable input price would be 0, exactly the same as the competitive price. Returning to our two-part pricing analogy, the firm sets the variable charge to marginal cost (zero) and extracts all consumer surplus in setting the price of the fixed input. In this case, tying does not achieve anything for the monopolist. However, if $\alpha > 1$, the monopolist's price for the variable input is now positive. The downside of this is that the maximum surplus that group 1 consumers will realize on variable input purchases (and therefore the maximum value of F if the firm wants to sell to both groups) now falls to $\frac{\left[A - \left(\frac{n_2}{n_1+n_2}\right)(\alpha - 1)A\right]^2}{2}$.

However, for group 1, this is partly (but not fully) offset by the fact that now the monopolist also earns $P^*(A - P^*)$ in profit from sales of the variable input. In addition, the monopolist also picks up an additional profit of $P^*(\alpha A - P^*)$ in variable input profits from group 2. For example, suppose that $n_1 = n_2 = n/2$. Then substitution of equation (6.40) into the profit function (6.39) implies a total profit for the monopolist of

$$\pi = \frac{nA^2}{2} + \frac{n(\alpha - 1)^2 A^2}{2} \tag{6.41}$$

So long as $\alpha > 1$, this clearly exceeds the no-tying profit of equation (6.38).

Why does tying permit additional profit? The reason is straightforward. At any given variable input price P, and fixed input fee F, each member of group 1 consumes fewer units of the service than each member of group 2. Denote these quantities as q_1 and q_2, respectively. Then, the average price per unit to each group is

$$\begin{aligned}\text{Average Unit Price } &= P + (F/q_1) \text{ for group 1 members} \\ &= P + (F/q_2) \text{ for group 2 members}\end{aligned} \tag{6.42}$$

Since $q_2 > q_1$, it follows that group 2 members are offered a lower unit price (i.e., there is a quantity discount). This discount existed even before the tying. However, by tying the purchase of the variable component to the fixed component, the monopolist has been able to harness the power of the quantity discount so that it works on her behalf. To complete our analogy with the analysis of price discrimination, $\alpha > 1$ requires that the monopolist employs second-degree price discrimination, but with the constraint that the firm employs a two-part pricing system.

6.3.3   Bundling/Tying, Policy, and Competition

A further result of tying has been to transform what was a competitive market for the variable input into a monopolized one. When the tied products are complements as in the present case, tying (and bundling) can be a means of driving current rivals out and preventing potential rivals from coming in. For example, in the 1920s, United Shoe had emerged as the dominant manufacturer of the various machines used to make shoes. However, while it had a near monopoly in some machine lines, it did not in others. When it began to stipulate in its contracts that the manufacturers could not use United Shoe machines in combination with those of rival shoe equipment makers, and also that the shoe manufacturers had to buy certain supplies exclusively from United Shoe, the government successfully sued. United Shoe was found guilty of violating the antitrust laws. A similar ruling in 1947 found International Salt guilty when that company refused to lease its salt processing machines unless the lessee also agreed to purchase all its salt from International Salt.[13]

Since these early cases, however, the courts have backed off from a nearly *per se* illegal approach to tying and bundling. One reason is that such contracts may expand the market for the complementary goods. To understand this argument, suppose that the market for the variable input was monopolized by another firm. In setting the variable input price, this firm would think only of its own profit and not recognize that as it raises P, it lowers the fee F that the firm producing the fixed input or component can charge. Because it ignores

---

[13]   *United Shoe Machinery Corp. v. United States*, 258 U.S. 451; *International Salt Co. v. United States*, 332 U.S. 392 (1947). Peterman (1979) argues that the fact that firms were allowed to use salt from producers other than International Salt if it was cheaper, suggesting that the real purpose of the tying was to reveal to International Salt the pricing practices of its rivals.

this effect, the variable component monopolist will set P even higher than the value in equation (6.40). By instituting a tying arrangement, then, the fixed component monopolist will set lower prices, even though the tying has the additional effect of excluding the variable unit rival.

Tying may also help insure product quality. Thus, the Court found in favor of the Jefferson Parish Hospital when it stipulated that to use its surgical services, it was necessary to use the group of anesthesiologists with whom the hospital had an exclusive contract. This finding was in part because the practice was justified as necessary for quality control.

More recently, Evans and Salinger (2005) and Evans (2006) have argued that bundling and tying are so ubiquitous that they must reflect some force other than a firm with market power either pursuing price discrimination or trying to exclude rivals. In their view, so many firms with very little market power engage in bundling and tying practices that the underlying explanation must have something to do with costs.

To understand the intuition of the Evans and Salinger (2005) argument, consider the case of head cold remedies. Suppose that there are 50 people whose cold symptoms are primarily headaches and sore throats and who therefore primarily seek a treatment of pain relief. Suppose that there are another 50 people whose primary symptom is sinus congestion and who therefore really want a decongestant in their cold remedy. Finally, let there be a third group of 100 people who want both a pain reliever and a decongestant. Let us also assume that to produce, package, and market each cold remedy drug for this market requires that a firm incur a fixed cost of $300. Further, assume that the marginal cost of producing and packaging either bottle of pain relief medicine or a package of decongestants is $4, but that there are some marginal cost savings in putting the two in one pill, so that the marginal cost of a combined pain reliever and decongestant product is just $7. There is just one cold remedy firm in actual operation, but entry is easy and costless; so that firm is constrained to offer its products at prices that just permit it to break even. Table 6.1 below shows the possible product offerings and the associated zero-profit prices.

Suppose that the firm just offers the pain reliever and the decongestant separately. The first group of consumers will buy the pain reliever, the second will buy the decongestant, and the third group will want to buy both products. So, demand for each product is 150, implying an average fixed cost for each drug of $300/150 = $2. When added to

Table 6.1 Pure bundling as the sustainable equilibrium

	Product		
	Pain Relief	*Decongestant*	*Bundle*
Demand Volume	50	50	100
Costs			
Fixed Cost	$300	$300	$300
Marginal Cost	$ 4	$ 4	$ 7
Possible Prices Under:			
Separate Goods	$ 6	$ 6	—
Pure Bundling	—	—	$ 8.5
Mixed Bundling	$ 10	$ 10	$ 10
Bundle and Good 1	$ 10	—	$ 9
Bundle and Good 2	—	$ 10	$ 9

the marginal cost of $4, the breakeven price is $6. However, this outcome is not an equilibrium. Any firm could enter the market and sell just the bundle for $10.00. This would attract all of the 100 consumers who want a combined medication, since they currently pay $6 + $6 = $12 to get both types of relief. In turn, the loss of these customers would make the continued offering of the two separate products at a price of $6 impossible, as the average cost of each of these would now rise to $10. Indeed, since this price is the same as the bundle price, we might imagine that some of these consumers will actually buy the bundle, as it gives them the relief they want plus a little something extra. As this happens, however, the bundle price falls further due to additional fixed-cost savings, while the individual prices must rise further. This will push all 200 customers to buy the bundle, at which point the breakeven price for the bundle drops to $8.50. This is, in fact, the only sustainable price and product combination. It is, therefore, the equilibrium in this imperfectly competitive but contestable market.[14]

The central elements in the foregoing example are worth noting. They are the scope and scale economies that attend the production and marketing of cold remedies. The Evans and Salinger (2005) and Evans (2006) papers thus make clear that when these elements are present, bundling and tying are necessary to achieve the least cost production that that competition requires. Such practices will therefore reflect the presence of competitive forces and not their absence.

6.4   EMPIRICAL APPLICATION
Price Discrimination, Product Variety, and Monopoly versus Competition

For the most part, we have set our discussion of price discrimination and product variety over the last few chapters in the framework of a monopolized market. Nevertheless, the strategies that we have described such as two-part pricing and quantity discounts are often practiced by firms that are far from a perfect monopoly. This is not to say that they are competitive in the sense of Evans and Salinger (2005). It is simply that competitive pressure and price discrimination will often go hand-in-hand. There are at least two reasons for this. We will show formally in Chapter 14 that when rival firms practice price discrimination, it tends to intensify the price competition between them.[15] Moreover, imperfectly competitive firms also have an incentive to pursue discriminatory pricing strategies, as Borenstein (1985) was one of the first to emphasize.

Consider a simple linear market on which two stores are located at opposite ends of the market and over which consumers are uniformly distributed. We will assume that while consumers have specific locations, they do not have transport costs. Second, we will assume that there are two types of consumers, both of which number N in total. For each group, the maximum willingness to pay is V. The difference is that the first type of consumers always shops at the store that is closest, no matter what the price at the alternative store. The second group is just the opposite. These consumers always shop wherever the price is lowest.

A little economic reasoning should convince you that a monopolist serving this market will set a price of V and serve all the $2N$ customers, half at each store. Clearly, the price cannot be higher than this, or no customer will buy the product. However, there is no

---

[14]   A review of Table 6.1 will make it clear why either mixed bundling or offering a bundle and one good separately also cannot be an equilibrium.

[15]   The interested reader can consult MacLeod (1988) et al. for the basic analysis.

need to reduce the price. The first set of consumers will not consider the price at any location other than the closest. The second group will consider alternative prices; but, since the price is V at each spot, this group also splits evenly between the two stores. The monopolist would then make a total profit of $2(V - c)N$, divided evenly between the two stores. No amount of price discrimination can increase this value.

Now, consider what would happen if the two stores were instead owned by two different firms, Firm 1 and Firm 2. If there were just the first type of consumers who are totally brand loyal to the nearest store, then each of these firms could again charge a price of V. Imagine that they are doing this. Now, consider the second group of consumers who always shop where the price is cheapest. At the current price V, these consumers would also be split evenly between the two shops. Each firm would then earn a profit of $(V - c)N$ just as did each of the monopolist's two stores. However, this outcome cannot be an equilibrium. A slight cut in Firm 1's price would lose very little profit from its existing customers. Yet because its price would now be less than Firm 2's price, it would gain all of the 2N consumers currently at Firm 2 who always shop where the price is lowest. Of course, if Firm 1 cuts its price, Firm 2 will respond with a price cut, also. Unfortunately for the firms, this brings the price down to all consumers, including the brand-loyal ones who do not care about the price. Indeed, at any common price $p_1 = p_2 > c$, each firm will have a strong incentive to cut price to attract the 2N price-sensitive consumer currently shopping at the rival's store. The result will be that prices are driven very close to marginal cost c, and each store's profit will be very low. In such a setting, we can easily see the incentives that each firm has to implement price discriminatory policies that permit it to cut the price to price-sensitive consumers while still charging V or at least a high price to the brand-loyal ones.

The foregoing simple example provides the basic intuition as to why we might observe price discrimination in more price-competitive markets. Price discrimination permits competing actively for those consumers who perceive alternatives to the firm's product while still charging a high price to those that do not. If there was only one other brand, only a few customers might be tempted to try it. As more brands are available, however, more of the firm's customers are likely to consider an alternative product. Being able to fight for these customers without lowering the price to the cadre of brand-loyal buyers then becomes all the more valuable.

The foregoing insight lies at the heart of the paper by Stavins (2001), which examines the influence of competition on the use of discriminatory pricing in the airline industry. For this purpose, she looked at price and other information for 5,804 tickets over 12 different routes on a specific Thursday in September 1995. Selecting a single day is useful, because it eliminates any price differentials due to flying on other days of the week, especially weekend days. A September choice also avoids both peak summer and winter demand periods. The key characteristics that Stavins (2001) looks at are (1) whether a Saturday night stay-over was required and (2) whether a 14-day advance purchase was required.

As discussed earlier, each of these restrictions serves as a means for airlines to identify and separate customers based on how they value their time and their need for flexibility. Prices for tickets requiring a Saturday night stay-over or that had to be purchased 14 days prior to departure should sell for less than other tickets. The hypothesis to be tested is that the price discount on these restricted tickets gets bigger the more competition there is on the route. Stavins (2001) constructs a Herfindahl-Hirschman Index H for each route to serve as a rough measure of that market's competitive pressure.

To test this hypothesis, Stavins (2001) runs two sets of regressions. The first of these serves to confirm that ticket restrictions do indeed translate into discriminatory price differentials. It takes the basic form

$$p_{ijk} = \beta_0 + \beta_1 R_{ijk} + \beta_2 H_i + \beta_3 S_{ij} + \beta_4 First_{ijk} + \beta_5 Days_{ijk} + \beta_6 Z_i + \varepsilon_{ijk} \qquad (6.43)$$

Here, p_{ijk} is the (log of) the price of the kth ticket sold by airline j in city-pair market i. R_{ijk} is a dummy variable equal to 1, if there was a restriction on the flight (Saturday night stay-over or pre-purchase requirement), and 0 otherwise. H_i is the Herfindahl-Hirschman Index for the ith market. S_{ij} is the market share of airline i in market j. $First_{ijk}$ is a dummy variable equal to 1 if the ticket was for first-class fare and 0 otherwise. $Days_{ijk}$ is the number of days prior to departure that the fare for that ticket was last offered. Z_i is a vector of other market i characteristics such as average income and population. The error term ε_{ijk} is assumed to be normally distributed with a mean of 0.

If ticket restrictions serve as a means of implementing price discrimination, then the coefficient β_1 on R_{ijk} should be negative. This would imply that passengers flying the same flight on the same airline paid lower prices if they accepted a requirement that they stay over Saturday night or that they purchase the ticket in advance.

However, simply finding that β_1 is negative only shows that price discrimination occurs. It does not tell us if there is any connection between the extent of such discrimination and the degree of competition in the market. To test this hypothesis, Stavins (2001) runs regressions of the basic form

$$p_{ijk} = \beta_0 + \beta_1 R_{ijk} + \beta_2 H_i + \beta_3 (H_i \times R_{ijk}) + \beta_4 S_{ij} + \beta_5 First_{ijk}$$
$$+ \beta_6 \, Days_{ijk} + \beta_7 Z_i + \varepsilon_{ijk} \qquad (6.44)$$

This is exactly the same as the previous regression, except that it now includes the interactive term $(H_i \times R_{ijk})$, the product of the concentration index and the restricted travel variables. If the coefficient on this term is positive, it says that the discount associated with, say, a Saturday night stay-over requirement declines as the level of concentration rises. Stavins' (2001) results are shown below.

The first four columns indicate that passengers do indeed pay different prices depending on the restrictions applied to their tickets. These effects are both statistically significant and economically substantial. For example, passengers who accepted the requirement that they

Table 6.2   Ticket Restrictions and Air Fares [Stavins (2001)]

Variable	Coefficient	t-statistic	Coefficient	t-Statistic	Coefficient	t-Statistic	Coefficient	t-statistic
Saturday-Night Stay-Over Required	0.249	−2.50	—	—	−0.408	−4.05	—	—
Saturday-Night Stay-Over × H	—	—	—	—	0.792	3.39	—	—
Advance Purchase Requirement	—	—	−0.007	−2.16	—	—	−0.023	−5.53
Advance Purchase Requirement × H	—	—	—	—	—	—	0.098	8.38

not return until after Saturday night paid 25 percent less on average than those who did not accept this restriction, even though they were otherwise getting the same flight service.

However, the real issue is how these discounts vary as the extent of competition in the market as measured by H varies. This is where the next four columns become relevant, as they show what happens when the term *interacting competition* or *concentration and ticket restrictions* is included. In both cases, the estimated coefficient on the interaction term is positive. This indicates that, while ticket restrictions still lead to price reductions, this effect diminishes as the airline route becomes less competitive or has high concentration.

Given the range of H values observed over the 12 routes Stavins (2001) studies, she estimates that in the most competitive markets, a Saturday night stay-over requirement led to a price reduction of about $253, whereas in the least competitive ones the same restriction led to a price reduction of only $165. Likewise, an advance purchase requirement was associated with a price reduction of $111 in the most competitive markets, but a cut of only $41 in the least competitive markets. The clear conclusion is that price discrimination and competition are positively linked in airline markets.

Summary

In this chapter, we have extended our discussion of price discrimination to cover cases where the firm offers differentiated products. Product differentiation can take two broad forms: *vertical differentiation* in which products are differentiated in terms of their quality, and *horizontal differentiation* in which firms are of similar quality but are differentiated in terms of their characteristics. In these settings, price discrimination is reflected in the fact that the firm prices its array of products differentially—that is, with a different price-cost margin—as it tries to reach different consumers with different preferences.

In the case of vertical differentiation, consumers agree on what makes one product better than another but disagree on their willingness to pay for higher quality, perhaps because their income or wealth is different. Whatever the source of these differences, however, the firm can exploit them by offering goods of different quality and prices to induce consumers to self-select according to their true willingness to pay for quality. This solves the information and arbitrage problems that would otherwise prevent effective price discrimination. Yet it does so at some cost, because the sorting and separating mechanism must also satisfy an incentive compatibility constraint. As a result, the vertically differentiated products will sell at prices that leave some surplus for those who buy high-quality products, but none for those who buy low-quality products. The analogy to the menu pricing analysis of Chapter 5 is clear and direct, including the results regarding efficiency.

With horizontal product differentiation, consumers agree about how much additional quality is worth, but disagree about exactly what makes for a better product. The easiest case to imagine is a spatial one in which consumers have location preferences, that is, they prefer shops that are closer to where they live. The firm located at a specific spot can respond to these preferences and reach out to more distant consumers by incurring transport cost to pick up and deliver the product to the consumer's address. Analogously, in a more general setting, we may imagine consumers located at different points in a product space while the firm with its own base location can modify its product at some cost into different versions that are closer to what different consumers prefer. If the firm knows the location or preferences of different consumers (the identification problem) and can prevent others from making the same modifications (the arbitrage problem), it can sell the different versions at different net prices. That is, the ability of the firm to price discriminate requires that two conditions be satisfied. Whether this discrimination favors consumers who are closer to (or those who are more distant from) the firm is determined by the precise form of the individual demand functions. However, the firm will generally find that it is optimal to select discriminatory prices for each variety that do not correspond precisely with the cost of producing that version.

Firms that produce more than one good can also implement price discrimination by bundling and tying. Bundling requires the consumer to buy the firm's products in specific proportions as in the case of a prix fixe menu. Tying requires simply that the use of one of the firm's products in any amount requires the purchase of another of the firm's products, as in the case of a Hewlett-Packard printer requiring the use of Hewlett-Packard printer cartridges.

Both bundling and tying exploit differences in consumers' relative valuations of the different products. In turn, this permits the firm to extract more surplus from the market. Bundling and tying may also serve as tactics to suppress rival firms. At the same time, however, both practices are sufficiently common that they likely reflect competitive pressures in the face of both scope and scale economies.

Although price discrimination tactics require market power they often are an expression of competitive pressures in settings of imperfect competition. Such tactics allow firms to compete for price-sensitive customers without lowering the price to less sensitive ones. As a result, we may actually observe greater price discrimination in markets with some rivalry as opposed to those that are a pure monopoly. Evidence from the airline industry in Stavins (2001) supports this hypothesis.

Problems

1. A monopolist produces a product of quality z according to a cost function $C(z, q) = z^2 q$. The inverse demand for the product is described by: $P(z, q) = z(1 - q)$.
    a. What quality will the monopolist choose, and what price will he sell at?
    b. Determine the choice of quality and price that would maximize social welfare.
    c. Compare your answers in 1a and 1b. Does the monopolist choose too high or low a quality relative to the efficient choice? Is the monopoly price above or below the socially optimal price?

2. A monopolist produces a product of two exogenous quality levels, $z = 1$ and $z - \sigma < 1$. The high-quality product costs c_H to produce. The low-quality good costs nothing to produce. All consumers consume either one unit of the good (either at quality $z = 1$ or $z = \sigma$) or none, and there are two types of consumers. High-value consumers have utility $\theta^H z - p$. Low-value consumers have utility $\theta^L z - p$. There are N_H high-value consumers and N_L low-value consumers.
    a. Under what conditions will the firm offer both qualities of the good, and what price will it charge for each?
    b. Assume that the conditions in 2a are met. Now consider a small, exogenous increase in the quality of either the low-quality or high-quality version. Which of these improvements will the firm prefer? That is, will the firm's profit increase more from a small increase in the quality of the high-quality good or from a similarly small increment in the low-quality good?

3. Consider again the market in Problem 2. Suppose regulation is passed that requires a minimum quality level $z = 1$.
    a. Under what conditions will the firm price its high-quality chip such that both high-value and low-value consumers will be willing to buy it?
    b. Does the regulation raise or lower social welfare relative to that obtained under the original equilibrium in Problem 2?

4. Mr. Clean is the only dry cleaner in Lineville. Lineville is a town with a population mass of M continuously distributed along the one-mile-long Main Street. Every consumer in the town has a utility function $V - p$, and will buy one unit of dry cleaning if this is positive (or 0) and no units if it is negative. Mr. Clean is located at address $b(0 < b < 1)$. His base cost for providing dry cleaning service is c. He can also provide pickup and delivery to a consumer at location x_i for a cost of $r|x_i - b|$. Assume that $V > r$.
    a. Taking Mr. Clean's location b as given, what price will Mr. Clean charge, and what proportion of the mass of M consumers will he serve?
    b. Determine Mr. Clean's profit as a function of his location b. What choice of b will maximize his profit?

5. Assume a monopolist has four consumers with reservation prices for each of two goods as described by the table below. The marginal cost of good 1 is $100. The marginal cost of good 2 is $150.

Consumer	Reservation Price For Good 1 ($)	Reservation Price For Good 2 ($)	Sum Of Reservation Prices
A	50	450	500
B	250	275	525
C	300	220	520
D	450	50	500

a. Determine the prices the monopolist will charge if she sells the goods unbundled and adopts simple monopoly pricing for each good.
b. What price will the monopolist charge if she sells the two goods as a bundle?
c. What prices will the monopolist choose if she chooses a mixed bundling strategy that sells each good separately as well as bundle comprised of each good?

References

Adams, W. J., and J. Yellen. 1976. "Commodity Bundling and the Burden of Monopoly." *Quarterly Journal of Economics,* 475 (May): 475–498.

Berry, S. and P. Jia. 2010. "Tracking the Woes: An Empirical Analysis of the Airline Industry." *American Economic Journal: Microeconomics*, 2: 1–43.

Borenstein, S. 1985. "Price Discrimination in Free-Entry Markets." *Rand Journal Economics,* 16 (Autumn): 380–397.

Ekelund, R. 1970. "Price Discrimination and Product Differentiation in Economic Theory: An Early Analysis." *Quarterly Journal of Economics,* 84: 268–278.

Evans, D. 2006. "Tying: The Poster Child for Antitrust Modernization." in R. Hahn (Ed.), *Antitrust Policy and Vertical Restraints*. Washington, D.C.: Brookings Institution Press, 65–88.

———, and M. Salinger. 2005. "Why Do Firms Bundle and Tie? Evidence from Competitive Markets and Implications For Tying Law." *Yale Journal on Regulation,* 22 (Winter).

Greenhut, M., G. Norman, and C. J. Hung. 1987. *The Economics of Imperfect Competition: A Spatial Approach*. Cambridge: Cambridge University Press.

Hotelling, H. 1929. "Stability in Competition." *Economic Journal,* 39 (January): 41–57.

Macleod, W. B., G. Norman, and J. F. Thisse. 1988. "Price Discrimination and Equilibrium in Monopolistic Competition." *International Journal of Industrial Organization*, 6: 429–446.

Maskin, E. and J. Riley. 1984. "Monopoly with Incomplete Information." *Rand Journal of Economics,* 15 (Summer): 171–196.

Mussa, M. and S. Rosen. 1978. "Monopoly and Product Quality." *Journal of Economic Theory,* 18: 301–317.

Peterman, J. 1979. "The International Salt Case." *Journal of Law and Economics,* 22: 351–364.

Phlips, L. 1983. *The Economics of Price Discrimination*. Cambridge: Cambridge University Press.

Shapiro, C. and H. R. Varian. 1999. *Information Rules*. Boston: Harvard Business School Press.

Stavins, J. 2001. "Price Discrimination in the Airline Market: The Effect of Market Concentration." *Review of Economics and Statistics,* 83 (February): 200–202.

Stigler, G. 1968. "A Note on Block Booking." In *The Organization of Industry*. Homewood, Illinois: Irwin.

Stiglitz, J. 1977. "Monopoly, Nonlinear Pricing, and Imperfect Information: The Insurance Market." *Review of Economic Studies,* 44 (April): 407–430.

Tirole, J. 1988. *The Theory of Industrial Organization*. Cambridge: MIT Press.

Part III
Oligopoly and Strategic Interaction

Chapters 7 through 10 introduce the student to game theory and formal analysis of two critical areas of concern for antitrust policy, namely, predation and price-fixing by firms with market power. Chapter 7 presents the formal concept of strategic interaction and the solution concept of a Nash equilibrium. It then describes the single-period Cournot and Bertrand models of oligopoly competition. In the case of Bertrand, we extend the analysis to the case of product differentiation. This also permits discussion of the Hastings (2004) study of product differentiation and consumer preferences in the Southern California retail gasoline market.

Chapter 8 introduces the reader to dynamic games. It begins with the Stackelberg model and the concept of a limit price or limit quantity. This discussion leads naturally to more extensive games and the issues of credibility and subgame perfection. Chapter 9 builds on this foundation to examine various models of predation, including those based on capacity commitments, asymmetric information, and long-term contracts. Chapter 10 then turns to the topic of collusion. Here again, the concept of dynamic games and repeated play is critical as it permits us to present the Folk Theorem for an indefinitely repeated game. Along with models demonstrating that both predation and collusion can be rational, profit-maximizing strategies, these chapters also include a discussion of public policy toward such behavior.

Students completing this section will have a formal understanding of strategic interaction and its use in modeling imperfect competition. They will also understand that there is a rich array of models demonstrating the feasibility of predatory and collusive behavior. Beyond all this, students will also gain further familiarity with the techniques of the new, empirical industrial organization as we present econometric evidence on predation (Ellison and Ellison 2009), the welfare cost of collusion (Kwoka 1997), and the use of leniency policies in countering price-fixing (Hinloopen and Soetevent 2006).

7

Static Games and Quantity versus Price Competition

In previous chapters, our focus has been markets dominated by a single firm whose strategies are designed to create and extract more surplus from consumers. However, such complete monopoly markets are relatively rare. Coca-Cola is one of the most successful companies in the history of American business with an almost iconic status in American popular culture. Nevertheless, Coca-Cola is far from the only major player in the soft-drink market. Instead, it has been in continual conflict with its archrival PepsiCo for almost 100 years, as well as having to worry about other, smaller beverage firms. Likewise, Hershey's, the largest firm in the North American commercial chocolate market, must continually worry about the actions of its nearly as large rival, Mars.

The soft-drink and chocolate markets are similar to many markets in that they are dominated by not one, but a small number of relatively large firms. These industries are oligopolies where firms have visible rivals with whom strategic interaction is a fact of life. Each firm is aware that its actions affect others and prompt *re*actions. Each firm must, therefore, take these interactions into account when making decisions about prices, output, new products or other business activities.

Since the pioneering work of von Neuman and Morganstern (1944), game theory has steadily evolved to become the analytical framework and language for understanding strategic interaction. Hence, game theoretic models have become the standard tools in the analysis of oligopolistic markets. The fact that we speak of models, and not just one model, merits some further discussion. There is more than one game-theoretic model of oligopoly. Oligopolistic markets have different defining features, and the model of strategic interaction that is appropriate for one market may not be appropriate for another. In this chapter, we introduce the basic one period or static game-theoretic models and leave consideration of dynamic, multiperiod games to later chapters.[1]

7.1 A BRIEF INTRODUCTION TO GAME THEORY

We begin with some terminology. In game theory, each player's plan of action is called a *strategy*. A list of strategies showing one particular strategy choice for each player is called a *strategy combination*. Any given strategy combination determines the *outcome*

---

[1] A good textbook that offers a more formal treatment of game theory and its applications to economics is Rasmusen (2007).

of game, which describes the payoffs or final net gains earned by each player. In the context of oligopoly theory, these payoffs are naturally interpreted as each firm's profit, though they may instead be proxied by market share or sales growth.

Since most firms will have more than one possible strategy choice, there will be more than one possible *strategy combination*, and more than one conceivable outcome to the game. Therefore, in order to predict what will happen in such settings, we need a way to select from the set of feasible strategy combinations those combinations that qualify as *equilibrium* outcomes. For this purpose, we use the equilibrium concept developed by Nobel Laureate John Nash (1950, 1951) and now generally referred to as the Nash equilibrium.

The formal statement of the Nash equilibrium concept is as follows. Let (S, π) be a game with n players where $S = S_1 x S_2 \ldots x S_n$ and S_i denotes the set of strategies available to player i, and $\pi = (\pi_1, \pi_2, \ldots, \pi_n)$ describes the set of payoffs for each player i that depend on a specific strategy combination $s = (s_1, s_2, \ldots, s_n) \in S$. Hence (S, π) is a complete description of the game's feasible outcomes. A pure strategy Nash equilibrium is a strategy combination $\hat{s} = (\hat{s}_1, \hat{s}_2, \ldots, \hat{s}_{i-1}, \hat{s}_i, \hat{s}_{i+1}, \ldots, \hat{s}_n)$ such that for each player $i, i = 1, 2, \ldots, n$:

$$\pi_i(\hat{s}_1, \hat{s}_2, \ldots, \hat{s}_{i-1}, \hat{s}_i, \hat{s}_{i+1}, \ldots, \hat{s}_n) \geq \pi_i(\hat{s}_1, \hat{s}_2, \ldots, \hat{s}_{i-1}, s_i, \hat{s}_{i+1}, \ldots, \hat{s}_n),$$

for any $s_i \in S_i$.

The formal definition says that a Nash equilibrium strategy combination is one in which no player has an incentive to *change* the strategy she is currently using, given that no other player changes her current strategy. If this is the case, then the combination of strategies across players will not change, since there is no incentive for any player to change her strategy.[2]

In the models of imperfect competition the players are firms. Each firm's strategy specifies a rule for choosing the value of a particular strategic variable. In this chapter, we focus on two possible strategic variables: output and price. However, there are many other strategic variables, such as advertising and research and development, which are important to firms. We use game theory to explore strategic interaction in these variables in later chapters.

Every game—and every case of strategic interaction—is governed by a set of rules that specify how the game is played. In the familiar children's game, Rock-Paper-Scissors, the rules specify the possible strategies for each player and the outcomes for any particular strategic combination such as Player 1 playing "Rock" and Player 2 playing "Paper." In that particular game, the rules also specify that play is simultaneous. Each of the two players announces their strategy choice at the same time. In contrast, the rules for playing card games such as poker and bridge specify sequential play. One player moves and then the next player takes her turn with the understanding that the moves made by the previous player cannot be changed once a card is played.

The rules also specify the information structure of the game. In games such as Tic-Tac-Toe, all relevant information is public. One player has no critical information unavailable to the other player and vice versa. However, card games like poker and bridge have a

---

[2]   Nash shared the 1994 prize with two other game theorists, R. Selten and J. Harsanyi. The award to the three game theorists served as widely publicized recognition of the importance game theory has achieved as a way of thinking in economic analysis.

very different information framework. In these games, each player has private information about his own cards that other players do not know. This more complex information structure permits signaling, bluffing, and other strategies that exploit the information asymmetries in the game.

A central insight of game theory is that the rules of the game matter a lot. The key features of the Nash equilibrium will depend on the game's rules. This is as true in real-world games as it is in board games and parlor amusements. The Nash equilibrium that results when firms compete in quantities is different from what happens when they compete in prices. Similarly, the equilibrium when one firm makes its strategic choice first and its rival knows that choice before the rival moves differs markedly from the equilibrium that arises when the firms choose strategies simultaneously.[3]

Whatever the rules of the game are, rational players will always need to think about the strategy choice of their rivals in determining their own strategic play. That is, each firm will wish to select the strategy that is optimal or profit-maximizing given the anticipated actions of its rivals. When each firm does this, and when each has, as a result of rational strategizing, correctly anticipated the choice of the others; we obtain a Nash equilibrium. In this chapter we will focus on solving for Nash equilibria in simultaneous or static games. To understand how one firm anticipates the strategy of another we begin by looking for dominant or dominated strategies.

7.2   DOMINANT AND DOMINATED STRATEGIES

Consider the case of two airlines, *Delta* and *American*, each offering a daily flight from Boston to London. Assume that each firm has already set a price for the flight, but that the departure time is still undecided, so that departure time is the strategy choice in this game. We also assume that the two firms choose departure times simultaneously. Neither can observe the departure time selected by the other before it makes its own departure time selection. However, each airline is aware that the other is also making a departure time decision and that each will learn of the other's decision at the same time. In other words, each airline is aware that they are both engaged in a strategic game of simultaneous moves.

Now consider consumer preferences. Suppose it is widely understood as the result of market research that 70 percent of the potential clientele for the flight would prefer to leave Boston in the evening and arrive in London the next morning, while the remaining 30 percent prefer a morning Boston departure. In addition, suppose as well that both airlines know that they split the market evenly when offering a flight at the same time and assume that each airline wants to maximize its share of the market.

This is a two-player game in which each player has two possible strategies, Evening Departure and Morning Departure. Consequently, there are four possible strategy combinations, each of which implies a different set of payoffs for the players. The payoff matrix in Table 7.1—typically referred to as the *normal form* of the game—is a simple description of this strategic interaction. For each strategy combination the matrix shows the payoff to each player, measured here as market share. Following convention, the payoff of the row player *Delta* is the first entry of each payoff pair.

---

[3]   This is, in fact, precisely what we mean when we use the term *simultaneous*. It refers to game settings in which each player (firm) moves without knowledge of the other player's choice. Moreover, each recognizes this mutual ignorance.

Table 7.1   Strategy combinations and firm payoffs in the flight departure game

		American	
		Morning	Evening
Delta	Morning	(15, 15)	(30, 70)
	Evening	(70, 30)	(35, 35)

Now the key to playing a game is to make an accurate guess of what one's opponent(s) will do. In the case of *American*, this means trying to determine *Delta's* strategic choice. A little thought reveals that this choice is clear. Suppose that *American* chooses a morning flight. In that case, if *Delta* also chooses a morning flight, then *Delta's* market share will be 15 percent; whereas if *Delta* chooses an evening flight, its market share will be a much higher 70 percent. Now consider *Delta's* response should *American* choose an evening flight. If *Delta* opts for a morning departure, its market share is 30 percent; whereas if it goes for an evening departure its market share is 35 percent. Once again, the evening departure gives a better payoff. In other words, no matter what *American* does, *Delta* will never wish to depart in the morning. As a result, *American* can safely anticipate that *Delta* will choose an evening flight. Knowing this, *American's* strategy is clear. Since it knows that *Delta* will choose an evening departure, and since in this case it gets a 35 percent market share if it also chooses an evening time but only 30 percent if it chooses a morning time, *American* will also choose an evening time.

We have now shown that both carriers will choose an evening departure and share equally the 70 percent of the potential Boston-to-London flyers. This outcome is a Nash equilibrium: neither firm has an incentive to change its strategy. For *Delta*, it will do best by choosing evening given that *American* is choosing evening. Likewise, given *Delta's* choice of evening, *American's* best response is also to play evening. Hence, neither carrier would want to change, since each is choosing its best response to the other carrier's choice. This is the verbal equivalent of our formal definition of a Nash equilibrium.

Solving the flight departure game was easy because each player had only two strategies; and for each player, one of the strategies—the evening flight—was better than all other strategies, no matter what choice the rival made. When one specific strategy gives the best outcome for all possible rival choices, we say that the strategy is *dominant*. In the flight departure game, evening is a dominant strategy for both firms. Conversely, morning is a *dominated* strategy because whatever strategy the rival selects, there is always an alternative strategy that does better. For a firm that has a dominant strategy, the choice is clear. Use it! Such a firm really does not have to think very much about what other firms do.

The existence of a dominant strategy greatly simplifies the solution of a game. However, it may be relatively rare to find a single strategy that is the best for all the possible choices of the rival. Nevertheless, the idea of dominance may help identify the Nash equilibrium. For example we could look for dominated strategies in the normal form of the game, that is, look for strategies that are never the best response to any rival's choice. Consider the modified version of the airline departure game described by Table 7.2. Here, we have adjusted the payoffs so that *Delta* has an advantage and typically does better than *American*, perhaps because of a frequent-flyer program. We have also added a third strategic choice, namely, a midday departure option.

Table 7.2 Strategy combinations and firm payoffs in the modified flight departure game

		American		
		Morning	Midday	Evening
Delta	Morning	(30, 18)	(25, 20)	(24, 40)
	Midday	(45, 25)	(35, 30)	(32, 32)
	Evening	(60, 30)	(33, 25)	(40, 24)

Table 7.3 Strategy combinations and firm payoffs in the modified flight departure game after elimination of *American's* dominated strategy

		American	
		Morning	Evening
Delta	Morning	(30, 18)	(24, 40)
	Midday	(45, 25)	(32, 32)
	Evening	(60, 30)	(40, 24)

As a little consideration quickly reveals, *American* will never use the midday departure strategy. *American* does best with an evening departure if *Delta* chooses either morning or midday. It does best with a morning departure if *Delta* leaves in the evening. Thus, for *American*, midday is a dominated strategy and will never be used. It follows that we can eliminate all the strategy combinations in the middle column from the game. Hence, the relevant description of the game now is that shown in Table 7.3 above.

With the elimination of *American's* dominated midday strategy, we can now see that *Delta* has a dominant strategy, namely, evening. Evening is not *Delta's* best response to *American* if the latter chooses a midday departure. However, since *American* never makes that choice, that consideration is no longer relevant. Focusing only on the relevant choices, *Delta* will choose evening, in which case a morning departure is clearly *American's* best strategy. In fact, evening/morning is the Nash equilibrium strategy combination for this game. Eliminating dominated strategies can greatly help in solving for a game's Nash equilibrium. The elimination of midday as choice for *American* immediately lets us rule out one-third of the feasible strategy combinations as potential Nash equilibria.[4]

Before leaving this brief introduction to game theory we wish to emphasize the fact that the Nash equilibrium is a solution concept. Settings of strategic interaction are typically characterized by a thought process that goes something like, "If I do this, then my rival will do that, in which case I would rather try that, but then my rival would do this, and so on and on." There must be some way of determining precisely where this thought process will ultimately lead. The Nash equilibrium is a mechanism for doing just that. While we define it as a setting in which no player wants to change her strategy given the strategy choices of her rivals, we should not let this definition obscure the deeper conceptual thinking behind the Nash concept. As we said at the start, in a setting of strategic interaction one must guess what the rival will do. The Nash equilibrium is in fact the logically consistent way of making that guess.

---

[4] Care must be taken in ruling out dominated strategies if they are *weakly* but not *strictly* dominated. See Mas-Colell et al (1995).

Consider, for example, the airline departure game described by Table 7.2. In that game, the only logically consistent guess for *Delta* is that *American* will choose a morning departure. Knowing that, *Delta* chooses the evening departure, which ensures that *American* will in fact do best by choosing the morning departure that *Delta* anticipated. If *American* ever thought that *Delta* was expecting *American* to choose a midday departure, *American* would realize that it ought to choose an evening departure, that is, something different from what it believes *Delta* expects. That sort of inconsistency is ruled out by the Nash equilibrium concept. In other words, the Nash equilibrium is a solution to a game that has the deeper logical consistency that each player is choosing the optimal strategy based on an expectation of rival strategies that are in fact optimal given the player's own strategic choice.

7.3   THE STATIC COURNOT MODEL

Game theory and the associated Nash equilibrium concept are 20th-century developments. They rank among the most important intellectual achievements in the social sciences in the last 150 years. Yet well before the work of Von Neuman and Morganstern (1944) and Nash (1950, 1951), economists began to face the difficult task of modeling oligopolistic interaction. Two particularly noteworthy early attempts are the model of Cournot (1836) and the alternative model of Bertrand (1883). The importance of these models is that they continue even now to lie at the heart of contemporary models of imperfect competition, and this is in no small part due to the fact that each achieves a solution that in fact meets the Nash equilibrium condition. In this section, we examine the Cournot model and its various extensions. We then turn to the Bertrand analysis in the following section.

The basic Cournot model is as follows. Let there be two firms, 1 and 2, each with a constant marginal cost c. The inverse demand function is given as: $P(Q) = P(q_1 + q_2)$ with $dP/dQ < 0$. Hence, profit for firm i, $\pi_i = [P(Q) - c]q_i$. Partially differentiating this with respect to q_i, we obtain the following first order necessary condition for profit maximization:

$$P(q_i + q_j) + q_i \frac{\partial P(q_i + q_j)}{\partial q_i} = c \quad \text{for} \quad i, j = 1, 2; i \neq j \tag{7.1}$$

Implicitly, equation (7.1) gives Firm i's optimal output q_i^* for any given value of its rival's production q_j. However, we cannot work out the explicit function governing that response, since we only have a general expression for demand. Nevertheless, we can determine the nature of the equilibrium implied when both firms follow the logic of this first order condition.

We start by rewriting (7.1) as

$$P(q_i + q_j) - c = -q_i \frac{\partial P(q_i + q_j)}{\partial q_i}; \quad i, j = 1, 2; \quad i \neq j \tag{7.2}$$

We then divide both sides of equation (7.2) by $P(q_1 + q_2)$, and also multiply and divide the right-hand side by Q. This yields

$$\frac{P(q_i + q_j) - c}{P(q_i + q_j)} = \frac{q_i}{Q} \frac{[\partial P(q_i + q_j)/\partial q_i]Q}{P(q_i + q_j)} \quad \text{for} \quad i, j = 1, 2; i \neq j \tag{7.3}$$

The left-hand side of (7.3) should be recognized as each firm's Lerner Index. The right-hand side should then be recognizable as a modified version of the demand elasticity ε confronting the firm. The differences are twofold. First, there is the term q_i/Q, which is just firm i's market share s_i. Second, the slope term in (7.3) $\partial P(q_1 + q_2)/\partial q_i$ is a partial derivative instead of total derivative. By definition, $dQ = dq_1 + dq_2$. Hence, holding q_j constant, $dQ = dq_i$. This means that, holding q_j constant, there is no difference between $\partial P(q_i + q_j)/\partial q_i$ and dP/dQ. Thus, the second right-hand term *is* equal to $1/\varepsilon$. Under the assumption that the two firms are symmetric and share the market evenly, equation (7.3) is

$$\frac{P - c}{P} = \frac{s_i}{\varepsilon} = \frac{0.5}{\varepsilon} \tag{7.4}$$

Recall now that the Lerner Index for the monopoly case is $(P - c)/P = 1/\varepsilon$. Thus, the Cournot model implies that in the symmetric duopoly case the same measure of the price-cost margin will be half as large. It will not be 0 as in the perfectly competitive case, but it will be significantly smaller than it would if there was only one firm in the market. The Cournot duopoly model thus yields an appealingly intuitive result. As a second firm comes into the market, the increased competition moves the market price closer to marginal cost.

The result just obtained may be easily generalized. Before doing that it is instructive to work out the duopoly Cournot Nash equilibrium for the case of linear inverse demand. Let demand be given by $P = A - BQ = A - B(q_1 + q_2)$, and again, let each firm have the identical and constant marginal cost c. Firm 1's profit is $\pi_1 = [A - B(q_1 + q_2) - c]q_1$, and the necessary first-order condition for profit maximization is

$$\frac{\partial \pi_1}{\partial q_1} = A - c - Bq_2 - 2Bq_1 = 0 \tag{7.5}$$

Equation (7.1) or the firm's first-order condition implicitly defines the best firm's best output choice (that is, its best strategy) in response to any specific output choice by its rival. By rearranging equation (7.5), Firm 1's best response function can be written as

$$q_1 = \frac{A - c}{2B} - \frac{q_2}{2} \tag{7.6}$$

Again, equation (7.6) describes Firm 1's best response for every strategy choice made by Firm 2. In the present case, strategy choices are synonymous with output choices, but that equivalency will not always hold. What will always be the case in a game-theoretic setting, however, is that there will be a decision rule describing each player's best strategy choice conditional on the choices of its rivals. For this reason, equation (7.6) is a specific case of what we will generally refer to as the firm's *best response function*. It is, in fact, what Cournot (1832) initially called the firm's reaction function. In the current duopoly setting, where there is just one other perfectly symmetric rival, it follows that we may write Firm 2's reaction or best response function as

$$q_2 = \frac{A - c}{2B} - \frac{q_1}{2} \tag{7.7}$$

If we now recall the definition of a Nash equilibrium, it should be clear that it requires that each firm be on its best response function simultaneously. If each firm is making its best strategic response to what the others are doing, then each will be unable to raise their payoff by choosing an alternative strategy. Accordingly, a market outcome in which each firm is on its best response function is one in which no firm has any incentive to change its strategy. The market outcome is a Nash equilibrium.

In the simple Cournot case of linear demand and two identical firms, the Cournot-Nash equilibrium therefore requires that both equations (7.6) and (7.7) hold simultaneously. Solving this two-equation system in the usual manner then yields

$$q_1 = q_2 = \frac{A - c}{3B} \tag{7.8}$$

In turn, this implies that the equilibrium market output and price are

$$Q = \frac{2}{3}\left(\frac{A - c}{B}\right); \quad \text{and} \quad P = \frac{A + 2c}{3} \tag{7.9}$$

This equilibrium is illustrated in Figure 7.1. Here, we label the best response functions of Firms 1 and 2 as $R1$ and $R2$, respectively. Note that the Cournot equilibrium occurs at the one point at which both firms are on their best response functions. This, of course, is a requirement for a Nash Equilibrium.

In this Cournot-Nash equilibrium, the Lerner Index or price cost margin will be

$$\frac{P - c}{P} = \frac{A - c}{A + 2c} \tag{7.10}$$

It is also straightforward to show that the demand elasticity at the equilibrium point is

$$\varepsilon = -\frac{P}{Q}\frac{dQ}{dP} = \frac{A + 2c}{2(A - c)} \tag{7.11}$$

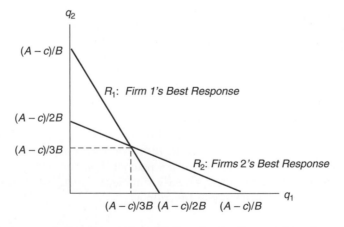

Figure 7.1   Best response functions and equilibrium for the Cournot duopoly model with linear demand

It follows immediately that the price-cost margin in this linear demand and constant marginal cost model satisfies the general condition in equation (7.4).

One advantage of working through the linear demand model is that it makes transparent an aspect of the Cournot model that continues to hold in the more general case, but is less easy to demonstrate there. Consider again the inverse demand function $P = A - BQ$, where $Q = q_1 + q_2$. If we define $A' = A - Bq_2$, we may rewrite the demand function as: $P = A' - Bq_1$. With this substitution, Firm 1's profit is

$$\pi_1 = [(A' - Bq_1) - c]q_1 \tag{7.12}$$

The necessary first-order condition for profit maximization is then

$$q_1 = \frac{A' - c}{2B} = \frac{A - c}{2B} - \frac{q_2}{2} \tag{7.13}$$

The expression $q_1 = \frac{A'-c}{2B}$ is, of course, identical to the expression in equation (7.6). Hence, this alternative approach does not in any way change our earlier results. What it does do is permit us to think of the Cournot model in a slightly different way. The inverse demand $P = A' - Bq_2$ is referred to as Firm 1's *residual demand*. In other words, equations (7.12) and (7.13) together say that the Cournot best response function of Firm 1 may be viewed as the behavior of a monopolist maximizing its profit with respect to it residual demand curve, that is, taking the output of Firm 2 as given. Of course, the same interpretation holds for Firm 2. Moreover, as noted earlier, while this interpretation is easier to see in the linear demand case, it really holds for all demand settings. The Cournot firm treats the output of other firms as given or anticipated and proceeds to maximize its profit with the residual demand that this implies. This is consistent with a Nash equilibrium solution concept because, in equilibrium, the output of one's rivals is given, as no one wants to change their production.

7.3.1   Cournot Variation 1: Many Firms

So far, we have used the Cournot model in a duopoly setting and it is natural to raise the question of whether the results may be generalized to many firms and what such a generalization might tell us. After all, we have already discovered that the Cournot outcome has the appealing feature that moving from a monopoly to a duopoly expands output and lowers the price toward the competitive price. Would introducing a third firm bring the industry still closer to the competitive ideal? What about a fourth? Or a fifth? Is the Cournot model consistent with the notion that, when there are many firms, the price converges to marginal cost?

Let us start with the linear demand case. From the viewpoint of Firm i, total output Q may be viewed as the sum of two components. One of these is Firm i's own output, q_i. The other is the output of all other not i firms, which we denote as Q_{-i}. That is, $Q = q_i + Q_{-i}$. As a result, Firm i's profit is $\pi_i = [A - B(q_i + Q_{-i}) - c]q_i$, and the necessary first-order condition for profit maximization is

$$\frac{\partial \pi_i}{\partial q_i} = A - c - BQ_{-i} - 2Bq_i = 0 \tag{7.14}$$

Rewriting the first-order condition, we then obtain Firm i's best response function:

$$q_i = \frac{(A - c)}{2B} - \frac{Q_{-i}}{2} \tag{7.15}$$

In a symmetric model, with each firm on its best response function, we have $Q_{-i} = (N - 1)q_i$. Substituting this result into equation (7.15), therefore, allows us to solve for the output of the representative firm:

$$q_i = \left(\frac{1}{N + 1}\right)\left(\frac{A - c}{B}\right) \tag{7.16}$$

It follows immediately that total and price are:

$$Q = \left(\frac{N}{N + 1}\right)\left(\frac{A - c}{B}\right); \quad \text{and} \quad P = \left(\frac{A + Nc}{N + 1}\right) \tag{7.17}$$

Equation (7.17) shows that the earlier intuition of the Cournot duopoly model continues to hold as we expand the number of firms. The first part of the equation is sometimes referred to as the $N - 1$ rule, since it implies that for this linear, constant cost case, the Cournot output is the fraction $(N - 1)/N$ of the competitive output. As the number of firms N grows, total output rises closer and closer to the competitive level $\frac{A-c}{B}$, and the price moves closer and closer to marginal cost c. Moreover, this intuitive link between structure and performance is not limited to the linear case but is in fact a general feature of the Cournot model.

7.3.2   Cournot Variation 2: Many Firms and Different Costs

So far, we have maintained the assumption that all firms are identical, that is, each has the same, constant marginal cost c. In real market settings, however, this is often not the case. Asian automakers have long been reported to have a cost advantage over U.S. rivals. Similarly, over the last two decades, older established airlines have increasingly found themselves competing against low-cost upstarts. These and many other common examples suggest that our assumption that unit cost c is the same for all firms is too restrictive. We now examine the Cournot model when each firm has its own unit cost c_i.

Consider the general inverse demand function $P(Q)$. Firm i views this demand as $P(q_i + Q_{-i})$. In turn, this implies a profit function $\pi_i = [P(q_i + Q_{-i}) - c_i]q_i$. The associated first-order condition, then, is

$$P(q_i + Q_{-i}) - c_i = -q_i \frac{\partial P(q_i + Q_{-i})}{\partial q_i} \tag{7.18}$$

Further, the logic of equation (7.3) still applies. That is, we may rewrite (7.18) as follows:

$$\frac{P(q_i + Q_{-i}) - c_i}{P(q_i + Q_{-i})} = \frac{q_i}{Q}\frac{[\partial P(q_i + Q_{-i})/\partial q_i]Q}{P(q_i + Q_{-i})} \tag{7.19}$$

In turn, this implies the following generalization of equation (7.4) for the case in which firms have different costs:

$$\frac{P - c_i}{P} = \frac{s_i}{\varepsilon} \tag{7.20}$$

Note that one implication of this equation is that firms with a higher marginal cost c_i will have a smaller market share s_i.

We can now no longer talk about one Lerner Index or one price-cost margin for the entire industry. However, we can construct a weighted-average price-cost margin $(P - \bar{c})\big/P$ using individual firm market shares s_i as the weights. This is

$$\frac{P - \bar{c}}{P} = \sum_{i=1}^{N} s_i \left(\frac{P - c_i}{P} \right) = \frac{\sum_{i=1}^{N} s_i^2}{\varepsilon} = \frac{H}{\varepsilon} \tag{7.21}$$

where H is the Herfindahl-Hirschman Index introduced in Chapter 4.

Reality Checkpoint
Production Commitment and Domestic Discomfort

The Cournot model of quantity competition makes the most sense for those industries in which production is so complicated that it must be set well in advance. Industries such as aircraft and automobile production are typically viewed in this manner. In such markets, firms must forecast demand and then plan their production schedules accordingly. Of course, demand forecasts may be wrong. Once the production from all firms hits the market, the price that equilibrates supply and demand may be very different from the price anticipated by firms when they chose their production levels. Yet, this does not alter the fact that it is that production that firms choose as their strategic variable.

When firms sell to different markets with different regulatory and other requirements, the precommitment of production can sometimes lead to unpleasant results. In the economic recovery following the burst of the dot com bubble and the September 11th terrorist attacks in the United States, both Boeing and Airbus—the two main manufacturers of commercial aircraft—committed the bulk of their new production to markets outside the United States. As a result, these years witnessed a substantial aging of the average U.S. commercial jet. American domestic passengers found they were flying on steadily older planes with fewer amenities and comforts. Engine noise was louder, bathrooms were dirtier, and breakdowns for mechanical reasons were rising. Over this time, airline finances improved but, given the uncertainties of oil prices and the American air travel market, the major aircraft producers scheduled the bulk of their production to meet the requirements of overseas markets. At the same time, U.S. airline prices rose—especially for business travelers—as airlines tried to recover from the financial difficulties that the recession and terrorism fears had caused them. Increasingly, American consumers felt that they were flying yesterday's planes at today's prices.

Source: J. Bailey, "U.S. Airlines Put Off Buying New Planes." *The New York Times* (27 October 2007), p. C1.

The generalized Cournot model with many firms and different costs implies that the industrywide price-cost margin will be directly related to market structure as measured by the Herfindahl-Hirschman Index. That is, the intuition of the $N - 1$ rule from the linear demand case extends to the generalized model, and establishes a clear link between the severity of the market price distortion and the extent of market power. For all these reasons, the Cournot-Nash model plays a central role in both theoretical and empirical industrial organization.

Marion et al (1979) collected price data for a basket of 94 grocery products, and market share data for 36 firms operating in 32 U.S. Standard Metropolitan Statistical Areas. They found food prices were significantly higher in markets with a higher Herfindahl Index. Likewise, Marvel (1989) found that for 22 U.S. cities, increases in the Herfindahl Index had a significant impact on the average retail price of gasoline.[5]

7.4   THE BERTRAND MODEL

The anticipation of the Nash equilibrium concept that characterizes Cournot's initial analysis is somewhat remarkable, given that it was developed more than 150 years ago. Yet some 50 years after its introduction, Cournot's model was harshly reviewed by Joseph Bertrand, a French mathematician, in an article in the *Journal des Savants*. Bertrand was skeptical that mathematical modeling in economics could be useful; and to prove his point, he analyzed the Cournot model in terms of prices rather than quantities. The legacy of Bertrand is not, however, his criticism of what he termed "pseudo-mathematics" in economics. Instead, Bertrand's contribution was the recognition that using price as a strategic variable is different from using quantity as the strategic variable, and that this difference is worth investigating.[6]

Let us rework the Cournot duopoly model, with each firm choosing the price it will charge rather than the quantity of output it will produce. We again start with the assumption that marginal cost is the same and equal to c for each firm. It is convenient to switch from expressing market demand in its inverse form to expressing it as $Q(P)$ where, as before, $Q = q_1 + q_2$. Because the goods that the two firms are selling are identical, the firm charging a lower price will win all the consumers willing to buy at that price, while the firm charging a higher price will sell nothing. If both firms charge the same price, we assume that customers randomly sort themselves out so that each firm meets half of the total market demand at that price. Hence, the demand facing Firm i can be written as:

$$q_i(p_i, p_j) = \begin{cases} 0 & \text{if } p_i > p_j \\ \frac{1}{2}Q(p) & \text{if } p_i = p_j \text{ for } i, j = 1, 2, i \neq j \\ Q(p_i) & \text{if } p_i < p_j \end{cases} \qquad (7.22)$$

The profit for Firm i is $\pi_i(p_i, p_j) = (p_i - c)q_i(p_i, p_j)$. It is straightforward to see that any price $p_i \geq p_j > c$, Firm i will wish to reduce its price. If $p_1 > p_2 > c$, Firm 1 will sell

[5]   Note that the Herfindahl Index is endogenous here as each firm's market share depends on its marginal cost.

[6]   Despite Bertrand's criticism, Friedman (1977) makes clear that Cournot's fate was not one of complete obscurity, owing to his friendship with the great French economist, Walras. The English economist Marshall was also influenced by Cournot.

no output and earn 0 profit. By reducing its price p_1, just a tiny amount below p_2, Firm 1 will sell $Q(p_1)$ and earn a profit of $(p_1 - c)Q(p_1) > 0$. Likewise, if $p_1 = p_2 > c$, Firm 1 can again reduce its price by a tiny amount and double its profit from $0.5\ (p_1 - c)Q(p_1)$ to $(p_1 - c)Q(p_1)$. Of course, these same conjectures can be made by Firm 2. On the other hand, if $p_i \leq p_j < c$, then Firm i will wish to raise its price above Firm j's price, so as to reduce its losses to 0 and not sell below cost.

The only Nash equilibrium for this price game is $p_1 = p_2 = c$. This is the only pair of prices at which neither firm has an incentive either to lower or raise its price. Yet, this implies that the market reaches the competitive outcome with price equal to marginal cost and output equal to $Q(c)$ with just two firms. It should be clear that adding more firms will not change this equilibrium outcome.

What if firms differed in their marginal cost? Imagine that there are N firms each with a different value of c_i. Without loss of generality, let us number these firms in order of their marginal cost. That is, Firm 1 has the lowest marginal cost c_1, Firm 2 has the next lowest c_2, and so on. In this case, the Nash equilibrium will drive the price to c_2, the second lowest of the two cost levels. Firm 1 will set $p_1 = c_2 - \varepsilon$, a shade lower than c_2 and serve roughly $Q(c_2)$ units to earn $(c_2 - c_1)Q(c_2)$ in profit. At that point, no other firm has an incentive to set p_i below c_2, as this would move them from 0 profit to actual losses. Conversely, no other firm can gain from raising its price since, if $p_i > c_2$, they would then just continue to serve 0 consumers and earn 0 profit. Firm 1 earns its maximum profit by charging the highest price it can without losing any customers to rivals.[7]

We now have a complete description of the Nash equilibria for N firms engaged in Bertrand or price competition when each sells an identical product and each has a possibly unique marginal cost c_i. In every case, the market price P falls to a level equal to the second lowest marginal cost c_2. If firms have identical cost c, this simply means that $P = c$ and output is at the competitive level $Q(c)$. No firm earns a positive profit. If firms have different marginal costs, then $P = c_2$ and output is $Q(c_2)$. Every firm earns 0 profit except for the lowest cost firm, which earns $\pi_1 = (c_2 - c_1)Q(c_2)$.

In general, Bertrand or price competition is more intense—tougher—than Cournot or quantity competition. This is trivially obvious when all N firms have the same marginal cost c, since in that case the Bertrand competition leads to price being set to the competitive level, while under Cournot the outcome is characterized by a price-cost margin of $(P - c)/P = 1/N\varepsilon$. For N firms each with a different cost c_i, Bertrand competition will again typically result in a more competitive outcome. Bertrand competition in this case leads to a price c_2, so only the lowest-cost firm earns a profit. Yet with Cournot competition, a firm can continue to earn a profit even when it does not have the lowest cost, because the price typically exceeds c_2.[8]

7.4.1 Bertrand Competition—Capacity Constraints

The dramatic difference of the Bertrand model and, in particular, difference in price-cost margins between this model and its Cournot cousin are a powerful testament to our earlier

---

[7] We assume here that the monopoly price $P^M > c_2$. If this is not the case, Firm 1 may wish to set a price lower than c_2 by more than a trivial amount, as this moves its price closer to the maximum level earned by a monopolist.

[8] Again, we are assuming c_2 (and perhaps the marginal cost of other firms as well) is below the monopoly price P^M.

Reality Checkpoint
Flat Screens and Flatter Prices

Perhaps one of the most dramatic examples of Bertrand competition comes from the market for flat screen TVs. Such screens use one of three basic technologies. These are liquid crystal display (LCD), digital light processing (DLP), and plasma. Initially, the technologies were such that LCD worked best on small screens, plasma worked best on medium-sized screens, and DLP worked best with large screens. In addition, DLP screens were not as flat. However, over time, the differences between the three types have diminished. The result has been the eruption of a severe price war. From mid-2003 to mid-2005, prices for new TVs based on these technologies fell by an average of 25 percent per year. Fifty-inch plasma TVs that sold for $20,000 in 2000 were selling for $4,000 in 2005. Nor has this pressure let up. In November 2006, Syntax-Brillian cut the price on its 32-inch LCD TV by 40 percent. Sony and other premium brands were forced to follow suit. Prices on all models fell further. Indeed, when Sony was rumored to be thinking of further reducing its 50-inch price to $3,000, James Li, the chief executive of Syntax-Brillian was quoted as saying, "If they go to $3,000, I will go to $2,999." Bertrand would have been proud.

Source: D. Darlin, "Falling Costs of Big-Screen TVs to Keep Falling" and "The No-Name Brand Behind the Latest Flat-Panel Price War." *The New York Times*, 20 August 2005, p. C1; and 12 February 2007, p. C1.

conclusion. The rules of the game matter. Strategic interaction when the choice variable is quantity of output leads to very different result from when the strategic variable is price.

At the same time, the Bertrand implications seem almost too powerful to be practical. The prediction that only two firms are needed to keep prices roughly equal to marginal cost and hence that there is no link between market structure and market conduct is at odds with much intuition as well as empirical evidence. Of course, the central driving force behind the Bertrand results is the fact that any price deviation between the two firms leads to an immediate and complete loss of demand for the firm charging the higher price. So for price-setting models we must somehow explain why this may not be the case.

There are two very sound reasons why a firm's decision to charge a price higher than its rival would not result in the complete loss of all its customers. One reason is that the rival firm may not have the capacity to serve all of the customers who demand the product or service at its low price.[9] The second is that consumers may not view the two products as identical or as perfect substitutes.

To see the importance of capacity constraints, consider again the Bertrand duopoly model in which marginal cost c is the same for both firms. Recall that in the Nash equilibrium for that case, each firm chooses $p_i = c$, and each serves half the market demand $Q(c)$ at that price. In that equilibrium, neither firm has an incentive to raise its price, because then it would lose all its customers to the rival. Yet for this to be the case, the rival needs to have the capacity to serve the entire market, or $Q(c)$. However,

[9] Edgeworth (1987) was one of the first economists to investigate the impact of capacity constraints on the Bertrand analysis.

if capacity has any cost, there seems to be little reason to invest in that capacity if in equilibrium a firm serves only $Q(c)/2$ customers.

When capacity constraints come into play, the game between the two firms becomes a two-stage game. In the first stage, the two firms choose capacity levels. In the second, they compete in price. If we work backwards, we must consider how firms will set prices knowing that there is an upper limit on the capacity to meet the demand at those prices.

Solving for the Nash equilibrium when capacity is chosen in advance is tricky. One issue that must be resolved is how a level of output for which there is excess demand is rationed. To return to our duopoly case, suppose that $p_1 < p_2$, but that $Q(p_1) > K_1$, where K_1 is Firm 1's maximum output capacity. The rationing question asks which of those customers willing to buy at price p_1 are permitted to do so. The conventional assumption is that firms practice what is known as *efficient rationing*. This means that if Firm 1 has capacity K_1, it sells its K_1 units of production to those consumers who value it most. That is, the firm successively works its way down the inverse demand curve until its capacity is exhausted.

Let us think through a few aspects of the possible price equilibria that could emerge under capacity constraints. First note that if both firms choose a capacity greater than or equal to the competitive level in stage 1 (i.e., if $K_1 \geq Q(c)$ and $K_2 \geq Q(c)$), then the Nash equilibrium in stage 2 is $p_1 = p_2 = c$. This is just the Bertrand equilibrium that we discussed earlier. Since the capacity cost has been sunk, each firm will have an incentive to undercut its rival's price so long as that price exceeds c.

Second, if neither firm has the capacity to meet the full demand at $p = c$ (i.e., if both $K_1 < Q(c)$ and $K_1 < Q(c)$), then $p_1 = p_2 = c$ cannot be the price outcome To see this, suppose Firm 1 sets $p_1 = c$. At that price potentially $Q(c)$ customers will wish to buy from Firm 1, but it can only serve $K_1 < Q(c)$. Hence, there will be $Q(c) - K_1$ excess demand. Firm 2 could also set $p_2 = c$ and serve these consumers but earn no net revenue on them. Alternatively, it could serve fewer of them, but at a price $p_2 > c$, and earn some positive profit. Clearly, the latter is the better choice, but this means that $p_1 = p_2 = c$ is no longer a Nash equilibrium.

Finally, it is instructive to consider the price equilibrium if each firm has chosen a capacity equal to its Cournot equilibrium output q^C. It is easy to see that full utilization of capacity by both firms will require $p_1 = p_2 = p^C$, where p^C is such that $Q(p^C) = 2q^C$. That is, the price that each firm would set to ensure that all its capacity was used would be the Cournot equilibrium price. Is this also a price equilibrium here? Clearly, neither firm has an incentive to lower its price. Neither can serve more consumers so this would simply lower its profit. Does either have an incentive to raise its price? The answer is no. Recall that in the Cournot equilibrium, each firm acts as a monopolist with respect to its residual demand curve. Since Firm 2's capacity is given at q^C, this is exactly the demand curve that Firm 1 faces should it raise its price. Yet, we know that the price p^C is precisely the price that maximizes Firm 1's profit when Firm 2 produces q^C. It follows that if each firm enters the second stage of the game with capacity equal to its Cournot output, the resultant equilibrium will be $p_1 = p_2 = p^C > c$. That is, each firm will set a price equal to the Cournot price. The total quantity demanded will be the Cournot production level, and this will just exactly use up all the available capacity.

Now consider the firms' prior choice of capacity and assume that capacity costs r per unit. Here, we begin with the observation that no firm will ever choose capacity $K_i > Q(c)$, that is, greater than the total market demand at the competitive price. To do so would be to guarantee that the firm has excess capacity since selling this much requires a price below marginal cost. Further, the choice $K_1 = K_2 = Q(c)$ cannot be an equilibrium either. To utilize fully their capacities would imply that firms set $p_1 = p_2 = c$. Hence, neither firm would earn any operating profit in this case. Since consumers split evenly between the two firms, each would lose $rQ(c)/2$. In this case, each firm would be able to reduce its loss by acquiring less capacity in stage 1. In other words, any first-stage Nash equilibrium in capacity choices will be characterized by both $K_1 < Q(c)$ and $K_2 < Q(c)$. Yet, as we have just seen, this means that prices will not be set equal to marginal cost.

What will be the Nash equilibrium? In light of the foregoing, perhaps it will not come as a surprise that Kreps and Scheinkman (1983) show that the equilibrium capacity choices are $K_1 = K_2 = q^C$. As we know, this then leads to a price equilibrium in which $p_1 = p_2 = p^C$. In other words, Bertrand competition with capacity precommitment replicates the Cournot model.

7.4.2   Bertrand Competition—Product Differentiation

Capacity constraints are one reason that Bertrand competition may not yield marginal cost pricing. A second reason is that the two firms may not, as Bertrand assumed, produce identical products. Think of hair salons, for example. No two hair stylists cut and style hair in exactly the same way. Nor will the salons have exactly the same sort of equipment or furnishings. Typically, they will differ in their locations. This in itself is often sufficient to generate a preference by some consumers for one salon or the other, even when different prices are charged. In short, differences in locations, furnishings, or cutting styles can each permit one salon to price somewhat higher than its rival without immediately losing all of its customers.

We briefly presented a spatial approach to product differentiation in Chapter 3. We now present a model of competition in a spatial setting. There are N consumers distributed uniformly along a line segment of unit length. Consumers are indexed by their position on this segment measured as the distance from the left or west end. Thus, consumer x_i is located x_i units from the left end of the segment and $1 - x_i$ from the right or east end of the segment. Firm 1 is located at the west end ($x = 0$). Firm 2 is located at the east end ($x = 1$). The marginal cost of production at each is c. Each consumer is willing to pay V per unit and will consume at most one unit of the good per period of time. Each also incurs a transport cost of t per round trip from their location to one of the two firms. Consumer utility from purchasing a unit of the good is given by

$$U_i = V - p_1 - tx_i \text{ if she buys from Firm 1; and}$$
$$U_i = V - p_2 - t(1 - x_i) \text{ if she buys from Firm 2} \tag{7.23}$$

We assume that the entire market of N consumers is served and both firms have positive market shares. It must then be the case that there is some marginal consumer x^m, who is indifferent between buying from either Firm 1 or Firm 2. Hence, we have

$$V - p_1 - tx^m = V - p_2 - t(1 - x^m) \tag{7.24}$$

Solving to find the location of the marginal consumer x^m, we obtain

$$x^m(p_1, p_2) = \frac{(p_2 - p_1 + t)}{2t} \tag{7.25}$$

At any set of prices p_1 and p_2, all consumers to the left of x^m buy from Firm 1. All those to the right of x^m buy from Firm 2. In other words, x^m is the fraction of the market that buys from Firm 1 and $(1 - x^m)$ is the fraction that buys from Firm 2. Therefore, the demand facing Firm 1 is

$$D_1(p_1, p_2) = x^m(p_1, p_2)N = \frac{(p_2 - p_1 + t)}{2t}N \qquad (7.26)$$

Similarly, Firm 2's demand function is

$$D_2(p_1, p_2) = (1 - x^m(p_1, p_2))N = \frac{(p_1 - p_2 + t)}{2t}N \qquad (7.27)$$

Unlike the initial Bertrand duopoly model, the demand function facing either firm here is continuous in both p_1 and p_2. A decision by Firm 1 to raise p_1 above p_2 does not cause Firm 1 to lose all of its customers. Some of its customers still prefer to buy good 1 even at the higher price, simply because they prefer that version of the good to the style (or location) marketed by Firm 2.[10]

The continuity in demand functions carries over into the profit functions. Firm 1's profit function is

$$\pi_1(p_1, p_2) = (p_1 - c)\frac{(p_2 - p_1 + t)}{2t}N \qquad (7.28)$$

Similarly, Firm 2's profits are given by

$$\pi_2(p_1, p_2) = (p_2 - c)\frac{(p_1 - p_2 + t)}{2t}N \qquad (7.29)$$

Focusing on Firm 1, the first-order necessary condition for profit maximization is

$$\frac{\partial \pi_1}{\partial p_1} = \frac{(p_2 - p_1 + t)N}{2t} - \frac{(p_1 - c)N}{2t} = 0 \qquad (7.30)$$

which implies

$$p_1 = \frac{c + t + p_2}{2} \qquad (7.31)$$

Equation (7.31) is Firm 1's best response function describing how it sets its optimal price for every choice of p_2 by its rival. By symmetry, Firm 2's best response function is

$$p_2 = \frac{c + t + p_1}{2} \qquad (7.32)$$

Substituting the result from (7.31) into (7.32) so that both firms are on their best-response functions yields the Nash equilibrium in prices. This is

$$p_1 = p_2 = c + t \qquad (7.33)$$

This equilibrium is illustrated in Figure 7.2. As before, each firm's best response function is labeled as R_1 and R_2, respectively. An equilibrium consistent with the Nash criterion

---

[10] Our assumption that the equilibrium is one in which the entire market is served is critical to the continuity result.

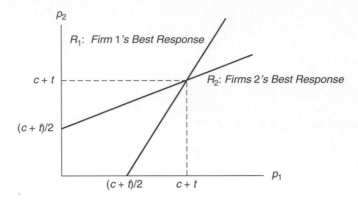

Figure 7.2   Best response functions and equilibrium for Bertrand duopoly model with imperfect substitutes

must lie at the intersection of the best response functions. As with the simple Cournot-Nash case, the equilibrium in this Bertrand duopoly model with differentiated products is unique.

Equation (7.33) shows that in equilibrium, each firm charges a price above marginal cost. Once again, the simple Bertrand analysis no longer holds. The source of supracompetitive pricing here is also clear. It is the transport cost or disutility t that consumers incur when they buy a product some distance from their most preferred type. When products are differentiated and consumers care about that differentiation, price competition does not lead to marginal cost pricing. It would do so, though, if $t = 0$ (i.e., if consumers saw no meaningful distinctions between brands so that all goods were perfect substitutes).

Moreover, it is easy to see that this spatial model also implies that prices become more competitive as the number of firms increases. This is because as more firms enter along the line segment, the distance between firms shrinks and goods become closer substitutes, forcing them to price more competitively. Suppose for example that there were three firms—one at each end of the line segment and one in the center, labeled successively as Firms 1, 2, and 3. As you are asked to show in the end-of-chapter problems, the equilibrium price then falls to $p_1 = p_2 = p_3 = c + t/2$.

In sum, when firms sell differentiated products, Bertrand competition no longer implies that prices are reduced to marginal cost even with just two firms in the market. Because a high-price firm now does not have to worry about losing all its customers to a lower-price rival, prices will be set at supracompetitive levels. However, as more firms enter and closer substitutes emerge for each product, the price-cost margin shrinks, and prices move closer to marginal cost.[11]

7.5   STRATEGIC SUBSTITUTES AND COMPLEMENTS

Best-response functions define the essence of a Nash equilibrium. Every player must be on her best-response function for an outcome to qualify as an equilibrium. Yet, an analysis of best-response functions does more than merely define the equilibrium outcome. In

[11]   We have assumed a symmetric location pattern for firms. However, this is not necessarily the case. See, for example, Eaton (1976), D'Aspremont, Gabszewicz, and Thisse (1979), Novshek (1980), and Economides (1989).

Reality Checkpoint
Unfriendly Skies: Price Wars in Airline Markets

Following general deregulation in 1977, the profitability of the airline industry has generally deteriorated and also become much more volatile. An important source of these developments has been the continued outbreak of price wars. Morrison and Winston (1996) define such conflicts as any city-pair route market in which the average airfare declines by 20 percent or more within a single quarter. Based on this definition, they estimate that over 81 percent of airline city-pair routes experienced such wars in the 1979–95 time period. In the wars so identified, the average fare in fact typically falls by over 37 percent—and sometimes falls by as much as 79 percent. These wars appear to be triggered by unexpected movements in demand and the entrance of new airlines on a route, especially low-cost airlines like Southwest. Morrison and Winston (1996) also find that the effect of such fare wars on industry profits is important. On average, they estimate that the intense price competition cost airlines $300 million in foregone profits in each of the first 16 years following deregulation. This amounts to over 20 percent of total net income over these same years. Of course, to the extent that this profit loss simply reflects movement toward the Bertrand outcome of marginal cost pricing, it shows up as a gain to consumers and a net improvement in efficiency. Judging from their comments in the press, however, airline executives appear to take little comfort in such gains.

Source: S. Morrison and C. Winston, "Causes and Consequences of Airline Fare Wars." *Brookings Papers on Economic Activity, Microeconomics, 1996* (1996): 85–124.

M. Maynard, "Yes, It Was a Dismal Year for Airlines. Now the Bad News." *The New York Times* (16 December 2002), p. C2.

particular, examining the properties of best-response functions can aid our understanding of how strategic interaction works and how that interaction can be made "more" or "less" competitive.

Recall the best-response functions of the Cournot duopoly model with linear demand (equations (7.6) and (7.7)). These are $q_i = \frac{A-c}{2B} - \frac{q_j}{2}$; $i, j = 1, 2$; and $i \neq j$. In contrast, the best response functions for the Bertrand duopoly model with product differentiation (equations (7.31) and (7.32)) are described by $p_i = (c + t + p_j)/2$; $i, j = 1, 2$; and $i \neq j$. Figure 7.3(a) and 7.3(b) show the best response functions for each case. In addition, they also show how Firm 2's best response R_2 shifts in each case in response to a rise in the firm's cost c.

One difference that is immediately apparent between Figures 7.3(a) and 7.3(b) is the difference in the slope of the best-response functions. In the Cournot quantity case of 7.3(a), these are *negatively* sloped—Firm 1's best response to an increase in q_2 is to *decrease* q_1. However, in the Bertrand case of 7.3(b) in which competition is in prices, the best-response functions are *positively* sloped. Firm 1's best response to an increase in p_2 is to increase p_1 as well.

Whether the best-response functions are negatively or positively sloped is quite important. The slope reveals much about the nature of competition in the product market. To see this, consider the impact of an increase in Firm 2's unit cost c_2. In the Cournot model, a rise in c_2 shifts Firm 2's best response curve *inward*. As Figure 7.3(a) indicates, this leads to a new Nash equilibrium in which Firm 2 produces less and Firm 1 produces more

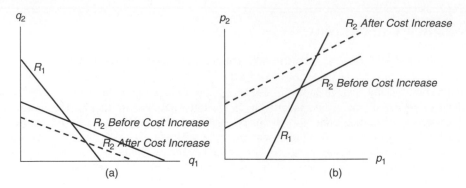

Figure 7.3   Strategic substitutes (Cournot) and strategic complements (Bertrand)
A rise in Firm 2's cost shifts its response function inward in the Cournot model, but outward in the Bertrand model. Firm 1 reacts aggressively to increase its market share in the Cournot case. It reacts mildly in the Bertrand price by *raising* its price.

than each did before c_2 rose. That is, in the Cournot quantity model, Firm 1's response to Firm 2's bad luck is a rather aggressive one in which it seizes the opportunity to expand its market share at the expense of Firm 2.

Consider now the impact of a rise in c_2 in the context of the differentiated-goods Bertrand model shown in Figure 7.3(b). The rise in this case shifts Firm 2's best response function *upward*. Given the rise in its cost, Firm 2 will choose to set a higher p_2 than it did previously in response to any given value of p_1. How does Firm 1 respond? The upward-sloping feature of Firm 1's response function tells us that here, unlike the Cournot case, Firm 1's reaction is less aggressive. The fact that Firm 2 is now less able to set a low price tells Firm 1 that the price competition from its rival is now less intense. Firm 1 now reacts by raising p_1.

When the best response functions are downward sloping, as in the Cournot case, we say that the strategies are *strategic substitutes*. When we have the alternative case of upward-sloping best-response functions, as in the Bertrand case, we say that the strategies are *strategic complements*.[12] As is evident from Figure 7.3, whether the strategic variables are substitutes or complements is quite important. In the Cournot case, one firm's reduction in output is offset somewhat by rival expansion, thereby lessening the blow to consumers. In the Bertrand case, one firm's price increase tends to spread throughout the market with consumers everywhere enduring some pain. As we will see in subsequent chapters, these differences have important market implications regarding the impact of mergers, advertising campaigns, or product innovations.

7.6   EMPIRICAL APPLICATION: BRAND COMPETITION AND CONSUMER PREFERENCES—EVIDENCE FROM THE CALIFORNIA RETAIL GASOLINE MARKET

Gasoline is typically produced by refiners and then shipped to a central distribution point. The gasoline is then bought either by an unbranded independent retailer, such as Race-Trac, or by service stations selling a branded product, such as an Exxon or Chevron

---

[12]   This terminology comes from Bulow, Geanakopolos, and Klemperer (1985).

station. In the latter case, a special additive unique to the brand has to be added. For example, to sell "Chevron" gasoline, a station has to have added Techron^{TM} to the fuel. Thus, each specific brand is differentiated by the use of its own additive. Independent stations, however, simply sell the basic gasoline without any additive. Here, we briefly describe a paper by Justine Hastings (2004) that examines the nature of price competition in the retail gasoline market in the Southern California.

The background to the study is as follows. In June 1997, the Atlantic Richfield Company (ARCO), a well-known refiner and retail brand, acquired control of about 260 gasoline stations that formerly had been operated by the independent retailer Thrifty in and around Los Angeles and San Diego. ARCO then converted these to ARCO stations—a process that was essentially completed by September of that same year. Thus, the ARCO-Thrifty acquisition resulted in the exit of a large number of independent service stations in Southern California, as these were replaced in large part by ARCO sellers.

Hastings (2004) asks what effect the ARCO-Thrifty deal had on retail gasoline prices. In principle, the effect could be either positive or negative, depending on consumer preferences. If consumers identify brands with higher quality and independents with lower quality, then conversion of the unbranded (low-quality) stations to the ARCO brand would mean that these stations now sell a closer substitute to the other branded products. This would intensify price competition and *lower* branded gasoline prices. However, if a large pool of consumers is unresponsive to brand labels because their willingness to pay for higher quality is limited and they only want to buy gasoline as cheaply as possible, then the loss of the Thrifty stations removes this low-cost alternative and *raises* gasoline prices.

To isolate the effect of the ARCO-Thrifty merger, Hastings (2004) looked at how prices charged by gasoline stations in the Los Angeles and San Diego areas differed depending on whether they competed with a Thrifty or not. Her data cover the prices charged by 699 stations, measured at four different times—February 1997, June 1997, October 1997, and December 1997. Notice that the first two dates are for prices before the conversion, while the last two dates are for prices after the conversion. She then defines submarkets in which each station's competitors are all the other stations within one mile's driving distance. A simple regression that might capture the effect of the merger would be

$$p_{it} = Constant + \alpha_i + \beta_1 X_{it} + \beta_2 Z_{it} + e_{it} \tag{7.34}$$

where p_{it} is the price charged by station i at time t; α_i is a firm-specific dummy that lets the intercept be different for each service station; X_{it} is a dummy variable that has the value 1 if station i competes with an independent (Thrifty) at time t (and 0 otherwise); and likewise Z_{it} is 1 if a competitor of station i has become a station that is owned by a major brand as opposed to a station that operates as a franchisee or lessee of a major brand (and 0 otherwise). This last variable Z_{it} is meant to capture the impact of any differential effects depending on the contractual relationship between a major brand and the station that sells that brand. The key variable of interest, however, is X_{it}. We want to know whether the estimated coefficient β_1 is negative—which would indicate that having independent rivals generally leads to lower prices—or is positive, which would indicate that the presence of independents softens competition and raises prices.

However, there is a potentially serious problem with estimating equation (10.12). The problem is that over the course of 1997, gasoline prices were rising generally throughout Southern California. Equation (10.12) does not allow for this general rising trend. Consider our key variable X_{it}. In the data, this will be 1 for a lot more stations before the merger (in

February and June) than it will be in October and December. As a result, the coefficient β_1 will likely be negative, because prices were lower in February and June (when there were a lot more independents) than in September and December (after the merger removed the Thrifty stations). That is, β_1 will be biased, because it will pick up time effects as well as the effects of independents.

In order to isolate the price effects that are purely due to independent rivals alone, Hastings (2004) puts in location specific time dummies for February, June, and September. (The effect of December is of course captured in the regression constant.) That is, she estimates an equation something like

$$p_{it} = Constant + \alpha_i + \beta_1 X_{it} + \beta_2 Z_{it} + \beta_3 T_i + e_{it} \qquad (7.35)$$

where T_i or time is captured not as a continuous variable, but rather, again, by time-specific dummies. Her results, both with and without the time dummies (but suppressing the firm specific intercepts), are shown below.

Consider first the column of results for the equation that includes the location time dummies. Here, the estimate of β_1, the coefficient on having a Thrifty or independent rival in a station's local market, implies that this led the station to lower its price by about 5 cents per gallon. The standard error on this estimate is very small, so we can be very confident of this measure. Note too how this contrasts with the effect measured in the regression results shown in the first column that leaves out the time effects. That estimate suggests a much larger effect of 10 cents per gallon decline when a station has independent rivals. Again, this is because in leaving out the time effects, the regression erroneously attributes the general rise in gasoline prices throughout the region to the merger when in fact prices were clearly rising for other reasons as well. We should also note that the coefficient estimate for β_2 is not significant in either equation. So, the type of ownership by a major brand does not seem to be important for retail gasoline prices.

One picture is often worth a large number of words. The graph below illustrates the behavior of Southern California gasoline prices over the period covered by Hastings's data for each of two groups: (1) the treatment group that competed with a Thrifty station; and (2) the control group of stations that did not.

Notice the general rise in prices in both groups through October. Clearly, this is a phenomenon common to the gasoline market in general and not the result of the merger per se. However, a close look at the data reveals that the merger did have some impact. In the months before the merger, stations that competed with a Thrifty had prices that

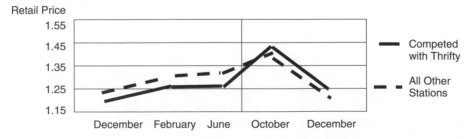

Figure 7.4 "Thrifty" competition and Gasoline prices in Southern California
Source: Hastings (2004).

Table 7.4   Brand competition and gasoline prices. Dependent variable = price per gallon of regular unleaded

Variable	*Without location-time dummies* Coefficient (Standard Error)	*With location-time dummies* Coefficient (Standard Error)
Constant	1.3465 (0.0415)	1.3617 (0.0287)
X_{it}	−0.1013 (0.0178)	−0.0500 (0.0122)
Z_{it}	−0.0033 (0.0143)	−0.0033 (0.0101)
LA*February		0.0180 (0.0065)
LA*June		0.0243 (0.0065)
LA*December		0.1390 (0.0064)
SD*February		−0.0851 (0.0036)
SD*June		−0.0304 (0.0036)
SD*December		0.0545 (0.0545)
R^2	0.3953	0.7181

were 2 to 3 cents *lower* than those in the control group. Starting about the time of the merger in June, however, and continuing afterwards, these same stations had prices 2 to 3 cents *higher* than those in the control group. It is this roughly 5-cent effect that is being picked up in the final column of Table 7.4 above. For both groups—those that initially competed with a Thrifty prior to the merger and those that did not—prices differ between the beginning of 1997 and the end. To isolate the effects of the merger, we need to look at how these differences over time were different between the two groups. If we recall that for the treatment group stations, $X_{It} = 1$ at first but 0 after the merger; while it is always 0 firms in the control group. The price behavior for the two groups is

	Before Merger	**After Merger**	**Difference**
Treatment group:	$\alpha_i + \beta_1$	$\alpha_i + time\ effects$	$-\beta_1 + time\ effects$
Control group:	α_j	$\alpha_j + time\ effects$	$time\ effects$

Thus, β_1 in our regression reflects the difference between the difference over time in the treatment group and that in the control group. For this reason, β_1 is often referred to as a *difference-in-differences* estimator.

Summary

In this chapter we have presented single-period models of competition. One of these is the Cournot model in which the variable of strategic choice for each firm is the quantity of production. The other set of models reflects the Bertrand approach in which the strategic choice variable is the price of the firm's product. Although each of these approaches was originally developed prior to the emergence of game theory, each reflects game theoretic principles and each can be cast in a modern game theoretic framework. We usually describe the outcome in these games as a Cournot-Nash equilibrium or a Bertrand-Nash equilibrium.

Both the Cournot and Bertrand approaches make clear the importance of firms' interdependence. The Cournot model also leads to the nice intuitive result that the degree of departure from competitive pricing may be directly linked to the structure of the industry as measured by the Herfindahl index. In addition, high cost firms can survive in a Cournot model of competition—although they will be less profitable than lower-cost rivals. This is not possible in the basic Bertrand model of price competition with identical products. In that case, only the lowest-cost producers can survive market competition.

However, the efficient outcome predicted by the simple Bertrand model depends upon two key assumptions. The first is that firms have extensive capacity so that it is possible to serve all a rival's customers after undercutting the rival's price. The second key assumption is that the firms produce identical products so that relative price is all that matters to consumers when choosing between brands. If either of these assumptions is relaxed, the efficiency outcome of the simple Bertrand model no longer obtains. If firms must choose production capacities in advance, the outcome with Bertrand price competition becomes closer to what occurs in the Cournot model. If products are differentiated, prices are again likely to remain above marginal cost, and given the fierceness of price competition, firms have a real incentive to differentiate their products.

One approach to modeling product differentiation is the Hotelling (1929) spatial model, which we first introduced in Chapter 3. This model uses geographic location as a metaphor for differences between versions of the same product. It thereby makes it possible to consider price competition between firms selling differentiated products. The Hotelling model makes it clear that Bertrand competition with differentiated products does not result in efficient marginal cost pricing. It also makes clear that the deviation from such pricing depends on how much consumers value variety among products. The greater value that the typical consumer places on getting her most preferred version of the product, the higher prices will rise above marginal cost. The spatial model of price competition has provided a useful framework for empirical work. Many policy makers are interested in investigating how a change in market structure—through entry or mergers or regulatory policy—will affect price competition.

Ultimately, the differences between Cournot and Bertrand competition reflect underlying differences between quantities and prices as strategic variables. The quantities chosen by Cournot firms are strategic substitutes—increases in one firm's production lead to decreases in the rival's output. In contrast, the prices chosen by Bertrand competitors are strategic complements. A rise in one firm's price permits its rival to raise price, too.

Our analysis of both quantity and price competition has been set in a static framework in which the market structure is taken as given. However, as we noted at the start of this book, the reality is that market structure is endogenous. Strategies that generate above normal profits for existing firms will induce new firms to enter over time. At the same time, incumbent firms may be able to take actions that deter such entry. In the following chapters, we extend our analysis to examine these issues.

Problems

1. Harrison and Tyler are two students who met by chance the last day of exams before the end of the spring semester and the beginning of summer. Fortunately, they liked each other very much. Unfortunately, they forgot to exchange addresses. Fortunately, each remembers that they spoke of attending a campus party that night. Unfortunately, there are two such parties. One party is small. If each attends this party, they will certainly meet. The other party is huge. If each attends this one, there is a chance they will not meet because of the crowd. Of course, they will certainly not meet if they attend separate parties. Payoffs to each depending on the combined choice of parties are shown below, with Tyler's payoffs listed first.

		Harrison	
		Go To Small Party	Go To Large Party
Tyler	Go To Small Party	(1,000, 1,000)	(0, 0)
	Go To Large Party	(0, 0)	(500, 500)

   a.   Identify the Nash equilibria for this problem.
   b.   Identify the Pareto optimal outcome for this "two-party" system.

2. Suppose that the small party of problem 1 is hosted by the "Outcasts," 20 men and women students trying to organize alternatives to the existing campus party establishment. All 20 Outcasts will attend the party. But many other students—not unlike Harrison and Tyler—only go to a party to which others (no one in particular, just people in general) are expected to come. As a result, total attendance A at the small party depends on just how many people X everyone *expects* to show up. Let the relationship between A and X be given by $A = 20 + 0.6X$.

   a. Explain this equation. Why is the intercept 20? Why is the relation between A and X positive?

   b. If the equilibrium requires that partygoers' expectations be correct, what is the equilibrium attendance at the Outcasts' party?

3. You are a manager of one of two identical widget-producing firms. Each firm produces the same good and faces the same costs of production described by the following cost function: Total Cost $= 1500 + 8q$ where q is the output of an individual firm. A market research company has found that market demand for widgets can be described as $P = 200 - 2Q$ where $Q = q_1 + q_2$, where q_1 is your output and q_2 is your rival's output. The board of directors has directed you to choose an output level that will *maximize* the firm's profit. If competition is Cournot, what output level will you choose? How will you explain your decision to the board of directors?

4. Assume that two firms sell differentiated products and face the following demand curves:

$$q_1 = 15 - p_1 + 0.5p_2 \text{ and } q_2 = 15 - p_2 + 0.5p_1$$

   a. Assume the firms choose prices and have equal and constant marginal cost $c = 0$. Derive each firm's best response function. Are prices strategic substitutes or complements?

   b. What is the equilibrium set of prices in this market? What profits are earned at those prices?

5. Consider the Bertrand model with spatially differentiated products along a line segment of unit length. Assume that there are three firms, each with an identical marginal cost of c. Assume that the three firms are symmetrically located with one at $x = 0$, one at $x = 1/2$, and one at $x = 1$. Derive the result suggested by the text that the equilibrium in this case is: $p_1 = p_2 = p_3 = c + t/2$. Do all three firms earn the same profit? Explain.

References

Bertrand, J. 1883. "Review," *Journal des Savants*, 68: 499–508, reprinted in English translation by James Friedman in A. F. Daughety (Ed.). 1988. *Cournot Oligopoly*. Cambridge: Cambridge University Press.

Bulow, J., J. Geanakopolos, and P. Klemperer, 1985. "Multimarket Oligopoly: Strategic Substitutes and Complements." *Journal of Political Economy*, 93 (June): 488–511.

Cournot, A. 1836. *Researches into the Mathematical Principles of the Theory of Wealth*. Paris: Hachette (English Translation by N.T. Bacon, New York: Macmillan, 1897).

D'Aspremont, C., J. Gabszewicz, and J. Thisse, 1979. "On Hotelling's Stability in Competition." *Econometrica*, 47 (September): 1145–1150.

Eaton, B. C. 1976. "Free Entry in One-Dimensional Models: Pure Profits and Multiple Equilibrium." *Journal of Regional Science*, 16 (January): 21–33.

Economides, N. 1989. "Symmetric Equilibrium Existence and Optimality in Differentiated Products Markets." *Journal of Economic Theory*, 27 (February): 178–194.

Friedman, J. 1977. *Oligopoly Theory*. Amsterdam: North Holland Press.

Hastings, J. 2004. "Vertical Relationships and Competition in Retail Gasoline Markets: Empirical Evidence From Contract Changes in Southern California." *American Economic Review*, 94 (March): 317–328.

Hotelling, H. 1929. "Stability in Competition." *Economic Journal*, 39 (January): 41–57.

Kreps, D. and J. Scheinkman. 1983. "Quantity Precommitment and Bertrand Competition Yield Cournot Outcomes." *Bell Journal of Economics*, 14 (Autumn): 326–337.

Marion, B. W., Mueller, W. F, Cotterill, R. W., Geithman, F. E. and Schmelzer, J. R. 1979. *The Food Retailing Industry Market Structure, Profits and Prices*. New York: Praeger.

Marvel, H. 1989. "Concentration and Price in Gasoline Retailing." In Leonard Weiss (Ed.). *Concentration and Price*. Cambridge, MA: MIT Press.

Mas-Colell, A., M. D. Whinston, and J. Green, 1995. *Microeconomic Theory*. New York: Oxford University Press.

Morrison, S. and Winston, C. 1996. "Causes and Consequences of Airline Fare Wars." *Brookings Papers on Economic Activity: Microeconomics*, 1996: 85–131.

Nash, J. 1950. "Equilibrium points in n-person games." *Proceedings of the National Academy of Sciences*, 36(1): 48–49.

———. 1951. "Non-Cooperative Games" *The Annals of Mathematics*, 54(2): 286–295.

Novshek, W., 1980. "Equilibrium in Simple Spatial (or Differentiated Products) Models." *Journal of Economic Theory*, 22 (June): 313–326.

Rasmusen, E., 2007. *Games and Information, An Introduction to Game Theory*. 4th Edition. Cambridge, MA: Basil Blackwell, Inc.

Schelling, T. 1960. *The Strategy of Conflict*. Cambridge Mass.: Harvard University Press.

Tedlow, R. 1996. *New and Improved: The Story of Mass Marketing in America*. 2nd Edition. Boston: Harvard Business School Press.

8

Dynamic Games and First and Second Movers

In 1928, after two years of product research and development, a previously small canning firm in Michigan called Fremont Canning, under the direction of Frank and Daniel Gerber, launched its new baby food line on a large scale. Gerber accompanied the new production with an advertisement in *Good Housekeeping* that included a coupon redemption program allowing parents to buy six tins of Gerber's soup and strained vegetables for $1.00 at a favorite grocer. Previously, the only prepared baby food on the market was a product made by a few small firms with annual production of less than 10,000 tins. It cost nearly three times the price Gerber offered and was sold only at special pharmacies.

Gerber's product launch was overwhelmingly successful. Within six months, the small Michigan firm had a national distribution. Its first-year sales reached 590,000 cans, with gross revenues of $345,000. Gerber had effectively created a new industry based on mass production and marketing. The firm changed its name to Gerber Products and introduced its famous logo, the Gerber baby. Of course, the company's monopoly did not last long. By 1935, more than 60 other manufacturers had introduced their own vitamin-rich, pressure-cooked, sealed baby foods. Yet Gerber retained its dominant position and to this day has a U.S. market share of over 75 percent, with the rest of the market split rather evenly between Beech-Nut and Heinz.

The development of the prepared baby food industry was sequential. Gerber introduced the product and sold it on a large scale. Other firms followed. Indeed, this sequential feature of the strategic interaction in this market may persist to this day among the three major surviving firms. Many claim that Gerber is still the industry leader, and that Heinz and Beech-Nut only make their move after Gerber announces its strategy.

The game in the baby food market appears to be quite different from the static, simultaneous games that we studied in the previous chapter. Games in which the players take their actions sequentially are dynamic games, and they are the focus of this chapter. In principal, these games can have many rounds of play. Here, we concentrate mostly on games with just two rounds or two periods of play and, for convenience, just two firms. Typically, one firm will play in the first round (the first mover) and the other will play in the second round (the second mover).

One difference between sequential and simultaneous games is that the order of play often confers an advantage to one player or another. When it is the player who goes first that gains, as is the case with some board games such as Tic-Tac-Toe and checkers, we say there is a first-mover advantage. Popular business literature is replete with stories about first-mover advantage in the business world and often gives advice as to how firms can establish a leadership position by moving first—much the way that Gerber did.[1]

Another classic example is the prepared soup industry. In the late 19th century, Campbell was the first entrant into the prepared soup market in the United States. In the early 20th century, Heinz was the first entrant in the U.K. market. Campbell entered the U.K. market after Heinz, and similarly Heinz entered the U.S. market after Campbell. Yet, the first mover in each market continues to dominate. Campbell has roughly 63 percent of the U.S. market, but only 9 percent of the U.K market; whereas Heinz has a 41 percent market share in the United Kingdom and a relatively minor market share in the United States.[2]

The observation that early entry into a market can confer substantial advantages relative to later entrants raises the possibility that an initial entrant's advantages are so great that it would be impossible for any subsequent firm to enter successfully. Since entry is a key part of a competitive market, we will address this important issue in both this chapter and the next. However, while the advantages of moving first are well-known, it is important to recognize that in many markets there is, instead, an advantage to playing second (i.e., a so-called second-mover advantage).

Our goal in this chapter is to examine the difference between sequential and simultaneous move games. Because simultaneous games are played at one point in time, they are sometimes referred to as static. In contrast, because sequential play must necessarily involve the passage of time between one move and the next, such games are dynamic.

In a market setting, static games can have an intertemporal component when the firms compete again and again, many times over. We call such games *repeated games*, and they have a different dynamic structure than the dynamic games we consider here. The dynamic games addressed in this chapter and the next are such that one player's choice establishes the environment in which a subsequent player moves. In contrast, in a repeated game, there need not be any link between the simultaneous play of one period and that of the next. We examine repeated games in Chapter 10.

We will see that an important issue in both dynamic and repeated games is the ability of a player to commit to a specific strategy in a way that rivals understand and believe. In other words, the commitment to a strategy has to be credible. In the marketplace, it is important to understand what commitment devices a firm might have.

8.1   THE STACKELBERG MODEL OF QUANTITY COMPETITION

When firms compete in quantity and the play is sequential we have the duopoly model of Stackelberg (1934). The firm that moves first and chooses its output level first is the leader firm. The firm that moves second is the follower firm. The sequential choice of output is what makes the game dynamic. However, the firms sell their goods on the market only once, and their interaction yields a "once-and-for-all" market-clearing outcome.

Let market demand again be represented by a continuous inverse demand function $P = P(Q) = P(q_1 + q_2)$ with $dP/dQ < 0$. Firm 1 is the Stackelberg leader who chooses output first, and Firm 2 is the follower who chooses its output *after* the choice of the

[1]   Lieberman and Montgomery (1988).
[2]   See Sutton (1991).

leader is made. Each firm has the same constant unit cost of production c. Total industry output Q equals the sum of the outputs of each firm, $Q = q_1 + q_2$.

Firm 1 acts first and chooses q_1. How should it make this choice? The answer is different from that of the Cournot analysis of Chapter 7. In that model, Firm 2 must make a (rational) guess of Firm 1's choice. In the current setting however, Firm 2 does not have to guess. It knows exactly what Firm 1 has done by the time that it makes its move. Equally, important, Firm 1 knows that Firm 2 will have this information.

Firm 1's profit is described by

$$\pi_1(q_1, q_2) = [P(q_1 + q_2) - c]q_1 \tag{8.1}$$

Firm 1 will recognize that Firm 2's choice will be on its best-response function, $R_2(q_1)$. As a result, Firm 1's maximization problem can be written as

$$\underset{q_1}{\text{Max}} \, \pi_1[q_1, q_2(q_1)] = P[q_1 + R_2(q_1)]q_1 - cq_1 \tag{8.2}$$

The solution is to choose q_1 such that the following condition holds:

$$P + q_1 \left[\frac{dP}{dQ}\right]\left[1 + \frac{dR_2(q_1)}{dq_1}\right] = c \tag{8.3}$$

We know from Chapter 7 that firms' output strategies are strategic substitutes and hence $dR_2(q_1)/dq_1 < 0$. More generally, the term $\left[1 + \frac{dR_2(q_1)}{dq_1}\right]$ must be less than $\frac{\partial Q}{\partial q_1}$, the change in total output due to a change in Firm 1's output level. Unlike the Cournot model in which Firm 1 takes Firm 2's output as given, the Stackelberg leader knows that as it expands output, the follower firm partly offsets this by reducing its output. This reduces the downward pressure on price that increases in Firm 1's output exert. Accordingly, Firm 1 now has a greater incentive to expand production than it did in the Cournot model. Yet if this is the case, then Firm 2 will produce less as a Stackelberg follower than it would as a Cournot duopolist; because, again, outputs are strategic substitutes so that the more Firm 1 produces, the less Firm 2 does. Since the two firms sell at the same price and have the same cost, there is clearly an advantage to being the Stackelberg leader rather than the follower. In other words, the Stackelberg game has a clear first-mover advantage. It therefore can serve as a starting point for explanations as to why early market pioneers such as Gerber continue their dominance for so long.

It is instructive to examine equation (8.3) in the case of a linear inverse demand function of the form $P = A - B(q_1 + q_2)$. Straightforward maximization reveals that Firm 2's best response function is

$$R_2(q_1): q_2 = \frac{A - c}{2B} - \frac{q_1}{2} \tag{8.4}$$

This implies that for the linear case

$$q_1\left(\frac{dP}{dQ}\right)\left(1 + \frac{dR_2(q_1)}{dq_1}\right) = -B\frac{q_1}{2} \tag{8.5}$$

Substituting both results into equation (8.3) then yields

$$A - B \left[q_1 + \frac{A - c}{2B} - \frac{q_1}{2} \right] - B \frac{q_1}{2} = c \tag{8.6}$$

Simplification then yields

$$q_1 = \frac{A - c}{2B}; \quad \text{and} \quad q_2 = \frac{A - c}{4B} \tag{8.7}$$

Equation (8.7) indicates that in the linear demand case, the Stackelberg leader produces twice as much output as the follower. Since both have the same cost and sell at the same price, this also implies that the leader earns twice the profit. The first-mover advantage in this case is relatively large.

There is something else that you might recognize in equation (8.7). The output of the leader is the same output as that chosen by a uniform pricing monopolist in this market. That is, the Stackelberg leader will in this case choose precisely the same output as would a textbook monopolist. The difference, of course, is that for the monopolist, there is no other firm and its output choice is also the total production level for the industry. In the Stackelberg model, the follower firm adds on to the leader's production, driving total output higher and prices lower. There is no doubt then that the Stackelberg duopoly model results in more output and lower prices than does the standard monopoly model. How does it compare with the equilibrium in the Cournot model?

If we start with the linear demand case just solved, the answer is straightforward. When demand is linear and unit cost is constant, a textbook monopolist produces half the competitive output. As we now know, this is also the output of the Stackelberg leader. Consequently, a review of equation (8.7) implies that the Stackelberg duopoly results in total industry output equal to three-fourths of the competitive level. By contrast, we know that the Cournot duopoly model with linear demand and constant unit cost yields two-thirds of the competitive output. The Stackelberg duopoly results in higher output and lower prices than does the Cournot duopoly model and so the Stackelberg duopoly is more efficient.

The foregoing finding is not limited to the simple, linear demand case. The Stackelberg duopoly will always yield output closer to the competitive level than will its Cournot counterpart for two closely related reasons. First, by going first, the first mover can claim a large output for itself—larger than that implied by its Cournot best-response function. Second, the follower's response to the leader's expansion is to reduce its output but by less than the first-mover's increase. Thus, total output rises closer to the competitive ideal.

Figure 8.1 shows the four possible industry equilibria for the linear demand and constant unit cost case. These are the monopoly output, the Cournot output, the Stackelberg output, and the competitive output, along with the total industry profit earned in each case. These illustrate an inverse relationship and a ranking that persists even for nonlinear demand settings. The competitive market has the greatest output and lowest total profit. The Stackelberg duopoly has less output and somewhat higher profit; the Cournot duopoly output falls further while industry profit rises; and the pure monopoly produces the least but generates the highest total profit of any of the market structures.

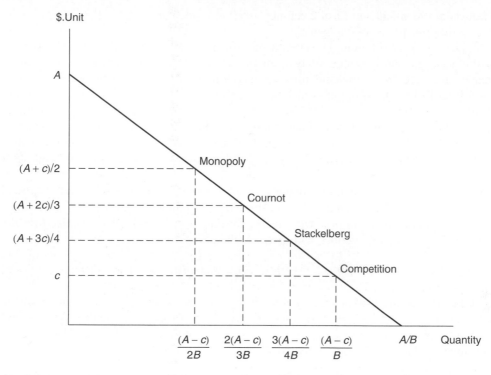

Figure 8.1   Monopoly, cournot duopoly, stackelberg duopoly, and competitive outcomes compared

8.2   SEQUENTIAL PRICE COMPETITION

What if the two firms—the leader and follower—in this dynamic game competed in price instead of quantity? If the firms are identical (that is, they produce the same product at the same cost unit), then the outcome to the sequential price-setting game is not much different from the simultaneous price game of the previous chapter. In a Nash equilibrium prices are set equal to marginal cost.

To see this, let us rework the Stackelberg quantity-setting model with instead each firm choosing the price it will charge. Firm 1 is the leader and sets its price first, and Firm 2 is the follower, setting its price second. The structural features of the market are the same as before. Each firm produces an identical good at the same constant marginal cost, c, and consumers will purchase the good at the lower-priced firm. If they set the same prices, then each firm will serve half the market demand.

In setting its price in stage 1, Firm 1 anticipates Firm 2's best response in stage 2. Clearly, Firm 2 will have an incentive to price below Firm 1's price any time that Firm 1 posts a price that is greater than marginal cost c. By undercutting, Firm 2 will serve the entire market and earn all the potential profits. On the other hand, if Firm 1 sets a price less than unit cost c, then Firm 2 will not match or undercut Firm 1's price, because Firm 2 has no interest in making any sales when each unit sold loses money. The leader's only choice is to set $p_1 = c$, a price that Firm 2 will not undercut. Since the products are identical and Firm 2 can never sell at a price $p_2 > p_1$, and $p_2 = p_1 = c$ are the equilibrium prices in this game.

Matters are very different, however, if the two firms are not selling identical products. In this case, not all consumers buy from the lower-priced firm. Product differentiation changes the outcome of dynamic price competition. To illustrate sequential price competition in a differentiated products market, we again use a variant of the Hotelling (1929) spatial model. There is a mass of N consumers distributed linearly along a line segment normalized to unit length. Each consumer is identified by her address x, which is the distance between the consumer's location and the left end of the segment, which is given the address 0. Hence, $1 - x$ is the consumer's distance from the right end of town.

Each of two firms are identified by the address s, where Firm 1 has $s = 0$ at the left-end point, while Firm 2 has address $s = 1$ at the right-end point. The firms have an identical unit cost c and compete in prices p_1 and p_2 for the consumers. Each consumer will buy at most one unit of the product, and each has the utility function

$$U(x, s) = V - p(s) - t|x - s|; \text{ with } s = 0, 1 \text{ and } p(0) = p_1 \text{ and } p(1) = p_2 \quad (8.8)$$

In order to find the demand facing the firms at prices p_1 and p_2, we assume that the market is fully served and each firm has positive market share. We identify the marginal consumer x^m, who is indifferent to buying from either Firm 1 or Firm 2. The marginal consumer's address must satisfy the condition

$$V - p_1 - tx^m = V - p_2 - t(1 - x^m) \quad (8.9)$$

Equation (8.9) implies that the address of the marginal consumer x^m is

$$x^m(p_1, p_2) = \frac{(p_2 - p_1 + t)}{2t} \quad (8.10)$$

When the market is fully served at prices, p_1 and p_2 all consumers to the left of x^m buy from Firm 1, and all those to the right of x^m buy from Firm 2. In other words, x^m is the fraction of the market buying from Firm 1 and $(1 - x^m)$ is the fraction buying from Firm 2. Since the mass of consumers N is uniformly distributed over the product space, the demand facing Firm 1 at price combination (p_1, p_2) is

$$q_1(p_1, p_2) = x^m(p_1, p_2)N = \frac{(p_2 - p_1 + t)}{2t}N \quad (8.11)$$

Similarly, Firm 2's demand function is

$$q_2(p_1, p_2) = (1 - x^m(p_1, p_2))N = \frac{(p_1 - p_2 + t)}{2t}N \quad (8.12)$$

We assume that Firm 1 is the price leader and sets its price p_1 anticipating Firm 2's best response to that price. As we showed in the last chapter, the best response function p_2 is

$$p_2 = \frac{p_1 + c + t}{2} = p_2(p_1) \quad (8.13)$$

Hence—conditional on the entire market being served—for a choice of price p_1, Firm 1's demand is

$$q_1(p_1, p_2(p_1)) = \frac{(p_2(p_1) - p_1 + t)}{2t} N = \frac{N}{4t}(c + 3t - p_1) \tag{8.14}$$

In turn, this implies that Firm 1's profit is

$$\pi_1(p_1, p_2(p_1)) = \frac{N}{4t}(p_1 - c)(c + 3t - p_1) \tag{8.15}$$

Maximizing (8.15) with respect to p_1 and setting $\frac{\partial \pi_1(p_1, p_2(p_1))}{\partial p_1} = 0$ yields

$$p_1 = c + \frac{3t}{2} \tag{8.16}$$

In turn, this implies that Firm 2's best response, as described by (8.13), is

$$p_2 = c + \frac{5t}{4} \tag{8.17}$$

The profit-maximizing prices in the simultaneous version of this game are $p_1 = p_2 = c + t$. A comparison of these prices with those in (8.16) and (8.17) reveals that prices in the sequential game are higher for both firms. Furthermore, substitution of (8.16) and (8.17) into equation (8.10) yields that the marginal consumer is located at address $x^m = 3/8$. Thus, Firm 1 charges the higher price and serves 37.5 percent of the market, while Firm 2 charges a lower price and serves 62.5 percent of the market. Profit for each firm is then

$$\pi_1(p_1, p_2) = (p_1 - c)x^m N = 0.5625Nt \tag{8.18}$$

$$\pi_2(p_1, p_2) = (p_2 - c)(1 - x^m)N = 0.78125Nt$$

The market outcome is described in Figure 8.2.

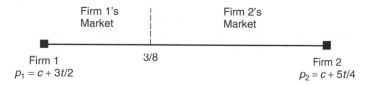

Figure 8.2 Sequential price competition: Firm 1 sets its price first, anticipating that Firm 2 will price below Firm 1's price

These results are very different from those obtained earlier in the quantity game. There, we found that the sequential Stackelberg duopoly produced more output and therefore sold at a lower market price than the simultaneous Cournot model. It also resulted in much greater profit for Firm 1, the first mover. However, moving from simultaneous to sequential play in a differentiated-product price game has led to an across-the-board rise in market prices—and greater profit for the follower firm.

The reasons for these differences are straightforward. Whereas quantities are strategic substitutes, prices are strategic complements. In the quantity game, Firm 2 reduces its output when Firm 1 raises its production. In a price game, the response function (8.13) makes clear that Firm 2 raises its price in response to a price hike by Firm 1. As a result, the price leader, Firm 1, knows that when it sets a high price, the falloff in business will be mitigated by the fact that the follower also raises her price—driving some consumers back to Firm 1. This softens the nature of the competition between the firms.

Although Firm 2 does raise its price in response to a price increase by Firm 1, it does not match the leader's increase fully. Instead, it raises its price, but by a smaller amount, so that Firm 2's price relative to Firm 1's price is less—attracting more customers and earning greater profit. Firm 1 is at a disadvantage in this case relative to Firm 2. Once Firm 1 makes a commitment to its price, Firm 2 is free to undercut it. While Firm 2 does not do this in an aggressive fashion—it does raise its price to some extent—the fact that it does not match Firm 1's price allows it to steal customers and profit for itself. Both firms are better off with sequential rather than simultaneous price competition; but the second mover is now advantaged relative to the first mover.

8.3   SEQUENTIAL QUALITY CHOICE

In Hotelling's (1929) spatial model, consumers agree on what they are willing to pay for their most preferred product, but they disagree on which product is the best or the highest quality. An alternative approach is one in which consumers agree on the ranking of product quality or what is the best but disagree regarding how much they are willing to pay for greater quality. In such a "vertically" differentiated product market, a firm's decision to produce either a high-quality or a low-quality product becomes important.

To understand the choice of quality in a sequential game, assume again that there are just two firms, 1 and 2, and two feasible qualities of some product. One is a high-quality product with quality index z_1. The other is low-quality and the index is $z_2 < z_1$. Define the quality difference $\Delta = z_1 - z_2$. Assume that Firm 1 produces the high-quality product, and Firm 2 produces the low-quality product. The unit cost of making a high-quality product is c_1, while the cost of making a low-quality product is c_2, with $c_1 > c_2$. We also assume that $\Delta > c_1 - c_2 > 0$, that is, that the increase in quality exceeds the increase in unit cost.

There is a mass of N consumers. Consumer i is indexed by the parameter θ_i, which we assume to be continuously and uniformly distributed from θ_L to θ_H. For convenience, we set $\theta_L = 0$ and $\theta_H = 1$. Each consumer buys at most one unit of the product and, if she does make a purchase, will choose the product whose quality and price gives the highest value of utility, given by

$$U_i = V + \theta_i z - p \tag{8.19}$$

Define the marginal consumer, θ_m. This value of θ solves the equation

$$\theta_m z_1 - p_1 = \theta_m z_2 - p_2 \geq 0 \tag{8.20}$$

It then immediately follows that

$$\theta_m = \frac{p_1 - p_2}{z_1 - z_2} = \frac{p_1 - p_2}{\Delta} \tag{8.21}$$

Note that we must have $p_1 > p_2$. Since everyone agrees that z_1 is of higher quality than z_2, no one will buy the low-quality product unless it has a lower price. Also, since $\theta_m \leq 1$, we must have that $p_1 - p_2 < \Delta$, otherwise no one will buy the high-quality product. Therefore, with $\Delta > p_1 - p_2 > 0$, those consumers with $1 \geq \theta_i \geq \theta_m$ will buy the high-quality product, and those consumers $0 \leq \theta < \theta_m$ will buy the low-quality product. Firm 1's demand will be

$$q_1(p_1, p_2) = N \int_{\theta_m}^{1} d\theta = N \left(1 - \frac{p_1 - p_2}{\Delta} \right) \tag{8.22}$$

Likewise, Firm 2's demand will be

$$q_2(p_1, p_2) = N \int_{0}^{\theta_m} d\theta = N \left(\frac{p_1 - p_2}{\Delta} \right) \tag{8.23}$$

The profit function for each firm is therefore

$$\pi_1(p_1, p_2) = (p_1 - c_1) N \left(1 - \frac{p_1 - p_2}{\Delta} \right) \tag{8.24}$$

$$\pi_2(p_1, p_2) = (p_2 - c_2) N \left(\frac{p_1 - p_2}{\Delta} \right) \tag{8.25}$$

The best-response function for Firm 1 is found by maximizing π_1 with respect to p_1 to yield

$$p_1 = \frac{(c_1 + \Delta + p_2)}{2} \tag{8.26}$$

Similarly, the best-response function for Firm 2 is

$$p_2 = \frac{(c_2 + p_1)}{2} \tag{8.27}$$

The Nash equilibrium with simultaneous pricing will then be

$$p_1 = \frac{2(c_1 + \Delta) + c_2}{3} \tag{8.28}$$

$$p_2 = \frac{2c_2 + c_1 + \Delta}{3} \tag{8.29}$$

Notice how the quality differential Δ raises the equilibrium price for *both* firms. As the difference in the quality of the two products grows, they become less and less of a substitute for each other. In turn, this softens the price competition between each firm and thereby permits each to charge a higher price. Again, prices are strategic complements. Therefore, factors that induce Firm 1 to charge a higher price will induce a similar response from Firm 2.

Substitution of the prices in equations (8.28) and (8.29) into the profit functions, (8.24) and (8.25), then implies that the profit for each firm is

$$\pi_1 = \frac{(2\Delta + c_2 - c_1)^2}{9\Delta} \tag{8.30}$$

$$\pi_2 = \frac{(\Delta + c_1 - c_2)^2}{9\Delta} \tag{8.31}$$

Given our assumptions that $\Delta > c_1 - c_2 > 0$, both profits are increasing in Δ. In addition, Firm 1 producing the high-quality product will have greater profit than its low-quality rival under the condition: $\Delta > 2(c_1 - c_2)$. If this condition does not hold, then the low-quality (and much lower-cost) firm will have the greatest profit.

We may now consider the sequential choice of product quality. The leader firm will choose to produce whichever product quality leads to the greatest profit. This will be the high-quality product if $\Delta \geq 2(c_1 - c_2)$, or the low-quality product if $\Delta < 2(c_1 - c_2)$. Whatever quality choice—high or low—is made by the leader, the opposite choice will be made by the follower. The follower will never wish to produce the same quality as the leader, as this would mean that they are producing identical products. In this case, competition in prices reproduces Bertrand's original model, where each firm earns zero profit.

8.4   COMMITMENT AND CREDIBILITY IN DYNAMIC GAMES

Whether the strategic variable is production level, price, or product quality, all of the above models assume that once the leader's choice is made, it will not be changed. In the Nash equilibrium for the Stackelberg game, the leader firm is not on its Cournot best-response function but, instead, is producing well beyond that output level. The follower firm is making its best response to the leader's extra production. Given the follower's low production level, the leader could do better and reduce its own production, returning to its best-response function. However if the leader firm could in fact change its output and the follower firm knew that this was possible, then the follower firm would anticipate this and not reduce its output level in the first instance. Instead, it will increase its production in anticipation of the leader's firm subsequent change. Ultimately, this anticipating output game will take us back to the Cournot-Nash equilibrium in the simultaneous game. If the leader firm is not committed to its first output choice, a change will be anticipated by the follower firm, and the game becomes analogous to the simultaneous move game.

The first mover or leader firm could announce publicly that it really intends to stay at the high output level of a Stackelberg leader. However, talk is cheap. If the leader simply announces an intention to produce the monopoly output without making any true commitment to that level, the follower has good reason to doubt that the leader will follow through with his announcement. Since the credibility of that first move is so crucial, we devote the rest of this chapter to developing a formal approach to credibility in game theory.

We begin by introducing a concept that is relevant to dynamic games—namely, that of a subgame. A subgame is a part of an entire game that can stand alone as a game in itself. A proper subgame is a game within a game. Simultaneous games cannot have proper subgames, but dynamic games can. A subgame in a two-period model could be price competition in the second period, which is a one-shot game nested within the larger two-period game.

Closely related to the notion of subgames is the concept of subgame perfection, first introduced by Nobel Prize winner Reinhard Selten (1978). It is the concept of subgame perfection that permits us to understand whether a firm's strategy is credible in a dynamic game. The term sounds very technical, but it is actually quite simple. Subgame perfection means that if a strategy chosen at the start of a game is optimal, it must be optimal to stick with that strategy at every later point in the game (or every subgame in the game).

Subgame perfection is a way of defining credibility for a game. If a player announces that he is adopting a strategy that is not subgame perfect, then the player's announcement

Reality Checkpoint

First-Mover Advantage in the TV Market: More Dishes and HigherPrice

We have emphasized that the analysis of first-mover advantage is complex. The consideration of the vertical quality model offers a case in point. When a firm markets a new good or service, its consumers are likely to be aware of the fact that it may not work that well. In particular, it may take time to learn how to use the good properly or to use it in such a way that one gets full use of all the features that the product or service contains. Think, for example, of such goods and services as personal computers, cellular phones, DVD players, online auctions, etc. It takes experience using an iPad or an Apple computer or purchasing a product on eBay before one really can get the most out of these products. Gabszewicz, Pepall, and Thisse (GPT) (1992) build on this idea to show how consumer learning may confer a first-mover advantage to the first firm to market a new product. Imagine a simple two-stage model. Firm 1 introduces its version of the new product, and a rival enters in the second stage with its own differentiated version of the same good. GPT argue that for those consumers who bought Firm 1's product in stage 1, they will know how it works, but they will not know that for Firm 2's new product. As a result, they will tend to prefer Firm 1's good, even if Firm 2 sells at a lower price.

Indeed, GPT show that the pricing implications can be quite novel. When Firm 1 introduces its product in stage 1, it foresees the later entry of Firm 2. Firm 1 will have an incentive to price very low in the first stage so as to induce a lot of consumers to try it and become experienced with its product before Firm 2 enters. This will create a large group of captive consumers for Firm 1 who will be willing to pay a higher price for its product in stage 2 now that they know how the product works. Thus, when Firm 2 enters, Firm 1 actually raises its price and still retains a larger number of consumers because they do not want to learn how to work with Firm 2's imperfect substitute. The first mover may not only have a large market share—we may actually see that firm raise its prices at the very time that new competition emerges—exactly the opposite of what simple textbook analysis often implies.

Evidence of the first-mover advantage suggested by GPT may come from the television market. Here, the initial new product was cable TV, which has rapidly spread so that now 70 percent of American homes receive cable service. The Telecommunications Act of 1996 essentially deregulated the cable TV industry, hoping that new firms, especially telephone companies, would provide competition to the local cable franchises. By and large, however, competition from alternative cable providers has remained weak. Instead, the major competition to cable that has emerged is from direct broadcast satellite (DBS) TV that consumers receive through a satellite dish. Textbook analysis would suggest that DBS competition would lead to lower cable prices. However, Goolsbee and Petrin (2004) find that, to the contrary, penetration of the market by DBS has led, on average, to an increase in the annual cable fee of about $34.68. The ability of cable firms to raise price as new rivals appear may reflect precisely the first-mover advantage noted by Gabszewicz, Pepall, and Thisse.

Source: Gabszewicz, J., L. Pepall, and J-F. Thisse. 1992. "Sequential Entry with Brand Loyalty Caused by Consumer Learning-By-Doing." *Journal of Industrial Economics*, 60 (December): 397–416; and Goolsbee, A., and A. Petrin, 2004. "The Consumer Gains from Direct Broadcast Satellite and Competition with Cable TV." *Econometrica*, 72 (March): 351–381.

lacks credibility and should not be believed. Why would a player take a future action that is not optimal at that point in the game, or for that subgame, and why should other players believe the player would take that action? The equilibrium concept for a dynamic game should be based on credibility or subgame perfection. When each player adopts a subgame-perfect strategy, the outcome is referred to as a subgame-perfect Nash equilibrium (SPNE).

To under how to apply the concept of subgame perfection, consider a simple game between two software firms. One is called Microhard (which is the incumbent firm already in the market) and the other is an upstart firm, Newvel, who wishes to enter the market. In this game, the potential entrant (Newvel) moves first, choosing either to enter Microhard's market or to stay out. If Newvel stays out, it earns a normal profit from being somewhere else in the economy, so economic profit is $\pi = 0$, and Microhard continues to earn a monopoly profit in the software market, say $\pi = 3$. If Newvel enters the market, then Microhard can choose either to accommodate the new entrant and share the market or to fight the new entrant by slashing prices. Microhard's Accommodation and Newvel's Entry results in each firm earning a profit $\pi = 1$. Fighting, however, leads to selling at a price below average total cost, in which case each firm earns $\pi = -1$.

A strategy for a dynamic game must specify decision rules for every possible point or move in the game. When a game extends over many periods of play, the strategy becomes more complex. However, for this simple dynamic game between Microhard and Newvel, we can use a payoff matrix to gain insight into which strategy pairs may yield a Nash equilibrium. Such a payoff matrix is shown in Figure 8.3 below.

Start with the combination (*Enter, Fight*). This cannot correspond to an equilibrium. Adopting *Enter* Newvel comes into the market. If Microhard has adopted the *Fight* strategy, it responds to entry very aggressively. Yet, as the payoff matrix makes clear, such an aggressive action is not Microhard's best response to entry by Newvel. By similar reasoning, the combination (*Stay Out, Accommodate*) cannot be a Nash equilibrium either. If Newvel knows that Microhard is ready to accommodate its entry, staying out is not in its best interest.

Now try (*Enter, Accommodate*). If Newvel chooses to enter, and if Microhard has adopted the strategy *Accommodate*, the associated outcome is a best response for both Newvel and Microhard. That is, if Microhard has adopted a strategy to *Accommodate*, then *Enter* is the best response for Newvel. Likewise, if Newvel enters, accommodating is a best response for Microhard. Therefore, the combination (*Enter, Accommodate*) is a Nash equilibrium.

What about the combination (*Stay Out, Fight*)? If Newvel chooses *Stay Out*, then the *Fight* strategy is a best response for Microhard; while if Microhard has chosen its *Fight* strategy, then *Stay Out* is a best response for Newvel. Therefore, (*Stay Out, Fight*) is a best response pair that seems to satisfy our concept of a Nash equilibrium. However, in this Nash equilibrium (*Stay Out, Fight*), Microhard never actually takes

		MICROHARD	
		Fight	Accommodate
NEWVEL	Enter	(−1, −1)	(1, 1)
	Stay Out	(0, 3)	(0, 3)

Figure 8.3   Payoff matrix for the Microhard and Newvel entry game

or implements a fighting action. Instead, it adopts a strategy that calls for it to do so if Newvel enters. It is the *threat* of such a fight that deters Newvel from entering. The Nash equilibrium concept is not based on what actions are actually observed in the market place, but rather upon what thinking or strategizing underlies what we observe.

By adopting the *Fight* strategy, Microhard may be interpreted as saying to Newvel, "I am going to price high so long as you stay out but, if you enter my market, I will cut my price and smash you." The problem is that this threat suffers a serious *credibility* problem. We already know that once Newvel has entered the market, taking action to fight back is not in Microhard's best interest. It does much better by accommodating such entry. Consequently, Microhard does not have an incentive to carry out its threat. So, why should Newvel believe that threat in the first place?

What we have really just discovered is that the combination (*Stay Out, Fight*) does not meet the criterion of subgame perfection. The game that takes place after Newvel makes its entry decision is a subgame of the game. In that subgame, Microhard will never wish to fight, therefore fighting is not a subgame-perfect strategy, and therefore (*Stay Out, Fight*) is not a subgame perfect Nash equilibrium (SPNE).

The fact that Microhard's *Fight* strategy is not subgame perfect is obscured in the payoff matrix (or normal form) of the game, because that characterization omits explicit consideration of the temporal nature of the game. It is for this reason that, for dynamic games, we prefer to use an extensive or tree representation that better captures the evolution of play over time. The extensive form of the game is shown in Figure 8.4 below.

With the Microhard and Newvel game in extensive form, it is easy to identify the unique SPNE for the game. A subgame is defined a single node by and all of the subsequent plays in the game from that node. Figure 8.4 shows two subgames. Again, a strategy combination is subgame perfect if the strategy for each player is a best response against the strategies of the other players for every subgame of the entire game. In the case at hand, it is readily apparent that for the subgame beginning at node M2, the best response strategy for Microhard is *Accommodate* and not *Fight*. Hence, the strategy combination (*Stay Out, Fight*) cannot be an SPNE. The only SPNE in this case is that of (*Enter, Accommodate*).

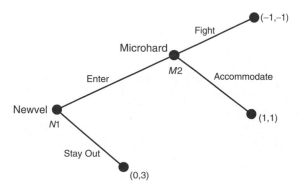

Figure 8.4   The extensive form of the Microhard-Newvel game

8.5   THE CHAIN-STORE PARADOX

In the Microhard and Newvel game, there is just one market and one potential entrant, and fighting the entrant was not an optimal response to entry. However, what if Microhard faced more than one entrant? Would it change matters if Microhard faced, say, 20 potential entrants in 20 different local markets? Perhaps protecting one market monopoly against entry is not worthwhile, but protecting 20 would be.

The fact that extension of the above game to many markets (distributed over time or space) and to other rivals may *not* lead to a different outcome is a famous result dubbed by Selten as *the Chain-Store Paradox*.[3] To see the logic of this puzzling result, consider a situation in which Microhard has established operating units in each of 20 markets, perhaps in 20 different cities. In each city, Microhard faces potential entry by a single competitor. At the moment, none of these potential competitors has the capital to start operations. However, as time goes on, one after another will raise the necessary funds. To make matters simple, assume that the payoffs in each of the 20 markets are given by the payoff matrix of the previous section. The question facing Microhard is how to react to this sequence of potential entrants. In particular, should Microhard adopt an aggressive response to the first entrant and drive it out of business?

Working backward can help us identify a subgame-perfect strategy. So, let us start with one possible scenario in which Microhard is facing the last potential entrant in the final, 20th market. For the moment, suppose that Microhard has followed through on its threat to cut prices and drive out any entrant—not just in the first market, but in all 19 previous markets. This is a feasible path in the game, and we are interested in seeing if such an aggressive response to entry can convince the last potential entrant to stay out, so that Microhard would be spared a fight in this final case.

Consider the viewpoint of the entrant to the 20th market. What happens in this market is, of course, a subgame. This firm will realize that because there are no subsequent entrants, this subgame is exactly like the one-period game we discussed in the previous section. Therefore, using the argument of that section, this last entrant will understand that Microhard has an incentive to accommodate its entry. Microhard's profit is greater if it follows a "live and let live" strategy in this last case. Accordingly, it will definitely accommodate the entry of a rival in this final market. Any threat to fight in the 20th market is *not* credible, and is not part of a subgame-perfect strategy.

Even though *Fight* cannot be part of Microhard's strategy for the 20th market, the question remains whether it still might be part of a strategy for the other markets. To see why this is not possible, consider now the potential entrant in the 19th rather than the 20th market. Once again, let us take the extreme case in which Microhard has taken predatory or fighting action in the prior 18 markets. Now, the potential entrant in the 19th market can reason as well as we can. As a result, this firm will work out the logic of the preceding case and rightfully conclude that Microhard will not fight in the 20th market. The entrant in the 19th or next-to-last market will then reason as follows: "Microhard will let the last rival firm survive, because it is pointless to cut prices at that point regardless of what happens in my market. That is, the last subgame's outcome is independent of what happens in the previous 19 markets. Because of this independence, the 19th market is effectively the final game. Yet, in that case, there is no reason for Microhard to fight

---

[3]   Selten (1978). We have limited ourselves here to consideration of finitely repeated games only.

my entry either. Doing so will not change what has already happened in the previous 18 markets and, as just noted, does not affect what happens in the following market." It follows that in the subgame starting with market 19, Microhard's strategy must be to play *Accommodate* in both remaining periods. Understanding this, the rival in the 19th market will enter, just as will the rival in the 20th.

We can continue in this fashion repeatedly, rolling back all the way to the initial market. At every stage, we will find that a strategy to fight after entry occurs is not subgame perfect and, accordingly, not credible. This will be just as true in the first market as in the last. There is no way for the incumbent to threaten credibly an aggressive low-price response to entry.

In the foregoing entry game the only SPNE is one in which entry occurs and fighting never happens. Microhard gains no advantage in any market even though it may be the first in the market when it comes to deterring entry. Instead, it has to accommodate and watch as its market position erodes as entry occurs in each of the 20 markets. This may lead you to think that being first to move does not really confer much benefit or even have much effect, and so wonder why being a first mover has received so much attention in the economics and business literature.

The point is not that the order of play is inconsequential. Instead, the key insight is the dual one that we stated at the outset—namely, that what makes the order of play important is the ability to commit credibly to a specific strategy. For example, return to the Microhard example above, but now suppose that entrants know that there are two types of incumbents but cannot tell which is which. Ninety percent are rational and pursue profit-maximizing strategies, just as we normally assume. However, 10 percent of incumbents are irrational and will fight to keep entrants out, even when it is not profitable to do so. Potential entrants now face uncertainty because they cannot know for sure what type Microhard is.

In this scenario, we can imagine that even a rational firm may wish to fight in some of the initial markets. Doing so may convince later potential entrants of its "craziness," that is, that it will retaliate aggressively against entry despite the fact that it is not profitable to do so in any one market. Faced with a 10 percent chance that the incumbent is of the irrational type, potential entrants may in fact decide that it is not worthwhile to enter. In other words, by "Fighting" in a few early markets, the incumbent Microhard may develop a reputation for "craziness" that in fact makes the threat of "Fighting" in later markets credible.

In this alternative game, Microhard does gain an advantage from moving in some markets before play occurs in others. It allows Microhard to take actions that, while costly, make its later promise to fight believable. The lesson is that unlike talk, credibility does not come cheap. It has to be earned, and that can be expensive. However, without such credibility, a firm cannot truly exploit its first-mover position.

The Stackelberg incumbent, the industry price leader, and the quality pioneer can only exploit their first mover advantage when their commitment to their strategy is credible. Often it requires a real expense to establish such credibility; but it can be worthwhile to incur this expense. In subsequent chapters, we will explore the mechanisms available to firms to establish the credibility in dynamic games.[4]

---

[4] Schelling (1960) contains early and lasting contributions to developing equilibrium notions for dynamic games. See also Tirole (1988) and Rasmusen (2007).

Summary

Dynamic games with sequential moves are different from simultaneous ones. The order of play is one of the rules of the game that has potentially large consequences, though the effects differ depending on whether the strategic variable of choice is quantity or price. The basic sequential-quantity game, typically known as the *Stackelberg model*, confers a large advantage to the firm that chooses production first. In the linear demand and cost case, the first mover in a Stackelberg game produces the monopoly output. The follower produces only half this much. Prices are lower than in the basic Cournot model, but the large market share of the first mover gives that firm an increase in profit over what it would earn in the simultaneous-production game.

Instead of quantity, firms may move sequentially in choosing price or quality. Here again, the order of play can be important. In the case of a sequential-price game in a differentiated-product market, the choice variables are strategic complements, and it is typically the second mover that does best. However, both firms are better off with sequential play in pricing than they would be with simultaneous play.

Crucial to the exploitation of the order of moves in a sequential game is the issue of commitment. In the linear Stackelberg game, for example, if a leader can easily reverse her first move, then her commitment to the monopoly output becomes suspect, since it is not on her best-response curve. Anticipating that the leader's first move will be reversed leads a follower to disregard any choice other than the Cournot one, and the game quickly reverts to the Cournot duopoly. Thus, a central issue that emerges regards the ability of firms to establish credibility regarding their strategy choices.

Typically, credibility comes with a cost. Firms have to demonstrate their commitment, and that usually requires some sacrifice. Yet, it is only when credibility has been established that firms can truly exploit the advantages that come from sequential play. In this light, the question is not simply whether credibility can be established, but also whether the cost in doing so is justified by the gains it yields. These issues are particularly important in considering entry deterrence or predation by large incumbents and in considering collusive agreements among firms that would otherwise compete. We address these topics in the next two chapters.

Problems

1. Consider a Stackelberg game of quantity competition between two firms. Firm 1 is the leader, and Firm 2 is the follower. Market demand is described by the inverse demand function $P = 1000 - 4Q$. Each firm has a constant unit cost of production equal to 20. Solve for the Nash equilibrium outcome.

2. Suppose, in the above problem, Firm 2's unit cost of production is $c < 20$. What value would c have to be so that in the Nash equilibrium the two firms, leader and follower, had the same market share?

3. In Tuftsville, everyone lives along Main Street, which is 10 miles long. There are 1000 people uniformly spread up and down Main Street, and each day they each buy a fruit smoothie from one of the two stores located at either end of Main Street. Customers ride their motor scooters to and from the store, and the motor scooters use $0.50 worth of gas per mile. Customers buy their smoothies from the store offering the lowest price, which is the store's price plus the customer's travel expenses getting to and from the store. Ben owns the store at the west end of Main Street, and Will owns the store at the east end of Main Street. The marginal cost of a smoothie is constant and equal to $1 for both Ben and Will. In addition, each of them pays Tuftsville $250 per day for the right to sell smoothies. Ben sets his price p_1 first, and then Will sets his price p_2. After the prices are posted, consumers get on their scooters and buy from the store with the lowest price including travel expenses.
   a. What prices will Ben and Will set?
   b. How many customers does each store serve, and what are their profits?

4. In Centipede[5] there are two players. Player 1 moves first, Player 2 moves second. After at most two moves, the game ends. The game begins with $1 sitting on a table. Player 1 can either take the $1 or wait. If Player 1 takes the $1, the game is over, and Player 1 gets to keep the $1. If Player 1 waits, the $1 quadruples to $4. Now it is Player 2's turn. Player 2 can either take the entire $4 or split the $4 evenly with Player 1.
   a. Draw the extensive form for the game of Centipede.
   b. What is the equilibrium to this game? Can Player 2's strategy of splitting the money ever be part of an equilibrium outcome to the game?

5. Now suppose that Centipede has three moves. Player 2 can now wait, split the money, or take the $4. If Player 2 waits, then the money on the table quadruples again and Player 1 can either take it all or split it. Draw the extensive form for the new game and solve for the equilibrium outcome.

6. Suppose that Firm 1 can choose to produce good A or good B or both goods or nothing. Firm 2, on the other hand, can produce only good C or nothing. Firms' profits corresponding to each possible scenario of goods for sale are described in the following table:

Products Marketed	Firm 1's Profit	Firm 2's Profit
A	20	0
A, B	18	0
A, B, C	2	−2
B, C	−3	−3
C	0	10
A, C	8	8
B	11	

   a. Set up the normal form game for when the two firms simultaneously choose their product sets. What is the Nash equilibrium (or equilibria)?
   b. Now, suppose that Firm 1 can commit to its product choice before Firm 2. Draw the extensive form of this game and identify its subgame perfect Nash equilibrium. Compare your answer to (a) and explain.

7. The Gizmo Company has a monopoly on the production of gizmos. Market demand is described as follows: at a price of $1,000 per gizmo, 25,000 units will be sold; whereas at a price of 600, 30,000 will be sold. The only costs of production are the initial sunk costs of building a plant. Gizmo Co. has already invested in capacity to produce up to 25,000 units.
   a. Suppose an entrant to this industry could capture 50 percent of the market if it invested in $10 million to construct a plant. Would the firm enter? Why or why not?
   b. Suppose Gizmo could invest $5 million to expand its capacity to produce 40,000 gizmos. Would this strategy be a profitable way to deter entry?

References

Gabszewicz, J., Pepall, L. and J-F. Thisse. 1992. "Sequential Entry with Brand Loyalty Caused by Consumer Learning-By-Doing." *Journal of Industrial Economics*, 60 (December): 397–416.

Goolsbee, A. and A. Petrin. 2004. "The Consumer Gains from Direct Broadcast Satellite and Competition with Cable TV." *Econometrica*, 72 (March): 351–381.

Hotelling, H. 1929. "Stability in Competition." *Economic Journal*, 39: 41–57.

---

[5] This game was first introduced by Rosenthal (1981).

Lieberman, Marvin B. and David B. Montgomery. 1988. "First Mover Advantages." *Strategic Management Journal*: 41–49.

Rasmusen, E. 2007. *Games and Information*. 4th Edition. Cambridge, MA: Basil Blackwell, Inc.

Rosenthal, R. W. 1981. "Games of Perfect Information, Predatory Pricing, and the Chain-Store Paradox." *Journal of Economic Theory*, 25 (August): 92–100.

Schelling, T., 1960. *The Strategy of Conflict*. Cambridge, MA: Harvard University Press.

Selten, R. 1978. "The Chain-Store Paradox." *Theory and Decision*, 9 (April): 127–159.

Stackelberg, H. von. 1934. *Marktform und Gleichgewicht*, Berlin and Vienna. English translation by A. T. Peacock (1952). London: William Hodge.

Sutton, J. 1991. *Sunk Cost and Market Structure*. Cambridge, MA: MIT Press.

Tirole, J. 1988. *The Theory of Industrial Organization*. Cambridge: MIT Press.

9

Entry Deterrence and Predation

Elementary microeconomics textbooks present monopoly power as a transient phenomenon. The argument is that whenever a firm acquires market power and earns supernormal profit, entry will occur, and the new entrants will reestablish a competitive market. Those who study actual real-life markets, however, know that this scenario may be more the exception than the rule. Campbell, for example, has held a dominant position with more than 70 percent of U.S. tinned canned soup sales for nearly a century. For 25 years, Microsoft has maintained control of over 90 percent of the market for operating systems software.[1] Sotheby's and Christie's have together controlled roughly 90 percent of the world auction market for two decades. These instances of sustained dominance are common. Moreover, such anecdotal evidence is buttressed by the work of Baldwin (1995) and Geroski and Toker (1996) who find that, on average, the number 1 firm in an industry retains that rank for somewhere between 17 and 28 years.

There is abundant evidence that, in contrast to the textbook representation, market power is lasting. This raises the question, then, as to how such firms can sustain their profit-winning position. Why don't new rivals emerge to compete away market share and profit? Are there strategies that the dominant firms can adopt to prevent this from happening? If so, what are these strategies, and what are their implications for market efficiency?

The questions just raised are the focus of this chapter. They are of much more than mere academic interest. The potential for large incumbent firms to eliminate or prevent the entry of rivals goes to the heart of what motivated the creation of the antitrust laws and their enforcement. It lay at the crux of the Microsoft antitrust case.[2] Section 2 of the Sherman Act deems it illegal to "monopolize or attempt to monopolize . . . any part of the trade or commerce." It follows that enforcement of this provision requires an understanding of what a firm can do in order to "monopolize" the market.

It can be useful to distinguish between two types of strategies by which dominant firms may preserve their dominance. One set of strategies aims at deterring rival firms from entering the market in the first place. A second set of strategies aims instead at driving existing rivals out. Practically speaking, the second set of strategies receives the most

---

[1] See "Squeeze Gently." *The Economist* (30 November 1996), p. 65–66.

[2] Indeed, each of the firms mentioned has been accused of unfair practices and has been the subject of antitrust scrutiny.

public policy attention, because these are cases in which there is an identifiable "victim" of the *predatory* conduct.[3] Of course, the two are not unrelated. A firm that establishes a reputation for driving out existing rivals may very well find that this also deters entry by others. In this chapter, we address both types of predatory conduct. Such conduct typically incurs costs for the predatory firm as well as its victim. Accordingly, it will only be pursued if the profit gain from insuring the dominant position outweighs these costs.

The Chain Store Paradox discussed in the previous chapter is relevant to the analysis of predatory conduct. As we saw there, predatory actions may not be part of a subgame-perfect strategy, because they are inconsistent with the firm's best response. A convincing model of predation must have some mechanism by which the predator can credibly commit to a predatory action that it would not otherwise take. The analysis of models that include precisely these features lies at the heart of this chapter.

9.1   MARKET STRUCTURE OVER TIME: RANDOM PROCESSES & STYLIZED FACTS

Before we begin to model incumbent firm strategies to deter rivals' entry and encourage rivals' exit, it is helpful to consider what theory and evidence can tell us about how an industry's structure might evolve over time. For example, consider an industry comprised of 256 firms, each with sales of $10 million. Suppose that in any period, sales at each firm will decline by 15 percent with probability 0.25, stay the same with probability 0.5, or rise by 15 percent with probability 0.25, regardless of the firm's size. (If these rates of growth or decline seem large, think of a period as three or four years long.) Table 9.1 shows the evolution of firm size over just four periods. We can see that even over this short amount of time, the distribution of firm sizes is becoming very unequal and skewed. The largest firm is now nine times as large as the smallest, and the top nine firms account for roughly the same amount of output as the bottom 37. This inequality is reflected in the fact that while the median firm size is still $10 million, the average size is now $10.7 million. This inequality will grow even larger as we let the process run over longer periods of time.

The trend toward increasing inequality is a common feature of all processes in which growth in any period is a random variable independent of firm size and previous growth rates. Robert Gibrat (1931) was the first to make this argument formally. His analysis

Table 9.1   Size distribution of firms after four years, starting with 256 equal-sized firms

	Sales (Millions)								
	$3.50	$4.55	$5.92	$7.69	$10	$13.0	$16.90	$21.97	$28.56
Period 0	0	0	0	0	256	0	0	0	0
Period 1	0	0	0	64	128	64	0	0	0
Period 2	0	0	16	64	96	64	16	0	0
Period 3	0	4	24	60	80	60	24	4	0
Period 4	1	8	28	56	70	56	28	8	1

[3]   See, for example, Fisher (1991).

proceeds as follows. Let X_t be a firm's size at time t. Let this be related to its size at t-1 by the following stochastic process:

$$X_t = (1 + v_t)X_{t-1} \tag{9.1}$$

Here, v_t is a random disturbance term that we assume is normally distributed and has mean μ and variance σ^2. Next, take the natural log of both sides. If the time interval between t and $t - 1$ is short, we may use the approximation that $\ln(1 + v_t) \approx v_t$. Using lower case letters to denote logs, we may then write

$$x_t = x_{t-1} + v_t \tag{9.2}$$

Denoting x at time $t = 0$ as x_0, we may then use repeated substitution to obtain

$$x_t = x_0 + v_t + v_{t-1} + v_{t-2} + v_{t-3} + \cdots + v_0 \tag{9.3}$$

This last equation says that the logarithm of the firm's size at time t will just be a random variable reflecting the accumulation of all the random growth shocks it has experienced up to that time. Each shock is itself a random variable drawn from the normal distribution. So, over k time periods, as the relative importance of x_0 approaches 0, x_t will converge to a random variable with mean $k\mu$ and variance $k\sigma^2$. In turn, since logarithmic transformations are nonlinear, this implies that the distribution of actual firm sizes will be heavily skewed.

Gibrat's (1931) approach suggests that oligopoly is an inevitable outcome how markets evolve over time. Even without consideration of mergers, dissolutions, bankruptcies, technical innovations, and predatory actions, Gibrat's assumed stochastic process shows that industries naturally converge to an oligopolistic structure in which a few firms dominate the market. Of course, the Gibrat process is a very bare-bones explanation of market structure evolution. Precisely what is in the assumed random shock terms is left out. However, subsequent attempts to put some flesh on those bones and to fill out the underlying mechanisms at play are in Jovanovic (1982), Nelson and Winter (1982), Sutton (1997), Klepper (2002), and Norman, Pepall, and Richards (2008). These papers confirm the insight that there are some strong underlying forces that tend to push industries toward an asymmetric oligopolistic structure. The important lesson to be drawn is that we should be cautious about concluding that the sustained dominance and asymmetric market structure, characteristic of so many markets, is largely the result of predatory actions by the largest firms.

The above papers are also consistent with four stylized empirical facts on entry and exit established over the last 20 years. The first of these is that *entry is common*. Dunne et al. (1988, 1989), using U.S. census data between 1963 and 1982, computed rates of entry in a wide cross section of two-digit SIC manufacturing industries. Their estimate of the average entry rate in manufacturing—defined as the number of *new* firms over a five-year period relative to the number of incumbent firms at the start of that period—ranged between 41.4 percent and 51.8 percent (about 8–10 percent on an annual basis). For the United Kingdom, Geroski (1995) estimated somewhat smaller (but still significant) annual rates of entry for a sample of 87 three-digit manufacturing industries. These ranged between 2.5 percent and 14.5 percent over the period 1974–1979. Cable and Schwalbach (1991) show that similar rates of entry obtain across a wide range of developed countries. More recently, Jarmin et al. (2004) show that rates of entry are even higher in the retail sector and may reach well over 60 percent, especially during periods of economic prosperity.[4]

The second stylized fact is that when entry occurs it is, by and large, *small-scale entry*. The studies by Dunne et al. (1988, 1989) showed that the collective market share of entrants in an industry ranged between 13.9 percent and 18.8 percent again over a five-year interval.[5] Similarly, in Geroski's (1995) U.K. study, the market share of entrants was found to be quite modest, ranging from 1.45–6.35 percent. In the United States, Cable and Schwalbach (1991) found that while new entrants typically constituted 7.7 percent of an industry's firms in any year, they account for only 3.2 percent of its output. The typical share of entrants in retailing is noticeably larger—closer to 25 percent according to Jarmin et al. (2004)—but they also find that this value has been declining over recent years.

The third stylized fact is that the *survival rate is relatively low*. Dunne et al. (1988, 1989) find that roughly 61.5 percent of all entrant firms exited within five years of entry and 79.6 percent exited within 10 years. The corresponding exit rates found in retailing by Jarmin et al. (2004) are very similar, between 59 percent and 82 percent. Birch (1987) used Dun and Bradstreet data for all sectors in the United States, including (but not limited to) manufacturing, and found that about 50 percent of all new entrant firms fail within the first five years.

Our final stylized fact that appears to hold in every study is that while rates of entry and exit vary across industries, *industries with high entry rates also have high exit rates*. In other words, entry and exit rates are strongly correlated. To take just one clear example, Cable and Schwalbach (1991) find that corresponding to an entry rate of 7.7 percent accounting for 3.2 percent of industry output, the exit rate is 7.0 percent—and, similarly, it accounts for 3.3 percent of industry output.

Taken together, the stylized facts suggest a sort of revolving-door setting in which mostly small firms enter, eventually fail, and exit, only to be replaced by a new cohort of small-scale entrants. In this light, the major difference across industries would be the pace at which this entry-fail-exit cycle proceeds. Moreover, the evidence is consistent with repeated attempts and failures of small firms aiming to penetrate the markets dominated by large incumbents. This would help explain the correlation between entry and exit rates. Incumbents in the most attractive markets may, for that very reason, fight the hardest against new entrants.

More formal support for the view that there is something special about long-standing incumbent firms is provided by Urban et al. (1984). They studied 129 frequently purchased brands of consumer products in 12 U.S. markets and found that market shares were a decreasing function of the order of entry of the brand. Earlier entrants enjoyed larger market shares, all else being equal. Similar results have been found by Lambkin (1988), Mitchell (1991), and Brown and Lattin (1994).[6] This finding is also consistent with the possibility that early (and surviving) entrants possess superior cost efficiency or offer

---

[4]   The Dunne et al. (1988, 1989) entry (and exit) estimates are generally higher than those obtained by other researchers, owing to the fact that they explicitly recognize the multiproduct and multiplant nature of firms.

[5]   Dunne et al. (1988) find that existing firms who enter a new market through diversification typically enter at a larger scale than new, or *de novo*, entrants do.

[6]   As Caves (1998) notes, though, there is regression toward the mean in firm growth rates. That is, really large firms tend to grow more slowly than small ones. This feature blunts the ever-increasing concentration tendency implied by Gibrat's Law.

better product or service quality due to experience. However, it is frequently alleged (especially by the failed entrants) that the ability of incumbents to sustain a dominant industry position also reflects predatory behavior aimed at both potential and actual new entrants. This is the primary issue to which we now turn.

9.2   DETERRING ENTRY

Consider the Stackelberg duopoly model of Chapter 8, in which each of the two firms has a constant marginal cost c and in which (inverse) demand is linear and described by the equation $P = A - Q$. We know from our previous analysis that the follower firm's best-response output q_F to any output choice q_L by the leader is given by

$$q_F = \frac{A - c}{2} - \frac{q_L}{2} \tag{9.4}$$

Knowing this response, the Stackelberg leader chooses output $q_L = \frac{A-c}{2}$ to maximize its profits, implying an output choice of $\frac{A-c}{4}$ for the follower firm. Profits for each firm are then

$$\begin{aligned}
\pi_L &= \frac{(A - c)^2}{8} \\
\pi_F &= \frac{(A - c)^2}{16}
\end{aligned} \tag{9.5}$$

This simple model gives a clear advantage to the firm that moves first. It produces twice as much output and earns twice as much profit as its rival. If we then interpret incumbency as the ability to move first, this simple model already gives us an explanation for the observed dominance of incumbent firms. Simply by exploiting its advantage to move first, the incumbent gains the ability to control a dominant share of the industry's output and earn a dominant share of the industry's profit. However, this first-mover advantage is rooted in the credibility of the leader's commitment to produce $q_L = \frac{A-c}{2}$. Without this commitment, the model reverts to the Cournot duopoly model, in which the firms have symmetric outcomes.

9.2.1   Limit Output and Limit Price Models

Because the Stackelberg leader chooses an output level that maximizes its profit if the rival firm enters, we cannot call its actions predatory. Predation is present when the dominant firm's actions are only profitable if they drive the rival out or, in this case, keep it from entering. However, with a little imagination, we can modify the analysis to accommodate predatory behavior. To do this we assume that the follower or potential entrant must incur a one-time sunk entry cost F to enter the market. This does not change the rival's best response to any output choice of the incumbent as described by equation (9.4). However, that equation only describes the follower firm's best response if it actually produces any output. If it turns out that, even with its best response, the follower earns a negative profit, it will choose not to enter at all.

Given the follower's best response, market price for any output choice q_L of the leader is

$$P = \frac{A + c}{2} - \frac{q_L}{2} \qquad (9.6)$$

This implies that the entrant's profit π_F will be

$$\pi_F = \left(\frac{A - c}{2} - \frac{q_L}{2} \right)^2 - F \qquad (9.7)$$

By choosing an output that makes this profit 0, the leader can thereby eliminate any incentive for the follower firm to enter. Thus, it would appear that the leader could deter entry by choosing

$$q_L^d = A - c - 2\sqrt{F} \qquad (9.8)$$

Note that the entry-deterring output of the leader is decreasing in the fixed costs F of the follower. Intuitively, it is easier for the leader to deter entry when the follower faces higher entry costs. More importantly, this implies that there is a value of fixed costs for the follower, above which entry is deterred without explicit strategic action by the leader. From (9.7), if the leader produces $(A - c)/2$, then profit to the follower is negative for any value of fixed costs greater than $(A - c)^2/16$. If the entrant's fixed costs of entry are greater than $(A - c)^2/16$, then entry to this market is *blockaded*—the incumbent need not take any explicit action to deter entry.

As a result, we should rewrite the entry-deterring output of the leader as

$$q_L^d = \max \left\{ \frac{A - c}{2}, A - c - 2\sqrt{F} \right\} \qquad (9.8a)$$

Second, it must be that entry deterrence is more profitable for the leader than accommodating entry and acting as a Stackelberg leader. Confine attention to the case where $F < (A - c)^2/16$, and entry deterrence requires explicit strategic action by the leader. Observe that if the follower's fixed costs are $F = 0$, then entry deterrence by the leader requires an output of $q_L^d = A - c$, in which case price is $P = c$ and the leader makes 0 profit. In these circumstances, it is better for the leader to accommodate entry. Now suppose that F is not 0. The entry-deterring output $q_L^d = A - c - 2\sqrt{F}$ results in a price of $P = c + 2\sqrt{F}$ and profit to the leader of

$$\pi_L^d = 2(A - c)\sqrt{F} - 4F \qquad (9.9)$$

Accommodating entry, by contrast, has the leader choosing output $(A - c)/2$ and earning profit, from (9.5), of $(A - c)^2/8$. For entry deterrence to be optimal for the leader it must be that

$$2(A - c)\sqrt{F} - 4F > (A - c)^2/8 \qquad (9.10)$$

This looks a bit complicated but can be made much more tractable using a simple substitution. In (9.9), make the substitution $\sqrt{F} = \alpha(A - c)/4$ with $0 \leq \alpha < 1$. As we have seen, when $\alpha = 0$, entry deterrence is unprofitable; while if $\alpha = 1$, entry would never happen. Substituting in (9.9) then gives $\pi_L^d = (A - c)^2 \alpha (2 - \alpha)/4$ and allows us to express the entry-deterring condition (9.10) as

$$2\alpha(2 - \alpha) > 1 \tag{9.11}$$

This condition holds for $\alpha > \alpha^d = 1 - 1/\sqrt{2}$ (recall that we need only consider values of $\alpha < 1$).

Intuitively, when the entrant's fixed costs are low enough ($\alpha < \alpha^d$), entry deterrence is not profitable. By contrast, if the entrant's fixed costs are higher ($\alpha > \alpha^d$), the leader finds it profitable to deter entry by increasing output to $q_L^d = A - c - 2\sqrt{F} = (A - c)(2 - \alpha)/2$.

In short, the incumbent leader firm can act strategically to limit entry. To begin with, its first-mover advantage permits it to stake out a dominant share of the market and thereby reduce the scale of any entry. That action is not predatory as the incumbent is simply pursuing the maximization of its own profit. However, there are market conditions under which the incumbent can do even better and preclude entry altogether by choosing output q_L^d. In that case, we may view the incumbent's action as a commitment that the market price will never be greater than $P = c + 2\sqrt{F}$. Following the work of Bain (1956) and Sylos-Labini (1962), it is conventional to call this price the *limit price* $\overline{P}$. By analogy then, we may call the entry-deterring output level the *limit output* $\overline{Q}$.

Two features of the limit output or limit price model are noteworthy. First, note that choosing to produce the limit output is only profitable because it prevents the follower firm from entering. Thus, this action *does* meet our requirement for true predation. Second, for the entry-deterring action to be effective, the incumbent firm must be able to commit to the limit output. A central question then emerges regarding how the incumbent may make such a commitment credibly.

9.2.2   Capacity Expansion as a Credible Entry-Deterring Commitment

In a key article, Spence (1977) recognized that what may make limit pricing a credible deterrent strategy is the incumbent firm's ability to make a prior and irrevocable investment in production capacity—specifically, an investment in the *capacity* to produce the limit output $\overline{Q}$. Subsequently, Dixit (1980) offered a complete model in which such behavior is subgame perfect or credible. We present the essentials of his model below.

We assume a dynamic or two-stage game between two firms. In the first stage, the incumbent firm moves first and chooses a capacity level $\overline{K}_1$ at a cost $r\overline{K}_1$. This capacity is measured in terms of output, and the cost r is the constant cost of one unit of capacity. By investing in capacity $\overline{K}_1$ in the first stage of the game, the incumbent firm has the ability in stage 2 of producing any output less than or equal to $\overline{K}_1$ at the cost of w per unit, reflecting the cost of variable inputs needed per unit of output in addition to plant capacity. The incumbent's capacity can be further increased in stage 2 of the game. However, it cannot be reduced. One may think of the capacity investment as the construction of, say, a sugar refining plant, for which any other industry has little use. If so, the plant cannot be resold if the firm decides it no longer needs it. In this sense, the $r\overline{K}_1$ spent on capacity investment in stage 1 is sunk.

The potential entrant is assumed to observe the incumbent's choice of capacity in stage 1. It is only after that observation that the potential entrant makes its entry decision in stage 2. If entry does occur in the second stage of the game, the two firms compete in quantities. Market demand for the product in stage 2 is described by $P = A - (q_1 + q_2)$. It is very important to note that the two firms simultaneously choose both their outputs (q_1, q_2) and their capacity levels (K_1, K_2) in stage 2. However, the capacity choice for the incumbent is constrained because its capacity in the second stage cannot be less than the capacity chosen in the first stage (i.e., $K_1 \geq \overline{K}_1$). The incumbent firm can increase its capacity in stage 2, but not decrease it.

We denote any sunk costs incurred by the incumbent other than those associated with its capacity choice $\overline{K}_1$ as F_1. We also assume that every unit produced requires variable inputs that cost w. Since the incumbent enters stage 2 with $\overline{K}_1$ units of capacity, the incumbent's marginal cost of production in stage 2 for output $q_1 \leq \overline{K}_1$ is w per unit. However, if the incumbent wishes to produce an output greater than q_1, then it must hire additional capacity, again at the price of r per unit. Hence, for every unit of output above $\overline{K}_1$, the incumbent's marginal cost is $w + r$. These relationships are reflected in the following description of the incumbent's cost function in stage 2 of the game:

$$
\begin{aligned}
C_1(q_1, q_2, \overline{K}_1) &= F_1 + wq_1 + r\overline{K}_1, \quad \text{for } q_1 \leq \overline{K}_1, \\
&= F_1 + (w + r)q_1, \quad \text{for } q_1 > \overline{K}_1,
\end{aligned}
\tag{9.12}
$$

The only difference between the entrant and the incumbent is that the entrant cannot invest in capacity in stage 1. Instead, the entrant must hire both labor and capital as they are needed to produce whatever output it selects in the second stage. Thus, the entrant's marginal cost is always $w + r$, no matter what output it chooses. If we denote any additional sunk cost the entrant incurs as result of participating in the market as F_2, its cost function in stage 2 is

$$
C_2(q_2) = F_2 + (w + r)q_2
\tag{9.13}
$$

The two firms thus face different *marginal* costs in stage 2 of the game. For the incumbent firm, the marginal cost of producing any output q_1 is equal to w so long as it is within its initial capacity (i.e., for $q_1 \leq \overline{K}_1$). However, because the entrant does not enjoy the first-mover advantage of being able to invest in capacity in stage 1, it faces a marginal cost equal to $(w + r)$ for all output levels. This difference is reflected in Figure 9.1, where we draw the marginal cost curves for both firms. The diagram suggests why investment in capacity can have a commitment value. The incumbent's commitment to produce at least as much as $\overline{K}_1$ is made more believable by the fact that, up to that production level, its marginal cost is *relatively* low.

To solve for a subgame-perfect equilibrium strategy for the incumbent firm, we need to determine how the incumbent's choice of capacity in stage 1 affects the market outcome when the two firms compete in stage 2. So, we start by working out what happens in stage 2 for any particular level of capacity chosen in stage 1. We then determine what happens in stage 1 by choosing the capacity that maximizes the incumbent's profits in stage 2.

In stage 2, the firms play a Cournot game in quantities. The incumbent firm's profit is

$$
\begin{aligned}
\pi_1(q_1, q_2, \overline{K}_1) &= [A - (q_1 + q_2)]q_1 - [wq_1 - r\overline{K}_1 - F_1] \quad \text{for } q_1 \leq \overline{K}_1 \\
\pi_1(q_1, q_2, \overline{K}_1) &= [A - (q_1 + q_2)]q_1 - [(w + r)q_1 - F_1] \quad \text{for } q_1 > \overline{K}_1
\end{aligned}
\tag{9.14}
$$

Equation (9.14) implies that the incumbent's best-response function has a discrete step in it at output level $q_1 = \overline{K}_1$. At this point, there is a discrete increase in its marginal cost

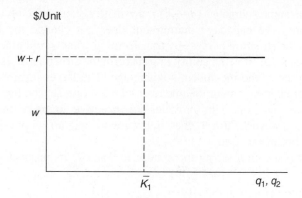

Figure 9.1   The effect of previously acquired capacity on current marginal cost
The incumbent has previously acquired capacity $\overline{K}_1$ and therefore incurs a marginal cost of only w up to this level of production. For greater levels, its marginal cost is $w + r$. The entrant has no previously acquired capacity. Its marginal cost is $w + r$ for all production levels.

from w to $w + r$. We derive this best-response function by maximizing the incumbent's profit in each case, taking the entrant's output as given. This yields

$$q_1 = \frac{(A - w)}{2} - \frac{q_2}{2} \quad \text{when } q_1 \leq \overline{K}_1; \quad \text{and}$$

$$q_1 = \frac{(A - w - r)}{2} - \frac{q_2}{2} \quad \text{when } q_1 > \overline{K}_1. \tag{9.15}$$

This best-response function described by equation (9.15) is illustrated in Figure 9.2. For output levels $q_1^* \leq \overline{K}_1$, the incumbent firm's response function is the solid line described by $L'L$, whereas for output levels $q_1^* > \overline{K}_1$ the reaction function shifts down to the lower solid line described by $N'N$. It is important to note that at any output q the incumbent's

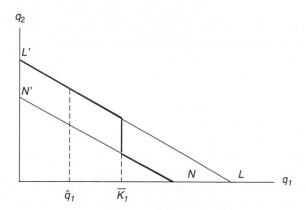

Figure 9.2   The incumbent's best response in stage 2 depends on stage 1 capacity
For output less than $\overline{K}_1$, the incumbent will have a low marginal cost and operate on the higher response function $L'L$. For output greater than $\overline{K}_1$, the incumbent will have a high marginal cost and operate on the lower best-response function.

total costs are the same, namely, $(w + r)q$ no matter what part of the best-response function is relevant. The capacity commitment does not change the firm's total cost. Instead, it changes the structure of costs by transforming what would otherwise be variable cost into sunk (fixed) cost. It is the ability to transform the structure of its costs in this way that is the true source of the incumbent's advantage. The larger Firm 1's initial capacity commitment, the greater the output volume over which it operates on the expanded portion of its best-response function. This provides an incentive to make the initial capacity investment large. However, Firm 1 does not want to end up with excess capacity for which it has paid but never used.

Now consider the situation facing the entrant in stage 2. Its profit is

$$\pi_2(q_1, q_2) = [A - (q_1 + q_2)]q_2 - [(w + r)q_2 - F_2] \tag{9.16}$$

This implies that the entrant's best-response function is

$$q_2 = \frac{(A - w - r)}{2} - \frac{q_1}{2} \tag{9.17}$$

However, we must once again note that equation (9.17) applies only in the case that the entrant chooses to produce a positive level of output, that is, so long as it is the case that the entrant's profit at that output is nonnegative. As in our earlier limit output model, the presence of the entry cost F_2, which is not taken into account in the marginal conditions underlying equation (9.17), raises the possibility that the entrant's best *positive* output response may not yield sufficient revenues to cover both its operating costs and its entry costs. In such cases, the output implied by equation (9.17) would result in a loss, and the entrant would be better off not to produce at all (i.e., not to enter).

The Nash equilibrium for the stage 2 game will occur at the intersection of the incumbent's and the entrant's best-response functions—provided, as just noted, that the entrant earns a nonnegative profit. This brings us back to the first stage. Understanding how competition works out in stage 2 allows the incumbent firm to manipulate this stage 2 equilibrium by its choice of $\overline{K}_1$ in stage 1. Naturally, the incumbent firm will choose $\overline{K}_1$ in the first stage to give itself the maximum profit possible in stage 2. Let us now investigate this choice and whether or not it implies the possibility that the incumbent firm will choose $\overline{K}_1$ to deter the second firm from entering.

We begin by drawing a diagram that describes all the possible equilibria for stage 2 of the game. In Figure 9.3 we draw the two-part best response function for Firm 1, one part corresponding to the low marginal cost of production w labeled $L'L$, and the other part corresponding to the higher marginal cost of production $(w + r)$ labeled $N'N$. We then add the response function for Firm 2, labeled $R'R$. We denote the point where Firm 2's reaction function meets $N'N$ by T. This point corresponds to stage 2 outputs for the incumbent and entrant of T_1 and T_2, respectively. Similarly, the point where $R'R$ meets $L'L$ is labeled V and corresponds to respective outputs of V_1 and V_2.

In the second stage, Firm 2 is either going to enter or stay out. Consider what happens if Firm 2 enters. In this case, the Nash equilibrium must lie somewhere between points T and V on Firm 2's best response function $R'R$. The actual point will depend on the capacity choice of the incumbent and, in particular, on the output level at which the incumbent shifts from response function $L'L$ to $N'N$. The minimum amount that Firm 1 will produce if its rival enters is T_1, and the maximum amount it will produce is V_1.

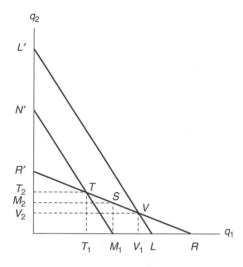

Figure 9.3   The rational bounds on the incumbent's initial choice of capacity, $\overline{K_1}$

The incumbent will choose an initial capacity investment somewhere in the interval from T_1 to V_1.

What if Firm 2 does not enter? First, think of what this means. If Firm 2 does not enter, it must be because no positive amount of production is possible given the output response of Firm 1. The incumbent will then be a monopoly. From equations (9.15), we can see that if Firm 1 is on the inner or lower portion of its best-response function, it will then wish to produce $q_1 = \frac{A-w-r}{2}$. This is the monopoly output in this market, when a firm has marginal cost $w + r$ and corresponds to the production level M_1 in Figure 9.3. Firm 1's profit in this case would be $\frac{(A-w-r)^2}{4} - F_1$. Recall, though, that if Firm 1 initially acquired $\overline{K}_1 = M_1$ initial capacity, so that it was operating on the outer portion of its best-response function, it could produce output M_1 at exactly the same cost and, again assuming no rival entry, earn precisely the same profit. Why might Firm 1 choose this option?

By choosing an initial capacity $\overline{K}_1 = M_1$, Firm 1 expands the range of outputs over which Firm 2 will not find entry profitable. Suppose, for example, that Firm 1 initially acquired T_1 units of capacity. Then it will only be a monopolist only if Firm 2 is unable to make a positive profit even in at T. But at T, Firm 2 produces its highest equilibrium output T_2. As we move down and to the right along Firm 2's best-response function, it is reducing its output by a half unit for every one unit increase in Firm 1's production. So, total output is rising and therefore price is falling at the same time that Firm 2's average cost is rising due to its lower volume of production. If Firm 2 cannot break even at T_2, then it cannot break even at any smaller output along its best-response function.

However, suppose that Firm 2 can in fact earn a positive profit at point T and can even break even at smaller outputs up to those just a little greater than M_2. In this case, an initial capacity of T_1 will not result in a monopoly for Firm 1. Quite to the contrary, it will mean that point T will be the Nash equilibrium, This corresponds to the Cournot duopoly outcome, in which each firm has marginal cost $w + r$, and thereby yields Firm 1 a profit substantially below the monopoly level. The way for Firm 1 to avoid this outcome is to instead invest initially in M_1 units of capacity. By doing so, it ensures that it will have a monopoly—and earn monopoly profit—in any case in which Firm 2 must produce at least M_2 units to break even.

Even if the investment of M_1 units of capacity will not prevent entry, it is still an attractive choice for Firm 1 because M_1 is the Stackelberg leader output as well, which we know is optimal for the incumbent if the entrant is going to enter. By investing in capacity of M_1, the incumbent makes a credible commitment to this output level. By doing so, it ensures that the intersection of the two response functions is at M, and that therefore the entrant will produce only the follower output $q_2 = \frac{(A-w-r)}{4}$, as indicated by equation (9.15).

What we have just shown is that the incumbent will never make an initial capacity investment less than M_1. If the entrant can only profitably enter at output levels greater than M_2, this investment will ensure that no entry occurs at all, and the incumbent will sell the M_1 units of output as a monopolist. If, on the other hand, the entrant can cover its costs at output levels below M_2, the investment of M_1 units of initial capacity will still guarantee the incumbent the output of a Stackelberg leader, which is the best it can do if Firm 2 is going to enter.

The question that arises now is whether the incumbent will ever choose an initial capacity greater than M_1. With this investment, after all, one of two outcomes must occur. Either the output M_1 deters any entry and the incumbent sells that output as a monopolist, or entry occurs and the incumbent does best by acting as a Stackelberg leader—in which case M_1 units of output is precisely its profit-maximizing choice.

However, there are in fact cases in which the incumbent may rationally choose to acquire more than M_1 units of capacity in stage 1 to deter Firm 2's entry in stage 2. To understand why, we refer to Figure 9.4.

As Figure 9.4 reveals, there are three possible equilibria for the game, and one of these has already been clearly identified. Whenever the entrant cannot earn a positive profit at output levels less than M_2, the incumbent will do best by initially investing in capacity of M_1. This is not predation, as it is the most profitable choice for the incumbent.

The easiest of the two remaining cases occurs when the entrant can operate successfully at production levels of V_2 and smaller (i.e., when its sunk entry cost F_2 is very small). In that case, it is simply not possible to prevent entry. All that the incumbent can do

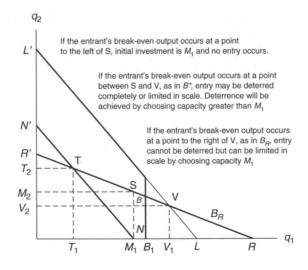

Figure 9.4   Possible locations of the entrant's break-even point

is limit entry optimally by again acquiring initial capacity M_1 and playing the role of a Stackelberg leader, forcing the entrant to produce at $q_2 = M_2$.

   The remaining case occurs when Firm 2's costs of production are such that its profit, as we move down its response function, is positive at M_2 but negative at V_2. This implies that the output combination where Firm 2 just breaks even lies between S and V, such as B. In this case, Firm 1 has a choice to make analogous to that described by equations (9.9) and (9.10) in the earlier limit output analysis. On the one hand, it can play the Stackelberg leader by initially installing capacity M_1 and producing at that level in stage 2, in which case Firm 2 will produce the follower output M_2. In this scenario, Firm 1 earns profit $\pi_1 = \frac{(A-w-r)^2}{8} - F_1$. On the other hand, Firm 1 can expand its initial capacity choice to the level B_1. While B_1 is not the optimal level that a monopolist would produce, this production choice is the one way that Firm 1 can guarantee its monopoly position. Here, Firm 1's profit is $\pi_1 = (A - B_1 - w - r)B_1 - F_1$. Thus, the incumbent will choose to deter entry rather than accommodate entry, albeit on a limited scale, if

$$(A - B_1 - w - r)B_1 - F_1 > \frac{(A - w - r)^2}{8} - F_1 \Rightarrow B_1 < \frac{1}{2}\left(1 + \frac{1}{\sqrt{2}}\right)(A - w - r)$$

$$(9.18)$$

The incumbent will more likely choose to deter entry if B_1 is not too large relative to the monopoly level $M_1 = (A - w - r)/2$. However, as the capacity choice or output required for entry deterrence rises, the incumbent is more likely to choose to limit the scale of such entry rather than to prevent it altogether.

   Let us briefly summarize the results of the limit output and capacity expansion models. In each, a monopoly incumbent faces the threat of rival entry. To the extent that the incumbent has a first-mover advantage, it can exploit that advantage by committing to a large output that either limits the scale of the rival's entry or prevents it altogether. We have seen that there are cases in which, even if the incumbent chooses to produce the monopoly level of output, entry will be deterred. In these cases, the incumbent's actions are not predatory. However, there are also cases in which the incumbent will find it profitable to commit to a higher production level that not only prevents entry, but also is optimal only if it has this effect. In these circumstances, the incumbent's strategy is predatory.

   All of these results depend critically on the incumbent having a means of making a credible commitment to a specific production level. Dixit's (1980) capacity expansion model provides such a mechanism by allowing the incumbent to alter the structure of its costs while leaving its total cost unchanged. Specifically, by investing in advance in productive capacity, the incumbent increases its fixed cost but lowers its marginal cost. This reduction in marginal cost increases the level of output the incumbent will optimally produce in response to any given output choice of the entrant and thereby makes credible the incumbent's promise to respond aggressively to entry and to utilize fully the acquired capacity.[7]

   Note that capacity expansion is credible as a deterrent strategy only to the extent that capacity, once in place, is a sunk cost. If unused plant capacity can be sold off for a fee

---

[7]   Spence's (1977) model, based on capacity expansion, envisioned equilibria in which the incumbent operated with unused capacity. Dixit's (1980) model has the advantage that in any equilibrium, the incumbent always utilizes its initial capacity fully.

Reality Checkpoint

The Alcoa Case: Do It First, Do It Right . . . and Keep On Doing It

In 1945, a U.S. Court of Appeals for the Second Circuit, under the direction of Judge Learned Hand, rendered one of the most famous decisions in U.S. antitrust history. The case involved the charge against the Aluminum Co. of America (Alcoa) that it had unlawfully monopolized the domestic market for aluminum and aluminum products. Alcoa had previously been involved in an antitrust case in 1912. At that time it was found guilty of restrictive and anti-competitive practices, including (1) signing contracts with electric power companies to obtain the large amount of electricity needed to process raw aluminum and including in those contracts covenants that prohibited the power companies from selling electricity to any other aluminum manufacturer; and (2) forming a cartel with foreign manufacturers to divide the world aluminum market into regions and restrict sales in any one region to primarily one member of the cartel. In part, the 1945 case was based on the allegation that these practices had continued despite the 1912 settlement.

However, the court's decision against Alcoa this time was predicated primarily on the view that Alcoa expanded capacity to keep out competitors. The court noted that Alcoa increased its capacity eightfold between 1912 and 1934. It noted that there had been "one or two abortive attempts to enter the industry, but Alcoa effectively anticipated and forestalled all competition." The court continued, saying that "we can think of no more effective exclusion than . . . to face every newcomer with new capacity already geared into a great organization."

Of course, much as the Microsoft case revealed 55 years later, the finding that a firm has illegally abused its market power does not make clear what the remedy to such abuse should be. Even a serious fine may seem too weak a penalty, because it leaves the firm intact and able perhaps to resume its illegal practices. Yet, breaking up a successful organization—as was done in the Standard Oil case—may seem overly harsh. In the Alcoa case, the government was fortunate to have an alternative remedy. The case was decided in the immediate aftermath of World War II. During that war, the government had operated a number of aluminum plants. The decision was made to sell these plants to two new firms, Kaiser and Reynolds, and thereby create more competitive market structure.

Source: *U.S. v. Aluminum Co. of America*, 148 F. 2d 416 (1945).

then capacity is actually flexible and acquiring it does not reflect any real commitment on the part of the incumbent. When such flexibility is not possible, which is often the case, then capacity investment is a much more effective entry deterring device. This is reminiscent of Schelling's (1960) analysis in which he states that "the power to constrain an adversary may depend on the power to bind oneself" (p. 22).

Now, think back to the empirical evidence on entry that we reviewed at the beginning of the chapter. Two of the stylized facts are (1) entry is commonly observed in a wide cross section of industries, and (2) market penetration as measured by market share is relatively low for the entrants. These stylized facts are consistent with this model. The incumbent has a strategic advantage in being the first to invest in capacity, and can use this advantage to strategically limit the impact of entry into its market—perhaps eliminating it altogether.

9.2.3   Evidence on Predatory Capacity Expansion

What evidence is there that dominant firms used capacity expansion or other methods to commit to a large output and thereby retain their dominance? To begin with, there is the stylized fact noted at the start of this chapter that the same firms continue to dominate their industries and earn superior profit for long periods of time. However, this could happen for a lot of reasons, including superior management or cost efficiency at such firms. The specific question is whether there is evidence of the maintenance of such market power explicitly by means of capacity expansion or preemptive investment.

Since investment commitment strategies are more likely to occur in more capital-intensive industries, we might expect profitability to be higher in such industries (all else equal), if preemptive expansion is the norm. An early study by Caves and Ghemawat (1986) does not find support for this result. Yet if preemptive expansion is not the norm, there does seem to be clear historic instances of its practice. The Alcoa case (see inset) is perhaps the best-known example, but there are others.

Weiman and Levin (1994) find that preemptive investment was an explicit tactic of Southern Bell Telephone (SBT) in its effort to monopolize the local phone service market in the central southern and eastern southern regions of the United States. Those markets had become intensely competitive after the expiration of the Bell patents; so by 1902, independent firms accounted for 60 percent of the local phone service in the region from Virginia to Alabama and Florida. Company archival records reveal that SBT's leader, Edward J. Hall, launched an aggressive capital expansion program to build a regional toll network in anticipation of market development, with the explicit goal of preempting rivals. Within four years, SBT had increased the geographic reach of its system from 2,000 to 8,600 pole miles. Even more impressively, its calling capacity (as measured by toll wires) grew from 5,000 to over 55,000 miles. All of this was accompanied by an aggressive price-cutting campaign, both in markets where it faced competition and those where it expected it. Among other features, this had the effect of restricting the investment funds available to competitors for their own expansion, whereas SBT was able to rely on heavy financing from its parent firm, AT&T. The plan worked. By 1912, SBT had virtually complete control of the southern local telephone market.

A more recent example is set in the town of Edmonton, Alberta, during the 1960s and early 1970s. The major retail grocer in Edmonton at that time was Safeway. However, in the early 1960s, a number of other grocery stores from other regions began to enter the Edmonton market. These included two Ontario firms, Loblaws and Dominion, and one Western Canada firm, Tom Boy. Between 1960 and 1963, these three firms opened 12 new stores in the Edmonton area. By 1964, they were operating a total of 21 stores—not far behind Safeway's (then) total of 25. Safeway could clearly see that continued entry by these and other firms was a real possibility, and it rapidly responded. It opened four new stores in 1963–64, another four new stores in 1965–66, and then five new stores in 1968. Moreover, Safeway chose the locations of these new stores quite carefully. It located them in areas where, due to increasing population and the fact that no other store was currently close by, it looked like a site of potential entry. In addition, just to drive home the seriousness of its intentions, Safeway also located some of its new stores almost right next to locations where its rivals also had a store. The strategy worked. By 1973, Safeway was operating 35 stores in the Edmonton area, whereas, due to closings, its three major rivals were operating just 10. Indeed, Safeway had so effectively established its credibility as a preemptive competitor that whenever its major rivals or even fringe firms opened up a new store, they typically located near each other (rather than in neighborhoods already served by Safeway) but sufficiently densely populated to permit room for a second store.[8]

Our final anecdote comes from the market for titanium dioxide. This is a chemical additive used as a whitener in such products as paint, paper, and plastics. It can be produced by three processes. One of these is a sulfate procedure that uses ilmenite ore. Another technique is a chloride process that uses rutile ore. Both of these processes are known and available to all producers. The third process, however, is a special chloride process that, because of legal restrictions, is known and available for use only by DuPont. Like the sulfate process, DuPont's procedure uses ilmenite ore. Yet, like the generic chloride process, DuPont's method emits little pollution. This is not the case with the sulfate procedure, which has bad pollution affects.

Seven domestic firms were active in the titanium dioxide market during the 1970s. DuPont was the largest of these, with about 34 percent of the market, but NL industries—which used the sulfate procedure—was a close second. Then, two events happened in the early 1970s that gave DuPont a decided advantage. First, rutile ore became more expensive, implying that other producers using the generic chloride technique might have to cut back. Second, strict pollution controls were imposed that also made the sulfate process very expensive. Suddenly, DuPont's proprietary chloride technique based on ilmenite ore gave the company an edge with respect to costs. A strategic firm would lose no time in exploiting that edge. It would know that those producers using sulfate were not likely to expand. It might also recognize that rutile could someday become cheap again (it did). If, in addition, the firm expected—as did all participants in the titanium oxide market—that demand would grow, a firm in DuPont's position might wish to expand capacity immediately. This would preclude those rivals using the rutile-based technique from expanding production when and if rutile prices dropped and, thus, permit the firm to capture the gap caused by market growth and the declining sulfate-based production entirely for itself.

In point of fact, DuPont increased its capacity by over 60 percent in the next five years, while the industry in general stagnated. By 1977, DuPont's market share had risen to 46 percent. Moreover, when rival Kerr-McGee began to construct a new plant in 1974, just before DuPont got its planned expansion going, DuPont reacted by trumpeting its plans to the whole industry. This likely precluded any further entry beyond that of Kerr-McGee's.[9]

In short, there is much anecdotal evidence that supports the use of capacity expansion to maintain market power. We should note that such evidence may be even greater when we use a spatial interpretation of expansion along the lines of the Hotelling model. It is sometimes claimed that General Motors' strategy of offering many different automobile varieties (and the ready-to-eat breakfast cereal manufacturers' strategy of selling a wide assortment of cereals) reflect attempts to "crowd out" any would-be rival by leaving it no market niche into which it can profitably enter.

---

[8]   Facing monopolization charges, Safeway signed a consent decree that, among other things, prohibited it from expanding its total square footage in Edmonton for three and a half years. See Von Hohenbalken and West (1986).

[9]   See Ghemawat (1984). See also Hall (1990) for evidence that DuPont's action was consistent with the Dixit model.

Reality Checkpoint
Take-Or-Pay ... And Win!

Firms typically have contracts with their key suppliers that stipulate the amount of the input to be bought and the price to be paid for the coming year. A common additional feature of such contracts, especially for suppliers of natural gas, electricity, and commodity raw materials, is a "take-or-pay" clause. A contract that includes a take-or-pay clause requires that the purchasing firm either uses all the amount of the input initially contracted—or, if it orders less than that amount, it still pays some amount, usually less than the full contract price, for the additional amount remaining.

Take-or-pay contracts stabilize both the production schedule and the revenues of supplier firms. However, as you should recognize, they also serve another purpose. They are a straightforward way to implement the Dixit entry deterrence strategy.

For example, Corning is one of the leading manufacturers of fiberoptic cables. One of its key suppliers is Praxair, a major producer of specialty gases. Suppose that Corning signs a contract with Praxair that calls for Corning to purchase 1,000,000 cubic feet of helium (which is used as a coolant in the production of fiberoptic cable) at $400 per 1,000 cubic feet. The contract also includes a take-or-pay contract where Corning has to pay $300 per 1,000 cubic feet for any amount of the 1,000,000 that it does not use. What this does is effectively transform the structure of Corning's costs. If Corning orders all of the 1,000,000 cubic feet, its helium bill will be ($400/1000) × 1, 000, 000 = $400,000. Suppose, though, that Corning only uses 900,000

cubic feet of helium (perhaps because a new rival steals some Corning customers). Because of the take-or-pay clause, it will still pay $300 per 1,000 cubic feet for the 100,000 cubic feet that it did not order. Hence, Corning's total helium cost in this case will be: ($400/1000) × 900, 000 + ($300/1000) × 100, 000 = $390,000. In other words, using the last 100,000 cubic feet of helium only raises Corning's total helium bill by $10,000. Effectively, the contract has changed the marginal cost of helium for Corning from $400 to $100 per thousand cubic feet. Note that it has not changed the total cost of using 1,000,000 cubic feet of helium. The contract has simply transformed some of those costs into fixed costs, so that up to the 1,000,000 volume, Corning has a very low marginal cost.

There is, of course, a downside to the take-or-pay contract. This is that if another large rival (e.g., the British fiberoptic producer Marconi) already exists, and both firms sign take-or-pay contracts with their helium suppliers, the industry could find itself in a nasty price war in which prices fall to the low levels of marginal cost (i.e., Bertrand competition). Some believe that this is part of what happened in the fiberoptic market following the burst of the telecommunications bubble.

Sources: Brandenburger, A. M., and B. J. Nalebuff. 1996. *Co-opetition*. New York: Doubleday; and Norris, F. "Disaster at Corning: At Least the Balance Sheet is Strong." *The New York Times* (13 July 2001), p. C2.

9.3   PREDATION AND ASYMMETRIC INFORMATION

The limit output or limit price and capacity expansion models have the common feature that the players have complete information. The incumbent knows the structure of demand as well as its own and rival's costs and can work out what it must do to prevent or limit entry. The entrant has the same information and therefore understands that the incumbent's commitment to a particular output is credible. In practice, though, such complete information is rare. Indeed, the analysis of situations of incomplete information has been perhaps the biggest growth area of economics over the last 30 years. A drug company may know the true quality of its new medication, but consumers may not. A startup firm's management may know the true state of the firm's finances, while investors remain uncertain. A home renovator may know that the project ran over budget because of his incompetence, but can convince the homeowner that the cause was due to faults discovered in previous work.

In all of the above situations, information is not only incomplete—it is asymmetric. Some players in the game know something that others do not. Because talk is cheap, the drug manufacturer will need to find some way to make its quality announcement credible if it wishes to convince consumers that its new drug is helpful. Similarly, the contractor may employ tactics that make it difficult for the homeowner to reach a conclusion of incompetence. What strategies (if any) might exist that permit players to signal credibly the information that they have so that the equilibrium outcome is the same as if information was complete? Another question that emerges concerns the nature of the equilibrium when no credible information signaling is possible (i.e., when uncertainty remains). Exploration of these issues has permitted a deeper understanding of many strategic interactions relevant to industrial organization. Below, we present two very different but related analyses of the role of asymmetric information and uncertainty in entry deterrence.

9.3.1   Asymmetric Information and Limit Pricing

In their classic paper, Milgrom and Roberts (1982) present a model in which asymmetric information may be exploited by an incumbent firm to establish a limit price that will preclude entry. Their analysis is based on the fact that a new entrant firm is unlikely to know the incumbent firm's cost of production. Clearly, however, the lower that cost is, the less likely it is that entry will be profitable. Thus, the incumbent may wish to set a low price to convince the entrant that it is a low-cost firm. The path-breaking model of Milgrom and Roberts (1982) explores the conditions under which such bluffing will and will not work.

The setting is a two-period game in which there is an incumbent and a potential entrant. Let's call the incumbent Microhard and the potential entrant Newvel. Microhard is alone in the market in the first period. During that period, Newvel observes Microhard's behavior, specifically the price that Microhard chooses to set in period 1, and then Newvel decides whether or not to enter the market in period 2. We assume the interest rate is 0, so that there is no discounting future profits.

Let us assume that both Microhard and Newvel know the structure of market demand and both Microhard and Newvel know Newvel's unit cost and this is common knowledge. However, Newvel does not know Microhard's unit cost. Instead, Newvel knows that Microhard must be one of two possible firm types. It is either a low-cost incumbent with probability q, or a high-cost incumbent with probability $1 - q$. This is the key informational asymmetry of the game. Microhard knows its true type with certainty. Newvel can only guess at this value.

In period 1 Microhard earns monopoly profit, which is a function of both the price it charges and its cost type. Denote the profit function for Microhard as a high-cost monopoly as $\pi_H^M(p^M)$, and its profit function as a low-cost monopoly as $\pi_L^H(p^M)$. In addition, denote the price that maximizes its monopoly profit when it is a high-cost firm as

p_H^M, and the price that maximizes its profit as a low-cost monopoly as p_L^M. Thus, Microhard's maximum profit when it is a high-cost firm is $\pi_H^M(p_H^M) = \pi_H^*$, while its maximum profit as a low-cost monopoly is $\pi_L^M(p_L^M) = \pi_L^*$, where $p_L^M < p_H^M$, and $\pi_H^* < \pi_L^*$.

If Microhard did not have to fear subsequent entry, it would simply set price at p_L^M if it were a low-cost firm and at p_H^M if it were a high-cost firm. However, if it always prices true to type in period 1, then its actions in that period fully reveal its type to Newvel, who is watching on the sidelines during that period. If, as seems likely, Newvel does much better against a high-cost firm than a low-cost one, then Microhard will be raising the likelihood of entry whenever it charges price p_H^M precisely because, if Microhard always sets prices consistent with its type, observing this price will completely inform Newvel that the incumbent is a high-cost firm. Hence, Microhard may not really wish to price according to its type and, in particular, may sometimes wish to set price p_L^M even when it is a high-cost firm so as to fool Newvel and prevent its entry.

To explore this possibility, we consider period 2 competition. If Newvel enters, then in period 2 the market is a duopoly. At that point, there is no reason for Microhard to set any price other than the duopoly price that is best for its type. Let Microhard's duopoly profit if it is a high-cost firm be D_H^M, and its profit if it is a low-cost firm be D_L^M. Similarly, let Newvel's duopoly profit if it faces a high-cost Microhard be D_H^N, and its profit when facing a low-cost Microhard be D_L^N. We assume that the following relationships hold:

$$D_L^M > D_H^M > 0 \tag{9.19}$$

$$D_H^N > 0 > D_L^N \tag{9.20}$$

Inequality (9.19) simply states that in the second-period duopoly Nash equilibrium, Microhard's profit is greater if it is a low-cost firm than if it is a high-cost one. Inequality (9.20) indicates that Newvel is profitable in the second period only if it is competing against a high-cost Microhard.

We have already noted the possibility that Microhard may decide to hide the fact that it is a high-cost firm in the first period by setting a price that is appropriate for a low-cost one. Such an outcome—in which the price observed in period one is the same regardless of the incumbent's type—is known as a pooling equilibrium. In contrast, if Microhard always sets price p_L^M when it is a low-cost firm and price p_H^M when it is a high-cost one, we have what is known as a *separating equilibrium*. Each of these possible equilibria are examples of what is known in game theory as a *Perfect Bayesian Equilibrium*.[10]

The reason for this terminology should not be hard to guess for those familiar with statistics and the Bayes Rule. An individual typically brings a set of prior expectations to any stochastic setting. Observing the data, the individual then updates those expectations in a manner consistent with the logic of the Bayes Rule. In this game Newvel is the player with some prior expectations of Microhard's true type. It then observes Microhard's first-period price, uses that information to update its belief about Microhard's type, and uses that updated belief in making its entry decision. The extra twist here is that for this process to be part of a Nash equilibrium, it must have the logical consistency that no player has an incentive to deviate from its particular strategy given the strategy of the other.

---

[10]   A full characterization of the equilibrium will also include a third possible equilibrium based on mixed strategies that will involve both pooling and separating equilibria. We omit consideration of this equilibrium in the present discussion.

In the absence of any information on the first-period price, it is reasonable for Newvel to believe that Microhard is a low-cost firm with probability q, and a high-cost one with probability $1 - q$. This is the known distribution of types and a natural choice for Newvel's prior beliefs. Denote Newvel's updated beliefs following its observation of Microhard's first period price by q' and $1 - q'$, respectively. Suppose then that Newvel adopts the following strategy to update its beliefs:

If Microhard's first period price is less than or equal to p_L^M, then $q' = 1$

If Microhard's first period price is greater than p_L^M, then $q' = 0$

$$\text{(9.21)}$$

Suppose further that Newvel enters when its expected profit based on those beliefs exceeds 0 and does not enter when its expected profit is less than 0. In other words, Newvel believes that Microhard's first-period price choice fully reveals its cost type. It then enters when evidence indicates Microhard is a high-cost firm, but stays out when its updated beliefs indicate that Microhard is a low-cost one. Understanding this, Microhard considers how to price in period 1. It can price according to its type just as Newvel expects. Alternatively, it can price against type. However, it is never reasonable for Microhard to set price above p_L^M if it is a low-cost type firm. This would not be the profit-maximizing monopoly price for a low-cost firm, and, given Newvel's beliefs, it invites entry in the second period. We therefore restrict Microhard's first-period choice either to pricing according to type, or setting price p_L^M regardless of whether it is a high-cost or low-cost firm.

Consider the case in which Microhard always sets a first-period price according to type. That is, Microhard adopts the first-period strategy

$p = p_L^M$, if Microhard is a low-cost firm;

$p = p_H^M$, if Microhard is a high-cost firm

$$\text{(9.22)}$$

If Microhard adopts this strategy, then Newvel's beliefs as described by (9.21) will be consistent. Newvel believes that Microhard's pricing accurately reveals its type, and Microhard's pricing does in fact reveal that information. However, for this to be a Nash equilibrium, it must be the case that no firm has a reason to deviate from this strategy. What happens, for example, if Microhard instead adopts the following strategy?

$p = p_L^M$, if Microhard is a low-cost firm;

$p = p_L^M$, if Microhard is a high-cost firm

$$\text{(9.23)}$$

In this case, Microhard always sets a low first-period price. If Newvel stays with its beliefs (9.21), this strategy will prevent Newvel from entering even when Microhard is a high-cost firm. Does Microhard have a reason to choose this strategy?

Denote Microhard's first-period profit when it prices low (even though its costs are high) as $\hat{\pi}_H = \pi_H^M(p_L^M) < \pi_H^*$. Thus, because it is not charging the optimal first-period price, this strategy imposes a first-period profit reduction of $\pi_H^* - \hat{\pi}_H$ on a high-cost Microhard. However, because it prevents entry given Newvel's beliefs in (9.21) it increases second period profit by the amount: $\pi_H^* - D_H^M$. Thus, a necessary condition for Microhard to price according to its type and not adopt the strategy in (9.23) is

$$\pi_H^* - \hat{\pi}_H \geq \pi_H^* - D_H^M \qquad \text{(9.24)}$$

Condition (9.24) is also a sufficient condition for Microhard to price according to type, given Newvel's beliefs as described by (9.21).[11] Thus, if (9.24) holds, then Newvel's beliefs in (9.21) and entering when it observes price any price above p_L^M (but not entering when it observes price p_L^M or lower), along with Microhard's strategy (9.22) of pricing according to type, is a perfect Bayesian Nash equilibrium. It is a separating equilibrium because Microhard sets a different price for each cost type. It prices high when its costs are high and prices low when its costs are low. As a result, Newvel's updating scheme is consistent with what is observed and leads to the profit-maximizing entry decision. So, Newvel has no reason to change its behavior. It is true that a high cost Microhard could prevent entry by changing its behavior and setting a first-period price of p_L^M; but condition (9.24) shows that this action loses more in first-period profit than it gains in second-period profit. So, Microhard, either cost type, has no reason to switch its behavior either.

What happens if condition (9.24) is not met? In that case, Microhard has an incentive to switch its price strategy (9.23) to always pricing low regardless of its type. But now Newvel only observes a low price p_L^M the first period and therefore recognizes that updating its beliefs according to (9.22) no longer makes sense. If Microhard always chooses a first-period price p_L^M, observing that price yields no information about Microhard's type to Newvel. Newvel sticks to its prior belief that Microhard has low costs with probability q and high cost with probability $1 - q$. In turn, this implies that its expected profit if it enters is $(1 - q)D_H^N + qD_L^N$. (Recall that $D_L^N < 0$.) It will therefore enter if

$$(1 - q)D_H^N + qD_L^N > 0 \tag{9.25}$$

However, if condition (9.25) is satisfied, then Microhard will not set a low first-period price when its costs are high, even though condition (9.24) is also satisfied. While condition (9.24) implies that such action would yield Microhard a net gain if the actions deter entry, condition (9.25) implies that no such entry-deterring will happen. Newvel's belief about Microhard's cost type after observing the first period price of p_L^M implies that entry will be profitable.

However, the situation will change if condition (9.25) is not satisfied and we instead have

$$(1 - q)D_H^N + qD_L^N \le 0 \tag{9.26}$$

as well as condition (9.24). In that case, we obtain a perfect Bayesian Nash equilibrium of a pooling type in which both a high-cost and a low-cost incumbent will always set a low first-period price p_L^M. The nature of such an equilibrium is as follows.

Newvel

If Microhard's first-period price $= p_H^M, q' = 0$. Microhard is a high-cost firm with certainty, and Newvel enters the market.

If Microhard's first-period price $= p_L^M, q' = q$. Expected profit from entering is $(1 - q)D_H^N + qD_L^N \le 0$ and Newvel does not enter.

---

[11] We have ruled out the possibility of a low-cost firm setting the high-cost firm's optimal price p_H^M.

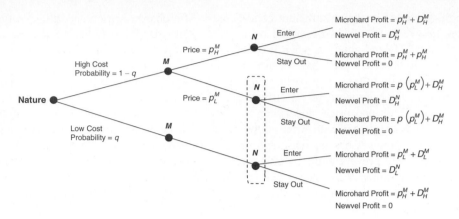

Figure 9.5   Extensive form of the sequential entry game with asymmetric information on cost

Microhard

First-period price $= p_L^M$ regardless of type
Second-period price $= p_L^M$ if it is a low-cost firm, but p_H^M if it is a high-cost firm

The extensive form for this example of the entry game is shown in Figure 9.5. Newvel's uncertainty about Microhard's cost is modeled by introducing the player Nature, who moves first and chooses the cost of the incumbent firm. With probability q, Nature chooses a low-cost incumbent, and with probability $(1 - q)$, Nature chooses a high-cost incumbent. Microhard moves next and sets either price p_L^M or price p_H^M in the first period. Then Newvel decides whether to enter and compete in period 2, or to stay out. At the end of each path, we show the total payoffs for each firm over the two periods depending on the choices about prices and entering. Microhard's total profit is the sum of its profit in each period. Newvel's profit is just that which it earns in the market for the final period.

Figure 9.5 shows the three possible paths for the dynamic game. In the first of these, Microhard is a high-cost firm and sets the corresponding first-period monopoly price p_H^M. In the second, Microhard is again a high-cost firm, but now chooses to set price p_L^M. The final possibility is that Microhard sets price p_L^M because it is truly a low-cost firm. In the separating equilibrium, the game proceeds down either the first or third path. Newvel's does not enter in the first of these, but does come into the market in the second. Both decisions are the correct ones and are identical to what would happen had Newvel known Microhard's cost type from the outset. In the pooling equilibrium, however, Newvel's observation of the first-period price p_L^M reveals no information. Hence, Newvel cannot know exactly which node it is at. This is why those two nodes are linked by a dotted-line box. Forced to revert to its prior on the distribution of firm types, Newvel chooses not to enter, even though this will be the wrong decision $1 - q$ of the time.[12]

---

[12]   We can introduce uncertainty on both sides of the game by permitting Newvel to be of two types and having Microhard uncertain about which type the potential entrant is. The basic idea that a high-cost incumbent may price low as a means of convincing the entrant that it is a low-cost firm and thereby deter entry remains. Note, too, that in the equilibria we have considered, a low-cost incumbent setting price p_L^M never faces rival entry. It is possible that this may not be the case. If so, a low-cost incumbent may set a price less than p_L^M that is too expensive for a high-cost incumbent to charge and thereby identify its true type and prevent entry.

It is important to recognize one further aspect of limit pricing. When it happens, it has the negative effect of deterring entry. Yet this blow is softened in that the incumbent is charging a price below the monopoly level. The welfare analysis of limit pricing is therefore complicated.

9.3.2   Predation, Asymmetric Information, and Financial Constraints

Thus far, the models that we have examined have focused on preventing entry rather than on eliminating existing rivals. However, as we noted at the outset, most public-policy debates focus on alleged attempts by dominant firms to eliminate existing rivals, typically by cutting prices to unsustainably low levels. Of course, the distinction is a fine one. After all, if a firm knows that its entry will lead the incumbent to take predatory actions that will drive the entrant out, why enter in the first place? Yet, just as a firm in the Milgrom-Roberts model needs to price low to convince rivals it has low costs, so an incumbent may be required to engage in predatory behavior in order to convince rivals of its cutthroat intent and deter others from entering.

Accusations of predatory behavior have been around a long time. Thanks to the popular work of Ida Tarbell (1904), such cutthroat predatory behavior is most frequently associated with the images of John Rockefeller and Standard Oil. Between 1870 and 1899, Standard Oil acquired more than 120 companies to establish itself as the dominant firm in the U.S. petroleum refining market, with a market share exceeding 90 percent. Tarbell's (1904) account, based in part on interviews with former Standard Oil executives, is that this growth was accomplished by Standard Oil's use of unfair practices—including, especially, the practice of selling below cost to make its rivals so unprofitable that they would gladly exit, typically by selling their firm to Rockefeller's company.[13] After achieving its market dominance in oil refining capacity and distribution, Standard Oil was accused of raising prices to oil consumers and acting like a textbook monopolist. It was in part these accusations that ultimately led to the prosecution of Standard Oil in the famous 1911 case that ended with the company's dissolution.

Yet, whatever the popular judgment about Standard Oil and other alleged predators may be, one must show that predatory actions are part of a rational (i.e., subgame-perfect) strategy to make a truly compelling case. One way to do this is by invoking a "deep pockets" argument.

Let us again consider two firms, Microhard and Newvel, with Microhard again in the role of the incumbent and Newvel as a recent new entrant in a two period game. Each firm has a fixed cost of F in each production period. This cost must be incurred at the start of each period, either by a cash payment or by borrowing. When both firms are in the market, each earns a duopoly profit $\pi^D - F > 0$. When Microhard is alone in the market, it earns a net profit of $\pi^M - F$. Microhard, however, can adopt a cutthroat pricing strategy of driving the market price sufficiently low that each firm earns ε less than F from its production and therefore a net income of $-\varepsilon$ overall. Because corporate law limits the liability of shareholders to the value of the firm, owners of Newvel stock will get nothing, and the lenders of the firm will incur the loss $F - \varepsilon$. Newvel is in the

---

[13]   There is extensive literature on the varied business practices used by Standard Oil during this period. Other practices include securing discriminatory rail freight rates and rebates, foreclosing crude oil supplies to competitors by buying up local pipelines, and allegedly blowing up competing pipelines. See also Yergin (1991).

market during the first period and must decide whether to stay into the second. In all that follows, we assume a 0 interest rate for convenience.

Clearly, Microhard will not adopt the cutthroat pricing policy in period 2. If Newvel is in the market at that time, trying to drive it out only reduces Microhard's profit in that period from $\pi^D - F$ to $-\varepsilon$ with no gain later to make that sacrifice worthwhile. Does this imply a similar outcome for the first period as in the Chain-Store Paradox?

One reason why the logic of the Chain-Store Paradox might break down here is that the two firms might differ in their ability to finance losses. We can imagine that, as a long-standing dominant firm, Microhard has "deep pockets." That is, it has internal funds (or access to capital markets) that allow it to cover any losses in the first period, so long as it has the expectation of positive profits in the second. In contrast, though, the newcomer Newvel only has access to external funds for one period. If it cannot cover its costs, then it has no ability to borrow the needed F funding at the start of the second period and therefore cannot operate at that time. In this asymmetric finance setting, there may indeed a reason for Microhard to pursue predatory behavior in period 1.

If Microhard accepts the presence of Newvel in period 1, it will earn $\pi^D - F$ in both periods. If it takes predatory action in period 1, however, it eliminates Newvel in period 2, and can then act as a monopolist in period 2. In that case, Microhard earns $-\varepsilon$ in the first period, but $\pi^M - F$ in the second period when, thanks to its predatory behavior, Newvel will be out of the market. Hence, Microhard will adopt cutthroat prices if

$$\pi^M - F - \varepsilon > 2\left(\pi^D - F\right) \text{ or } \pi^M - \varepsilon > 2\pi^D - F \tag{9.27}$$

Satisfying condition (9.27) thus appears to be all that is needed to generate predatory action.

The trouble with the "deep pockets" argument as presented above, however, is that it does not explain why Newvel should have trouble with funding in the second period. Yes, it lost money in period 1, but that is history at the time the second period starts. Anyone lending to Newvel in period 2 can work out that there will be no predation at that time, just as we did. Hence, Newvel will earn π^D from its production in the second period, and this is more than enough to fund its fixed costs F. Thus, a firm that lends F to Newvel at the start of period 2 knows that it will be repaid in one period. Why then is Newvel unable to get funding in period 2?

An answer to that question has been provided by Bolton and Scharfstein (1990). Their model builds uncertainty into the analysis along with a reasonable element of asymmetry between borrowers and lenders. As a result, their model gives plausibility to the "deep pockets" argument.

We assume again a two-period game but, for the moment, focus on the upstart firm Newvel and ignore the presence of Microhard. We introduce uncertainty into the model by assuming that Newvel's profit from production in any period is random and may take on either of two values: a low value π_L^N, with probability θ, or a high value π_H^N with probability $1 - \theta$. As before, Newvel requires financing of F at the start of each period if it is to operate. We assume that

$$\pi_L^N < F < \pi_H^N \tag{9.28}$$

and that

$$\overline{\pi}^N = \theta \pi_L^N + (1 - \theta)\pi_H^N > F \tag{9.29}$$

Thus, if Newvel earns only the lower profit π_L^N, its creditors will incur a loss as before, but the expected value of Newvel's operating profit is sufficient to cover a loan of F.

Newvel's creditors may suffer a loss even if Newvel earns the higher profit π_H^N. The reason is that we also assume an information asymmetry in that the true level of Newvel's profit is known only to Newvel's management and not to its creditors. If the loan contract runs only one period, Newvel's management will always report π_L^N, even when the truth is π_H^N, because they then only have to pay π_L^N to the creditors instead of the higher amount of F. Note that this would mean that creditors would never write a one-period loan contract with Newvel, as they would be certain to lose $F - \pi_L^N$. Hence, the only viable loan contracts must run for two periods. There is still however, the question of what that two-period loan contract should look like.

From the lender's viewpoint, certain aspects of the problem are clear. First, in any situation in which it actually puts up funding of F in both periods, the second-period loan will definitely not be paid in full. Since the true state of Newvel's profit in the second (and last) period cannot be verified, Newvel will always report the lower profit π_L^N at that time. Hence, if she hopes to be repaid, the lender must somehow earn a surplus on the first-period loan. To do this, however, requires that Newvel have some motivation to report the higher profit π_H^N at the end of period 1 when that is in fact the case. How can the lender induce this behavior? One way is to make the extension of a loan in the second period contingent upon Newvel's profit performance in the first. Specifically, the lender can write a contract that makes it less likely that it will extend funds to Newvel at the start of period 2, unless Newvel reports some threshold level of earnings at the end of period 1, and then transfers an amount at that time that compensates the lender both for the loan that she made for period 1 and for the additional extension that she will now make in period 2.

The general contract design is as follows. At the start of period 1, the lender extends F dollars to Newvel. At the end of that period, Newvel report its first-period earnings. If it reports the low value π_L^N, the lender collects what it can from Newvel, namely, π_L^N. If, however, Newvel reports the higher value π_H^N, the lender demands a payment R_H^N and with probability β extends F dollars again to finance Newvel for the second period. At the end of that period, the lender knows that she will be forced to settle for π_L^N as repayment. Thus, from the lender's point of view, the value V of the two-period loan contract is

$$V = -F + \theta \pi_L^N + (1 - \theta) \left[R_H^N + \beta(\pi_L^N - F) \right] \qquad (9.30)$$

The lender's problem is to pick the two loan parameters—R_H^N, the amount it collects at the end of period 1 when Newvel reports high profits, and β, the probability that it then extends a loan for period 2—so as to maximize this value. In choosing these parameters, however, the lender must satisfy two constraints.

First, the contract must give Newvel an incentive to report accurately at the end of period 1. If operating profit in period 1 is π_H^N and Newvel instead reports π_L^N, it pays the latter amount to the lender and keeps the difference, but loses any chance at a second-period loan. So, the gain is $\pi_H^N - \pi_L^N$. If instead, Newvel truthfully reports that profit was the higher value π_H^N, it pays the lender R_H^N and, with probability β gets a second loan. On average, it will then earn $\overline{\pi}^N$ in period 2 and, as we know, pay back π_L^N. Hence, the gain from telling the truth is $\pi_H^N - R_H^N + \beta(\overline{\pi}^N - \pi_L^N)$. Therefore, in order to induce Newvel to reveal truthfully when it earns π_H^N in the first period, the contract parameters must be chosen such that

$$\pi_H^N - R_H^N + \beta \left(\overline{\pi}^N - \pi_L^N \right) \geq \pi_H^N - \pi_L^N \qquad (9.31)$$

In an optimal contract, this constraint will be binding, which means that it will be a strict equality. Hence, we can write

$$R_H^N = \pi_L^N + \beta \left(\overline{\pi}^N - \pi_L^N \right) \qquad (9.32)$$

The second requirement is that Newvel actually be willing to take the contract, that is, that Newvel's expected income is non-negative. Given the contract's terms, Newvel knows that with probability θ it earns π_L^N in period 1, all of which it pays to the lender—after which no further loans are forthcoming. Hence, in this case, Newvel's net earnings are 0. However, with probability $1 - \theta$, Newvel earns π_H^N in period 1 and pays R_H^N to the lender. Thereafter, it obtains a second-period loan with probability β, earns $\overline{\pi}^N$ on average, and always pays back π_L^N. So, for Newvel's expected income under the contract to be positive requires that:

$$(1 - \theta) \left[\pi_H^N - R_H^N + \beta(\overline{\pi}^N - \pi_L^N) \right] \geq 0 \qquad (9.33)$$

It can be shown that this condition will not be binding and so will hold as a strict inequality.

If we substitute the incentive compatibility requirement of equation (9.32) into the lender's objective function, the latter becomes a function of the probability of loan renewal β, alone, and the problem becomes

$$\text{Max } V = -F + \pi_L^N + (1 - \theta)\beta(\overline{\pi}^N - F) \text{ subject to: } 0 \leq \beta \leq 1 \qquad (9.34)$$

Since both $(1 - \theta)$ and $(\overline{\pi}^N - F)$ are given, and since each term is positive, the solution for the maximization problem in (9.34) is the corner solution of setting $\beta = 1$. In this case, it follows from the incentive compatibility constraint (9.32) that the repayment at the end of the first period if Newvel reports earnings of π_H^N is $R_H^N = \overline{\pi}^N$. Hence, the optimal contract specifies that Newvel only gets a second-period loan if it reports earnings of π_H^N for period 1, in which case it must then pay the lender $\overline{\pi}^N$ at that time. It is easy to check that this results in a positive expected income for Newvel, so that Newvel will accept these terms.[14]

We now have an explanation as to why Newvel may find it difficult to get funding in the second period. Realizing that borrowers have an incentive to lie, lenders must rely on a two-period contract that induces honesty by making future loans contingent on past performance. Yet, we also know that this sort of contract makes an entrant like Newvel vulnerable to predation from an incumbent such as Microhard with "deep pockets." How would the optimal contract differ if we now allow it to recognize this possibility of predation?

---

[14]   We assume that the optimal contract is profitable for the lender since, if it cannot make money under the optimal contract, it will not make the loan in any case, and the problem is not interesting. Note that the contract parameters are also such that Newvel will also never report the high profit level when first-period profits are actually low (i.e., the parameters induce complete honesty in Newvel's reporting).

Since the contract specifies that the loan will be terminated after one period if Newvel reports earnings of π_L^N, the incumbent, Microhard, may now find it worthwhile to take action that raises the likelihood that Newvel will earn a low profit π_L^N in period 1. Recall that, in general, the lender extends a second-period loan with probability β, and that the inherent probability of Newvel earning only π_L^N in any period is θ. Thus, the probability that Microhard is a monopolist in period 2 is $(1 - \beta) + \theta\beta$. Define Microhard's monopoly profit as π_M^M and its duopoly profit as π_D^M. Suppose that by incurring a cost C, Microhard can take predatory actions that raise the inherent probability that Newvel earns π_L^N from θ to $\theta + \delta$. Hence, it raises the probability of Newvel's exit to $(1 - \beta) + (\theta + \delta)\beta$. This action will be worthwhile if

$$\delta\beta(\pi_M^M - \pi_D^M) - C > 0 \tag{9.35}$$

It is immediately apparent from condition (9.35) that the loan contract can be used to lessen the likelihood of predation by lowering the value of β, the probability of loan renewal following Newvel's report of high earnings. Without any concern for predation, we have seen that the lender sets β equal to its maximum value of 1. However, if the lender wishes to mitigate the likelihood of predatory attacks against its borrower, it needs to reduce β below this value. This may seem counterintuitive. Newvel's disadvantage relative to Microhard is that the latter has deeper pockets and does not have to rely on external funding. Yet paradoxically, if the lender wishes to prevent this, she does so by *reducing* the likelihood that Newvel will receive funding in period 2, effectively making Newvel's pockets even shallower.[15]

Why does the contract aimed at preventing or limiting predation have this feature? Why does it reduce Newvel's access to funding even more than a contract that ignores the predatory threat? The answer is that as β gets smaller, the more likely it becomes that Newvel will be denied second-period funding and have to leave even with no predation on Microhard's part. This is perhaps easiest to see in the extreme case of $\beta = 0$. In that case, Newvel will not get financing in period 2 regardless of its performance in period 1. In that case, there is absolutely no reason for Microhard to incur a cost of C to drive Newvel out, because Newvel is not going to survive in any case.

Recall that in the absence of predation $\beta = 1$ was the parameter value that maximized the value of the loan contract to the lender. Reducing β below this value therefore deters predation only by making the contract less valuable to the lender. Again, the extreme case of $\beta = 0$ is illustrative. Since this implies no second-period loan in any circumstance, it is equivalent to the one-period loan case we examined at the outset. We know, however, that this results in a certain loss for the lender; therefore, the lender will not make any loans to Newvel. Yet without any loans, Newvel will not enter in the first place. More generally, the lender's expected loan value when the value of β is such that predation is deterred is

$$V = \theta(\pi_L^N - F) + \beta(\overline{\pi}^N - F) \tag{9.36}$$

As β is reduced to deter entry, so is the lender's reward for granting the loan. It is entirely possible that the β required to prevent predation is such that the lender prefers not to make any loan at all.

---

[15]   Here, we assume that the contract is observable to Microhard. Otherwise, the contract parameters will not affect Microhard's decision to engage in predation.

Let us briefly recap. We have built a two-period model of market competition based on the assumption that an entrant firm needs external financing. We then showed that when the entrant's earnings are uncertain and known only to the entrant's management, a problem of "moral hazard" emerges for the lender requiring that it offers a contingent two-period loan that conditions the extension of funds for the second period on the entrant's achievement of high profit in the first period. This, however, opens the door to predation, because by taking actions that make it less likely that the entrant will achieve the required first-period profit, the incumbent also makes it less likely that the entrant will survive to compete in period 2. The lender can possibly deter such predation by reducing the likelihood that it extends second-period financing even when the entrant achieves a high first-period profit. This works because it makes it less likely that the entrant will survive in any event, implying that there is little need for the incumbent to be predatory. However, this same strategy lowers the value of the loan to the lender and therefore reduces its incentive to finance the entrant at all. In this last case, the entrant simply may not enter.

We now have a plausible "deep pockets" model of predation that is rooted in strategic behavior under uncertainty. Moreover, the model is consistent both with actual predation in which a small upstart firm is driven from the market or, alternatively, entry deterrence in which the threat of predation can only be countered by a contract that makes lending (and therefore entry) untenable. In this last respect, the Bolton and Scharfstein (1990) model is similar to an earlier one by Saloner (1987) in which the threat of predation serves to improve the contractual terms of a buyout of the entrant. This is precisely the behavior of which Standard Oil was accused. It is also a strategy that appears to have been used by American Tobacco in the late 1890s and early 1900s. During that time, American Tobacco acquired 43 rival cigarette firms. A study by Burns (1986) finds that the strategy used by American Tobacco was to identify the target rival that it wished to buy and introduce a competing brand at a low price in the target's market. The resultant drop in the target firm's profit would induce it to settle for a lower acquisition price. Burns (1986) estimates that such a predatory episode preceding a takeover bid lowered acquisition costs by about 25 percent.[16]

The ability to use predation—or the threat of predation—to alter contract terms and, in particular, the terms of a merger or buyout is important because it helps address a further counterargument against claims of predation made by the economist John McGee (1958, 1980). In his classic 1958 article, *"Predatory Price Cutting: The Standard Oil Case,"* McGee argued that predatory pricing only makes sense if two conditions are met. The first is essentially the requirement that the predation be subgame perfect. This requirement is met by Dixit (1980), Milgrom and Roberts (1982), and the Bolton and Scharfstein (1990) models above, as well as by other modern analyses. Yet, McGee also noted that there was a second requirement that a predation strategy would have to meet. This is that there is *no more profitable strategy* to achieve the same outcome. It was this second point that drew McGee's attention. He argued that a merger is always more profitable than predatory pricing. Hence, predatory pricing should not occur.

---

[16] In 1911, immediately following the Standard Oil decision, the Supreme Court found American Tobacco guilty of monopolizing the cigarette and tobacco product market, and cited predation to induce rivals to sell out as evidence of illegal monopolistic intent. A district court ordered that American Tobacco be dissolved and reconstituted as separate firms, the big three being American Tobacco, Ligget and Myers, and Lorillard.

McGee's argument, placed in a game-theoretic framework, is that predatory pricing is a dominated strategy; hence, it is one that will never be used. We can illustrate this point using the Stackelberg model.

The Stackelberg leader is the potential predator, and the follower is the intended prey. Suppose that each firm has a constant average and marginal cost c. The inverse market demand curve is $P = A - Q = A - (q_L + q_F)$. Here, q_L is the output of the Stackelberg leader, and q_F is the output of the follower. The Nash equilibrium outcome is $q_L = (A - c)/2$, and $q_F = (A - c)/4$, which leads to an industry price $p = (A + 3c)/4$. At this price, each firm earns a positive profit. The leader earns the profit $(A - c)^2/8$, while the follower earns half this amount. The leader's profit is still less than that earned by a pure monopolist, namely, $(A - c)^2/4$.

We now allow for two market periods, thus giving scope for the leader to engage in predatory behavior. Imagine that for the first market period, the leader is fully committed to producing an output so large that it can only all be sold at a price just equal to its average cost of c. Since the follower can only sell additional units by driving the market price below c (and therefore losing money), the follower will exit—or not enter. In the second market period, the leader is now a monopolist and can set the monopoly price and earn the monopoly profit $(A - c)^2/4$.

The trouble with this strategy, as McGee pointed out, is that a better one is available. Under the predatory strategy just described, the leader or predator earns a stream of profit of 0 in the first market period and then $(A - c)^2/4$ in the second. The follower anticipates a stream of 0 profit in both periods. McGee's point is that it would be more profitable for the leader to buy out or merge with the follower at the start of the first period. The merged firms can then act as a monopoly and earn the monopoly profit $(A - c)^2/4$ in both market periods. Even if the leader has to share this first period profit with the follower, say on a 50-50 basis, *both* firms still do better than they did under predation, when both the predator and prey earned a 0 profit in period 1. Since the second period profit is unchanged by the merger, it seems clear that the merger strategy dominates the predatory one.

Of course, McGee's (1958) argument ignores the fact that the antitrust authorities may disapprove and prevent the merger he envisions. It also ignores another moral hazard problem—that once a dominant firm is seen as willing to buy out any rival, it will likely face a stream of entrants who enter just for the profitability of being purchased.[17] Most importantly, it ignores the issue just raised that while merger may be a superior strategy, predatory actions or threats of action may in fact work to make the terms of any such buyout much more favorable to the incumbent, predatory firm.[18] At the same time, we should recognize that McGee's (1958) suggested strategy has been observed with some frequency in recent years. As the Reality Checkpoint on the pharmaceutical industry points out, many brand name drug manufacturers have adopted something like a buyout strategy relative to new generic competitors—paying these potential rivals not to enter the market.

---

[17]   Rasmussen (2007) explores this possibility.

[18]   This point was made by Yamey (1972): "[T]he aggressor will, moreover, be looking beyond the immediate problem of dealing with its current rival. Alternative strategies for dealing with that rival may have different effects on the flow of future rivals."

Reality Checkpoint
Getting to the Heart of the Matter—McGee on Drugs

Millions of Americans, including Vice-President Dick Cheney, suffer from hypertension (high blood pressure) and coronary heart disease or angina. Two major prescription drugs used to treat these conditions are Cardizem CD, produced by Aventis (formerly Hoechst Marion Roussel); and Hytrin, produced by Abbott Laboratories. These drugs are protected by patents and therefore protected from competition by generic or unbranded substitutes. However, the Hatch-Waxman Act of 1984 does provide some conditions under which a firm is permitted to market a generic substitute to a patented drug even before the patent expires. The generic producer must claim either that the new substitute does not really infringe on the patent, or that the patent was not really valid in the first place. If the patent holder challenges this claim, then entry of the generic drug is automatically delayed for 30 months to decide the issues. Such delay clearly makes life more difficult for the generics. As partial compensation aimed at promoting generic entry, the Hatch-Waxman Act has another provision. The *first* generic to enter obtains, after entry, a 180-day immunity against all other generics. That is, once one firm is granted the right to sell a generic substitute to the patented product, no other firm is allowed to do so for at least 180 days.

In the mid 1990s, the pharmaceutical firm, Andrx, applied for permission to market a generic substitute for Cardizem CD. Another firm, Geneva (a division of Novartis), requested authorization to market a generic substitute for Hytrin. Both Aventis and Abbott challenged these applications, and the automatic 30-month delay began. As the end of the 30 months drew near, and with the cases still not resolved, each incumbent was faced with the imminent entry of a rival. Presumably, each firm could have pursued predatory pricing to deter such entry. But each instead went the route proposed by McGee. They bought out the potential competitor.

Aventis forged an agreement to pay Andrx $10 million per quarter in return for *not* entering the Cardizem market, starting in July 1998 when Andrx gained FDA approval.

Aventis also agreed to pay an additional $60 million per year from 1998 until the end of the ongoing patent trial if Andrx eventually won that litigation. A similar agreement between Abbott and Geneva required that Abbott pay $4.5 million per month in return for Geneva agreeing to stay out of the Hytrin market. A common feature of both agreements was that Andrx and Geneva each also agreed not to transfer their 180-day immunity to any other firm. Since no other generic could enter the relevant market until 180 days after Andrx or Geneva entered, and since each of these two firms had agreed not to enter at all, these agreements had the effect of blocking all generic entry in these markets. Thus, neither Aventis nor Andrx had to face the prospect of paying off an endless stream of entrants.

A somewhat related case involves Mylan laboratories, the maker of two major anti-anxiety drugs, Lorazepam and Clorazepate. Both drugs use a key ingredient produced by a European firm, Cambrex. Starting in 1998, Mylan paid Cambrex not to sell this ingredient to any other firm. As a result, no other firm could compete with Mylan. Once in effect, Mylan raised the price of its drugs on the order of 2,000–3,000 percent.

Pursuant to a complaint filed by the FTC, Abbott agreed to terminate its agreement with Geneva. Mylan also settled with the FTC and agreed to pay $100 million into a fund designed to reimburse those who paid the exorbitant prices. Aventis pursued the matter in the courts, but both a federal district court and an appellate court found its agreement with Andrx to be a violation of the antitrust laws. It has so far paid out over $200 million in settlements with drug wholesalers and individual states.

Source: Guidera, J., and R. T. King, Jr. 2000. "Abbott Labs, Novartis Unit Near Pact with FTC Over Agreement on Hytrin." *Wall Street Journal* (14 March 2000), p. B6; M. Schroeder, 2000. "Mylan to Pay $100 Million to Settle Price-Fix Case." *Wall Street Journal* (13 July 2000), p. A4. See also various press releases at the FTC website, www.ftc.gov.

9.4   LONG-TERM CONTRACTS AS A BARRIER TO ENTRY

Our discussion of predation has now revealed how predatory actions may be used to alter contractual terms such as a rival's financing or the terms on which a rival may be bought. However, recent analysis has gone one step further to examine how contracts themselves may be a tool of predation and/or entry deterrence. This has a practical policy importance. While the Microsoft antitrust trial primarily focused on Microsoft's practice of bundling its *Internet Explorer* web browser for free with its *Windows* operating system as a possible case of predatory pricing aimed at Netscape, other predatory practices were also alleged. One of these was that Microsoft used its contracts with PC makers to foreclose other rivals from entering the operating systems market.

This possibility has a long tradition in antitrust history, dating back at least 50 years to the ruling in the famous United Shoe Machinery Corporation antitrust case in the early 1950s. The judge found that United Shoe, which then controlled about 85 percent of the shoemaking equipment market, consciously used the contracts by which it leased its machinery to shoe manufacturers as a tool to prevent entry into the market for shoe machinery.

Perhaps not surprisingly, the Chicago School has traditionally been skeptical of the use of contracts as a predatory device. The simple logic of this counterargument is well expressed by prominent antitrust scholars Bork (1978) and Posner (1976). Buyers do not have an incentive to sign contracts that disadvantage them with respect to a monopolist. Any contract signed must give not just the supplier but also the buyer some benefit—say, by way of increased service or repair—and therefore a step toward greater efficiency. These proponents of the Chicago School emphasize the efficiency grounds for observed contracts, rather than the predatory motive. Again, however, more recent theory has provided consistent arguments supporting the view that predation can occur in this rational world. We briefly present two such analyses below. The first is due to Aghion and Bolton (1987). The second is due to Rasmussen, Rasmeyer, and Wiley (1991).

9.4.1   Long-Term Contracts, Penalty Fees, and Entry Deterrence

Aghion and Bolton (1987) consider a two-period market with N identical customers, each of whom has a perfectly inelastic demand. Each is willing to pay V for the product and will buy exactly one unit, so long as the price $P \leq V$. In the first period, there is an incumbent monopoly, which we will again refer to as Microhard. The incumbent has a unit cost $c^M = V/2$. In the second period, a new rival may enter the market, which we will name Newvel. The new rival's unit cost c^N is drawn randomly from a uniform distribution between 0 and V with expected value $V/2$. In period 2, the firms compete in prices. If Newvel's cost $c^N > V/2$, it recognizes that it cannot win the price competition and does not enter. Hence the probability of entry is 0.5.

If there are no long-term contracts, Microhard will set the first-period price $P_1 = V$ and earn $N(V - V/2) = NV/2$ in first-period profit. In the second period, it will face a lower-cost rival with a probability of 0.5. If Newvel does enter, it is because its unit cost $c^N < V/2$. In that case, Newvel can profitably win the price competition with a price of $V/2$, in which case Microhard earns 0 second-period profit. If entry does not occur, however, Microhard can again sell to each of the N customers at price $P_2 = V$, and again earn $NV/2$ in profit. Thus, without any long-term contracts, the relevant market features will be as follows:

$P_1 = V$; $E(P_2) = 0.5V + 0.5V/2 = 0.75V$

Microhard Expected Profit $= NV/2 + 0.5(NV/2) = 0.75NV$ $\qquad$ (9.37)

Probability of Newvel Entry $= 0.5$

Now, consider how Microhard might use long-term contracts to improve its competitive position. Let it again set a first-period price of $P_1 = V$, but also offer each customer a contract to buy the product in period 2 at a price of $0.75V$. The only catch is that the customer is obligated to buy from Microhard at this contracted price. If it does not and instead buys it from a rival, it must pay Microhard a "breach of contract" penalty fee of $V/2$.

If consumers accept this contract, Newvel's chances of entry fall dramatically. A customer who has accepted Microhard's contract will only switch to Newvel if the price Newvel offers provides the customer enough savings relative to Microhard's price to cover the breach-of-contract penalty as well. The contract price is $0.75V$. If Newvel enters and offers a second-period price P_2^N, a customer who switches to Newvel will pay $P_2^N + V/2$. For this to be attractive, it must be the case that $P_2^N + V/2 \leq 0.75V$, which requires that $P_2^N \leq V/4$. Accordingly, Newvel will now only be able to enter if its unit cost $c^N \leq V/4$. However, the probability that this will happen is just one-fourth, which is now the, lower probability of entry.

Two questions then arise. First, is the contract profitable for Microhard? To see that it is, recall that Microhard's expected profit over two periods in the no-contract setting is $0.75NV$. With the contract, Microhard will continue to earn $0.5NV$ in period 1. In period 2, Microhard will now earn $(0.75V - c^M)N = (0.25V)$ with a 75 percent probability. With a probability of 25 percent, it will cede the market to a very low-cost Newvel. However, in this case, Microhard will receive the penalty fee $V/2$ from each of the N customers. Hence, Microhard's two-period expected profit $\mathrm{E}(\pi^M)$ is

$$\mathrm{E}(\pi^M) = NV/2 + 0.75(0.25V)N + 0.25N(V/2) = 0.8125NV > 0.75NV \qquad (9.38)$$

Hence, offering the contract does raise Microhard's expected profit. Accordingly, Microhard will find it attractive to offer the contract. However, this brings us to a second question—namely, will consumers find this contract attractive? Does the contract offer consumers enough compensation for the fact that as a result of signing it, they will now have a much lower chance of buying from a lower-cost rival?

Looking ahead to the second period, a rational customer will recognize that if she does not take the contract, she will either buy from Microhard at a free-standing price of V or from Newvel (if it enters) at a price of $V/2$ for an expected price of $0.75V$, exactly the same as in the contract offered by Microhard. On the other hand, accepting the contract means that a consumer will never pay a second-period price $P_2 > 0.75V$. Moreover, with probability 0.25, the customer will pay a lower fee even accounting for the penalty it must incur if it breaks the contract. Specifically, consumers will pay $0.75V$, three-fourths of the time. The remaining one-fourth of the time they will pay the penalty fee of $V/2$ and, on average, a price to Newvel of $0.125V$ (the mean of the distribution over which Newvel enters). Hence, consumers will pay an expected second-period price of $0.75(0.75V) + 0.25(V/2 + 0.125V) = 0.7185V < 0.75V$. Accordingly, customers will sign willingly.

From a social viewpoint, however, the contract is inefficient. Microhard's expected profit rises by $0.0625NV$. Consumer's surplus rises by $0.0315NV$. However, Newvel's expected profit falls from $0.25NV$ to $0.125NV$. Hence, the gain enjoyed by Microhard and consumers is more than offset by the loss incurred by Newvel. This model therefore offers a response to the Chicago counterargument. It is possible for consumers and the incumbent firm to benefit from entry-deterring practices that nonetheless reduce social welfare.

Reality Checkpoint
Coke Takes Out A Contract on Texas Rivals

Dangerfield, Texas, gets awfully hot. The summertime temperature can regularly top 100 degrees Fahrenheit, and shade is hard to find. That's probably one reason that Dangerfield residents and their neighbors drink a lot of soft drinks every year. Indeed, for convenience stores in the area, it is estimated that as much as half of their sales are from beverages. In the years just before 1992, the stores received their soft-drink supplies from a number of small soft-drink firms and bottlers, as well as from Coca-Cola and Pepsi. However, that all began to change after 1992.

Bruce Hackett, a former Coke employee and owner of Hackett Beverages, supplied ice-filled barrels to a number of stores that were also stoked with his soft-drink bottles. The barrels were usually displayed just outside the cash register line so that customers could easily grab a cold beverage and pay for it on the way out. However, starting in 1992, Hackett found more and more of his barrels turned upside down and left at the side of the road. In four years, he went from having barrels in 52 stores to barrels in just 2. Other independent bottlers and small beverage firms had similar experiences. They found stores abandoning the refrigerator units they gave them to display their products, dumping their fresh soda dispensing and vending machines, and even refusing them any shelf space.

The reason for these changes was easy to find. Coca Cola had started an aggressive marketing campaign in which it paid store owners to display its products *exclusively* and refused to give them access even to non-Coke drinks handled by Coca-Cola bottlers

if they did not. Thus, one contract offered a bonus of $2 million to a regional supermarket chain, Brookshire's, in return for just selling Coke products alone. Another contract required that "Coca Cola products will occupy a minimum of 100 percent of total soft-drink space" in the store.

The case went to trial before a Texas court in 2000. Coke's defense was that the stores wanted the contract deals it was offering. They argued that the stores felt they had little to offer in the soft-drink category unless they offered the national Coke brand at the best terms possible. Coke argued that the contracts it offered allowed the stores to do just that. However, it was indisputable that as the smaller firms were driven from the market, Coke prices went up. At Nu-Way, a popular Dangerfield convenience store that still offers Royal Crown Cola, a 20-ounce container of the Royal Crown product sells for 69 cents, while the same size container of Coke sells for 92 cents. However, at E Z Mart, another convenience store a short distance away, there is no Royal Crown alternative, and Coke sells for $1.09. Whether this was a case of predation or not is a question of judgment. However, a comment by Coca-Cola spokesperson Polly Howes probably did not help Coke's cause. In a widely distributed statement, Ms. Howes said that far from "a lack of competition. There was too much competition." The Texas jury found Coca-Cola guilty of violating the antitrust laws.

Source: C. Hays. 2003. "How Coke Pushed Rivals Off the Shelf." *The New York Times* (6 August 2003), Section 3, p. 1.

9.4.2 Naked Exclusion

Rasmussen, Rasmeyer, and Wiley (1991) offer a different model in which exclusive contracts that reward customers for agreeing not to purchase from an alternative supplier can be used by an incumbent to exploit the difficulty that consumers have in acting in coordination with the result that entry is again deterred. To understand their analysis, we again suppose a two-period model with, as before, N identical customers each with an inelastic demand for one unit of a good so long as price is less than V. In addition, we again suppose an incumbent firm, Microhard, and a potential rival, Newvel. However, we now modify our cost assumptions to permit some limited scale economies. In this case, each firm finds that its average cost declines as its output expands up to some level Q^*, after which unit costs are constant at c_{min}. When both firms are in the market, competition is in prices. If both charge the same price, customers randomly assign themselves to one or the other so that each firm gets half of the market. We also assume that $Q^* < N/2$, which implies that it is possible for both firms to be in the market and operating at minimum average cost.

First note that any equilibrium that has both firms in the market implies the price c_{min}. If both are in the market, price competition will lead each to cut its price to a minimum. Since this results in 0 profit, Microhard has a large incentive to try to keep Newvel from entering. Because it is in the market already, one way it can do this is to offer a contract that ties customers to its product before period 2 starts. However, customers are rational and forward-looking, too. So, we need to work out why they might agree to sign such a contract.

Suppose that N_S customers have signed the contract. Those $N - N_S$ consumers who have not are free to buy from any firm that is in the market. Likewise, each firm is free to compete for the patronage of these $N - N_S$ consumers. Note though that if $(N - N_S)/2 < Q^*$, Newvel cannot profitably enter and compete for these remaining customers. The reason is that if $(N - N_S)/2 < Q^*$, Newvel cannot operate at minimum average cost c_{min}, while Microhard can. If both firms charge the price c_{min} to the unsigned customers, each will serve $(N - N_S)/2$ of them. In addition, Microhard will serve the remaining N_S customers. It will therefore serve $(N + N_S)/2 > Q^*$ in total. Newvel, however, will be producing less than Q^*. As a result, it will not be able to compete against Microhard and, foreseeing this, will not enter.

Of course, if Newvel does not enter, those without a contract will have no alternative to buying from Microhard. Therefore, Microhard will be able to charge them V. It can therefore make it somewhat attractive for customers to accept the exclusive contract by offering them a price less than V. Accordingly, assume that at the end of period 1, Microhard offers all those who sign an exclusive agreement not to purchase from any firm other than itself a price of $V - X$, where $X \in [0, V - c_{min}]$. This offer puts each customer in something of a bind. If one customer declines the contract but N_S others accept it to the extent that $(N - N_S)/2 > Q^*$, then the one customer will have passed up the opportunity to buy at the price $V - X$, and be forced to buy at price V. On the other hand, a consumer that signs the exclusive contract and agrees to buy at price $V - X$ runs the risk that the number N_S who do so is such that $(N - N_S)/2 > Q^*$, so that Newvel can enter and the price to all those outside the contract falls to c_{min}. There is then a coordination problem in that each consumer has to make a decision without knowing what others are doing, while each would be better off if they could all coordinate their buying decisions.

In fact, the game actually has two Nash equilibria in pure strategies. One is for no customer to sign the contract. In that case, Newvel will enter and the second period price will be c_{min}. Neither Newvel nor Microhard can improve their lot by changing their behavior. Hence, neither has an incentive to change. The same is true for every customer. If any consumer were to change unilaterally, that consumer would only find that she has agreed to pay $V - X$ instead of the lower value c_{min}. The same is true in the alternative equilibrium outcome in which all consumers sign the contract. Here, if any single consumer declines the exclusive contract given that all others have signed, that consumer will simply find that in period 2 he pays V instead of $V - X$.

The naked exclusion model does not generate predatory entry deterrence as a unique outcome. However, it does make clear that such predatory behavior is a real possibility. It happens because the decisions of customers are decentralized. If consumers could band together and make one decision that would bind them all, they would reach the no-signing equilibrium and all would pay c_{min} in period 2. Yet because they cannot do this, each consumer has to worry that if others sign and she does not, she may be left out in the final period and forced to pay the monopoly price V. In this equilibrium, each consumer signs the contract because she believes others will—and with each signing, that belief is consistent with the outcome.

9.5   PREDATORY CONDUCT AND PUBLIC POLICY

Should there be public policies that restrain the conduct of firms who have acquired or are likely to acquire a dominant position in the marketplace? In the wake of the Standard Oil and American Tobacco antitrust cases, and continuing as late as the 1960s, the consensus answer to this question was yes. The fear of large corporations taking every opportunity to drive small entrepreneurs out of business was widespread and led to many court cases in which large firms were found guilty of antitrust violations. The expression of this view reached its apex perhaps in the infamous *Utah Pie*[19] case decided by the U.S. Supreme Court in 1967. In that case, a local dominant bakery, Utah Pie, that had over two-thirds of the Salt Lake City market complained against the practices of three national firms, Continental Bakeries, Pet, and Carnation, when they all entered the Utah market. Their entry resulted in a one-third decline in the price and a halving of Utah Pie's market share to just 33 percent. Yet, while its market share fell, Utah Pie's sales grew steadily after the entry of these large rivals and so did its net worth. Many economists believed that Utah Pie's real complaint was more about preserving its initial near-monopoly position—and the high prices that market power permitted—than it was about predatory tactics.

In the end, however, the Supreme Court found in favor of Utah Pie in a decision that was widely decried (and later repudiated). This ushered in a period of deep skepticism about allegations of predatory behavior and the ascendancy of the Chicago School view. This view was reflected in the work of McGee (1958, 1980), Koller (1969), Posner (1976), Bork (1978), and Easterbrook (1984) along with others. It served to make clear that many firms achieve dominance, not because of predation, but because of their superior competitive skill, and that the response of such firms to rival entry was not predatory but simply the normal response of any market when competitive pressures are intensified. The Chicago School view received something like an official blessing in the 1986 *Matsushita* case when the Supreme Court wrote, "For this reason, there is a consensus among commentators that predatory pricing schemes are rarely tried, and even more rarely successful."[20] A few years later, in the *Brooke* case of 1993, the Court went even further and outlined stringent evidentiary standards that had to be met before a predation claim would be supported.[21]

---

[19]   *Utah Pie Co. v. Continental Baking Co. et al* 386 U.S. 685 (1967).
[20]   See *Matsushita Electronic Industrial Co., Ltd v Zenith Radio Corporation et al.*, 475 U.S. 574 (1986).
[21]   *Brooke Group v. Brown & Williamson Tobacco* 509 U.S. 209 (1993). Interestingly enough, Brooke actually won the initial jury trial but lost in subsequent appeals to the federal courts.

The Brooke Group (also known as Ligget) was a small cigarette manufacturer that began selling a generic brand in 1980 at prices well below those of the major brands. When consumers responded favorably to the introduction of these cheap cigarettes, Brown & Williamson and other large tobacco companies responded with vigorous price cuts. In its effort to undersell Brooke, it seems clear that Brown cut prices so low that it sustained millions of dollars of losses over a period as long as a year or more. Ultimately, however, Brooke could not keep pace. It raised the price on its cigarettes. Almost immediately thereafter, Brown & Williamson and other cigarette manufacturers did the same.

The Supreme Court did not find the foregoing evidence conclusive. As noted, the Court had moved to a view that there was an economics consensus that predatory pricing was irrational. The court then established two broad requirements for a successful prosecution of a predatory pricing case. The first was evidence of selling below some measure of cost. The second, and really new element, introduced by the court was evidence that the predator had a reasonable expectation of recouping the losses endured during the predatory period. Just how strong the new requirements were can be seen in the fact that there was not one successful prosecution of predatory action in the first 40 cases that followed the Brooke decision. It was not until the important case of Microsoft that a finding of "guilty" was made.

The consensus to which the Supreme Court referred in *Matsushita* no longer exists—if it ever did. As we have seen in this chapter, capacity expansion, credible threats, and contractual exclusions are all tactics that can be part of a rational predatory strategy. Moreover, with respect to recoupment, it is important to recognize that successful predation has important reputation effects. Once a firm is successful in eliminating one rival, it sends a message to all other potential competitors. Thus, in measuring the ability of a firm to recover its losses, one has to include in the calculations all the profits secured by the deterrent effect that the firm's reputation has on other would-be entrants.

However, the Court's statement of necessary evidence does speak to an important issue. The recognition that predation can be rational and can happen does not carry any clear policy implications unless we have a clear standard by which predatory actions can be identified and distinguished from conduct that is truly procompetitive. Any entry will generally evoke some reaction from the incumbent firms. Typically, this may come in the form of lower prices or other expanded consumer benefits. Most such responses are not predatory in nature. To the contrary, they are exactly the conduct that we expect and hope that markets will promote. Similarly, when any firm, large or small, first comes into a market as a new entrant, it may want to set a low initial price—lower than the short-term, profit-maximizing one—as a way to induce consumers to forego their usual brand and try the entrant's relatively unknown product. Once established, the firm may then raise the price. Clearly, the intent of this kind of promotional pricing is not to drive a rival from the market. Yet, it may be difficult empirically to distinguish this pricing strategy from predatory pricing.

In other words, to the extent that antitrust enforcement seeks to prevent predatory practices, policymakers need to create workable legal standards that are able to distinguish procompetitive from anticompetitive conduct. Ideally, we would like such policy to be governed by a simple rule that could be used to detect the presence of predation. This would permit all parties to understand just what is and what is not legal. Yet, in the area of predation, simple rules rarely work.

Of the various rules that have been proposed, the most widely recognized and applied is that of Areeda and Turner (1975), which essentially finds any price to be predatory if it is below the firm's short-run average variable cost standing in as a proxy for marginal cost. Unfortunately, it is not a very good proxy. In actual practice, average variable cost can be significantly less than short-run marginal cost, so a firm could set a price below its current marginal cost yet still above its average cost. In so doing, the firm would be acting within the legal range permitted by the Areeda and Turner rule, even though a price below short-run marginal cost would likely be judged as predatory by many economists. Hence, as Scherer (1976) was quick to point out, the use of the average-cost standard could still permit serious predation.[22] Moreover, if there are important learning curve effects so that average cost falls with a firm's cumulative production over time (as opposed to scale economies in which average cost falls with the volume of production per unit of time), predation can occur by means of a vigorous output expansion without prices ever falling below cost.[23]

Despite its shortcomings, the Areeda and Turner rule has been applied in many U.S. antitrust cases. It has been frequently relied upon by Supreme Court Justice Stephen Breyer.[24] It was also used to exonerate IBM against predatory price-cutting charges in *California Computer Products, Inc., et al. v. International Business Machines* (613 F. 2d 727 (9th Cir. 1979)). Perhaps the clearest statement is that of Judge Kaufman who, in *Northeastern Telephone Company v. American Telephone and Telegraph Company et al*, (651 F. 2d 76 (2nd Cir. 1981)), wrote: "We agree with Areeda and Turner that in the general case, at least, the relationship between a firm's prices and its marginal costs provides the best single determinant of predatory pricing."

The weaknesses in the Areeda and Turner rule have led many economists to propose modified alternatives. These include rules proposed by Baumol (1979, 1956), Williamson (1977), Joskow and Klevorick (1979), Ordover and Willig (1981), and Bolton, Brodley, and Riordan (2001). However, none of the proposed predatory standards is simple or easily translated into a courtroom proceeding. The difficulty of distinguishing between good, fierce competition on the one hand and predatory efforts on the other is substantial. Moreover, as tough as this distinction is to make in the case of pricing, it may be even more difficult to achieve in considering other actions, such as contractual "lock ins." Thus, while the post-Chicago view that predation can be rational and does happen is now widespread among economists, the difficulties in separating predatory actions from normal competitive responses has meant that few allegations of such behavior have been sustained by the courts.

9.6   EMPIRICAL APPLICATION
Entry Deterrence in the Pharmaceutical Industry

While legal cases and anecdotal examples of entry deterrence can be easily found, empirical work testing systematic entry deterrence has been limited. The reason for this is that the data requirements necessary to identify consistently any systematic predatory behavior across a set of market data points are fairly demanding. For example, in a paper on shipping cartels, Scott Morton (1997) finds some supportive evidence that established

---

[22]   See Scherer's (1976) exchange with Areeda and Turner (1976) on this and other points.
[23]   See Cabral and Riordan (1997) for an elaboration of this point.
[24]   See, for example, his decision in *Barry Wright Corporation v. ITT Grinnell Corporation, et al.*, 724F. 2d 227 (1st Cir. 1983).

Reality Checkpoint
Cut-rate or Cutthroat Fares?

In 1994, Sun Jet Airlines began offering service between Dallas-Fort Worth airport and a select few other cities including Tampa, Florida and Long Beach, California. Its entry was subsequently followed by that of Vanguard Airlines flying between Dallas and Kansas City, and Western Pacific offering flights between Dallas and Colorado Springs. All three airlines are small startup carriers whose operating costs are widely recognized to be well below those of the major, established airlines. Indeed, it was this cost advantage that gave these small startups their only hope of surviving in the Dallas-Fort Worth market. This is because the Dallas-Fort Worth airport is a central hub for American Airlines. American carries 70 percent of all the passengers who travel from any city nonstop to Dallas and 77 percent of all those nonstop passengers originating in Dallas. It has concessions from local businesses and has already sunk the costs necessary to operate its gates, ticketing desks, and so on. Internal documents obtained from American by the Justice Department reveal that these and other advantages made the firm confident that its dominance would not be challenged by another major airline. However, those same documents suggest that American

was concerned about the entry of low cost startups, especially after observing how much market share such firms had taken from other major carriers at their hub airports.

American responded aggressively to the three startups. It greatly expanded its flight offerings in the challenged markets and lowered its fares. In each of the three markets shown, this strategy ultimately led the startups to exit the market. Immediately thereafter, American cut its flights and raised fares back to or above earlier levels. This is shown for the case of three markets in the table below.

Was this a case of predatory pricing? The Justice Department thought so. It claimed that during the battle with the startups, American lost money on each flight. The actual losses are claimed to be even greater because to offer the additional flights, aircraft were diverted from profitable routes to these unprofitable ones. American won an initial decision in district court. In July 2003, a three-judge Appeals Court upheld the lower court's decision.

Source: D. Carney and W. Zellner, "Caveat Predator: The Justice Department is Cracking Down on Predatory Pricing". *Business Week* (22 May 2000), p. 116.

	Before entry		During conflict		After exit	
	Daily flights	Price	Daily flights	Price	Daily flights	Price
Kansas City	8	$108	14	$80	11	$147
Long Beach	0	—	3	$86	0	—
Colorado Springs	5	$150	7	$81	6	$137

cartels in the late 19th and early 20th century engaged in predatory pricing to deter new shipping entrants, especially when the entrants were small or had poor financial resources. However, in an another paper, Scott Morton (2000) finds little evidence that pharmaceutical firms successfully use advertising to deter generic entry as the end of the incumbent's patent nears.

One reason that econometric work on predation is so tricky is that such work must somehow identify cases where an incumbent both regarded entry as a real threat *and* felt that there was a way to prevent it. Suppose, for instance, that the data set includes two kinds of markets. One type is characterized by a high likelihood of entry by several new firms and that by taking a costly action X the incumbent can reduce the number of entrants. The second type market is characterized by a very low probability of entry and by at most one new rival. Finally, suppose that post-entry competition is Cournot, so the fewer new entrants the better from the viewpoint of the incumbent.

In such a setting, we may find that incumbents only take action X in the first type of market, because entry is so unlikely in the second kind of market that incurring the cost of action X is not worthwhile. If this is so, the data will be divided into two groups. In one set of cases, the incumbent takes action X and there is some entry (though less than otherwise would have been the case). In the other set of cases, the incumbent does not take action X, yet there is no entry. Thus, on balance, the data will show that there is *more* entry when the predatory tactic X is used than when it is not. Unless care is taken to identify such markets *a priori*, it will be hard to conclude from such data that predation is a serious threat.

Another difficulty that the researcher must overcome is identifying the entry-deterring strategy. This, too, is trickier than it may at first appear. Consider the first-mover, consumer learning-by-doing model of Gabszewicz, Pepall, and Thisse (1992) discussed in Chapter 8. Recall that in the first period of that model, when the incumbent is alone, it prices low to "buy up" a cohort of customers who will be loyal to its product after the second-period entry of a rival, because these customers have learned how to work with the incumbent's brand. On the one hand, then, such aggressive pricing may seem as if it deters entry because it limits the number of customers for whom the later entrant can compete. On the other hand, however, the fact that it has such a loyal and price-insensitive cohort encourages the incumbent to charge a high price when entry occurs, and this allows the entrant to gain more consumers at a high price as well. Of course, this latter effect makes entry more likely.

A recent paper that tries to sort all these issues out is Ellison and Ellison (2010). They look at the advertising and pricing behavior of pharmaceutical companies in the case of 64 drugs about to lose their patents over the years 1986–92. They first do a simple regression to determine which markets are most vulnerable to entry. For this purpose, they code each market as to whether or not there was any generic entry within three years after the expiration of the incumbent's patent. This procedure creates a 1, 0 variable for each market called *Entry*, where the variable is 1 if there was entry and 0 if there was none. Ellison and Ellison (2010) then try to explain this entry variable with an equation that includes three right-hand side variables that should be related to entry. These are Rev_i, the average annual revenue earned by the incumbent over the three years prior to patent expiration; $Hosp_i$, the fraction of revenues from the drug due to hospital sales in the year prior to patent expiration; and $Chronic/Acute_i$, which takes on the value 0 if the drug treats an acute condition but 1 if it treats a chronic condition. Their estimated equation then is

$$Entry_i = constant + \beta_1 Rev_i + \beta_2\ Hosp_i + \beta_3\ Chronic/Acute_i + \varepsilon_i \qquad (9.39)$$

where ε_i represents random factors that may affect entry in the ith market.

Because the dependent variable is not continuous but, instead, is either 1 or 0, equation (9.39) cannot be efficiently estimated by ordinary least squares (OLS) regression. The linear feature of OLS means that it is quite likely that for plausible values of the independent variables, the OLS estimates of the β_k coefficients will predict a value for entry outside the 0–1 interval.

Instead, Ellison and Ellison (2010) use an alternative regression procedure called Probit. This procedure effectively transforms the data so that for any value of the right-hand side variables, the coefficient estimates give rise to a value for Entry that lies between 0 and 1. This predicted value is then a measure of the probability of entry given the market features. In turn, this allows them to classify each of their 64 markets as one of three types: (1) low probability of entry; (2) intermediate probability of entry; and (3) high probability of entry.

Ellison and Ellison (2010) next consider the strategic use of advertising to deter entry in these markets. They start by noting that, in these cases, advertising by one firm has considerable spillover to the products of another. In particular, advertising by an incumbent calls attention to the specific functions of the drug, its potential benefits, its proper use, and so on, in a way that is likely to inform consumers of the benefit of later generic rivals. This is particularly the case with drugs, since doctors are smart enough to realize that the active ingredients in branded medications and generics are chemically identical. It is even more the case in those states in which pharmacies are required by law to fill a prescription with a cheaper generic medication if one is available and the doctor has not explicitly forbidden it. In other words, Ellison and Ellison (2010) assume that advertising by an incumbent today will *help* tomorrow's generic entrant. Hence, if incumbents wish to deter entry, they should *reduce* advertising in the period prior to the expected emergence of a rival.

Of course, whether or not incumbents wish to deter entry will depend in part on how likely entry is. A key insight of the Ellison and Ellison (2010) paper is that the relationship between the probability of entry and strategic deterrence efforts is likely to be nonmonotonic. This is because entry deterrence is probably not worth the cost either in markets where entry is highly probable or in markets where it is very unlikely. In the first case, no amount of deterrence is likely to prevent entry. In the second case, no deterrence is really necessary. Thus, Ellison and Ellison (2010) predict that deterrence efforts will first rise (relative to what they would otherwise be) as the probability of entry rises from a low value to an intermediate one; and then fall, as the probability of entry rises still further to a high value. In terms of advertising, this means that incumbents will *lower* their advertising in those markets that their Probit regression results characterize as having an intermediate probability of entry but exhibit no advertising response to the threat of entry in either low or high probability of entry markets. Again, this is because Ellison and Ellison (2010) assume that advertising by the incumbent also has strong benefits for the generic entrant. Reducing advertising prior to the period of potential entry can then make that entry less likely. To some extent, this is precisely what they find.

Consider so-called detail advertising. By this we mean the promotional efforts of pharmaceuticals to influence physicians' prescribing practices by visiting doctors and health care providers and making direct presentations in their offices. Ellison and Ellison (2010) look at the time trend in the value of detail advertising relative to its average in the three years prior to patent expiration for each month, starting 36 months before that expiration and continuing for 12 months after by estimating the regression equation:

$$\frac{\text{Advertising}_{it}}{\text{Average Advertising}_i} - 1 = (\beta_1 \text{ Low Entry}_i + \beta_2 \text{ Intermed Entry}_i$$
$$+ \beta_3 \text{ High Entry}_i)\text{Time} + \varepsilon_{it} \tag{9.40}$$

Table 9.2   Detail advertising trend by category of entry probability, 64 pharmaceutical markets

Coefficient	Estimated Value	Standard Error
β_1	−0.007	0.013
β_2	−0.032	0.009
β_3	0.009	0.007

The *Time* variable is just a trend term that increases by 1 as one moves a month closer to expiration date. The dependent variable is the ratio of advertising in the ith market in month t relative to average monthly detail advertising in that market. LowEntry, IntermedEntry, and HighEntry are each a 1,0 dummy variable indicating what entry category market i is in. The hypothesis is that β_2 will be significantly less than either β_1 or β_3, reflecting the efforts of incumbents in these markets to reduce advertising as a means of deterring entry. The estimated results are shown in the table below.

As you can see, the estimate of β_2 is noticeably smaller (algebraically) than either of the other two coefficients. That is, the results imply that while the incumbent's detail advertising declines by less than 1 percent per month relative to the norm in high entry markets (β_1) and actually rises a bit in low entry markets (β_3), it falls by over 3 percent per month in markets with an intermediate chance of entry. Thus, Ellison and Ellison (2010) provide some interesting evidence of strategic deterrence efforts in U.S. pharmaceutical markets in the late 1980s.

Summary

Allegations of pricing below cost to drive out a competitor and other comparable predatory strategies have been part of antitrust concerns for over 100 years. However, these fears faced increasing skepticism by the courts in the last part of the 20th century. This development partly reflected an increased understanding of the evolution of market structure, which often produced sustained dominance without any predatory actions by incumbents to destroy new entrants. It also reflected the growing influence of the Chicago School view that predation is irrational. In the language of game theory, the Chicago view is that predation is neither a subgame-perfect strategy nor a dominant strategy. Accordingly, few charges of predatory activity have been successfully prosecuted in the last 20 years, although the *Microsoft* case stands as a notable exception.

At the same time, history seems to offer many examples of actual predatory conduct. As a result, an important question in contemporary industrial organization theory has been whether we can construct plausible models in which predatory actions are rational. The answer turns out to be yes, and numerous game-theoretic models have now been developed that overturn the logic of the Chain Store Paradox and have established a post-Chicago understanding of strategic predation.

An important common feature in many of these models is asymmetry. Dominant incumbent firms have an advantage over smaller potential and actual entrants in that they can commit via capacity expansion to high levels of output, rely on internal financing, and establish contracts with current customers that inhibit rival expansion. Yet, despite the widespread recognition that predation can be part of a rational and successful strategy for a dominant firm, the proper role of public policy remains clouded.

The principal problem for policymakers is one of distinguishing aggressive pricing and other competitive strategies from ones that are truly predatory—profitable only if they succeed in driving a rival out of business. Some antitrust enforcement—especially those cases prosecuted under the Robinson-Patman Act in the first 35 years after it was passed—appear to have been misguided efforts to protect competitors and not competition. Both economists and the courts continue to struggle with the implementation of a workable definition of predation. Empirical work testing systematic entry deterrence has been challenged by the data requirements necessary to identify predatory behavior across a set of market data points. Nevertheless, this is an active research area in empirical industrial organization, holding promise for policymakers seeking to implement and enforce antitrust laws on predatory behavior.

Problems

1. Let the domestic market for small, specialized calculators and similar office equipment be currently served by one firm, called Firm I. This incumbent's total cost is: $\text{TC}(q_I) = 0.025q_I^2$. Inverse market demand is $P = 50 - 0.1Q$. Initially, Q is equal to q_I, because the only firm in the market is the incumbent Firm I.

   a. Suppose now that a foreign producer of calculators is considering exporting to the U.S. market. Because of transportation costs and tariffs, this foreign firm faces some cost disadvantage relative to the domestic incumbent. Specifically, the foreign firm's cost schedules are $\text{TC}(q_E) = 10q_E + 0.025q_E^2$. Suppose that the incumbent firm is committed to the monopoly level of output. What demand curve is faced by the potential entrant? Facing this demand what level of output will the foreign firm actually export to the domestic market? What will be the industry price?

   b. To what level of output would the incumbent firm have to commit in order to deter the foreign firm from entering the market? What is the incumbent firm's profit?

   c. Competition in this market is in quantities (Cournot). In this light, is it reasonable to believe that the incumbent is committed to the output q^* needed to deter entry? Why or why not?

2. Suppose that the inverse demand function is described by $P = 100 - 2(q_1 + q_2)$, where q_1 is the output of the incumbent firm and q_2 is the output of the entrant. Let the labor cost per unit be $w = 20$ and capital cost per unit be $r = 20$. In addition, let each firm have a fixed cost of $F_1 = F_2 = \$100$.

   a. Suppose that in stage 1, the incumbent invests in capacity $\overline{K}_1$. Derive the best response function of both the incumbent and the entrant.

   b. Show that if the incumbent commits to a production capacity of $\overline{K}_1 = 15$, the entrant will do best by producing 7.5 and earn a profit of \$12.5, while the incumbent earns a profit of \$125.

   c. Show that if the incumbent instead commits in stage 1 to a production capacity $\overline{K}_1 = 16$, then the entrant's best stage two response is to produce $q_2 = 7$, at which output the entrant does not earn a positive profit. What profit level for the incumbent does this imply?

3. An incumbent firm operates in a local computer market, which is a natural monopoly. That is, there is room for only one firm to sell profitably in this market. Market demand for the good is estimated to be $Q^D = 100 - P$. Another firm would like to enter this market, but only if the incumbent firm has a higher unit cost than it does. Specifically, there is a 25 percent chance that the incumbent is a low-cost firm, with a unit cost equal to 20, and there is a 75 percent chance that the incumbent is a high-cost firm with a unit cost of 30. The entrant's unit cost is 25. The entrant knows its costs, but not that of the incumbent. The incumbent does know its unit cost. Market demand is common knowledge to both firms. The entrant, however, does get to observe the current or preentry market price at which the incumbent sells its goods. If the entrant decides to enter the market, it incurs a setup cost of \$1,000. Does the high-cost firm have an incentive to set a low price in order to masquerade as a low-cost firm?

4. Let inverse demand be: $P = 100 - Q$ and let the incumbent's cost be: $C_I = 100 + 1.5q_I^2$. Recently, an upstart firm has entered the market. The upstart has the cost function $C_U = 100 + 110q_U$. Suppose the incumbent sets a price of \$74 and meets all the demand at that price.

    a. Does the incumbent's behavior violate the Areeda-Turner rule of selling below marginal cost?

    b. Does the incumbent's behavior violate the Areeda-Turner rule when average variable cost is used as a proxy for marginal cost?

5. (Preemption game) Suppose that two firms are in a race to enter a new market. For each firm, there is an advantage to taking time and perfecting its product, because then consumers will pay more for it and it will be more profitable. However, there is also a disadvantage in waiting; this has an interest opportunity cost of r. Let the time to enter t vary from 0 to 1 (year), and denote the choice of Firm 1's entry and Firm 2's entry be t_1 and t_2, respectively. The (symmetric) profit functions are:

$$\pi^1(t_1, t_2) = \begin{cases} e^{(1-r)t_1} & \text{if } t_1 < t_2 \\ e^{(\frac{1}{2} - rt_1)} & \text{if } t_1 = t_2 \\ e^{(1-t_2)-rt_1} & \text{if } t_1 > t_2 \end{cases}$$

$$\pi^2(t_1, t_2) = \begin{cases} e^{(1-r)t_2} & \text{if } t_2 < t_1 \\ e^{(\frac{1}{2} - rt_2)} & \text{if } t_1 = t_2 \\ e^{(1-t_1)-rt_2} & \text{if } t_2 > t_1 \end{cases}$$

Show that the Nash equilibrium entry times are $t_1 = t_2 = 1/2$.

References

Aghion, P., and P. Bolton. 1987. "Contracts as a Barrier to Entry." *American Economic Review*, 77 (June): 388–401.

Areeda, P. E. and D. F. Turner. 1975. "Predatory pricing and related practices under section 2 of the Sherman Act." *Harvard Law Review*, 88 (February): 697–733.

———. 1976. "Scherer on Predatory Pricing: A Reply." *Harvard Law Review*, 89 (March): 891–900.

Bain, J., 1956. *Barriers to New Competition: Their Character and Consequences in Manufacturing Industries.* Cambridge, MA: Harvard University Press.

Baldwin, J. 1995. *The Dynamics of Industrial Competition.* Cambridge: Cambridge University Press.

Baumol, W. J. 1979. "Quasi-Permanence of Price Reductions: A Policy for Prevention of Predatory Pricing." *Yale Law Journal*, 89: 1–26.

———. 1996. "Predation and the Logic of the Average Variable Cost Test". *Journal of Law & Economics*, 39 (April): 49–72.

Birch, D. 1987. *Job Creation in America: How our Smallest Companies Put the Most People to Work.* New York: MacMillan, Free Press.

Bolton, P. and D. Scharfstein. 1990. "A Theory of Predation Based on Agency Problems in Financial Contracting." *American Economic Review*, 80 (March): 93–106.

Bork, R. 1978. *The Antitrust Paradox.* New York: Basic Books.

Brandenburger, A. B. and B. J. Nalebuff. 1996. *Co-opetition.* New York: Doubleday.

Brodley, J., P. Bolton and M. Riordan. 2001. "Predatory Pricing: Strategic Theory and Legal Policy." *Georgetown Law Review*, 88 (August): 2239–2330.

Brown, C. and J. Lattin. 1994. "Investigating the Relationship between Time in Market and Pioneering Advantage." *Management Science*, 40 (October): 1361–1369.

Burns, M. R. 1986. "Predatory pricing and the acquisition cost of competitors." *Journal of Political Economy*, 94, (April): 266–296.

Cable, J. and J. Schwalbach, 1991. "International Comparisons of Entry and Exit." In P. Geroski and J. Schwalbach (Eds.). *Entry and Market Contestability*. Oxford: Blackwell Publishers.

Cabral, L. M. B., and M. J. Riordan. 1997. "The Learning Curve, Predation, Antitrust, and Welfare." *Journal of Industrial Economics*, 45 (June): 155–169.

Caves, R. E. 1998. "Industrial Organization and New Finding on the Turnover and Mobility of Firms." *Journal of Economic Literature*, 36 (December): 1947–1982.

Caves, R. E., and P. Ghemawat. 1986. "Capital Commitment and Profitability: An Empirical Investigation." *Oxford Economic Papers*, 38 (July): 94–110.

Dixit, A. 1980. "The Role of Investment in Entry Deterrence." *The Economic Journal*, 90 (January): 95–106.

Dunne, T., M. J. Roberts, and L. Samuelson. 1988. "Patterns of firm entry and exit in U.S. Manufacturing Industries." *RAND Journal of Economics*, 19 (Winter): 495–515.

_____. 1989. "The Growth and Failure of U.S. Manufacturing Plants." *Quarterly Journal of Economics*, 104 (November): 671–698.

Easterbrook, F. H. 1984. "The Limits of Antitrust." *The Texas Law Review*, 63 (January): 1–40.

Ellison, G., and S. Ellison. 2010. "Strategic Entry Deterrence and the Behavior of Pharmaceutical Incumbents Prior to Patent Expiration." American Economic Journal, *Microeconomics*, (forthcoming).

Fisher, F. 1991. *Industrial Organization, Economics and the Law*. Cambridge MA: MIT Press.

Genesove, D. and W. Mullin. 1998. "Testing Static Oligopoly Models: Conduct and Cost in the Sugar Industry, 1890-1914." *Rand Journal of Economics*, 14 (Summer): 355–377.

Geroski, P. A. 1995. "What do we know about entry?" *International Journal of Industrial Organization*, 13 (December): 421–440.

Geroski, P. A., and S. Toker. 1996. "The Turnover of Market Leaders in UK Manufacturing Industries, 1979–86." *International Journal of Industrial Organization*, 14 (June): 141–158.

Ghemawat, P. 1984. "Capacity Expansion in the Titanium Dioxide Industry." *Journal of Industrial Economics*, 33 (December): 145–163.

Gibrat, P. 1931. *Les inegalities economiques; applications: aux inegalities des richesses, a la concentration des enterprises, aux populations des villes, aux statistiques des familles, etc., d'une loi nouvelle, la loi de l'effet proportionnel*. Paris: Librairie du Recueill Sirey.

Hall, E. A., 1990. "An Analysis of Preemptive Behavior in the Titanium Dioxide Industry." *International Journal of Industrial Organization*, 8 (September): 469–484.

Hohenbalken, B. von, and D. West. 1986. "Empirical Tests for Predatory Reputation." *Canadian Journal of Economics*, 19 (February): 160–178.

Jarmin, R. S., S. D. Klimek, and J. Miranda. 2004. "Firm Entry and Exit in the U. S. Retail Sector: 1977–1997." Working Paper 04-17, Center for Economic Studies, Bureau of the Census.

Joskow, P. L. and A. K. Klevorick. 1979. "A Framework for Analyzing Predatory Pricing Policy." *Yale Law Journal*, 89 (December): 213–270.

Jovanovic, B. 1982. "Selection and the Evolution of Industry." *Econometrica*, 50 (May), 649–70.

Kalecki, M. 1945. "On the Gibrat Distribution." *Econometrica*, 13 (April): 161–170.

Klepper, S. 2002. "Firms Survival and the Evolution of Oligopoly." *Rand Journal of Economics*, 33 (Summer): 37–61.

Koller, R. H. II. 1971. "The Myth of Predatory Pricing: An Empirical Study." *Antitrust Law & Economics Review*, 4 (Summer): 105–143.

Lambkin, M. 1988. "Order of Entry and Performance in New Markets." *Management Science*, 9 (Summer): 127–140.

McGee, J. S. 1958. "Predatory Price Cutting: the Standard Oil (N.J.) case." *Journal of Law and Economics*, 1 (April): 137–169.

_____. 1980. "Predatory pricing revisited." *Journal of Law and Economics*, 23 (October): 289–330.

Milgrom, P., and J. Roberts. 1982. "Limit Pricing and Entry Under Incomplete Information: An Equilibrium Analysis." *Econometrica*, 50 (March): 443–460.

Mitchell, W. 1991. "Dual Clocks: Entry Order Influences on Incumbent and Newcomer Market Share and Survival When Specialized Assets Retain Their Value." *Strategic Management Journal*, 12 (February): 85–100.

Nelson, R., and S. G. Winter. 1982. *An Evolutionary Theory of Economic Change*. Cambridge, MA: Harvard University Press.

Ordover, J., and R. Willig. 1981. "An Economic Definition of Predation: Pricing and Product Innovation." *Yale Law Journal*, 91: 8–53.

Posner, R. 1976. *Antitrust Law: An Economic Perspective*. Chicago: University of Chicago Press.

Rasmussen, E. 2007. *Games and Information*. 4th Edition. Cambridge, MA: Basil Blackwell, Inc.

Rasmussen, E., J. M. Rasmeyer, and J. Wiley. 1991. "Naked Exclusion." *American Economic Review*, 81 (December): 1137–1145.

Saloner, G. 1987. "Predation, Mergers and Incomplete Information." *Rand Journal of Economics*, 18 (Summer): 165–186.

Scherer, F. M. 1976. "Predatory Pricing and the Sherman Act: A Comment." *Harvard Law Review*, 89 (March): 869–890.

Scott Morton, F. 1997. "Entry and Predation: British Shipping Cartels, 1879–1929." *Journal of Economics and Management Strategy*, 6 (Winter): 679–724.

_____. 2000. "Barriers to Entry, Brand Advertising, and Generic Entry in the U.S. Pharmaceutical Industry." *International Journal of Industrial Organization*, 18 (October): 1085–1124.

Spence, A. M. 1977. "Entry, Investment, and Oligopolistic Pricing." *Bell Journal of Economics*, 8 (Fall): 534–544.

Sylos-Labini, P. 1962. *Oligopoly and Technical Progress*. Cambridge, MA: Harvard University Press.

Sutton, J. 1997. "Gibrat's Legacy." *Journal of Economic Literature*, 35 (March): 40–59.

Tarbell, I. 1904. *The History of The Standard Oil Company*. McClure, Phillips and Co.

Urban, G., T. Carter, S. Gaskin, and Z. Mucha. 1984. "Market Share Rewards to Pioneering Brands." *Management Science*, 32 (June): 645–659.

Weiman, D., and R. C. Levin. 1994. "Preying for Monopoly? The Case of Southern Bell Telephone Company, 1894–1912." *Journal of Political Economy*, 102 (February): 103–126.

Williamson, O. E. 1977. "Predatory Pricing: A Strategic and Welfare Analysis." *Yale Law Journal*, 87 (December): 284–340.

Yamey, Basil, S. 1972. "Predatory price cutting: notes and comments." *Journal of Law and Economics*, 15 (April): 129–142.

Yergin, D. 1991. *The Prize*. New York: Simon and Schuster.

10

Price Fixing and Repeated Games

In November 2009, the European Union Competition Directorate jointly fined Akzo, Ciba, Elf Aquitaine and seven others €173 million ($260 million at the time) for fixing the price of plastic petrol additives. In that same month, U.S. authorities jointly imposed fines totalling $585 million on LG Display of South Korea, Sharp of Japan, and Chunghwa Picture Tubes of Taiwan after the three pleaded guilty to price fixing in the market for flat screens used in computers, televisions, and cell phones. The European fines came almost a year from the date that the Competition Directorate imposed fines nearly as large on four companies for being members of a cartel that engaged in illegal market sharing agreements and discussed target market prices for delivery of auto glass in the European Union.[1] Notably, in this last case, the fine imposed on Asahi/AGC was reduced by 50 percent to €113.5 million in return for that firm's cooperation with the cartel investigation and their providing information that helped expose the cartel.

The good news is that all of the above conspirators were caught and prosecuted. The bad news is that collusive agreements serving as evidence are not that uncommon. In 2007, for example, European regulators fined five elevator manufacturers a total of €992 million (approximately $1.4 billion) for operating a cartel that controlled prices in Germany, Belgium, Luxembourg, and the Netherlands. The elevator case came just one month after another case involving gas insulated switch-gear projects, in which the Commission imposed fines totaling €750 million on 11 companies for their part in a price-fixing cartel. Earlier in the decade, the U.S. Department of Justice imposed a total of more than $732 million on companies operating a cartel to control the pricing of dynamic random access memory (DRAM). As Table 10.1 and Figure 10.1 make clear, many other price-fixing conspiracies have been detected and stopped—the most infamous of which may still be the lysine and vitamin conspiracies.[2] For its role in the latter of these, the Swiss pharmaceutical company Hoffman-LaRoche alone was fined $500 million.

An interesting feature of many of the recent conspiracies is that a number were caught because at least one of the members decided to confess to the authorities in response to leniency policies that have been adopted in recent years. Under such a policy, the first firm

---

[1] Details of the European Union cases can be obtained at http://ec.europa.eu/comm/competition/antitrust/cases/index.html.
[2] Details can be found at http://www.usdoj.gov/atr.

Table 10.1   Violations yielding a corporate fine of $20 million or more since 2000

Firm	Year	Product	Fine (millions)
LG, Sharp, and Chungwha	2009	LCDs	$585
Air France, KLM	2008	Air Cargo	$350
Korean Air Lines	2007	Air Cargo/Passenger	$300
British Airways	2007	Air Cargo/Passenger	$300
Samsung	2006	DRAM	$300
Hynix Semiconductor Inc.	2005	DRAM	$185
Infineon Technologies AG	2004	DRAM	$160
Mitsubishi Corp.	2001	Graphite Electrodes	$134
Cargolux Airlines	2009	Air Cargo	$119
JAL	2008	Air Cargo/Passenger	$110
Lan Cargo Brazil	2009	Air Cargo	$109
Elpida Memory, Inc.	2006	DRAM	$84
Dupont Dow Elastomers L.L.C.	2005	Chloroprene Rubber	$84
Bayer AG	2004	Rubber Chemicals	$66
Qantas Airways	2008	Air Cargo	$61
Cathay Pacific Airways	2008	Air Cargo	$60
Bilhar International Establishment	2002	Construction	$54
Daicel Chemical Industries, Ltd.	2000	Sorbates	$53
ABB Middle East & Africa Participations AG	2001	Construction	$53
SAS Air Cargo	2008	Air Cargo	$52
Asian Airlines	2009	Air Cargo	$50
Crompton	2004	Rubber Chemicals	$50
Nippon Air Cargo	2009	Air Cargo	$45
Sotheby's Holdings Inc.	2001	Fine Arts Auctions	$45
Odfjell Seachem AS	2003	Parcel Tanker Shipping	$43
Martinair Holland	2008	Air Cargo	$42
Solvay	2006	Hydrogen Peroxide	$41
Bayer Corporation	2004	Polyester Polyols	$33
Philipp Holzmann AG	2000	Construction	$30
Irving Materials, Inc.	2005	Ready Mix Concrete	$29
Arteva Specialties	2003	Polyester Staple	$29
Jo Tankers, B.V.	2004	Parcel Tanker Shipping	$20
El Al Airlines	2009	Air Cargo	$16
Merck KgaA	2000	Vitamins	$14
Degussa-Huls AG	2000	Vitamins	$13
Akzo Nobel Chemicals, BV	2001	Monochloracetic Acid	$12
Hoechst Aktiengesellschaft	2003	Monochloracetic Acid	$12
Ueno Fine Chemicals Industry, Ltd.	2001	Sorbates	$11
Zeon Chemicals L.P.	2005	NBR	$11
De Beers Centenary AG	2004	Industrial Diamonds	$10
Morganite, Inc.	2003	Carbon Products	$10

Source: U.S. Department of Justice, Antitrust Division, www.usdoj.gov/atr.

Figure 10.1   Criminal antitrust fines for fiscal years, 2001–08 (millions of dollars)
Source: U.S. Department of Justice, Antitrust Division, www.usdoj.gov/atr.

in a conspiracy to confess and "fink" on its co-conspirators gets a much reduced penalty. In fact, the finking firm in the switch-gear case, ABB Switzerland, was granted full immunity and paid no penalties in return for its confession and provision of information to the authorities. That reflects a considerable savings from the €215 million it would otherwise have had to pay as a repeat offender.

The evidence is then that cartels happen. There appears to be no shortage of firms that enter into collusive agreements to fix prices and avoid competition. However, forming and maintaining a cartel is not easy. The cooperative monopoly outcome is rarely (if ever) a Nash equilibrium to the strategic game being played by the firms. Each member of a cartel must have reasons for resisting the temptation to cheat on the agreement. When every other firm is charging high prices or restricting its output, any one firm cannot help but realize that it can reap more than its agreed share of the cartel profits by charging a somewhat lower price or by putting more output on the market. Further, each firm not only recognizes this temptation for itself but also understands that other cartel members face the same temptation. The fear that others will cheat acts as a powerful incentive for a cartel member to deviate from the agreement.

Further, if cartels are less than rare, detection and prosecution are also relatively common. The historical experience in both Europe and the United States confirms the ability of the legal authorities to uncover and prosecute cartel conspirators successfully. Thus, the many cartels found (and those not caught) arise despite the many difficulties conspiring firms must overcome in order to implement such collusion, and despite the fact that both the antitrust laws of the United States and the legal framework established in Europe's Treaty of Rome, not to mention the laws of most other nations, are explicit in making such collusion illegal.[3]

Why break the law by forming a cartel, risking fines and imprisonment? The answer is obvious—because doing so is profitable. Firms that would otherwise be in potentially

---

[3] If anything, the language of European Union law is even stronger in that it also treats "concerted practices" based upon a "concordance of wills" as illegal per se. In practice, however, the U.S. and European policies are nearly identical.

fierce competition recognize that they may be able to get close to the monopoly outcome that maximizes their joint profits by limiting competition.

If forming a cartel were not illegal, the firms in the cartel could make their agreement legally enforceable. However, in the language of U.S. antitrust law, price-fixing agreements are, per se, illegal. The firms cannot formulate some "reasonable explanation" for the collusion or argue that price fixing is necessary to prevent ruinous competition that would otherwise lead to the industry being monopolized.[4]

To see why this argument might be valid, suppose that market demand is $q(p) = 10 - p$ and that each potential entrant's costs are $c_i(q_i) = F + 2q_i$. Furthermore, suppose that in the absence of a price-fixing agreement, entry leads to Bertrand competition, with price driven down to marginal cost. Only one firm will enter (since with more than one entrant no firm is able to cover its fixed costs), the industry is monopolized, and price is 6. The monopolist has profit $16 - F$, consumer surplus is 8, and total surplus is $24 - F$.

Suppose, by contrast, that two potential entrants communicate with each other and in doing so they agree to set a price of 4, perhaps anticipating that setting the monopoly price will undermine their proposed defense that the price on which they have agreed is "reasonable." Each firm earns profit $6 - F$ and consumer surplus is 18, giving a total surplus of $30 - 2F$. Total surplus with the agreement is greater than without it, provided that $F < 6$, which is also necessary for the entry of the second firm to be profitable in the presence of the price fixing agreement.

In other words, the per se treatment of price fixing should be seen as an argument that, while a "ruinous competition" or, more generally, "socially beneficial" defense is theoretically possible, it is highly unlikely to be justified by the facts on the ground. In these circumstances, the per se rule avoids the high costs that would otherwise be incurred in the investigation of the impact of price fixing, since now prosecution would have to satisfy a rule of reason criterion.

Given that cartel members cannot use the law to enforce their agreements, how can firms effectively enforce and execute any collusive agreement that they make? The goal of this chapter is to determine the conditions under which cartels are likely to happen and how best to detect and prevent them.

10.1   THE CARTEL'S DILEMMA

By forming a cartel, firms can coordinate their actions to become something like a monopoly, achieving the maximum joint profit that the industry can generate. They can then develop a profit-sharing mechanism that makes them all better off than they would be in the absence of the cartel agreement. As we have just seen, however, a major challenge to this agreement is the inevitable temptation that each firm has to cheat. While each may only wish to shave its price or raise its output a little bit, if every cartel member acts in this manner, the aggregate increase in output or fall in price will not be small, and the cartel agreement will break down. On top of all this, as we have also noted, the sustainability of the cartel is further complicated by the possibility of discovery, prosecution, and the need to pay potentially heavy legal penalties if successfully prosecuted.[5] As a result, any agreements that the firms make must necessarily be covert as opposed to overt

---

[4]   This argument was tried but rejected in the *Trans-Missouri* case, 166, US 290 (1897).

[5]   Posner (1970) found that cartels were more active when the regulatory authorities were relatively lax in their enforcement of antitrust legislation.

to reduce the likelihood of being caught. Yet, the more secretive the agreement is, the more opportunities arise for firms to cheat on the agreement.

Even if the cartel is overt, it is not immune from the temptation to cheat. Consider the international OPEC cartel. The members come from different countries (or are countries) at least some of which have governments that support the cartel. While such cartels violate antitrust laws, prosecution is difficult because it requires that one country reach into the sovereign affairs of others.[6] Nevertheless, even OPEC has to worry about members cheating on the agreement, because there is no supranational authority to enforce their collusion.

Stories of cheating and cartel breakdown have accompanied virtually all of the major cartels such as the electrical conspiracy of the 1950s, OPEC, and the NASDAQ pricing agreement (see Reality Checkpoint, next page). In developing an insight into how cartels might work, it is useful to begin by understanding why they might not.[7]

The simplest place to start is with the Bertrand model that was introduced in Chapter 7. Suppose that the market contains N firms, each producing a homogeneous product and each operating with an identical constant marginal cost of c. In the absence of cooperation, prices will be competed down to marginal cost c, and each firm will just break even.[8]

Assume that the firms agree to coordinate their prices at $p^a > c$, generating aggregate profit π^a that the firms share equally, each firm earning π^a/N. Now, consider the choice by one firm to undercut this price by a small amount ε. The undercutting firm gains the whole market, increasing its profit to π^a. The cartel is, indeed, unstable in the absence of some enforcement mechanism. Every firm has a stronger profit incentive to cheat on the cartel agreement than to stick with it. This is illustrated in Table 10.2, for the duopoly case. Of course, if both firms undercut, then price will ultimately be driven down to marginal cost. Indeed, it is easy to confirm that the noncooperative Nash equilibrium for this game is for both firms to price at $p = c$.

Table 10.2 Payoff matrix for a Bertrand duopoly cartel game

		Strategy for Firm j	
		Cooperate	Undercut
Strategy for Firm i	Cooperate	$\pi^a/2, \pi^a/2$	$0, \pi^a$
	Undercut	$\pi^a, 0$	$0, 0$

Consider instead the Cournot model of Chapter 7. Suppose that there are N identical Cournot firms, each with constant marginal cost of c, jointly supplying a market with linear aggregate inverse demand $P = a - Q = a - \sum_{i=1}^{N} q_i$, where q_i is the output of Firm i. Profit of firm i is $\pi_i = (P - c)q_i = \left(a - q_i - \sum_{j \neq i} q_j - c \right) q_i$. Maximizing profit with respect to q_i gives us Firm i's best-response function:

$$\frac{\partial \pi_i}{\partial q_i} = a - 2q_i - \sum_{j \neq i} q_j - c = 0 \Rightarrow q_i = \frac{a-c}{2} - \frac{1}{2} \sum_{j \neq i} q_j \tag{10.1}$$

[6] It is worth noting, however, that the United Sates has become increasingly active in pursuing international cartels.

[7] A terrific guide to the intuition underlying the cartel problem and, indeed, all of game theory is Schelling (1960).

[8] We assume that there are no fixed costs.

Reality Checkpoint

"I Am the Broker, You Are the Brokee!"

Once upon a time, two economists named Paul Schultz (of Ohio State) and William Christie (of Vanderbilt) were talking about stock prices for trades in the over-the-counter market quoted by the National Association of Securities Dealers Automated Quotation (NASDAQ) system. The NASDAQ securities market is a computerized market in which dealers list the prices at which they will buy (the "bid" price) and sell (the "ask" price) various stocks. The difference between the bid and ask prices is the "spread," and it is a major source of dealer profits. Over time, the two economists noticed something odd. The spread was rarely less than 75 cents and always expressed as a multiplier of 25 cents, even though stocks themselves are priced in odd eighths (e.g., 20 and 3/8, or 24 and 5/8). The two economists subsequently published a research paper suggesting that NASDAQ prices could only come about as a result of a price-fixing agreement.

The paper caused an immediate stir and, ultimately, led to an investigation by the antitrust division of the Justice Department. Some time later, the Justice Department filed a civil complaint against two dozen securities dealers. The complaint documented the earlier findings of Schultz and Christie. It also showed that cheating was a potential problem that the dealers dealt with by harassment and verbal assault of the culprit. For example, consider this recorded conversation of one dealer complaining to a second dealer that the latter employed a trader who was not maintaining a spread divisible by 25.

(First trader): "He's trading it at one-eighths and embarrassing your firm."
(Second trader): "I understand."
(First trader): "You know, I would tell him to straighten up his act, stop being a (expletive deleted) moron!"

The agreement did not require the two dozen dealers involved to admit guilt or pay a fine. But it did require the dealers to cease and desist the practice and to randomly tape 3.5 percent of all trader conversations to ensure compliance.

Source: Lohse, D., and A. Raghavan. "Will NASDAQ Accord Lead to Better Prices?" *The Wall Street Journal* (18 July 1996), p. C1.

We know that in the Cournot-Nash equilibrium, all firms produce the same output, so that $q_j = q_i$. Substituting into (10.1) and solving for q_i gives the Cournot-Nash output for each firm of $q_c = (a - c)/(N + 1)$, aggregate output $Q_c = N(a - c)/(N + 1)$, equilibrium price $P_c = (a + Nc)/(N + 1)$, and profit to each firm is

$$\pi_c = \frac{(a - c)^2}{(N + 1)^2} \tag{10.2}$$

Now, suppose that the firms form a cartel and agree to produce the monopoly output, $Q_m = (a - c)/2$, which will sell at the monopoly price $P_m = (a + c)/2$ and earn each firm an equal share of the monopoly profit:

$$\pi_m = \frac{(a - c)^2}{4N} \tag{10.3}$$

It is easy to confirm from (10.2) and (10.3) that the cartel is, indeed, profitable for all firms.

With the cartel agreement in place, each firm is producing its share of the monopoly output. But then we can see from (10.1) that this is not a best response for Firm i. Given that all of the other firms stick with the cartel agreement and each produce the agreed output $q_m = (a - c)/2N$, Firm i will prefer to deviate from the agreement, increasing its output to

$$q_{i,d} = \frac{(N + 1)(a - c)}{4N} \tag{10.4}$$

This will result in an increase in aggregate output to $(3N + 1)(a - c)/4N$, as a result of which price falls to $P_d = [(N + 1)a + (3N - 1)]/4N$. The profit of the deviating Firm i increases to

$$\pi_{i,d} = \frac{(N + 1)^2(a - c)^2}{16N^2} \tag{10.5}$$

while the profit of each of the other firms, given that they abide by the cartel agreement, falls to

$$\pi_{j,nd} = \frac{(N + 1)(a - c)^2}{8N^2} \tag{10.6}$$

Comparison of (10.5) and (10.3) confirms that Firm i increases its profit by deviating from the cartel agreement, given that the remaining firms are expected to abide by the agreement. Once again, the cartel is unstable.

The Cournot duopoly case is illustrated in Table 10.3. As in the Bertrand case, it is easy to confirm that the only noncooperative Nash equilibrium for this game is for both firms to deviate from the agreement and to increase output from the monopoly to the Cournot-Nash output.

Table 10.3 Pay-off matrix for a Cournot duopoly cartel game

| | | Strategy for Firm j | |
		Cooperate	Deviate
Strategy for Firm i	Cooperate	$\dfrac{(a - c)^2}{8}, \dfrac{(a - c)^2}{8}$	$\dfrac{3(a - c)^2}{32}, \dfrac{9(a - c)^2}{64}$
	Deviate	$\dfrac{9(a - c)^2}{64}, \dfrac{3(a - c)^2}{32}$	$\dfrac{(a - c)^2}{9}, \dfrac{(a - c)^2}{9}$

The games we have illustrated in Tables 10.2 and 10.3 are classic examples of "prisoners' dilemma" games (one of the earliest illustrations of this type of game involved dealings between a prosecutor and two suspects). The firms have a mutual interest in cooperating, but there is a conflict. If one firm is expected to stick to the agreement, then the other firm can do much better by deviating, producing more output in the Cournot case, or lowering price in the Bertrand case. Each firm can be expected to reason as follows: "If I cooperate and the other firm cooperates, then we share the monopoly profit.

Reality Checkpoint

School for Scandal—Bid Rigging by Suppliers to New York City Schools

On June 1, 2000, almost all of the companies that supply food to New York City's schoolchildren were charged in a bid-rigging scheme that overcharged the city at least $21 million for frozen goods and fresh produce. Twelve of the officials and six of the companies involved immediately pled guilty. Some of these defendants were also charged with rigging the bids to supply schools in Newark as well. The defendants reportedly designated which of the companies would be the low bidder on several contracts with the New York Board of Education. The system of schools supervised by the Board services a student population of nearly 1.1 million and serves about 640,000 lunches and 150,000 breakfasts every day. The school board buys more food than any other single U.S. customer except the Defense Department. The conspirators allegedly agreed on prices to bid for supplying such standard items as French fries, meat, and fish sticks. One firm would be designated as the low bidder and all others would either refrain from bidding or submit intentionally high or complementary bids on the contracts. The cartel also allegedly paid potential suppliers not to bid competitively, including a payment of $100,000 to one produce company.

Source: Smith, A. "N.Y. Schools' Food Suppliers Accused of Bid-Rigging." *The Washington Post* (2 June 2000), p. A8.

If, on the other hand, I don't cooperate and the other firm does, then I make a lot of money; and if the other firm does not cooperate, then it's as if we were playing noncooperatively anyway. No matter what the other firm does, I am better off not cooperating."

In the language of game theory, noncooperation is a dominant strategy. This is the prisoners' dilemma. Together, both firms are worse off not cooperating than if they cooperate. Individually, however, each firm gains by not cooperating. Unless there is some way to overcome this conflict, it would appear that the antitrust authorities need not be terribly worried about cartels because, logically, they should not happen—and if they do, they should be expected to be short-lived. Yet, as we have seen, cartels do happen and they do survive. There must be some way that firms can create incentives that work to sustain their cartel agreements.

10.2   REPEATED GAMES

In the last 30 years, economists have come to understand that there are ways to escape the prisoners' dilemma. These require that firms recognize that they interact not just once, but many times. In other words, the static framework that we have been using in this section should be changed to a dynamic one in which strategic interaction is repeated over time. This is, of course, a perfectly reasonable change. Firms considering the formation of a cartel are very likely to have been competing with each other for some time—otherwise, how did they meet in the first place? More importantly, it seems reasonable to assume that they believe that their market interactions will continue into the future—again, otherwise why would they seek to cooperate?

Recognizing this "shadow of the future" fundamentally alters the incentives that firms have to defect on collusive agreements. When market interaction is repeated over and over again, it is possible for the firms to adopt strategies that are conditional on the history of play. In our specific context, firms that are party to a collusive agreement can reward "good" behavior by sticking with the agreement and punish "bad" behavior by guaranteeing a breakdown in the cartel.

In order to work out what such a strategy might look like, we need to analyze what is called a *repeated game*. Repeated games are dynamic games in which a simultaneous market interaction is repeated at each stage of the dynamic game. By moving from one period to many, we change the rules of the game. The appropriate strategies therefore also change.

We shall show that a key question is whether the interaction is repeated over a finite (though perhaps large) number of periods, or whether it goes on indefinitely. In other words, we separate repeated games into two classes: (1) those in which the number of repetitions is finite *and known to the potentially colluding firms*, and (2) those in which the number of repetitions is infinite.

10.2.1   Finitely Repeated Games

One can think of at least three situations in which it is reasonable to assume that the number of times that the firms interact is finite and known to both firms. First, it may be that the firms exploit an exhaustible and nonrenewable resource such as oil or natural gas. Second, the firms might operate in a market with proprietary knowledge protected by patents. All patents are awarded for a finite period—in the United States, the duration is 20 years from the date of filing the application. Once the patent expires, a market protected from entry suddenly becomes competitive. For example, as the patents on serotonin-based antidepressants Prozac, Zoloft, and Paxil expire, the manufacturers of these drugs can expect a major increase in the number of competitors in this market, ending the market interaction of the original three firms that had previously applied. Finally, while we conventionally equate the players in the game with firms, the truth is that it is ultimately individuals who make the output or price decisions. The same management teams can be expected to be around for only a finite number of years. When there is a major change in management at one or more of the firms the game is likely to end. Often this end can be foreseen.

Whatever the reason that the number of plays is limited, it turns out that what happens in a one-shot or stage game gives us a very good clue to what is likely to happen in a repeated game when the number of repetitions is finite. After all, a one-period game is just one that is very finite. Consider a simple extension of our Cournot game from one period to two, so that we now have a repeated (albeit briefly so) game.[9] It is straightforward to show that this two-period repeated game has the same noncooperative outcome in each round as the earlier one-shot game. To see why, consider the following alternative strategy for Firm 1:

First play: Cooperate
Second play: Cooperate if Firm 2 cooperated in the first play, otherwise defect.

---

[9]   Even though the game lasts for two market periods, we will keep things simple and assume that profits in the second period are not discounted. In other words, we will assume that the discount factor $R = 1$ or, equivalently, the interest rate $r = 0$ percent. See the discussion of discounting in Chapter 2.

The idea behind this strategy is clear enough. Start off on a friendly footing. If this results in cooperation in the first round, then in the second round, Firm 1 promises to continue to cooperate. However, should Firm 2 fail to reciprocate Firm 1's initial cooperation in the first round, then in the second round, Firm 1 will "take the gloves off" and fight back.

The problem with this strategy is that it suffers from the same basic credibility problem that afflicted many of the predatory threats that we discussed in Chapter 9. To see why, suppose Firm 2 chooses to cooperate in the first round with a view of earning the cooperative profit. Now think of Firm 2's position at the start of its second and last interaction with Firm 1. The history of play to that point is one in which both firms adopted cooperative behavior in the first round. Furthermore, Firm 2 has a promise from Firm 1 that, because Firm 2 cooperated in the first round, Firm 1 will continue to do so in the second. Unfortunately, this promise is worthless. When Firm 2 considers the payoff matrix for the last round, the firm cannot fail to note that—regardless of Firm 1's promise—the dominant strategy for Firm 1 in the last round is not to cooperate. This breaks Firm 1's promise, but there is nothing Firm 2 can subsequently do to punish Firm 1 for breaking its promise. There is no third round in which to implement such punishment. Firm 2 should rationally anticipate that Firm 1 will adopt noncooperative behavior in the last round.

Selten's Theorem

Firm 2 has just discovered that any strategy for Firm 1 that involves playing the cooperative strategy in the final round is not credible (i.e., it is not subgame perfect). The last round of the game is a subgame of the complete game, and a strategy that calls for Firm 1 to cooperate in this last period cannot be part of a Nash equilibrium in that period. No matter what has transpired in the first round, Firm 1 can be counted upon to adopt noncooperative behavior in the final period of play. Of course, the same is true viewed from Firm 1's perspective. Firm 2's dominant strategy in the last round is likewise not to cooperate. In short, both firms realize that the only rational outcome in the second round is the noncooperative equilibrium.

Now, return to the first round. The foregoing logic will not be lost on the two firms. Each will realize that the noncooperative outcome is inevitable in round 2. Nothing they do in round 1 can change the profit either will earn later. Consequently, each will try to maximize profit in round 1. In other words, we have identified the subgame-perfect equilibrium for the entire game. Both firms adopt strategies that call for noncooperative behavior in *both* period 1 and period 2. Running the game for two periods produces outcomes identical to that observed by playing it as a one-period game.

What happens if we extend the number of plays to any finite number of plays T? The reasoning that we have just developed can be extended to these cases. No strategy that calls for cooperation in the final period is subgame perfect. Therefore, no such strategy can be part of the final equilibrium. In the last period, each firm always chooses not to cooperate regardless of the history of the game to that point. This implies that the penultimate $T - 1$ period is the effective final period. But the only possible reason for Firm 1 or Firm 2 to cooperate in period $T - 1$ is the promise of cooperation in period T, and such a promise is not credible. Both firms adopt noncooperative behavior in both periods $T - 1$ and T.

We can repeat this logic for periods $T - 2$, $T - 3$, and so on. The outcome will always be the same Nash equilibrium of mutual noncooperation no matter how many times the game is played, so long as that number is finite and known. The one-shot Nash equilibrium is just repeated T times, with each firm taking noncooperative action in every period.

This is by no means a special case relating to our specific examples. Rather, our analysis is an example of a general theorem first proved by Nobel Prize winner Reinhard Selten (1973).

> *Selten's Theorem:* If a game with a unique Nash equilibrium is played finitely many times, its solution is that equilibrium played each and every time. Finitely repeated play of a unique Nash equilibrium is the Nash equilibrium of the repeated game.[10]

Introducing repetition into a game-theoretic framework adds history as an element to the analysis. What Selten's Theorem demonstrates is that history—and the rewards and punishments it makes possible—really do not play a role in a finitely repeated game in which the one-shot play has a unique Nash equilibrium.

Again, though, we know that effective collusion does occur in the real world. So there must be some way to escape the logic of Selten's Theorem. As with any theorem, the devil lies in the details. The "solution" is suggested by the theorem itself. There are two important qualifications in Selten's Theorem. First, the theorem holds only when the Nash equilibrium to the stage game is unique. What if there are multiple equilibria? Second, we have so far limited our analysis to finitely repeated games in which the firms understand exactly when their interactions will end. What if, instead, the firms believe that their interactions will be repeated over and over, indefinitely? Because it gives an insight into indefinite play and yet still falls under the category of a finitely repeated game, we consider the non-uniqueness issue here and address the case of indefinitely repeated games in the next section.

In demonstrating the feasibility of sustaining collusion in finitely repeated games with more than one Nash equilibrium, we focus on a simple example outlined in Table 10.4.[11] This game has three essential features. First, it has two Nash equilibria to the one-shot game, (A, A) and (B, B). Second, both firms agree that (B, B) is preferable to (A, A). Third, the firms do better with the strategy combination (C, C) than either (A, A) or (B, B), but such a strategy combination is not a Nash equilibrium.

Finitely Repeated Games with Multiple Nash Equilibria

Suppose that the firms expect to play this game twice and assume that both firms have a discount factor of R. We will now show that in this case, repetition—even if it is only

Table 10.4 A game with more than one Nash equilibrium

		Strategy for Firm 2		
		A	B	C
Strategy for Firm 1	A	6, 6	8, 5	9, 4
	B	5, 8	8.5, 8.5	10, 5
	C	4, 9	5, 10	9.5, 9.5

[10] A formal proof can be found, for example, in Eichberger (1993).
[11] The full, formal analysis is rather complex, although the underlying idea is quite simple. See, for example, Benoit and Krishna (1985).

for a finite number of periods—opens up the possibility of another equilibrium. For the two-period case, the strategy that does this is as follows:

First Period: Play C
Second Period: If the history from the first period is (C, C) then play B, otherwise play A.

To show that this is a subgame-perfect equilibrium, it is necessary to show that the strategy for each firm is a best response to the strategy of the other firm. This is obvious for the second period, since each player, in playing B, is playing a Nash equilibrium of the one-shot game. So we need only consider the first period. Consider Firm 1. If Firm 1 is going to cheat in the first period, then the best that it can do is to play B, giving a payoff in this period (given that Firm 2 plays C) of 10. Of course, Firm 1 then knows that according to the stated strategy, Firm 2 will play A in the second period, in which case Firm 1 must also play A (since (A, A) is a Nash equilibrium to the stage game). Recalling the discount factor R defined in Chapter 2, the payoff to Firm 1 from defecting is $10 + 6R$.

By contrast, if Firm 1 does not cheat but rather plays C in the first period, the history of play going into the second period is (C, C), and Firm 2 is expected to play B. Unlike the prisoners' dilemma game, Firm 2 has no incentive to break its promise, since (B, B) is a Nash equilibrium, so Firm 1 also plays B. The payoff to Firm 1 from cooperating is $9.5 + 8.5R$.

For cooperation to hold in period 1, therefore, we need

$$9.5 + 8.5R > 10 + 6R \Rightarrow R > 0.2 \tag{10.7}$$

So long as the firms have sufficiently high discount factors (or sufficiently low discount rates), cheating on the cartel in the first period is not profitable.

Of course, this result is a product of the specific example that we have constructed,[12] but the main lesson can be simply stated. When the one-shot Nash equilibrium is not unique, repetition of the game may enable the firms to sustain a stable cartel agreement for at least part of the time, even if the number of repetitions is finite. Indeed, Benoit and Krishna (1985) show that this outcome becomes a certainty, provided that the number of times that the game is played is "sufficiently many" and the firms' discount factors are "sufficiently close to unity."

There are then ways to escape the logic of Selten's Theorem, and our example with multiple Nash equilibria reveals exactly what this requires. It is the presence of credible threats that is essential to the maintenance of any successful cartel. The existence of multiple Nash equilibria introduces the possibility of punishing defection and rewarding cooperation in ways that are not possible when the Nash equilibrium is unique. Such credible or subgame-perfect strategies are also possible in infinitely repeated games, as we shall see in the next section.

10.2.2 Infinitely or Indefinitely Repeated Games

There are situations in which the assumption of finite repetition makes sense. However, for many—perhaps most—situations, it does not. Firms may be regarded as having an

---

[12] While we have limited the multiple equilibrium example to a simple two-period case, the logic of the argument extends to the case of a large but still finite number of periods.

infinite or, more precisely, an indefinite life. Microsoft may not last forever, but nobody inside or outside the software giant works on the assumption that there is some known date T periods from now at which time Microsoft will cease to exist. The more likely situation is that after any given period, the firms see some positive probability that the game will continue one more round. So, while firms may understand that the game will not last forever, they cannot look ahead to any particular period as the last. As long as there is some chance of continuing on, it makes sense to treat Microsoft and other firms as if they will continue indefinitely.

Why is this important? Recall the argument that we used to show that repetition does not lead to cooperation in a finite game. That argument turns on our using backward induction. Cooperation is not an equilibrium in the final period T, and so is not an equilibrium in $T - 1$, and in $T - 2$, and so on. With infinite or indefinite repetition of the game, this argument fails *because there is no known final period*. So long as the probability of continuing into another round of play is positive, there is, probabilistically speaking, reason to hope that the next round will be played cooperatively and so reason to cooperate in the present. Whether that motivation is strong enough to overcome the short-run gains of defection, or can be made so by means of some reward-and-punishment strategy, will depend on certain key factors that we discuss below. The point is that once we allow for the strategic interaction to be repeated indefinitely, another route to successful collusion is opened.

In developing the formal analysis of an infinitely repeated game, we must first consider how a firm values a profit stream of infinite duration. The answer is simply that it will apply the discount factor R to the expected cash flow in any period. Suppose a firm knows that its profits are going to be π in each play of the game. Suppose also that the firm knows that in each period, there is a probability p that the market interaction will continue into the next period. Then, starting from an initial period 0, the probability of reaching period 1 is p, the probability of reaching period 2 is p^2, of reaching period 3 is $p^3, \ldots$ of reaching period t is p^t, and so on. Accordingly, the profit stream that the firm actually expects to receive in period t is $p^t \pi$.

Now, apply the firm's discount factor R. The expected present value of this profit stream is given by

$$V(\pi) = \pi + pR\pi + (pR)^2\pi + (pR)^3\pi + \cdots + (pR)^t\pi + \cdots \tag{10.8}$$

To evaluate $V(\pi)$, we use a simple trick. Rewrite equation (10.8) as

$$V(\pi) = \pi + pR[\pi + pR\pi + (pR)^2\pi + \cdots + (pR)^t\pi + \cdots] \tag{10.9}$$

Now, note that the term in brackets is just $V(\pi)$ as given by (10.8), so (10.9) can be rewritten

$$V(\pi) = \pi + pRV(\pi) \tag{10.10}$$

Solving this for $V(\pi)$ then gives us

$$V(\pi) = \frac{\pi}{1 - pR} = \frac{\pi}{1 - \rho} \tag{10.11}$$

where $\rho = pR$ can be thought of as a "probability-adjusted" discount factor. It is the product of the discount factor reflecting the interest rate and the belief the firm holds regarding the probability that the market will continue to operate from period to period.

At first sight, consideration of games that are infinitely or indefinitely repeated, which are often referred to as supergames, may seem hopeless. Repetition allows history to figure in strategy making, and with infinitely repeated play, the number of possible histories also becomes infinite. It turns out, though, that the actual strategies on which firms rely to secure compliance with cartel policy can be made remarkably simple. The type of strategy that will work is called a *trigger strategy*. A player plays the cooperative action upon which the players have agreed, so long as all the players have always stuck to the agreement. However, if any player deviates from the agreement, then the player reverts to the Nash equilibrium forever.

To see how a trigger strategy might work, suppose that there are N firms and that they formulate a price-fixing agreement that gives them each profits of π_m. Each firm knows that if it deviates optimally from this agreement, it will earn a profit of π_d in the period of deviation. Finally, the Nash equilibrium profit to each firm if the agreement breaks down is π_n. Common sense and our Cournot and Bertrand examples tell us that $\pi_d > \pi_m > \pi_n$. Now, consider the following trigger strategy:

Period 0: Cooperate

Period $t \geq 1$: Cooperate if all firms have cooperated in every previous period. Switch to the Nash equilibrium forever if any player has defected in any previous period.

It should be clear why strategies of this type are called trigger strategies. Firm i's switch to the Nash equilibrium is triggered by a deviation from the agreement by any firm. The threat to make this switch is credible precisely because it simply requires that Firm i moves to the noncooperative Nash equilibrium.

Suppose that at the beginning of the game all firms announce the trigger strategy just described. Now consider a possible deviation from the agreement by Firm i. Firm i can increase its profit to π_d in the current period by defecting but that gain lasts for only one period. In the next period, the other firms retaliate by switching to the Nash equilibrium, in which case Firm i's best response is to do the same. One period of higher profit π_d is followed by an endless number of periods in which its profit is only π_n. This represents a real cost to Firm i since, had it not broken the agreement, it could have enjoyed its share of the cartel profit, π_m, indefinitely. In short, the trigger strategy means that Firm i realizes both a gain and a loss if it breaks the cartel agreement.

The only way to compare the gain with the loss is in terms of present values. The present value of profit to Firm i from sticking to the agreement is, using equation (10.11)

$$V_m = \pi_m + \rho\pi_m + \rho^2\pi_m + \cdots = \frac{\pi_m}{1 - \rho} \tag{10.12}$$

Now, consider the present value of the profits that Firm i makes if it deviates. We can always number the period in which Firm i deviates as period 0 (today). Its profit stream from deviation is then

$$V_d = \pi_d + \rho\pi_n + \rho^2\pi_n + \rho^3\pi_n + \cdots$$
$$= \pi_d + \rho[\pi_n + \rho\pi_n + \rho^2\pi_n + \cdots] = \pi_d + \frac{\rho\pi_n}{1 - \rho} \tag{10.13}$$

Cheating on the cartel is not profitable, and so the cartel is *self-sustaining*, provided that $V_m > V_d$, which requires that

$$\frac{\pi_m}{1-\rho} > \pi_d + \frac{\rho\pi_n}{1-\rho} \Rightarrow \pi_m > (1-\rho)\pi_d + \rho\pi_n \Rightarrow \rho(\pi_d - \pi_n) > \pi_d - \pi_m \qquad (10.14)$$

In other words, the critical value of ρ above which defection from the cartel does not pay and firms find it in their own self-interest to stick by the agreement is

$$\rho > \rho^* = \frac{\pi_d - \pi_m}{\pi_d - \pi_n} \qquad (10.15)$$

Equation (10.15) has a simple intuition. Cheating on the cartel yields an immediate, one-period gain of $\pi_d - \pi_m$. In every subsequent period, the punishment for cheating is a loss of profit of $\pi_m - \pi_n$. The present value of that loss is $\rho(\pi_m - \pi_n)/(1-\rho)$. Cheating is unprofitable if the gain is less than the cost when both are measured in present value terms, that is, if $\pi_d - \pi_m < \rho(\pi_m - \pi_n)/(1-\rho)$. It is easy to show that this condition is identical to that in equation (10.15).

Equation (10.15) also allows us to state a strong result. Because $\pi_d > \pi_m > \pi_n$, it follows that $\rho^* < 1$. *There is always a probability-adjusted discount factor above which a cartel is self-sustaining.*

Consider our two duopoly examples in Tables 10.2 and 10.3. In the Bertrand game, we have $\pi_m = \pi^a/2$, $\pi_d = \pi^a$ and $\pi_n = 0$. Substituting into (10.15) gives the critical probability adjusted discount factor above which our Bertrand duopolists can sustain their cartel as $\rho_B^* = 0.5$. In the Cournot case, $\pi_m = \frac{(a-c)^2}{8}$, $\pi_d = \frac{9(a-c)^2}{64}$ and $\pi_n = \frac{(a-c)^2}{9}$. Substituting into (10.15) gives the critical probability adjusted discount factor, above which our Cournot duopolists can sustain their cartel as $\rho_C^* = 0.529$. The threat of much fiercer competition that characterizes Bertrand actually works to make a price-setting cartel more stable than a quantity-setting cartel.

We may also illustrate another general point. Suppose that both firms playing the Cournot game believe that their interaction will always be repeated with certainty, so that $p = 1$. Then the critical probability adjusted discount factor ρ_C^* corresponds to a pure discount factor of $R = 0.529$. That is, if $p = 1$, neither firm will deviate so long as the firm's discount rate r does not exceed 89 percent. Suppose instead that both firms believe that there is only a 60 percent probability that their interaction lasts from one period to the next (i.e., $p = 0.6$). Now the cartel agreement is self-sustaining only when the pure discount factor $R > 0.529/0.6 = 0.882$. That is, successful collusion now requires that the discount rate r does not exceed 14.4 percent, which is a more restrictive requirement. This points to another general result. *An indefinitely lived cartel is more sustainable the greater the probability that the firms will continue to interact and the lower the discount rate.*

10.2.3   Some Extensions

We have illustrated our analysis using quite standard duopoly examples. However, it is easy to show that our analysis easily extends to cases where the number of firms is more than two. All we need do is to identify the three firm-level profits π_d, π_m, and π_n for each firm and substitute these values into equation (10.15) to identify the critical probability-adjusted discount factor for each firm. So long as $\pi_d > \pi_m > \pi_n$ (which seems perfectly reasonable), the trigger strategy preserves cooperative behavior so long as the firms' discount factors are sufficiently close to unity.

However, there are two objections to trigger strategies. First, these strategies are based on the assumption that cheating on the cartel agreement is detected quickly and that punishment is swift. What if, as seems likely, it takes time for cartel members to discover a firm that is cheating and additional time to retaliate?

The fact that detection and punishment of cheaters takes time certainly makes sustaining the cartel more difficult. Delay allows the defector to enjoy the gains for more periods, and this strengthens the incentive to engage in cheating behavior. Nevertheless, this does not necessarily make collusion impossible. Trigger strategies can still work even if detection of cheating on the agreement takes more than one period, and even if it takes the remaining cartel members some time to agree on the proper punishment.

A second and related objection to the trigger strategy is that it is harsh and unforgiving because it does not permit mistakes. For example, suppose that market demand is uncertain, but known to fluctuate over a specific range, and that the cartel has agreed to set a price P_m or has agreed to production quotas that lead to that market price. In this setting, a cartel firm that observes a decline in its sales cannot tell whether this reduction is due to cheating by one of its partners or to an unanticipated reduction in demand. Yet, under the simple trigger strategies we have been discussing, the firm is required quickly and permanently to move to the retaliatory behavior. This will lead to some regret if the firm later discovers that its partners were innocent and that it has needlessly started a damaging price war.[13]

This objection too can be overcome. The trick is to adopt a modified trigger strategy. For instance, the firm might only take retaliatory action if sales or price fall outside some agreed-upon range. The firm refrains from retaliation against minor infractions. A different modification would impose punishment swiftly after any deviation from the cartel agreement is observed, but limit the period of punishment to a finite period of time. Thus, we can envision a trigger strategy of the form "I will switch to the Nash equilibrium for $\tau \geq 1$ periods if you deviate from our agreement, but will then revert to our agreed cooperative strategies." This approach may mistakenly punish innocent cartel members, but by limiting the period of such punishment, it permits reestablishment of the cartel at a later date.

The point is that in an infinitely repeated game, there are many trigger strategies that allow a cartel agreement to be sustained. Indeed, in some ways, there are almost too many. This point is made clear by what is known as the *folk theorem* for infinitely repeated games (Friedman 1971):[14]

Folk Theorem: Suppose that an infinitely repeated game has a set of payoffs that exceed the one-shot Nash equilibrium payoffs for each and every firm. Then any set of feasible payoffs that are preferred by all firms to the Nash equilibrium payoffs can be supported as subgame-perfect equilibria for the repeated game for some discount factor sufficiently close to unity.

---

[13]   Two different views of oligopolistic behavior with uncertain demand that makes detection difficult may be found in Green and Porter (1984) and Rotemberg and Saloner (1986).

[14]   The term "folk theorem" derives from the fact that this theorem was part of the "folklore" or oral tradition in game theory for years before Friedman wrote down a formal proof.

We can illustrate the folk theorem using our Cournot duopoly example. If the two firms collude to maximize their joint profits, they share aggregate profits of $2\pi_m = \frac{(a-c)^2}{4}$. If they act noncooperatively, they each earn $\pi_n = \frac{(a-c)^2}{9}$.

The folk theorem says that any cartel agreement in which each firm earns more than $\frac{(a-c)^2}{9}$ and in which total profit does not exceed $\frac{(a-c)^2}{4}$ can, at least in principle, be sustained as a subgame-perfect equilibrium of the infinitely repeated game.

The folk theorem does not say that firms can always achieve total industry profit equal to that earned by a monopoly. It simply says that firms can do better than the noncooperative Nash equilibrium. The reason that exact duplication of monopoly may not be possible is that duplicating the monopoly outcome gives members a tremendous incentive to cheat unless the probability-adjusted discount factor is fairly large. However, the incentive to break the monopoly agreement does not mean that no cartel can be sustained. Firms can still earn profits higher than the noncooperative equilibrium by means of a sustainable cartel agreement, even if they cannot earn the highest possible profits that the industry could yield. This is what the folk theorem says.

Before leaving this discussion of the feasibility of collusion we note that the foregoing analysis implicitly assumes that a fair bit of information is available to all the firms, including typically information on rivals' prices. However, many if not most cartels involve upstream markets where the colluders are suppliers selling to industrial firms. In such cases, prices are often privately negotiated and therefore unobservable although market share data may be collected. Nevertheless, recent work by Athey and Bagwell (2001) and Harrington and Skrzypacz (2007) show that collusion may still be sustained in such cases *if* punishments can be imposed asymmetrically so that the likely cheaters are treated more harshly than other firms unlike the symmetric punishments applied in the trigger strategies above.[15] In sum, once we consider a framework of infinitely or indefinitely repeated interaction between firms, there is a real possibility for sustainable collusive behavior among these firms, so long as the discount factor is not too low and the probability of their continued interaction is not too low.

10.3   EMPIRICAL APPLICATION 1
Estimating the Effects of Price-Fixing

We have seen that both theory and evidence imply that the threat of cartels is a real one. Even so, that threat may be minimal from a policy viewpoint if, when they happen, cartels have only minor effects on prices and quantities. As we noted above, the folk theorem does not assert that the cartel can duplicate the monopoly profit. It only asserts that the cartel members can do better than the one-shot Nash outcome. This leaves open the possibility that while cartels may be successful in raising prices above the noncooperative level, they may not raise them much higher. If that is the typical outcome, then there may still be little need to devote much effort to detecting and prosecuting such cartels.

---

[15]   An example would be the punishment scheme adopted in the lysine cartel in which a firm that exceeded its production quota was required to buy that excess back from the other colluding firms. See Connor (2001).

Table 10.5   Summary statistics for the auction cartel

	Mean	*Minimum*	*Maximum*
P	$25,800	$8,800	$44,800
K	$30,500	$10,800	$47,300
N	4.63	2	9
K/P	1.28	1.02	2.46

This is not, however, the full impact of the cartel, since we know that $V = K + S$. Moreover, it can be seen from Table 10.5 that there is considerable variance in K/P. Kwoka, therefore, estimated equation (10.19) directly, obtaining the results in column (a) of Table 10.6.

In the regression in column (a), observe that the coefficients on the two terms P and $P(N-1)/N$ are significant, have the expected signs, and the fit is remarkable. In addition, the coefficient on P is (just) insignificantly different from unity, as required by equation (10.19). The coefficient on $P(N-1)/N$ is an estimate of $f - 1$, giving $f = 1.86$. Since $P/V = 1/f$, this tells us that $P/V = 0.54$. In other words, the cartel results in public bid prices 46 percent lower than the true valuation of the properties being auctioned.

Kwoka then estimated two refinements on the simple model of equation (10.19). First, of the 30 properties in his sample, 19 were foreclosure auctions and 11 were nisi auctions held under court supervision as a condition to further legal action. It is possible that the cartel members would be more careful in their public auction bidding with a court watching. Suppose, therefore, that on nisi auctions we have that $V/P = f - d$. If we introduce a dummy variable D that takes the value of unity for nisi auctions and 0 otherwise the reduced form to be estimated then becomes

$$K = P + (f - 1)P\frac{(N-1)}{N} - dDP\frac{(N-1)}{N} \tag{10.20}$$

The results are given in column (b) of Table 10.6. The coefficient on $DP(N-1)/N$ is the estimate of d. It has the correct sign (negative) but is statistically insignificant.

The second refinement modifies the mechanism by which losing bidders in the cartel were compensated. In some auctions, losing bidders were compensated equally, while in others the compensation was based on each losing bidder's final (but losing) bid.

Table 10.6   Regression results

	(a)	(b)	(c)
P	0.519	0.520	0.703
	(2.18)	(2.15)	(4.47)
$P(N-1)/N$	0.860	0.879	0.481
	(2.58)	(2.58)	(2.01)
$DP(N-1)/N$		−0.045	0.014
		(0.51)	(0.23)
UNEQUAL			3,501
			(3.08)
R^2	0.979	0.980	0.995
S	667	433	694

The impact of unequal compensation is potentially ambiguous. On the one hand, it might make bidders more aggressive to secure them a higher share. On the other hand, aggressive bidding might result in a bidder winning an auction that she did not want to win. To test for this impact, Kwoka added a dummy variable UNEQUAL to equation (10.20) and ran the regression for the 18 auctions in which it was possible to distinguish the compensation mechanism.

The results are given in column (c) of Table 10.6. The coefficient on UNEQUAL is positive and significant, implying that unequal compensation increased the subsequent knockout price. Moreover, the coefficient on $P(N-1)/N$ gives a revised estimate for $1/f$ of 1.48, implying that the cartel rigged the public auction prices to 32.5 percent below the true property values. From this and the rest of Kwoka's (1997) results, this cartel is seen to have had an unambiguous and significant impact on the prices at which these properties were traded in the public auctions.

Kwoka's (1997) findings are broadly consistent with those of many other researchers. For example, Froeb, Koyak, and Werden (1993) found that a price-rigging scheme involved in supplying frozen fish to the U.S. military raised prices by 23 to 30 percent. Connor (2001) found that the lysine cartel raised the market price by 17 percent, while Morse and Hyde (2000) argue the effect was twice as high at 34 percent. In the most exhaustive and complete review of the evidence that we have seen, Connor and Lande (2005) find that the median cartel price effect over all time periods and across all cartel types is 22 percent. They estimate that this effect is 18 percent for domestic cartels and 32 percent for international cartels.[18]

10.4   CARTELS IN PRACTICE: FACILITATING FACTORS AND PRACTICES

It seems clear in light of the foregoing that the threat of significant price distortion due to collusive behavior is a real one. In principle, a cartel can occur in almost any market. However, one suspects that it is more likely to occur in some markets than in others. Since the antitrust agencies have limited resources that make it impossible to patrol every industry and every market, they must focus on those settings where collusion is most likely to occur.

Thus, a natural question to ask is, what industry characteristics are most conducive to firms achieving a cooperative outcome? What market practices facilitate cooperative pricing? Such questions have been the focus of considerable theoretical and empirical research.[19] We review some of the major findings of this research below.

10.4.1   Factors that Facilitate Collusion[20]

What factors make collusion easier and, therefore, more likely? Any factor that facilitates collusion must do one of two things. It must either reduce the critical probability-adjusted

---

[18]   Sproul (1993) is the one contrary study finding that industry prices rise slightly *after* an indictment, which he interprets as evidence that cartels keep costs low. Apart from notable data problems, Sproul's (1993) analysis suffers from the difficulty that indictments only come after a long investigation. If the investigation itself triggers a breakdown in the cartel, then prices will fall long before the indictment. What happens at the indictment date then gives little guidance as to the actual cartel price effect.

[19]   Stigler (1964) is a classic in this field.

[20]   Motta (2004) provides an excellent and detailed discussion of these factors.

discount factor ρ^* above which the cartel is potentially self-sustaining, or it must reduce the likelihood of profitable cheating by cartel members. We examine specific industry features to see whether and how they meet these criteria.

i. High Industry Concentration

We are more likely to find collusion in more concentrated markets for at least two reasons. First, increased concentration typically reduces the critical probability-adjusted discount factor ρ^*. Take, for instance, a simple Bertrand model with N identical firms in the market. Each has profit π_m/N per period if it participates in the cartel. However, if one firm deviates, it can undersell all the others at just a bit lower price than the collusive one and therefore earn a one-period total monopoly profit π_m. Deviation is not profitable, therefore, if

$$\frac{\pi_m}{N}(1 + \rho + \rho^2 + \ldots) = \frac{\pi_m}{N(1 - \rho)} > \pi_m \Rightarrow \frac{1}{N} > 1 - \rho \Rightarrow \rho(N) > 1 - \frac{1}{N} \quad (10.21)$$

Clearly, $\rho(N)$ is increasing in N: $\rho^*(2) = 0.5$ as we noted above, $\rho^*(4) = 0.75$, and $\rho^*(10) = 0.9$. The intuition is clear. A firm in the cartel has to share the cartel's profits with other cartel members. As a result, the returns to collusion fall as the number of cartel members increases. By contrast, the reward for deviation is π_m regardless of the number of firms N. The net gain from deviation is, in other words, more profitable as industry concentration falls. This result extends to the Cournot case as well as to the Bertrand case. Note, too, that detecting noncooperative behavior by any one firm is more difficult when there are many firms. Since detection of cheating is essential for the success of the cartel, high concentration again makes collusion more likely.

Hay and Kelley (1974) provide compelling support for the proposition that industry structure matters for the likelihood of collusive arrangements. Their analysis of successful prosecutions of 62 cartels by the U.S. Department of Justice from 1963–72, summarized in Table 10.7, shows that the extent of collusive behavior depends substantially on the number of active firms.[21]

ii. Significant Entry Barriers

Easy entry undermines collusion. Suppose that an entrant does not join the cartel. Ease of entry weakens the ability of the cartel to maintain its goal of higher profit. Suppose,

Table 10.7 Cartels and industry concentration

Number of Conspirators	2	3	4	5	6	7	8	9	10	11–15	16–20	21–25	>25	Total
Number of Cases	1	7	8	4	10	4	3	5	7	5	2	–	6	62
Trade Association	–	–	1	–	4	1	–	1	3	1	1	–	6	18

	Concentration Ratios			
Concentration (percentage)	0–25	25–50	51–75	76–100	Total
Number of Cases	3	9	17	21	50

Source: Hay and Kelley (1974).

---

[21] Concentration ratios were available for only 50 of these cartels. We comment on the importance of trade associations.

Reality Checkpoint
The Guild Trip

European guilds first appeared in the 11th century as a result of growing commercial activity and urbanization. Merchants from the same city traveling to distant markets protected themselves by banding together in a caravan, called a Gilde or Hansa in the Germanic countries and a caritas or fraternitas in Latin-speaking ones. Caravan members had specific duties for defense if the caravan were attacked, and were also required to support each other in any legal disputes. Since the members of a hansa or fraternitas remained in touch with each other when they returned to their home city, they also began to assume rights and privileges in regard to trade within their local community—rights often supported by the authorities. This led in time to the merchant guilds monopolizing all of the industry and commerce of the city; nonguild members were only permitted to sell goods at wholesale.

Guilds based on specialized crafts replaced the earlier merchant guilds by the fourteenth century. The members of the craft guilds were all those engaged in any particular craft. They monopolized the making and selling of a particular commodity within the cities in which they were organized.

They did this in two ways: (1) by preventing goods from other cities being imported, and (2) by controlling local entry to membership in the craft guild. All those fortunate enough to be accepted as members were required to establish both uniform hours for all shops making the same commodity and uniform wages for workers in the same industry. Similarly, the number of people to be employed in each shop, the tools to be used, and the prices to be charged were all strictly regulated and enforced by close supervision. No advertising was allowed; and improvements in techniques of production, which might give one artisan a cost advantage, were also prohibited. Both the merchant and craft guilds were based in the cities of their day. These were small by our standards. This size coupled with the "everyone knows everyone else's business" aspect of medieval life meant that the setting was one of frequent, repeated encounters extending over an indefinite future.

The decline of the craft guilds came in the 16th century with the emergence of capitalist methods of production. This made possible the manufacture of goods on a larger scale at one point and shipping them to many others. Competition now came not from one's fellow local craftsmen but from anonymous sources further away. Policing and enforcement became impossible, and the new, more efficient production methods gradually forced the craft guilds out of existence.

Source: Weber, M. 1961. *General Economic History*. New York: Collier.

---

alternatively, that the entrant joins the cartel. Then our analysis above applies: there are now more cartel members, making the cartel harder to sustain. Moreover, such accommodation is likely to attract even more new entrants! Levenstein and Suslow (2006) note that "the most common cause of cartel breakdown in (their) nineteen case studies was entry" (p. 76). We can put this another way. For a cartel to succeed, it will need either to create strategic barriers to entry or to have structural ones in place.

iii. Frequent and Regular Orders

An industry in which firms receive infrequent and irregularly timed orders is not one that is conducive to price-fixing. The critical discount factor ρ^* is a per-period discount factor (day, week, month, etc.) that can be converted into an annual discount factor if we know the relevant time period. The longer the time between orders, the higher the annual discount factor. Suppose, for example, that orders are monthly, and $\rho^* = 0.9$. This is equivalent to an annual discount factor of $0.9^{12} = 0.28$. If, by contrast, the period between orders is six months, then the annual discount factor is $0.9^2 = 0.81$. Simply put, with infrequent orders, it takes longer to punish a firm that cheats on the cartel agreement, making cheating more attractive.

That regular orders aid collusive efforts is also easily illustrated. Take again the simple Bertrand case as an example, but suppose that in the current period ($t = 0$) a large order is received that has profit $\lambda\pi_m$, with $\lambda > 1$, while all later aggregate profits are expected to return to π_m per period. A slightly altered equation (10.21) gives the condition for the cartel to be self-sustaining in the face of this large order:

$$\frac{\pi_m}{N}(\lambda + \rho + \rho^2 + \cdots) = \frac{\pi_m}{N}\left(\lambda + \frac{\rho}{(1-\rho)}\right) > \lambda\pi_m \Rightarrow \lambda + \frac{\rho}{(1-\rho)} > \lambda N \quad (10.22)$$

Solving this for ρ gives the critical probability-adjusted discount factor

$$\rho(\lambda, N) = \frac{\lambda(N-1)}{1 + \lambda(N-1)} \quad (10.23)$$

It is easy to check that $\rho(\lambda, N)$ is increasing in the parameter λ and decreasing in N. In other words, the temptation to "steal" the profits from a one-time increase in demand can be sufficiently great to undermine the cartel. The same argument can be applied in analyzing random shocks to expected demand.[22] A positive demand shock "looks like" a large unexpected order, and we have just shown that this makes the cartel harder to sustain. By contrast, a negative demand shock can provide an incentive for the cartel to stick together.

iv. Rapid Market Growth

Cartels are more likely to be sustainable in growing markets and more likely to be unstable in declining markets. Returning once more to the N-firm Bertrand case, suppose that the market is forecast to grow by a factor g each period. That is, aggregate cartel profit in period t is forecast to be $\pi_m g^t$. For the cartel to be self-sustaining, it is necessary that

$$\frac{\pi_m}{N}(1 + g\rho + g^2\rho^2 + \ldots) = \frac{\pi_m}{N(1 - g\rho)} > \pi_m$$

$$\Rightarrow \frac{1}{N} > 1 - g\rho \Rightarrow \rho(g, N) > \frac{1}{g}\left(1 - \frac{1}{N}\right) \quad (10.24)$$

Clearly, $\rho(g, N)$ is decreasing in g. Take $g = 1$, or no growth, as our base case. With the market forecast to be unchanging over time, $\rho(1, N) = 1 - 1/N$ as in equation (10.23). However, when $g < 1$, so that the market is forecast to decline, we have that $\rho(g, N) > \rho(1, N)$ and the cartel is harder to sustain. By contrast, when $g > 1$, we have

[22]   Rotemberg and Saloner (1986) provide a more formal analysis.

$\rho(g, N) < \rho(1, N)$ and the cartel is easier to sustain. When growth is positive, the one-period gain from cheating meets a more severe punishment, since the future cooperative profits that are lost get larger over time.

v. Technological or Cost Symmetry

Symmetry among industry firms in terms of technology and cost is another market feature that can support cartel formation. Basically, a firm is more able to formulate a collusive agreement with a firm that "looks like" itself, rather than with one that does not. In addition, detailed negotiations over prices and market shares are much more straightforward when firms are similar. This is especially so when marginal cost s is rising at each firm. In this case, the maximum aggregate monopoly profit—denoted as π^M—is only reachable when each firm is producing the precise amount that minimizes the cost of producing the output associated with that maximum aggregate profit. As we saw in Chapter 3, such cost minimization requires that marginal cost be the same at each firm. Yet, if the firms have different cost structures, this will imply that each produces a different output level and therefore each earns a different profit.

The situation is illustrated in Figure 10.2. Here, the curve $\pi_1^* \pi_2^*$ describes the *profit possibility frontier* for two firms, 1 and 2. This frontier defines the maximum profit Firm 1 can achieve for any specific profit level assigned to Firm 2. The profit levels at M and other points on the frontier are achieved by an appropriate choice of output at each firm. Thus, if Firm 2 is assigned 0 profit (0 output), the maximum profit possible for Firm 1 is π_1^*. Similarly, if Firm 1 is assigned 0 profit or 0 output, the maximum amount of profit Firm 2 can earn is π_2^*. In constructing this example, we have assumed that marginal costs are increasing for both firms, but that Firm 2's costs rise more rapidly than Firm 1's costs.

There is one point on the profit frontier that generates the highest total profit π^M for both firms. This is point M. It is identified by the fact that a straight line with slope -1, that is, the line $\pi^M \pi^M$ is just tangent to the frontier at this point. This implies that at M production has been allocated such that marginal cost is equal at both firms,

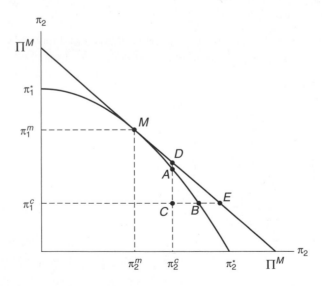

Figure 10.2   A collusive agreement between firms with different costs

and this equalized marginal cost is equal to industry marginal revenue. Note, though, that at this point, Firm 1's greater cost efficiency means that it earns the greater profit π_1^m, while Firm 2 earns the lesser amount π_2^m. The sum of these two profit levels is just π^M. Note that neither firm can earn this profit level by itself. That is, both π_1^* and π_2^* are less than π^M. Again, this is because achieving π^M requires that production be allocated such that the marginal cost is the same at each firm. If Firm 1 were to do all the production by itself, marginal cost would rise to a sufficiently high level that it could not earn π^M. The same is true for Firm 2. As we move to other allocations of production across the two firms, costs rise inefficiently, and the maximum profit achievable along the frontier falls below π^M. The two firms need each other if they are to achieve the joint maximum at M.

Unfortunately for Firm 2, not only is its profit at M smaller than Firm 1's profit, but it is also below the level Firm 2 earns in the Cournot-Nash equilibrium at point C, which we note does not lie on the curve $\pi_1^* \pi_2^*$. There is, then, a serious potential conflict between the firms that can make it difficult for them to collude. The conflict can be overcome, but getting to a point closer to M will generally require a side payment from Firm 1 to Firm 2. That is, Firm 1 will have to share the fruits of its greater productive efficiency with Firm 2 if the latter is to be persuaded to join a cooperative agreement. Both firms produce the outputs necessary to achieve the industry maximum at M. Then Firm 1 transfers some of the large profit it makes at M to Firm 2. In principle, such a transfer allows the firms to move along the $\pi^M \pi^M$ line to somewhere on the interval DE. However, negotiating and collecting side payments is never easy, and they serve as evidence that can make the cartel easier to discover. To be sure, points along the AB section of the frontier are possible without side payments. Yet, even these may be a challenge if the discount factor is sufficiently small.

The foregoing analysis should also make clear why collusion is more likely to be sustainable when the colluding firms are of roughly equal size, as they will tend to be when they have similar production capabilities. Once again, the Bertrand model provides a useful means by which this can be illustrated. Suppose that there are N firms in the cartel and that the profit share of firm i is s_i. For convenience, we number the firms in decreasing order of their profit shares, so that $s_1 \geq s_2 \geq s_3 \geq \cdots \geq s_i \geq \cdots \geq s_N$ with, of course $s_1 + s_2 + \cdots + s_N = 1$. For Firm i to be willing to remain in the cartel, the condition is

$$s_i \pi_m (1 + \rho + \rho^2 + \cdots) = \frac{s_i \pi_m}{(1 - \rho)} > \pi_m \Rightarrow s_i > 1 - \rho \Rightarrow \rho(s_i) > 1 - s_i \qquad (10.25)$$

If all the firms have equal profit shares $s_i = 1/N$, this simplifies to our "standard" Bertrand case of equation (10.21). By contrast, when profit shares are different, the firm with the lowest profit share determines the binding probability-adjusted discount factor used in equation (10.25). The smaller the share of the smallest firm, the higher the discount factor has to be for collusion to be sustainable.

vi. Multimarket Contact

It is tempting to suspect that when rival firms compete simultaneously in several distinct markets, their interaction is analogous to when they compete in one market over several periods. This intuition would then suggest that multimarket contact should be a feature that facilitates collusion. Unfortunately, the space and time analogy is somewhat misleading.

In the multimarket case, a firm can cheat on all of its collusive arrangements across different markets at one point of time. So, if there are no future periods, cooperation will be difficult regardless of the number of market contacts. However, an alternative argument does support the notion that multimarket contact can encourage collusion, at least when the firms have asymmetric market shares in the different markets in which they compete.[23]

For example, suppose that two firms A and B each operate in two markets, 1 and 2. Assume further that aggregate cartel profits in each market is π_m per period. The profit share for Firm A in each of these markets is, respectively, s_{A1} and s_{A2}, and we assume that $s_{A1} > 1/2$ while $s_{A2} < 1/2$. Of course, we have that $s_{B1} = 1 - s_{A1} < 1/2$ and $s_{B2} = 1 - s_{A2} > 1/2$. In other words, Firm A is the "large" firm in Market 1 and Firm B is the "large" firm in Market 2. As an example, A might be a U.S. firm and B a European firm, with market 1 being the U.S. and market 2 being the European market. To keep matters simple, further assume that the two firms have the same time preferences and the same discount rates. In other words, they have the same probability-adjusted discount factors.

If we treat the two markets separately, we know from our discussion in the previous section that collusion is sustainable in Market 1 only if the probability-adjusted discount factor for each firm is greater than $1 - s_{B1} > 1/2$, and in Market 2 only if the probability-adjusted discount factor for each firm is greater than $1 - s_{A2} > 1/2$. Now consider the two markets together. Take Firm A. Firm A knows that if it deviates from the collusive agreement in either market, then it will be punished in both. So if Firm A is contemplating deviation, it should deviate in both markets. In these circumstances, for deviation *not* to be profitable, it must be that

$$(s_{A1} + s_{A2})\pi_m(1 + \rho + \rho^2 + \cdots) = \frac{(s_{A1} + s_{A2})\pi^M}{(1 - \rho)} \geq 2\pi_m$$

$$\Rightarrow (s_{A1} + s_{A2}) > 2(1 - \rho) \Rightarrow \rho(s_{A1}, s_{A2}) \geq 1 - \frac{(s_{A1} + s_{A2})}{2}$$

(10.26)

The analogous result applies for Firm B: $\rho(s_{B1}, s_{B2}) \geq 1 - \frac{(s_{B1} + s_{B2})}{2}$.

A simple but instructive example is to suppose that Firm A has profit share s in Market 1 and $1 - s$ in Market 2, with $s > 1/2$ to reflect asymmetric positions. Analogously, Firm B has profit share $1 - s$ in Market 1 and s in Market 2. From (10.26), the cartel between Firms A and B is sustainable when they operate in both markets for any probability-adjusted discount factor greater than or equal to 1/2 (which is the standard Bertrand result again). However, the probability-adjusted discount factor would have to be greater than s, which by assumption is greater than 1/2, if the firms collaborate in only one market.

Multimarket contact can, indeed, support cooperation. What is necessary is, first, that the colluding firms have asymmetric positions in the markets in which they jointly operate; and second, that the asymmetry is reduced when all the markets in which they compete are considered. In our example, each firm has a share in excess of 1/2 in any one market. However, aggregated across both markets each firm has a share of 1/2.

vii. Product Homogeneity

The empirical evidence reported in Hay and Kelley (1974) and the conventional wisdom of government authorities and the courts is that collusion is easier to sustain when the

---

[23] See Bernheim and Whinston (1990) for a more complete analysis of this insight.

cartel members produce homogeneous or nearly homogeneous products. Again, there is an intuitive basis for this finding that stems from the complexity of the cartel agreement. First, with homogeneous products, a price-fixing cartel, in principle, has to set and monitor only one price; by contrast, collusion in pricing differentiated products requires agreeing and monitoring a different price for each product. This raises a second issue. Setting such a set of distinct prices requires that the cartel members agree on the degree to which their products are differentiated. This is a far-from-simple matter, especially as its resolution will largely determine each firm's share of the cartel profits. Third, punishment of deviation becomes more complex in a differentiated products context. Should all nondeviating firms punish a deviant, or should punishment be confined to those whose products are the closest substitutes to the deviant's product? If the latter, can punishment be targeted to affect only the deviant firm, or will there be spillover effects to other members of the cartel? Beyond all these arguments there is the likelihood that heterogeneous products will be associated with differential costs and other asymmetries that further hinder cooperative behavior.[24]

10.4.2   Facilitating Practices

In addition to market conditions, there are certain practices that also facilitate the formation and continuation of cartel agreements by making prices *observable*. We consider a number of these, starting with *basing-point-pricing*.

i. Basing-point-pricing

Basing-point-pricing is a pricing practice, now largely abandoned, that was used in a number of industries, most notably steel and plywood. The system worked by choosing one or a few production locations as basing points. Then, all prices of delivered goods were quoted as if they shipped from the basing point, regardless of where they actually originated. In the steel case in the United States, for example, Pittsburgh was the basing point. Hence, a consumer in Columbus, paid the same price for delivered steel—the mill price plus the transportation cost *from Pittsburgh*—whether the delivery actually came from Pittsburgh or from Birmingham, Alabama. This is in contrast to *free-on-board* or *fob* pricing in which the delivered price reflects the mill price plus the transport cost from the actual production location.

Basing-point pricing considerably simplified collusion by streamlining the price structure and making it easier to detect cheaters. It also made it easier to punish cheaters. Suppose that there are just two steel plants—one in Pittsburgh and one in Birmingham—and that the two firms aim to set a cooperative monopoly price. Under fob pricing, prices are set at the mill. If one firm cheats, retaliation by the other firm requires a reduction in that firm's mill price. Since this reduces its profit on sales to *all* customers, it means that meting out punishment is costly. By contrast, with basing-point pricing, a price cut can be made by shading the delivered price to just the area or areas in which the noncooperative firm violated the agreement. As a result, the retaliation can be more surgically precise and, most importantly, less costly, discouraging cheating in the first place. It is not surprising that basing-point pricing schemes have now been declared illegal in the United States.

---

[24] Note though that if products are differentiated and each brand has strong consumer loyalty, then the temptation to cheat by offering a secret price reduction to a rival's customer will be reduced.

ii. Most-favored Consumer and Meet-the-Competition Clauses

More modern business practices such as *most-favored customer* and *meet-the-competition clauses* may also help to maintain a price-fixing agreement among firms.[25] *Most-favored customer clauses* guarantee that if the seller offers the same product to another buyer at a lower price, the first buyer will receive a rebate equal to the difference in the two prices, whereas *meet-the-competition clauses* guarantee that a firm will match any lower price offered by another seller. Why might these practices maintain cartel discipline?

First, consider *meet-the-competition clauses*. These make the process of detecting cheating particularly effective, since now the firms offering these guarantees have vast numbers of unpaid market watchers in the person of every consumer who has bought the product. Second, such clauses effectively bind the hands of the firms that offer them. Third, retaliation can be made specific to particular customers. Finally, the rewards to deviation are significantly reduced.

To get some idea as to just how powerful this effect can be, consider the simple one-period pricing game between two firms shown in Table 10.8. The one-shot nature of the game leads the firms to the Nash equilibrium in which both firms price low. Now, consider what happens when we permit both firms to publish meet-the-competition guarantees that are legally and instantaneously binding.[26] These guarantees render the off-diagonal price pairs in Table 10.8 unattainable. There is no opportunity to undercut one's cartel partner when each firm has announced a meet-the-competition policy that goes into effect immediately. Because the combinations of one firm pricing low and the other firm pricing high are unattainable, neither firm has any incentive to deviate from the Price High policy. The cartel works even in this simple one-period setting. This has led Motta to suggest that "the pro-collusive impact of meeting-competition clauses seems so strong that anti-trust authorities should probably put them under a *per se* prohibition rule." (Motta, 2004, p. 158)

Now, consider the role of *most-favored customer clauses*. Admittedly, such a contract severely restricts the temptation of any seller to reduce its price, since the price reduction has to be offered to all previous buyers as well. On the other hand, the contract also makes the response to deviation more costly. Punishment is now more difficult since the clause requires that the lower price be offered to all customers and not just those of the cheating firm. The ultimate effect then depends on how these forces balance out although Motta argues that he knows of "no model where (most-favored customer) is found to increase sustainability of collusion in an infinite horizon game." (Motta, 2004, p. 157 fn 53.)

Table 10.8 Payoff matrix for a 2 × 2 pricing game

		Strategy for Firm 2	
		Price High	Price Low
Strategy for Firm 1	Price High	(12, 12)	(5, 14)
	Price Low	(14, 5)	(6, 6)

---

[25] See Salop (1986) for more details on these competition clauses.

[26] This is perfectly legal, since the price-matching guarantees are offered to buyers rather than communicated to other sellers.

Reality Checkpoint

Most-Favored Customer Policy Was a Bad Prescription for Medicaid

The Omnibus Budget Reconciliation Act of 1990 (OBRA 90) contained a Most-Favored Customer clause that applied to reimbursement for pharmaceuticals purchased under Medicaid. Medicaid is a very large program that accounts for nearly 15 percent of the prescription drug market sales in the United States. The drug companies routinely offered other large buyers of drugs, such as HMOs and drug store chains, quantity discounts. However, because Medicaid did not purchase the drugs directly in bulk itself but instead reimbursed hospitals and pharmacies on an individual basis, it never received these discounts.

OBRA 90 included a number of steps that Congress hoped would alleviate this problem. On the one hand, it required that the drug price charged Medicaid had to be no more than 12.5 percent *less* than the average price charged all customers. Moreover, a most-favored customer clause further required that if a firm charged any customer a price more than 12.5 percent below the average, that same price had to be extended to all Medicaid customers.

Yet the analysis presented in this chapter raises the possibility that these well intentioned regulations may well have backfired. The most-favored customer clause tends to soften price competition. If a firm tries to cut its price in one market to gain competitive advantage there, the most-favored customer clause requires that it will have to cut its price in all other markets, too. This acts as a disincentive to aggressive price competition. Indeed, the legislation also required that the Office of Inspector General monitor all firms so that there would be no secret price discounts that were not passed on to Medicaid. Of course, this meant no secret price discounts at all and, as a result, a further weakening of price competition.

Economist Fiona Scott Morton (1997) studied the impact of OBRA 90 on cardiovascular drug prices in the two years starting with January 1, 1991—the date that the regulations went into effect. She found that prices for well-known brand drugs, which had been facing tough price competition from generic substitutes, actually rose by over four percent. This finding supports the view that most-favored customer clauses, like meet-the-competition clauses, facilitate collusive behavior aimed at reducing price competition.

Source: Morton, Fiona Scott. 1997. "The Strategic Response by Pharmaceutical Firms to the Medicaid Most Favored Customer Rules." *Rand Journal of Economics*, 28 (Summer): 269–290.

If meet-the-competition and (possibly) most-favored customer clauses have anticompetitive effects, why are consumers lured by such guarantees? The answer lies in the fact that there is a difference between what is good for an individual consumer and what is good for consumers overall. A price-matching clause is valuable to any one buyer who is assured of getting the very best deal possible. However, because that buyer then becomes implicitly a monitor of prices on behalf of the colluding firms, there is an externality to the buyer's purchase of which she may be unaware. Moreover, such monitoring will lead to prices being set higher (albeit identical) for all consumers. So in fact, the equilibrium outcome will be one in which all buyers are worse off.

iii. Centralized Sales Agency and Trade Associations

One way for a cartel in an unstable market to reinforce the trigger strategy is to establish a *centralized sales agency*, as in the De Beers diamond cartel, or a *trade association*. Either institutional arrangement can monitor and report upon both market conditions and individual firm performance. For government contracts, this monitoring is often made easier by regulations that require government agencies to publish the bids they have received. Trade associations can be particularly helpful, then, for monitoring private-sector contracts where no such disclosure is required. The Hay and Kelley study noted above (Table 10.6) provides evidence of the importance of such trade associations in sustaining "large number" cartels.

10.5   ANTITRUST POLICY TOWARD CARTELS: DETERRENCE AND DETECTION

In the preceding sections, we have shown that there are conditions and practices that foster cartel formation, as well as strong theoretical arguments and empirical evidence that cartels with substantial power to raise prices can and do arise. This brings us to the issue of policy. Given the potentially serious effects of an illegal cartel, what type of policy response will best limit cartel formation? We begin with a general analysis of the broad policy parameters regarding the likelihood of investigation and the fines imposed for illegal behavior. We then examine how these broad considerations are altered by the use of leniency or amnesty programs.

10.5.1   Antitrust Policy: Investigation versus Fines

Assume that a potentially self-sustaining cartel exists as defined by equation (10.15). Now introduce an antitrust authority, which is charged with looking for and attempting to prosecute cartels. In any given period, assume that there is a probability a that the authority will investigate the cartel. If no investigation is instituted, the cartel continues to the next year. The investigation takes one period, and we assume that there is a probability s that it leads to successful prosecution, in which case the cartel members are subjected to a fine of F and the cartel breaks down.[27] If the investigation is unsuccessful, the cartel continues.

We denote the expected present value of the profits that each cartel member receives as V_m. To evaluate this expected value, we need to consider three possibilities.

(i) With probability $1 - a$, there is no investigation in period 0, and the cartel continues. Expected profit is

$$V_1 = (1 - a)(\pi_m + \rho V_m) \tag{10.27}$$

---

[27]   Note that Motta and Polo (2003) assume in contrast that the cartel begins again after one period of punishment. We prefer our approach since, in the former case, the antitrust authority, having once found a cartel, could simply keep on investigating the same firms. We are aware, of course, that the evidence shows that there are repeat offenders; but in those cases, the offenders have joined different cartels rather than reconstituted the cartel that was prosecuted.

The first term in the second bracket is profit in the current period given that the cartel is active. The second term uses the same reasoning as in equation (10.11). Given that there is no investigation, the "cartel game" begins again in period 1 and so has expected profit V_m, which has to be discounted one period.

(ii) With probability $a(1-s)$, there is an unsuccessful investigation in period 0. The cartel continues, and expected profit is

$$V_2 = a(1-s)(\pi_m + \rho V_m) \tag{10.28}$$

Similar to equation (10.27), the second term in the second bracket reflects the fact that the cartel game begins again in period 1 after an unsuccessful prosecution.

(iii) With probability as, there is a successful prosecution. Each cartel member is fined and the cartel collapses after the prosecution. Expected profit is

$$V_3 = as \left(\pi_m - F + \frac{\rho}{1-\rho} \pi_n \right) \tag{10.29}$$

Putting together all the possibilities in (10.27), (10.28), and (10.29) gives us the expected present value of profit for a cartel member, $V_m = V_1 + V_2 + V_3$. This is

$$V_m = (1-a)\pi_m + a(1-s)\pi_m + as\pi_m - asF + \frac{as\rho}{1-\rho}\pi_n + (1-a)\rho V_m$$

$$+ a(1-s)\rho V_m = \pi_m - asF + \frac{as\rho}{1-\rho}\pi_n + (1-as)\rho V_m \tag{10.30}$$

Solving for V_m gives the expected profit of each firm in the cartel:

$$V_m = \frac{\pi_m - asF + \frac{as\rho}{1-\rho}\pi_n}{1 - \rho(1-as)} \tag{10.31}$$

Comparing (10.31) with (10.12) confirms, as we would have expected, that the introduction of an antitrust authority reduces the expected profit from cartel formation. This is true even if the authority merely breaks up the cartel while imposing no fines.

Equation (10.31) makes clear that antitrust policy has two major tools. The first and most obvious tool is the fine F. As F increases, the expression in equation (10.31) decreases for any positive values of a and s. Even with small detection probabilities, a large enough fine would deter cartel formation. However, this tool is limited. The antitrust authorities cannot impose fines of arbitrary magnitude, but must instead relate any fine to the damage that the cartel is estimated to have inflicted.[28]

The second tool is the probability of investigation and successful prosecution as. As this term increases, the expression in equation (10.31) becomes smaller. In the extreme case of $as = 1$, the expression becomes $\pi_m - F + [\rho/(1-\rho)]\pi_n$. For this expected profit to exceed the gains from cheating on a collusive agreement, or $\pi_d + [\rho/(1-\rho)]\pi_n$, requires that $\pi_m - F > \pi_d$—which, of course, is not possible even if the fine F is 0. In other words, a sufficiently high rate of successful cartel discovery and prosecution would end cartel formation, even if there were no penalty.

[28]   Detailed analyses of the EC assessment of damages can be found at http://ec.europa.eu/competition/antitrust/actionsdamages/study.html.

The final question is whether the introduction of the antitrust authority affects the ability of a cartel to be self-sustaining. For this to be the case, V_m from (10.31) should be greater than V_d from (10.13). Take the case of a 0 fine. A bit of manipulation indicates that the critical probability adjusted discount factor ρ^A for this case is

$$\rho > \rho^A = \frac{\pi_d - \pi_m}{(1 - as)(\pi_d - \pi_n)} \tag{10.32}$$

Comparison of equations (10.15) and (10.32) confirms that $\rho^A > \rho^*$ and that ρ^A rises as either a or s increases. The underlying reason is that there are now two forces that can cause the cartel to fail. One of these is the ever-present pursuit of self-interest that induces individual cartel members to cheat on the agreement. The other is the newly introduced force stemming from the possibility of successful prosecution by the authorities.

Take our Bertrand duopoly example. We know that $\pi_m = \pi^a/2$, $\pi_d = \pi^a$, and $\pi_n = 0$. Substituting into (10.32), the critical probability adjusted discount factor for this cartel to be self-sustaining in the presence of an antitrust authority (which causes cartel breakdown but does not impose a penalty) is $\rho^A = 1/2(1 - as)$. If there had been no investigative effort ($as = 0$), then ρ need only be greater than 1/2 for the cartel to be self-sustaining. However, as a or s rises, the likelihood that the cartel can survive declines. For $as \geq 1/2$, no cartel can be self-sustaining.

Which tool—fines or increased probability of apprehension and conviction—should the authorities use? Uncovering and prosecuting price-fixing conspiracies requires careful surveillance and legal work, which is expensive. In contrast, fines may be imposed at little cost. This suggests that a heavy reliance on substantial punishment is likely to be the more cost-effective strategy. In turn, this helps to explain why the law imposes treble damages in private antitrust lawsuits. However, unlike detection efforts, fines can never be used by themselves as part of a deterrence strategy. The reason is simple. If either a or s is 0, then the probability of getting caught and paying the fine is also 0, and hence, a fine will have no deterrent effect no matter how large it is.

Note as well that whether the authorities rely on investigations or fines, much of what antitrust enforcement is about is deterrence. The policy works by preventing cartels from forming in the first place and not just by breaking them up once they have been uncovered. Such deterrence means that we may have difficulty in evaluating the full impact of antitrust efforts, because we cannot easily measure the number of cartels that would have formed were it not for these deterrent effects. Here again, the extreme case is insightful. Suppose that because of a combination of investigative efforts and punishments, as and F are set such that firms never find it worthwhile to form a cartel. Because no cartels are ever observed, it may seem to an outsider that price-fixing penalties are not necessary and that the funds spent on detection (as) are wasted. Yet in fact, it is precisely because of those expenditures and punishment policies that cartels have been eliminated.

10.5.2   Antitrust Policy: Detecting Cartels

Investigation of suspected collusion is time consuming and costly. Furthermore, unless it uncovers convincing evidence, an investigation may not lead to an indictment—let alone a conviction. The conspiring firms are entitled to their "day in court" and have an informational advantage over any government agency. They are the ones that know the nature of market demand as well as the costs of production and transportation.

The best the authorities can do is to infer this information from data provided by the very same firms who are being investigated. Somewhat surprisingly, it can be very difficult to distinguish collusive behavior from competitive actions. This problem has been termed the *indistinguishability theorem* by Harstad and Phlips (1990).[29].

To show the indistinguishability theorem in action, we consider a case in which the European Commission ultimately rendered a verdict against ICI and Solvay, the two firms that control the European market for soda ash, which is a raw material used in glass manufacture. ICI and Solvay had operated a number of cartel agreements for many years. Solvay supplied continental Europe while ICI supplied the United Kingdom, Ireland, and the British Commonwealth. These explicit agreements terminated in 1972, but there was no subsequent market interpenetration by the two producers. In the 1980s, prices in the United Kingdom rose some 15 to 20 percent above those in continental Europe, which the Commission argued was greater than the transport costs across the English Channel. The Commission judged that the lack of market invasion by either firm into the other's historic regional market—especially in the face of such price differentials—was strong evidence of continued tacit collusion by the two firms.

While the Commission's judgment may appear to be sound, there is a counterargument. If each firm has the same marginal cost schedule and if each sets its price equal to marginal cost plus the cost of transportation across the Channel, no cross-market penetration will ever occur. Such pricing behavior would reflect true rivalry—would lead to prices well below the collusive level—and yet there would be no market invasion of one firm by the other. Unless the regulatory agency has independent data on transportation costs, the nature of demand on each side of the Channel, and on production costs, it cannot make a definitive case that the continued market segmentation of the market is the result of collusive action.

Similar considerations apply when defending companies who are being charged with collusion because of evidence that they changed their prices in parallel. MacLeod (1985) shows that when firms' profit functions are not known to each other, there is no systematic difference in the response of collusive and noncollusive equilibrium prices to exogenous shocks. This is relevant to a 1984 judgment by the European Commission against a number of North American, Finnish, and Swedish companies who exported wood pulp to Europe for use by paper manufacturers. The Commission determined that these companies had to pay fines of between 50,000 and 500,000 ECU because they had announced and enforced parallel seasonal price changes. The judgment was thrown out on appeal in 1993 to the European Court of Justice because, as the MacLeod analysis suggests, such parallel price responses do not necessarily imply collusion.

Fortunately, the situation facing government authorities is not hopeless. Studies by Porter and Zona (1993, 1999) are good illustrations of work that uncovers signs of collusion that perhaps one can look for *ex ante*. In the first of these, Porter and Zona reviewed bidding on highway paving projects on Long Island in the early 1980s. This was a case in which the product (government-designed highway construction) was homogenous, and bidders and the winning bid were known by all of the (relatively few) bidders. Hence, conditions were ripe for cartelization and, indeed, in 1984 one of the largest firms in this industry was convicted of price-fixing along with four other unindicted co-conspirators, mainly as the result of a confession by one executive.

---

[29]   For a much more detailed exposition of the indistinguishability theorem, see Phlips (1995a). See also LaCasse (1995).

Looking back at the data uncovered by the government, Porter and Zona (1993) ranked separately the cartel firms and the noncartel firms by order of their unit costs. They then compared this ranking with the ranking of the submitted bids. For the noncartel firms, the ranking of bids and costs were similar. The lower a firm's cost, the lower its bid. This was not the case for the cartel firms. For these firms, there was little relationship between their cost and bid ranks. The choice by the cartel firms as to who among them will be the low bidder had little to do with cost, but was simply rotated among cartel members to keep each one happy. Once the winning firm and its bid were chosen for a specific project, all the other cartel members did was to bid a bit higher, whether their costs were low or high.

In their study of school milk procurement auctions with an active cartel, Porter and Zona (1999) again looked at the behavior of noncartel members. Here they were able to show that while noncartel members' bids increased with distance from the firm to the school district, as would be expected, cartel members' bids often decreased with distance. The explanation is that the cartel members were bidding competitively in distant districts not covered by the cartel, but cooperatively in proximate districts they controlled.[30]

Osborne and Pitchik (1987) propose another test for detecting collusion. Recall our discussion in Chapter 9 of the Spence (1977) and Dixit (1980) models in which a large firm invests in extra capacity as a means to discipline a new rival. Osborne and Pitchik argue that extra capacity may play a similar disciplinary role in cartels.[31] For example, we know that Bertrand price competition cannot yield the competitive outcome unless each firm has the capacity to serve the entire market. In the case of a cartel, however, acquiring such large capacity affords the firm the means to threaten the other firms with the competitive outcome if either one cheats on the collusive agreement. Osborne and Pitchik (1987) show that in this case, cartel members have an incentive to acquire a larger amount of capacity.

However, it is likely that the firms choose their capacities before the collusive agreement is implemented, and so the collusive agreement covers only their pricing behavior. Because the capacity choice is made noncooperatively, it is unlikely that each will choose exactly the same amount of capacity. Accordingly, when collusion subsequently begins, the price/marginal cost distinction may be the same for each firm, but the profit per unit of capacity will be greater for the firm with the smaller amount of capacity. Not only will the smaller firm have a higher profit per unit of capacity, but Osborne and Pitchik (1987) also show that this difference will increase as the total amount of excess capacity grows. By contrast, if there is no collusion, the profits per unit of capacity will be identical across firms.

Phlips (1995b) shows how this analysis can be used to examine the behavior of the two British producers of white salt, British Salt and ICI Weston Point. Many analysts suspected these two firms of collusion, even after they abandoned an earlier explicit price agreement when the United Kingdom adopted its Restrictive Practices Act in 1956. Based on the analysis shown in Table 10.9, Phlips claims:

---

[30]   In a related piece, Hendricks and Porter (1988) examine bids for offshore oil and gas leases. They find that firms with tracts adjacent to the tract being auctioned often lose to non-neighboring firms even though the latter are, presumably, less well informed and therefore, should bid more cautiously. This suggests that neighboring firms are colluding to keep bids low.

[31]   Davidson and Deneckere (1990) offer a similar analysis.

Table 10.9   The great salt duopoly

	1980	1981	1982	1983	1984
BS Profit	7065	7622	10489	10150	10882
WP Profit	7273	7527	6841	6297	6204
BS Profit per Unit of Capacity	8.6	9.3	12.7	12.3	13.2
WP Profit per Unit of Capacity	6.6	6.9	6.3	5.8	5.7
Industry Capacity/Total UK Sales	1.5	1.7	1.7	1.9	1.9

Throughout the period under investigation, both British Salt (BS) and ICI Weston Point (WP) had excess capacity. BS had a given capacity of 824 kilotons, WP had a given capacity of 1095 kilotons. All I had to do was to divide the yearly profits by the capacities and to divide the sum of the capacities by total sales, to find the . . . numbers [shown in Table 10.9]. Not only was BS's profit per unit of capacity larger than WP's: it also increased relative to WP's as their joint capacity increased relative to market demand. None of these numbers is disputable. . . . This beats the indistinguishability theorem: I wish more such tests were available. (Phlips, 1995b, p. 15)

10.5.3   Antitrust Policy: Leniency/Amnesty Programs

We have argued that the prospect of getting caught and fined can serve as a major deterrent to cartel formation, but that the ability to distinguish collusive from competitive behavior can make successful prosecution quite difficult, even with careful analysis of the evidence. The framework underlying our discussion so far, however, is one in which the cartel members play a game against the antitrust authorities. As noted earlier, many of the recently prosecuted cartels have been discovered as the result of "finking" by a specific cartel member. In some cases, the informer has been a firm in the industry either unhappy with the share it was allocated, or upset because it was excluded altogether. Sometimes it has been a former employee of a cartel member who has blown the whistle because of a dispute with his employer.[32] Whatever the reason, all of these cases suggest that the possibility of investigation and being caught often reflects some sort of conflict or game between the participating firms themselves. In recent years, policy makers have relied on so-called leniency/amnesty programs to exploit such conflicts.

While the actual programs enacted in different regions differ in their details, they typically have the following form: "The first member of a cartel to provide evidence that leads to successful prosecution of the cartel receives lenient treatment. Everybody else is subject to heavy fines." Even if an investigation has been started, a lighter sentence or even total amnesty might still be offered to the first firm coming forward with evidence, if this evidence proves central to successful prosecution of the cartel.

[32]   A classic example of this is the garbage-hauling business in New York, which was controlled by a trade association between firms who carved up the city between them. Any firm attempting to enter this industry was met with threats of arson and physical violence. If a firm in the cartel took business away from another member, then the association forced the offending company to pay compensation amounting to "up to 40 times the monthly pickup charge." Ex-mobsters who had been the victims of the financial penalties and violence provided some of the evidence necessary to break the cartel. (S. Raab, "To Prosecutors, Breakthrough after 5 Years of Scrutiny." *The New York Times* (23 June 1995), p. 3.

Since the other conspirators remain subject to heavy fines and perhaps imprisonment for their executives, the program creates a strong incentive for firms to be the first to confess.

This new program has been very successful in aiding the prosecution of cartels. As the Antitrust Division of the U.S. Department of Justice has said:

> Today, the Amnesty Program is the Division's most effective generator of large cases, and it is the Department's most successful leniency program. Amnesty applications over the past year have been coming in at the rate of approximately two per month—a more than *20-fold increase* as compared to the rate of applications under the old Amnesty Program. Given this remarkable rate of amnesty applications, it certainly appears that the message has been communicated. (http://www.usdoj.gov/atr/public/speeches/2247.htm)

On first sight, it would appear that these leniency programs put the prisoners' dilemma to work. However, as Motta and Polo (1999) and Spagnolo (2004)—among others—have pointed out, such programs are a double-edged sword. The good news is that leniency encourages confessions once an investigation is underway. The bad news is that it also raises the possibility of getting out of the cartel free of prosecution altogether and thereby increases the expected net gains from starting a cartel in the first place. Indeed, evidence that more cartels are being successfully prosecuted since the advent of leniency programs might simply be the result of more cartels being formed so that with the same or even lower detection rate more conspiracies are caught! We now examine this complicated tradeoff.

Consider a duopoly industry. Assume that a price-fixing agreement gives each cartel member profit π_m, while optimal deviation from the agreement gives profit π_d, and the noncooperative Nash equilibrium profit to each firm is π_n. Both firms have probability-adjusted discount factors of ρ. Now consider the following game.[33] Each firm can adopt one of three strategies:

(1) *(Collude, Not Reveal)*: Form a cartel and do not reveal evidence of the existence of the cartel if it is investigated. This is the strategy that we analyzed in Section 10.5.1. We know from equation (10.31) that the value V_{NR}^C of expected profit is

$$V_{NR}^C = \frac{\pi_m - asF + \dfrac{as\rho}{1-\rho}\pi_n}{1 - \rho(1-as)} \tag{10.33}$$

where a is the probability that the antitrust authorities launch an investigation; s is the probability that the investigation leads to successful prosecution given that the members of the cartel do not provide evidence of the cartel's existence; and F is the maximum legal fine that can be levied on successful prosecution.

(2) *(Collude, Reveal)*: Form a cartel, but reveal its existence once an investigation has been started. Assume that the investigation takes one period and that the cartel firms maintain the cartel until the investigation is "nearly" complete. Each firm earns the cartel

---

[33]   This game is a highly simplified version of the game presented in Motta and Polo (2003); see also Motta (2004) p. 195 ff.

profit for one period, but then both confess and the cartel collapses. To evaluate expected profit V_R^C for this strategy, we consider two possibilities:

a. With probability $1 - a$, no investigation is initiated in period 0. In this case, the cartel continues, and expected profit is

$$V_1 = (1 - a)(\pi_m + \rho V_R^C) \tag{10.34}$$

The first term in the second bracket is cartel profit in the current year, after which the "game" with the authorities resumes with expected profit V_R^C discounted by one period.

b. With probability a, an investigation is initiated in period 0. In this case, the cartel continues until the investigation is nearing completion, at which point the firms confess and pay a reduced fine of $0 \leq L < F$. The cartel then collapses. Expected profit is:

$$V_2 = a \left(\pi_m - L + \frac{\rho}{1 - \rho} \pi_n \right) \tag{10.35}$$

Summing (10.34) and (10.35) gives the expected profit from the strategy **(Collude, Reveal)** $V_R^C = V_1 + V_2$. Solving for V_R^C then gives:

$$V_R^C = \frac{\pi_m - aL + \dfrac{a\rho\pi_n}{1 - \rho}}{1 - (1 - a)\rho} \tag{10.36}$$

Equation (10.36) shows the potential downside of a leniency program. Expected profit is decreasing in the fine L. In other words, the more generous the leniency program—the smaller is L—the more profitable is (Collude, Reveal) and so the more likely it is that a cartel will be formed.

(3) *(Defect)*: on the cartel in period $t = 0$, in which case, of course, the cartel breaks down—or, more accurately, is never effectively formed. We know from equation (10.11) that the value of expected profit in this case is

$$V_d = \pi_d + \frac{\rho\pi_n}{1 - \rho} \tag{10.37}$$

We need some further assumptions to complete the analysis. If both firms defect, then no cartel is ever formed, and each firm has profit $V_n = \pi_n/(1 - \rho)$. If one firm defects while the other does not, the defecting firm earns V_d while the non-defecting firm makes "very low" profits V_l. If one firm reveals while the other does not, the revealing firm earns V_R^C as above, while the nonrevealing firm earns $V_R^C - D$, where $D > 0$ can be calculated by substituting F for L in equation (10.36). This gives the payoff matrix of Table 10.6, in which Firm 1's payoffs are listed first.

Inspection of Table 10.10 reveals that it potentially has a number of possible Nash equilibria. **(Defect, Defect)** is, of course, one of these. The noncooperative Nash equilibrium to the one-shot game repeated over and over is always one of the potential equilibria

Table 10.10   Payoff matrix with a leniency program

		Strategy for Firm 2		
		Defect	Collude, Reveal	Collude, Not Reveal
Strategy for Firm 1	Defect	(V_n, V_n)	(V_d, V_l)	(V_d, V_l)
	Collude, Reveal	(V_l, V_d)	(V_R^C, V_R^C)	$(V_R^C, V_R^C - D)$
	Collude, Not Reveal	(V_l, V_d)	$(V_R^C - D, V_R^C)$	(V_{NR}^C, V_{NR}^C)

to the repeated game. As Table 10.10 shows, however, there are also other and more interesting equilibrium possibilities. In particular,

1. **(Collude, Reveal)** for both players is an equilibrium provided that $V_R^C > V_d$;
2. **(Collude, Not Reveal)** for both players is an equilibrium provided that $V_{NR}^C > \max \{V_R^C, V_d\}$

Indeed, an interesting feature of this game is that if $V_{NR}^C > V_R^C > V_d$, then there are actually three equilibria. These are: both Defect, both play (Collude, Reveal) and both play (Collude, Not Reveal). It seems reasonable to make the following assumption:

Equilibrium Selection: If the firms are able to form a cartel, they will do so; and they will choose the most profitable strategy combination for the cartel.

In our example with $V_{NR}^C > V_R^C > V_d$ the result of our equilibrium selection assumption is that both firms will play (Collude, Not Reveal).

To make the analysis more concrete, consider the impact of the leniency program in the context of a Bertrand model with: $\pi_m = 1,800, \pi_d = 3,600$ and $\pi_n = 0$. Our prior analysis then implies

$$V_{NR}^C = \frac{1,800 - asF}{1 - (1 - as)\rho}; \quad V_R^C = \frac{1,800 - aR}{1 - (1 - a)\rho}; \quad V^D = 3,600 \qquad (10.38)$$

The antitrust authority can use its scarce resources to affect three parameters in our model: (1) the probability a that an investigation is initiated; (2) the probability s that the investigation is successful in identifying the cartel; and (3) L, the strength of the leniency program. The maximum penalty F paid in litigation that results in a conviction is, on the other hand, determined by the courts. Given that we know F and ρ, we can illustrate how the parameters a and s determine the equilibrium for a given value of L. For convenience (and without being too unrealistic), we set $\rho = 0.8$. We also assume that $F = \$3,600$, or twice the per-period excess cartel profit. (Recall that private antitrust lawsuits pay treble damages to successful plaintiffs.)

Table 10.11 gives the profits for each of the three strategies for any values of a and s and for two values of L, namely, $L = 0$ (complete amnesty); and $L = \$600$ (one-third of the cartel profits). From the table, we then have

(i) $V_R^C > V^D$ if $a < a_{CR}(L) = 3/8$ if $L = 0$ and $= 9/29$ if $L = 600$;

(ii) $V_{NR}^C > V^D$ if $a < a_{CNR}(s) = 1/6s$; and

(iii) $V_{NR}^C > V_R^C$ if $a < a_{ES}(L, s) = (2 - 3s)/4s$ if $L = 0$ and $(13 - 18s)/20s$ if $L = 600$

Table 10.11   Profits for the Leniency Program Game

	$L = 0$	$L = 600$
V_R^C	$\frac{9{,}000}{1+4a}$	$\frac{3{,}000(3-a)}{1+4a}$
V_{NR}^C	$\frac{9{,}000(1-2as)}{1+4as}$	$\frac{9{,}000(1-2as)}{1+4as}$
V_d	3,600	3,600

The subscript *ES* in (iii) stands for "equilibrium selection" when both (Collude, Reveal) and (Collude, Not Reveal) are Nash equilibria. Given our equilibrium selection assumption, (Collude, Reveal) is the equilibrium for $a \in [a_{ES}(L, s), a_{CR}(L)]$, (Collude, Not

---

Reality Checkpoint
Leniency Program Succeeds—Only Too Well

The Competition Directorate of the European Commission introduced its leniency program in 2002 and updated the program in December 2006. The new program guidelines include the following provisions:

- Fines are up to 30 percent of the sales value affected by the cartel, multiplied by the number of years over which the cartel operated;
- Cartel members will also be fined an "entry fee" for joining the cartel, which will be between 15 and 25 percent of annual sales in the sectors affected by the cartel;
- Repeat offenders can have their fines doubled for a second offense, tripled for a third offense, and so on;
- Fines can be further increased for companies that do not cooperate with the Commission's investigation and for the ringleader in the cartel;
- Fines can be decreased if a company fully cooperates with the cartel investigation.
- Companies that "blow the whistle" on the cartel receive full immunity from punishment.

The problem is that this policy appears to be almost too successful. The lure of immunity has generated more than 200 applications since 2002. While this has led to a series of high-profile successes, it also runs the risk of overwhelming the 70 specialist investigators. Even with evidence provided by immunity applicants, cartel investigations currently take at least three years to complete. The flood of immunity applications threatens to drag this out even more. In response, the competition commissioner Neelie Kroes has floated the idea of offering "direct settlements:" reduced fines in return for cooperation with the cartel investigation and the promise not to appeal the Commission's final ruling. However, this proposal faces many practical and legal obstacles, so for the time being it looks as if the investigators will have soldier on with their increased workload—unless, of course, some of the rapidly growing revenues from fines are used to hire additional investigators!

Source: "Cartels Feel Pain Of Kroes Crusade." *Financial Times* (29 March 2007, Thursday). Companies International.

Reveal) is the equilibrium for $a < \min \{a_{ES}(L, s), a_{CNR}(s)\}$, and no cartel is formed otherwise.

These Nash equilibria are illustrated in Figure 10.3(a) and highlight the conflicting effects of the leniency program. Look first at Figure 10.3(a), which assumes that the leniency program offers compete amnesty or $L = 0$. If no leniency program exists, a cartel will be formed only if the probability of an investigation $a < a_{CNR}(s)$, and these cartels will not reveal evidence if they are investigated. There is no incentive to do so if there is no hope of leniency.

The leniency program extends the parameter region in which cartels form. If a and s lie in region CR_1, cartels form using the strategy (Collude, Reveal), whereas without the leniency program no cartels form in this region. On the other hand, cartels in the region CR_2 that follow the policy (Collude, Not Reveal) in the absence of a leniency program now switch to (Collude, Reveal), potentially making the antitrust authorities' detection problems somewhat easier. In other words, the leniency program encourages more cartels to be created, but also makes them easier to find and prosecute.

The same conflict arises when we compare the generous leniency program of Figure 10.3(a) with the less generous program of Figure 10.3(b), in which $R = 600$. In region (1), cartels that would form with the generous program do not form with the less generous program. On the other hand, in region (2), cartels that would adopt (Collude, Reveal) with the generous program adopt (Collude, Not Reveal) with the less generous program. A less generous leniency program creates fewer cartels, but makes them harder to find.

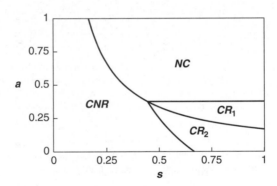

Figure 10.3(a)   Equilibria with a leniency program; $L = 0$

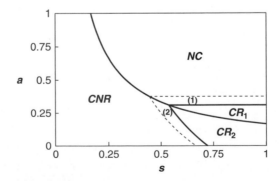

Figure 10.3(b)   Equilibria with a leniency program; $L = 600$

10.6   EMPIRICAL APPLICATION
An Experimental Investigation of Leniency Programs

If theory does not provide a definite judgment on the net impact of leniency programs, perhaps evidence can. Unfortunately, the usual empirical approaches, such as regression analysis of observed data, may not be reliable in this case. The only actual cartel evidence we can ever have comes from those cartels that have been successfully prosecuted. Thus, if the leniency policy leads to many more cartels being formed and many of these avoid detection, relying on data actually observed will not be very informative. In recent years, however, economists have turned to an alternative source of economic data—namely, using individuals to conduct laboratory simulations of actual economic interactions. While such controlled experiments are contrived, when done carefully they can nonetheless offer important insight into real-world settings.

In this section, we report on an experiment designed by Hinloopen and Soetevent (2006)—HS hereafter—in which they assess the impact of leniency programs on cartel formation, effectiveness, and duration.[34] Test subjects play a repeated Bertrand game and are randomly assigned to one of four different treatments or settings. The BENCHMARK case is just the Bertrand pricing game without communication between players. COMMUNICATION is the same game, except that players are allowed to communicate before setting prices via computer screens. ANTITRUST introduces a 15 percent probability in each period that any cartel or communication that is formed is detected. Finally, LENIENCY gives cartel members the option of reporting the cartel in return for a reduced penalty. Throughout the experiment, all communications between players take place through computer screens.

The precise play of the game is that in each period, each of the three subjects acts like a firm and sets price by choosing an integer in the range 101–10. Those members of a group who set the lowest price p receive net earnings of $(p - 100)/L$, where L is the number of group members setting the lowest price. All other group members earn nothing. In each treatment or setting, the game is played for at least 20 periods, and this is known from the start. The subjects are informed that after period 19, each next period will be the last one with probability 20 percent so that finite period effects are weakened.

The one-shot equilibrium for this pricing game is for all players to set a price of 101. The indefinitely repeated equilibrium is for all players to set a price equal to 110, provided that players are sufficiently patient (HS provide a formal proof of these results). In each round of play, the subjects in the LENIENCY treatment have the most steps. There are seven steps as follows:[35]

Step 1: Decide whether or not to communicate with the other group members. If all three choose to communicate, move to step 2; otherwise, move to step 3.

[34]   A revised version of this working paper can be found at "Laboratory evidence on the effectiveness of corporate leniency programs," Jeroen Hinloopen and Adriaan R. Soetevent (2008), *RAND Journal of Economics*, 39: 607–616.
[35]   Detailed descriptions of subject instructions are provided in the Hinloopen and Soetevent (2006) paper.

Step 2: Communicate by suggesting minimum and maximum prices. Players have one minute to reach an agreement through repeated iteration on these prices.

Step 3: Each player in the group sets a market price. This need not be the price agreed upon in step 2, since agreements are unenforceable, giving players the option to defect on an agreement.

Step 4: Market price is revealed. Market price is equal to the minimum price submitted by the three group members in Step 3.

Step 5: If a cartel is formed in step 1, players are given the option of reporting the cartel. Reporting costs one point. The first player to report receives full amnesty; the second, a 50 percent reduction in the fine; and the third, no reduction. The point deduction for nonreporting group members (or the third member to report) is 10 percent of gross earnings for the relevant period.

Step 6: If no report is submitted in step 5, there is a 15 percent probability that the cartel is detected, in which case all players pay the full point deduction.

Step 7: Close of the game for this period, when players are notified of their earnings (points) for this period, whether a reporting decision was made, and how many players in the group reported.

In contrast to the LENIENCY group, those in the BENCHMARK treatment are restricted to only three steps: Steps 3, 4, and 7. Those in the COMMUNICATION treatment have five steps, omitting Steps 5 and 6, while those in the ANTITRUST treatment have six steps, omitting Step 5.

In all treatment groups, the subjects can, at any time, review the entire history of their rivals' play on a scrollable screen. At the end of the experiment, the profit points accumulated by a player are converted into euros at an exchange rate of one point for €0.25.

The experiment was conducted over the period June 13–17, 2005, at the University of Amsterdam, with subjects drawn from a large pool of undergraduates across all subject fields. There were approximately 40 subjects in each treatment. This allows running that scenario with different sets of players.

Table 10.12 summarizes the overall intention to form a cartel among players in each of the three settings in which formation is possible. (Recall that in the BENCHMARK group, no communication is allowed.) The first row shows the average fraction of players in that treatment group who wanted to form a cartel in any given period. The next two rows show the fraction of players in a treatment group who either (a) always wanted to form a cartel in every period, or (b) never wanted to form a cartel in any period. The final row shows the average number of cartels formed for each group.

On average, 78 percent of those who had the opportunity to collude on price without fear of any antitrust prosecution were interested in forming a cartel. This falls to

Table 10.12 Cartel formation

	COMMUNICATION	ANTITRUST	LENIENCY
Cartel intention	78.08	64.74	62.26
Always	30.77	20.51	23.81
Never	0.00	0.00	9.52
Cartel formation	47.31	27.31	12.86

65 percent when an antitrust authority with a 15 percent detection rate is introduced. Perhaps somewhat surprisingly, introducing a LENIENCY program does not noticeably reduce this willingness any further.

Since unanimity is an important element in a cartel's success, the actual number of cartels formed is much less than the average fraction of players interested in forming one. In this experiment not only does the presence of an active antitrust agency cut cartel formation by 20 percentage points, but the augmentation of that agency's policy to include a LENIENCY program reduces cartel formation by a further 15 percentage points. Thus, this initial evidence suggests that fears that LENIENCY works to encourage cartel formation may be overstated. Moreover, with LENIENCY there is a small group of subjects that is persistent in their unwillingness to participate in a cartel at all, which the authors interpret as the first indication that the LENIENCY program is working to break down trust among potential cartel members.

Of course, the fact that cartel formation declines with the emergence of a LENIENCY program does not necessarily give us a complete description of the effect of that program. It may be that even though there are fewer cartels, the ones that form are more aggressive in that they set a higher cartel price. Evidence on this point is provided in Tables 10.13 and 10.14. A quick inspection of the first of these indicates, however, that there is no significant difference across treatments in the average agreed-upon price. A similarly quick inspection of Table 10.14 indicates that the average market price actually established is somewhat lower with a LENIENCY program. There is in this experiment little evidence that the beneficial effect of a LENIENCY program in reducing cartel formation is offset by higher prices in those instances in which cartels are actually formed. If anything, the LENIENCY program seems to have a procompetitive effect on prices. In addition, the average defection size—the difference between the agreed-upon price and the market price—is greatest in the LENIENCY treatment. It would appear that in this treatment, defectors want to be more certain of capturing the entire market, a second indication that the LENIENCY program is working to undermine trust between cartel members.

We now return to the question about the role of LENIENCY programs in detecting collusive agreements. Table 10.15 presents the HS results regarding cartel breakdowns using, as a unit of analysis, both cartels themselves and also actual cartel members.

Table 10.13   Agreed-upon prices

	Mean	Median	Minimum	Maximum
COMMUNICATION	109.40	110	102	110
ANTITRUST	109.12	110	103	110
LENIENCY	109.60	110	105	110

Table 10.14   Average market prices

	BENCHMARK	COMMUNICATION	ANTITRUST	LENIENCY
All	103.24	103.31	103.04	101.38
Cartels	*	105.43	104.82	103.39
Non-Cartels	103.24	101.40	102.38	101.08

Table 10.15 Cartel breakdown

	Fraction of Cartels			Fraction of Cartel Members	
	Defection	Detection	Reporting	Defection	Reporting
COMMUNICATION	0.67	*	*	0.52	*
ANTITRUST	0.68	0.17	*	0.50	*
LENIENCY	0.94	0.03	0.78	0.72	0.40

The evidence indicates that a large fraction of cartels—roughly two-thirds—suffer at least a temporary breakdown. In some cases, 94 percent of cartels break down. The HS evidence also shows that when a LENIENCY program exists, a sizable percentage of cartel defection is accompanied by members reporting to the antitrust authorities in order to take advantage of the LENIENCY offer. This evidence thus suggests that LENIENCY programs actually do enhance the discovery of illegal cartels. In turn, the findings suggest that another reason for the high rate of defection when LENIENCY is introduced is that LENIENCY leads cartel members to defect before they can be reported, a third indication that the LENIENCY program undermines trust among cartel members.

HS conclude that the evidence from their experiments imply that LENIENCY programs lower prices for three reasons. These are:

1. Cartel formation is made more difficult.
2. Defection is more likely and more frequent.
3. Defection is more severe insofar as there is a greater difference between the agreed-upon price and the undercutting price. In short, LENIENCY programs undermine trust among potential cartel members.

HS also use statistical analysis to illuminate the dynamics of prices over the course of a cartel. As Sproul (1993) found in a number of real-world cartel cases, HS find that their laboratory-generated cartel prices tend to rise at the moment of detection. The reason for this in the HS generated data is equally clear. Because in the basic ANTITRUST treatment group, there is a constant 15 percent chance of detection in any period, the cartels most likely to be caught are those that are most successful and last the greatest number of periods. However, these are precisely the ones in which the price is likely to be highest. Thus, while the statistical data may show a correlation between cartel detection and high prices, any inference that cartels work to keep costs (and therefore prices) down is clearly wrong. That correlation is present in the HS simulations, even though it is clear from the way the experiment is set up that the only role of cartels in this setting is to raise prices.

Summary

At least since the time of Adam Smith, there has been the fear that firms in the same industry may try to collude and set a price close to the monopoly price rather than vigorously compete. The good news over the last 15 years or so is that a large number of such collusive cartels have been caught and successfully prosecuted in the courts, both in Europe and North America. The bad news is that this same evidence also reveals that cartels happen and that they often raise prices by 20 percent or more over what would have been the case otherwise.

It is the repetition of firm interaction that makes cartels potentially stable and sustainable. When rivalry occurs only once, each firm can cheat on the collusive agreement without fear of later punishment, especially since the agreement is not legally enforceable. If, however, the game is repeated over a number of periods, the scope for cooperation widens considerably. Now, a firm can threaten to "punish" any cheating on the collusive agreement in one period by being more aggressive in later periods.

Repetition by itself is not sufficient. In addition to the game being repeated, one of two conditions must apply. Suppose first that the cartel game is played a finite number of times. For the cartel to be sustainable over some number of these repetitions it is necessary that the stage game have a "good" and a "bad" Nash equilibrium. Absent this condition, Selten's Theorem makes clear that a finitely repeated game with a unique Nash equilibrium will simply result in that Nash equilibrium being the outcome in each period. By contrast, a non-unique Nash equilibrium introduces the possibility of credible punishment of deviation from the cartel agreement.

Suppose by contrast that the game has an indefinite end point. That is, in any given period, there is always a positive probability that the game will be played one more time. Now the cartel can be sustained by a trigger strategy provided only that the cartel members are "sufficiently patient". This is true even in cases where cartel members have limited information about rivals' prices. However, the trigger strategy in these cases will likely have to be asymmetric and punish more harshly those firms who most likely cheated. The frequency of real world cartels suggests that one or other of these conditions is a common feature of the corporate battlefield.

When the fact of continued cartel formation is coupled with the persistent finding that such cartels raise prices on the order of 20 percent or more above what they otherwise would be, the implication is that there is a clear need for an active antitrust authority charged with finding and prosecuting cartels. It should therefore come as no surprise that uncovering and prosecuting cartels is a major policy goal in both the United States and Europe. In turn, this requires a careful policy design with the right mixture of monitoring and penalties or fines. It also requires knowing the conditions most likely to foster cartel formation and a thoughtful analysis of business practices. Theory suggests that markets in which collusive agreements are likely to succeed are ones with relatively high concentration, substantial barriers to new entry, relatively homogeneous products, similar cost functions across firms, and relatively stable market conditions. Evidence confirms that these are indeed common features of those markets in which actual cartels have been uncovered.

In recent years, the authorities have implemented leniency programs that grant reduced or even no penalty to the first member of a cartel that confesses. The aim is to create a "race to confession," since being the second firm to confess—even if only a little after the first—achieves little. Such policies appear to have been successful in that they have played a role in many of the recent successful cartel prosecutions. However, the promise of ultimate immunity that leniency programs offer may lead firms to create more cartels than they would have done in the absence of such programs. Thus, the net impact of leniency programs on cartel formation is not clear from theory. However, recent experimental evidence suggests that the deterrence and detection effects dominate. If this is the case, then the authorities are indeed justified in their use of leniency programs as a tool against price-fixing conspiracies.

Problems

1. Suppose that two firms compete in quantities (Cournot) in a market in which demand is described by $P = 260 - 2Q$ and that each firm has a constant marginal cost of 20 while incurring no fixed costs. What is the probability adjusted discount factor that can sustain the collusive agreement in an indefinitely repeated setting?

2. Suppose again that market demand is given by $P = 260 - 2Q$ and that firms again have a constant marginal cost of 20, while incurring no fixed cost, but now assume that the firms are

Bertrand competitors. What probability adjusted discount factor is necessary now in order to maintain the collusive agreement in an indefinitely repeated setting?

3. Compare your answers in problems 1 and 2. Based on this comparison, which market setting do you think is more amenable to cartel formation?

4. Once again, assume Cournot competition in an industry in which market demand is described by: $P = 260 - 2Q$ and in which each firm has a marginal cost of 20. However, instead of two firms, let there now be four.
   a. If the market game is repeated indefinitely, what is the probability adjusted discount factor that can sustain the collusive agreement?
   b. Compare your answers to that for question 1. Based on this comparison, what do you infer about the ability of firms to sustain a collusive agreement as the number of firms in the industry expands?

5. Assume that the market demand for lysine has a price elasticity of 1.55. In the 1990s, the noncooperative structure of that market and the (assumed to constant) marginal cost per pound for each firm are shown below:

Firm	Market Share	Marginal Cost
Ajinomoto	32%	$0.70
Archer Daniels Midland	32%	$0.70
Kiyowa Hakko	14%	$0.80
Sewon/Miwon	14%	$0.80
Cheil Sugar	4%	$0.85
Cargill	4%	$0.85

   a. Use elasticity, market share, and cost data above to determine the weighted-average industry equilibrium price if the firms are competing in quantities.
   b. Under the lysine cartel, the world price of lysine rose to an average of $1.12 per pound. Total world production at this time was about 100 thousand metric tons per year. A metric ton $= 2,200$ pounds. Calculate the percentage price increase and the welfare loss resulting from the cartel.

6. When highway departments receive bids from construction firms, they regularly open the sealed bid tenders and announce the identity and the bid of the winning bidder. Do you think that this practice facilitates or hinders collusion among the construction firms?

7. Suppose that a cartel has just been created and it includes both large and small firms, each having different average and marginal cost curves. The cartel agreement is for each member to reduce its output by 20 percent from the current level. Suppose that the current level of industry output approximates the competitive output level. Will this 20 percent reduction rule maximize the cartel's profit? Why or why not?

8. Cartel firms often maintain excess capacity. Members of OPEC (especially Saudi Arabia), conspirators in the 1950s electric turbine conspiracy, and the firms in the international lysine conspiracy typically produced below the capability of their plants. One explanation of this is that the success of the cartel inevitably leads the members to reinvest their profits in new capacity. In this view, the cartel sows the seeds of its own destruction. Based on the analysis of this chapter, can you give an alternative explanation? What implications does your explanation have for the long-run viability of the cartel?

9. Assume two firms compete in prices in a market in which demand is given by $P = 150 - 2Q$. Each firm has a constant marginal cost of $c = \$30$. Show that if they collude, each firm earns

$1,800, while if one cheats on the agreement, the defector earns $3,600 and the other earns $0. Assume $\rho = 0.8$ and that a firm caught colluding pays a fine of $3,600.

a. Assume a program with complete amnesty ($L = 0$). If a is the probability that an investigation is launched and s is the probability that it is successful, determine the range of a and s values for which the equilibrium strategy is: (a) Defect; (b) Collude and Reveal; and (c) Collude and Not Reveal.

b. Repeat your analysis above assuming now a limited amnesty of $L = \$600$.

References

Athey, S., and K. Bagwell. 2001. "Optimal Collusion with Private Information." *Rand Journal of Economics*, 32 (Autumn): 428–465.

Baker, J. B., and D. L. Rubinfeld. 1999. "Empirical Methods in Antitrust Litigation: Review and Evidence." *American Law and Economics Review*, 1 (Fall): 386–435.

Benoit, J. P., and V. Krishna. 1985. "Finitely Repeated Games." *Econometrica*, 53 (July): 905–922.

Bernheim, B. D., and M. D. Whinston 1985. "Common Marketing Agency as a Device for Facilitating Collusion." *Rand Journal of Economics*, 16 (Summer): 269–281.

Connor, J. M. 2001. *Global Price Fixing: Our Customers Are the Enemy*. Boston: Kluwer Academic Publishers.

Connor, J. M., and Robert H. Lande. 2005 (20 April). "How High Do Cartels Raise Prices? Implications for Reform of the Antitrust Sentencing Guidelines." American Antitrust Institute Working Paper. Available at SSRN: http://ssrn.com/abstract=787907.

Davidson, C., and R. Deneckere. 1990. "Excess Capacity and Collusion." *International Economic Review*, 31 (August): 521–542.

Dixit, A. 1980. "The Role of Investment in Energy Deterrence." *Economic Journal*, 90 (January): 95–106.

Eichberger J. 1993. *Game Theory for Economics*. New York: Academic Press.

Eichenwald, K. 2000. *The Informant*. New York: Random House.

Froeb, L., R. Koyak, and G. Werden. 1993. "What Is the Effect of Bid Rigging On Prices?" *Economics Letters*, 42 (April): 419–423.

Green, E. J., and R. Porter. 1984. "Noncooperative Collusion Under Imperfect Price Information." *Econometrica*, 52 (January): 87–100.

Harsanyi, J. C. 1973. "Games with Randomly Distributed Payoffs: A New Rationale for Mixed Strategy Equilibrium Points." *International Journal of Game Theory*, 2 (December): 1–23.

Harrington, J. and A. Skrzypacz. 2007. "Collusion with Monitoring of Sales," *Rand Journal of Economics*, 38 (Summer) 2007: 314–331.

Harstad, R. M., and L. Phlips, 1990. "Perfect Equilibria of Speculative Futures Markets." In R. Selten, eds. *Game Equilibrium Analysis*, *Vol. II*. Berlin: Springer, 289–307.

Hay, G., and D. Kelley, 1974. "An Empirical Survey of Price-Fixing Conspiracies". *Journal of Law & Economics*, 17 (April): 13–38.

Hendricks, K., and R. H. Porter. 1988. "An Empirical Study of an Auction with Asymmetric Information." *American Economic Review*, 78 (December): 865–883.

Hinloopen, J. and A. R. Soetevent. 2006. "Trust and Recidivism: The Partial Success of Corporate Leniency Programs in the Laboratory." Tinbergen Institute Discussion Paper, 06-067/1.

Kwoka, J. 1997. "The Price Effect of Bidding Conspiracies: Evidence from Real Estate 'Knockouts'." *Antitrust Bulletin*, 42 (Summer): 503–516.

LaCasse, C. 1995. "Bid Rigging and the Threat of Government Prosecution". *Rand Journal of Economics*, 26 (Autumn): 398–417.

MacLeod, W. B. 1985. "A Theory of Conscious Parallelism." *European Economic Review*, 27 (February): 25–44.

Morse, B. A., and J. Hyde. 2000. "Estimation of Cartel Overcharges: The Case of Archer Daniels Midland and the Market for Lysine." Purdue University, Department of Agricultural Economics, Staff Paper 00-8.

Motta, Massimo, and M. Polo. 1999. "Leniency Programs and Cartel Prosecution" (May 1999). IGIER Working Paper No. 150. Available at SSRN: http://ssrn.com/abstract=165688.

_____. 2004. *Competition Policy: Theory and Practice*. Cambridge: Cambridge University Press.

Osborne, M. J., and C. Pitchik. 1987. "Cartels, Profits, and Excess Capacity." *International Economic Review*, 28 (June): 413–428.

Phlips, L. 1995a. *Competition Policy: A Game-Theoretic Perspective*. Cambridge, UK: Cambridge University Press.

_____. 1995b. "On the Detection of Collusion and Predation." EUI Working Papers in Economics, no. 95/35. Florence, Italy: European University Institute.

Porter, R. H. and J. D. Zona. 1993. "Detection of Bid Rigging in Procurement Auctions." *Journal of Political Economy*, 101 (June): 518–538.

_____. 1999. "Ohio School Milk Markets: An Analysis of Bidding." *Rand Journal of Economics*, 30 (Summer): 263–288.

Posner, R. 1970. "A Statistical Study of Cartel Enforcement." *Journal of Law and Economics*, 13 (October): 365–419.

Rotemberg, J. and G. Saloner. 1986. "A Supergame-Theoretic Model of Pricing Wars During Booms." *American Economic Review*, 76 (June): 390–407.

Salop, S. 1986. "Practices that (Credibly) Facilitate Oligopoly Coordination." *New Developments in the Analysis of Market Structure* J. Stiglitz and F. G. Mathewson, Cambridge: MIT Press, 265–290.

Schelling, T. 1960. *The Strategy of Conflict*. Cambridge, MA: Harvard University Press.

Scott Morton, F. 1997. "The Strategic Response by Pharmaceutical Firms to the Medicaid Most Favored Customer Rules". *Rand Journal of Economics*, 28 (Summer): 269–290.

Selten, R. 1973. A Simple Model of Imperfect Competition Where 4 Are Few and 6 Are Many. *International Journal of Game Theory*, 2 (December): 141–201. Reprinted in R. Sultan. 1988. *Models of Strategic Rationality*. Amsterdam: Kluwer Academic Publishers.

Spagnolo, G. 2004. "Divide et Impera: Optimal Deterrence Mechanisms Against Cartels and Organized Crime." CEPR Discussion Paper No. 4840.

Spence, A. M. 1979. "Entry, Investment, and Oligopolistic Pricing." *Bell Journal of Economics*, 8 (Spring, 1979): 1–19.

Sproul, M. 1993. "Antitrust and Prices." *Journal of Political Economy*, 101 (August): 741–754.

Stigler, G. 1964. "A Theory of Oligopoly." *Journal of Political Economy*, 72 (February): 44–61.

Part IV
Contractual Relationships between Firms

Part IV focuses on formal contractual agreements between firms. Chapters 11 and 12 start with the most complete of such contracts, namely, merger agreements. Chapter 11 examines the issues surrounding horizontal mergers. It begins with the well-known merger paradox that mergers in a symmetric, Cournot setting are not likely to be profitable (Salant, Switzer, and Reynolds 1983). We then consider possible efficiency and sequential merger arguments that may help to resolve this paradox. Since horizontal mergers are common despite the theoretical paradox that they may not be profitable, we also demonstrate the power of modern analysis by presenting the basic elements of empirical merger simulations.

Chapter 12 discusses vertical mergers and the gains from avoiding double marginalization. This chapter permits a return to models of predation and "price squeezing" of rivals. It also includes an empirical application based on the study of vertical integration in the ready-mix concrete market by Horteçsu and Syverson (2009).

Chapter 13 examines both price and nonprice vertical constraints. These include the familiar restrictions of resale price maintenance, exclusive dealing, and exclusive territories. We consider the potential pro- and anticompetitive effects of these restrictions. Here again, we present empirical evidence based on Sass's (2005) study of vertical restrictions in the U.S. beer industry.

Students completing Chapters 11, 12, and 13 will understand why contract theory has emerged as such a critical topic in modern economic analysis. They will also have deepened their ability to apply the modeling tools of imperfect competition, including the derivation of upstream demand and the analysis of settings with uncertain demand.

Contractual Relationships between Firms

11

Horizontal Mergers

The merger mania that transformed much of corporate America through the 1990s largely disappeared in the wake of the terrorist attack of September 11, 2001; the corporate scandals at Enron, Tyco, HealthSouth and WorldCom; and the bursting of the dot.com bubble. However, after quieting down for a few years, merger activity bounced back sharply in 2004, when over 10,000 deals were transacted in the United States for a total value of $823.2 billion. In 2005, there were more than 11,000 deals with a total value of $1.235 trillion. In 2006, the number of mergers rose still further to over 11,750 with a total value of nearly $1.5 trillion.[1] It is only with the financial meltdown that began in 2007 that we see a reduction in merger activity. In other words, while merger activity appears to exhibit cycles, as illustrated in Figure 11.1 (next page), the desire to grow and to reorganize corporate activity via mergers and acquisitions is ever present.

One possible motivation for merging is to exploit scope or scale economies, perhaps by eliminating wasteful duplication or by improving information flows within the merged organization. Similarly, a merger may lead to more efficient pricing and/or improved services to customers in cases in which a firm sells complementary products such as cameras and film. In such instances, mergers can benefit consumers as well as producers.

However, mergers can also be an attempt to create legal cartels. The new corporate entity that a merger creates now controls what were formerly separate and independent production units with a view to achieving the joint profit-maximizing outcome. By placing such separate units within the boundaries of one firm, a merger can legitimize precisely the kind of coordinated behavior that would have been illegal had the two firms remained separate. In this light, mergers can be viewed as an undesirable attempt to create and exploit monopoly power.

Mergers therefore pose a difficult challenge for antitrust policy. Policymakers need to be able to distinguish between anticompetitive mergers on the one hand, and those that are not injurious to competition on the other. This tension is openly acknowledged in the Overview to the U.S. Merger Guidelines. "While challenging competitively harmful

---

[1]   *Mergerstat Review*, January 2006 and 2007.

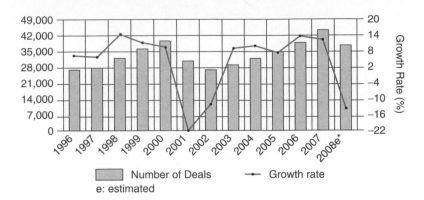

Figure 11.1 Fluctuations in the Level and Growth Rate of Merger Activity since 1996
Source: Thomson Financial, Institute of Mergers, Acquisition and Alliances (IMAA)

mergers, the Agency seeks to avoid unnecessary interference within the larger universe of mergers that are either competitively beneficial or neutral."[2]

In this chapter and the next, we examine what economic theory can tell us about the rationale for mergers. By way of introduction, it is useful to recognize that mergers are of different types depending on the relationship that existed between the merging firms prior to their combination. First, there are horizontal mergers. Such mergers combine two or more firms that, so far as their buyers are concerned, market substitute products. The 2009 merger of Delta and Northwest Airlines is one example of a horizontal merger.

Vertical mergers are a second type. These may involve firms at different stages in the vertical production chain. For example, the purchase of Capital Cities/ABC by the Disney Company involved a major producer of films and television programs acquiring a major distributor and network that airs such material. Likewise, the 2006 purchase of Murphy Farms, a major hog farming enterprise, by Smithfield Foods (the largest pork company in the world) is a vertical combination. Unlike horizontal mergers that involve firms producing substitute goods, vertical mergers involve firms that produce complementary goods. Thus, if ABC raises the price it charges for television advertising time, it reduces both the demand for such time *and* the related demand from advertisers for showing Disney films on television. In terms of economic impact, this is analogous to the situation that now exists between Hewlett-Packard and Compaq, which HP acquired in 2002. If Compaq raises the price of computers, it reduces demand for HP software, printers, and scanners. Accordingly, while such mergers are typically referred to as vertical in nature, we should recognize that they need not be limited to firms either upstream or downstream in a specific production chain.

Finally, there are conglomerate mergers. These involve the combination of firms without either a clear substitute or a clear complementary relationship. General Electric, a firm that produces aircraft engines, electric products, financial services and, until recently, television programming via NBC, is one of the world's most successful conglomerate firms. Recent examples of conglomerate mergers include the purchase of Duracell Batteries by Gillette and, in turn, the purchase of Gillette by Procter & Gamble; the purchase of Snapple (iced

---

[2] The DOJ/FTC Merger Guidelines can be read at http://www.ftc.gov/bc/docs/horizmer.htm Section 2 on the potential adverse effects of mergers is particularly relevant.

tea) and Gatorade (a sports drink) by Quaker Oats; and the merger of CUC International, a health and home shopping company with HFS, a major hotel firm.

In this chapter we focus on horizontal mergers. Since these reflect combinations of two or more firms in the same industry, they raise the most obvious antitrust concerns. Vertical and conglomerate mergers are discussed in the next chapter.

11.1 HORIZONTAL MERGERS AND THE MERGER PARADOX[3]

Horizontal mergers replace two or more former competitors with a single firm. The merger of two firms in a three-firm market changes the industry to a duopoly. The merger of two duopolists creates a monopolist. The potential for a horizontal merger to create monopoly power is clearly an issue in such cases. Our first order of business is therefore rather surprising. It is to discuss a phenomenon known as the *merger paradox*. The paradox is that it is, in fact, quite difficult to construct a simple economic model in which there are sizable gains for firms participating in a horizontal merger *that is not a merger to monopoly*.[4] We illustrate the paradox using the Cournot model of Chapter 7.

We begin with a general illustration of why a merger might be unprofitable for the merged firms. Assume that the market contains n identical Cournot competitors. Designate as "insiders" those firms that intend to merge and as "outsiders" those firms that intend to remain independent. Let $R_O(Q_I)$ in Figure 11.2 (next page) be the aggregate output that the outsiders choose to produce for any given aggregate output Q_O of the insiders. This function is obtained by first identifying the residual demand function for the outsiders—market demand minus the aggregate output Q of the insiders—then computing the Cournot-Nash equilibrium for each outsider given this residual demand, and finally summing these equilibrium outputs. Let $R_I^{NC}(Q_O)$ in Figure 11.2 be the aggregate output that the insiders will produce prior to the merger for any aggregate output Q_O of the outsiders. This function is identified in a manner similar to $R_O(Q_I)$. Identify the residual demand for the insiders—market demand minus Q_O—compute the Cournot output for each insider premerger and add these up. The resulting Cournot-Nash equilibrium is at point A in Figure 11.2, with aggregate output Q_I^{NC} by insiders and Q_O^{NC} by outsiders.

A merger of the insiders changes this equilibrium. The outsiders' best response function $R_O(Q_I)$ is, of course, unaffected by the merger since this function is identified no matter how the output Q_I is produced. By contrast, the best-response function for the insiders shifts downwards to $R_I^C(Q_O)$. The intuition for this shift is simply explained. We know from our discussion of the Cournot model that competition leads each firm to overproduce compared to the monopoly outcome because the firms do not internalize the losses that they impose on each other. For any given output Q_O of the outsiders, the merged firms can internalize these losses by coordinating their output choices. In doing so, they reduce their aggregate output—again, for any given output Q_O of the outsiders. The postmerger equilibrium must therefore be at a point such as B, where the aggregate output of the insiders has decreased while that of the insiders has increased.

Figure 11.2 makes clear the potentially adverse consequences that merging can have for the newly combined firms. As we have just shown, the merger leads to a rise in outsider output and a decline in insider production. Recall though that total insider profit

---

[3]   This section draws on the seminal analysis by Salant, Switzer, and Reynolds (1983).
[4]   A merger to monopoly is when all the firms in an industry combine into a single monopoly producer.

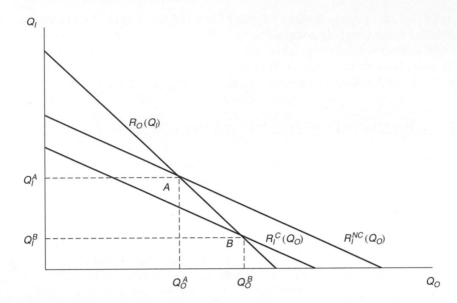

Figure 11.2 Impact of a merger on insider and outsider firms

The merger shifts the collective best response of the insider firms downward from the noncooperative $R_I^{NC}(Q_O)$ to the cooperative $R_I^C(Q_O)$, while leaving the collective best response of those outside the merger $R_O(Q_I)$ unchanged. As a result, the industry equilibrium moves from A to B. Outsider output expands from Q_O^A to Q_O^B. Insider output falls from Q_I^A to Q_I^B.

is $(P - c)Q_I$. From this it is clear that the reduction in production can lead to a fall in insider profit even if, as we will shortly show, the merger leads to a rise in $P - c$. As it turns out, this is a precisely the most likely outcome in a conventional Cournot model.

To make the analysis more explicit, assume that the market contains $N > 2$ firms, each of which produces a homogeneous product and acts as a Cournot competitor. For simplicity, assume that the firms have identical costs given by the total cost function

$$C(q_i) = cq_i \quad \text{for } i = 1, \dots, N \tag{11.1}$$

where q_i is output of Firm i. Market demand is linear and, in inverse form, is given by

$$P = A - BQ = A - B(q_i + Q_{-i}) \tag{11.2}$$

where Q is aggregate output produced by the N firms and Q_{-i} is the aggregate output of all firms except Firm i; that is, $Q_{-i} = Q - q_i$. The profit function for Firm i can then be written as

$$\pi_i(q_i, Q_{-i}) = q_i[A - B(q_i + Q_{-i}) - c] \tag{11.3}$$

In a Cournot game, firms choose their output levels simultaneously to maximize profit. Standard analysis (see Chapter 7) then tells us that the resulting output and profit to each firm in the noncooperative Cournot-Nash equilibrium is

$$q_I^{NC} = q_O^{NC} = \frac{A - c}{B(N + 1)} \quad \text{and} \quad \pi_I^{NC} = \pi_O^{NC} = \frac{(A - c)^2}{B(N + 1)^2} \tag{11.4}$$

Suppose now that $M \geq 2$ of these firms decide to merge. In order to exclude the case of merger to monopoly, we assume that $M < N$. Such a merger therefore leads to an industry in which there are now $N - M + 1$ firms competing in the industry. Since all firms still have identical costs, we can think of the merged firm as comprised of firms 1 through M.

The newly merged firm picks its postmerger output q_m to maximize profit, which is given by

$$\pi_m(q_m, Q_{-m}) = q_m \left[A - B(q_m + Q_{-m}) - c \right] \tag{11.5}$$

where $Q_{-m} = q_{m+1} + q_{m+2} + \cdots + q_N$ denotes the aggregate output of the $N - M$ firms that have not merged. Each of the outsider firms chooses its output to maximize profit given, as before, by

$$\pi_i(q_i, Q_{-i}) = q_i \left[A - B(q_i + Q_{-i}) - c \right] \tag{11.6}$$

In this case, the term Q_{-i} now denotes the sum of the outputs q_j of each of the $N - M$ outsider firms excluding outsider Firm i, plus the output of the merged firm q_m.

The only difference between equations (11.5) and (11.6) is that in the former we have a subscript m, while in the latter we have a subscript i. In other words, the fact that the merger leaves cost unchanged means that, after the merger, *the merged firm is just like any one of the other firms in the industry*. Each of these identical $N - M + 1$ firms then must have the same profit-maximizing production level in equilibrium and therefore earn the same profit. Hence, in the postmerger Cournot-Nash equilibrium, it must be the case that the output and profit of the merged firm, q_m^C and π_m^C, is the same as the output and profit of each outsider firm. Using the equations for a market with $N - M + 1$ firms, these are, respectively

$$q_I^C = q_O^C = \frac{A - c}{B(N - M + 2)} \quad \text{and} \quad \pi_I^C = \pi_O^C = \frac{(A - c)^2}{B(N - M + 2)^2} \tag{11.7}$$

Equations (11.4) and (11.7) allow us to compare the output and profit of the firms before and after the merger. It is clear that $q_O^C > q_O^{NC}$. Each outsider firm increases its output after the merger. For the insiders, aggregate premerger output is $M(A - c)/B(N + 1)$, while postmerger output is $(A - c)/B(N - M + 2)$. Thus, the merger reduces the merged firms' aggregate output provided that $M(N - M + 2) > N + 1$, which is always true since $M \in [2, N]$. Moreover, if we put the two foregoing results together, we see that aggregate output premerger, $N(A - c)/B(N + 1)$, is greater than aggregate output postmerger, $(N - M + 1)(A - c)/B(N - M + 2)$. As a result, the merger increases the consumer price. Since it has not increased cost, it follows immediately that the profit of each outsider is increased by the merger. Each sells more output and does so at a higher margin $P - c$ per unit.

What about the insiders? For the merger to be profitable, it must increase the insiders' aggregate profit, which from (11.4) and (11.7) requires

$$M\pi_I^{NC} < \pi_I^C \Rightarrow M\frac{(A - c)^2}{B(N + 1)^2} < \frac{(A - c)^2}{B(N - M + 2)^2} \Rightarrow (N + 1)^2 > M(N - M + 2)^2 \tag{11.8}$$

Before evaluating this condition, note that it does not include any of the demand parameters or the firms' marginal costs. That is, equation (11.8) tells us about the profitability of *any* M firm merger so long as demand is linear and the firms each have the same constant marginal costs.

As a little reflection will quickly reveal, however, condition (11.8) turns out to be very difficult to satisfy, even when more than two firms merge, as long as the merger does not result in a monopoly. To see this, suppose that we substitute $M = aN$ in equation (11.8), with $0 < a < 1$. That is, a is the fraction of firms in the industry that merge. We can then work out how large a has to be for the merger to be profitable. A little manipulation of condition (11.8) shows that for a merger to be profitable, we must have $a > a(N)$, where[5]

$$a(N) = \frac{3 + 2N - \sqrt{5 + 4N}}{2N} \tag{11.9}$$

Table 11.1 gives $a(N)$ and the associated minimum number of firms $\underline{M}$ that have to merge for the merger to be profitable for a range of values of N, the number of firms in the industry.

Together, equation (11.9) and Table 11.1 illustrate what has come to be termed the 80 percent rule. At least 80 percent of the firms in the market have to merge for a merger to be profitable in our simple Cournot world of linear demand and identical constant costs. Of course, the merger authorities would be very unlikely to allow a merger of this magnitude. Moreover, note that while the merger is unlikely to benefit the merging firms, each outsider firm unequivocally gains. This establishes a free-rider problem that makes mergers even less likely. Why go through all the trouble of organizing a merger of uncertain profit, rather than let other firms do that work and enjoy the certain profit increase of an outsider?

The merger paradox then is that many, if not most, horizontal mergers are unprofitable when viewed through the lens of our standard Cournot model, especially when compared with the profit of nonmerging firms. Moreover, this result is not dependent on the particular demand and cost specification that we have used. Farrell and Shapiro (1990) work with quite general demand and cost relationships and show that no merger that does not generate a substantial cost reduction is likely to be profitable in a Cournot setting.

The possibility that a merger generates sufficient cost savings to make it profitable is worth exploring. As the events of the 1990s and more recent years tell us, horizontal mergers appear to happen all the time. Our analysis above makes the critical assumption that when firms merge the newly combined firm is fundamentally just like any of the remaining firms that did not merge. Hence, each outsider firm, after the merger, has equal status to the merged firm, even though it now faces the combined strength of its previous

Table 11.1   Necessary condition for profitable merger

N	4	5	10	15	20
$a(N)$	80.2%	80%	81.5%	83.1%	84.5%
$\underline{M}$	4	4	9	13	17

---

[5]   You can check this equation by direct substitution of $a(N)$ in equation (11.8).

rivals. One cannot help but suspect that, for a merger of any substantial size, the newly merged firm is different in some material sense from its unmerged rivals. Lower costs may be the source of one such difference. Other sources might include changes in "the rules of the game" that govern strategic interaction in the market. In what follows we explore such possible modifications.

11.2   MERGERS AND COST SYNERGIES

In developing the merger paradox, we assumed that all firms in the market have identical costs and that there are no fixed costs. What happens if we relax these assumptions? It seems reasonable to suppose that if a merger creates sufficiently large cost savings, it should be profitable. In this section we develop an example to show that this can indeed be the case.[6]

Suppose that the market contains three Cournot firms. Consumer demand is given by

$$P = A - BQ \tag{11.10}$$

where Q is aggregate output—which, premerger, is $q_1 + q_2 + q_3$. Two of these firms are low-cost firms with a marginal cost of c, while the third firm is potentially high cost with marginal cost γc, where $\gamma \geq 1$ is a measure of the cost disadvantage of Firm 3. Total costs at each firm are

$$C_1(q_1) = f + cq_1; C_2(q_2) = f + cq_2; C_3(q_3) = f + \gamma cq_3 \tag{11.11}$$

where f represents fixed costs associated with overhead expenses such as marketing or maintaining corporate headquarters. We now consider the effect of a merger of Firms 2 and 3.

11.2.1   Fixed-Cost Savings

Consider first the case in which $\gamma = 1$ so that all firms have the same marginal cost of c. Suppose, however, that after the merger, the merged firm has fixed costs af with $1 \leq a \leq 2$. This will arise if the merger allows the merged firms to economize on overhead costs—for example, by combining the headquarters of the two firms, eliminating unnecessary operational overlap, combining R&D functions, and economizing on duplicated marketing efforts. These are, in fact, typical cost savings that most firms claim will result from a merger.

Because the merger leaves marginal costs unaffected, we know that in the premerger market the two insider firms have aggregate profit of $(A - c)^2/8B - 2f$. In the postmerger market with just two firms, the outsider, Firm 1, earns a profit of $(A - c)^2/9B - f$, while the merged firm earns $(A - c)^2/9B - af$. For this merger to be profitable, it must be the case that $(A - c)^2/9B - af > (A - c)^2/8B - 2f$, which requires that $a < 2 - (A - c)^2/72fB$. What this says is that a merger is more likely to be profitable when fixed costs are relatively high and the merger gives the merged firm the ability to make "substantial"

[6]   This is a special case of the much more sophisticated analysis by Farrell and Shapiro (1990) to which we refer above.

savings in these costs. Note, however, that even if the merger is profitable for the merging firms, consumers are worse off as a result of the higher equilibrium price. That same higher price also raises the profit of the outsider firm and the merged firm loses market share postmerger.

11.2.2   Variable Cost Savings

Now, consider the case in which the source of the cost savings is not a reduction in fixed costs, but is instead a reduction in variable costs, which we capture by assuming that $\gamma > 1$. In other words, Firm 3 is a high variable cost firm. Now a merger with Firm 3 can generate variable cost savings, because its high-cost operations will either be shut down or its plants will be redesigned to use the low-cost technology.

To make matters as clean as possible, we assume that there are no fixed costs ($f = 0$). The outputs and profits of the three firms prior to the merger are

$$q_1^{NC} = q_2^{NC} = \frac{A - 2c + \gamma c}{4B}; q_3^{NC} = \frac{A - 3\gamma c + 2c}{4B}$$

$$\pi_1^{NC} = \pi_2^{NC} = \frac{(A - 2c + \gamma c)^2}{16B}; \pi_3^{NC} = \frac{(A - 3\gamma c + 2c)^2}{16B} \tag{11.12}$$

The equilibrium premerger price is $P^{NC} = \frac{(A+2c+\gamma c)}{4}$, and the low-cost Firms 1 and 2 each produce more than their high-cost rival, Firm 3. Note that this equilibrium exists only if there is a limit on the cost disadvantage γ for Firm 3. Specifically, Firm 3's premerger output will be positive only if $\gamma < (A + 2c)/3c$; otherwise, it will not operate in this market in the first place.

Now, suppose that Firms 2 and 3 merge. Since $\gamma > 1$, it is always more expensive to produce a unit of output at Firm 3 than it is at Firm 2, so all production will be transferred to Firm 2's technology. The result is that the market now contains two identical firms, 1 and 2, each with marginal costs of c. Accordingly, in the postmerger industry, each firm produces $(A - c)/3B$ units, the product price is $(A + 2c)/3$, and each firm has profit of $(A - c)^2/9B$.

Is this a profitable merger? For the merger to increase aggregate profit of the merged firms, it must be the case that

$$\frac{(A - c)^2}{9B} > \left[\frac{(A - 2c + \gamma c)^2}{16B} + \frac{(A - 3\gamma c + 2c)^2}{16B} \right] \tag{11.13}$$

You can check that this simplifies to

$$\left(\frac{A + 2c}{3c} - \gamma \right) \left(\gamma - \frac{A + 14c}{15c} \right) > 0 \tag{11.14}$$

We have already noted that the first bracketed term in (11.14) has to be positive for Firm 3 to have been in the market in the first place. So the merger is profitable, provided that the second bracket is also positive, which requires that $\gamma > (A + 14c)/15c$. In other words, *a merger between a high-cost and a low-cost firm will be profitable provided that the cost disadvantage of the high-cost firm prior to the merger is "large enough."* However, as we have already demonstrated, whether the merger is profitable or not, the price rises, and consumers are made worse off.[7]

Together, our analysis of a merger that generates fixed-cost savings and one that generates variable-cost savings makes clear that mergers can be profitable when the cost savings are great enough. However, there is no guarantee that consumers gain from such a merger. Admittedly, the merger removes a relatively inefficient technology, but it also reduces competitive pressures between the remaining firms. Farrell and Shapiro (1990) demonstrate that in the Cournot setting used here, the cost savings necessary to generate a gain for consumers are much larger than those needed simply to make the merger profitable. In turn, this suggests that we should be skeptical of cost savings as a justification of the benefits to consumers of horizontal mergers.

Research by both Lichtenberg and Siegel (1992) and Maksimovic and Phillips (2001) finds that merger-related productivity gains (and, therefore, marginal cost savings), while real, are typically no more than 1 to 2 percent. Salinger (2005) expresses even more doubt that fixed-cost savings are substantial. Beyond all this, it is worth noting that even with cost savings, part of our initial paradox still remains, since large profit gains continue to accrue to the outsider firms that do not merge. Why should a firm incur the headaches of merging if it can enjoy many of the same benefits by free-riding on other mergers?[8]

11.3   MERGED FIRMS AS STACKELBERG LEADERS

If cost efficiencies are not a likely way to resolve the merger paradox, then perhaps a resolution can be found in some other change that gives the merged firm an advantage. One possibility is that merged firms become Stackelberg leaders in the postmerger market.[9] Recall from our discussion in Chapter 8 that the source of a Stackelberg leader firm's advantage is its ability to commit to an output before output decisions are taken by the follower firms. This permits a leader to choose an output that takes into account the reactions of the followers.

Assume that when two firms merge, they acquire a leadership role. Certainly, such a role seems plausible. After all, the new firm has a combined capacity twice that of any of its nonmerged rivals, and so might well be able to act as a Stackelberg leader. Will this be enough to make a merger profitable? If so, what will be the response of other firms? Will they also have an incentive to merge? If they do, will their merging undo the profitability of the first merger and thereby—if firms are foresighted—discourage them from merging in the first place?

Suppose that demand is of the usual linear form: $P = A - BQ$. There are $N + 1$ firms in the industry, and each of the $N + 1$ firms has a constant marginal cost of c. Standard

[7] You can easily check that the price rises as a result of the merger if $\gamma < (A + 2c)/3c$, which we know must be the case.

[8] Perry and Porter (1985) assume that each firm's cost schedule declines with the total amount of capital it owns. Hence, by merging and gaining more capital, a firm lowers its costs. The scarcity of capital makes it difficult for other firms to do this and, because of rising costs, to free-ride as much on the merger of rivals.

[9] This analysis draws on A.F. Daughety (1990), who first suggested this role for the merged firms.

Cournot analysis tells us that the premerger equilibrium is described by the following equations:

$$q_i = \frac{(A-c)}{B(N+2)}; \quad Q = \frac{(N+1)(A-c)}{B(N+2)}; \quad P = \frac{A+(N+1)c}{N+2}; \quad \pi_i = \frac{(A-c)^2}{B(N+2)^2}$$

$$(11.15)$$

Suppose now that two of these firms merge and, as a result, become a Stackelberg leader. There will then be $F = N - 1$ follower firms and one leader firm so that we have N firms in total. The Stackelberg leader is able to choose its output first in a two-stage game. In stage 1, the leader chooses its output Q^L. In the second stage, the follower firms independently choose their outputs in response to that chosen by the leader.

To find the equilibrium, we work through the game backward. Consider the second stage of the game in which the follower firms make their output decisions in response to the output choice Q^L of the leader or merged firm. Denote by Q_{F-f} the aggregate output of the follower firms *other than f*, and denote the output of follower firm f by q_f. Then aggregate output of *all* firms is $Q = Q^L + Q_{F-f} + q_f$ and profit of follower firm f is

$$\pi_f = \left(A - B\left(Q^L + Q_{F-f} + q_f\right) - c\right)q_f \tag{11.16}$$

Taking the derivative with respect to q_f and solving for q_f gives us firm f's best-response function:

$$q_f = \frac{A-c}{2B} - \frac{Q^L}{2} - \frac{Q_{F-f}}{2} \tag{11.17}$$

Since all the followers are identical, symmetry demands that, in equilibrium. the output of each of the follower firms must be identical. The group of followers excluding firm f has $F - 1 = N - 2$ firms, so $Q_{F-f} = (N-2)q_f$. Substituting in (11.17) and solving for q_f gives us

$$q_f = \frac{A-c}{BN} - \frac{Q^L}{N} \tag{11.18}$$

Aggregate output of the followers as a function of the output of the leader firm is

$$Q^F = (N-1)q_f = \frac{(N-1)(A-c)}{BN} - \frac{(N-1)Q^L}{N} \tag{11.19}$$

Now, consider the Stackelberg leader. Its profit is $\pi^L = (A - B(Q^L + Q^F) - c)Q^L$. Substituting from (11.19) and simplifying gives

$$\pi^L = \frac{Q^L(A - BQ^L - c)}{N} \tag{11.20}$$

Maximizing with respect to Q^L gives

$$Q^L = \frac{A-c}{2B} \tag{11.21}$$

You should recognize by now that the output level in equation (11.21) is just the output that would be chosen by a uniform-pricing monopolist. This is, of course, a standard result for a single-leader model with linear demand and constant costs. In turn, it implies the following industry equilibrium values:

$$q_f = \frac{A - c}{2BN}; Q^F = \frac{(N - 1)(A - c)}{2BN}; Q = Q^L + Q^F$$

$$= \frac{(2N - 1)(A - c)}{2BN}; P = \frac{A + (2N - 1)c}{2N} \qquad (11.22)$$

Profits for the leader (merged) firm and for each follower firm are respectively

$$\pi^L = \frac{(A - c)^2}{4BN}; \pi_f = \frac{(A - c)^2}{4BN^2} \qquad (11.23)$$

Comparison of (11.23) with (11.15) indicates that for any industry initially comprised of three or more firms and characterized by symmetric Cournot competition, a two-firm merger that creates a Stackelberg leader is profitable. This seems to resolve the merger paradox. Equations (11.23) and (11.15) also show that the unmerged firms who have become followers are definitely worse off as a result of the merger. The leadership power of the merged firms prevents the outsider firms from free-riding on the merger. As a result, we might expect some response from these firms.

Now, compare the market price and output in (11.15) with (11.22). While the merger has raised the profit of the merging parties, it also has lowered price. Hence, the merger is good for consumers. We may have replaced one paradox with another. We now have a model in which a merger is profitable, but the model would also appear to remove a principal reason why the antitrust authorities should object to such a merger. This presumes, however, that there will be only one two-firm merger.

Consider the response of the outsider firms to the merger. Since leadership confers additional profit, they, too, have an incentive to merge and try to become a leader. This raises the question of what happens if there is a second or third two-firm merger. Daughety's (1990) model answers this question by assuming that there can be more than one leader firm and merging is the ticket to entry into the club of such leaders. That is, imagine a market that may be divided into two groups of firms: followers and leaders. The first of these groups compete as Cournot rivals over the demand remaining after the leaders make their output decisions. The leaders anticipate this reaction. They compete against each other as Cournot rivals, but with the knowledge that they act first and the followers take their production decisions as given.

To analyze this two-stage competition, we extend the model developed above. Instead of assuming N firms with one leader and $N - 1$ followers, let us assume that there are N firms with L leaders and $N - L = F$ followers. Since followers simply take their cue from the total leader output Q^L, regardless of whether it is produced by one firm or many, equation (11.17) still describes the best response of the typical follower firm. The only difference is that, since there are $N - L$ such firms, $Q_{F-f} = (N - L - 1)q_f$. Substituting into (11.17) and solving for q_f gives us

$$q_f = \frac{(A - c)}{B(N - L + 1)} - \frac{Q^L}{(N - L + 1)}; Q^F = \frac{(N - L)(A - c)}{B(N - L + 1)} - \frac{(N - L)Q^L}{(N - L + 1)}$$

$$(11.24)$$

Now consider the leader firms. Denote the output of any one leader firm as q_l and that of all the leaders *other than Firm l*, as Q_{L-l}. Profit of a leader Firm l is then

$$\pi^L = \left[A - B\left(Q^F + Q_{L-l} + q_l\right) - c\right] q_l \tag{11.25}$$

Substituting for Q^F from (24), noting that $Q^L = Q_{L-l} + q_l$, and simplifying gives us

$$\pi^L = \frac{(A - c - B(Q_{L-l} + q_l))}{(N - L + 1)} q_l \tag{11.26}$$

Differentiating with respect to q_l and solving gives

$$q_l = \frac{A - c}{2B} - \frac{Q_{L-l}}{2} \tag{11.27}$$

We can take advantage of the fact that, since all of the leader firms have the same costs, they will each produce the same level of output in equilibrium. Because there are $L - 1$ leaders other than Firm l, this gives the symmetry condition $Q_{L-l} = (L - 1)q_l$—which, when substituted into equation (11.27), allows us to solve for the output chosen in stage 1 by each merged firm in the leader group and for the aggregate output of the leaders:

$$q_l = \frac{A - c}{B(L + 1)}; Q^L = \frac{L(A - c)}{B(L + 1)} \tag{11.28}$$

Contrast this with the single-leader case of equation (11.21). Competition between the leaders increases the aggregate output that they produce. This in turn reduces the output of the followers. Substituting from (11.28) into (11.24), we find the individual and aggregate outputs of the follower firms:

$$q_f = \frac{A - c}{B(L + 1)(N - L + 1)}; Q^F = \frac{(N - L)(A - c)}{B(L + 1)(N - L + 1)} \tag{11.29}$$

Aggregate output of leaders and followers and the equilibrium price are

$$Q^T = Q^L + Q^F = \frac{(N + NL - L^2)(A - c)}{B(L + 1)(N - L + 1)}; P = \frac{A - c(N + NL - L^2)}{(L + 1)(N - L + 1)} \tag{11.30}$$

Finally, the price and output equations imply that, in an industry comprised of N firms in total (L of which are leaders), the price-cost margin $(P - c)$ and the profits for the typical leader firm $(P - c)q_l$ and typical follower firm $(P - c)q_f$ are

$$P - c = \frac{A - c}{(L + 1)(N - L + 1)}$$

$$\pi_l(N, L) = \frac{(A - c)^2}{(L + 1)^2(N - L + 1)}; \pi_f(N, L) = \frac{(A - c)^2}{(L + 1)^2(N - L + 1)^2} \tag{11.31}$$

The profits indicated by equations (11.31) show that the leader firms are more profitable than the followers. However, this is not the real issue facing two firms that are contemplating merger. The question is whether *one more merger* is profitable. We cannot check this by differentiation of the profit equations in (11.31). Rather, we have to recognize that if there is another merger, there will then be one more leader, two fewer followers, and one less firm in total. This is why we have written the profit expressions as functions of N and L. The point is that an additional merger sets up two countervailing forces. On the one hand there are fewer firms in total, which ought to increase profits; but there are also more leaders, which ought to decrease the profits of the leaders. Which force is greater?

Suppose there is an additional merger of two followers, so that the newly merged firm and all other leaders earn profit given by (11.31), with N replaced by $N - 1$ and L replaced by $L + 1$ to give us $\pi^L(N - 1, L + 1)$. For there to be an incentive to merge, this must exceed the combined profit earned by the two follower firms prior to the merger, which is $2\pi^F(N, L)$. The merger will be profitable if

$$
\begin{aligned}
\pi^L(N - 1, L + 1) &= \frac{(A - c)^2}{B(L + 2)^2(N - L - 1)} > 2\pi^L(N, L) \\
&= \frac{2(A - c)^2}{B(L + 1)^2(N - L + 1)^2}
\end{aligned}
$$

which simplifies to the condition

$$
(L + 1)^2(N - L + 1)^2 - 2(L + 2)^2(N - L - 1) > 0 \tag{11.32}
$$

Note that this condition does not include the demand parameters A and B or the marginal cost c. In other words, the profitability (or lack thereof) of this type of merger depends only on the number of leaders and followers, not on the precise demand and cost conditions.

We can show that the condition in (11.32) is always met. To see why, note the following: define $x = L + 1$ and $y = N - L - 1$. Then we need to show that

$$
x^2(y + 2)^2 \geq 2(x + 1)^2 y.
$$

The derivative $d(y + 4 + 4/y)/dy = 1 - 4/y^2$ is negative for $0 < y < 2$ and positive for $y > 2$, so for $y > 0$ we have

$$
y + 4 + 4/y \geq 2 + 4 + 4/2 = 8
$$

with equality only for $y = 2$. For $x \geq 1$, this inequality can be rewritten

$$
(y + 2)^2 \geq 8 \geq 2(1 + 1/x)^2 y = 2((x + 1)/x)^2 y
$$

giving $x^2(y + 2)^2 \geq 2(x + 1)^2 y$ as required.[10]

Starting from any configuration of leaders and followers, *an additional two follower firms always wish to merge*. This is encouraging and offers one way to resolve the merger paradox. A merger raises the profit of the two merging firms by allowing them to take a position as one of perhaps several industry leaders. Moreover, the fact that such a merger is always profitable also helps us to understand better the domino effect so often observed within an industry. Once one firm merges and becomes a leader, the remaining firms will wish to do the same, rather than watch their output and profits be squeezed.

[10] We are grateful to our colleague Professor Boris Hasselblatt of the Tufts University Mathematics Department for this proof.

This raises the question of whether such mergers are in the public interest. Is there some point at which further mergers are harmful to consumers? The answer to this question can be most easily derived from the price-cost margin $P - c$ of equation (11.31). Any rise or fall in P will be reflected in a rise or fall of $P - c$.

With L leaders and $N - L$ followers, the price-cost margin is $\frac{A-c}{(L+1)(N-L+1)}$, while with $L + 1$ leaders and $N - 1$ firms in total, the price-cost margin is $\frac{A-c}{(L+2)(N-L-1)}$. For such a merger to benefit consumers, it must be the case that

$$\frac{A - c}{(L + 2)(N - L - 1)} < \frac{A - c}{(L + 1)(N - L + 1)} \tag{11.33}$$

$$\Rightarrow (L + 1)(N - L + 1) < (L + 2)(N - L - 1) \Rightarrow N - 3(L + 1) > 0$$

An additional two-firm merger benefits consumers only if $N > 3(L + 1)$ or, equivalently, $L < N/3 - 1$. In other words, *a two-firm merger that increases the number of leaders benefits consumers only if the current group of leaders contains fewer than a third of the total number of firms in the industry*. We know from equation (11.32) that a two-firm merger that creates a leader will always be profitable. However, such a merger will be harmful to consumers once the leader group includes one-third or more of the industry's firms. In other words, some mergers are bad—at least for consumers. Accordingly, we now have a model that both resolves the merger paradox and explains why the antitrust authorities are correct to worry about anticompetitive mergers.

Daughety's (1990) model solves the merger paradox and gives rise to a merger wave by assuming an asymmetry between newly merged firms and their remaining unmerged rivals. The former gain membership in the club of industry leaders. However, this is a rather strong assumption. While some mergers may create corporate giants with an ability to commit to large production levels, it is far from obvious that every two-firm merger should result in this leadership role, regardless of which two firms merge and irrespective of the number of leaders already present. In principle, Daughety's (1990) model implies that in an industry of 10 firms there could be, say, 8 leaders. It is difficult to imagine a configuration with so many leaders and so few followers. Moreover, what happens if two leaders merge? Does this create a superleader?

It is also worth noting that while production is sequential in Daughety's model, merging is not. Leader firms choose production first. Yet, it is not accurate to describe the decision to merge in a sequential way. The model simply says that for any market configuration, if a two-firm merger creates an industry leader, all follower firm pairs will wish to merge as well. One pair does not merge only after it sees another pair merge. Instead, at any single point in time, merging is a dominant strategy and, absent any antitrust intervention, all follower firms will pursue it. Again, this is not because of any new cost savings or product development. It is simply because merging confers leadership status. Daughety's model, therefore, does not give rise to the sporadic merger waves that we often see as much as it suggests an ever-present tendency for an industry to become more concentrated.

11.4   SEQUENTIAL MERGERS

To capture the idea that merger decisions may be explicitly sequential, that is, that the decision of one firm pair to merge is a catalyst for another pair to do the same, a number of papers—including Nilssen and Sørgaard (1998), Fauli-Oller (2000), and Salvo (2006)—have recently presented models in which asymmetry in cost or product qualities give rise to merger opportunities that are only profitable if other mergers also occur. It is difficult for this to happen in a simultaneous game, because each potential merger pair cannot be sure if others will also merge. However, in a sequential game, some firms get to make their merger decision knowing for certain that others have already merged. This greatly enhances the likelihood of a successful merger.

We illustrate the sequential merger model with a simplification of the Fauli-Oller (2000) model. Consider a four-firm industry characterized by Cournot competition. Initially, all four firms are high-cost firms with constant unit cost $c^h = c$. Suppose that Firms 1 and 2 have a technical breakthrough that allows them to become low-cost firms with low constant unit cost $c^l = 0$. Industry demand is described by $P = A - Q$.

Now, consider the following sequential scenario. In period 1, low-cost Firm 1 decides whether to merge with one of the high-cost firms (3 or 4). Without loss of generality, suppose that Firm 1 chooses whether or not to merge with Firm 3. In period 2, low-cost Firm 2, having observed Firm 1's decision, decides whether or not to merge with the remaining high-cost Firm 4. The game ends after period 2. To determine the subgame-perfect equilibrium, we need the payoffs detailed in Table 11.2. Clearly, for these to make sense, we must have the *cost assumption*: $A > 3c$.

First, note that a merger in period 1 between Firms 1 and 3 or 2 and 4 *not* followed by a merger in period 2 will be profitable only if $\frac{(A+c)^2}{16} > \frac{(A+2c)^2+(A-3c)^2}{25}$. It is straightforward (but tedious) to show that this requires that $7A/61 < c < A/3$. That is, c must be less than the value necessary for a high-cost firm to be viable, but not so low as to make the disadvantage of being a high-cost firm trivial. We now need to show that assuming mergers to be sequential expands the range of c for which mergers are profitable.

The extensive form of the game is illustrated in Figure 11.3 (next page). In formulating the game, we assume that a merger offer will not be made unless the postmerger profit of the merged entity is greater than the aggregate profit of the two firms premerger. If this were not the case, no merger offer could be made that is satisfactory to both firms. As usual, we solve this game backward.

Suppose first that Firm 1 has chosen not to merge. Firm 2 will choose to merge so long as $(A + c)^2/16 > [(A + 2c)^2 + (A - 3c)^2]/25$, which requires $7A/61 < c < A/3$. (This is just the condition that we identified above.) Now, suppose that Firm 1 has chosen to merge. Firm 2 will choose to merge so long as $A^2/9 > [(A + c)^2 + (A - 3c)^2]/16$. Again, it is tedious but straightforward to show that this requires, $A/15 < c < A/3$. Note also that $A^2/9 > [(A + c)^2 + (A - 3c)^2]/25$ for $0 < c < A/3$. Two mergers are better than none. We can now identify the solution to the game.

(a) Suppose that $c \in (7A/61, A/3)$. If Firm 1 chooses to merge with Firm 3, then Firm 2 will merge with Firm 4, and the merged Firm 1–3 earns $A^2/9$. If, by contrast,

Table 11.2 Pay-offs for the sequential merger game

Number of Mergers	Profit of Low-Cost Firm	Profit of High-Cost Firm
No Mergers	$\dfrac{(A + 2c)^2}{25}$	$\dfrac{(A - 3c)^2}{25}$
One Merger	$\dfrac{(A + c)^2}{16}$	$\dfrac{(A - 3c)^2}{16}$
Two Mergers	$\dfrac{A^2}{9}$	NA

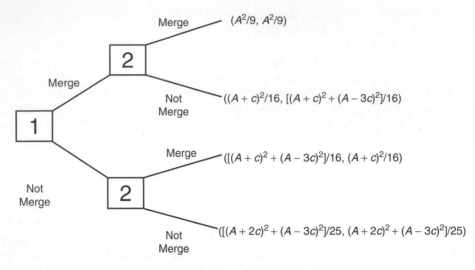

Figure 11.3   Sequential Cournot mergers

Firm 1 chooses not to merge, Firm 2 will choose to merge, and Firms 1 and 3 have combined profits $[(A + c)^2 + (A - 3c)^2]/16$. Firm 1 will choose to make a merger offer.

(b) Suppose that $c \in (A/15, 7A/61)$. If Firm 1 chooses to merge with Firm 3, Firm 2 will merge with Firm 4, and the merged Firm 1–3 earns $A^2/9$. If, by contrast, Firm 1 chooses not to merge, Firm 2 will also choose not to merge, and Firms 1 and 3 have combined profits $[(A + 2c)^2 + (A - 3c)^2]/25$. Firm 1 will choose to make a merger offer.

(c) Suppose that $c \in (0, A/15)$. If Firm 1 chooses to merge with Firm 3, Firm 2 will not merge with Firm 4, and the merged Firm 1–3 earns $(A + c)^2/16$. If Firm 1 chooses not to merge, Firm 2 also chooses not to merge, and Firms 1 and 3 have combined profits $[(A + 2c)^2 + (A - 3c)^2]/25$. Firm 1 chooses not to make a merger offer.

To summarize, if $c < A/15$, there will be no mergers; while if $c > A/15$, Firms 1 and 3 will merge in period 1 and Firms 2 and 4 will merge in period 2. Thus, allowing for sequential mergers does, indeed, expand the range of marginal costs c for which mergers are profitable. Such a merger wave is, however, not good for consumers. The equilibrium price premerger is $(A + 2c)/5$, and after the merger wave it is $A/3$. The market price rises so long as $A > 3c$, which is true from our cost assumption.

The foregoing story is not limited to just two mergers or to models of Cournot competition. Once cost asymmetries or product quality differences are introduced, we can construct sequential merger models that lead to merger waves for a large number of firms in a variety of settings (e.g., Nilssen and Sørgaard (1998) and Salvo (2006)), and these mergers are also anticompetitive. This approach offers another resolution to the merger paradox because it demonstrates not only why mergers may happen, but also why they often happen in sequential waves. As with Daughety's (1990) model, these models also justify concern over the impact that mergers may have on consumer prices.

11.5   HORIZONTAL MERGERS AND PRODUCT DIFFERENTIATION

Our analysis of mergers has so far been set in the Cournot framework of identical products and quantity competition. However, many firms expend considerable effort differentiating their products, and this differentiation gives them some latitude in setting their prices. Accordingly, we need to consider the incentives for (and the impact of) mergers in industries in which firms produce and market differentiated products.

It is particularly important to explore the merger phenomenon in differentiated product markets for at least two reasons. First, firms are often price setters in differentiated product markets, and the nature of competition is different under price competition than with quantity competition. In quantity competition firms' best-response functions are downward sloping (i.e., quantities are strategic substitutes). Thus, when merging occurs, the nonmerged firms want to *increase* their outputs in response to the lower output produced by the merger. This response undermines the effectiveness of the merger. By contrast, under price competition, best-response functions are upward sloping, as prices are strategic complements. A merger leading to an increase in the merged firms' prices will encourage the nonmerged firms also to increase their prices, potentially strengthening the effectiveness of the merger.

Second, we saw that one reason for the merger paradox under Cournot competition is that the merged firm looks no different from a nonmerged firm. If m firms merge, effectively $m-1$ of them disappear. This is not the case with differentiated products. Merger allows coordination of the product prices *and also* allows the merged firm to keep all m products on the market.

We develop this intuition more explicitly using two different approaches to product differentiation. The first approach is to extend our standard linear demand representation of consumer preferences to incorporate product differentiation. The second is to adopt the spatial model of horizontal differentiation first introduced in Chapter 3 and revisited in Chapter 8.[11]

11.5.1   Bertrand Competition with Linear Demand

Suppose that there are N firms in the market, each producing a single differentiated product, and that demand for product $i = 1, \ldots, n$ is given by[12]

$$q_i(p_1, \ldots, p_N) = V - p_i - \gamma \left(p_i - \frac{1}{N} \sum_{j=1}^{N} p_j \right) \tag{11.34}$$

In this specification, γ is an inverse measure of the degree of product differentiation. When $\gamma = 0$, the products are totally differentiated; and as γ approaches infinity, the products become perfect substitutes. Effectively, equation (11.34) states that the demand

---

[11]   We earlier introduced the linear version of the spatial model formulated by Hotelling (1929). In this chapter, we use an alternative circular space version due primarily to Salop (1979). See Greenhut, et al. (1991) for an application of this model to analysis of transport services deregulation.

[12]   This section draws on Deneckere and Davidson (1985). The demand specification was suggested by Shubik (1980).

for product i is decreasing in its own price and in the extent to which its price is greater than the average price on the market.

To keep the analysis (reasonably) simple, we assume that each firm has constant marginal costs c normalized to 0.[13] As a result, the profit of Firm i is

$$\pi_i = p_i \left(V - p_i - \gamma \left(p_i - \frac{p_i}{N} - \frac{1}{N} \sum_{\substack{j=1 \\ j \neq i}}^{N} p_j \right) \right) \tag{11.35}$$

This gives the first-order condition

$$\frac{\partial \pi_i}{\partial p_i} = V - 2p_i - 2\gamma p_i + \frac{2\gamma}{N} p_i + \frac{\gamma}{N} \sum_{\substack{j=1 \\ j \neq i}}^{N} p_j = 0 \tag{11.36}$$

We can take advantage of our assumption that the firms are symmetric, as a result of which in equilibrium $p_i = p_j = p_0$. Substituting into (11.36) and solving gives the Bertrand-Nash premerger equilibrium prices

$$p_0 = \frac{NV}{2N + \gamma(N - 1)} \tag{11.37}$$

It is straightforward to check that, as we would expect, p_0 is decreasing in N and γ.

Now, suppose that M of these firms merge. Without loss of generality, we can assume that these are firms $1, \ldots, M$. There is no reason for the merged firm to remove any of the M products that it offers. On the other hand, merger does allow the merged firm to coordinate the prices of these products. Indeed, the objective of the merged firm is to set prices $p_1, \ldots, p_M$ to maximize aggregate profit $\sum_{m=1}^{M} \pi_m$. As a result, the first-order condition for product m of the merged firm is

$$\frac{\partial \sum_{k=1}^{M} \pi_k}{\partial p_m} = \frac{\partial \pi_m}{\partial p_m} + \sum_{\substack{k=1 \\ k \neq m}}^{M} \frac{\partial \pi_k}{\partial p_m} \tag{11.38}$$

You can check from equation (11.35) that $\partial \pi_k / \partial p_m = \gamma p_k / N$. The first-order condition for a nonmerged firm, on the other hand, is still give by equation (11.36).

Once again we appeal to a symmetry assumption. In equilibrium each merged product will sell at the same price p_m and each non-merged firm will set price p_{nm}. Hence, for a non-merged Firm i, the sum of rival prices that determines the base against which its own price will be compared is:

$$\sum_{\substack{j=1 \\ j \neq i}}^{N} p_j = Mp_m + (N - M - 1)p_{nm} \tag{11.39}$$

---

[13]   It is simple but tedious to show that prices are always a function of $V-c$, so this assumption loses us no generality.

Similarly, for a merged firm m, the relevant sum of rival prices is:

$$\sum_{\substack{j=1 \\ j\neq m}}^{N} p_j = (M-1)p_m + (N-M)p_{nm} \tag{11.40}$$

Note also that

$$\sum_{\substack{k=1 \\ k\neq m}}^{M} \frac{\partial \pi_k}{\partial p_m} = \frac{(M-1)\gamma p_m}{N} \tag{11.41}$$

Substituting equation (11.39) into (11.36), noting that $p_i = p_{nm}$, and simplifying gives the first-order condition for a nonmerged firm:

$$\frac{\partial \pi_i}{\partial p_{nm}} = V - (2+\gamma)p_{nm} + \frac{\gamma}{N}(Mp_m - (M-1)p_{nm}) = 0 \tag{11.42}$$

Note that the implied best response function for p_{nm} is upward sloping in the merged price p_m. Again, prices are strategic complements.

Substituting equations (11.36), (11.40), and (11.41), with $p_i = p_m$, into (11.38) and simplifying gives the first-order condition for a merged firm:

$$\frac{\partial \sum_{k=1}^{M} \pi_k}{\partial p_m} = V - 2(1+\gamma)p_m + \frac{\gamma}{N}((N-M)p_{nm} + 2Mp_m) \tag{11.43}$$

Again, the implied best-response function is upward sloping.

Equations (11.42) and (11.43) are linear in p_m and p_{nm} and so can be solved for the equilibrium prices. The results (see also Deneckere and Davidson, 1985, p. 477) are:

$$p_m = V - \frac{2N + \gamma(2N-1)}{4N + 2\gamma(3N-M-1) + \gamma^2\left(\dfrac{N-M}{N}\right)(2N-M+2)}$$

$$p_{nm} = V - \frac{2N + \gamma(2N-M)}{4N + 2\gamma(3N-M-1) + \gamma^2\left(\dfrac{N-M}{N}\right)(2N-M+2)} \tag{11.44}$$

Comparison of the numerators of these two equations tells us that the merged firm sets higher product prices than the nonmerged firms. This reflects the ability of the merged firm to at least partly internalize the impact that a change in any one of its product prices has on the profits of the other products that the merged firm controls.

Comparison of equations (11.44) and (11.37) confirms that the merger increases the prices set by both nonmerged and merged firms. Since prices are strategic complements, a rise in the prices set by the merged firm induces its rivals to raise their prices as well. What about the merger's effect on the profitability of the merged and nonmerged firms? As Deneckere and Davidson (1985) show, in a market containing N firms any merger of $M \geq 2$ firms is profitable for the merged firms and even more profitable for the nonmerged firms.

To see why, note that the merger results in all nonmerged firms increasing their prices from p_0 to p_{nm}. This raises demand for the merged firm's products since, from (11.34), all products are substitutes. The prices p_0 are no longer profit-maximizing, so raising them to p_m must benefit the merged firm (since p_m is a best response to the non-merged prices p_{nm}). What about the nonmerged firms? Each such firm shares $N - 2$ competitors with each product of the merged firm ($N - M - 1$ nonmerged firms and $M - 1$ merged firms). The remaining competitor is part of the merged firm and so sets price p_m. By contrast, for each product of the merged firm, the remaining competitor is a nonmerged firm that sets a lower price p_{nm}. In other words, each product of the merged firm faces tougher competition than each nonmerged firm and so must earn lower profits. Finally, mergers are increasingly profitable—a merger of $M + 1$ firms is more profitable for both merged and nonmerged firms than a merger of M firms.[14]

To summarize: this (relatively) simple framework of price setting in a product differentiated market avoids the merger paradox, suggesting that mergers are both profitable and of potential concern to antitrust authorities unless accompanied by cost efficiencies.

11.5.2   Mergers in a Spatial Market

In the spatial model, a merger between two firms may well bring increased profit for reasons similar to those in the previous section. Here again, while merging means that the firms lose their separate identity, it does not mean they lose the ownership or control of the product varieties they can offer. For example, the merger of two major banks, Bank of America and Fleet Bank, results in a single new corporate entity. Yet, it does not require that the new firm give up any of the locations at which either Bank of America or Fleet operated prior to the merger—or that it lose control over the choice of moving some of those locations.

Further, consideration of a firm's product line points to a second source of potential profit increase. The merged firms can now coordinate not just the prices, but also the design of their product line. In the context of the spatial model, these decisions are reflected in the firm's location choices. A firm controlling two or more products can coordinate their locations to enhance its profit in the same manner that the Bank of America and Fleet can coordinate the services they offer.

To investigate the impact of a merger in the spatial model, we begin by recalling the basic setup of the model.[15] There is a mass of N consumers uniformly distributed over a linear market whose length is normalized to 1. Again, we can think of this as Main Street in Littlesville. However, one small problem with the Main Street analogy is that outlets at either end of the market can only reach consumers on one side. This restriction introduces an asymmetry in the model, which we would like to avoid. To make the product differentiated market symmetric, we replace our straight line with a circle of unit circumference. If we use the spatial model to represent, for example, departure times in the differentiated airline market, the circle represents the 24 hours of the day about which consumers differ in terms of their most preferred time of departure. In all other respects, the spatial model remains as before.

---

[14]   As we would expect, profitability is a decreasing function of the product differentiation parameter γ, since a higher value of γ is equivalent to less product differentiation.

[15]   A more general, but much more complicated, version of this analysis can be found in Brito (2003).

Each consumer's "address" or location on the circle indicates her most preferred product type. Each is willing to buy at most one unit of a differentiated good. The consumer's reservation price for her most preferred good is denoted by V. Different varieties of the good are offered by the firms that are also located on Main Street—or, more appropriately, Main Circle.[16] A consumer buys from the firm that offers the product to her at the lowest price, taking into account the costs of transporting the good from the firm's address to the consumer's address. Transport costs are linear in distance d, and equal to td where t is the transport cost per unit distance.

Suppose that there are M firms. We assume that these are located symmetrically around the circle so that the distance between firms is $1/M$. Each firm has identical costs given by $C(q) = F + cq$, where F is fixed cost and c is (constant) marginal cost. As in the previous section, we can normalize marginal costs $c = 0$ without loss of generality.[17]

No Price Discrimination

We start by considering the case in which firms do not engage in price discrimination. This means that each firm sets a single mill price m that consumers pay at the firm's store or mill location. The consumer then pays the fee for transporting the product back to her location. The full price paid by a consumer who buys from Firm i is $m_i + td_i$ where m_i is Firm i's mill price and td_i is the consumer's transport cost (or the utility lost by this consumer in buying a product that is not "ideal"). Since marginal cost is 0, the net revenue or profit margin earned by Firm i on every such sale is m_i. Consumers buy from the firm offering the product at the lowest full price. As a result, for any set of mill prices across the M firms, the market is divided between the firms as illustrated in Figure 11.4 for the case in which $M = 5$. The short lines indicate the market division between the firms. Firm 3, for example, supplies all consumers in the region (r_{23}, r_{34}).

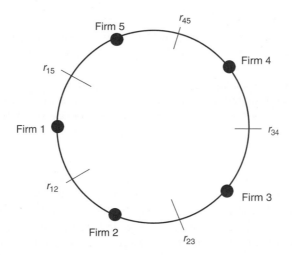

Figure 11.4   Product differentiation—no price discrimination

<hr>

[16]   It bears repeating that the spatial or geographic interpretation of this model is only the most obvious one. See the discussion in Chapter 3.

[17]   If the reader is interested in working out the outcome for the case of $c \neq 0$, note that in each case that we examine, the equilibrium price m that we derive should be replaced by $c + m$.

We assume that the reservation price V is sufficiently large that the market is covered. That is, every consumer buys from some firm. Hence, the marginal consumers for any firm are those who are just indifferent between buying from that firm and buying from its nearest neighbors.[18] We can take any one of the firms as typical of the others. So consider Firm i. Demand for this firm from consumers to its left is $Nr_{i,i-1}$, where $r_{i,i-1}$ is the marginal consumer given by

$$m_i + tr_{i-1,i} = m_{i-1} + t\left(\frac{1}{M} - r_{i-1,i}\right) \Rightarrow r_{i,i-1} = \frac{m_{i-1} - m_i}{2t} + \frac{1}{2M} \qquad (11.45)$$

Similarly, demand from consumers to the right of Firm i is

$$r_{i,i+1} = \frac{m_{i+1} - m_i}{2t} + \frac{1}{2M} \qquad (11.46)$$

Firm i's profit, therefore, is

$$\pi_i = Nm_i(r_{i-1,i} + r_{i,i+1}) = Nm_i\left(\frac{m_{i-1} - m_i}{2t} + \frac{m_{i+1} - m_i}{2t} + \frac{1}{M}\right) \qquad (11.47)$$

Maximizing with respect to m_i gives the first-order condition for Firm i:

$$\frac{\partial \pi_i}{\partial m_i} = N\left(\frac{m_{i-1} + m_{i+1}}{2t} - \frac{2m_i}{t} + \frac{1}{M}\right) = 0 \qquad (11.48)$$

Since the firms are identical, in equilibrium it must be that $m_i = m_{i-1} = m_{i+1} = m^*$. Substituting into equation (11.48) and solving for m^* gives $m_i^* = t/M$. At this price, the profit earned by each firm is

$$\pi_i^* = \frac{Nt}{M^2} - F \qquad (11.49)$$

Now consider a merger between some subset of these firms. Taking store locations or product choice as given, *such a merger will have no effect unless it is made between neighboring firms* because competition is localized between each firm and its two nearest neighbors. A merger, for example, between Firms i and $i+2$ leaves prices and market shares unaffected. More generally, a merger has no effect on the market outcome unless the market areas of the merging firms have a common boundary. The merging firms gain by softening price competition between them and this will happen only if, prior to the merger, they actually compete for some of the same consumers.

It is more tractable (and no insight is lost) if we consider a merger in the context of a precise value for the number of premerger firms M.[19] Therefore, consider the case in which $M = 5$, and in which there is a merger between Firms 2 and 3. Suppose that after the merger, the firms do not change either the locations of their existing products or the number of products they offer. Acting now as a single corporate firm with stores in two locations, the merged firm has an incentive to set prices to maximize the joint profits of

[18]   We assume no firm prices so low as to lure buyers from beyond its two immediate neighbors.

[19]   It is possible to analyze the general case of M firms, but this presents formidable technical challenges. To see why, note that if a merger causes the merged firms to increase their product prices, this will lead to an increase in prices of the nearest neighboring firms, which will in turn lead to (lesser) increased prices at the second-nearest neighbors and so on. Calculating this chain effect is complex and adds little to the basic insights of the model.

both products 2 and 3, while the remaining firms continue to price non-cooperatively. Of course, Firms 1, 4, and 5 also take account of the fact that the merger has taken place. Since Firms 2 and 3 are now cooperating divisions of the merged firm, they no longer compete for the consumers located between them and so have an incentive to raise the prices of products 2 and 3.[20] This will likely lead to the loss of some consumers, namely, those just on the boundaries identified by the points r_{12} and r_{34}. But provided that the merged firm does not raise prices too much, the loss of market share will be more than offset by the increased profit margins on their "captive" consumers—the consumers between the two merging firms. Moreover, the increased prices set by the merged firm will induce a similar increase in prices set by Firms 1, 4, and 5. Such a response reduces the loss of market share that the merged firm actually suffers, making the price increase all the more profitable.

Working with the case of $M = 5$, we can identify the profits of each firm by changing the labels in equation (11.47) to give

$$\pi_1 = Nm_1 \left(\frac{m_5 - m_1}{2t} + \frac{m_2 - m_1}{2t} + \frac{L}{5} \right)$$

$$\pi_2 = Nm_2 \left(\frac{m_1 - m_2}{2t} + \frac{m_3 - m_2}{2t} + \frac{L}{5} \right)$$

$$\pi_3 = Nm_3 \left(\frac{m_2 - m_3}{2t} + \frac{m_4 - m_3}{2t} + \frac{L}{5} \right) \qquad (11.50)$$

$$\pi_4 = Nm_4 \left(\frac{m_3 - m_4}{2t} + \frac{m_5 - m_4}{2t} + \frac{L}{5} \right)$$

$$\pi_5 = Nm_5 \left(\frac{m_4 - m_5}{2t} + \frac{m_1 - m_5}{2t} + \frac{L}{5} \right)$$

After the merger, the merged firm chooses m_2 and m_3 to maximize aggregate profit $\pi_2 + \pi_3$, while the remaining firms choose their prices to maximize their individual profits. This means there are five first-order conditions to solve:

$$\frac{\partial \pi_1}{\partial m_1} = N \left(\frac{m_5 + m_2}{2t} - \frac{2m_1}{t} + \frac{L}{5} \right) = 0$$

$$\frac{\partial (\pi_2 + \pi_3)}{\partial m_2} = N \left(\frac{m_1 + m_3}{2t} - \frac{2m_2}{t} + \frac{L}{5} \right) + N\frac{m_3}{2t} = 0$$

$$\frac{\partial (\pi_2 + \pi_3)}{\partial m_3} = N \left(\frac{m_2 + m_4}{2t} - \frac{2m_3}{t} + \frac{L}{5} \right) + N\frac{m_2}{2t} = 0 \qquad (11.51)$$

$$\frac{\partial \pi_4}{\partial m_4} = N \left(\frac{m_3 + m_5}{2t} - \frac{2m_4}{t} + \frac{L}{5} \right) = 0$$

$$\frac{\partial \pi_5}{\partial m_5} = N \left(\frac{m_4 + m_1}{2t} - \frac{2m_5}{t} + \frac{L}{5} \right) = 0$$

[20] If the merger leaves products 2 and 3 under the control of separate, competing product divisions, prices will not change. It is important, in other words, that the merged firms take advantage of the opportunity they now have to coordinate their prices.

Solving these equations simultaneously[21] gives the equilibrium prices

$$m_2^* = m_3^* = \frac{19tL}{60}; m_1^* = m_4^* = \frac{14tL}{60}; m_5^* = \frac{13tL}{60} \tag{11.52}$$

As expected, the merger increases all five product prices. Profit to each product is

$$\pi_2^* = \pi_3^* = \frac{361NtL^2}{7,200} - F; \quad \pi_1^* = \pi_4^* = \frac{392NtL^2}{7,200} - F; \quad \pi_5^* = \frac{338NtL^2}{7,200} - F \tag{11.53}$$

Comparison of the profit levels in equation (11.53) with those in (11.49) confirms that this merger is profitable for the merging firms. In addition, the nonmerged firms get a free ride.

The equilibrium we have identified assumes that the merged firms leave their product lines unchanged after the merger. What do we expect to happen if we relax this assumption? This turns out to be a far from straightforward question. If the merged firms move their locations nearer to Firms 1 and 4, these firms in turn might be expected to move closer to Firm 5, with the result that the merged firm gains market share. However, this comes at the expense of tougher competition with Firms 1 and 4, leading to lower mill prices for the merged firm and a loss of revenue from its captive consumers. By contrast, if the merged firm moves its products closer to each other, it loses market share to Firms 1 and 4 but softens competition with these firms, leading to higher mill prices and so higher revenues from its captive customers.

There is no simple way to resolve this tradeoff. Posada and Straume (2004), for example, show that while a merger will generally induce the merger participants to relocate, the direction of relocation is ambiguous, dependent on the degree of convexity in the consumers' transportation cost function. In general, the issue of product design in the postmerger market remains a complicated but perhaps vitally important one. Indeed, when products are vertically instead of horizontally differentiated, the postmerger product selection by the newly-combined firm can critically affect the impact of the merger on consumer welfare. (See Reality Checkpoint, next page.)

A merger between two firms in our spatial market is clearly advantageous to the merging firms, but is disadvantageous to consumers, because a merger raises prices throughout the industry. Both merged and unmerged firms enjoy greater profit and consumers obtain less surplus. The only possible benefit to consumers is if the merger leads to cost savings that permit lower prices. Here, it is important to remember that the two merged products, while not identical, are close substitutes. They might be, for example, low-sugar and high-sugar versions of a soft drink. Consequently, we might expect there to be some cost complementarities in the production of these products. If so, then production of both goods by one firm will be cheaper than production of both by two separate firms. In short, we should not be surprised if, in a product-differentiated market, production of many closely related product lines exhibits economies of scope.[22]

---

[21]   We cannot take the approach we adopted in the previous section of taking one first-order condition for a merged firm and one for a nonmerged firm, because there is every reason to believe that the nonmerged firms will adopt different prices.

[22]   Refer to Chapter 3 for a definition and explanation of economies of scope.

Reality Checkpoint
Baby, Baby, Where Did that Brand Go?

Cost savings have always been a possible justification for horizontal mergers. Such efficiencies took on increased importance after 1997 when the U.S. Federal Trade Commission (FTC) and Department of Justice amended their well-known merger guidelines to give greater weight to such cost efficiencies as a rationale for what otherwise might be a questionable merger. The intuition is that while there may be potential harm to consumers from the monopoly power that the merger creates, this will often be offset by the lower prices that result from the lower costs that the merger makes possible.

Evaluation of the cost-efficiency defense is therefore important. It is also tricky. Besides the question of how real the cost savings may be, there is the further question as to whether the cost savings will be passed on to consumers in the form of lower prices.

Consider the proposed acquisition of Beech-Nut Baby Food by Heinz in 2001. Along with Gerber, these two companies controlled the bulk of the jarred or prepared baby food market. Gerber was the industry giant with a market share between 65 and 70 percent. The remaining 30 to 35 percent was split fairly evenly between Heinz and Beech-Nut.

The FTC sought to block the merger arguing that it would significantly decrease competition in the baby food industry. Heinz and Beech-Nut responded that the merger would actually increase competition. Their analysis relied heavily on cost savings. In brief, the merging parties argued that Beech-Nut has a superior brand image but very old and costly production techniques relative to Heinz. They further argued that the merger would permit the two firms to offer a single product of the higher Beech-Nut quality but at the lower Heinz cost. As a result, this product would enable the merged firm to really put pressure on the industry giant, Gerber. Given Gerber's large size, and market share, a fall in its price would bring large gains to consumers.

Heinz and Beech-Nut backed up their claims with statistical evidence. Using a model of the baby food industry that is similar in spirit to the circular spatial model used here, they provided simulations of the postmerger market that implied a fall in baby food prices. These simulations took the assumptions of a 15 percent cost savings as given and suggested that between 50 and 100 percent of these savings would be passed through to consumers as lower prices.

The claim that much of the cost savings would be passed on to consumers depends critically on the nature of competition in the postmerger market. As noted, Heinz and Beech-Nut assumed that that market could be described as a spatial one of the type used in this chapter. Horizontal differentiation is not the only type of product differentiation that we observe, however. An alternative approach is to view the market as vertically differentiated (Chapter 6) with each brand representing a different level of quality and consumers differing in how much they are willing to pay for quality. Gerber would be the highest quality, Beech-Nut the next highest, and Heinz (well-known as the discount brand) would be the least highest. In this set-up it is the Beech-Nut quality that directly competes with the Gerber premium brand. If this is the case, then Heinz and Beech-Nut have a strong incentive to discontinue the Beech-Nut brand after the merger. This would allow the firms postmerger to soften price competition in the market by producing the brand that is maximally differentiated (furthest) from Gerber. If so, consumers could be hurt in two ways. Not only would prices rise but consumers would also suffer a loss in choice as one brand was removed from the market. Moreover, removal of a brand in the postmerger market means that the demand estimates made for the pre-merger market (the ones relied on by Heinz and Beech-Nut in their simulations) might not be relevant.

Norman, Pepall, and Richards (2002) show that the foregoing concern is very real. Indeed, they show that no matter what the cost savings, a merger of two lower quality brands will always lead to the removal of the higher quality one and a rise in consumer prices on the remaining brands. They show that this is true even when there is potential competition from a later entrant.

Sources: G. Norman, L. Pepall, and D. Richards, "Product Differentiation, Cost-Reducing Mergers, and Consumer Welfare," *Canadian Journal of Economics*, 38 (November 2005): 1204–1223. See also J. Baker (2001), "Efficiencies and High Concentration: Heinz Proposes to Acquire Beech-Nut," in J. Kwoka and L. White (Eds.), *The Antitrust Revolution*. Oxford: Oxford University Press, 2004: 150–169; and Ghandi, et al. (2008), "Post-Merger Product Repositioning," *Journal of Industrial Economics*, 56 (March): 49–67.

Scope economies provide a strong incentive to merge by allowing the new firm to operate as a multiproduct company exploiting the cost-savings opportunities this generates. These savings may be reflected in a reduction in fixed costs. For example, the firms can combine their headquarters, research and development, marketing, accounting, and distribution operations. If, in addition, the merger leads to a reduction in variable costs of production, then this change will be reflected in lower prices. Moreover, even if scope economies are not present, it is still possible that one of the merging firms has a more effective purchasing division or a superior production technology that, following the merger, will be extended to its new partners. The greater are such cost synergies, the more likely it is that consumers will benefit from the merger. In evaluating mergers in a spatial context then, a key issue will be to balance the potential for price increases due to softened competition against the potential for cost decreases due to the exploitation of economies of scope.

Price Discrimination

Firms that operate in a spatial or product-differentiated setting clearly have some monopoly power. That is, the firms on our circle do not lose all of their customers if they raise the price a little bit. Given that the firms have some market power, we might expect them to adopt some of the price discrimination strategies that we developed in earlier chapters. We now consider how price discrimination affects the effect of mergers in a product differentiated market.

Suppose that firms adopt first-degree or personalized discriminatory pricing policies (Chapter 5), but maintain at the same time all the remaining assumptions of our spatial model. The noncooperative price equilibrium is then easy to identify. Consider a consumer located midway between two firms. For any such consumer, the two goods are perfect substitutes as the transport cost is the same in either direction, equal to $t/2M$. We know from Chapter 7 that when two firms compete in price with identical products, the price is driven to marginal cost, including the transport cost. Thus, if Firms i and $i+1$ can compete freely for the consumers located midway between them without this imposing any constraint on the prices they charge other consumers, the price at this point—located $1/2M$ distance from either firm—must be $c + t/2M$.

Now consider the consumer who is ε closer to Firm i than to Firm $i+1$, that is, the consumer located the distance $1/2M - \varepsilon$ from i and therefore $1/2M + \varepsilon$ from Firm $i+1$. Firm i can charge this customer a price as high as $c + t/2M + t\varepsilon$ without fear of losing this consumer's business. Any higher price, however, will allow Firm $i+1$ to compete profitably with Firm i for such a consumer. By extension, we can see that Firm i's personalized price to each consumer rises linearly as the consumer's preferred location moves closer to Firm i and further from Firm $i+1$. For those consumers closest to Firm i, that is, for those located at exactly the same position as i, the nearest alternative in any direction is $1/M$ units away. Firm i can charge these consumers a price as high as $c + t/M$ without losing their patronage. In short, for any Firm i, the price it can charge rises linearly from $c + t/2M$ to customers $1/2M$ units away to $c + t/M$ to those whose preferred variant is the same as Firm i's location. With each firm pursuing this policy, each will serve N/M customers.

The heavy shaded line in Figure 11.5 illustrates this price equilibrium, again returning to our example in which $c = 0$ and $M = 5$. Firm 2 is the lowest-price supplier (including transport cost) for all consumers in the region (r_{12}, r_{23}). Therefore, Firm 2 supplies all consumers in this market region, charging its consumers on the left one cent less than Firm 1's costs of supplying them, and its consumers on the right one cent less than Firm 3's costs of supplying these consumers. By adopting this pricing strategy, each firm earns a gross profit (profit before deducting fixed cost) given by the shaded areas for their market regions in Figure 11.5. This gives profit to each firm of

$$\pi_i = \frac{Nt}{2M^2} - F = \frac{Nt}{50} - F \quad \text{with } c = 0 \text{ and } M = 5 \tag{11.54}$$

There are two interesting features of the discriminatory prices. First, the highest price now paid by any consumer is $c + t/5$. This was the *lowest* price paid by any consumer when firms did not practice price discrimination! Price discrimination in this oligopolistic market unambiguously benefits consumers. Why is this? In effect, personalized pricing turns each customer into an individual battlefield. With nondiscriminatory pricing, when a firm reduces the price to one consumer, it has to reduce the price to every consumer—an expensive prospect. By contrast, price discrimination allows the firm to lower the price necessary to win any specific customer without that placing any constraint on the price it sets to any other customer. In turn, this means that price discrimination weakens each firm's ability to commit to a set of higher prices, making price competition between the firms much fiercer and so leading to the lower prices that we have just identified. This leads to the second interesting feature. Price discrimination lowers each firm's profit compared to nondiscriminatory pricing, in sharp contrast to the profit effect for a monopolist.[23]

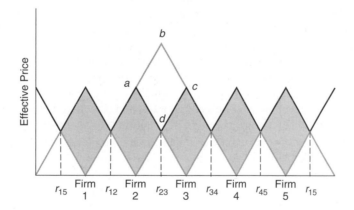

Figure 11.5   Price equilibrium with price discrimination

---

[23]   These results are discussed in Norman and Thisse (1996). They show that with a given number of firms, discriminatory pricing always benefits consumers and harms the firms. They also show, however, that the much more competitive environment of discriminatory pricing may cause enough firms to want to leave the market that prices actually increase for some consumers. In our example, there is no incentive to exit the market.

We can now consider the effect on this equilibrium of a merger between two of these firms, say Firms 2 and 3, as before. Two points should be clear. First, as in the no-price discrimination case, a merger of non-neighboring firms has no effect. Second, the merged firm's ability to coordinate the formerly separate pricing strategies is particularly valuable in this discriminatory setting. This is because prior to the merger these firms were engaged in nearly cutthroat price competition. By merging, the two firms can avoid this expensive conflict, at least with respect to each other. From the perspective of the merged firm, the nearest competitor for consumers in the region between Firm 2's location and r_{23} is now Firm 1. Similarly, for consumers in the region between Firm 3's location and r_{23}, the nearest competitor is now Firm 4. As a result, the merged firm can raise prices to all consumers located between Firms 2 and 3, as indicated by the line abc in Figure 11.5. A merger of Firm 2 and Firm 3 increases the profits of the merging firms by an amount given by the area $abcd$, which is just $Nt/50$—half the combined profits of the merged firms (ignoring fixed costs) prior to the merger. Also, in the personalized pricing case shown here, the effects of the merger are now completely localized to the set of consumers for which the two merging firms previously competed. That is, *the merger only (and favorably) affects the merging firms*. Prices and profit increase for these former competitors. However, all other prices are unaffected, and so the profits of the nonmerging firms are unaffected by the merger.

We could also consider issues regarding the merged firm's product location strategies. However, the basic point has been made. Our conclusions for the no-price discrimination case hold all the more strongly when firms engage in discriminatory pricing. Prices to consumers rise and the merging firms are more profitable. There is absolutely no paradox about merging in this case. From the viewpoint of the partner firms a merger can be a highly profitable venture.

Why is it that mergers with price competition in a product-differentiated market do not run into the merger paradox that so bedeviled our earlier analysis with homogenous products and quantity-setting firms? The first part of the answer has already been suggested. Prices are strategic complements, whereas quantities are strategic substitutes. With price competition, therefore, the strategic responses of nonmerged firms are potentially beneficial to the merged firms, whereas with quantity competition they are potentially harmful.

The second part of the answer is equally important and is related to the notion of credible commitment discussed in Chapters 8 and 9. The reason why mergers are profitable in the spatial or differentiated products context is that the merged firms can credibly commit to produce some particular *range* of products—that is, the commitment required in the spatial context is a commitment to particular locations or to continue marketing the products of the previously independent firms. By contrast, the commitment necessary with homogenous products and quantity competition must be in terms of production *levels*. The merging firms must be able to commit to a high volume of output following the merger. Generally, this is not credible, because such a high volume of production is not the merged firm's best response to a Cournot output decision by the other firms. It is only if the merged firm becomes a Stackelberg leader that the commitment to a high level of postmerger output is credible.

11.6   PUBLIC POLICY AND HORIZONTAL MERGERS

U.S. public policy with respect to horizontal mergers has changed dramatically over the last 40 years. The differences between the first Merger Guidelines issued by the Justice Department in 1968 and the Merger Guidelines currently in force are dramatic. In broad terms, this evolution has reflected a movement away from a rigid approach based on market structure considerations to a more sophisticated approach that has increasingly recognized the complexity of strategic interaction.

The heavy reliance on market structure that characterized the 1968 Merger Guidelines reflected the great influence of the Structure-Conduct-Performance paradigm at that time. Mergers would be challenged in any industry in which the four-firm concentration ratio[24] exceeded 75 percent and the merging firms each had a market share of as little as 4 percent. In markets with a four-firm ratio below 75 percent, mergers would be challenged if the two firms each had market shares of 5 percent or more. Thus, under the 1968 Guidelines, a combined share of as little as 10 percent would be sufficient in many cases for the government to challenge a merger. This approach had in fact been operative for some time before the Guidelines were formally adopted. Indeed, the rigidity of this framework had already been revealed in a number of court cases including one of the most controversial merger cases ever, *U.S. v. Von's Grocery* (1966). In that case, the Supreme Court upheld the government's prohibition of a merger between two grocery store chains in Los Angeles that, in combination, had less than 10 percent of the market.

Perhaps it is not surprising in the wake of that controversy and others that the courts began to deviate from the rigid, structure-based Guidelines of 1968 almost as soon as they were adopted. One early such case was the acquisition by General Dynamics of another coal producer, which was ultimately allowed by the Supreme Court in 1974—despite the fact that the combined market shares of the two firms clearly exceeded the permissible levels set forth by the then (1968) Merger Guidelines. As the courts permitted a number of similar mergers, it soon became clear that the 1968 Guidelines were no longer guiding policy. This eventually led to the Justice Department issuing of a new set of Merger Guidelines in 1982.

Under the new rules, reliance on the four-firm concentration ratio was abandoned in favor of the Herfindahl-Hirschman Index (H). The threshold for intervention now became an H of 1,800 (a little more concentrated than an industry comprised of six equally large firms). Mergers in less concentrated industries would only be challenged if they raised the H by more than 100 points—and even then only if the industry H already exceeded 1,000. Subsequent amendments to the Guidelines in 1984, 1992, and 1997 relaxed even more the constraints on mergers by specifying and enlarging the appeal to merger-generated cost efficiencies as a merger justification.

There is no doubt that these changes ushered in a more permissive policy toward mergers. Major consolidations such as those of the Union Pacific and Southern Pacific (railroads), AOL and Time Warner (telecommunications), Chase Manhattan and J. P. Morgan (finance), Exxon and Mobil and also British Petroleum and Amoco (both petroleum

---

[24] Refer to Chapter 4 for a discussion of concentration ratios.

mergers), Westinghouse and Infinity Broadcasting (radio), Aetna and U.S. Healthcare (health services), and Maytag and Whirlpool (home appliances) have been allowed that would certainly have been denied under the 1968 Guidelines. Whether, on balance, this more permissive approach has strengthened or weakened market competition may not be entirely clear. However, there is no doubt that these developments have reflected an increasing awareness of modern industrial organization theory. We should add as well that any impact on competition has not been reflected in higher profit margins. A long list of studies, including Mueller (1982), Ravenscraft and Scherer (1987), Lichtenberg and Siegel (1992), Loughran and A. Vijh (1997), Andrade, Mitchell, and Stafford (2001), and Maskimovic and Phillips (2001) have found that mergers are not terribly profitable—especially for the acquiring firm. Indeed, many acquisitions are later reversed by "spin-offs."[25]

Nevertheless, it would be wrong to characterize current merger policy as simply more permissive. In some ways, the greater number of mergers allowed in fact reflects a more interventionist approach in that the authorities now often require the merging firms themselves to take actions aimed at mitigating antitrust concerns. First, the antitrust authorities have increasingly used a "fix-it-first" approach centered on divestiture of some of the assets of the merging parties to another, third firm so as to ensure that competitive pressures are maintained. If, for example, the two firms operate in several towns across the country, but in one town they are the only two such suppliers, then the government may permit the merger so long as one of the firms sells off its operations in the town in question to a new, rival entrant firm. This principle was applied in both of the petroleum mergers mentioned above, and it is often used in the case of media mergers, where newspaper and broadcasting firms have been required to sell their operations in certain locations before being permitted to conclude a merger.

Second, merger approval has increasingly been subject to behavioral constraints on the merging firms, followed by active monitoring by government agents. Typically, these consent agreements require the firms to take specific actions and to avoid engaging in certain practices. In monitoring these agreements, the regulatory agencies can always count on a reliable source of outside help, namely, the competitors of the merged firms and other parties who opposed the merger. They are always quick to report violations of the consent agreement. Since 1992, the number of consent decrees issued by the FTC and the Justice Department has dramatically increased.

Divestiture does have some problems. Cabral (2003) notes that divestiture allows the merging firms to dictate the entry position for new rivals. If we think of the circle spatial model described above, if two firms merge but sell the locations of some of their stores to a formerly excluded entrant, it means that the entrant enters in the same locations in which the initial stores existed, rather than elsewhere on the circle which would be better for consumers.

We should also note that merger-generated cost efficiencies are not necessarily completely beneficial once entry possibilities are considered. If a merger generates lower marginal costs, then any potential entrant will know that *if it enters* price competition will be relatively fierce. If the entrant has fixed costs, this will mean that the market will need to be larger for entry to be profitable. In other words, for a given market size,

---

[25] Note, though, that these findings also raise doubts about any cost savings that mergers are alleged to generate.

merger-generated cost efficiencies make postmerger entry less likely. Thus, cost savings can have two price effects. One is the downward pressure on prices exerted by lower costs, and the other is the upward pressure exerted by the reduced likelihood of rival entry. Cabral (2003) shows that it is possible that the former outweighs the latter.

11.6.1   Coordinated Effects of Mergers

Two other issues that are important considerations in the analysis of mergers deserve mention. The first has to do with a merger's so-called *coordinated effects*. So far, we have focused in this chapter on the *unilateral effects* of a merger. That is, we have focused on how the merger enhances the ability of the merging firms themselves to enhance their own profits. However, it is also possible that a merger may change the competitive environment in the industry and, in particular, alter the ability of firms to collude successively. These changes are often referred to as the coordinated effects of a merger, although in formal European proceedings they fall under the semiofficial category of *collective dominance*.

For example, in 2001, H. J. Heinz and BeechNut proposed to merge their baby food operations. At the time, these two firms accounted for between 30 and 40 percent of the jarred baby food market with the almost all of the remainder going to Gerber. Hence, the merger would have replaced a triopoly with a duopoly. The FTC opposed the merger on the grounds that a reduction from three to two firms would greatly enhance the opportunities for tacit collusion in the industry. In *FTC v. H. J. Heinz*, the Appellate Court agreed and the merger was effectively blocked.[26] A similar ruling was made earlier by the European Commission when it blocked the proposed merger of two of the largest platinum (and rhodium) producers, Gencor and Lonrho.[27] Together, the newly combined firm and its principal remaining rival, Amplats, were estimated to account for about 70 percent of world platinum production (and more, once Russia's meager supplies were depleted). Here again, the decision was rooted in the view that the merger would transform the market into a duopoly and thereby greatly increase the possibility of collusive practices.

In reaching a decision on whether or not a merger raises coordinated effects issues, authorities generally use the intuitive criteria discussed in Chapter 10 as the conditions that facilitate collusive behavior. That is, the authorities consider the number of firms, the homogeneity of products and of cost structures across firms, the extent of entry barriers, and the frequency of orders in an effort to gauge the ability of firms to reach and enforce cooperative agreements in the postmerger market. We agree that this is a sensible procedure, but note that the little formal empirical evidence that does exist on this topic does not necessarily support these broad theoretical generalizations.

How might one test the impact of mergers on collusive behavior? The one formal test with which we are familiar is a recent study by Ganslandt and Norbäck (2004) focusing on the retail gasoline industry in Sweden. Their basic framework is familiar to us from our analysis of the Cournot model. Recall that we showed there that the industry-average Lerner Index (LI) may be written as

$$LI = \frac{P - \overline{c}}{P} = \frac{H}{\varepsilon} \tag{11.55}$$

---

[26]   See *F.T.C. v. H.J. Heinz*, 246 F.3d 708 (D.C. Cir 2001).
[27]   See *Gencor/Lonrho*, M.619 OJ 1997 L11/30.

where $\bar{c} = \sum_{i=1}^{k} s_i c_i$ is the weighted-average marginal cost over all k firms in the industry. Note that we may alternatively write equation (11.55) by defining the elasticity-adjusted Lerner Index LI_ε

$$LI_\varepsilon = \varepsilon LI = H \tag{11.56}$$

Ganslandt and Norbäck (2004) replace this relationship with the more general one that $LI_\varepsilon = \alpha H^\eta$. Taking logs and adding in a random shock term v, we then have

$$\ln LI_\varepsilon = \alpha + \eta \ln H + v \tag{11.57}$$

Here, η measures the elasticity of the adjusted Lerner Index with respect to concentration. If the basic Cournot hypothesis is correct, η (and also α) should be one as in equation (11.56). However, if a merger that leads to a significant increase in concentration makes coordinated activity more likely, then η should be greater than one.

Ganslandt and Norbäck (2004) estimate equation (11.57) via regression analysis using time series data from Sweden's retail gasoline market over the years 1986–2002, having first obtained time-varying estimates of both the elasticity of demand ε, and the basic Lerner Index LI. These years witnessed some major mergers and, hence, some major increases in the Herfindahl Index H. There was also a period of a major dissolution and therefore a decline in H. Therefore, the data contain considerable variation in H that should allow some inference about how it influences the price-cost margin. Using a quadratic specification for industry demand, they find that one cannot reject the hypothesis that $\eta = 1$. The results for other specifications are cloudier but in no case could they find evidence that η is significantly greater than one. In general, nothing in their data suggests that the mergers in the Swedish retail gasoline market had coordinated effects that enhance the ability of firms to collude. This is not a definitive study, of course. However, it does suggest that one needs to be cautious about attributing important coordinated, as opposed to unilateral, effects for a proposed merger.

11.6.2   Consumer versus Producer versus Total Surplus

The second issue that has recently emerged in merger policy concerns the appropriate target for antitrust policy more broadly. As noted in Chapter 2, the basic economic complaint against market power is that it leads to inefficiency in that it reduces the combined producer and consumer surplus below what it would be in a competitive market. This total surplus measure is the common measure economic analysis uses to evaluate all social arrangements. In that respect, there is little or no formal concern over the individual components of that surplus, that is, over either consumer or producer surplus separately.

However, the U.S. (and European) practice has been to focus on consumer welfare explicitly. In the case of merger policy, the explicit question asked is whether or not the merger will harm consumers, regardless of its impact on producers. If one thinks about our early discussion of the merger paradox, one can easily see how this focus can conflict with the larger goal of economic efficiency. As we saw there, a large cost reduction is necessary to render a merger profitable in a Cournot setting, and an even larger one is necessary to make consumers better off. Yet as we also saw, the nonmerging firms in such a setting enjoy a healthy profit increase even if the merging firms and consumers are worse off. It is entirely possible that the gains of nonmerging firms can more than offset any losses to the merging parties and consumers, especially if the merger is profitable. In such cases, focusing on consumer surplus alone will lead authorities to block a proposed merger that would, if permitted, raise total surplus.

Consider, for example, the merger of Superior Propane and IGC Propane in 2003. These were two of Canada's largest propane suppliers who, together, controlled more than 70 percent of the propane market. Extensive research by the Canadian Competition Bureau suggested that the merger would result in a 9 percent rise in prices via unilateral effects and a consequent loss in consumer surplus of about $3 million. However, the cost efficiencies associated with the merger were far larger and generated increased profit for the two firms of close to $29 million. Although the Competition Bureau opposed the merger, the law under which it operates seems clearly to favor a total surplus measure. Eventually, the Canadian courts ruled that the law trumped the Bureau's concerns and the merger was allowed to proceed. As mentioned above, economic analysis is rooted in a total surplus standard. What justification can there be then for the U.S. and European approaches that focus primarily on just consumer surplus?

There are three possible reasons for favoring a consumer-surplus-only standard. One of these is a distributional one. Pittman (2007) is perhaps the most forceful advocate of this view. Based on data from a number of empirical studies, he concludes that the standard finding in merger research is that the transfer from consumers to producers is usually several times any total surplus gain. Again, though, while such distributional effects may be common, economists generally are wary of justifying policy on distributional concerns since there is no clear and generally agreed-upon standard as to what constitutes a "good" distribution of income or wealth. This is especially the case in mergers where the merging firms often produce intermediate goods, and the "consumers" in question may themselves be other firms.

Apart from distributional concerns, there are two further arguments in support of a consumer-surplus-only standard. First, as noted in the text, merging firms may well exaggerate the cost efficiencies stemming from the merger. Focusing on consumer surplus alone will diminish the incentives to do this, since the profits that result from such cost savings will not help to justify the merger. Since consumers are not well represented at these proceedings, there may be merit in giving less weight to the claims of producers.

Second, even when total surplus is the real goal, focusing on consumer surplus may still prove a useful selection criterion. Suppose that a firm is considering two different mergers. Each will raise total surplus by X. However, the first will raise producer surplus by $X + e$ while reducing consumer surplus by e. By contrast, the second merger will raise both producer and consumer surplus by $X/2$. Under a total surplus standard, the firm will choose the first merger. Under a consumer-surplus-only standard, it will choose the second. In short, a consumer surplus criterion may serve as a useful instrument to guide firms' choice of merger possibilities even when total surplus is the real target.[28]

---

[28] For a discussion of the appropriate standard motivated explicitly by the IGC Propane case, see Ross, T. and R. Winter. (2003) "Canadian Merger Policy following *Superior Propane*." *Canadian Competition Record*, For a discussion of how a consumer-surplus-only policy might be useful even when the goal is maximization of total surplus, see Armstrong and Vickers (2010) and Lyons (2002).

11.7   APPLICATION
Evaluating the Impact of Mergers with Computer Simulation

The key issue in merger evaluation is to understand the nature of the postmerger market. For this purpose, policymakers have increasingly relied on merger simulation. This procedure requires two steps. The first is to obtain relevant information on key variables using econometric techniques. The second step is to use this evidence to run computer-simulated models of the market in question both before and after a proposed merger. In effect then, merger simulation allows economists to conduct laboratory experiments to examine a merger's likely effects. While not necessarily conclusive, such experiments can be very helpful as an evaluative tool.

To understand merger simulation better, consider an industry with four firms, each of which produces a differentiated product and competes in prices against its rivals. For any one firm, we know that the first-order condition for profit maximization is

$$\frac{p_i - c}{p_i} + \frac{1}{\eta_{ii}} = 0 \quad i = 1 \text{ to } 4 \tag{11.58}$$

Here, η_{ii} is the (negative of) the elasticity of Firm i's demand with respect to its own price. If we denote the price-cost margin term as μ_i, Firm i's market share as s_i, and then multiply through by the elasticity of demand, equation (11.58) becomes

$$s_i + s_i \eta_{ii} \mu_i = 0 \tag{11.59}$$

If two firms merge, however, the first-order condition will change, as we saw in Section 11.5. Now, the merged firm will coordinate the prices of its two separate products by taking account of the cross demand effects between the two products. Specifically, assume that Firms 1 and 2 merge. Then it is straightforward to show that for the merged firm, the first-order condition is

$$s_1 + s_1 \eta_{11} \mu_1 + s_2 \mu_2 \eta_{21} = 0$$
$$s_2 + s_2 \eta_{22} \mu_2 + s_1 \mu_2 \eta_{12} = 0 \tag{11.60}$$

where η_{ij} is the cross-price elasticity of good i with respect to the price of good j. It is clear from equations (11.59) and (11.60) that measures of the own and cross-price elasticities for each good are critical to estimating the impact of a proposed merger. Indeed, once these elasticities are known, it is relatively straightforward to work out the implied postmerger equilibrium and, therefore, the postmerger prices.

In order to estimate the elasticities, one needs a model of market demand. One commonly used such model is derived from what is referred to as the Almost Ideal Demand System (AIDS) as first described by Deaton and Mulbauer (1980). Essentially, such a system describes the demand facing each firm as a function of its own price and the prices charged by other firms, similar to the linear demand that we used to describe our initial model of Bertrand competition with differentiated products. In the case of our four-firm example above, a conventional approach would be to describe market demand with a system of equations something like the following:

$$s_1 = a_1 + b_{11} \ln p_1 + b_{12} \ln p_2 + b_{13} \ln p_3 + b_{14} \ln p_4$$

$$s_2 = a_2 + b_{21} \ln p_1 + b_{22} \ln p_2 + b_{23} \ln p_3 + b_{24} \ln p_4$$

$$s_3 = a_3 + b_{31} \ln p_1 + b_{32} \ln p_2 + b_{33} \ln p_3 + b_{34} \ln p_4 \tag{11.61}$$

$$s_4 = a_4 + b_{41} \ln p_1 + b_{42} \ln p_2 + b_{43} \ln p_3 + b_{44} \ln p_4$$

The b_{ij} coefficients in the above system are directly linked to the demand elasticities needed to run the merger simulation. Thus, econometric estimation of those coefficients is the first step in obtaining a simulated outcome.

Not counting the a_i coefficients or intercepts, this still leaves 16 b_{ij} coefficients to estimate, even in our small four-product example. In general, unless some restrictions are imposed on the nature of the own and cross-price effects, there will be on the order of n^2 coefficients to estimate in a general n-product demand system of the type illustrated above. This is a rather large number of estimates to make with any degree of precision. To simplify matters, it is common to impose restrictions that reduce the number of parameters to be estimated directly.

For example, suppose that our four-firm example is characterized by $q_1 = 250$; $q_2 = 100$; $q_3 = 100$; and $q_4 = 50$, or $s_1 = 50$ percent; $s_2 = s_3 = 20$ percent; and $s_4 = 10$ percent. One way to proceed is to calibrate the model under the assumption of proportionality. As developed by Epstein and Rubinfeld (2002), Proportionally Calibrated AIDS (PCAIDS) assumes that the output loss for good 1 caused by an increase in p_1 will be allocated to the other products in proportion to their market shares. Suppose that the overall elasticity of market demand $\eta = -2$ and the own price elasticity of good 1 is $\eta_{11} = -4$. If we think of the overall industry price as the share-weighted-average price across the four firms, then a 1 percent increase in Firm 1's price p_1 translates into a 0.5 percent increase in the industry price, all else equal. Firm 1's price increase will then reduce industry output by one-half of 2 percent, or by 1 percent, which in this case is five units. Firm 1's own output will fall by 4 percent, or 10 units. Thus, five of these 10 units will be picked up in the demand for the other firms if the net industry demand decline is to be just five units. The proportionality assumption is that $[0.2/(0.2 + 0.2 + 0.1)] \times 5$ (or 2) units will be diverted to each of Firms 2 and 3, while the remaining one unit will be diverted to Firm 4. Note that this implies that a 1 percent increase in Firm 1's price will raise the demand at each of the other firms by 2 percent, that is, the cross elasticities η_{21}, η_{31}, and η_{41} are -2 in each case.

What we have just shown is that with the proportionality restriction, the knowledge of just the market demand elasticity and Firm 1's own price elasticity has permitted us to deduce three other of the elasticity measures needed for simulation. As it turns out, we can go much farther. In fact, the proportionality assumption permits the complete derivation of all the relevant elasticities once the elasticity is known for the market and for one firm. To put it slightly differently, knowing the market elasticity and own-price elasticity of one firm permits complete calculation of all the b_{ij} coefficients in equation (11.61). The proportionality assumption reduces the number of parameters to be estimated from n^2 to just 2. Once that estimation is complete, we may use the resulting elasticity and market share data to solve the first-order conditions in (11.60) and (11.61) for both the premerger and postmerger market. We can then evaluate the price effects of the merger.

Of course, proportionality is a strong assumption. Other techniques for simplifying the estimation procedure also exist. Unfortunately, the resultant simulations are fairly sensitive to the demand specification imposed. For example, the linear demand function that we use in most of the examples in this text implies that demand becomes more elastic as prices rise. This imposes a constraint on postmerger prices, even if a merger raises market power because it means that consumers become increasingly sensitive to such price increases. In contrast, a log-linear demand function implies a constant price elasticity of demand that will yield a notably higher price rise for the same market power increase.

Unfortunately, it is often far from clear what precise specification is most appropriate and, as noted, this can greatly alter the findings. Slade (2007), for example, in examining a beer merger in the United Kingdom, found a range of price effects that varied by a factor of almost 2.4 to 1. Furthermore, even when the proper specification can be identified, estimation is tricky at best so that the resultant elasticity estimates have somewhat large confidence intervals. This raises further issues, since the model's price predictions are also sensitive to small changes in the assumed elasticities. Own price elasticities, for instance, are typically on the order of 1.5. Hence, a 10 percent increase in the estimate would take such an estimate to 1.65, while a similar decrease would reduce it to 1.35. Walker (2005), however, shows how such small changes can lower the predicted price increase from 12.5 to 8 percent, in the first case, or raise it from 12.5 to 24 percent in the second case.

Our view is that merger simulation is a very useful tool despite the foregoing limitations. Its principal advantage is that it forces one to think clearly and with precision about the modeling of a market. As a result, it makes it easier to determine what assumptions are driving the different results and also to test these for reasonability. Simulation, in other words, provides a useful starting point, but cannot be the final word.

Summary

Horizontal mergers that unite former rivals within an industry raise obvious antitrust concerns. It may be somewhat surprising, then, to discover that such mergers are typically unprofitable in the Cournot framework that economists often—though not exclusively—use to model imperfect competition. This result is frequently referred to as the merger paradox. The paradox is not easily resolved by permitting the merger to generate cost efficiencies unless they are very large. Instead, it requires some means of credibly committing the newly merged firm to a strategy that was not available without merging. This can be done by allowing the merged firm to take on the role of Stackelberg leader or by introducing a sequential feature to merger decisions. Either of these approaches is capable of generating profitable mergers that also have adverse consequences for consumers. The sequential merger approach can also help explain the "domino effect," often observed, by which a merger of two firms in an industry is quickly followed by similar marriages among other firms in the same industry.

The merger paradox can also be resolved by moving the setting to one of differentiated products in which firms compete in prices. In these markets, the merging firms can more easily commit to product variety and design choices that are typically sufficient to make merger profitable.

The ambiguous effects of mergers found in economic theory are also found in empirical analysis. To date, there is little clear evidence that mergers have systematically resulted in greatly enhanced profits for firms and losses for consumers. Even if such outcomes were common, however, the policy implications would be ambiguous, since total surplus might still increase. Indeed, a lively debate has recently emerged as to precisely what welfare criterion should be used in evaluating a proposed merger. Yet, whatever criterion is chosen, the central issue in any merger case is the likely effect the merger will have on the postmerger market—especially postmerger prices. Increasingly, economists have used sophisticated computer simulations to model the postmerger market as a means of resolving this question. However, the sensitivity of such simulations to seemingly innocuous changes in the specification of market demand, or to small variations in the estimated elasticity parameters, makes them less than conclusive as an analytical tool. This is an area where experienced judgment is likely to remain important as a guide to more formal econometric investigation and economic modeling.

Problems

1. Consider a spatial market comprised of a mass of N consumers distributed continuously around a circle of unit circumference. Each consumer buys at most one unit per period. If she does buy a good from a firm located at position x on the circle, a consumer located at position s on the circle earns utility $U(x, s) = V - p(x) - t|x - s|$, where t is the transport cost per unit of distance. There are M firms located $1/M$ distance apart symmetrically around the circle. Each firm has a production cost: $C(q) = F + cq$, where F and c are both positive

   a. Assume there is no price discrimination. Work out the equilibrium price and the equilibrium number of firms M, assuming each firm earns zero-profit (i.e., each earns just enough revenue to cover its fixed plus variable cost).

   b. Assume there is a computer innovation that allows personalized pricing or first-degree price discrimination. Work out the equilibrium average price and the equilibrium number of firms M, now under this alternative arrangement.

   c. Comparing 1a with 1b, what can you say about the ability of market structure to capture the intensity of price competition?

2. Suppose that one looks over the historical record of antitrust enforcement and finds that while the authorities have permitted some mergers and blocked others, the industry's average price has tended to fall whenever a merger has been permitted and occurred. Is it correct then to infer that the antitrust authorities should have been more lenient and permitted more mergers? Why or why not?

3. Assume an industry characterized by Cournot competition and populated by M identical firms, each with a marginal cost of c. Inverse demand $P = P(Q)$, with $P'(Q) < 0$, and $P'(Q) + QP''(Q) < 0$.

   a. Define $R_i = dq_i/dq_j$ as Firm i's best output response to an increase in Firm j's output. Show that

   $$R = \frac{dq_i}{dq_j} = -\frac{P' + q_i P''}{2P' + q_i P''} < 0$$

   b. Show that $-1 < R \leq 0$.

   c. Define Q_{-i} as the output of all firms other than Firm i. Consequently, the change in total industry output dQ is $dQ_{-i} + dq_i$. Use the result in 3a to show that we may then write

   $$dq_i = \frac{R}{1 + R} dQ = -\lambda dQ, \text{ where } \lambda = -\frac{R}{1 + R} > 0.$$

4. The result in 3b indicates how the optimal response of an individual firm in this Cournot setting will be related to a rise in total industry output. In turn, that rise in total output will be in response to some exogenous shock to Firm i's output.

   a. Recalling that $dQ = dQ_{-i} + dq_i$, show that when all firms respond optimally to an exogenous shock in Firm i's output, the change in total industry output is $\dfrac{dQ}{dq_i} = \dfrac{1}{1 + (N-1)\lambda}$.

b. Show that 4a implies that total output moves in the same direction as the change in the output of the firm whose production is exogenously shocked (Firm i) but by a smaller amount. That is, show that $0 < \dfrac{dQ}{dq_i} < 1$.

5. The results in problem 4 imply that a merger of, say, Firms 1 and 2 will raise total output—and therefore lower price—if the output of the merged firm exceeds the combined output of the two separate firms in the premerger market. Denote total premerger output as Q^0 and the premerger output of Firms 1 and 2 as q_1^0 and q_2^0, respectively. In addition, let the merged firm's new marginal cost be $c_M < c$. For the merged firms to wish to expand their total output beyond its premerger level, it must be the case that marginal revenue at that output level now exceeds the new lower marginal cost, c_M. That is, we must have: $P(Q^0) + (q_1^0 + q_2^0)P'(Q^0) > c_M$.

   a. Recalling that in the premerger market, it must be the case that $P(Q^0) + q_1^0 P'(Q^0) = c$; and also that $P(Q^0) + q_2^0 P'(Q^0) = c$; show that the condition for the merged firm to expand output (and so for price to fall) is $P(Q^0) - c_M > 2\left[P(Q^0) - c\right]$. In other words, for price to fall, the merged firm's margin of premerger price less its new unit cost must be twice the margin that the firms had in the premerger market.

   b. Show that we may alternatively write the necessary condition in 5a as $c - c_M > P(Q^0) - c$.

   c. Recall from Chapter 7 that in the premerger market with N symmetric firms, $\dfrac{P(Q^0)-c}{P(Q^0)} = \dfrac{1}{N\varepsilon}$ where ε is the elasticity of demand. Use this relationship to show that for the merger to lower the market price, we must have $\dfrac{c_M}{c} < \dfrac{1 - \frac{2}{N\varepsilon}}{1 - \frac{1}{N\varepsilon}}$. Use this expression to determine the percentage decline in unit cost that a merger must generate if it is to result in lower prices when there are initially five firms and the elasticity of demand is 1.

References

Andrade, G., M. Mitchell, and E. Stafford. 2001. "New Evidence and Perspectives on Mergers." *Journal of Economic Perspectives*, 15 (Spring): 103–120.

Armstrong, M. and J. Vickers. 2007. "A Model of Delegated Project Choice with Application to Merger Analysis." *Econometrica*, 78 (January): 213–244.

Baker, J. 2004. "Efficiencies and High Concentration: Heinz Proposes to Acquire Beech-Nut (2001)." In J. Kwoka and L. White, eds., *The Antitrust Revolution*. Oxford: Oxford University Press, 150–169.

Brito, D. 2003. "Preemptive Mergers under Spatial Competition." Working Paper, FCT, Universidade Nova de Lisboa.

Cabral, L. 2003. "Horizontal Mergers with Free Entry: Why Cost Efficiencies May Be a Weak Defense and Assets Sales A Poor Remedy." *International Journal of Industrial Organization*, 21 (May): 607–623.

Daughety, A. F. 1990. "Beneficial Concentration." *American Economic Review*, 80 (December): 1231–1237.

Davidson, C., and R. Deneckere. 1985. "Long-Run Competition in Capacity, Short-Run Competition in Price, and the Cournot Model." *The RAND Journal of Economics*, 17 (Autumn): 404–415.

Deaton, A., and J. Mulbauer. 1980. "An Almost Ideal Demand System." *American Economic Review*, 70 (June): 312–326.

Epstein, R., and D. Rubinfeld. 2002. "Merger Simulation: A Simplified Approach with New Applications." *Antitrust Law Journal*, 69: 883–920.

Farrell, J., and C. S. Shapiro. 1990. "Horizontal Mergers: An Equilibrium Analysis." *American Economic Review*, 80 (March): 107–126.

Gandhi, A., L. Froeb, S. Tschantz, and G. Werden. 2008. "Post-Merger Product Repositioning." *Journal of Industrial Economics*, 41 (March): 49–67.

Ganslandt, M., and P-J. Norbäck. 2004. "Do Mergers Result in Collusion?" Working Paper, Research Institute of Industrial Economics, Stockholm, Sweden.

Greenhut, J., G. Norman, and M. L. Greenhut. 1991. "Aspects of Airline Deregulation." *International Journal of Transport Economics*, 18 (January): 3–30.

Hotelling, H. 1929. "Stability in Competition." *Economic Journal*, 39 (January): 31–47.

Judd, K. 1985. "Credible Spatial Preemption." *Rand Journal of Economics*, 16 (Summer): 153–166.

Lichtenberg, F. and D. Siegel. 1992. "Takeovers and Corporate Overhead." In F. Lichtenberg, ed., *Corporate Takeovers and Productivity*. Cambridge, MA: MIT Press.

Lyons, B. 2002. "Could Politicians Be More Right Than Economists? A Theory of Mergers Standards." University of East Anglia, Center for Competition Policy, Working Paper 07-03.

Maskimovic, V., and G. Phillips. 2001. "The Market for Corporate Assets: Who Engages in Mergers and Assets Sales and Are There Efficiency Gains?" *Journal of Finance*, 56 (December): 2019–2065.

Mueller, D. C. 1985. "Mergers and Market Share." *Review of Economics and Statistics*, 67 (May): 259–267.

Norman, G., and J. F. Thisse. 1996. "Product Variety and Welfare under Soft and Tough Pricing Regimes." *Economic Journal*, 106 (January): 76–91.

Norman, G., J. F. Thisse, L. Pepall, and D. Richards. 2005. "Product Differentiation, Cost-Reducing Mergers, and Consumer Welfare." *Canadian Journal of Economics*, 38 (November): 1204–1223.

Perry, M., and R. Porter. 1985. "Oligopoly and the Incentive for Horizontal Merger." *American Economic Review*, 75 (January): 219–227.

Pittman, R. 2007. "Consumer Surplus as the Appropriate Standard for Antitrust Enforcement." Working Paper 07-9, Department of Justice, Economic Analysis Group.

Posada, P., and O. D. Straume. 2004. "Merger, Partial Collusions and Relocation." *Journal of Economics*, 83 (December): 243–265.

Ravenscraft, D. J., and F. M. Scherer. 1989. "The Profitability of Mergers." *International Journal of Industrial Organization*, (Special Issue) March: 101–116.

Reitzes, J. D., and D. T. Levy. 1995. "Price Discrimination and Mergers." *Canadian Journal of Economics*, 28 (May): 427–436.

Ross, T.W., and R.A. Winter. (2003). "Canadian Merger Policy following Superior Propane." *Canadian Competition Record*, 21 (May): 7–23.

Salant, S., S. Switzer, and R. Reynolds. 1983. "Losses from Horizontal Merger: The Effects of an Exogenous Change in Industry Structure on Cournot–Nash Equilibrium." *Quarterly Journal of Economics*, 98 (May): 185–213.

Salinger, M. 2005. "Four Questions About Horizontal Merger Enforcement." Remarks to ABA Economic Committee of Antitrust Section: 14 September.

Salop, S. C. 1979. "Monopolistic Competition with Outside Goods." *Bell Journal of Economics*, 10 (Spring): 141–156.

Schmalensee, R. 1978. "Entry Deterrence in the Ready-to-Eat Breakfast Cereal Industry." *Bell Journal of Economics*, 9 (Autumn): 305–327.

Slade, M. 2007. "Merger Simulations of Unilateral Effects: What Can We Learn from the UK Brewing Industry?" forthcoming in B. Lyons (Ed.), *Cases in European Competition Policy: The Economic Analysis*. Cambridge: Cambridge University Press.

Walker, M. 2005. "The Potential for Significant Inaccuracies in Merger Simulation Models." *Journal of Competition Law and Economics*, 1 (3): 473–496.

Werden, G., and L. Froeb. 1994. "The Effects of Mergers in Differentiated Products Industries: Logit Demand and Merger Policy." *Journal of Law, Economics, and Organizations*, 10 (October): 407–426.

————. 2002. "The Antitrust Logit Model for Predicting Unilateral Competitive Effects." *Antitrust Law Journal*, 70: 257–260.

12

Vertical and Conglomerate Mergers

In the fall of 2000, General Electric and Honeywell International announced that the two companies would merge, with GE acquiring Honeywell. GE is a major supplier of jet engines for commercial aircraft; its chief competitors are Rolls Royce and Pratt-Whitney. Honeywell had developed into a major aerospace firm whose products included electric lighting, ventilation units, and braking systems for aircraft and also starter motors for aircraft engines of the type GE builds. The deal was approved in the United States. However, in July 2001, the European Commission, following the recommendation of Competition Commissioner Mario Monti, blocked the merger.

The proposed GE-Honeywell merger was a marriage of firms manufacturing vertically related products. Any aircraft engine such as those that GE sells needs a starter motor and other related aircraft items such as those that Honeywell makes. Vertical mergers explicitly join firms operating at different levels of the production chain, say, a wholesaler and a retailer. In such cases, the joint interest between both firms in maximizing the sales of the final product is clear. However, the mutual interest when firms sell complementary goods like computer hardware and software or nuts and bolts is qualitatively the same as the vertical relation between Honeywell and GE. In all of these cases, two or more products are combined to yield the final good or service. Because a vertical relationship is just one of the many types of complementary relationships that may exist between firms, the term *vertical merger* has come to have the more general interpretation of any merger between firms that produce complementary products.

The separate production of complementary goods by firms with monopoly power reduces the joint profit of the firms and imposes an efficiency loss on firms and consumers. The intuition behind this result is straightforward. Each firm's pricing decision imposes an externality on the other firm(s). This suggests that cooperation (for example, through merger) by internalizing the externality leads to lower prices *and* higher profits—a Pareto improvement.

Precisely the same issues arise when the firms occupy different stages in the vertical production chain. This is important because it sheds light on how vertical mergers affect competition and consumer welfare. In the 1980s, the realization that vertical mergers can improve efficiency led to something of a revolution in antitrust policy. In the decades prior to 1980, vertical mergers were often seen as anticompetitive because of the fear that such mergers would facilitate foreclosure. That is, the merged firms would, after the merger, refuse to supply their products to other firms and thereby either drive them out of the market or otherwise adversely affect them.

Economists primarily associated with the Chicago School challenged this negative view of vertical mergers. They argued that vertical mergers could also achieve complementary efficiencies and that "vertical integration was most likely pro-competitive or competitively neutral" (Riordan 1998, p. 1232). By the 1980s, the Chicago School approach began to gain in the courts, and vertical mergers were treated increasingly favorably by the antitrust authorities. However, by the mid-1990s the pendulum once more began to swing the other way. A post-Chicago approach emerged based on game-theoretic analysis in which, once again, the potential for anticompetitive harm is real.

We begin this chapter by developing an analysis of how vertical mergers may enhance efficiency and also be used to facilitate price discrimination. The next three sections then present various models in which vertical mergers can lead to anticompetitive effects of precisely the nature the European Commission feared in the GE-Honeywell case. This is followed by a reappraisal of that decision and a more recent statistical study of the impact of vertical integration on prices and welfare. We also devote some brief attention to those mergers that involve neither substitute nor complementary products, namely, conglomerate mergers.

12.1   PROCOMPETITIVE VERTICAL MERGERS

When firms occupy different stages of the vertical chain, the convention is to label the firms farthest from the final consumer of the product as upstream and those closest to the consumer as downstream. These firms supply each other with *complementary* goods and services, since each firm in the vertical chain provides an essential service to other firms in the chain. Such vertical or complementary relationships between firms with monopoly power lead to a loss of economic efficiency in the absence of some mechanism to coordinate the decisions of the firms. In the case of vertically related firms, this is referred to as the *problem of double marginalization*.

To see why, suppose that we have a single upstream supplier, the manufacturer, who sells a unique product to a single downstream firm, the retailer. The manufacturer produces the good at constant unit cost, c, and sells it to the retailer at a wholesale price, r. The retailer resells the product to consumers at the market-clearing price, P. For simplicity, we assume that the retailer has no other retailing cost. Assume that consumer demand for the good is given by the linear inverse demand function $P = A - BQ$, where we assume of course that $c < A$.

Given that the retailer purchases Q units from the manufacturer at wholesale price r and resells these Q units to consumers at price $P = A - BQ$, the retailer's profit is

$$\pi^D(Q, r) = (P - r)Q = (A - BQ)Q - rQ \qquad (12.1)$$

It follows immediately that the profit maximizing output for the retailer is

$$Q^D = (A - r)/2B \qquad (12.2)$$

Substituting Q^D into the inverse demand function gives the market-clearing retail price $P^D = (A + r)/2$. From (12.1) the retailer's profit is, therefore, $\pi^D = (A - r)^2/4B$.

What about the manufacturer? What wholesale price should be charged? Equation (12.2) makes clear that the wholesale price determines the number of units the upstream supplier sells to the retailer. At the wholesale price r, the retailer sells $Q^D = (A - r)/2B$ units and so purchases this number of units from the manufacturer. In other words, $Q = (A - r)/2B$ describes the relationship between the wholesale price r set by the manufacturer and the quantity of his product demanded by the retailer. But this means that when the retailer has no marginal costs other than the input price charged by the manufacturer, the inverse demand facing the upstream manufacturer at wholesale price r is $r = A - 2BQ$, which is also the marginal revenue function facing the retailer.[1]

The manufacturer's profit is:

$$\pi^U(Q) = (r - c)Q = (A - 2BQ - c)Q \qquad (12.3)$$

Maximizing with respect to Q and substituting in the manufacturer's inverse demand function gives the profit-maximizing output and price for the manufacturer:

$$Q^U = \frac{A - c}{4B}; \quad r^U = \frac{A + c}{2} \qquad (12.4)$$

When the upstream manufacturer sets the price $r^U = (A + c)/2$, the downstream retailer charges a price $P^D = (A + r^U)/2 = (3A + c)/4$. The retailer sells $Q^D = (A - c)/4B$ units, which is, of course, precisely the amount the upstream manufacturer anticipated it would sell when it set its upstream price $r^U = (A + c)/2$. The profit of the manufacturer is $\pi^U = (A - c)^2/8B$, the profit of the retailer is $\pi^D = (A - c)^2/16B$, and the combined profit of the two firms is $3(A - c)^2/16B$. These results are illustrated in Figure 12.1.

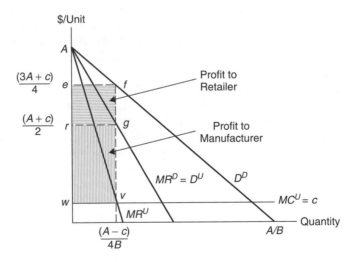

Figure 12.1   Upstream and downstream profit maximization without vertical integration
The retailer's marginal revenue curve MR_B is the manufacturer's demand curve D_U. Double marginalization results when the manufacturer sets its optimal wholesale price $r = (A + c)/2$ above marginal cost c, after which the retailer adds a further markup by setting retail price $P = (3A + c)/4$. Retail profit is area $refg$. The manufacturer's profit is area $wrgv$.

---

[1]   If, by contrast, the retailer has additional marginal costs of c^D, then the inverse demand facing the manufacturer is $r = (A - c^D) - 2BQ$.

Suppose now that the two firms merge so that the manufacturer becomes the upstream division of an integrated firm, supplying its output to the downstream retail division of the same parent company. This transforms the integrated firm into a simple monopoly whose goal is to maximize monopoly profit through its choice of retail price P. Profit is total revenue PQ minus total cost cQ, which is

$$\pi^I = (A - BQ - c)Q \tag{12.5}$$

The profit-maximizing output of the integrated firm and the retail price that the firm sets to consumers are then

$$Q^I = \frac{A - c}{2B}; \quad P^I = \frac{A + c}{2} \tag{12.6}$$

These outcomes are illustrated in Figure 12.2. The merger of the manufacturer and retailer results in consumers benefiting from a lower price and so consuming a greater quantity. Moreover, the profit earned by the integrated firm is $\pi^I = (A - c)^2/4B$, which is greater than the aggregate premerger profit of the manufacturer and the retailer. From a social welfare point of view, *integrating the two monopoly firms has benefited everyone*. Both total profit and consumer surplus increase.

Merger of vertically related firms generates an all-around efficiency gain, because it allows the related activities to internalize the externality that each imposes on the other. In the absence of coordination, the final product price reflects double marginalization. The independent manufacturer marks up its price to the retailer, who then adds a further markup in setting a price to the consumer. This is the basis of the old saying, "What is worse than a monopoly? A chain of monopolies!"

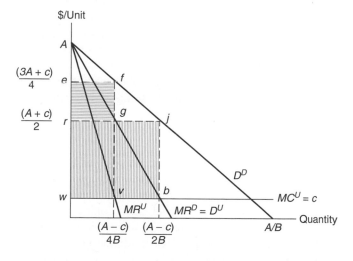

Figure 12.2 Upstream and downstream profit maximization with vertical integration
An integrated manufacturer-retailer sets a retail price to consumers at $P = (A + c)/2$. The area *refg* that would have been profit for a nonintegrated retailer now becomes part of consumer surplus. However, the increased sales volume generates a more than offsetting profit gain of area *gjbv*. Total profit for the integrated firm is *rjbw*.

There is, however, one qualification that we should mention. The benefits of vertical merger just described assume that the downstream firm uses a fixed amount of the upstream firm's product for every unit of output that the downstream firm sells. In our example of a manufacturer and a downstream retailer, this assumption makes sense. The retailer has to have one unit of the manufacturer's product for every unit it sells to its customers. But in other situations, this assumption could be too strong. For example, if the upstream firm is a steel producer and the downstream firm is an automobile manufacturer, the steel firm's decision to charge the car manufacturer a price that includes a high markup may induce the automaker to substitute aluminum or fiberglass for steel. The potential gains of the car manufacturer integrating backward into the steel market are then less dramatic.

Yet, the qualitative flavor of the analysis generally carries through. Vertical and, more generally, complementary mergers permit the correction of a market failure that results when independent firms fail to internalize the external effects of their strategic actions. While these benefits most clearly arise when the downstream firms have no ability to substitute for the complementary or upstream inputs, the general problem tends to persist whenever input substitution is limited.

12.2   VERTICAL MERGERS, PRICE DISCRIMINATION, AND COMPETITION

The foregoing analysis suggests that the antitrust authorities should be less concerned about the welfare impact of vertical mergers than of horizontal mergers. However, we have assumed that there is a single market in which the final output is sold and that there is monopoly at each stage in the vertical chain. Before coming to the general conclusion that vertical mergers are good for firms and consumers, we should check on the effects of relaxing these assumptions.

There are many cases in which downstream firms differ in their willingness to pay for an upstream firm's product. Examples include a wholesaler supplying retailers in different cities, a manufacturer of motorcar parts supplying automakers in different countries, a consultant advising different firms in different industries, and so on. In these settings, the upstream firm will wish to price discriminate across these different buyers.

Our earlier discussions of price discrimination noted that successful price discrimination has two requirements. First, the firm must be able to identify buyers of different types. Second, the firm must somehow prevent arbitrage, or resale of its product among its buyers. For now, we assume that the firm has somehow solved the identification problem. What can the firm do to surmount the arbitrage problem?

The simplest approach would be for the upstream firm to write a no-resale contract with its buyers. In many circumstances, however, such contracts are unenforceable—for example when the client firms are in different legal jurisdictions—in which case some other approach is necessary. One such approach is for the upstream firm to merge with some or all of its downstream customers.

To make matters simple, suppose that the upstream firm supplies two downstream firms in separate markets. Each downstream firm has different and independent final product demands but we assume that the upstream firm cannot prevent arbitrage between its downstream buyers. If financing were unlimited, the upstream supplier could integrate into both markets, but we will instead imagine that there are binding financial constraints that limit the upstream firm to integrating forward into only one of these markets.

Assume that the upstream firm has constant marginal costs of c^U. Further assume, as in our earlier example, that each downstream firm requires exactly one unit of the upstream firm's product to make a unit of final output. The downstream firms each have constant marginal cost, for all inputs other than the input supplied by the upstream firm, of c^D. Inverse demand in the two final product markets is

$$P_1 = A_1 - B_1.Q_1; \; P_2 = A_2 - B_2.Q_2 \tag{12.7}$$

(i) No Integration

Consider first the situation in which the upstream firm does not integrate forward into the downstream. Because the firm cannot prevent arbitrage between the downstream firms it must charge them the same input price r. Profit to each downstream firm is

$$\pi_i = \left(P_i - c^D - r\right)Q_i = \left(A_i - B_i Q_i - c^D - r\right)Q_i \qquad i = 1, 2 \tag{12.8}$$

Downstream, Firm i chooses output Q_i to maximize profit, which from equation (12.8) gives

$$Q_i = \left(A_i - c^D - r\right)/2B_i \qquad i = 1, 2 \tag{12.9}$$

The aggregate derived demand facing the upstream firm, $Q_1 + Q_2 = Q^U$, is then, in inverse form

$$r = \frac{A_1 B_2 + A_2 B_1 - (B_1 + B_2)c^D}{B_1 + B_2} - \frac{2B_1 B_2}{B_1 + B_2}Q^U \tag{12.10}$$

Profit of the upstream firm is

$$\pi^U = \left(r - c^U\right)Q^U \tag{12.11}$$

Substituting from (12.10) and maximizing with respect to Q^U gives the profit-maximizing aggregate output and retail price for the upstream firm:

$$Q^U = \frac{A_1 B_2 + A_2 B_1 - (B_1 + B_2)\left(c^U + c^D\right)}{4B_1 B_2};$$

$$r^U = \frac{A_1 B_2 + A_2 B_1 - (B_1 + B_2)\left(c^D - c^U\right)}{2(B_1 + B_2)} \tag{12.12}$$

Profit of the upstream firm is

$$\pi^U = \frac{\left(A_1 B_2 + A_2 B_1 - (B_1 + B_2)\left(c^U + c^D\right)\right)^2}{8B_1 B_2(B_1 + B_2)} \tag{12.13}$$

Substituting equation (12.12) into (12.9) gives the output of each downstream firm. Then from equation (12.7), the final product price that each downstream firm charges

$$Q_i^D = \frac{A_i\left(2B_i + B_j\right) - A_j B_i - \left(B_i + B_j\right)\left(c^U + c^D\right)}{4B_i\left(B_i + B_j\right)}$$

$$\qquad\qquad\qquad\qquad\qquad\qquad\qquad\qquad i, j = 1, 2, i \neq j \quad (12.14)$$

$$P_i^D = \frac{A_i\left(2B_i + 3B_j\right) + A_j B_i + \left(B_i + B_j\right)\left(c^U + c^D\right)}{4\left(B_i + B_j\right)}$$

Profit of each downstream firm therefore is

$$\pi_i^D = \frac{\left(A_i\left(2B_i + B_j\right) - A_i B_j - \left(B_i + B_j\right)\left(c^U + c^D\right)\right)^2}{16B_i\left(B_i + B_j\right)^2} \qquad i, j = 1, 2, i \neq j \quad (12.15)$$

The difference between the two downstream prices is

$$P_i^D - P_j^D = \frac{A_i - A_j}{2} \qquad i, j = 1, 2, i \neq j \qquad\qquad\qquad\qquad (12.16)$$

Price is higher in the downstream market with the higher reservation price A_i.

The comparison of profits is more complicated. Suppose that the inverse demands in the downstream markets have the same slope $B_1 = B_2 = B$. Then

$$\pi_i^D - \pi_j^D = \frac{\left(A_i - A_j\right)\left(A_i + A_j - 2\left(c^U + c^D\right)\right)}{8B} \qquad i, j = 1, 2, i \neq j \qquad (12.17)$$

Suppose, by contrast, that the inverse demands in the downstream markets have the same maximum reservations prices $A_1 = A_2 = A$. Then

$$\pi_i^D - \pi_j^D = \frac{\left(B_j - B_i\right)\left(A - c^U - c^D\right)^2}{16B_i B_j} \qquad i, j = 1, 2, i \neq j \qquad (12.18)$$

Not surprisingly, profit is higher in downstream market i if it has a higher maximum reservation price A_i and a lower slope B_i since then market i is in some sense larger than market j. By contrast, profit in market i may be higher or lower than profit in market j if it has a higher (resp. lower) reservation price and a higher (resp. lower) slope.

(ii) Integration Forward into Market i

Recall that we assumed that financial constraints limit the upstream firm to integrating into only one downstream market. The firm must then strategically choose the market into which it will integrate. Suppose that the upstream firm integrates forward into downstream market i. Since we have assumed that the downstream markets are independent of each other, the upstream firm will supply its downstream division i at marginal cost c^U and will set a wholesale price r to downstream firm j. The arbitrage problem is solved since the integrated firm can refuse to supply its final product to buyers in market j.

Profit to the integrated firm from supplying the integrated market i is

$$\pi_i = \left(P_i - c^U - c^D\right)Q_i = \left(A_i - B_i Q_i - c^U - c^D\right)Q_i \qquad\qquad (12.19)$$

Maximizing with respect to Q_i gives the quantity, price, and profit:

$$Q_i = \frac{A_i - c^U - c^D}{2B_i}; \quad P_i = \frac{1}{2}(A_i + c^U + c^D); \quad \pi_i = \frac{(A_i - c^U - c^D)^2}{4B_i}. \quad (12.20)$$

Profit of the downstream firm in the nonintegrated market j is

$$\pi_j^D = (P_j - c^D - r)Q_j = (A_j - B_j Q_j - c^D - r)Q_j \quad (12.21)$$

Maximizing with respect to Q_j gives the derived inverse demand for the upstream firm's product:

$$r = A_j - c^D - 2B_j Q_j^U \quad (12.22)$$

The upstream firm's profit from supplying market j is: $\pi_j^U = (r - c^U)Q_j^U$. So, substituting from equation (12.22) and maximizing with respect to Q_j^U yields the complete solution for the output, wholesale price and profit that the upstream firm earns in this market:

$$Q_j^D = \frac{A_j - c^U - c^D}{4B_j}; \quad r_j^U = \frac{1}{2}(A_j + c^U - c^D); \quad \pi_j^U = \frac{(A_j - c^U - c^D)^2}{8B_j} \quad (12.23)$$

Finally, by substituting the above into equations (12.7) and (12.21), we obtain the price and profit for downstream firm j:

$$P_j^D = \frac{1}{4}(3A_j + c^U + c^D); \quad \pi_j^D = \frac{(A_j - c^U - c^D)^2}{16B_j} \quad (12.24)$$

What is the impact of this merger? For consumers in the integrated market i, comparison of equations (12.20) and (12.14) gives us

$$Q_i - Q_i^D = \frac{A_i B_j + A_j B_i - (B_i + B_j)(c^U + c^D)}{4B_i(B_i + B_j)} > 0 \quad (12.25)$$

These consumers gain from the merger. What about consumers and the downstream firm in the nonintegrated market j? Both will gain if the merger reduces the wholesale price charged to firm j, since this will lead to a lower final product price and higher profits. Hence, we compare equations (12.12) and (12.23). This comparison reveals that

$$r_j^U - r^U = \frac{B_j(A_j - A_i)}{2(B_j + B_i)} \quad (12.26)$$

Consumers and the final-product firm in nonintegrated downstream market j gain (lose) from the merger if the reservation price in market j is lower (higher) than that in market i.

This raises the question of which market the upstream will choose when it integrates forward.[2] From equations (12.20) and (12.24), the aggregate profit for the integrated firm, if it integrates into downstream market i and sells strategically to market j, is

$$\pi_i^a = \pi_i + \pi_j^U = \frac{1}{8} \left(\frac{2\left(A_i - c^U - c^D\right)^2}{B_i} + \frac{\left(A_j - c^U - c^D\right)^2}{B_j} \right) \quad i, j = 1, 2, i \neq j$$

(12.27)

Denote $\tilde{A}_i = A_i - c^D - c^U$. Then, equation (12.27) implies that the difference in profit from integrating into downstream market i rather than j is

$$\pi_i^a - \pi_j^a = \frac{1}{8} \left(\frac{\tilde{A}_i^2}{B_i} - \frac{\tilde{A}_j^2}{B_j} \right)$$

(12.28)

Suppose that final product demands have the same slope. In that case, the upstream firm will prefer to integrate forward into the market with the higher reservation price. From equation (12.26), consumers and the nonintegrated firm in the nonintegrated market lose from such a merger. Is it possible for a merger to benefit all consumers and the independent firm even if $A_i > A_j$? The upstream firm will choose to integrate into downstream market j if

$$B_j < B_i \left(\tilde{A}_j / \tilde{A}_i \right)^2$$

(12.29)

Simply put, for the upstream firm to choose to integrate into downstream market j—in which demand is more elastic, since we assume $A_i > A_j$—it is necessary that the slope of the final-product inverse demand function in market j is "small enough."

Is a merger that is intended to facilitate price discrimination efficient? If the condition in equation (12.29) is satisfied, then the answer is yes. In that case, all parties gain from the merger. However, if this condition is not satisfied, matters are less clear-cut. The merger increases profit for the merged firm and removes double marginalization in one group of markets. However, it increases prices and reduces profit in the remaining markets. In other words, some consumers (and firms) gain and others lose from the vertical merger. The overall effect is uncertain and can be resolved only when we have more information on the precise nature of demand in the various markets.

12.3   VERTICAL MERGERS, OLIGOPOLY, AND FORECLOSURE

So far, we have assumed that there is monopoly in both upstream and downstream markets.[3] This is important because, had we instead assumed either a competitive manufacturing sector or a competitive retail sector, no double marginalization would occur.

---

[2]   We need not worry about whether the merger is profitable for the integrated firms. After all, the worst that the upstream firm can do postmerger is to replicate the premerger, nondiscriminatory wholesale price.

[3]   In our price discrimination analysis we assumed that the downstream markets are independent, effectively making the downstream firms monopolists in their respective markets.

When competitive manufacturers sell to a retail monopolist, they sell at marginal cost. So, any markup added at the retail level will not come on top of an already existing one. Similarly, if an upstream monopolist sells to a competitive retail sector, the upstream firm's markup will be the only one, since competition now drives the dealers to sell at cost. In either of these cases, then, no double marginalization can occur, and there is no efficiency gain to vertical integration.

Of course, both pure monopoly and perfect competition are relatively rare in the real world. It therefore seems reasonable to consider vertical mergers in the more realistic setting in which both upstream and downstream markets are oligopolies. Perhaps not surprisingly, we find that, while there may be gains from a vertical merger in this setting due to a reduction in the degree of double marginalization, there is now another motive for vertical integration that is more clearly anticompetitive. This is the possibility of *market foreclosure*. The integrated company may choose to deny downstream rivals a source of inputs—or upstream competitors a market for their products. If so, the impact of vertical mergers in this case is much less clear.

Consider a hypothetical case in which two suppliers of computer chips compete for sales to two downstream computer manufacturers who in turn sell to the general public. We assume all competition is in prices and that the chips of the two upstream firms are identical. However, the two downstream firms are assumed to occupy different locations—either in geographic or product space—so that each can sell positive amounts at different prices. The assumption of identical chips together with price competition implies, of course, that each chipmaker sells at marginal cost and earns no economic profit. The assumption that the downstream manufacturers sell differentiated products and compete in prices means that each has an upward-sloping best-response function (prices are strategic complements), as well as implying that each will earn a positive surplus.

The intuition as to why a vertical merger might, in this case, be anticompetitive is relatively straightforward. Suppose that a chipmaker and a computer firm merge. The integrated computer producer can still acquire chips at marginal cost (internally now). So, in this respect, the market equilibrium has not changed. However, this integrated firm might refuse to sell any of its chips to its rival in the computer business (i.e., it might foreclose this chip supply to its rival). Why? How does this change anything if the remaining independent computer maker still has the ability to buy chips from the remaining independent chip firm?

The answer to these questions is straightforward. True, foreclosure does not eliminate the independent computer firm's access to all chip supplies. There is still the one independent chip firm remaining. What foreclosure does do, though, is give that surviving chipmaker a *monopoly* in dealing with the independent computer manufacturer. This supplier will, accordingly, set a higher wholesale price for its chips knowing now that it is freed from pricing at marginal cost. Faced with a higher cost, the independent computer firm will be forced to raise its downstream price. In turn, this permits the merged firm to raise its downstream computer price and earn more profit. The merger does not generate any cost savings. The integrated firm still buys at cost. However, by changing the relationship between the now independent firms, the merger has introduced an inefficiency. Indeed, it has introduced double marginalization where none previously existed. The upstream chipmaker can now charge a price that includes a markup over cost. Subsequently, the downstream computer firm marks the wholesale price up further.

Consumers face higher computer prices on both counts. This vertical integration clearly reduces welfare.[4]

Fears of foreclosure are common. The telecommunications industry in both the United States and in Europe has historically been one in which a local telephone network is monopolized by a firm that also provides long-distance service in competition with other long-distance firms. Since a long-distance provider has to gain access to its potential customers by connecting to the local network, the local network provider has the potential to price its long-distance competitors out of the market by charging them a very high price for network access or, in an extreme case, denying them access to the local network at all. Accordingly, a major concern of the regulatory authorities has been the prices that suppliers of local telephone networks are allowed to charge for access to the local network.[5]

Similarly, Alcoa has often been accused of using its near-monopoly position in the aluminum ingot market to squeeze or foreclose its rivals in downstream markets such as the aluminum sheet market. It has also been accused of the similar practice of making contractual arrangements with power companies to prevent them from supplying vital electricity to competing aluminum producers. Such examples can be multiplied many times over. They not only reflect a fear that the vertical merger may lead to a welfare loss with consequent disadvantages for consumers, but—as the telephone and aluminum examples suggest—also reflect the fear that monopoly power in one market may be leveraged into power in another.

Yet, while the fear that a vertical merger may lead to foreclosure and harm competition is common, it must be justified by more than the intuitively appealing computers-and-chips scenario that we gave above. That analysis does not provide anything like a formal proof that the merger will lead to foreclosure. Nor does it consider the obvious response by the remaining independent firms, namely, to merge and acquire the benefits of vertical integration as well. In the following two sections, we describe two models that directly address these concerns. The first, due to Salinger (1988), is based on Cournot competition. The second, due to Ordover, Saloner, and Salop (1990), is set in a differentiated-products framework and assumes Bertrand competition.

12.3.1   Vertical Integration and Foreclosure in a Cournot Model

Consider a market with N^U upstream intermediate-goods producers and N^D downstream final-goods producers. Let n of these firms be vertically integrated, so that there are $N^U - n$ independent upstream producers and $N^D - n$ independent downstream producers. Each upstream firm has a constant marginal cost of c^U and each downstream firm a constant marginal cost of c^D. Inverse demand for the final good is linear and given by $P = A - BQ_F$, where Q_F is aggregate output of the final good. Exactly one unit of the intermediate good is needed to make one unit of the final good. For simplicity, we normalize the model by setting $A = B = 1$.

The formal model is a two-stage game. In the first stage, the upstream firms choose their outputs. This determines the intermediate-good price P^U that is charged to the independent downstream firms. In the second stage, the downstream divisions of the integrated

---

[4]   For a description of ways that an integrated firm can impose a cost squeeze, see Krattenmaker and Salop (1986).

[5]   Chipty (2001) describes how foreclosure can happen in the cable TV industry.

firms and independent downstream firms choose their outputs taking P^U as given. This yields the equilibrium final good price P^D.

Imagine now that the game has been played and we can observe the equilibrium just described. We first check whether the integrated firms would choose to foreclose on the intermediate product market, that is, whether they would neither buy this good from an external supplier nor sell it to an independent downstream rival. First, note that for independent upstream firms to be in business, it must be the case that $P^U > c^U$. Analogously, for independent downstream firms to be in business, we must have $P^D > P^U + c^D$. The first inequality makes clear that an integrated firm loses profit if it buys the intermediate product from an independent upstream firm rather than making the product itself. Likewise, the second inequality implies that the integrated firm will not sell the intermediate product to an independent downstream rival. However, understanding this implication requires a proof by contradiction.

To this end, suppose that the integrated firm actually did supply rivals with the intermediate good. Specifically, imagine that it currently sells X units of its intermediate good to independent rivals at price P^U. What would happen if instead it withdrew these units and sold them internally to its own downstream division, so that total output and therefore price in the downstream market remain unchanged? In withdrawing the units from the market, the integrated firm loses profit per unit of $P^U - c^U$. However, it gains profit per unit of $P^D - (c^U + c^D)$ on the new internal sales. Hence, it will be profitable to stop selling to downstream rivals (i.e., to foreclose) if $P^D - (c^U + c^D) > P^U - c^U$. Yet all that this requires is that $P^D > (P^U + c^D)$. However, as noted above, this condition has to hold, given that independent downstream rivals are in business. So, foreclosure is a rational action for integrated firms.

In equilibrium, we now know that integrated firms source their intermediate inputs internally, while nonintegrated downstream firms buy from independent upstream firms. Now consider the downstream market and suppose that the integrated firms are firms $i = 1, \ldots, n$. Furthermore, assume that $c^U = c^D = 0$. The profit of the downstream division of integrated Firm i is

$$\pi_i^D = P^D q_i^D = \left(1 - (q_i^D + Q_{-i}^D)\right) q_i^D \qquad i = 1, \ldots, n \tag{12.30}$$

where Q_{-i}^D is aggregate output of all downstream producers other than Firm (or downstream division) i. The profit of nonintegrated downstream Firm j is

$$\pi_j^D = \left(P^D - P^U\right) q_j^D = \left(1 - (q_j^D + Q_{-j}^D) - P^U\right) q_j^D \, (j = n + 1, \ldots, N^D) \tag{12.31}$$

where Q_{-j}^D is aggregate output of all downstream producers other than Firm j.

The first-order conditions for the two types of downstream firm are

$$\frac{\partial \pi_i^D}{\partial q_i^D} = 1 - Q_{-i}^D - 2q_i^D$$

$$\qquad \qquad i = 1, \ldots, n; \, j = n + 1, \ldots, N^D \tag{12.32}$$

$$\frac{\partial \pi_j^D}{\partial q_j^D} = 1 - P^U - Q_{-j}^D - 2q_j^D$$

Of course, the choice of outputs must be symmetric. All integrated divisions choose the same outputs, and all nonintegrated firms choose the same outputs. As a result, we can write both that $Q^D_{-i} = (n-1)q^D_i + (N^D - n)q^D_j$ and that $Q^D_{-j} = nq^D_i + (N^D - n - 1)q^D_j$. Substituting these results into equation (12.32) then yields two linear equations in two unknowns. These are

$$1 - (n+1)q^D_i - (N^D - n)q^D_j = 0$$

$$1 - P^U - nq^D_i - (N^D - n + 1)q^D_j = 0 \qquad i = 1, \ldots, n; \; j = n+1, \ldots, N^D \qquad (12.33)$$

Solving for the equilibrium outputs q^D_i and q^D_j gives

$$q^D_i = \frac{1 + (N^D - n)P^U}{(N^D + 1)}$$

$$\qquad i = 1, \ldots, n; \; j = n+1, \ldots, N^D \qquad (12.34)$$

$$q^D_j = \frac{1 - (n+1)P^U}{(N^D + 1)}$$

Since one unit of the intermediate good is needed to produce one unit of the final good, aggregate demand Q^U for the intermediate good supplied by the nonintegrated upstream producers is $Q^U = (N^D - n)q^D_j$. Solving for P^U then gives the derived inverse demand function for the upstream product:

$$P^U = \frac{1}{n+1} - \frac{(N^D + 1)}{(n+1)(N^D - n)} Q^U \qquad (12.35)$$

This is a linear function of the form $P = a - bQ$, where $a = 1/(n+1)$ and $b = (N^D + 1)/(n+1)(N^D - n)$. Standard Cournot analysis (Chapter 7) tells us that with our cost normalization and with $N^U - n$ independent upstream firms, the equilibrium upstream price is $P = a/(N^U - n + 1)$. That is

$$P^U = \frac{1}{(n+1)(N^U - n + 1)} \qquad (12.36)$$

We can check on how this is affected by additional mergers by differentiating with respect to n to obtain[6]

$$\frac{\partial P^U}{\partial n} = \frac{2n - N^U}{(n+1)^2(N^D - n + 1)^2} \qquad (12.37)$$

As an inspection of equation (12.37) quickly reveals, the analysis implies that for an additional vertical merger to reduce the intermediate product price, no more than half of the upstream firms should be divisions of vertically merged firms. While this result is interesting, we need to recognize that a reduction in the intermediate product price is not a sufficient condition for a vertical merger to benefit consumers. Nevertheless, the result in equation (12.37) is useful, and we will return to it later in the analysis.

---

[6]   In contrast to the Daughety (1990) analysis of Chapter 11, an additional vertical merger does not change the number of upstream and downstream firms N^U and N^D; it merely changes their types.

Standard analysis also tells us that the Cournot equilibrium output of each nonintegrated upstream firm is $a/b(N^U - n + 1)$. So output and profit of each independent upstream firm are, from equation (12.35)

$$q_j^U = \frac{(N^D - n)}{(N^D + 1)(N^U - n + 1)};$$

$$\pi_j^U = \frac{(N^D - n)}{(n + 1)(N^D + 1)(N^U - n + 1)^2} \qquad j = n + 1, \ldots, N^U$$

(12.38)

Substituting the intermediate product price from equation (12.36) into the downstream output equations (12.34) gives the equilibrium outputs for each integrated downstream division and nonmerged downstream firm:

$$q_i^D = \frac{1}{(N^D + 1)}\left(1 + \frac{(N^D - n)}{(n + 1)(N^U - n + 1)}\right)$$

$$i = 1, \ldots, n; j = n + 1, \ldots, N^D \qquad (12.39)$$

$$q_j^D = \frac{1}{(N^D + 1)}\left(1 - \frac{1}{(N^U - n + 1)}\right)$$

As we would expect, the integrated downstream firms produce more output than the nonintegrated firms, since they have lower input costs. Aggregating equations (12.39) over the n integrated and $N^D - n$ nonintegrated firms gives aggregate output and the equilibrium final product price

$$Q^D = \frac{N^D}{N^D + 1}\left(1 - \frac{(N^D - n)}{N^D(n + 1)(N^U - n + 1)}\right)$$

$$P^D = \frac{1}{N^D + 1}\left(1 + \frac{(N^D - n)}{(n + 1)(N^U - n + 1)}\right)$$

(12.40)

Since unit cost is 0, the profit of an integrated downstream firm[7] is $P^D q_i^D$, while the profit of a nonintegrated downstream firm is $(P^D - P^U)q_j^D$. Substituting from equations (12.36), (12.39), and (12.40) gives these two different profit levels:

$$\pi_i^D = \frac{1}{(N^D + 1)^2}\left(1 + \frac{(N^D - n)}{(n + 1)(N^U - n + 1)}\right)^2$$

$$i = 1, \ldots, n; j = n + 1, \ldots, N^D \qquad (12.41)$$

$$\pi_j^D = \frac{(N^U - n)^2}{(N^D + 1)^2(N^U - n + 1)^2}$$

Equation (12.41) makes clear that each additional vertical merger—each increase in n—reduces the profit of the remaining nonmerged downstream firms. In addition, we

[7]   Since the integrated firm supplies the intermediate product at marginal cost, this is also aggregate profit for the integrated firm.

know that since each integrated downstream firm has greater output and wider price-cost margins than does each nonmerged downstream firm, the integrated downstream firms are more profitable than their nonintegrated rivals.

We may now evaluate the impact that additional mergers have on the final product price and therefore on consumers. In general, this will depend on the interplay between two forces. One of these forces is what we might call the *competition effect*. A vertical merger and market foreclosure reduces the number of independent upstream suppliers. It therefore reduces upstream competitive pressure and so raises upstream prices—and, hence, downstream prices as well. The opposing force is what we might call the *efficiency effect*. A vertical merger eliminates double marginalization for the merged firms and, by reducing their input costs, makes them fiercer competitors in the downstream market. This effect tends to reduce consumer prices. We can see how the balance of these forces plays out by differentiating equation (12.40) with respect to n to obtain

$$\frac{\partial P^D}{\partial n} = \frac{1}{N^D + 1}\left(\frac{2nN^D - N^U\left(N^D + 1\right) - n^2 - 1}{(n+1)^2\left(N^U - n + 1\right)^2}\right) \tag{12.42}$$

The sign of this expression is fully determined by the numerator $Z = 2nN^D - N^U(N^D + 1) - n^2 - 1$. Note that this is clearly negative if $2n < N^U$. Recall that this is also the condition for a merger to reduce the intermediate-product price noted earlier in equation (12.37). Thus, we now can conclude that any vertical merger that lowers the price in the intermediate-good market will also reduce the final product price.

Next, note that if $N^D = N^U = N$, then Z can be written $Z = -(1 + N) - (N - n)^2 < 0$. Thus, an additional vertical merger will reduce the final product price whenever there is the same number of upstream as downstream firms. More generally, Salinger notes that $Z < 0$ if $N^D < N^U + 1$. In other words, for an additional vertical merger to benefit consumers, there must be at least as many upstream as downstream firms. The intuition is reasonably straightforward. The final product price increases when the competition effect outweighs the efficiency effect; but when there are "many" upstream firms, the competition effect is weakened.

Thus, Salinger's model shows that vertical mergers will generally be associated with foreclosure and also reveals the conditions (when $Z > 0$) under which, partly as a result, such a merger will raise prices to final consumers. This is no small accomplishment. At the same time, there are two important strategic issues that remain to be addressed. First, since integrated firms are more profitable than are their nonintegrated rivals, one wonders why all firms do not pursue vertical integration. A clue to at least part of the answer may lie in equation (12.41), which shows that any additional merger that reduces the downstream product price also reduces the profits of the integrated firms. This then raises a second strategic issue, namely, whether the integrated firms take steps to limit other firms from also joining vertically. To address this point, as well as to explore other features of vertical mergers, we now consider the Ordover, Saloner, and Salop (1990) (OSS) model.

12.3.2   Vertical Mergers in a Differentiated Products Setting

The OSS model is in some ways simpler and in others more complex than the Salinger model. It is simpler in that we confine the analysis to a market in which there are two upstream firms and two downstream firms. It is more complex in that we treat the relationships between upstream and downstream firms more strategically.

The upstream firms incur constant marginal cost c^U. One unit of the upstream product is needed for every unit of downstream production; the downstream firms have no other production costs. In contrast to the Salinger model, firms compete in prices in both markets. The upstream product of the two firms is homogeneous, but the downstream products are differentiated. We capture this feature by letting the demand for downstream product $i = 1, 2$ be

$$q_i^D = A - p_i^D + B(p_j^D - p_i^D) \qquad (i = 1, 2; 0 < B < \infty) \tag{12.43}$$

In equation (12.43), B is an inverse measure of the degree of product differentiation in the downstream market. If $B = 0$, the two products are totally differentiated. However, as B approaches infinity the two products become increasingly similar. As in the Salinger model, we can normalize $A = 1$ and $c^U = 0$, without loss of generality.[8]

In order to consider the explicitly strategic aspects of vertical mergers, OSS develops a four-stage game. In the first stage, one of the downstream firms can choose to acquire one of the upstream suppliers. If such a merger takes place, we assume—again, without loss of generality—that it is between $U1$ and $D1$ and results in the merged firm $F1$.

In the second stage, input prices are set. If no merger occurs, then the upstream firms compete in prices. If a merger has occurred, then in the second stage two possibilities are considered. First, $F1$ refuses to supply $D2$, that is, foreclosure. Second, $F1$ sets an upper bound on the input price to be paid by $D2$ by offering to supply it at price c_{12}, with $F1$ setting c_{12} before $U2$ sets its input price. In the third stage, if there has been a merger in the first stage, Firms $U2$ and $D2$ decide whether or not to merge. We then proceed to the fourth stage. Here, downstream prices are set, given the input prices and organizational structures that have been determined in the previous stages. As usual, we solve this game by working backward from stage 4.

The profit of downstream Firm i, given that it pays c_i for the upstream product, is

$$\pi_i^D = \left(p_i^D - c_i\right)q_i^D = \left(p_i^D - c_i\right)\left(1 - p_i^D + B\left(p_j^D - p_i^D\right)\right) \quad (i, j = 1, 2; i \neq j) \tag{12.44}$$

Differentiating with respect to p_i^D gives the first-order conditions

$$1 + (1 + B)c_i + Bp_j^D - 2(1 + B)p_i^D = 0 \quad (i, j = 1, 2; i \neq j) \tag{12.45}$$

Solving for the downstream prices gives

$$p_i^D(c_i, c_j) = \frac{2 + 3B + (1 + B)(2(1 + B)c_i + Bc_j)}{(2 + 3B)(2 + B)} \quad (i, j = 1, 2; i \neq j) \tag{12.46}$$

Substituting these prices into the downstream demand functions of equations (12.43) gives the equilibrium downstream outputs:

$$q_i^D(c_i, c_j) = \frac{(1 + B)(2 + 3B - (2 + 4B + B^2)c_i + B(1 + B)c_j)}{(2 + 3B)(2 + B)} \quad (i, j = 1, 2; i \neq j) \tag{12.47}$$

---

[8] We cannot normalize B, since this is a measure of the degree of product differentiation that affects the outcome of the model.

Next, substituting equation (12.46) into (12.44) and simplifying gives each downstream firm's profit:

$$\pi_i^D(c_i, c_j) = \frac{(1+B)(2+3B-(2+4B+B^2)c_i + B(1+B)c_j)^2}{(2+3B)^2(2+B)^2} \quad i,j=1,2; i \neq j$$

(12.48)

An important point to note for subsequent analysis is that the profit of downstream Firm i is decreasing in its own input cost c_i and increasing in its rival's input cost c_j.

Now consider the third stage. If there was no merger in stage 1, there is no merger in stage 3; and the independent upstream firms, acting as Bertrand competitors, supply the upstream product at marginal cost c^U. In this case, equation (12.48) with $c_i = c_j = c^U = 0$, implies a downstream profit of:

$$\pi_i^D(c^U, c^U) = \frac{(1+B)}{(2+B)^2} \quad (i = 1, 2)$$

(12.49)

Suppose, by contrast, that there has been a merger of $U1$ and $D1$ in stage 1 to form Firm $F1$. As we noted above, we then consider two possibilities in stage 2 of the game. The first of these is that $F1$ forecloses on $D2$. The second is that $F1$ sets its input price c_{12} before $U2$ sets its input price.

Suppose that $F1$ forecloses in stage 2. If, in stage 3, Firms $U2$ and $D2$ do not merge, this effectively makes $U2$ a monopoly supplier to $D2$. Since one unit of the upstream product is required to make one unit of the final product, profit of $U2$ if it sets input price c_m is $\pi_2^U(c_m, c^U) = (c_m - c^U) q_2^D(c_m, c^U)$, where q_2^D is given by (12.47) with $c_2 = c_m$ and $c_1 = c^U = 0$. Maximizing with respect to c_m then gives the optimal upstream product price:

$$c_m = \frac{2+3B}{2(2+4B+B^2)}$$

(12.50)

Substituting the above result into π_2^U and π_2^D and simplifying gives aggregate profit for $U2$ and $D2$:

$$\pi_2^A(c_m, c^U) = \frac{(1+B)(3+6B+2B^2)}{(2+B)^2(4+8B+2B^2)}$$

(12.51)

Now, consider what happens if instead $U2$ and $D2$ merge to form Firm $F2$. Both $F1$ and $F2$ will then obtain the upstream product at marginal cost. As a result, the profits of $F1$ and $F2$ are each given by equation (12.49), which is greater than that shown in equation (12.51). In other words, if $F1$ forecloses, $U2$ and $D2$ will wish to integrate.

As we suggested near the end of our discussion of the Salinger (1990) model, those who belong to the club of vertically integrated firms may wish to exclude others from joining. Facing vertically integrated rivals means competing against firms with low input costs, and this can lead to intense price competition. So, suppose that $U1$ and $D1$ have merged to form $F1$, but want to prevent $U2$ and $D2$ from doing the same thing. Is there a strategy that might work to achieve this goal?

One possibility is that in stage 2, $F1$ offers to supply $D2$ at unit input price c_{12}. Since, by assumption, $F1$ sets c_{12} before $U2$ sets its input price, $U2$ can win $D2$'s business by just undercutting c_{12}. Yet, by committing to price c_{12}, $F1$ puts a ceiling on the price that $U2$ can charge $D2$ and thereby limits the gains from a merger. To see this more clearly, consider the following analysis.

Profit to $D2$ given that $F1$ supplies its downstream division at marginal cost $c^U = 0$ and that $U2$ just undercuts c_{12} is given by equation (12.48) with $c_1 = 0$ and $c_2 = c_{12}$, which is

$$\pi_2^D\left(c_{12}, c^U\right) = \frac{(1+B)\left(2+3B-\left(2+4B+B^2\right)c_{12}\right)^2}{(2+3B)^2(2+B)^2} \tag{12.52}$$

Profit to $U2$ given that it supplies $D2$ at input price c_{12} is $c_{12}q_2^D\left(c_{12}, c^U\right)$, where $q_2^D(c_{12}, c^U)$ is given by equation (12.47) with $c_i = c_{12}$ and $c_j = c^U = 0$:

$$\pi_2^U\left(c_{12}, c^U\right) = \frac{(1+B)c_{12}\left(2+3B-\left(2+4B+B^2\right)c_{12}\right)}{(2+3B)(2+B)} \tag{12.53}$$

Aggregate profit of $U2$ and $D2$ therefore is $\pi_2^A(c_{12}, c^U) = \pi_2^U(c_{12}, c^U) + \pi_2^D(c_{12}, c^U)$. From equations (12.52) and (12.53), this aggregate profit $\pi_2^A\left(c_{12}, c^U\right)$ is quadratic in c_{12}. Of course, we also know that $\pi_2^A\left(c^U, c^U\right) = \pi_2^D(c^U, c^U)$ from equation (12.49). Moreover, it is straightforward to show that $\frac{\partial \pi_2^A\left(c_{12}, c^U\right)}{\partial c_{12}}\Big|_{c_{12}=c^U=0} > 0$. Finally, $\pi_2^A\left(c_m, c^U\right) < \pi_2^D(c^U, c^U)$ from comparison of (12.50) and (12.48).

The function $\pi_2^A(c_{12}, c^U)$ is shown in Figure 12.3. As that figure makes clear, there is always a strategic input price $c_{12} = c^* \in (c^U, c_m)$ that $F1$ can set to make $U2$ and $D2$ jointly more profitable as separate firms than they would be if they merged. In preventing their merger, F_1 not only preserves itself as the lone vertically integrated firm, but also

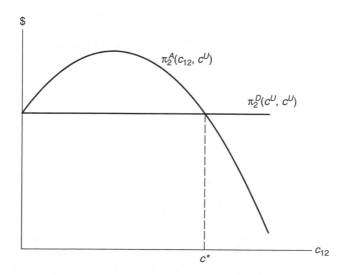

Figure 12.3 Strategic supply price

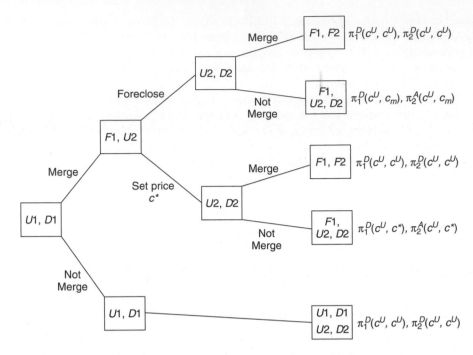

Figure 12.4   The OSS Extensive-form game with $c_{12} = c^*$

ensures that it continues to face a high-cost rival in the downstream market rather than the low-cost one it would face if $U2$ and $D2$ merged.

Figure 12.4 shows the extended form of the OSS four-stage game. Suppose that $U1$ and $D1$ merge in stage 1 to form $F1$. If $F1$ chooses to Foreclose in stage 2, it is simple to prove from equations (12.49) and (12.51) that $\pi_2^D(c^U, c^U) > \pi_2^A(c_m, c^U)$. In other words, if $F1$ forecloses in stage 2, then $U2$ and $D2$ will choose to merge in stage 3, as a result of which $F1$ has profit $\pi_1^D(c^U, c^U)$. Suppose by contrast that $F1$ sets c^*, which $U2$ just undercuts. By construction of c^*, we know that $\pi_2^A(c^*, c^U) > \pi_2^D(c^U, c^U)$, so $U2$ and $D2$ choose not to merge. As a result, $F1$ has profit $\pi_1^D(c^U, c^*)$. We know that, since $c^* > c^U$, $\pi_1^D(c^U, c^*)$ $> \pi_1^D(c^U, c^U)$. It follows that $F1$ prefers to set price $c_{12} = c^*$ rather than to foreclose. So if $U1$ and $D1$ Merge in stage 1, the merged firm will offer to supply $D2$ at price c^* in stage 2, as a result of which $U2$ and $D2$ choose not to merge in stage 3 and $F1$ earns $\pi_1^D(c^U, c^*)$.

Now, suppose that $U1$ and $D1$ choose not to merge in stage 1. Then the upstream firms compete in prices and set input price at marginal cost c^U, as a result of which the downstream firms, in competing in prices, earn $\pi_i^D(c^U, c^U)$. Clearly, $U1$ and $D1$ prefer to merge.

Note that the strategy of offering to supply its rival at price $c_{12} > c^U$ is much closer in spirit to the "squeeze" pricing that phone companies and Alcoa have been accused of than it is to outright foreclosure. The merged firm does not actually refuse to supply its unintegrated downstream rival. However, the conditions on which it stands ready to supply are chosen specifically to ensure that no sales are actually made to the independent downstream firm. Note too that by preventing the merger of $U2$ and $D2$, and thereby preserving the existence of double marginalization and a high-cost rival, $F1$'s strategy of offering to sell to $D2$ at price c_{12} also leads to higher prices for consumers. It is an action designed to thwart the outbreak of competition and is therefore truly anticompetitive. In all these ways, the OSS model has an air of realism about it.

Chen (2001) extends the OSS analysis, starting from the empirical regularity that fore-closure seems to be a rarity in practice. He shows that whenever the wholesale price offered by the integrated firm and independent producer $U2$ are the same, the independent downstream firm $D2$ will prefer to buy from the integrated producer. Why? Because in so doing, $D2$ gives the integrated firm another source of profit—a source that rises as $D2$ sells more downstream. As a result of selling to $D2$, the integrated firm will price less aggressively in the downstream market because this would cut into its profit on input sales to $D2$. Of course, less aggressive downstream pricing also helps $D2$, and that is precisely why $D2$ would prefer to buy from the integrated firm rather than from $U2$. Indeed, Chen suggests that if there are cost efficiencies associated with the vertical merger so that c^U falls at the integrated firm, the merger could lead to a different sort of foreclosure altogether. Instead of cutting off independent downstream firms from a source of supply, the vertical merger may leave independent upstream firms without any customers.[9]

12.4   A REAPPRAISAL: THE GE-HONEYWELL MERGER ONCE MORE

Let us return to the GE-Honeywell merger described at the start of this chapter. As noted, the European Commission eventually ruled against the merger. Their reasoning is summarized in the following extract from the Commission's report (paragraph 355):

> Because of their lack of ability to match the bundle offer... [independent] suppliers will lose market shares to the benefit of the merged entity and experience an immediate damaging profit shrinkage. As a result, the merger is likely to lead to market foreclosure on the existing aircraft platforms and subsequently to the elimination of competition in these areas.[10]

There are several points to make in regard to this judgment. First, the "bundling" that the commission feared would give GE-Honeywell an unfair competitive advantage is nothing more than the elimination of double marginalization that we have described above. Packaging jet engines with engine starter motors is economically equivalent to combining the upstream manufacturing with the retail services of a downstream dealer. In this sense, there is some legitimacy in the Commission's fear that a GE-Honeywell merger would, by itself, give the combined firms some advantage over independent rivals.

Whether the merger would lead to foreclosure or a price squeeze, and (if so) whether this would raise final prices, is another matter. In part, that would depend on the nature of initial competition. In this respect, it is fair to say that neither premerger market was competitively structured. Estimates of GE's share of the jet engine market for large commercial aircraft range from 28 to 52 percent, and it had just two major rivals, the Pratt-Whitney division of United Technologies and the Rolls Royce Group. Likewise,

---

[9]   Pepall and Norman (2001) offer a similar analysis to Chen in which vertical foreclosure is never an equilibrium, precisely because, again, this leads to competition between multiple vertically integrated firms.

[10] The full decision is available at: http://ec.europa.eu/comm/competition/mergers/cases/decisions/ m2220_en.pdf

Honeywell's share of the avionics market was on the order of 50 percent, and it had just three rivals: Rockwell Collins (25 percent); Thales (15 percent); and Smiths Industries (5 percent). In reaching its decision, the European Commission appears to have been persuaded that the preeminence of GE and Honeywell made subsequent integration by their rivals impossible. As a result, and as the quote above makes clear, the Commission feared foreclosure of GE's competitors and the ultimate loss of competition in the jet engine market.

Yet, while the Commission's view that competition could not be relied on may be warranted, its judgments regarding both the inability of firms outside of GE-Honeywell to integrate and the likelihood of foreclosure are more questionable. Certainly, on the face of it, there do not appear to be large obstacles to integration by the remaining firms. In any event, as discussed above in the context of the Salinger (1990) model, even when integrated firms choose to foreclose independent rivals, it is still possible that the merger puts downward pressure on the final price to consumers. These considerations suggest why many economists thought the ruling a mistake.[11]

12.5   A NOTE ON CONGLOMERATE MERGERS

Before considering a recent empirical study of vertical integration, we mention briefly a third type of merger: the conglomerate. Such mergers bring under common control firms whose products are neither direct substitutes nor complements. The result is a set of firms producing a diversified range of products with little or nothing in common. Because these products are neither substitutes nor complements, the competitive impact of such mergers is limited. For much the same reason, however, it is difficult to provide an economic rationale for conglomerate mergers at all.

Scope economies and savings on transaction costs are two possible advantages that may accrue to conglomerate firms. However, the data on conglomerates do not appear to support the idea that these firms exhibit significant scope economies. Nathanson and Cassano (1982), for example, found that there are at least as many conglomerate firms that produce goods with little in common as there are firms that have relatively low product and market diversity.

By transaction costs we mean the costs that are incurred by firms when they use external markets in order to procure goods and services.[12] These include, for example, the costs of searching for the desired inputs, negotiating supply contracts, monitoring and enforcing these contracts, and the risk associated with unforeseen changes in supply conditions. However, the argument that economies based on transaction costs underlie conglomerate mergers is also suspect. Part of the reason is that, again, such economies would most likely be present if there were some commonality in the production lines. This is not the case for conglomerate firms. Moreover, as Teece (1982) and others have argued, conglomeration is not necessary even when potential transaction cost economies

---

[11]   For a similar analysis of the GE-Honeywell case—but one that is set in a framework of differentiated products—see Nalebuff (2004). To be fair, the Commission also expressed other fears besides foreclosure. One of these was that GE already had an unfair advantage in that its large financial operations allowed it to package financing with jet aircraft engines in a way that Pratt-Whitney and Rolls Royce could not. In addition, there was a horizontal element to the case in that GE and Honeywell were the only two suppliers of engines for large regional jets.

[12]   For an excellent discussion of transaction costs, see Besanko, Dranove, Shanley, and Schaefer (2007).

exist. There are various contracts between firms that would achieve this goal, but that stop far short of merger.

Instead of cost efficiencies, two alternative factors may lie behind the formation of conglomerate firms. One of these reflects the internal organization of the firm, specifically, the nature of executive compensation. In any reasonably large public company, ownership, which essentially resides with the shareholders, may be separated from control, which essentially resides with the management team. This separation would not matter too much if management and shareholder interests were the same. However, whereas shareholders care about the company's value, managers are likely to be most concerned with their own remuneration—just like any other employee. It is precisely the recognition of this potential conflict that leads firms to establish compensation systems such as payment with stock options or profit-based bonuses that more closely tie management's pay to the firm's profit performance.[13] Yet, while these practices work to ally management's interest more closely to that of the stockholders, they also increase the risk that management faces. As profits go up and down, management's compensation rises and falls irrespective of whether the profit results were management's fault or not. To protect against such fluctuations, management may seek to diversify the sources of the firm's income by pursuing conglomeration. This smoothes the firm's income stream, because with many product lines operating, positive and negative shocks tend to cancel each other out. The derived income stream of the firm's executives is also smoother. Even shareholders might prefer this approach if, in the absence of such diversification, the firm would have to pay its executives higher salaries to compensate them for the greater risk. This may be particularly true for managers who are heavily invested in the firms, so that not only their labor income but also their capital income is subject to the same risk.

Some evidence in support of diversification as a means of spreading managerial risk is found in studies by Ahimud and Lev (1981) and by May (1995). The first of these studies finds that when no shareholder owns 10 percent or more of the stock and management control is high, firms tend to be more diversified. May (1995) finds in a comparison of CEOs in terms of the proportion of their wealth invested in the firm that as this proportion rises, CEOs tend to favor conglomeration.[14]

A second possible rationale for conglomeration—one more in the spirit of this text—reflects external considerations based on the firms strategic interaction with rivals. Recall our discussion of collusion in Chapter 10 and the features that make cooperation among firms more likely. One of these was multimarket contact. While facing a common rival across many different settings will not necessarily lead to a more collusive agreement in every one of these markets, it does enrich the strategy space beyond that available to the case in which each of these battlefields is a separate conflict fought by independent firms. Thus, conglomerate mergers may offer firms a means of achieving this multimarket contact and thereby fostering more cooperative pricing across these various markets. Empirical work by Feinberg (1985) and experimental work by Phillips and Mason (1992) lends some support to this hypothesis.

[13] Boeing, for instance, paid top executives with options linked to the firm's share price over the next five years. See F. M. Biddle, "Boeing Links Managers' Stock Options to Five-Year Performance of Shares." *Wall Street Journal* (26 February 1998), p. B12.

[14] Alternatively, management may pursue a conglomerate structure to make it more difficult for shareholders to monitor the firm's performance and assess accountability. If it is more difficult to replace the CEOs of a complex firm, conglomeration may also be a way for management to acquire greater job security. See Aggarwal and Samwick (2003).

In sum, conglomerate mergers pose something of a puzzle. The economic motivation that gives rise to such combinations is not obvious, since the merged enterprises typically exhibit neither substitute nor complementary features. There is some evidence that conglomeration may reflect management's goal of stabilizing its compensation when such compensation is based on market performance. Alternatively, conglomerate mergers may be attempts by firms to create rivals with many points of contact and thereby facilitate cooperative behavior. If this last factor were the dominant one, it would of course mean that conglomerate mergers present some of the same challenges for analysis and policy as do horizontal and vertical ones.

12.6   EMPIRICAL APPLICATION: VERTICAL INTEGRATION IN THE READY-MIXED CONCRETE INDUSTRY

Ready-mixed concrete is one of the most widely used construction materials. It is comprised mainly of cement, water, and aggregates such as sand and gravel. Of these, cement is clearly crucial as the binding agent that hardens the aggregates into a solid mass. Almost invariably, cement comprises 12 percent of the concrete mixture by weight. Hence, cement and ready-mixed concrete match the assumptions of the Salinger (1988) and Ordover, Saloner, and Salop (1990) models in that cement is an upstream product used in fixed proportion per unit of the downstream product, ready-mixed concrete. This makes it an ideal industry in which to study the effects of vertical integration.

Ali Hortaçsu and Chad Syverson (2007) point out that there is a further aspect of the concrete business that makes studying vertical integration in that industry interesting. Due in part to the fluctuations in U.S. merger policy over the last 50 years, vertical integration between upstream cement-makers and downstream concrete firms has fluctuated a good bit, as shown in Table 12.1 below. As a result, the data reveal a lot of variation in the extent of integration over time. Because these data include observations in which the extent of integration is low and observations in which integration is widespread, they can be used in determining the various effects of such integration.

Of course, transport costs are far too high for there to be a single national market for ready-mixed concrete. Using Commerce Department data, Hortaçsu and Syverson (2007) identify 348 local markets over the years 1963–97. They then use this data to determine whether the differences in ready-mixed concrete prices across markets are systematically related to the extent of vertical integration in those markets. A simple regression aimed at answering this question might have the form $P_{it} = A + \beta VI_{it} + e_{it}$, where P_{it} is the average concrete price (measured in logs) in Market i in Year t; A is an intercept term; VI_{it} is the market share of output accounted for by vertically integrated firms in Market

Table 12.1   Time pattern of vertical integration of cement and ready-mixed concrete firms

Year	1963	1967	1972	1977	1982	1987	1992	1997
Fraction of Cement Sales Accounted for by Vertically Integrated Firms	25.2	51.2	48.4	41.0	49.5	51.3	75.1	55.4

i in Year t; and e_{it} is a random error term centered on 0. Such a simple model, however, leaves out many other variables that are likely to be important in determining concrete prices in any given market year, and therefore would lead to a biased estimate of the coefficient β.

To begin with, the average price over time might be different in each market. There might be something about the Chicago market, for example, that makes its price of cement always relatively high. This effect can be handled by letting the intercept term vary across each market. Then, too, industrial organization theory suggests that market structure, as measured by the Herfindahl Index (HI), could also be important for the behavior of prices, as might be the level of demand coming from the local construction industry in that year. In fact, given our discussion of antitrust policy, we might also think that the precise year is important as well, because firms might try to keep prices low in years when antitrust pressure is more intense than in years when it is lenient. We need to control for such time-specific factors and the many other forces that could affect concrete prices if we are to isolate the influence of changes in vertical integration alone. The easiest way to do this is to include measures of concentration and local demand and put in a dummy variable for each market and each year.

Hortaçsu and Syverson (2007) make these adjustments (and some others as well) to estimate regressions explaining the variation in concrete prices across markets and time. Their central results are shown below.

Results for regressions explaining ready-mixed concrete prices in the US

Independent Variable	Dependent Variable: Weighted Average Market Price (log)	Dependent Variable: Weighted Average Market Price (log)	Dependent Variable: Weighted Average Market Price (log)
Market Share of Vertically Integrated Firms	−0.090*[15] (0.041)	−0.086*[16] (0.041)	−0.043 (0.039)
Market Share of Multiple Plant Firms	—	−0.015 (0.022)	0.001 (0.024)
Weighted-Average Total Factor Productivity	—	—	−0.293* (0.054)
R^2	0.433	0.434	0.573

*Significant at 5 percent level.

In all the regressions, results for the time and market dummies are suppressed—as are those for the HI and construction demand, which are never significant. The first column shows the results when, apart from the control variables just mentioned, the only explanatory variable is the extent of vertical integration in the local market. This effect is both negative and statistically significant. It is also economically meaningful. For their entire sample, Hortaçsu and Syverson find that, on average, vertically integrated firms account for 31.5 percent of the typical market. The estimated coefficient shown in the first column then implies that ready-mixed concrete prices would be 4 percent lower in such a market than they would be in a market with no vertically integrated firms. Thus, this result suggests that the efficiency results of vertical integration typically outweigh any anticompetitive effects so that consumers benefit.

The next two columns test additional variables that may be important for concrete prices. In column 2, a second independent variable is added for the fraction of firms that operate more than one plant. This includes all the vertically integrated firms plus all those that operate multiple plants horizontally. Including this variable in the regression is a means of testing whether the vertically integrated variable is really capturing efficiencies that come from coordinating different plants—for example, better-timed production and lower transport costs—rather than from vertical integration per se. However, this variable is insignificant and does not materially affect the results in column 1.

The third column is perhaps the most interesting. Here, Hortaçsu and Syverson include as an additional regressor a measure of average productivity in the local market. This is clearly an important variable. Including it reduces the magnitude of the effects of vertical integration and eliminates their statistical significance. What are the implications of this finding?

First, it makes intuitive sense that concrete prices will be lower in markets where firms are more productive. In this sense, the results in column 3 are not surprising. Second, we should recall that vertical integration has (potentially) two effects: a price-reducing effect due to greater efficiency and a price-increasing effect due to foreclosure-type forces. Including the productivity variable should control for any efficiency effects so that the vertical integration term now picks up only the price-increasing impact of vertical mergers. The findings in column 3 suggest that once this control for efficiency effects is included, the price-increasing effects appear very weak. Finally, Hortaçsu and Syverson (2007) produce other evidence to show that vertically integrated firms have higher productivity. If vertical integration in this industry has an impact on prices, it does so through the efficiency effect. Overall, these results imply that vertical integration has been welfare enhancing and good for consumers, at least in the ready-mixed concrete business.

Summary

This chapter has examined the economics of vertical mergers. Unlike horizontal mergers in which the firms involved produce substitute products, a vertical merger is a merger between two firms whose products are complements. The prototypical case is a merger of two firms operating at different stages of production in the same product line (e.g., a manufacturer and a retailer). However, the same issues arise in other cases whenever the goods are complements (e.g., computers and computer printers).

Vertical mergers raise complicated issues. On the one hand, such mergers can benefit firms and consumers by eliminating double marginalization. On the other hand, they may be a means to foreclose either upstream or downstream markets to rivals—or at least to squeeze rivals with higher input prices. Vertical mergers can also facilitate price discrimination.

There is no simple way of determining which of these forces is likely to be the strongest. Some argue that vertical foreclosure itself sets up a countervailing force that will induce remaining independent companies to integrate. If so, this can reduce—perhaps eliminate—the inefficiencies associated with foreclosure. However, vertically integrated firms may have both the means and the motive to prevent such subsequent mergers. Resolution of these issues in any particular case must, as always, depend on careful evaluation of the realities of the specific situation.

It is worth noting, however, that even when a vertical merger leads to foreclosure or a price squeeze for independent rivals, it may be the case that final consumers are made better off. Policy makers should therefore not be too hasty in condemning a vertical merger simply because it disadvantages rival firms. The goal of antitrust policy is to preserve the benefits of competition, not the fortunes of competitors. Indeed, we presented evidence from the ready-mixed concrete industry that vertical integration has, in general, been beneficial for both firms and consumers.

Problems

1. A downstream monopoly retailer $D1$ buys from an upstream monopoly producer $U1$. $D1$ faces a downstream demand described in inverse form as $P = A - Q$. $U1$ has a constant marginal cost of $c = 0$. $D1$'s only cost is the price it pays for units from $U1$. Instead of buying units from $U1$ individually at some unit price r, however, $D1$ makes a take-it-or-leave-it offer to buy a package of x units for some lump sum amount V.

   a. If $D1$ can do this—that is, if $D1$ can credibly commit to no renegotiation how many units x will $D1$ ask for, and what will be the value V that it offers to pay for the package?

   b. Now, imagine that it is $U1$ that gets to make a take-it-or-leave-it offer to sell a bundle of x units to $D1$ at a bundle price of V. What value of x will $U1$ choose, and what price V will it sell the package for?

2. Consider a simple Cournot model in which final demand is given by $P = A - Q$. The downstream market is a duopoly in which each of the two firms produces output q using an intermediate good x as an input according to the production technology, $q_i^D = x_i^D$. Every unit of x costs r, where r is the price established in the upstream market for intermediate goods. This is the only cost incurred by downstream firms (i.e., $C_i = rx_i^D$). Similarly, the upstream market is also a Cournot duopoly. Here, each firm has a unit cost of zero.

   a. Determine the equilibrium profit earned by each upstream and each downstream firm.

   b. Assume that one upstream firm merges with a downstream firm, but that the remaining upstream and downstream firms continue to operate independently. Determine the profit earned by the integrated firm and the remaining upstream and downstream independent operators.

   c. Now, assume that the second pair of firms merges so that the market is comprised of just two firms, each with a 0 cost. Determine the equilibrium profit of each of these two firms.

3. Consider a monopolist upstream supplier $U1$ selling to two downstream producers $D1$ and $D2$ engaged in Cournot competition. Downstream demand is described by: $P = A - Q$ and marginal cost upstream is zero while downstream it equals the wholesale price.

   a. Show that if the monopolist could sell directly to the downstream market, she would set a price $P = A/2$ and earn profit $= A^2/4$.

   b. Imagine a contract by which $U1$ sells $A/4$ units as a package to each of $D1$ and $D2$ at a bundle price of $A^2/8 - \varepsilon$, where ε is an arbitrarily small number. Each downstream firm can either accept the package or reject it. Show that if firms choose simultaneously, and each has full information about the other's possible actions and payoffs, the Nash Equilibrium is for each to accept this offer.

4. Ginvir and Sipep are Bertrand competitors selling differentiated products in the carbonated-drinks market. The demands for the products of the two firms being given by the inverse demand functions

$$p_G = 25 - q_G - 0.5 q_S$$
$$p_S = 25 - q_S - 0.5 q_G$$

Here, p_G and q_G are the price and quantity for Ginvir, and p_S and q_S are the price and quantity for Sipep, respectively. Both companies need syrup to make their drinks that is supplied by two competing companies, NorSyr and BenRup. These companies incur unit costs of $5 per unit in making the syrup. Both Ginvir and Sipep can use the syrup of either supplier.

   a. Confirm that Bertrand competition between NorSyr and BenRup leads to the syrup being priced at $5 per unit.

   b. What are the resulting equilibrium prices for Ginvir and Sipep, and what are their profits?

5. Now suppose that Ginvir and NorSyr merge, and that NorSyr no longer competes for Sipep's business.

   a. What price will Benrup now charge Sipep for the syrup?

   b. What are the resulting profits to the three postmerger companies?

   c. Do Benrup and Sipep have an incentive also to merge?

References

Aggarwal, R. K., and A. Samwick. 2003. "Why Do Managers Diversify Their Firms? Agency Reconsidered." *Journal of Finance*, 58 (February): 71–118.

Ahimud, Y., and Lev, B. 1981. "Risk Reduction as a Managerial Motive for Conglomerate Mergers." *Bell Journal of Economics*, 12 (Autumn): 605–617.

Besanko, D., D. Dranove, and M. Shanley. 1996. *Economics of Strategy*. New York: John Wiley & Sons.

Chen, Y. 2001. "On Vertical Mergers and Their Competitive Effects." *Rand Journal of Economics*, 32 (Autumn): 667–685.

Chipty, T. 2001. "Vertical Integration, Market Foreclosure, and Consumer Welfare in the Cable Television Industry." *The American Economic Review*, 91 (June): 428–453.

Daughety, A. 1990. "Beneficial Concentration." *American Economic Review*, 80 (December): 1231–1237.

Feinberg, R. M. 1985. "'Sales at Risk': A Test of the Mutual Forebearance Theory of Conglomerate Behavior." *Journal of Business*, Vol. 58 (Spring): 225–241.

Hortaçsu, Ali, and Chad Syverson. 2007. "Cementing Relationships: Vertical Integration, Foreclosure, Productivity, and Prices." *Journal of Political Economy*, 115 (February): 250–301.

Krattenmaker, T., and S. Salop. 1986. "Anticompetitive Exclusion: Raising Rivals' Costs to Achieve Power Over Price." *Yale Law Journal*, 96: 209–295

May, D. O. 1995. "Do Managerial Motives Influence Firm Risk-Reduction Strategies?" *Journal of Finance*, 50 (November): 1291–1308.

Nalebuff, B. 2004. "Bundling: GE-Honeywell." In J. Kwoka and L. White (Eds.). *The Antitrust Revolution*. 4th ed. Oxford: Oxford University Press, 388–412.

Nathanson, D. A., and J. Cassano. 1982. "What Happens to Profits When a Company Diversifies?" *Wharton Magazine*, 24: 19–26.

Ordover, J. A., G. Saloner, and S. Salop. 1990. "Equilibrium Vertical Foreclosure." *American Economic Review*, 80 (March): 127–142.

Pepall, L., and G. Norman. 2001. "Product Differentiation and Upstream Downstream Relations." *The Journal of Economics and Management Strategy*, 10 (Summer): 201–233.

Phillips, O. R., and C. F. Mason. 1992. "Mutual Forbearance in Experimental Conglomerate Markets." *Rand Journal of Economics*, 23 (Autumn): 395–414.

Salinger, M. A. 1988. "Vertical Mergers and Market Foreclosure." *Quarterly Journal of Economics*, 103 (May): 345–356.

Salop, S. C. 1979. "Monopolistic Competition with Outside Goods." *Bell Journal of Economics*, 10 (Spring): 141–156.

Teece, D. 1982. "Towards an Economic Theory of the Multiproduct Firm." *Journal of Economic Behavior and Organization*, 3 (March): 39–63.

13

Vertical Restraints

Seagate is the largest single supplier of hard disk drives to Dell. AK Steel is the major supplier of steel to General Motors. Mattel Toys sells its Barbie, Fisher-Price, and Hot Wheels products through retailers such as Toys "R" Us and Walmart. Each of these examples describes a vertical transaction. An upstream firm sells its good to another firm further downstream or closer to the final consumer. More importantly, each of these transactions and virtually all vertical relationships are governed by contracts. These contracts do not simply set the terms for payment for the supplied goods. Instead, they almost always include additional restrictions on the behavior of one party or the other. These restrictions can focus on price, such as a specification of a maximum retail price or a nonbinding manufacturer's suggested retail price. Alternatively, the contract may include a "quantity forcing" clause requiring that a minimum number of units be bought by the downstream firm. In addition, there will often be nonprice restraints, such as an exclusive dealing requirement that prohibits the downstream firm from using other suppliers, or an exclusive territory clause that allows (and limits) the downstream firm to sell in a particular geographic region.

The economic analysis of these price and nonprice vertical restraints lies at the heart of this chapter. Our goal is to understand the reasons for such agreements and their economic effects. Because there has perhaps been no area of antitrust policy that has been more continuously litigated, our discussion inevitably carries over into policy analysis. We begin by focusing on vertical price restraints and will then turn to consider nonprice restraints.

13.1   VERTICAL PRICE RESTRAINTS AND ANTITRUST POLICY: A BRIEF HISTORY

Vertical price restrictions usually fall under the heading of Resale Price Maintenance (RPM). Because they are explicitly an agreement on price, all such contractual provisions were found to be a per se violation of the U.S. antitrust laws in the *Dr. Miles* case decided by the U.S. Supreme Court in 1911.[1] Notably, the per se violation was found

---

[1]   *Dr. Miles Co. v. John D. Park and Sons, Co.*, 220 U.S. 373 (1911).

regardless of whether the contract specified a minimum or a maximum downstream price. However, this rigid approach began to erode fairly rapidly. First, in the *Colgate* case of 1919, the Supreme Court ruled that if a producer unilaterally announced that it would terminate any firm that sold below a specified retail price, it could proceed to do just that and to cut off downstream firms that violated that pricing policy, because the unilateral quality of the decision meant that there really was no price agreement.[2] Then in the wake of the Great Depression, the U.S. Congress passed the Miller-Tydings Act of 1937, which explicitly exempted RPM agreements from antitrust prosecution. This was later followed by the 1952 McGuire Act, which permitted the enforcement of an RPM agreement even on firms who had not signed on to the arrangement, provided at least one retailer and manufacturer had agreed to it.

The one loophole in the Miller-Tydings and McGuire legislation was that it required participation by state legislatures to make it effective. Some states, however, continued to prohibit RPM agreements. Over time, this led to considerable discounting of prices in these states relative to those with pro-RPM legislation. Consumers willing to drive across the state line, or just willing to deal with a mail-order firm, were able to gain access to discount stores with lower prices. Such competition put tremendous pressure on firms participating in RPM agreements. In 1975, in the wake of the substantial inflation induced by OPEC's fourfold increase in the price of crude oil, both the Miller-Tydings and the McGuire Acts were repealed. This reestablished the presumed illegality of RPM agreements, but it did not remove manufacturers' ability, established by the *Colgate* decision, to cut off discount dealers.

Three subsequent legal cases have greatly expanded the ability of manufacturers to impose retail price restrictions. In the *Sharp Electronics* case,[3] the Court broadened its *Colgate* exception by permitting the manufacturer to terminate a discount dealer even if this was the result of other dealers' complaints. Later, in the 1997 *State Oil vs. Khan* case, the Court explicitly renounced any per se illegality for RPM agreements establishing a maximum price or a price ceiling. Most recently, in the *Leegin* case of 2007, the Court has reversed the *Dr. Miles* per se ruling and held that all resale price agreements, maximum or minimum, should be subject to a rule of reason test.

Nonprice vertical restraints have traditionally been treated more leniently in the U.S. courts than have price restrictions such as RPM agreements. The *Schwinn* bicycle case of 1967 marked a turn toward very strict prohibitions of nonprice as well as price restraints, almost to the point that nonprice restraints became as much per se illegal as price restraints then were.[4] However, this tough stance softened over time. The current view seems well reflected in the *Toys "R" Us* case of 1997 (see Reality Checkpoint, p. 377).[5] It is a policy stance that is somewhat lenient in general, but one in which the authorities will challenge vertical restraints when they take place in a setting in which firms have substantial market power and maybreak abuse it.

Although it is much more recent, European antitrust policy regarding vertical restrictions has come largely to mirror that of the United States. Article 81(1) of the European Communities Treaty does include a clause permitting nonprice restraints when they promote greater efficiency or innovation. This potentially large loophole has not resulted in

---

[2]   *United States v. Colgate & Co.*, 250 U.S. 300 (1919). This exception is often referred to as the *Colgate Doctrine*.

[3]   *Business Electronics Corp. v. Sharp Electronics Corp.* 488 U.S. 717 (1988).

[4]   *United States v. Arnold, Schwinn & Co.*, 388 U.S. 365 (1967).

[5]   *Toys 'R' Us, Inc. v. FTC*, 221 F.3d 928 (7th Cir. 2000) (Wood, J.).

Reality Checkpoint
Yesterday's News

Resale price maintenance contracts have both a variety of motivations and a variable legal history. One clear motivation, however, is to resolve the double marginalization problem and, in particular, to insure that retailers do not set downstream prices too high. The important case of *Albrecht v. The Herald Co.*, settled in 1968, nicely illustrates this point.

The Herald Co. was a newspaper firm publishing, among others, the St. Louis *Globe Democrat*. In turn, the company hired various carriers to deliver the morning paper to subscribers. Each carrier was given an exclusive territory from which all other carriers were excluded. On the newspaper itself, Herald printed its suggested retail price for the *Globe Democrat*.

Albrecht was one of the carriers hired by the newspaper who served about 1,200 customers. In 1961, Albrecht began charging his customers a newspaper price above that recommended by Herald. The company quickly objected. When its several requests that Albrecht lower the price back to the suggested retail charge were rejected by Albrecht, Herald took decisive action. It contacted Albrecht's customers and offered to deliver the paper to them itself at the lower price. Subsequently, it contracted with an alternative carrier to "invade" Albrecht's exclusive territory, again, delivering the paper at the lower recommended price. Albrecht's response was thoroughly American. The firm sued Herald for breach of contract and for attempting to fix prices in violation of the Sherman Act.

In its 1968 decision, the U.S. Supreme Court found in Albrecht's favor. The decision found that Herald's efforts to force a specific price on Albrecht amounted to price-fixing and was, therefore, per se illegal in keeping with the court's treatment of all price-setting agreements. Thus, once it was determined that Herald was in fact trying to enforce a price restraint there was no defense.

The *Albrecht* case did not sit well with many economists and others who recognized the double-marginalization problem and, more broadly, the possibility that some vertical price arrangements might actually be good for consumers as well as for firms. Gradually, this learning spread to the courts as well. The *Sharp* case of 1988 expanded the *Colgate* exception to the per se ruling. However, the major break came with the court's ruling in *State Oil v. Khan*.

Barkat Khan was a midwestern gasoline dealer supplied by State Oil. The oil firm required that all dealers who set a markup of more than 3.25 cents per gallon would have to rebate the excess markup to the company itself. Much like Albrecht, Khan began to exceed this maximum; and when State Oil complained, Khan filed suit. As the case progressed to the Supreme Court, it generated enormous interest. Newspapers, auto manufacturers, and the U.S. Department of Justice were among the many urging the court to reverse the *Albrecht* decision and eliminate the per se status of vertical price agreements. On the other side, associations representing auto dealers and service station owners, as well as 33 states' attorney generals, filed briefs urging the court to hold to the *Albrecht* finding.

The court's decision was dramatic. Not only did it find in favor of State Oil, but it also made an explicit statement that vertical price agreements stipulating *maximum* prices would no longer be per se illegal. This is not to say they would be automatically legal. However, they would be subject to a rule of reason and therefore permitted if it could be shown that there was a legitimate justification for their use—and if they did not substantially lessen competition. What made the decision particularly compelling was that it was unanimous—a rarity in Supreme Court cases. However, while the court opened the door to resale price arrangements that limited *maximum* prices, the per se illegality of agreements setting *minimum* prices was maintained. The court was not quite ready to address that question in 1997.

Sources: Albrecht v. The Herald Co., 390 U.S. 150 (1968), and *State Oil v. Khan*, 522 U.S. 3 (1997). See also L. Greenhouse, "High Court, in Antitrust Ruling, Says Price Ceilings Are Allowed." *The New York Times* (5 November 1997), p. A1.

an "anything goes" policy framework, however. Because the free flow of goods between the many European Union countries is so important, the Commission has been very quick to prosecute territorial restrictions, especially when these are used to block imports across country lines. RPM agreements have been generally subject to a *per se* prohibition.[6]

13.2   VERTICAL PRICE RESTRAINTS AND SUPPRESSED COMPETITION

The brief history just outlined is enough to make clear both that the debate over vertical price restraints is long-standing and that policy toward such agreements has varied between periods of strict prohibition and periods of leniency. One constant, though, has been the central fear of those in favor of making all such agreements illegal per se that, at their root, RPM agreements are essentially a means to suppressing price competition.

The fear underlying the resistance to any legal justification for RPM agreements is, of course, that they amount to either explicit or implicit collusion. Imagine a market of two upstream firms, each with a constant unit cost of c_U; and two downstream dealers, each with a constant unit cost of c_D. Suppose that the upstream goods are identical as are the retail service, and that final demand is, in inverse form, $P = A - Q$. Then, price competition at each level implies a final price to the consumer of $c_U + c_D$, and each firm breaks even. Suppose, however, that the two downstream dealers can persuade the upstream firms to adopt contracts forbidding resale below the monopoly price:

$$P^M = \frac{A + c_U + c_D}{2} \tag{13.1}$$

In this case, if the downstream firms continue to buy at the same upstream cost c_U, they can share the market and each earn half the monopoly profit downstream, while the upstream firms are no worse off. What makes this a particularly attractive option is that it puts responsibility for the implementation and the enforcement of the price fixing agreement on the manufacturers, thereby protecting the retailers from any prosecution.

The RPM agreement thus has the potential to act as a facilitating device for collusion. It is also easy to see how some or all of the profit from this collusion may instead accrue to the upstream firms. For example, a simple two-part contract similar to the nonlinear pricing that we described in Chapter 5 (in which the upstream firm sells to the downstream firm at cost, but collects an upfront fee for giving the dealer the right to sell the product downstream) will do the trick.

The fact that it is a binding and legally enforceable contract is what makes an RPM agreement a potentially powerful mechanism for collusive behavior. The fear that this end is precisely the motivation behind RPM agreements is, in turn, at least partially justified by the historical record. Pro-RPM legislation such as the Miller-Tydings and McGuire Acts has traditionally drawn its biggest support from downstream retailers at both the federal and state levels. In addition, as documented by both Overstreet (1983) and Steiner

---

[6]   See Rey and Vergé (2008).

(1985), the vast majority of RPM legal cases have been those in which the contracts set a minimum retail price, not a maximum price. Similar evidence for the United Kingdom has been presented by Pickering (1966).

Thus, the historical evidence is certainly consistent with the view that RPM agreements are seen by the firms involved in such contracts as a means to achieve higher price-cost margins. Accordingly, policymakers are right to be concerned about the anticompetitive effects of RPM agreements. At the same time, it is important to recognize that manufacturers and retailers may have other, more legitimate incentives to restrict a retailer's pricing decision besides suppressing retail competition. In turn, recognizing these other motivations may reveal that RPM contracts can enhance consumer as well as producer surplus. We consider some of these issues in the next section.

13.3   ARGUMENTS IN SUPPORT OF VERTICAL PRICE RESTRAINTS

Any examination of RPM agreements must start with the recognition that firms enter such contracts voluntarily. That is, while legislation and judicial interpretation may permit such contracts, it has never mandated them. Yet if firms enter into such a contract willingly, then it must presumably be in their interest to do so. However, the firms in turn earn their profit from the patronage of consumers. So, it is entirely possible that the motivation behind the price restraint ultimately reflects an aim of providing consumer benefits as well from which the firm can draw profits. We now consider a variety of arguments that proceed along these lines.

13.3.1   Vertical Price Restraints as a Response to Double-Marginalization

One of the earliest arguments concerns the problem of double marginalization that we discussed in the previous chapter and which we review briefly here. Consider a monopoly manufacturer that sells to a single or monopoly retailer. As before, the manufacturer produces the good at constant unit cost c_U. It then sells it at a wholesale price w to the retailer who, in turn, incurs a marginal cost of c_D in reselling the product to consumers at price P. Consumer demand for the good is described by the demand function $Q = A - P$. Hence, as above, the total marginal cost of producing and retailing the product is $c_U + c_D$, which implies the maximal monopoly profit that can be earned jointly by the two firms is achieved by a retail price of $P^M = \frac{A + c_U + c_D}{2}$, as in equation (13.1). At this price, the two firms earn a combined profit of

$$\pi^M = \frac{[A - (c_U + c_D)]^2}{4} \tag{13.2}$$

However, if the two firms price independently of each other, they will not achieve this outcome. Consider first the retail firm. At any wholesale price $w \geq c_U$ set by the upstream producer, downstream profit π^D is

$$\pi^D = [P - (w + c_D)][A - P] \tag{13.3}$$

Reality Checkpoint
Leather Cuts All Too Deep

On December 7, 2006, the United States Supreme Court agreed to hear the case *Leegin Creative Leather Products, Inc., v. PSKS, Inc.*, No. 06A179. In accepting this case, the court signaled that is was ready to review its century-old policy on resale price maintenance. The court's decision in the case could give manufacturers and franchisors considerably more leeway in controlling the retail prices paid by consumers.

Leegin is a manufacturer of a line of women's accessories. In 1997, it initiated a new marketing policy designed to encourage retailers to promote its brand in a separate section of their stores. In order to participate in this program, retailers had to pledge to adhere to Leegin's suggested prices at all times. One of those retailers was PSKS. However, while it initially agreed to participate in Leegin's marketing initiative, PSKS found in mid-2002 that the product was not selling as hoped. Therefore, it placed its entire line of Leegin's products on sale. On discovering this, Leegin suspended its shipments of product to PSKS.

PSKS demonstrated at trial that its sales and profits decreased substantially as a result of Leegin's action. It argued that it was not bound by Leegin's promotion agreement and, specifically, by that part of the agreement that required that it not price below Leegin's stipulated minimum, because such agreements are per se unlawful. While the *Colgate* decision would allow Leegin's not to supply PSKS, the per se rule makes the agreement invalid. Under that rule, once the conduct is proven, liability is found without the need to show an adverse impact on competition. The jury agreed with PSKS and awarded the firm $1.2 million in damages, which was then trebled, plus attorneys' fees of approximately $350,000.

On appeal, Leegin did not contest the finding that there had been an unlawful agreement. Rather, it challenged the application of the per se rule to vertical minimum resale price maintenance. However, the U.S. Court of Appeals for the Fifth Circuit affirmed the district court's decision. The case then went to the Supreme Court.

As noted previously, the Supreme Court had recently decided that *maximum* resale price agreements would no longer be subject to the per se rule, but would instead be evaluated under the rule of reason. That decision, however, left intact the per se unlawful status of *minimum* resale price agreements. On June 28, the Supreme Court issued its decision. In *Leegin Creative Leather Products, Inc. v. PSKS, Inc.*, 551 U.S. (2007), the court overturned the nearly century-old *Miles* case precedent. The ruling meant that now minimum as well as maximum resale price maintenance agreements would be subject to a rule of reason test.

Source: S. LaBaton, "Century-Old Ban Lifted on Minimum Retail Pricing." *The New York Times* (29 June 2007), p. A1.

Maximization of this with respect to the retail price P implies

$$P = \frac{A + w + c_D}{2} \tag{13.4}$$

So, faced with wholesale price w, the dealer sets the retail price of equation (13.4), which clearly exceeds w for the dealer to earn a profit. In turn, this implies a total demand of

$Q = \frac{A-(w+c_D)}{2}$. This is, therefore, the demand facing the upstream manufacturer. Upstream profit is then

$$\pi^U = [w - c_U]\frac{A - (w + c_D)}{2} \tag{13.5}$$

This is maximized at a wholesale price of

$$w = \frac{A - c_D + c_U}{2} > c_U \tag{13.6}$$

The difficulty is that each firm considers only the impact of its price decision on its own profit and not on the profit of its vertical partner. As a result, the unit cost is marked up twice—once at the wholesale level as $w > c_U$ and again at the retail level $P > w + c_D$—hence, the name, double marginalization. Because each firm ignores the impact of its decision on the other's profit, the combined profit of each firm is less than the combined profit possible.

An RPM agreement is one way to resolve this issue. The optimal agreement will restrict the ability of the retailer to charge a price greater than P^M. With this constraint, the manufacturer can then set its wholesale price $w = P^M - c_D$.[7] As is easily verified, this greatly exceeds the wholesale price implied by equation (13.6). Freed from the fear of a second markup, the upstream firm can set a wholesale price that effectively claims all the monopoly profit for itself.

We have just shown that the double marginalization problem provides a motivation for the manufacturer to restrain the pricing of the retailer by setting a ceiling on the price consumers pay. As the *Albrecht* and *Khan* cases (see Reality Checkpoint, p. 353) illustrate, this motivation is quite real. Yet, it cannot be the driving force behind most vertical price restraints. To begin with, no double marginalization occurs if either the upstream or downstream market is competitive. If the upstream market is competitive, the wholesale price will be $w = c_U$, in which case equation (13.4) implies that the optimal retail price will be the same as the joint profit-maximizing price of equation (13.1). Likewise, if the downstream market is competitive, the retail price will be $P = w + c_D$. Effectively, the demand facing the manufacturer is the same as the retail demand—so again, the optimal price is given by equation (13.1).

Further, while RPM is one solution to the double marginalization issue, it is not the only one. One alternative is to merge the two firms. Making both firms part of a joint effort to maximize the merged firm's profit will resolve the externality issue—although, as noted in the previous chapter, it does so at the expense of losing the gains from having firms specialize. Alternatively, the upstream firm can sell to the retailer under a two-part tariff with a unit price of c_U. Since this unit price includes no markup, there will be no double markup problem. The retailer will optimally set a final price of P^M to earn the monopoly profit, and the fixed payment or up-front fee will share this profit between the two firms.

In short, to the extent markets are competitive or that firms can rely on nonlinear price contracts, the double marginalization problem is resolvable without resort to an RPM

---

[7] Equivalently, the manufacturer can specify that the retailer must buy $A - P^M$ units if it buys any at all. This number of units will clear the market at the optimal price P^M, and the manufacturer can again charge $P^M - c_D$ per unit to claim the monopoly profit for itself.

arrangement. Thus, we should not expect that most such agreements are motivated by a fear that retail prices are set above P^M. In fact, Lafontaine and Slade (2008) have presented evidence that most vertical price restraints are motivated by the participating firms' fear that without such restraints, retail prices will be too low. On the face of it, this seems to support the contention that RPM agreements are meant to suppress retail competition. However, there are sound theoretical arguments behind the argument that RPM agreements may make everyone, including consumers, better off even when they result in higher prices for at least some consumers. We now turn to these arguments.

13.3.2 RPM Agreements and Retail Competition with Price Discrimination

As just shown, an upstream producer selling to a perfectly competitive retail market can set the wholesale price w that implies the monopoly retail price without fear of any additional markup. We have also shown that even if the retail market is not perfectly competitive, two-part pricing contracts may still resolve the double marginalization problem without any recourse to a vertical price restraint. However, we know from our work in Chapters 5 and 6 that imperfectly competitive firms often have the ability to price discriminate. When this is the case, Chen (1999) has shown that the upstream manufacturer may find that an RPM agreement is the only way it can achieve its goals.

To illustrate Chen's (1999) argument, consider again the case above with demand described by: $Q = A - P$. Let there be a monopoly upstream producer with unit cost c_U and two downstream retailers (Firm 1 and Firm 2) with unit cost equal to the wholesale price w plus an additional retailing unit cost of c_D. The one difference from the earlier market setting that we now impose is that the total market demand can be segmented. In particular, $1 - \alpha$ of consumers are entirely mobile comparison shoppers who regard products sold at either store as perfect substitutes. These shoppers will simply buy from whatever firm has the lowest price. The remaining α consumers are evenly divided between the two firms. These are immobile local consumers who will buy only from their local firm. Thus, total demand is

$$Q = \frac{\alpha}{2}(A - p_1) + (1 - \alpha)[A - \min(p_1, p_2)] + \frac{\alpha}{2}(A - p_2) \tag{13.7}$$

We assume that the retail firms compete in prices for the mobile or comparison shoppers and divide these shoppers evenly at any common price. Hence, this Bertrand competition will result in a retail price equal to $w + c_D$ for the $1 - \alpha$ of comparison shoppers. However, because they can prevent resale between comparison and local consumers, each firm can act as a monopolist with respect to its local patrons. The demand segment from local consumers facing each firm is

$$q_i = \frac{\alpha}{2}(A - p_i); i = 1, 2 \tag{13.8}$$

It is straightforward to show that the profit-maximizing price charged the immobile consumers is the same as in equation (13.4). That is

$$p_i = \frac{A + w + c_D}{2}; i = 1, 2 \tag{13.9}$$

The dilemma facing the upstream firm should now be clear. If it sells to the two dealers under a contract that simply requires they pay a specific wholesale price w per unit, it cannot achieve the maximum profit of equation (13.2). Although there will be no second markup on the goods sold to comparison shoppers, there will be one on the goods sold to local shoppers. If, for example, it sets w to achieve the maximum profit from comparison shoppers, it will choose $w = P^M - c_D = \frac{A+c_U-c_D}{2}$. However, each firm will set a retail price for local consumers that does include a second markup over that wholesale cost, and this will reduce the joint profit below the maximum level—the more so the larger is α.

Unfortunately, selling to the two dealers under a two-part contract cannot resolve this issue either. Let us denote any such contract as (w, F). Because the producer cannot write the contract to be different depending on whether a local or comparison shopper buys the product, it cannot simultaneously keep the unit price low for sales the retailer makes to local shoppers while pushing it higher for sales to comparison shoppers.

The best the firm can do is to recognize that at any wholesale price w, all retail profit from sales to comparison shoppers will be competed away. Hence, each retailer will only realize a low profit π_L^i from sales to local customers. Given the local demand in (13.8) and the optimal pricing relation in (13.9), this profit will be

$$\pi_L^1 = \pi_L^2 = \alpha \frac{[A - (w + c_D)]^2}{8} \tag{13.10}$$

Thus, setting F equal to the value in equation (13.10) implies that $\alpha \frac{[A-(w+c_D)]^2}{4}$ is the total amount from both firms that the upstream producer can recover with a fixed fee. However, the manufacturer can earn additional profit by setting w above c_U. Therefore, the total profit π^U of the upstream firm will be

$$\pi^U = (1 - \alpha)(w - c_U)[A - (w + c_D)] + (w - c_U)\alpha \left(\frac{A - w - c_D}{2} \right) \tag{13.11}$$

$$+ \alpha \frac{[A - (w + c_D)]^2}{4}$$

Maximizing this with respect to w yields the optimal

$$w^* = \frac{2(1 - \alpha)(A - c_D) + 2 \left(1 - \frac{\alpha}{2}\right) c_U}{4 - 3\alpha} \tag{13.12}$$

It is easy to verify that as α goes to 0 so that all shoppers are comparison shoppers, the value in equation (13.12) converges to the wholesale price $w = \frac{A+c_U-c_D}{2}$ that is optimal for this case. Likewise, as α goes to 1, w^* converges on c_U, precisely the value necessary to maximize the joint profit in this alternative. For all values of α between 0 and 1, w^* will be less than the former price but greater than the latter price. Because the downstream firms price discriminate so that their prices include two different markups, the manufacturer has to accept a second-best solution in which her optimal wholesale price is a compromise between the high value needed to maximize profit in a competitive retail market and the low value needed when the retailer is a monopolist who will add a second markup. In turn, this means that no two-part contract (w, F) can achieve the first-best or joint profit-maximizing outcome. Chen (1999) shows that because any sort of price discrimination leads to varying retail markups, this will be a quite general result.

However, with the help of a RPM agreement, the first-best profit outcome is attainable. For example, a two-part tariff contract $\{c_U, \frac{[A-(c_U+c_D)]^2}{8}\}$, together with a vertical price restraint that neither retailer sell at a price less than P^M, will do the trick. With the wholesale price equal to c_U, both retailers will want to charge a price of P^M to local consumers. Competition would, of course, push the price to comparison shoppers below P^M, but the RPM agreement prevents this from happening. As a result, the retailers sell at the joint profit maximizing price P^M to all consumers, and each earns a profit of $\frac{[A-(c_U+c_D)]^2}{8}$ —which, of course, is the value of the fixed fee. Hence, the joint profit realized across all firms is its maximum value $\frac{[A-(c_U+c_D)]^2}{4}$.

Notice that the adoption of the RPM agreement will result in a lower retail price for local consumers but a higher one for comparison shoppers. That is, it does benefit some consumers. However, from the viewpoint of consumers used to searching retail firms for the best price, the RPM agreement will surely look like a mechanism meant to repress competition and raise prices. In this respect, it is interesting that in the *State Oil vs. Khan* case the Supreme Court removed the per se presumption against RPM agreements specifying a maximum price. State Oil Co. had imposed a maximum retail price on its distributors, one of whom (Barkat Khan) tried to exceed that price. However, Khan's actual pricing strategy was more complex. He did want to raise the price to premium buyers, but he wanted to lower the price to consumers of regular grade fuel. That is, Khan wanted to price discriminate. The RPM agreement subsequently legitimized by the Supreme Court appears to have been motivated in part by State Oil's need to prevent such price discrimination. In turn, this suggests that this motivation may well be important in promoting RPM contracts in general.

13.3.3   RPM Agreements to Ensure the Provision of Retail Services

In the preceding two sections, we have treated retailing as simply an extra stage that occurs between production and final consumption. This approach has allowed us to gain some important insights into the downstream pricing issues that the retailing stage raises. However, retailers such as supermarkets, discount chains, and department stores form the crucial link between those who make goods and those who use them, and these retailers provide many services that are valuable to the manufacturers. Not only do they gather information about customer satisfaction and desired changes in the manufacturer's product, but they also provide such valuable services as the provision of desirable shelf space, pleasant shopping environments, advertising, and product demonstration. These services can be crucial to the marketing and sales of the manufacturer's product.

Consider the magazine industry. Supermarkets and discount chains presently account for over 55 percent of single-copy sales of U.S. magazines. Because such sales are made at the full, nonsubscription price, they are profitable and quite important to publishing firms. Yet the publishers must rely heavily on the efforts of the retailers to sell their magazines. A prominent display near the checkout register, for example, can greatly increase sales. So can advertising or a promotional visit to the store by a celebrity. Publishers have a deep interest in making sure that retailers undertake such efforts. In recent years, publishers of *People* and other magazines such as *Cosmopolitan* and *Harper's Bazaar* have had tense negotiations with retailers like Walmart and Winn Dixie supermarkets over the display and promotion of these publications.[8]

---

[8]   G. Knecht, "Big Retail Chains Get Special Advance Looks at Magazine Contents." *The Wall Street Journal* (22 October 1997), p. A1.

Thus, the relationship between a manufacturer and its retailers should address the upstream manufacturer's interest in the provision of retail services—and the motivation for the retailer to incur the expense of such services. Promotion, product demonstration, and simply providing a pleasant place to shop are costly. Moreover, it is extremely difficult for the manufacturer to monitor the provision of such services. Taken together, these two facts mean that a manufacturer cannot simply specify the level of retail services that it wants for its product and assume that they will be provided. What is required is an enforceable contract that specifies the obligations of both the manufacturer and the retailer. It is this aspect of the vertical contract—that pertaining to the provision of retail services—that we now wish to examine.

Let us begin by describing how demand is affected by retail services. Denote by $Q(p, s)$ the amount of the good demanded at price p with retail service level s. Increases in the level of services s raise the quantity demanded at any price or, alternatively, raise the willingness to pay of each consumer. We assume that this effect takes the form shown in Figure 13.1. In this case, an increase in the service level from, say, s_1 to s_2 raises most the marginal consumer's willingness to pay. An example of a demand curve that captures this effect is $Q(p, s) = s(A - p)N$, where N is the number of consumers in the market. In inverse form, this is $p = A - Q/sN$. The top price anyone is willing to pay for the product is A, no matter the service level s, and more is bought as s rises.

Providing retail services is costly. Let the cost of supplying s retail services per unit of the good sold be described by a function $\phi(s)$. We will assume that the provision of retail services is subject to diminishing returns, so that raising the service level s raises the cost of providing such services and does so at an ever-increasing rate. For a given level of services s, the retailer's marginal cost of selling the manufacturer's product is $w + \phi(s)$. This is the sum of the wholesale price paid to the manufacturer w plus the cost of providing s retail services per unit sold, $\phi(s)$.

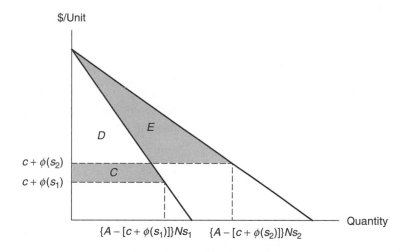

Figure 13.1 The effect of services on demand, costs, and the social surplus
Demand is given by $P = A - Q/sN$. This means that as the level of services rises from s_1 to s_2, the demand curve rotates up and to the right. At service level s_1, marginal cost $= c + \phi(s_1)$. If price equals marginal cost, total demand is $\{A - [c + \phi(s_1)]\}Ns_1$, and social surplus is the sum of areas C and D. At service level s_2, marginal cost $= c + \phi(s_2)$. In this case, equality of price and marginal cost implies that total output $= \{A - [c + \phi(s_2)]\}Ns_2$, and the social surplus is $D + E$.

Optimal Provision of Retail Services

We start with a determination of the efficient level of services that would maximize the combined consumer and producer surplus. Recall that efficiency in a market requires that price equal marginal cost. We assume that marginal production cost for a given level of services is constant at c_U. Hence, we have that $p = c_U + \phi(s)$ is a requirement for efficiency. Note that if this condition holds, there is no producer surplus. As shown in Figure 13.1, the social surplus at any price equal to $c_U + \phi(s)$ is just the triangular area above the cost line but below the demand curve. Accordingly, the optimal choice of service level s is the level of s that maximizes the area of this triangle. By definition, this area is given by $\{A - [c_U + \phi(s)]\}^2(Ns)/2$. To find the surplus maximizing value of services, denoted by s^*, we take the derivative of this expression with respect to s, and set it equal to zero. This yields

$$(A - [c_U + \phi(s^*)]\}^2 N/2 - Ns^*\{A - [c_U + \phi(s^*)]\}\phi'(s^*) = 0. \tag{13.13}$$

In turn, this implies that s* must satisfy

$$(A - c_U)/2 = \phi(s^*)/2 + \phi'(s^*)s^*. \tag{13.14}$$

Suppose, for instance, that $N = 100$, $c_U = 5$, $A = 10$, and $\phi(s) = s^2$. Then, a small bit of algebra will reveal that the social optimum calls for a service level of $s^* = 1$. (Remember, s is an index, and so it is measured in some arbitrary unit.) At this level of service, optimality would require that the price be equal to $c_U + \phi(s) = 6$.

Now, consider what the outcome would be if the monopolist could operate as a vertically integrated manufacturing and retailing business. Certainly, the price will be higher. The monopolist will not make a profit at a price equal to cost. But what about the integrated firm's choice of service level s? How would this compare to the optimum described in equation (13.14)?

The profit of the integrated firm depends upon the price it sets and the service level it provides. It is

$$\pi(p, s) = p(A - p)Ns - [c_U + \phi(s)](A - p)Ns \tag{13.15}$$

To maximize profit, the firm must choose both the profit-maximizing price p and the service level s. We take the derivative of the profit function with respect to each of these variables and set it equal to 0, yielding

$$\frac{\partial \pi(p, s)}{\partial p} = (A - 2p)Ns + [c_U + \phi(s)]Ns = 0 \tag{13.16}$$

and

$$\frac{\partial \pi(p, s)}{\partial s} = p(A - p)N - [c_U + \phi(s)](A - p)N - Ns\phi'(s)(A - p) = 0 \tag{13.17}$$

Equation (13.16) may be simplified to read

$$p^I = [A + c_U + \phi(s)]/2 \tag{13.18}$$

Here, p^I is the integrated firm's optimal price conditional upon a given service level s. Equation (13.18) implies that, as usual, the integrated monopolist will set a price of obtaining a unit of the good along with a given service level that exceeds the marginal cost of providing the good and the associated service cost $c_U + \phi(s)$. This is shown in Figure 13.2.

The next step is straightforward. Substitute the optimal price value from equation (13.18) into condition for the profit-maximizing service level shown in equation (13.17). Simplification then yields the following necessary condition for the profit-maximizing service level s^I:

$$(A - c_U)/2 = \phi(s^I)/2 + \phi'(s^I)s^I \tag{13.19}$$

Comparing equations (13.19) and (13.14), it is clear that they are the same. Although the integrated monopoly firm sets too high a price, the service level s^I that it chooses is the same as the socially optimal service level s^*. As it turns out, this specific result reflects the particular demand and cost relationships that we assumed and is not fully general. Nevertheless, the result is useful, because it does show that the manufacturer's interest in providing retail services is often in harmony with the public interest as well. As we shall see shortly, this is why vertical price restrictions can play a potentially welfare-enhancing role.

The Case of a Monopoly Retailer and a Monopoly Manufacturer

Let us next examine the case where the retailing of the good is done by an independent monopoly downstream retailer. The manufacturer sells the product to the monopoly retailer at wholesale price w, after which the retailer sells the good to final consumers at retail price p^M and provides s^M retail services. Keeping with the values of our earlier example, the downstream retailer's profit is

$$\pi^R(p^M, s^M, w) = [p^M - w - \phi(s^M)]Q(p^M, s^M) \tag{13.20}$$
$$= [p^M - w - \phi(s^M)]Ns^M(A - p^M).$$

As in the case of the integrated firm, the retailer must choose the two strategic variables, price p and the level of services s. The retailer in this case has exactly the same

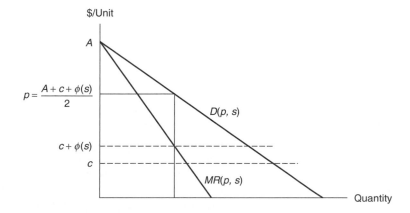

Figure 13.2   The integrated firm's optimal price as a function of the service level, s

profit-maximizing problem as did the integrated firm of the previous discussion, except that the retailer faces a marginal cost w that may differ from the true production cost c_U, depending on the upstream firm's price choice. So, we can work out the monopoly retailer's choices just by replacing c_U with w in equations (13.18) and (13.19). This yields the choices p^M and s^M satisfying

$$p^M = \frac{A + w + \varphi(s^M)}{2} \tag{13.21}$$

and

$$(A - w)/2 = \phi(s^M)/2 + \phi'(s^M)s^M. \tag{13.22}$$

Because $w > c_U$, the price implied by equation (13.21) exceeds that implied by equation (13.18). This is simply the double-marginalization problem again. At any given service level, the monopoly retailer adds her markup to the markup already reflected in the manufacturer's wholesale price. Yet, as a comparison of equations (13.19) and (13.22) also makes clear, having $w > c_U$ means that this double-markup is now compounded by a further problem, namely, a suboptimally low level of retail services. A careful examination of these two equations reveals that when $w > c_U$, then the level of retail services chosen by the retailer s^M is less than the level s^* that is optimal from the viewpoint of both society and the upstream manufacturer. The intuition behind this outcome is straightforward. Providing retail services is costly and this, along with the fact that the manufacturer charges a wholesale price w above marginal production cost, puts the squeeze on the retailer's profit. In response, the retailer tries to recapture some of her surplus by cutting back on services.

The failure to coordinate the actions of the manufacturer and the retailer leads to a less than desirable outcome—both for the firms and for consumers. Clearly, the manufacturer will not be happy with this situation. From his perspective, the retail firm is charging too high a price and offering too few retail services. Both of these actions reduce the final consumer demand facing the retailer and the profit to the manufacturer. Coordination of the upstream and downstream operations would result in lower prices and better services, increasing the joint profits of the two firms and making consumers better off. In the absence of vertical integration, what can be done to improve the outcome for both manufacturer and retailer?

We again consider two possible solutions. The first is a RPM agreement. The second is a two-part pricing strategy comprised of a fixed franchise fee T and a constant wholesale price w charged to the monopoly retailer.

In general, resale price maintenance will not solve the upstream manufacturer's problem. It is true that under an RPM agreement, the manufacturer can require the retailer to sell the product at the price p^* and thereby solve the double-marginalization problem. However, since there is no franchise fee, the manufacturer will only make a profit by charging a wholesale price w to the retailer that is greater than marginal cost c_U. Because the contract still leaves the retailer free to choose the level of services s the retailer will react to this profit squeeze by cutting its service provision below s^*.

What happens if the manufacturer adopts a two-part pricing mechanism? To begin with, we know that the manufacturer will set w equal to marginal production cost, or $w = c_U$. Only when w is equal to c_U is it possible for the retailer's final retail price and level of services to be exactly the same as those chosen by the integrated firm. Accordingly, the manufacturer must set a wholesale price equal to c_U.

Faced with a wholesale price of $w = c_U$, however, the retailer is in exactly the same position as our integrated firm was earlier. Hence, it will make the identical choices regarding the price to consumers p^I and the service level s^I. The downstream retailer's profit π^D prior to paying any franchise fee T will therefore be

$$\pi^D = [\mathrm{p}^I - c_U - \phi(s^I)]\mathrm{s}^I(\mathrm{A} - p^I)\mathrm{N} \qquad (13.23)$$

where p^I and s^I now take on those values that maximize the joint profit of the manufacturer and retailer together, namely, the values described by equations (13.18) and (13.19). Of course, if $w = c_U$, the manufacturer earns nothing and all profit goes to the retailer. As usual, this is where the franchise fee T comes in. By setting a fee equal to the integrated firm's profit, the manufacturer can capture all that profit for itself. Of course, if the retailer is truly a monopoly without which the manufacturer cannot bring its good to market, then the retailer is unlikely to agree to such a high franchise fee. Some profit sharing would have to occur. Again however, the point is that this arrangement can yield the optimal service outcome.

The foregoing argument suggests that franchising agreements are superior to RPM agreements as a means to achieve the provision of retail services. However, this argument rests critically on our assumption that the downstream retail market is monopolized. As we show below, matters change greatly if there is retail competition.

The Case of Competitive Retailing

Let's now consider the (perhaps) more likely case of a competitive retailing sector. One might think that this is a market structure that should work to the manufacturer's benefit. When there is only one retailer, the manufacturer's reach into the retail market is limited, as is its bargaining power with respect to claiming any of the additional profit that coordination yields. When there are many retailers, both the manufacturer's reach and bargaining power are enhanced. Competition among the retailers downstream will bring the retail price-cost margin to 0, and therefore, minimize the problem of double marginalization. The issue of the provision of promotional or retail services, however, still remains. We want to determine the level of services s^c provided by a competitive retail sector and compare that level with the manufacturer's preferred amount s^*.

We assume that all the downstream retailers are identical. Each buys the manufacturer's product at a wholesale price w and incurs the cost $\phi(s)$ per unit of output for retail service s. A little thinking leads us to two quick results. First, we know that retail competition will drive the retail price down to marginal cost. In other words, the price to final consumers will have to be $p = w + \phi(s)$. Second, that same competitive pressure will also force every retailer to offer, at that price, the level of services most preferred by consumers. Any retailer who offered a lower service level would quickly lose all his customers. Accordingly, competitive pressure will lead each and every retailer to offer the same retail price and the same service package. The competitive retail price will be $p^C = w + \phi(s^C)$, and the competitive service level s^C will be the level that maximizes consumer surplus given the price p^C. In Section 13.4.1, we showed that when the price of the good is equal to its true marginal cost (i.e., when $p = c_U + \phi(s)$), consumer surplus is $\{A - [c_U + \phi(s)]\}^2 Ns/2$. It follows that when price $p = w + \phi(s)$, consumer surplus is just $\{A - [w + \phi(s)]\}^2 Ns/2$. Maximizing this with respect to s yields the service level under competitive retailing, s^C

$$(A - w)/2 = \phi(s^C)/2 + \phi'(s^C)s^C \tag{13.24}$$

Comparison of the value s^c that satisfies equation (13.24) with the manufacturer's efficient level of services (s^* in equation (13.14) or s^I in (13.19)) reveals that the competitive outcome will again provide too low a level of services, so long as the wholesale price w exceeds the production cost c_U. Since the manufacturer can only earn a profit if $w > c_U$, we once again have the problem that, from the manufacturer's point of view, the retail sector—now organized competitively—will provide too low a level of retail services. As always, the source of the problem is that the profit that results from providing increased service flows to the upstream manufacturer. As a result, each competitive retailer focuses only on the cost of services and ignores the extra profit that they bring to the upstream manufacturer.

Is there a solution to this problem of suboptimal service provision in the case of a competitive retail sector? If there is, it will not be reached by means of the two-part tariff strategy that worked before. The reason for this is straightforward. Competition among retailers drives the price-cost margin to 0. Consequently, there is no profit margin in the retail sector from which the manufacturer can extract the lump sum fee T. The only way that the manufacturer can earn any profit is to set $w > c_U$. However, unless it takes some additional steps, this will also raise retailing costs, thereby creating an incentive to cut services further.

The solution is to impose a carefully designed RPM agreement by working backward from the desired outcomes. The manufacturer wants a retail price equal to the integrated price of p^I. Hence, it should impose a RPM agreement that stipulates p^I at the retail level. The manufacturer also wants a level of services equal to the integrated level of s^I. If the retail price is p^I, then the wholesale price w should be set less than p^I by just enough to cover the cost of providing the desired service level s^I. In an effort to win consumers, retailers will provide as much service as they can afford given the difference between p^I and r. By setting $p^I - w = \phi(s^I)$, the manufacturer can count on retail competition in services to result in service provision at the desired level s^I.

Free Riding and the Provision of Retail Services

Retail product services enhance the consumer's experience with a product and raise the demand for it. They are, in this sense, a complement to the product itself, much the way roadways and service stations are to automobiles. However, because the provision of those services is costly and because the reward for providing them is not always transferred to the firm that incurs the cost, standard linear-price contracts might not ensure the optimal level of service provision. Instead, we have seen that firms will typically need a nonlinear price contract and, quite possibly, a RPM agreement to obtain a proper service level.

Although we have not been explicit, our discussion has basically assumed that the retail services we are considering are tangible items, such as parking, or pleasant store accommodations, or perhaps repair parts. However, one of the most important services that retailers provide is information. In this case, the argument for RPM agreements becomes even stronger.

The reason that securing the provision of informational services requires strong vertical price restraints is straightforward. Such information is a pure public good. It can typically be consumed freely by consumers whether they purchase the good or not. As a result, there is the potential for a serious free-riding problem in the retail sector.

Think about it for a moment. A consumer electronics shop may keep experts on hand to assist a customer in choosing the digital camera that best meets her needs in terms of portability and convenience, works most effectively with her computer and other peripherals, and fits best within her budget. Similarly, wine shops may employ personnel to advise customers regarding the quality of a particular vintage or the food that best accompanies a given wine.

Providing such presale or point-of-sale services is costly. Unfortunately, there is no obligation for the consumer, once educated by the store's expert staff, to buy from that specific establishment. Quite to the contrary, once fully informed, the consumer has a strong incentive to go to the "no frills" electronics shop down the street or to the discount wine shop around the corner and purchase what she now knows to be the proper digital camera and the appropriate wine at a lower price. Even worse, she is free to share her information with friends, who can then use this knowledge to bypass the specialty shops altogether and go directly to the low-price, low-service outlets.

Because information—including information about a product and its uses—is a public good, it is hard to deny it even to those who do not pay for it. As a result, low-price discount dealers can "free ride" on the hard work that specialty shops do. Of course, over time, this will mean that the specialty shops will be less profitable; so the likely outcome of this process, if left unattended, is a market in which few informational retail services are provided by any firm.

To be sure, the information externality that we are now introducing is qualitatively different from the service externality addressed in the previous sections. There, the externality was a vertical one in that retailers tended to overprice and underservice the products of an upstream manufacturer because they ignored the impact on the manufacturing firm's profit, whether the retail sector itself was monopolized or competitive. In the current case, though, we are talking about a problem that is explicitly related to the presence of retail competition. If retailing were monopolized, then no free riding would be possible because there would be no potential free riders, although in either case, the externality has ramifications for the upstream firm.

In addressing the horizontal externality presented by informational services, the advantage of a RPM agreement should be clear. It prevents one retailer from undercutting another and, hence, stifles the emergence of discount stores. In turn, this implies that consumers will visit the retailer who provides the best services, since they will not find a lower price elsewhere. In other words, RPM agreements in this view do suppress price competition; but this deleterious effect is offset by the fact that they encourage service competition.

Telser (1960) was one of the first to articulate the efficiency-enhancing potential of vertical price restraints and, specifically, RPM agreements. While this view was initially associated with the Chicago School approach, it has come to be widely recognized among economists of all persuasions. This is not to say that the fear that RPM agreements may principally work to suppress price competition has evaporated. It is just to acknowledge that offsetting benefits may also be realized. Indeed, the free-riding justification for RPM agreements can be valid, even when the information provided by retailers is not an explicit communication from staff to customers about product features or about which products are easiest to repair. This is because one of the services that retailers provide is a screening one. That is, top stores such as Bloomingdales, Neiman-Marcus, and Bergdorf Goodman play an important role in identifying and then selling "what's hot" or in fashion. Here again, providing this service is not cheap. Prestigious retail stores must spend considerable resources to build up their reputation for being on the "cutting edge" of fashion trends. Thus, when the store carries a manufacturer's fashion line, the store's reputations stands behind the quality or fashionability of the garment. If a consumer can go window shopping at a prestigious store to find out "what's in" this season and then buy the apparel at a discount store, we again have the problem of free riding. Here, too, the problem can be sufficiently severe that, absent RPM protection, no store would find it worthwhile to screen and identify the fashionability and quality of products.[9]

13.4 RETAIL PRICE MAINTENANCE AND UNCERTAIN DEMAND

We have been discussing the way in which pressures in the retail market can reduce the profit of the manufacturer and the welfare of consumers by creating disincentives to provide customer services. However, retail competition can be destructive in other ways as well. Consider the case of Nintendo, one of the dominant players in the video games market. When Nintendo first introduced its video game players and cartridges in the late 1980s, it faced one very serious obstacle. This was the recent history of the video game market. Led by Atari, that market grew from $200 million in 1978 to over $3 billion in 1982. However, the market then crashed even more rapidly, with sales falling to just $100 million in 1983. In that year, retailers found themselves with excessive inventories and cut prices drastically in order to liquidate this stock. Atari itself went bankrupt.

The boom-bust cycle of the video game market in the early 1980s, and especially the sizable losses incurred in 1983, made retailing firms highly skeptical about the prospects for any new video game product. Nintendo representatives found that department and toy stores were almost totally unwilling to talk to them about their product. Nobody wanted to buy Nintendo's games and risk getting caught with an inventory that could only be sold at distressed prices as in the previous video game cycle. Eventually, of course, Nintendo prevailed. Along with Sony and Microsoft, it is a dominant player in the video game market, earning a generous profit as a result. However, that victory was not guaranteed. Nintendo's product—so obviously valued by consumers—might never have survived had it not been for Nintendo's pricing strategy.

The Nintendo story was used by Deneckere et al. (1997) to offer another explanation for RPM agreements when retailing is competitive. When retail firms need to stock their shelves with inventory by ordering goods from the manufacturer in advance, the uncertainty of demand places them at a risk of holding excessive stock that can only be sold at a loss. In this case, a RPM agreement may again benefit both producers and consumers.[10]

The basic argument proceeds as follows. Let demand be given by:

$$Q = A - P \text{ with probability 0.5; and}$$
$$Q = \theta(A - P) \text{ with probability 0.5; } \theta > 1$$

$$(13.25)$$

[9] Matthewson and Winter (1983) make a similar argument that resale price maintenance can benefit consumers by economizing on consumer search costs, since consumers will no longer spend time trying to find out which retailer sells at the lowest price. This argument assumes, however, that no other means is available to inform consumers about retail prices.

[10] See also Marvel and McCafferty (1984).

Because we wish to focus on the impact of demand uncertainty, we will work with the simplest case possible, namely, one where $c_U = c_D = 0$. That is, we normalize both production and retail cost per unit to be 0. This does not lose any generality of the analysis, but it does make it easier to see the exact nature of the problem.

Consider first the profit-maximizing calculations of an integrated monopolist. If the firm knew demand was going to be low (given by $Q = A - P$), it would wish to set a price of $P = A/2$ and produce and sell $A/2$ units. If instead it knew that demand was going to be high (given by $Q = \theta(A - P)$), it would still wish to set a price of $P = A/2$, but now produce and sell $\theta A/2$ units. Suppose, though, that the firm does not know what demand will be and, furthermore, that it has to set its production in advance. What should the firm do?

Clearly, the firm will never wish to produce more than $\theta A/2$, the maximum it would produce in the high demand state. Would it ever wish to produce less than this amount? The answer in this case is no. If it produces less than $\theta A/2$, then—if demand is high—it will not have enough inventory to yield the maximum profit in this case. Since this event happens with strictly positive probability, producing less than $\theta A/2$ imposes some expected revenue loss. However, since production is costless, this revenue loss is not offset by any savings in production cost. From the integrated firm's viewpoint, it may as well produce $\theta A/2$ and be prepared to meet all of the forthcoming demand at $P = A/2$, rather than produce an amount ε less (which does not save any money) and take a chance of earning only $(\theta A/2 - \varepsilon)[(A/2) + (\varepsilon/\theta)]$.

What if demand is low? It does not matter. In that case, the firm will simply maximize its revenue by setting a price of $P = A/2$ and also selling $A/2$ units. Yes, this will leave it with $(\theta - 1)A/2$ extra units, but it did not cost anything to produce these units and they can be thrown away with no loss.

In other words, forced to produce before it knows the true state of demand, the integrated firm produces $\theta A/2$ units. When the state of demand is realized, the firm then chooses price $P = A/2$ regardless of whether demand is high or low. Because costs are sunk, the firm wishes to price where marginal revenue is 0 and simply discard excess units, rather than try to sell more, which would lower price so much that revenue would actually fall. The manufacturer's expected profit is therefore

$$\pi^I = 0.5 \left[\left(\frac{A}{2} \right) \left(\frac{A}{2} \right) \right] + 0.5 \left[\left(\frac{A}{2} \right) \left(\frac{\theta A}{2} \right) \right] = \frac{(1 + \theta)A^2}{8} \tag{13.26}$$

Now, consider what happens if the firm sells at a wholesale price w to a set of competitive retailers. To keep all else equal, we assume that, like the integrated producer, the retailers must order their stock before the state of demand is known. A critical difference that introducing a competitive retail sector brings is the implication of any excess inventory. If at price $P = A/2$, the integrated firm had any excess supply, it simply threw it away. At that price, the marginal revenue from another unit is 0. Selling any more would therefore push into the region where marginal revenue is negative, reducing total revenue (and, of course, total profit as well). However, for each individual competitive firm, the marginal revenue *is* the price. So long as this is positive and the firms have units to sell, they will sell them. To be sure, when all firms do this, the price falls; but from the viewpoint of any one firm, its decision to sell has no impact on price. Hence, each will continue to sell and try to earn more revenue given that they have already incurred the sunk cost of their inventory.

There are two cases to consider. First, suppose that θ is large enough that when demand is strong, it is much greater than when it is weak. In this case, the manufacturer has a great incentive to try to get the retailers to stock $\theta A/2$ units to make sure that she does not miss such a great profit opportunity when it arises. The difficulty, though, is that for any $\theta > 2$, stocking this many units means that if demand is low, the efforts of competitive retailers will be to sell all their excess inventory, which will make the retail price fall to 0. In that case, the retailers will earn no revenue at all. On the other hand, if the retailers have bought an initial stock of $\theta A/2$, then when demand is strong, the market will clear at a price of $A/2$. Thus, half the time the retailers will earn $A/2$ per unit, and half the time they will earn nothing. If they are to buy the $\theta A/2$ units that the manufacturer wishes to sell them, they must be offered a wholesale price that allows them to break even. Hence, $w = A/4$. At this price, the retailers buy the $\theta A/2$ units from the manufacturer. Hence, the manufacturer's profit π^M is

$$\pi^M = \theta A^2/8 \tag{13.27}$$

In the above case, the quantity demanded when demand is strong is sufficiently high that the manufacturer is willing to sell at a low wholesale price in order to get retailers to stock $\theta A/2$ units knowing that they will then earn zero profit if demand is weak. A higher wholesale price will lead to fewer units ordered by the wholesalers, and therefore less possibility that the price will be driven to 0 if demand is weak. This may be preferable if θ is not so large.

Let the amount of inventories ordered by the retailers in total be Q^L. When demand is strong, selling this level of inventories will lead to a price $P = A - Q^L/\theta$. When demand is weak, selling this volume will imply a price of $P = A - Q^L$. The competitive equilibrium requires that the expected price just equals the wholesale price w. Hence, for this second case, we must have

$$w = A - 0.5 \left(\frac{1+\theta}{\theta} \right) Q^L \tag{13.28}$$

At this wholesale price, the manufacturer will earn a profit of

$$\pi^M = AQ^L - 0.5 \left(\frac{1+\theta}{\theta} \right) (Q^L)^2 \tag{13.29}$$

The profit in equation (13.29) can be maximized with respect to Q^L to yield the optimal Q^L level of inventories that the manufacturer wants the retailer to buy. This value is: $Q^L = \frac{\theta A}{1+\theta}$. When this value is substituted for Q^L in (13.29), we find that the manufacturer's profit in this case is

$$\pi^M = 0.5 \frac{\theta A^2}{1+\theta} \tag{13.30}$$

It is easy to verify that the profit in equation (13.30) is less than that in equation (13.27) for all values of $\theta > 3$, but rises above the earlier value for $\theta < 3$. Thus, if $\theta > 3$, the manufacturer will set a wholesale price $w = A/4$ and sell $\theta A/2$ units. For lower values of θ, however, the manufacturer will set the wholesale price w given by equation (13.28) and sell $\frac{\theta A}{1+\theta}$ units. Note, though, that the profit in either case—as given by either (13.27) or (13.30)—is less than the profit of the integrated manufacturer shown in equation (13.26).

The dimensions of the manufacturer's problem are now clear. The first-best profit-maximizing inventory level is $\theta A/2$. If that turns out to be excessive, the integrated firm will just sell $A/2$ and throw away the extra units. Competitive retailers, however, will not throw away the extra units. Instead, they will compete to sell them and in so doing, will push sales to the point where marginal revenue as a whole is negative, and possibly to the point where the retail price is 0. The independent manufacturer can therefore get retailers to stock the optimal amount $\theta A/2$, but only by setting a low wholesale price $w = A/4$. Alternatively, if θ is not too large, the upstream firm can charge a higher wholesale price as given by equation (13.28), but this leads retailers to stock less than the integrated optimum $\theta A/2$. In either case, the manufacturer's profit falls below what it would earn in the integrated case.

A carefully designed RPM agreement can, however, save the day. The reason is that setting a floor retail price prevents the destructive competition among retailers that might otherwise drive the retail price to 0. The price floor P^F must replicate the price charged by the integrated firm. The wholesale price w must be such that the competitive retailers just break even when they buy the optimal amount $\theta A/2$ but sell only $A/2$ in a low demand period. Hence

$$P^F = A/2 \tag{13.31}$$

and

$$w = \frac{(1+\theta)A}{4\theta} \tag{13.32}$$

In fact, something like a RPM arrangement seems to have been the source of Nintendo's ultimate victory. It closely monitored inventories and cut off dealers who sold below Nintendo's suggested retail prices. Nintendo was forced in 1991 to sign a consent decree with the FTC under which it promised not to engage in any further implicit RPM behavior. By that time, however, Nintendo was well established in the video game market.

Since the RPM contract induces retailers to hold greater inventories, it can benefit consumers as well as producers. It depends on how much of the inventory is sold relative to sales in the absence of the agreement. Deneckere et al. (1997) show that in general, the RPM contract helps consumers so long as demand is not "too" variable.[11] However, it is also possible that without a RPM contract retailers will stock no goods at all if demand is extremely variable, as the Nintendo case illustrates.

13.5   NONPRICE VERTICAL RESTRAINTS

Beyond restrictions on prices, contracts between firms in a vertical relationship often include nonprice restraints. For example, both public and private schools often sell beverages produced by Coca-Cola or Pepsi. In return for providing the soft drinks, the beverage

---

[11]   The RPM contract always helps the manufacturer. In our example, For $\theta > 3$, the contract does not change sales if demand is high but lowers sales and consumer surplus if demand is low. For $1 < \theta \leq 3$, the contract lowers sales and consumer surplus if demand is high but raises both if demand is low. The latter effect can dominate.

firm will frequently include in its contract a prohibition against the school selling the drinks of a rival beverage producer. In addition, school personnel are often required to keep the vending machines stocked, and so on.

Requiring the school to sell no other soft drink is known as an *exclusive dealing requirement*. Such contracts are common not just between soft-drink makers and schools, but also between manufacturers of many products and their dealers. Lafontaine and Slade (2008) estimate that some such sort of exclusive dealing covers one-third of sales by independent retailers in the United States. Other nonprice vertical restraints, such as those granting dealers exclusive territories, are also common. As we saw in Chapters 9 and 12, nonprice vertical restraints can be instruments of predation and work to suppress competition. However, just like vertical price restraints, they can also be useful arrangements that benefit both manufacturers and consumers.

There are a number of arguments that may be used to justify exclusivity in vertical contracts. We present two of them here. The first has to do with free riding. The second has to do with commitment issues.

13.5.1   Exclusivity to Limit Free Riding

Household products companies such as Procter and Gamble, cosmetic manufacturers such as Revlon, and appliance firms such as Whirlpool/Maytag are just some of the many manufacturers that extensively advertise their products. Such advertisements may well increase demand for the manufacturer's brand. They may also increase demand for the product category in general.

Consider, for example, advertisements for Tylenol, the well-known nonaspirin pain reliever. Undoubtedly, such advertising helps raise the consuming public's awareness of both Tylenol in particular, and of the benefits of nonaspirin pain relievers in general. However, it is expensive. To recover the cost of the advertising, Johnson & Johnson, Tylenol's manufacturer, will have to raise Tylenol's price. We can easily imagine the following transaction between a pharmacy owner and a customer searching for Tylenol. When asked why she wants Tylenol, the consumer will say it is because she needs nonaspirin medication for pain and fever. The pharmacist may say that Tylenol will work fine but that he also can offer a lower-cost, unadvertised brand that is the chemical equivalent of Tylenol. The price of this alternative may not be a lot below the Tylenol price—just enough to persuade the customer to switch to this brand.

It is precisely because the pharmacist can sell the alternative nonaspirin pain reliever at a price relatively close to the price of Tylenol that the pharmacist has an incentive to inform the consumer of the alternative. From the perspective of Tylenol, however, the pharmacist is free-riding on Tylenol's advertising. Tylenol now makes no sale, even though it was the Tylenol advertising that may have induced the customer to ask for a nonaspirin pain reliever in the first place.

An exclusive dealing agreement offers a solution to this problem because it permits the manufacturer to prevent the retailers of its product from making such substitutions.[12] This is particularly important in the case of goods in which the retailer plays a role something similar to that of a doctor whose recommendation acts like an informal guarantee of the product's quality. Many intermediate goods sold between firms, e.g., chemical products,

---

[12]   Marvel (1982) is among those who have stressed this argument.

have this feature. At the retail consumer level, automobile dealers are among retailers who may serve this function.

A similar argument may justify the award of an exclusive territory to each dealer. Indeed, in a number of settings, it is the dealers that do the most advertising and promotional work. However, as we saw with informational services, the enhanced demand that the content of the advertising message generates does not have to accrue to the dealer that pays for that advertising. Thus, advertisements that promote the improved mileage of the Ford Focus (or its new 6-speed, dual-clutch automated manual transmission) may bring customers to many Ford dealers and not just the ones that incurred the cost of running the ads.

The award of an exclusive territory is one way to limit such free riding. So long as the territory is fairly large so that the nearest dealer is some distance beyond the audience for which the advertisement is targeted, the restriction helps the dealer who pays for the promotional effort also to be the one who reaps the benefits of those efforts. Without such a restriction, we might see retailers providing much less information about the various features and availability of their products.

13.5.2   Exclusivity and the Suppression of Competition

As we have just seen, exclusivity for both dealerships and territories can help solve important free rider problems. In the absence of these nonprice vertical restraints, firms might not provide the promotional (and especially informational) services that enhance both producer and consumer welfare. However, as our discussion in Chapter 12 showed, exclusivity can lead to foreclosure and other outcomes that inhibit market competition to the detriment of consumer and social welfare. We now describe two further ways in which this suppression of competition may be achieved.

Exclusivity as a Commitment Device

Consider two upstream manufacturers, Firm 1 and Firm 2, each of which sells its product through a related network of dealers, $D1$ and $D2$. Consumers regard products of Firm 1 to be the same no matter which dealer in network $D1$ sells it. Similarly, every unit of Firm 2 is regarded as identical regardless of the particular retailer in network $D2$ that is offering it. However, goods 1 and 2 are not perfect substitutes. In general, the demand for the two goods within any potential territory is

$$q_i = A - p_i + \mathrm{B}p_j; i = 1, 2 \text{ and } i \neq j \text{ and } 0 < \mathrm{B} < 1 \qquad (13.33)$$

Again, it is easiest to keep matters simple by normalizing $c_U = c_D = 0$, that is, by setting both the production and retailing unit cost to 0. Thus, for dealers, their only cost is the wholesale price w_1 or w_2 set by the manufacturer.

Now consider what happens if each manufacturing firm (1 and 2) does not grant exclusive territories to the dealers in its network. Competition among the dealers of Firm 1's product will result in $p_1 = w_1$. Similarly, competition among the dealers of Firm 2's product will imply $p_2 = w_2$. Accordingly, profit for each upstream firm is

$$\pi^i = Aw_i - w_i^2 + Bw_iw_j; i = 1, 2; \text{ and } i \neq j \qquad (13.34)$$

The best-response function for each manufacturer then is

$$w_1 = \frac{A + Bw_2}{2} \tag{13.35a}$$

$$w_2 = \frac{A + Bw_1}{2} \tag{13.35b}$$

From this, it follows that the equilibrium wholesale price w and upstream profit π^M are

$$w_1 = w_2 = \frac{A}{2 - B} \tag{13.36}$$

$$\pi_1^M = \pi_2^M = \left(\frac{A}{2 - B}\right)^2 \tag{13.37}$$

Now, consider what happens if Firm 1 assigns each of its dealers a monopoly in selling good 1 over a specific area by granting each the exclusive rights to sell good 1 over that area. Effectively, this means that the typical good 1 dealer faces the demand curve in (13.33) and a cost of w_1. The retailer profit will therefore be $\pi_1^R = (p_1 - w_1)(a - p_1 + Bw_2)$. This implies the following best response function for the Firm 1 retailers:

$$p_1 = \frac{A + Bw_2 + w_1}{2} > w_1 \tag{13.38}$$

Comparison of equation (13.38) with (13.35a) reveals immediately the impact of granting each dealer in network $D1$ an exclusive territory. On the one hand, there is a double marginalization, as a good 1 dealer now sets p_1 above w_1. On the other hand, this means that for any given wholesale price w_2 by Firm 2, the sellers of Firm 1 respond less aggressively than they did before. In turn, knowing this allows Firm 2 to raise its wholesale price, because prices are strategic complements.

The latter effect is the critical one for our purposes. What it means is that by limiting competition among its own dealers to sell its own product, Firm 1 also commits to pricing less aggressively relative to the dealers selling Firm 2's product. In other words, granting exclusive territorial rights to its dealers is a way for Firm 1 to soften price competition with its rival manufacturer, Firm 2. Of course, Firm 2 can do the same thing. When both firms establish exclusive dealers, the equilibrium wholesale prices are

$$w_1 = w_2 = \frac{A(2 + 3B)}{(4 - B - 2B^2)} \tag{13.39}$$

In turn, given the markup that the retailers make, this leads to final sales q_1 and q_2 of

$$q_1 = q_2 = \frac{A(2 + 3B)(2 - B^2)}{(4 - B^2)(4 - B - 2B^2)} \tag{13.40}$$

Hence, both firms enjoy a profit of

$$\pi_1 = \pi_2 = \frac{A^2(2 + 3B)^2(2 - B^2)}{(4 - B^2)(4 - B - 2B^2)} \tag{13.41}$$

This is greater than the profit in equation (13.37). The granting of exclusive territories has allowed each firm to set higher wholesale prices that more than compensate for the loss that the consequent double marginalization imposes. Consumers, of course face, higher prices and so are worse off.

Exclusive Dealing and Entry Deterrence

We know from our earlier work in Chapter 12 that contract clauses can be used to foreclose markets and deter new entrants—even when those new entrants are, on average, more cost-efficient than the existing incumbent. This can be achieved in some instances by appropriate breach-of-contract fees (Aghion and Bolton 1987) and in other situations by the strategic playing of one downstream firm against the other (Rasmussen, Ramseyer, and Wiley 1991). Comanor and Rey (2000) present another way in which this outcome can be achieved by appropriate use of exclusive contracts. We sketch their argument out briefly here.

Let there be an incumbent upstream firm with unit cost c_U and an incumbent retailer with unit cost c_D. The demand for the product is perfectly inelastic and equal to 100 units, so long as the final price is less than V. Hence, the firms will sell at $P = V$ and their joint profit $\pi^U + \pi^D$ will be

$$\pi^U + \pi^D = 100(V - c_U - c_D) \tag{13.42}$$

Suppose now that there is an alternative manufacturer that could enter with unit cost $c_U - \varepsilon$, that is, lower than the current manufacturer. Suppose as well that there is a potential retailer entrant with unit cost $c_D + \lambda$, that is, higher than the current retailer. If it is free to choose, the current retailer will switch to the cheaper upstream producer so that these two firms together will have a combined unit cost of $c_U - \varepsilon + c_D$. If this happens, the incumbent manufacturer will have no choice but to partner with the less efficient retailer. This partnership will have a combined unit cost of $c_U + c_D + \lambda$. This less efficient team will, of course, not be able to sell any units given the competition from the lower-cost rival combination. Therefore, each member of this less efficient team will earn 0 profit.

However, while the high-cost team earns no profit, its presence does set an upper limit on the price that the more efficient team can charge. That is, the final price can now no longer be V but must instead be $P = c_U + c_D + \lambda$ if, as we assume, $\lambda < V - c_U - c_D$. As a result, the cost-efficient combination will earn a profit of

$$\pi^U + \pi^D = 100(c_U + c_D + \lambda - (c_U - \varepsilon) - c_D) = 100(\varepsilon + \lambda) \tag{13.43}$$

Of this total, it is natural to suspect that the new, more efficient manufacturer will earn the portion that comes from its cost advantage, namely 100ε, while the initial incumbent retailer will earn the portion that comes from its relative efficiency, 100λ. In the post-entry equilibrium, then, the combined profit of the two initial incumbents—0 for the manufacturer and 100λ for the retailer—will be less than it was previously:

$$100\lambda < 100(V - c_U - c_D) \tag{13.44}$$

The attraction of an exclusive dealing arrangement between the initial incumbent manufacturer and retailer is now clear. The contract can institute a mutually beneficial agreement that raises both incumbents' profit above what it will be if entry occurs. This, of course, will reduce both consumer surplus and—by precluding the entry of a more efficient manufacturer—producer surplus as well.[13]

Mathewson and Winter (1987) present a similar model in which upstream firms compete for exclusive representation at downstream dealers. The market power of the product that obtains this exclusivity is enhanced. However, the competition to win that prize often is won by selling to the dealer at a very low wholesale price. The result is that consumers lose the option of buying the excluded good—but they get the product that is sold at a very low price. As Mathewson and Winter (1987) show, the net effect of exclusive dealing for social welfare is somewhat ambiguous in this case.[14]

13.6   AFTERMARKETS

The vertical restrictions that we have examined so far primarily reflect constraints on the sale of the same product as it moves through the chain from the upstream producer to the downstream dealer. In recent years, a different kind of vertical restriction has caught the interest of economists—one that is closely related to the tying arrangements that we considered in Chapter 6. This restriction effectively involves an exclusive selling arrangement in what are known as *aftermarkets*.

The key legal case in the aftermarkets debate is the *Kodak* case. The specifics of that case are as follows. Kodak was one of a number of manufacturers of micrographic equipment—used for creating, viewing, and printing microfilm and microfiche—and office copiers. This was the primary market (or *foremarket*). However, Kodak also provided repair parts and services to these machines through a nationwide network of technicians. Kodak advertised the quality of this network as a means of persuading consumers to buy its machines in the first place. Because no one needs micrographic or copier parts and services if they have not already purchased a micrographic machine or copier, the parts and services market is referred to as the *aftermarket*.

Just as in the foremarket, Kodak had competition in the aftermarket. There were many independent firms providing parts and services to firms using Kodak's office machines. However, to the extent that these independent firms needed replacement parts, they relied on Kodak to provide them. Kodak was happy enough to do so until it lost a service contract with Computer Service Corporation (CSC) to an independent firm, Image Technical Services (ITS). After that, Kodak announced a new policy of not providing replacement parts to any independent service provider. Effectively, Kodak agreed to an exclusive selling arrangement with its service network. It would only sell its repair parts to that group. As Kodak enforced the new policy more and more strictly, ITS and other independents filed a lawsuit contesting Kodak's action.

In court, Kodak asked for a summary dismissal of the plaintiffs' case. Kodak's basic argument ran along the following lines. There were many other producers of photographic

---

[13]   The foreclosure argument has been a recurrent topic in industrial organization. Bernheim and Whinston (1990) show that when there are two brands produced by two upstream firms and a single retailer, there are no incentives to adopt exclusive dealing. The retailer will always be a common dealer of both products. In the case of several retailers, O'Brien and Schaffer (1994) and Besanko and Perry (1994) find that exclusive dealing is always adopted. However, in the last two models, foreclosure is explicitly ruled out as an option

[14]   See Besanko and Perry (1994) for a similar model along these lines.

Reality Checkpoint

Trouble in Toyland: "It's Toys "R" Us or Them!"

On September 30, 1997, an administrative law judge ruled against the toy retailer Toys "R" Us on a charge of anticompetitive exclusive dealing. Three years later, a U.S. appeals court upheld this decision. The crux of the case was a government charge that Toys "R" Us had made informal agreements with America's leading toy makers, notably, Mattel and Hasbro. The nature of the agreement was that Toys "R" Us agreed to sell these manufacturers' products only if the manufacturers in turn refused to sell their products to large discount firms such as Sam's Club. This exclusive arrangement may have helped both Toys "R" Us and the toy makers by creating downstream profits that could be shared among them.

Toys "R" Us did not deny the charges. Indeed, at the time of the decision, it had already settled an earlier suit brought by 44 states by agreeing to stop the practice and paying a settlement fee of $50 million. Mattel and Hasbro also agreed to stop the practice, and each had paid a fee of $5 million.

Instead of disputing the allegation, Toys "R" Us argued that the practice was "perfectly lawful" as the firm's lawyer, Michael Feldberg, said. Mr. Feldberg continued that "[We] simply posed a choice to the manufacturers: It's us or them. If you sell an item to the warehouse clubs, we may not buy it." The justification for this policy was that Toys "R" Us screened what toys were in high demand and did the bulk of the promotional work for these items. In this view, the discount stores simply used Toys "R" Us to identify the hottest products and free rode on its advertising. There may be some merit to this contention, as we have seen. However, the case had the additional unusual twist of horizontal collusion. Instead of just offering an exclusive dealing contract to all toy firms, there was evidence that Toys "R" Us had worked to make the deal go through by coordinating with Mattel and Hasbro. In particular, it brokered a deal whereby Mattel agreed to the restriction of not selling to the discount clubs on the condition that Hasbro would do the same (so that Mattel would not be disadvantaged). Likewise, Hasbro agreed to the restraint on condition that Mattel would as well. As noted in the text, there are sound theoretical reasons to worry that vertical restrictions may facilitate horizontal collusion. The Toys "R" Us case suggests that those theoretical concerns also have some basis in fact.

Source: W. M. Bullkeley and J. R. Wilke, "Toys Loses a Warehouse-Club Ruling with Broad Marketing Implications." *The Wall Street Journal* (1 October 1997), p. B10; and T. Hall, "Toys "R" Us Loses Ruling." *The New York Times* (2 August 2000). For further details, consult the Federal Trade Commission website at http://www.ftc.gov.

office equipment. Kodak faced competition in the foremarket. As a result, Kodak argued it could not possibly exert monopoly power in the aftermarket. Before making a purchase in the foremarket, consumers consider the full cost of, say, a copier—both the price at the initial time of purchase and the price of services later in time. If Kodak were to try to charge a high price in the aftermarket for services, it would only attract foremarket customers if it reduced its machine prices by a corresponding amount. Hence, Kodak argued that it could not impose monopoly pricing in the aftermarket. The Supreme Court rejected Kodak's contention. Later, a jury turned in a verdict against Kodak.

The Kodak case has been followed by a number of similar cases (see Reality Checkpoint). Again, the central issue is whether and how a firm can exercise monopoly power

Reality Checkpoint
Aftermarkets After Kodak

The controversy over the aftermarkets issue raised in the Kodak case has continued to this day. Two cases subsequently decided by different circuit courts amply illustrate the continuing tension.

The case of *Alley-Myland v. IBM* 33 F.3d 194 (3rd Cir. 1994) involved a suit filed by an independent firm, Allen-Myland, that specialized in the maintenance and upgrading of IBM mainframe computers. The upgrade market was a substantial one—in some years as valuable as the mainframe market itself. At one point, Allen-Myland had half the upgrade market. Then IBM introduced a set of new policies. Specifically, IBM began to offer lower installation prices for firms that committed to use only IBM's upgrade services. Subsequently using an independent like Allen-Myland would then involve a financial penalty for breaking this contract. IBM also started to require customers to return used parts to them, thus drying up a potential alternative source of parts. Although the district court originally ruled for IBM, the appeals court overturned the ruling, noting that IBM could have substantial power in the upgrade market.

In *PSI v. Honeywell*, 104 F.3d 811 (6th Cir. 1997), the Court considered the case of PSI Repair Services, Inc., an independent firm engaged in the repair of computer systems. PSI filed suit under the Sherman Act against the computer manufacturer Honeywell, Inc. The basis of the suit was the fact that Honeywell forced computer chipmakers to refrain from selling parts unique to Honeywell computers to any independent repair services such as PSI and also to any Honeywell customers. PSI contended that this practice was precisely what was found to be illegal in the *Kodak* case.

After losing in the district court, PSI appealed to the Sixth Circuit U.S. Court of Appeals. That court also rejected PSI's claims citing two reasons. First, the Court noted that, unlike Kodak, Honeywell's refusal to deal was not a change in policy but something that it had always done. Second, the Court rejected the assertion of aftermarket power based on "lock-ins." The Court instead said that the relevant market was not the aftermarket for Honeywell parts, but rather the equipment market shared by Honeywell and its competitors. Consumers were free to purchase computers from other sources with different servicing policies.

Sources: Antitrust Litigation Reporter, 5 June 1997; and G. Graham. 1994. "IBM Sent Back By Appeals Court To Face Retrial In Anti-Trust Suit." *Financial Times* (19 August), p. 6.

in the aftermarket if it does not have such power in the foremarket. It seems clear that this will not happen if buyers find it easy to switch service providers in the aftermarket in the face of any price increase by one such supplier. In other words, there must be some sort of lock-in or switching cost such that once a buyer has a Kodak copier, the buyer cannot easily switch to another copier by selling its Kodak machine in a used-machine market and buying an alternative machine for which no service companies are excluded from obtaining parts. This seems a reasonable assumption in many cases, so long as the used machine market is not very well developed.

However, if buyers are forward looking, the presence of lock-in or switching cost effects may not be enough to permit the exercise of pricing power in an aftermarket. If buyers understand that buying a Kodak machine also means later buying expensive Kodak parts and service, Kodak will only sell its machine by cutting its price below that of its rivals, for whose machines cheaper service is available. Thus, Kodak and other companies as well have argued that they have no incentive to raise aftermarket prices, because it will simply require that they lower the price in the primary market by an offsetting amount.

We think that there are at least two reasons to suspect that the lock-in effect may translate into the ability to raise price above cost in the aftermarket. The first is simply that buyers may not be so forward looking as to consider the machine and its subsequent service as one integral purchase. To do so would require that they acquire information regarding their future service needs and future service costs over many years ahead—and, moreover, that they do this across all machine brands. This is both difficult and expensive. Yet, if buyers do not do this, then a firm with a lock-in technology can raise its aftermarket price without lowering its primary market price.

The second reason is more subtle. It is that firms such as Kodak may have no credible way to commit to a low service price far into the future, because there are always some locked-in customers who have recently bought the machine and who can be exploited. To see this point in a simple context, consider the following scenario.

Imagine that there are two producers of copying machines. Each type of machine lasts potentially for two periods. A machine runs without problems in the first period but has a 50 percent chance of breaking down in the second period. When it breaks down, the buyer can have it repaired, but only by using the repair service of the company that manufactured the machine. For simplicity, we will assume that the costs of producing the machine and also of repairing it are each 0.

Buyers are assumed to derive $50 of value from the machine for each period that it runs well. However, once a buyer buys a particular brand and integrates it into their production, the cost of switching to an alternative brand, setting up and reintegrating it into the buyer's operations midway through the machine's expected life is at least $50. In any given period, there are equal numbers of buyers who are in the market for new machines and buyers who have already owned a machine for one period.

If buyers are forward-looking, they will be willing to pay $75 for a new machine. This is the expected surplus they will receive over the machine's two-period life. With 50 percent probability, the machine will run fine for two periods and generate $100 worth of value. With an equal probability, it will break down in the second period, at which point switching to an alternative machine is not worthwhile given the switching cost.

Of course, the price of a new machine will be far less than $75. Indeed, competition between the two firms will likely lower this price quite close to cost. However, the price for repairs is another story. For those unlucky buyers who have bought a machine that has broken down after one period, they either have to do without a machine (and lose $50 of value) or get their machine fixed. As long as the cost of fixing the machine is less than $50, these buyers will be willing to pay for the repairs.

There is a time inconsistency in the firm-customer relationship in that buyer behavior changes once a machine is bought. By the second period, whatever price buyers paid for the machine initially becomes an irrelevant sunk cost. As a result, the firm always has some motivation to raise the repair price and extract some surplus from these buyers. Note that even if the repair price rises to close to $50, consumers with a broken machine will still be willing to pay to have it fixed since they get $50 of value from the machine working. In other words, even with that high a repair price, the expected value of a machine when it is first purchased remains at least at $75 so long as the price for repairs is less than $50. However, $50 is well above the cost of repairs. Thus, the equilibrium will be one in which the repair price exceeds marginal cost and everyone, including consumers, understands that this will be the case.

Although the model just presented is a simple one, its basic point can be generalized as Borenstein, Mackie-Mason, and Netz (2000) have shown. Recent work by Gabaix and Laibson (2006) suggests that the presence of some unsophisticated consumers can interact with the lock-in effects just described to make firms unwilling to announce low aftermarket prices, even when they can and even when competition is strong.

Suppose that while most buyers are rational, there are a few unsophisticated ones who, if repairs are needed, do not look at the alternative of buying and integrating a new machine, but just purchase the repairs as long as these cost $50 or less. Suppose, however, that—unlike our earlier case—the cost of switching to a new machine and integrating it with current operations is only $25. Rational or sophisticated buyers will foresee the possibility of machine failure and the need to switch. Competition may then lead to market entry until all profits are exhausted, implying that the price of machine and repairs *together* would have to be close to cost. This does not mean, though, that the equilibrium prices of both the machine and repairs have to fall to their respective marginal costs, which are here assumed to be 0. Instead, the outcome is likely to be one in which each firm sells its machine below cost but sells repairs well above cost, say at $50. Firms will lose money on rational consumers because these consumers will buy the machine at a price below cost and, if it breaks down, pay $25 in switching costs. However, the firms will recoup these losses from unsophisticated consumers who pay $50 for repairs rather than switching.

What is noteworthy about the above outcome is that each firm has little incentive to announce a low repair price. If it does, it will only lose the demand of forward-looking or sophisticated buyers. These buyers did not pay the high repair price in the first place. When they discover that the firm is lowering its repair fees, sophisticated buyers will recognize that this is only possible if the price for the initial machine is raised. As a result, at least some will switch their initial purchases to other firms. Even worse, the lower repair price will reduce the profits earned from unsophisticated buyers. For example, hotels often charge a low room price but set high fees for use of the phone and the minibar. Similarly, rental car firms may set a low rent for the car itself, but charge hefty rates for insurance and gasoline. In neither case do the firms compete by announcing low prices in these associated aftermarkets. They have no incentive to do so. Profits may be low overall, but that is because the foremarket price is inefficiently too low and the aftermarket price is inefficiently too high.

13.7   EMPIRICAL APPLICATION
Exclusive Dealing in the U.S. Beer Industry

The impact of exclusive dealing and exclusive territorial contracts has been the subject of many studies. The emerging consensus from these studies is that such contracts are beneficial, both for firms and for consumers, when they are not mandated by the government but, instead, are the result of private negotiations. A recent study by Tim Sass (2005) on exclusive dealing in the U.S. domestic beer market is an example of the kind of study that finds support for private vertical contracts.

The United States has a three-tiered beer market. At one end of the stream are the beer producers or breweries such as Anheuser-Busch (AB), Miller, and Coors. In the case of a foreign beer, the domestic firm importing that beer plays the role of a producer. Besides producing the beer, brewers also engage in a good bit of advertising and product promotion.

The brewers sell to the next tier, which is comprised of distributors. These sales are usually made at a constant price per unit, that is, they typically do not set franchise fees or use two-part tariffs. The distributors warehouse the product, do local advertising and promotion, and also monitor local beer quality. They sell to the third tier, the retailers from whom consumers make their purchases of beer. Again, sales to retailers usually employ linear pricing.

All of the major breweries have exclusive dealing contracts with at least some of their distributors. They also typically assign exclusive territories. The latter means that there is little *intra*brand competition among distributors. However, there is a fair bit of *inter*brand competition. It is very rare that a single distributor possesses a monopoly in a regional market.

Sass (2005) first tries to determine what factors lead to the use of exclusive contracts in the beer market. Data from a *1996/1997 Distributor Brand-Equity Survey* provides evidence on 381 distributor contracts, 69 of which include an exclusive dealing clause (most of these are AB distributors). If foreclosure is a motivation for such contracts, then they should become less likely as market size grows. This is because foreclosure basically works by denying the rival a sufficiently large sales base to permit exploiting scale economies, and this is harder to do when the market is large. Sass (2005) uses two variables to capture potential market size. One is the population (*POP*) of the distribution region. The other is the state-level market share (*MSD*) of the brewery that is the primary supplier of the distributor.

Another factor has to do with the local market information that the distributor has acquired. A distributor who has a lot of information about local consumer tastes and price responsiveness will likely be less willing to sign an exclusive dealing contract, because this limits that distributor's ability to profit from her information. Sass (2005) proxies this information by the number of years (*YRS*) that the distributor has been owned by the same family.

Finally, brewers may want to have exclusive dealing when they have large promotional expenses themselves that raise retail demand for beer in general—but which, in the absence of an exclusive arrangement, the distributor might meet by selling an alternative brand. To capture the importance of such non-brand specific advertising, Sass (2005) uses the national advertising of the brewer's primary supplier (*ADS*) and a (1, 0) variable indicating whether or not there is a state ban on billboard or sign advertising (*BAN*). If protecting its advertising against free riding is a motivation for the brewer, the first should have a positive effect and the second should have a negative effect.

Since a contract is either classified as an exclusive deal or not, the independent variable is either 1 or 0. Hence, Sass (2005) estimates this regression using the Probit procedure described in Chapter 9. Therefore, the estimated coefficients indicate how much a change in the explanatory variable will raise or lower the *probability* of using an exclusive contract. The results are shown in Table 13.1 (next page).

Overall, the evidence on the determinants of where exclusive dealing contracts are used in the U.S. beer market implies that these contracts are not used to harm competition. Instead, they appear to be used for the beneficial reason of protecting brewers' investments in their own product promotion. For example, increases in market size as measure by both *POP* and *MSD* raise the likelihood of an exclusive dealing clause, and the *t*-statistics

Table 13.1   What explains the use of exclusive dealing in U.S. beer distributor contracts?

Explanatory Variable	Estimated Coefficient	t-Statistic
POP	0.0001	(1.87)
MSD	0.0079	(2.79)
YRS	−0.0017	(−2.10)
AD	−0.0002	(−0.38)
BAN	−0.0955	(−2.12)

indicate that both of these effects are statistically significant. This suggests that these contracts are not being used to foreclose markets to rivals. There is some evidence that the real motive is to protect the brewer's generalized advertising efforts against free riding. While *AD* is not statistically significant, the presence of a ban against beer advertising on billboards and signs does have a negative effect on exclusive dealing. When there is less promotion, there is less need to protect it with an exclusive dealing contract. Finally, there is also evidence that as distributors gain experience and knowledge of the local market, they are less willing to sign an exclusive dealing contract that might restrict their ability to profit from that information. The coefficient on *YRS* is negative and significant.

Having examined the factors that lead to exclusive dealing, Sass (2005) then turns to examining the market effects that such contracts have. He considers four possible variables that might be affected. These are (1) the average price paid by the distributor to brewers, *PB*; (2) the price the distributor charges retailers for its primary brand, *PD*; (3) the quantity of the primary brand sold, *QPRIMARY*; and (4) the quantity of all brands sold, *QTOTAL*, each measured in logarithms.

Prices, of course, should reflect both supply (i.e., cost) and demand pressures. Assuming that production costs are roughly the same for the brewers, the cost differences in supplying a distributor will reflect shipping costs or the distance from the nearest plant *DIST*; the level of excise taxes *TAX*; and, possibly, the presence of a ban on outside advertising *BAN*, which could raise promotional costs. If these variables affect the price paid by the distributor, then they should also affect the price paid by the retailer. That price, in turn, should affect sales of both the primary brand and of all brands. Thus, these three variables belong in all four equations.

To capture demand effects, Sass (2005) uses three variables. These are (1) per capita income in the distribution territory, *INC*; (2) population in the distribution territory, *POP*; and (3) the percent of the population that is of prime drinking age, *AGESHARE*. Of course, the primary variable of interest is whether or not the distributor in question operated under an exclusive dealing contract, *EXDEAL*. This is a binary variable equal to 1, if there was an exclusive dealing contract, and 0 if there was not.

The four regressions suggested by the variables just described are as follows:

$$PB = \text{CONSTANT} + a_1 EXDEAL + a_2 DIST + a_3 TAX + a_4 BAN +$$
$$a_5 INC + a_6 POP + a_7 AGESHARE + \varepsilon_{PB}$$
$$PD = \text{CONSTANT} + b_1 EXDEAL + b_2 DIST + b_3 TAX + b_4 BAN +$$
$$b_5 INC + b_6 POP + b_7 AGESHARE + \varepsilon_{PD}$$

$$QPRIMARY = CONSTANT + c_1EXDEAL + c_2DIST + c_3TAX +$$
$$c_4BAN + c_5INC + c_6POP + c_7AGESHARE + \varepsilon_{QPRIMARY}$$
$$QTOTAL = CONSTANT + d_1EXDEAL + d_2DIST + d_3TAX +$$
$$d_4BAN + d_5INC + d_6POP + d_7AGESHARE + \varepsilon_{TOTAL}$$

These are the basic regressions that Sass (2005) estimates. However, in both the first and the fourth equations, he includes market share data for three of the major brands to see how their presence affects the brewer's price to the dealer and final total sales. Sass also recognizes that the distributor's costs—and, hence, the price to retailers—may reflect both the distributor's business savvy, as captured by the number of years the family has owned the distributorship, and an additional cost factor based on the average number of retailing shops the distributor must visit per week. Hence, Sass's final regressions are

$$PB = CONSTANT + a_1EXDEAL + a_2DIST + a_3TAX + a_4BAN +$$
$$a_5INC + a_6POP + a_7AGESHARE + MARKET\ SHARE$$
$$EFFECTS + \varepsilon_{PB}$$
$$PD = CONSTANT + b_1EXDEAL + b_2DIST + b_3TAX + b_4BAN +$$
$$b_5INC + b_6POP + b_7AGESHARE + OTHER\ COST$$
$$FACTORS + \varepsilon_{PD}$$
$$QPRIMARY = CONSTANT + c_1EXDEAL + c_2DIST + c_3TAX +$$
$$c_4BAN + c_5INC + c_6POP + c_7AGESHARE + \varepsilon_{QPRIMARY}$$
$$QTOTAL = CONSTANT + d_1EXDEAL + d_2DIST + d_3TAX + d_4BAN +$$
$$d_5INC + d_6POP + d_7AGESHARE + MARKET\ SHARE$$
$$EFFECTS + \varepsilon_{TOTAL}$$

We are mainly interested in the impact of exclusive dealing. Before discussing that effect, however, it is worth noting two features of this system. These are reduced-form equations. That is, they are not equations that describe the full supply and demand structure. Instead, they describe the outcome for the dependent variable in terms of the basic factors that underlie supply and demand. In each case, the final term represents the influence of random factors that may affect the brewer's price, the distributor's price, primary brand sales, or total brand sales.

In principle, each of these regressions could be run alone using ordinary least squares (OLS). However, it seems likely that the random factors that, for example, raise total demand may also affect primary brand demand—and, in turn, feed into prices. In other words, while the regressions may seem independent of each other, there is a correlation between the random forces affecting each one (i.e., $\varepsilon_{PB}, \varepsilon_{PD}, \varepsilon_{QPRIMARY}$, and ε_{TOTAL} may all be correlated). If they are, then information about the nature of this correlation can be used to estimate the regression coefficients more precisely. To do this, Sass (2005) employs a regression technique known as Seemingly Unrelated Regression. This approach estimates the four regressions simultaneously by applying an estimate

Table 13.2   Effect of exclusive dealing on market outcomes

Dependent Variable							
PB		PD		QPRIMARY		QTOTAL	
EXDEAL Coefficient	t-Statistic	EXDEAL Coefficient	t-Statistic	EXDEAL Coefficient	t-Statistic	EXDEAL Coefficient	t-Statistic
0.0630	(2.73)	0.0368	(2.13)	0.3241	(3.09)	0.2816	(2.74)

of the correlation across the error terms to construct generalized least squares (GLS) estimates. The estimated effect of exclusive dealing in each of the four regressions is shown in Table 13.2 above.

In every case, the effect of an exclusive dealing clause is positive and highly significant. It raises the unit price set by brewers by about 6 percent and the price set by distributors by about 5 percent. Despite these increases, final sales of both the primary producer's brand and of all brands also rise under exclusive dealing. These effects are particularly large. Demand for the brewer's product rises by 32 percent as the result of exclusive dealing. Yet, this does not come at the expense of other brands. Instead, their sales rise as well, by over 28.1 percent. In further regressions, Sass finds that exclusive dealing by one brewer (AB, in particular) does not significantly decrease rival brewers' prices.

The implications of these findings are relatively straightforward. The fact that exclusive dealing rises with the size of the market seems inconsistent with the idea that it is used as an anticompetitive foreclosure device. This inference is strengthened by the finding that such restrictions also do not tend to force rivals to lower their prices. Instead, the fact that exclusive dealing restraints rise with both market size and the presence of restrictions on outdoor advertising is more consistent with the notion that such contracts are used to mitigate conflicts between the brewery and its distributors.

Since the price to the distributor and the distributor's price to the retailer rise, and sales volume also rises, there is no doubt that the surplus of brewers and distributors is enhanced by exclusive dealing. What happens to retailers and consumers is less clear. However, the rise in sales volume is sufficiently large that there is a strong supposition that their surplus also goes up. In short, the results of Sass (2005) strongly indicate that exclusive dealing in the U.S. beer industry is welfare enhancing.

Summary

Consumers buy most of their products from retailers such as department stores, supermarkets, automobile dealers, and gasoline stations. In these and many other cases, the retailer from which the consumer buys is not the firm that originally made the product. The manufacturer lies further upstream in the chain of production.

Because a manufacturer relies on retailers to get his goods to the market, the manufacturer must hope that the retailers will share his views about the appropriate price to consumers and the proper amount of promotional and other services to provide. Yet this is rarely the case. Double marginalization and other problems lead to a divergence of interests between the manufacturer and the retailer. However, contractual agreements governing this vertical relationship can resolve some of these differences. Unfortunately, such agreements can also facilitate price collusion and suppress competition, among either manufacturers or retailers.

The contradictory effects to which vertical restraints give rise invariably mean that no rigid public policy rules can be applied uniformly to every case. Instead, each restraint can only be appraised in the context of the market in which it is observed. In this light, the recent decisions in *State Oil v. Kahn* and *Leegin v. PSKS* replacing the legal presumption that vertical price arrangements are per se illegal with a more nuanced rule of reason are welcome developments. However, the rule-of-reason approach does run the risk of capriciousness, as each vertical restraint is judged differently by different courts.

Problems

1. ABC, Inc. is a monopolist selling to competitive retailers. It faces a constant marginal cost of 10. Demand at the retail level is described by $P = 50 - Q$.
   a. What wholesale price maximizes ABC's profit? What retail price does this imply?
   b. What is consumer surplus if ABC sets a profit-maximizing wholesale price?
   c. What is ABC's maximum profit?

2. Assume that the actual number of retailers the monopoly ABC sells to is ten but that they act as perfect competitors. ABC now requires that each retailer spends $100 on services, which shifts demand to: $P = 90 - Q$.
   a. ABC decides to implement a RPM agreement with retailers. Under this agreement, what retail price should ABC specify? How many units will retailers sell at this price?
   b. What is consumer surplus under the RPM agreement?

3. Under the RPM agreement and the price specified in 2(a), what is the maximum wholesale price that ABC can set? What is its profit at this wholesale price? Did adoption of the RPM agreement improve social welfare?

4. Consider a market with two downstream dealers that compete in prices and face a retail demand of $Q = A - P$. Their only cost is the wholesale price set in the upstream market. That market also has two firms but these firms compete in quantities. Each has a marginal cost of zero.
   a. Derive the equilibrium retail and wholesale prices and the profit of each firm in this market.
   b. What would be the retail and wholesale prices if the upstream market were monopolized?
   c. Suppose that one retailer offers an exclusivity contract to both upstream producers in which it is the only retailer allowed to handle either manufacturer's product, but still pays a per unit wholesale price determined by upstream competition. Will all three participants in this arrangement be better off?

5. Most McDonald's hamburger outlets are owned by individual entrepreneurs who pay franchise fees to McDonald's for the right to use the McDonald's name and recipes. Recipes for food at least as good as McDonald's are easy to find and often cost less than the fees these entrepreneurs pay to McDonald's. Why are franchise holders willing to pay so much money to the franchiser corporation?

6. What are the incentives for McDonald's to require franchisees to buy hamburger buns, meat, napkins, and other supplies from the company rather than from other (possibly) lower-cost local suppliers—other than the incentive of removing double marginalization?

7. Two firms compete in quantities (Cournot) in a market in which final demand is given by: $Q = A - P$. However, rather than compete directly, the two firms compete through franchises in a two-stage process. In stage 1, Firm 1 and Firm 2 choose the number of franchises—n_1 and n_2, respectively—that each will operate in stage 2. Each such franchise incurs a one-time setup cost of K. Then the market opens and each of the $n_1 + n_2$ franchises chooses how much output to produce given that each has a unit cost of c.

a. Show that each franchise will earn an operating profit (apart from the setup cost of K) equal to

$$\pi_i = \frac{(A - c)^2}{(n_1 + n_2 + 1)}$$

b. The result in 7a implies that firm i's total profit π_i net of setup costs is

$$\pi_i = n_i \frac{(A - c)^2}{(n_1 + n_2 + 1)} - n_i K$$

What is the equilibrium number of franchises that each firm will operate?

c. Is your answer in 7(b) the number of franchises that would maximize the firms' joint profit? Explain.

References

Aghion, P., and P. Bolton. 1987. "Contracts As A Barrier To Entry." *American Economic Review,* 77 (June): 388–401.

Bernheim, B. D., and M. Whinston. 1990. "Multimarket Contact and Collusive Behavior." *Rand Journal of Economics,* 21 (Spring): 1–26.

Besanko, D., and M. K. Perry. 1994. "Exclusive Dealing in a Spatial Market of Retail Competition." *International Journal of Industrial Organization,* 12 (Fall): 297–329.

Bonanno, G., and J. Vickers. 1988. "Vertical Separation." *Journal of Industrial Economics,* 36 (March): 257–265.

Borenstein, S., J. Mackie-Mason, and J. Netz. 2000. "Exercising Market Power in Proprietary Aftermarkets." *Journal of Economics and Management Strategy,* 9 (Summer): 157–188.

Bork, Robert. 1966. "The Rule of Reason and the Per Se Concept: Price Fixing and Market Division." *Yale Law Journal,* 75 (January): 399–441.

Chen, Yongmin. 1999. "Oligopoly Price Discrimination and Resale Price Maintenance." *Rand Journal of Economics,* 30 (Autumn): 441–455.

Comanor, W., and P. Rey. 2000. "Vertical Restraints and the Market Power of Large Distributors." *Review of Industrial Organization,* 17 (Spring): 135–153.

Deneckere, R., H. P. Marvel, and J. Peck. 1997. "Demand Uncertainty and Price Maintenance: Markdowns as Destructive Competition." *American Economic Review,* 87 (September): 619–641.

Gabaix, X., and D. Laibson. 2006. "Shrouded Attributes, Consumer Myopia, and Information Suppression in Competitive Markets." *Quarterly Journal of Economics,* 121 (May): 461–504.

Lafontaine, F., and M. Slade. 2008. "Exclusive Contracts and Vertical Restraints: Empirical Evidence and Public Policy." *Handbook of Industrial Economics*. Cambridge: MIT Press, Inc., 391–414.

Marvel, Howard. 1982. "Exclusive Dealing." *Journal of Law and Economics,* 25 (April): 1–25.

Marvel, Howard, and S. McCafferty. 1984. "Resale Price Maintenance and Quality Certification." *Rand Journal of Economics,* 15 (Autumn): 346–359.

Mathewson, G. F., and R. A. Winter. 1987. "The Incentives for Resale Price Maintenance under Imperfect Information." *Economic Inquiry,* 62 (June): 337–348.

————. 1987. "The Competitive Effects of Vertical Agreements: Comment." *American Economic Review,* 77 (December): 1057–1062.

Overstreet, T. 1983. *Resale Price Maintenance: Economic Theories and Empirical Evidence*. Washington, DC: Federal Trade Commission Bureau of Economics Staff Report (November).

Pickering, J. F. 1966. *Resale Price Maintenance in Practice*. New York: August M. Kelley Publishers.

Posner, R. 1981. "The Next Step in the Antitrust Treatment of Restricted Distribution: Per se Legality." *University of Chicago Law Review,* 48 (Winter): 6–26.

Rasmussen, E., J. Ramseyer, and J. Wiley. 1991. "Naked Exclusion." *American Economic Review,* 81 (December): 1137–1145.

Rey, P., and T. Vergé. 2008. "The Economics of Vertical Restraints." *Handbook of Industrial Economics*. P. Buccirossi, ed. Cambridge: MIT Press, 353–390.

Steiner, Robert L. 1985. "The Nature of Vertical Restraints." *Antitrust Bulletin,* (Spring): 143–197.

Telser, L. 1960. "Why Should Manufacturers Want Free Trade?" *Journal of Law and Economics,* 3 (October): 86–105.

Sass, T. 2005. "The Competitive Effects of Exclusive Dealing: Evidence from the US Beer Industry." *International Journal of Industrial Organization,* 23 (April): 203–225.

Whinston, Michael. 1990. "Tying, Foreclosure, and Exclusion." *American Economic Review,* 80 (September): 837–859.

....

Part V
Topics in Nonprice Competition: Advertising and Research and Development

Chapters 14, 15 and 16 present analyses of nonprice competition. Chapter 14 focuses on advertising and begins with a derivation of the basic Dorfman-Steiner condition. It then considers the informational role of advertising, beginning with the quality signaling approach initiated by Nelson (1970) and pursued by others such as Bagwell and Riordan (1991), as well formal explanations of suppressed informational content such as Anderson and Renault (2006). We also examine the competitive effect of advertising in a spatial market conditional on the assumption that advertising does provide some information.

Chapters 15 and 16 address, respectively, R&D competition and patent races. We distinguish between drastic and nondrastic innovations and between product and process innovations. We derive formal models of the impact of market competition on technological progress, beginning with Arrow's (1962) classic paper. This permits identification of the replacement and efficiency effects that complicate the relationship between market power and the incentive to innovate. We then build a broader model and consider the impact of technological competition in the Cournot framework of Dasgupta and Stiglitz (1980). We also contrast the outcomes of technological competition in Cournot and Bertrand settings. Because there are likely to be positive externalities to any one firm's R&D, Chapter 15 also presents a formal analysis of R&D competition in the presence of such "spillovers." Chapter 16 discusses patent races and patent policy. We begin with the analysis of optimal patent breadth and length, working through such important contributions as Nordhaus (1969), Gilbert and Shapiro (1990), and Klemperer (1990). We then consider models of patent races—starting with Reinganum's (1989) important paper—and "sleeping patents." The implications of all these analyses are then examined in two final sections on patent policy, including licensing issues.

Each of these chapters includes an empirical application. Chapter 14 presents Ackerberg's (2001) study of the Yoplait advertising in South Dakota and Missouri. Chapter 15 presents Keller's (2002) analysis of technology spillovers, and Chapter 16 presents the Hall and Zedonis (2001) study of the effect of patent law on innovation.

After this section, students will understand that the formal tools of game theory and optimization also apply in a nonprice setting. In addition, they will understand that the choice of modeling strategy has important implications for the conclusions one reaches. Their experience with (and understanding of) formal hypothesis testing will also be enhanced.

14

Advertising, Market Power, and Information

Advertising is ubiquitous. It airs on our television sets and radios and is displayed all over the Internet. It accounts for many of the pages in magazines and daily newspapers, dots the landscape and cityscape with billboards, looks down on us from city buses and subway cars, flashes on shirts and other apparel, and is now beginning to turn up on cell phones. The ubiquity of advertising is reflected in the large amount of advertising expenditure. In 2008, advertising expenditures in North America were well over $200 billion.[1] A 30-second spot aired during either Super Bowl XLIII in 2009 or XLIV in 2010 cost on the order of $3 million.

The large volume of advertising expenditures and the cost of individual advertising campaigns are strong evidence that advertising is an important component of corporate strategy. Moreover, the different strategic environment in which firms find themselves is likely why advertising strategies and expenditures differ across industries. For example, the consumer goods giant Procter & Gamble was the largest U.S. advertiser in 2008, spending a total amount of close to $5 billion on advertising in that year. In contrast, Dell Computers spent only $538 million, or little more than one-tenth as much. Of course, part of the explanation behind these differences lies in different firm sizes. Yet, considerable variation among firms remains even when the basis of comparison is not total advertising expenditure, but rather the ratio of advertising expenditure as a percentage of sales revenue, that is, the advertising-to-sales ratio. GM, similar to most car companies, has an advertising expenditure that is roughly 3 percent of its total sales. This is well below the ratio at pharmaceutical firms (such as Pfizer), which typically spend over 10 percent of sales revenue on advertising.[2]

Economists have long been interested in understanding the role of advertising in the marketplace. Some of the earliest writings on advertising (e.g., Kaldor 1950, Galbraith 1958, and Solow 1967), took a negative view of this role. This early research treated advertising as an effort by the firm to persuade consumers that there are few, if any, substitutes for the firm's products. To the extent that this effort is successful, the firm will then enjoy a degree of monopoly power; it will not lose its customers to a rival should the firm raise its price. Yet, while beneficial for the firm, these efforts in persuasion are bad

---

[1] Data on advertising expenditures are from Advertising Age Data Center, adage.com.
[2] *Ibid.*

for consumers not only because of the monopoly power and resultant deadweight loss, but also because these advertising efforts themselves are costly. Since the differentiation achieved by advertising is not considered to be "real" but instead an artificial distinction created in the consumer's mind, the resources expended on advertising were seen as wasted. Accordingly, they would be better used to produce real goods and services.[3]

Industrial economists working in the Structure-Conduct-Performance framework coupled this analysis with the observation that the advent of wide-scale advertising in the second half of the 20th century was closely associated with the advent of mass production and the realization of large-scale economies. If advertising enabled manufacturing firms to expand their markets and thereby realize scale economies, then advertising should lead to a more concentrated market structure. Even worse, if advertising were persuasive, it could deter potential competition and new entry even when there was no real product differentiation. Established firms with a history of advertising would possess a market identity for their products that any new entrant would find difficult to overcome. As a result, the incumbent firm would be more immune to competitive entry.

The fear that advertising would confer monopoly power also found early empirical support. There was anecdotal as well as more formal evidence to support the hypothesis that wide-scale advertising enhances a firm's market power and its ability to raise prices above cost. The casual evidence was found in local drugstores and supermarkets, where comparisons of the price of a nationally advertised brand with that of its generic, or private label, substitute repeatedly showed (and still shows) that national brands sell at a significant premium. The formal evidence was provided by many early statistical studies that found a significant positive relationship between advertising and industry profitability across a wide range of consumer goods industries. An early study by Nichols (1951) offered statistical evidence that the major cigarette brands relied heavily on advertising to differentiate their products and thereby insulate them from price competition, especially that of "penny cigarettes." Many other studies followed; perhaps the best known is that of Comanor and Wilson (1967). Their basic finding that industries with high profitability are associated with high advertising to sales ratio has been replicated many times since, both for different time periods and different countries.[4]

14.1   ADVERTISING AND MONOPOLY POWER: THE DORFMAN-STEINER CONDITION

Advertising is costly. Profit-maximizing firms will only engage in advertising if it yields revenues sufficient to cover these costs. In other words, advertising must shift the firm's demand curve outwards. From this perspective, it is easy to see that perfectly competitive firms will not engage in advertising. Perfectly competitive firms face a horizontal or infinitely elastic demand curve and can sell all they want at the existing price. It must instead be firms that face a downward-sloping demand (i.e., firms with market power) that advertise in order to sell more. Such firms face a downward-sloping demand curve; so, in the absence of a shift of the demand curve, an increase in sales must be accompanied by a fall in price. Note that in this simple observation, the causality runs from monopoly

---

[3]   Viewed in this light, advertising is much like rent-seeking behavior. See, for example, Posner (1975).
[4]   See, for example, Lambin (1976), Geroski (1982), and Round (1983).

power to advertising. This should serve as a cautionary note to those who might otherwise assert that it is the advertising that causes the monopoly power.

More formally, assume that the firm's demand is described by $Q(P, \alpha)$ where P is the product price and α is the amount of advertising messages sent, measured for example as seconds of television or radio time, or perhaps as page space in newspapers or magazines per period. We assume $\partial Q/\partial P < 0$; and $\partial Q/\partial \alpha > 0$. We further assume that the cost per unit of α is constant at m,[5] and that marginal production cost is constant at c. The firm's maximization problem may then be stated as

$$\text{Max } \pi(P, \alpha) = (P - c)Q(P, \alpha) - m\alpha$$

The necessary first-order conditions are

$$\frac{\partial \pi}{\partial P} = Q(P, \alpha) + (P - c)\frac{\partial Q}{\partial P} = 0 \tag{14.1}$$

and

$$\frac{\partial \pi}{\partial \alpha} = (P - c)\frac{\partial Q}{\partial \alpha} - m = 0 \tag{14.2}$$

Equation (14.1) may now be easily expressed in terms of the Lerner Index. Specifically, the equation implies

$$(P - c) = -\frac{Q(P, \alpha)}{\partial Q/\partial P} \Rightarrow \frac{P - c}{P} = -\frac{Q}{P}\frac{\partial P}{\partial Q} = \frac{1}{\varepsilon} \tag{14.3}$$

We may similarly manipulate (14.2). Thus, we have

$$P - c = \frac{m}{\partial Q/\partial \alpha} \Rightarrow \frac{P - c}{P} = \frac{m}{P(\partial Q/\partial \alpha)} = \frac{Qm\alpha}{QP(\partial Q/\partial \alpha)\alpha}$$
$$= \frac{\alpha m}{PQ}\left(\frac{Q/\alpha}{(\partial Q/\partial \alpha)}\right) = \frac{\alpha m}{PQ}\left(\frac{\partial \alpha/\alpha}{\partial Q/Q}\right) \tag{14.4}$$

We know from equation (14.3) that $(P - c)/P = 1/\varepsilon$, where ε is the absolute value of the elasticity of demand. Turning to the right-hand side of equation (14.4), the first term is the ratio of advertising expenditures αm to total sales revenue PQ. The second right-hand side term reflects the influence of another elasticity term. If we define the elasticity of demand with respect to advertising as $\eta = (\partial Q/\partial \alpha)/(Q/\alpha)$, this term is the inverse of this advertising elasticity (i.e., it is $1/\eta$). Accordingly, Equation (14.4) may be rewritten thus:

$$\frac{\alpha m}{PQ} = \frac{\eta}{\varepsilon} \tag{14.5}$$

We now have a key result. A firm with market power maximizes profits by choosing a price and a level of advertising such that the ratio of advertising expenditure to sales is

---

[5]   This assumption may not always hold. Often there is considerable quantity discounting when air time, network time, or magazine space is purchased by a firm for advertising.

just equal to the ratio of the advertising elasticity of demand to the price elasticity of demand. That is, profits are maximized when

$$\frac{\text{Advertising Expenditure}}{\text{Sales Revenue}} = \frac{\alpha m}{PQ} = \frac{\eta}{\varepsilon} \tag{14.6}$$

Equation (14.5) is usually referred to as the Dorfman-Steiner condition, after the pioneering paper on advertising written by Dorfman and Steiner in 1954. It states that a firm with market power maximizes profit by choosing to spend a proportion of its revenue on advertising that is just equal to the ratio of the advertising elasticity of demand to the price elasticity of demand. That is, the firm will advertise until the ratio of dollar advertising to dollar sales equals the ratio of the advertising elasticity of demand to the price elasticity of demand. Note that the *less* price-elastic demand is, or the smaller ε is, the *more* the firm should spend on advertising; and the *more* advertising-elastic demand is, or the greater η is, the *more* the firm should spend on advertising.

The Dorfman-Steiner condition is a useful reference point in the analysis of advertising behavior. It helps us see the relationship between the firm's profit margin and the extent of advertising as an outcome of market power. Equation (14.6) confirms our earlier intuition that advertising will be more intense the more market power there is in the industry and, in particular, that the causality runs from market power, as measured by the Lerner Index, to advertising rather than the reverse.

A second insight of the Dorfman-Steiner condition is what it says about how the firm's advertising-to-sales ratio changes in response to changes in the cost of advertising. The condition in equation (14.6) shows that unless the change in cost alters the ratio of the two elasticities (the price elasticity of demand and the advertising elasticity of demand), the profit maximizing advertising-to-sales ratio will be constant. Even if the cost of advertising increases, the firm's advertising-to-sales ratio will not change if these elasticities are unaffected. This result suggests that the ratio of advertising expenditure to sales across industries will not be greatly affected by changes in the cost of advertising.

14.2   ADVERTISING AS CONSUMER INFORMATION

The textbook model of consumer choice assumes that consumers are perfectly informed about the kinds of goods and services available and their prices. However, consumers typically do not know which brands of products are available, or how quality varies across brands, or which stores sell which brands at the lowest prices. It is the marketing efforts of firms that inform consumers about a product's attributes, availability, and price. It was Gerber's launch of a major advertising campaign in *Good Housekeeping* in the late 1920s that made consumers aware of the availability of the new prepared baby food product—and simultaneously propelled Gerber to the dominant position in that market ever since. In recent years, pharmaceutical companies have spent billions to advertise drugs on television, frequently including commercials for drugs that treat conditions such as Peripheral Artery Disease, which few consumers knew about.

The Gerber (and perhaps the pharmaceutical) commercials make clear that advertising can often be associated with substantial market power. Yet, these and other advertising make equally clear that an important function of advertising is to provide consumers with information. As such, advertising plays a useful role in helping consumers learn of the choices available to them. Because information is in many respects the purest of all public goods, the private provision of such information may be particularly valuable. It is difficult to imagine that many markets would function if firms had no way of communicating with consumers via promotional activities.

At the same time, even a cursory survey of advertisements in the major media is enough to reveal that the explicit informational content of many commercials is very small. A car commercial may show a young woman driving along the California coast on a beautiful evening but say very little about the price, durability, or safety features of the car. A commercial for Kellogg's *Sugar Frosted Flakes* in which its cartoon tiger, Tony, says "They're great!" appears to be little more than an effort in persuasion. However, persuading consumers which products to buy is different from informing them of what goods they can buy. Persuasive advertising raises the possibility that consumers do not know their own preferences as assumed by standard economics models but instead have their preferences shaped by clever advertising.[6] Hence, there is a good deal of debate regarding precisely what information advertising actually conveys.

14.2.1 Advertising and Quality Signaling

An early—if somewhat speculative—answer to the informative content of advertising was offered by Philip Nelson (1970, 1974) in two seminal articles written in the 1970s. Nelson began answering the question by first posing another. "What do consumers *know* about a product *before* they purchase it?" Specifically, can consumers identify the quality of the product before they try it?

For certain goods, specifically ones such as salt or china dishes, Nelson argued that the answer is surely yes. Consumers can more or less ascertain the quality of these goods before they decide to buy them. The only issue remaining, then, is the search to find the lowest price. Following his suggestion, we might refer to these goods as *search goods*.

Nelson argued that many goods were, however, *experience goods*. For this class of goods, which might include health care products, electrical appliances, restaurant meals, and other services, consumers need to use them to learn their true quality. It was regarding these goods that Nelson suggested advertising could play a significant role.

The intuition of Nelson's argument is quite straightforward. The manufacturer of an experience good knows whether it is a high-quality or a low-quality product, that is, she knows whether or not the consumer will be satisfied with the product after purchasing it. The problem is that the consumer does not have this information and can only acquire it by perhaps painful experience. How can the producer—particularly one who knows that she is selling a high-quality product—get this information across to potential customers? Advertising is the key.

In Nelson's model, the role for advertising emerges because the manufacturer of, for example, an analgesic does not want the customer's business only once, but also hopes

---

[6] If advertising changes preferences, evaluating its welfare effects is very difficult. Dixit and Norman (1978) attempt to do so by using both preadvertising demand and postadvertising consumer behavior. If on the basis of both sets of tastes one gets the same welfare effects, they argue that the effect of persuasive advertising on welfare is clear. As noted by Fisher and McGowan (1979), however, this approach compares welfares before and after advertising using either one set of preferences or the other for both equilibrium outcomes, when it should compare the preadvertising equilibrium using preadvertising tastes to the postadvertising equilibrium using postadvertising tastes. But this raises the familiar problem of interpersonal comparison of utility levels.

to gain that patronage on a repeated basis. As long as experience with the pain reliever is satisfactory, the typical consumer will very likely continue to purchase that same product repeatedly, rather than start all over searching for an alternative brand. This is not the case, though, for an ineffective pain relief product. The consumer who buys a low-quality product will, in all probability, switch to an alternative brand the next time she goes shopping. Accordingly, only makers of high-quality goods have any hope of earning repeat purchases.

Nelson (1970, 1974) then argues that a firm's advertising expenditures are incurred up front, while the revenues from sales come later in the current period—and, possibly, in future periods. Accordingly, the advertising expenditures can only be financed by borrowing against these subsequent revenues. However, producers of good and bad products will differ in this respect. Those with bad products know that even if the advertising works to induce one sale, it will not lead to any subsequent sales. In contrast, producers of good products know that once they induce a first purchase, later purchases will follow. Accordingly, producers of good products can afford more initial advertising than those offering bad products. If this is the case, then consumers can infer a product's quality by the amount of advertising. That is, advertising serves as a reliable signal of quality, with firms doing heavy advertising being precisely those selling high-quality goods. Indeed, it is the extent of advertising and not its content that conveys this signal. Thus, there is in this view no need for advertising to have significant information content. It is the fact of advertising, perhaps heavily, that signals quality. Advertising can be informative even if specific commercials appear to have little informational content.

Nelson's (1971) argument can be illustrated as follows. Let Nature choose the quality of product with probability ρ that it is good and $1 - \rho$ that it is bad. Let $L < 0$ be the loss consumers suffer from buying a bad product and G the gain. When a firm's behavior reveals nothing about the quality of the product, consumers use these probabilities to determine the expected utility of purchasing the product as $E\left(U\right) = \rho G + (1 - \rho)L < 0$. The assumption that—conditional only on Nature's probability—the expected utility is negative implies that, absent any additional information, consumers will not purchase the product at any positive price.

However, additional information may come in the form of advertising. Specifically, let Z_1 be the present value of current and future profits, exclusive of advertising costs, for a firm marketing a bad product that consumers will not purchase more than once. Similarly, let Z_2 be the present value of current and future profits if the firm markets a good product that consumers will return to buy after having tried it once. Because firms marketing good products enjoy repeat sales and those marketing bad products do not, we have $Z_2 > Z_1$.

Now, imagine that advertising expenditure is a discrete choice (making it continuous would not materially affect the analysis). In particular, imagine that a firm can choose to spend 0, K_1, or K_2 on advertising, with $Z_1 > K_1 > 0$ and $Z_2 > K_2 > Z_1$. Clearly, a firm can afford to spend K_1 on advertising regardless of its type. Thus, spending K_1 or less provides no information to consumers about the product type, in which case they base their expected utility calculations on the probabilities ρ and $1 - \rho$. Given these probabilities, no sale will occur for a firm spending K_1 or less on advertising. A firm marketing a high-quality product, however, can afford to spend the larger amount K_2 on advertising. If it does, it will earn a net profit of $Z_2 - K_2 > 0$. In contrast, a firm with a low-quality product cannot afford to spend K_2 on advertising because this will result in a net profit of $Z_1 - K_2 < 0$. Knowing this, consumers rationally update their initial beliefs about the product's quality. Specifically, any product for which advertising is less than

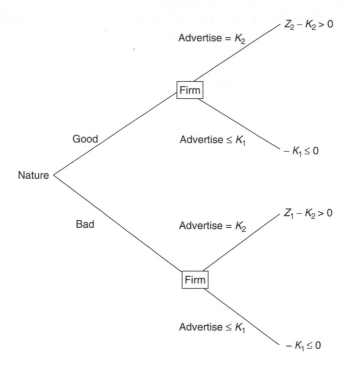

Figure 14.1   Advertising as a signal of product quality

or equal to K_1 is believed with certainty to be a poor-quality product (which is not worth buying), whereas a product for which the advertising expenditure is K_2 is believed with certainty to be a good product.

Figure 14.1 illustrates the advertising game just described. The firm has developed its product, and Nature randomly selects the product's quality to be good with probability ρ and bad with probability $1 - \rho$. This outcome is initially known only to the firm. At that point, the firm then determines its advertising expenditure as either 0, K_1, or K_2. A firm with a low-quality product can either choose an expensive advertising campaign that will win consumers initially but, because there will be no repeat purchases, lose money overall in the amount of $Z_1 - K_2$; or it can choose to spend 0 on advertising, which, given consumer beliefs, means that it will sell no goods and, consequently, also earn 0 profit. As $0 > Z_1 - K_2$, the obvious choice is to spend nothing on advertising. By contrast, a firm with a high-quality product can either choose to spend K_2 and earn a profit (in present value terms) of $Z_2 - K_2 > 0$, or spend K_1 or 0, in which case the best it can achieve is 0 profit. Here, the profit-maximizing choice is to spend K_2.

In short, we have a separating equilibrium in which consumers rationally believe that firms choosing an expensive advertising campaign have higher-quality products than firms that advertise only a little—and in which firms' profit-maximizing advertising decisions precisely confirm that belief. Note that we have said nothing about the content of the advertising. It is instead the fact that advertising is occurring—and at a high level—that signals that a product is of high quality. This is the essential idea behind the Nelson model.

For the next 15 years, Nelson's insight into advertising and signaling set the agenda for a great deal of theoretical work on advertising. An important early paper in this regard is Schmalensee (1978). That paper raises the point that Nelson's argument that a firm offering a "good deal" has a stronger incentive to advertise than a firm offering a "bad deal" depends quite a bit on the price-cost margin of a "good deal" relative to that of a "bad deal." In our framework, for example, we assume that $Z_2 > Z_1$. However, this need not be the case. While it is true that the good-quality product will enjoy greater repeat sales, it may also cost more to make and therefore have a lower price-cost margin. For example, suppose a high-quality pain reliever can be produced at a cost of 10 cents per dosage; while a worthless pain reliever, made from a commonly available extract of carrot roots, costs only a penny per dose to make. In this case, a firm offering the carrot root painkiller may find that it can earn a very high markup on each bottle sold. Even if no repeat purchases occur, the firm may earn enough on every first-time purchase to justify considerable advertising expense. Quite possibly, this expense will exceed the amount the maker of the high quality pain reliever will spend.

Yet, despite Schmalensee's cautionary point, the signaling possibility raised by Nelson remained the subject of investigation, and much additional work was done.[7] Among the more important papers in the signaling literature are those by Kihlstrom and Riordan (1984) and Milgrom and Roberts (1986). Kihlstrom and Riordan (1984) develop a two-period model in which a firm's advertising alone in the first period determines whether consumers believe the good to be a high- or low-quality product. Given consumer beliefs about quality, prices are then determined in a traditional demand-and-supply manner. The important result of the Kihlstrom and Riordan (1984) paper is that they also find a strong incentive for high-quality producers to lure "repeat buyers" by advertising heavily in the first period, just as Nelson (1970, 1974) found in his earlier and much simpler analysis. The contribution of Milgrom and Roberts (1986) is to show that both pricing and advertising can serve as a quality signal. Because both advertising and pricing can indicate product quality, the extent to which either is used is very complicated. Using a high price to signal quality is, however, often a cheaper alternative for the firm than advertising, with the result that the Milgrom and Roberts (1986) paper weakens the theoretical link between advertising and product quality. However, the Milgrom and Roberts signaling model is a monopoly or single-firm model. Fluet and Garella (2002) show that when the firm competes in price with other firms, it may be necessary to use advertising, not price, to signal quality.[8]

With regard to empirical evidence regarding Nelson's hypothesis, casual observation suggests that it is not easy to validate. To begin with, if Nelson's insight that costly advertising serves as a signal for high product quality is correct, we should see firms explicitly informing consumers just how costly their ad campaign is. Yet this is rarely (if ever) done. Similarly, if the Nelson hypothesis holds, then it should not be necessary to continue advertising extensively after many or most consumers have tried the good and experienced its high quality. Again, however, what we observe in practice is that firms who market established and well-known brands, such as Coca-Cola, Miller Lite, Chevrolet, and Rice Krispies, continue to launch expensive advertising campaigns.

---

[7]   The interested reader can refer to Bagwell and Riordan (1991) and Schwartz and Wilde (1985).

[8]   Remember, we are assuming again that firms care about repeat business. If not, and if consumers always inferred that high quality meant high price, every producer would raise its price whether it made a high-quality or a low-quality product.

Table 14.1   Price and quality in the upright vacuum cleaner market

Brand/Model	Model Quality Rating (0–100)	Price
Kenmore Progressive	74	$300
Hoover Wind Tunnel	69	$250
Eureka Boss	68	$150
Electrolux Oxygens	67	$400
Kirby Sentria	67	$1350
Riccar Superlite	66	$350
Bissell Healthy	64	$300
Oreck XL21	63	$750
Panasonic MV-V7720	63	$200
Dyson DC 14	62	$550

Formal empirical analysis has been nearly as critical. Kotowitz and Mathewson (1986) examined the quality-advertising relationship for both automobiles and whole life insurance. In neither case did they find evidence that the higher the advertising the better the deal. Similarly, Archibald, Haulman, and Moody (1983) examined running shoes and again found that neither price nor advertising levels for 187 brands were strongly correlated with the quality rankings, which were published in the magazine *Runner's World*. However, these authors did find that the magazine's quality ratings, once publicized and circulated, were very positively correlated with the extent of advertising done *after* those rankings were published. Firms with a high ranking were anxious to let consumers know this fact, while those with a low ranking were less interested in calling attention to a review that displayed their product's deficiencies.[9]

A study of 196 different industries by Caves and Green (1996) also found few discernible tendencies in the relation between advertising and brand quality. For many industries, these authors find that the quality-advertising expenditure correlation approaches a negative one—the exact opposite of Nelson's prediction. They do, however, find a positive relationship between advertising and quality in the case of new or innovative goods. They also find a weaker, but still positive, correlation between advertising and the quality of those goods in their sample that might be called "experience goods." The Caves and Green evidence on Nelson's hypothesis may then be best described as mixed.

As a final, but less formal, bit of evidence on this issue, we offer in Table 14.1 (above) an analysis of upright vacuum cleaners recently reported by *Consumer Reports*.[10] The table lists the top 10 models and their prices. It is quite clear that the correlation between price and quality is very weak. One of the lowest-ranked brands, the Oreck XL21, sells for nearly $300 above the average of $460. A medium-quality model, the Kirby Sentria, sells for nearly three times the average and four times the most highly ranked model. Moreover, while Kenmore and Hoover both advertise extensively, it is not clear that they advertise more than Eureka, Bissell, or Oreck.

[9]   *Runner's World* allows manufacturers to quote their rankings in advertisements. *Consumer Reports* does not.
[10]   *Consumer Reports.org*, Upright Vacuum Ratings, May 2007.

14.2.2   Suppressed Information Advertising Content

One way to interpret the work by Nelson (1970, 1974) is that the content of an advertising message is much less important than the fact of advertising itself. Because it is the existence of advertising that informs consumers that the product is of high quality, what the advertising message actually says does not really matter. This is important because, as noted above, much advertising seems to have very little informational content. A well-known review of the evidence from some 60 studies by Abernethy and Butler (1992) found that based on a 14-point measure, where 14 indicates complete information, the typical television advertisement scored 1.06, that is, it contained less than 8 percent of the possible information cues that could have been transmitted. Magazine advertising was slightly better with an average score of 1.56. The view that much advertising has little explicit information appears well founded.

Anderson and Renault (2006) also consider the Abernethy and Butler (1992) evidence, but offer a somewhat different explanation. They recognize that once the consumer has traveled to the store to make a purchase, that travel cost is sunk. This can lead to a so-called "holdup" problem for consumers. Suppose, for example, that consumers are interested in buying a differentiated widget, and each consumer's willingness to pay for each type of widget is shown in Table 14.2 below.

Each consumer also incurs a transport cost of $5.01 to visit the store. That cost is sunk once a consumer actually visits a store. A store is equally likely to have either red, yellow, or blue widgets. If consumers know only that a store has widgets, they infer a probability of one-third that the store has widgets of any specific color. Assume that the store incurs 0 cost per widget.

Consider two advertising strategies for a store that has only red widgets. The store can advertise that it has red widgets or the store can advertise simply that it has widgets. Which strategy will the store prefer? First, observe that the store will never set a widget price below $15, the minimum valuation of any consumer. Now, consider the first strategy of advertising that the store has only red widgets. If the retailer does this, consumer types 2 and 3 will not come to the store. The $5.01 in transport cost will mean that the effective price for them will never be less than $20.01. So, it is not worthwhile for either of these two types to come. Of course, the store knows this, too. So, if it advertises its "Red Widgets" alone, it knows that the only buyers who show up are Type 1 consumers. Since, for these consumers, the $5.01 in transport cost is a sunk cost once they are at the store, the owner can then charge them their full willingness to pay of $40 for the widgets. Foreseeing this outcome, type 1 consumers will not respond to a red widget advertisement either. Advertising that the store only has red widgets will therefore not attract any customers.

However, if the shop announces that it simply has widgets in general, consumers can reason as follows. Faced with a crowd of all consumer types, but not knowing who is

Table 14.2   Consumer types and widget demand

widget type	Consumer 1	Consumer 2	Consumer 3
Red	$40	$15	$20
Yellow	$20	$40	$15
Blue	$15	$20	$40

who, the shopkeeper will set a price of $15 per widget. This will permit the store to sell one (red) widget to each type and earn profit of $45 from each threesome rather than set a price of $40 and sell only to one type, or a price of $20 and sell to types 1 and 3 (each of which yields profit of $40 per threesome). Moreover, since consumers infer that the probability associated with each color is one-third, all three types will in fact respond to the ad by showing up at the store, knowing that the store owner will keep the price at $15.

A consumer will work out that for a price of $15 and a transport cost of $5.01, she will receive either a red, yellow, or blue widget (each with probability 0.3333) whose value therefore is 0.3333($40 + $20 + 15) =$25, implying a net value of $5 regardless of what the consumer's most preferred type is.

More formally, let there be a mass of N consumers each with a willingness to pay v for a particular type of widget that is uniformly distributed from 0 to V, the value depending on how the consumer's taste matches the variety of widget offered. The cumulative distribution of v is $F(v) = v/V$. Assume as well that each consumer will buy either one widget or none, depending on how the variety of widget offered matches her tastes and the price charged. Ignoring the transport cost, the demand for the firm's widgets at any price P will simply be that fraction of the N consumers whose willingness to pay v exceeds the price (i.e., it will be $N[1 - F(P)] = \left(1 - \frac{P}{V}\right)N$). Again, we normalize the product cost to 0 so that the shop's profit is given by

$$\pi = P\left(1 - \frac{P}{V}\right)N \tag{14.7}$$

Maximizing this profit with respect to the price P yields the optimal price as

$$P^* = V/2 \tag{14.8}$$

At price $P^* = V/2$, each consumer can calculate her expected surplus (exclusive of any transport cost) from visiting the store as

$$E(S) = \int_{P*}^{V} (v - P^*)\frac{1}{V}dv = V/8 \quad \text{where } p* = V/2 \tag{14.9}$$

So long as the transport cost is less than $V/8$, consumers will come to the store once they know the firm has the basic product. Let us make the assumption here that this is the case. Specifically, let us assume that the transport cost is $T = \alpha V$, with $0 < \alpha < 1/8$. Then, not knowing the product's precise characteristics, all N consumers will expect to earn a positive net surplus of $(1/8 - \alpha)V$ by visiting the store. When they arrive, $N/2$ will find it worthwhile to pay the $V/2$ the firm is charging and the firm will therefore earn $VN/4$ in profit. Hence, so long as the cost of advertising is less than this amount, it pays for the firm to advertise that it has widgets. However, as the colored-widget example shows, it does not pay for the firm to give detailed information such that it identifies precisely those consumers for whom the product is a perfect match (i.e., those for whom the willingness to pay is $v = V$). If it does, only those consumers will show up. Knowing that, the firm would then charge price $P = V$, which the consumers will pay, having already sunk the transport cost.

Before going further, let us note some of the interesting features of Anderson and Renault (2006). First, the model definitely identifies a motive for firms to suppress the informative content of their advertising. Indeed, the suppression of this informational content can raise welfare. A law that required full disclosure so that the widget shop had to advertise that it had only red widgets—or, more generally, that firms had to provide detailed information sufficient for each consumer to identify the value of their match—could lead to a complete breakdown of the market.

Second, in the cases at hand, it is also a matter of indifference whether the advertising includes any price information. In our example, the firm could mention that $P = V/2$, but even if it does not, consumers will use their knowledge of the market to work out that the price will be $V/2$ in order to work out their expected surplus. Hence, in this case, advertising need not contain any price information.

Finally, note that if the sunk transport cost T rises, the firm may have an incentive to provide more (but still less than complete) information. Suppose, for example, that in the case just discussed, $\alpha = 7/50 > 1/8$. Substitution then reveals that the price would have to fall to $0.4708V$ for the expected surplus generated by equation (14.9) to be sufficient to attract all N consumers.

However, advertising does permit an alternative strategy. In particular, suppose that the firm can advertise in such a way that all those for whom $v \leq 0.4V$ are made aware that visiting the store is not in their interest. The relevant distribution of consumer valuations then ranges from $0.4V$ to V, so that the relevant cumulative distribution is $F(v) = \frac{v - 0.4V}{0.6V}$ [for $0.4V \leq v \leq V$]. As can easily be verified, the profit-maximizing price therefore remains at $V/2$. For this restricted pool of potential customers, application of the expected surplus calculation (14.9) using the new distribution implies a positive expected surplus. Advertising that partially informs consumers, so that the 40 percent for whom the product is not a good deal drop out of the market, will result in the remaining 60 percent coming to the store. Five-sixths of this group—the same 50 percent of consumers who bought in the previous case—will then find it worthwhile to purchase the product at a price of $V/2$, having already sunk the T transport cost. That is, the firm sells at the same price to the same consumers it did earlier. This, of course, is really why $V/2$ is still the profit-maximizing price. By sending out advertising that includes some (but still incomplete) information regarding how the product matches with consumer preferences, the firm has been able to reach the same customers and earn the same profit even as transport costs have risen.[11]

14.3   ADVERTISING, INFORMATION, AND COMPETITION

The models of advertising and information that we have explored so far have been set in a market that is basically a monopoly. While the insights may to some extent be generalized to a more competitive framework, we have yet to analyze the role of advertising in strategic interaction. We now present two models that include competition.

---

[11]   Ellison and Ellison (2005) present a somewhat related argument regarding search engines on the Web. While e-tailers may want to attract search engines as a means to reach potential customers, they also wish to avoid revealing information that hurts the e-tailer's competitive position and profit. Thus, an e-commerce company has some reason to thwart the search engine, even though it may like the fact that the search engine or shopbot brings customers to its site. It may therefore resort to tactics such as listing a low product price that the search engine sees but then charging a very high transport price that the search engine does not see or similarly offer only very slow delivery.

14.3.1   Advertising, Information, and Competition in a Product-Differentiated Market

In the context of firm rivalry, the informational role of advertising takes on a new role as it becomes a means by which consumers can discover the availability of rival products. Armed with this knowledge, consumers can compare prices which, in turn, can make price competition more intense. Grossman and Shapiro (1984) present a useful model that illustrates this point. We present a modified version of their analysis below.

The model is set in the now familiar Hotelling (1929) spatial competition framework. There are two firms located at opposite ends of the Hotelling line. Firm 1 is located at the left end and markets brand 1, while Firm 2 is located at the right end and markets brand 2. A mass of N consumers is distributed continuously along this line, and each consumer's location indicates that consumer's most preferred version of the product. For product varieties located at other addresses, the consumer incurs a disutility cost equal to t per unit of distance the alternative is located from the consumer's most preferred point. Each consumer buys at most one unit of the product per period. If a consumer's location is x_i and she buys a product, her utility is

$U_i = V - p_1 - tx_i$ if she buys from Firm 1; and

$U_i = V - p_2 - t(1 - x_i)$ if she buys from Firm 2.

We first work out the outcome (see also Chapter 7) when all consumers are perfectly informed about each of the two products. Assuming that V is sufficiently large, or the prices of the brands p_1 and p_2 are sufficiently low that all consumers find it worthwhile to buy one of the two brands, and both brands have positive market share at these prices, then there must be a consumer whose preferred brand is located at some distance x^m from brand 1, and who is indifferent between buying brand 1 at price p_1 and buying brand 2 at price p_2. This implies that

$$V - p_1 - tx^m = V - p_2 - t(1 - x^m) \tag{14.10}$$

In turn, this implies that the location of the marginal consumer must satisfy

$$x^m(p_1, p_2) = \frac{(p_2 - p_1 + t)}{2t} \tag{14.11}$$

Brand 1 is purchased by $x^m N$ consumers, while brand 2 is bought by the remaining $(1 - x^m)N$ consumers. Hence, the demand facing each firm is

$$q_1(p_1, p_2) = x^m(p_1, p_2) N = \frac{(p_2 - p_1 + t)}{2t} N \tag{14.12}$$

$$q_2(p_1, p_2) = \left(1 - x^m(p_1, p_2)\right) N = \frac{(p_1 - p_2 + t)}{2t} N \tag{14.13}$$

This, in turn, implies profit functions for each firm of

$$\pi_1(p_1, p_2) = (p_1 - c) \frac{(p_2 - p_1 + t)}{2t} N \tag{14.14a}$$

and

$$\pi_2 (p_1, p_2) = (p_2 - c) \frac{(p_1 - p_2 + t)}{2t} N \qquad (14.14b)$$

Maximizing Firm 1's profit with respect p_1 then yields its best-response function $p_1 = p_2 + c + t/2$. When this is combined with the symmetrical best-response function for Firm 2, the resultant Nash equilibrium in prices is

$$p_1 = p_2 = c + t \qquad (14.15)$$

Grossman and Shapiro (1984) introduce an informational role for advertising in this model by assuming that a consumer knows the important information about a brand (i.e., its location and price) only when the consumer receives an advertisement from the firm selling that brand. In addition, the probability that each consumer actually receives that message is less than 1. This is not unreasonable. When a firm airs a commercial, it is quite likely that some consumers will not hear it, and so not everyone is informed in this market.

Formally, each firm chooses a level of advertising aimed at informing a fraction θ of the N consumers distributed uniformly along the line so that each consumer has the same chance of receiving an advertisement about a brand. Hence, a proportion θ_1 of the N consumers receives an advertisement about brand 1, while a proportion θ_2 receives an advertisement about brand 2. The fraction θ_1 that receives an advertisement for brand 1 may be further divided into two groups. One group is the proportion $\theta_1\theta_2$ who also received an advertisement for brand 2, and the remaining group is the fraction $\theta_1(1 - \theta_2)$ who received the message from Firm 1 but did not hear a commercial for brand 2. There is also a fraction of consumers $(1 - \theta_1)(1 - \theta_2)$ who receive no advertisement from either firm. We assume that this last group of consumers simply does not participate in the market—that is, consumers who receive no commercial from either firm do not buy either brand 1or brand 2.

If $\theta_1 = \theta_2 = 1$, the situation would be the full-information setting already considered. However, the fact that both θ_1 and $\theta_2 < 1$ implies that the set of consumers characterized by any amount of information is still uniformly—but less densely—distributed along the line segment or "Main Street." Thus, from the viewpoint of Firm 1, only two subsets of the original N customers may actually purchase the firm's product. The first group is comprised of that fraction of customers $\theta_1(1 - \theta_2)N$ distributed uniformly along the line who have heard only the commercial of Firm 1. The other set of potential customers for brand 1 are those who have heard the commercials of both firms. These $\theta_1\theta_2 N$ consumers are also distributed uniformly along the line. Symmetrically, Firm 2 also faces two groups of potential consumers: the $\theta_2(1 - \theta_1)N$ who have heard only its message, and the same $\theta_1\theta_2 N$ consumers that have heard both messages.

Because firms cannot tell what information a consumer has when she visits their store, each firm must charge the same price to all consumers. Accordingly, it is the competition for those $\theta_1\theta_2 N$ consumers informed about both products that determines the market prices. Specifically, we can define a marginal consumer with an address of $x^m(p_1, p_2) = \frac{(p_2 - p_1 + t)}{2t}$.

The foregoing analysis implies that the demand for brand 1 is comprised of two parts. The first part is the $\theta_1(1 - \theta_2)N$ consumers who have heard only Firm 1's commercial and who we assume buy Firm 1's product. The second part comes from the $\theta_1\theta_2 N$ consumers who have heard commercials for both products and for whose patronage the two firms must compete through the prices they set. Hence, the demand for brand 1, denoted by q_1, is given by the equation

$$q_1(\theta_1, \theta_2, p_1, p_2) = \theta_1(1 - \theta_2)N + \theta_1\theta_2 x^m N = \left(\theta_1(1 - \theta_2) + \theta_1\theta_2\frac{(p_2 + t - p_1)}{2t}\right)N \tag{14.16}$$

Where $x^m(p_1, p_2) = \frac{(p_2 - p_1 + t)}{2t}$.

If advertising were costless, equation (14.16) makes clear that Firm 1 would want to raise θ_1 to the maximum value of 1, since this raises the firm's demand and therefore its profit so long as $p_1 > c$. Unfortunately, advertising is not free. We capture this formally by assuming that Firm 1's total advertising costs depend on the fraction of consumers θ it reaches with its message, as described by the following function:

$$A(\theta_1)N = \frac{1}{2}\alpha\theta_1^2 N \tag{14.17}$$

Firm X's profit function is therefore

$$\pi_1(\theta_1, \theta_2, p_1, p_2) = [p_1 - c]\left[\theta_1(1 - \theta_2)N + \theta_1\theta_2 x^m N\right] - \frac{1}{2}\alpha\theta_1^2 N \tag{14.18}$$

Maximization of this profit function requires that the firm choose two variables, namely, its price p_1 and the fraction θ_1 that it tries to reach via advertising. The two corresponding first-order conditions are

$$\frac{\theta_1\theta_2(p_2 + t - p_1)N}{2t} + \theta_1(1 - \theta_2)N - \frac{\theta_1\theta_2(p_1 - c)N}{2t} = 0 \tag{14.19}$$

and

$$(p_1 - c)\left[(1 - \theta_2) + \theta_2\left(\frac{p_2 - p_1 + t}{2t}\right)\right]N - \alpha\theta_1 N = 0 \tag{14.20}$$

There are, of course, corresponding conditions for Firm 2. However, we may take a shortcut to the equilibrium by relying on the symmetry of the firms in equilibrium leading to $p_1 = p_2 = p^*$ and $\theta_1 = \theta_2 = \theta^*$. With this requirement, the first of the two first-order requirements becomes

$$p^* - c = -t + \frac{2t}{\theta^*} \tag{14.21}$$

Similarly, the second first-order condition now becomes

$$(p^* - c)\left(1 - \frac{\theta^*}{2}\right) = \alpha\theta^* \tag{14.22}$$

These two conditions may then be jointly solved to yield

$$p^* = c + \sqrt{2\alpha t} \tag{14.23}$$

and

$$\theta^* = \frac{2}{1 + \sqrt{\frac{2\alpha}{t}}} \tag{14.24}$$

Because we assumed that some of the initial N consumers in the market remain uninformed,[12] we must make sure that the equilibrium value of each firm's advertising effort θ^* is less than 1. To guarantee that $\theta^* < 1$, we assume that the cost of advertising, reflected in the parameter α, is sufficiently large relative to consumers' preference for variety, reflected in the parameter t, that $\alpha > t/2$ holds.[13] When $\theta^* < 1$, we have in equilibrium a fraction $2\theta^*(1 - \theta^*)$ of consumers who know only about one brand, a fraction θ^{*2} who know about both brands, and a fraction $(1 - \theta^*)^2$ who do not know about either brand.

The market outcome that we have just derived yields a number of insights regarding advertising as a tool of competitive strategy. First, note that our assumption that $\alpha > t/2$ implies that the equilibrium price will now be greater than $c + t$—the price that prevailed under the fully informed equilibrium. In part, the higher price is necessary to fund the advertising that provides consumers with the information that they need in order to participate in the market. However, the higher price also partly reflects the fact that some of those customers do not know about the rival brand, and this lack of complete information dampens the competitive intensity relative to the fully informed case.

A further insight from our analysis is that an increase in the degree of specialization in consumer tastes—an increase in t—causes both price and advertising to increase. The more those differences in product brands matter to consumers, the higher the prices and the larger the advertising expenses. Here is yet another case in which it is important to understand that advertising does not play a causal role. Advertising is not the force that causes consumers to have specialized tastes, nor is it the factor that enables firms to set high prices. Instead, it is the fact that consumers have specialized tastes to begin with that both encourages firms to advertise extensively and that permits price to be set above marginal cost.

The final insight is the relationship implied between profitability and the cost of advertising. Substituting our results from equations (14.23) and (14.24) for the optimal price and advertising efforts into the profit function of equation (14.18), we find that, in equilibrium, each firm will earn a profit, π^*, equal to

$$\pi^* = \frac{2\alpha}{\left(1 + \sqrt{\frac{2\alpha}{t}}\right)^2} N \tag{14.25}$$

Inspection of equation (14.25) reveals that each firm's profit is increasing in the parameter α, the cost of advertising. In other words, the model yields the somewhat paradoxical result

---

[12]   Indeed, it is this implicit assumption that explains why the equilibrium price shown in equation (14.23) does not converge to the equilibrium when one lets α take on the value $t/2$ necessary to make α equal to 1. Having derived the equilibrium under the assumption that $\theta < 1$, and the market is imperfectly informed, we cannot now impose on that equilibrium result the contrary assumption that $\theta = 1$ and the market is perfectly informed.

[13]   However, the cost of advertising should not be so high that firms advertise only a little and there are too few consumers who know of both brands. In that case, it will not be profitable for the firms to compete in price for these consumers.

that profit of both firms rises as advertising grows more expensive. Although the result seems strange, the reason behind it is straightforward. When α increases, it becomes more costly to advertise to consumers. So, firms reduce their advertising levels. As a result, consumers in the market are now less informed about the alternatives that are available, and so each firm can raise the price of its brand with less fear of losing customers to its rival. The increase in the price-cost margin outweighs the increase in the overall cost of advertising.

In sum, viewing advertising in a framework of strategic interaction allows us to see that advertising provides information about the availability of rivals' products. The more consumers are aware of such substitutes, the more intense is the price competition and the closer price is driven to marginal cost. Price must exceed marginal production cost in order to provide firms with the funds to finance the advertising expenditure; but this is, to some extent, the cost of maintaining an informed marketplace. Perhaps more importantly, a setting of strategic interaction permits one to recognize that advertising is an endogenous choice of profit-maximizing firms made in response to market parameters—but does not causally determine them.

14.3.2 Advertising and Wasteful Competition

Careful examination of the Grossman and Shapiro (1984) model reveals that advertising is profitable in part because, by making consumers of a rival's product aware that a firm offers an alternative, the firm can induce some of these consumers to switch their purchase when its product is closer to their preferred variety. Yet, while this is beneficial to the firm that wins the consumer, it is, in equilibrium, a zero-sum game for the industry. Since each firm is charging the same price and each has the same cost, one firm's profit gain is the other's loss; and industry revenue remains unchanged even as the advertising expenditure rises. Thus, advertising competition has the potential to be wasteful—a point made early on by a number of economists, including Kaldor (1950), Galbraith (1950), and Solow (1967).

This insight can be easily illustrated by means of a simple game. Suppose Firms 1 and 2 sell differentiated products in a market and compete in prices and advertising. If neither firm advertises, price competition results in each firm earning a given level of profit Z. Incurring advertising costs then serves to raise market size and the pool of profit as described by the equations below:

$$\pi_1 = Z(1 + A_1 - bA_1A_2 - 0.5A_1^2) \tag{14.26a}$$

$$\pi_2 = Z(1 + A_2 - bA_1A_2 - 0.5A_2^2) \tag{14.26b}$$

where A_i is the level of advertising effort of Firm i, and b is a positive parameter.

As can be easily verified, the first-order conditions then yield the following best-response functions:

$$A_1 = 1 - bA_2 \tag{14.27a}$$

$$A_2 = 1 - bA_1 \tag{14.27b}$$

The Nash equilibrium is, therefore, $A_1 = A_2 = 1/(1 + b)$. Note that if b is large—if Firm 1's advertising largely offsets Firm 2's advertising—then the net effect of both firms' advertising is small. If, for example, $b = 10$, then the combined effects of optimal

Reality Checkpoint
The Brush War in Hog Heaven

A classic example of a "prisoner's dilemma" advertising war comes from the rivalry between Braun (owned by Gillette) and Optiva (owned by Philips), the two biggest makers of electric toothbrushes. For years the two firms engaged in a "no holds barred" PR war, each side taking extreme measures to convince households and dentists that its brush is best.

A most extraordinary round in this fight occurred in 1999. Optiva was vigorously pursuing market share for its Sonicare brand. It conducted tests purporting to show that Sonicare toothbrushes were both less abrasive to tooth enamel and far better at attacking bacteria below the gumline than Braun's Oral B Plaque Remover model. Under a Swiss dental scientist, researchers compared the two brushes by repeatedly brushing the teeth of 3,000 dead pigs. This was expensive. It required the purchase of pigs' heads from slaughterhouses and arranging for their transportation and refrigeration. Further expenses arose from ensuring that the tests were completed before decay set in.

Braun's response was quick and forceful. It sent a team of scientists to Kansas where it contracted with farmers to brush the teeth of a similarly large number of live pigs. For this, it not only had to pay the farmers but also arrange to sedate the swine, since hogs don't like their teeth cleaned electronically. Braun also had to pay its researchers extra to enter the sties and squat in the muck to brush the hogs' teeth. Unsurprisingly, Braun claimed the tests on live pigs demonstrated Oral B's superiority.

The whole affair was very expensive. It is hard to know how relevant the brushing of pigs' teeth is to human oral hygiene. Moreover, the resultant claims and counterclaims led to yet another court battle. Doubtless, both sides would have preferred a ceasefire to avoid these costs. Yet each found it difficult to halt its aggressive behavior unilaterally. It seems these tests yielded little gain for consumers. Since they also appear to be jointly unprofitable for producers, the advertising expenses must be considered largely wasteful—unless one thinks a hog's healthy smile is worth a lot, even if it's dead!

Source: M. Maremount, "Braun, Sonicare Brush Up on Their Legendary Feud." *The Wall Street Journal* (30 April 1999), p. A1.

advertising by both firms is to shift the market size and total profit pool up by just 0.4 percent of what it would have been if neither firm advertised at all.

The problem is that the two firms are caught in a "prisoners' dilemma" game, spending extra resources on advertising in a struggle to steal consumers from each other. If they cooperated, each would choose a much smaller advertising effort level of $1/(1+2b)$—a reduction of nearly half in the case of $b = 10$. Thus, while advertising provides information, it may nonetheless be excessive.

14.4   COMPLEMENTS, ADVERTISING, AND BRAND NAMES

The availability of software greatly enhances the demand for computers. Likewise, the building of roads greatly increases the sales for automobiles which, in turn, raises the appetite for gasoline. All these cases are examples of complementary relationships in which demand for one product rises as more of another good or service is consumed. Since advertising also raises the demand for a product, it may be useful to view advertising as part of a complementary relationship as well—as a complement to the advertised good. This carries the implication that advertising is something consumers would willingly pay for. This is the subtle argument made by Becker and Murphy (1993).

Providing information about the availability or quality of the good, even if that information is not complete, may be one way that advertising serves as a complement. Such information is valuable to consumers. As they acquire it, their demand for the product being promoted rises. The phenomenon of brand names may be related to this complementary function. Soft drinks, consumer electronics, automobiles, and, indeed, just about all goods and services are generally sold with specific brand names attached. A restaurant diner may order a "Coke." Someone searching for a digital music player will ask for an "iPod." A consumer in the market for a luxury car may look for nearby locations of Mercedes dealers. These and countless other examples make clear that brand names have value to consumers. Brand value is often a major intangible asset on a firm's balance sheet. In turn, this implies that the brand conveys something for which consumers are willing to pay. This is why street vendors typically claim to be selling a genuine "Gucci" or true "Versace" product.

Because brand names are a part of the advertising message, it seems likely that whatever value branding brings to the market, advertising is a means of exploiting that value. Having Brand X is more valuable to the consumer precisely because the complementary effect of advertising is explicitly tied to that brand. This effect may be because advertising provides information or identifies the product in a way that makes it easy for consumers to interact with others.[14] Another way that brand name advertising can be a complement to the product advertised is that it may convey information, not about the product's price, or quality, or location, but rather about how to use the good or service more effectively.

For example, the food manufacturing giant General Mills operates a Web site for its brand name Betty Crocker. Among other offerings, this site includes a link to "Betty's Recipes—What's on Hand?" Here, the interested browser is asked to list the ingredients that are available for that night's meal. Then, the site provides a number of "Betty's Favorite Recipes" which utilize those very ingredients. The recipes include both preparation steps and nutritional information. However, when listing the ingredients necessary for each dish, the site always gives a plug for the General Mills brand of that product (e.g., Gold Medal all-purpose flour).

An important aspect of the complementary approach to advertising is that it is consistent with the fact that consumers who have already tried an experience good and know its quality continue to respond to advertising. By advertising, the firm is providing something (perhaps at no cost to consumers) that consumers value. That extra value will be reflected in a shift in the demand curve for the advertised product. However, it turns out that the precise nature of the demand shift induced by advertising is of some importance. We now consider the two different ways in which this shift may occur.

---

[14] Clark and Horstmann (2001) show that if consumers care about wearing the "right" clothes or eating the "right" food, then firms can use advertising to coordinate consumer purchases. Consumers believe that a firm advertising more will have more purchases and a more valued product. This builds on the Bagwell and Ramey (1994) idea that advertising is a coordinating mechanism.

14.4.1   Advertising and Building Brand Value

Consider a firm that sells a product, such as a car, a new book, a film video, or a spring coat, of which each consumer typically wishes to buy only one unit. Assume there is a mass of N potential consumers who differ principally in the value v that they place on the product. In the absence of advertising, this valuation is distributed uniformly between a minimum of 0 and a maximum value denoted by V. For a given level α of advertising, this value is scaled up by the factor $v\ (\alpha)$, so that the distribution of values is now uniform from 0 to $v(\alpha)V$. Each consumer buys either one unit or none, where one unit is bought if the willingness to pay exceeds the unit price p.

To derive the demand curve facing the firm, we proceed in the usual fashion of identifying a marginal consumer who is just indifferent between buying and not buying. For this consumer, it will be the case that her value of the product just equals the price, that is

$$v(\alpha)V = p \tag{14.28}$$

Together, these assumptions imply that market demand for the product is

$$Q(p, \alpha) = N \int_{p}^{v(\alpha)V} \left(\frac{1}{V}\right) dV = N \left(1 - \frac{p}{v(\alpha)V}\right) \tag{14.29}$$

The total demand for the firm's product is negatively related to the price it charges p, but positively related to the extent of advertising α. Note that the demand function is linear in price, so that it can be represented by the general form $Q(p, \alpha) = A - \frac{B}{v(\alpha)}p$. As advertising or α increases, so does the factor $v(\alpha)$; hence, the demand curve rotates outward as shown in Figure 14.2.

Note though that the outward shift in the demand function that advertising induces in this case has a particular feature. In particular, the willingness to pay of those consumers who really like the good, that is, the relatively high V or inframarginal consumers, increases proportionately more than that of other consumers. We refer to this case as the *building value case*, because advertising does not work to expand the maximum number of consumers N that might possibly buy the product. Instead, the complementary

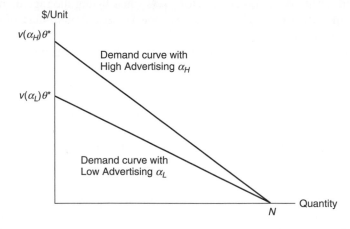

Figure 14.2   Effect of advertising services α on firm's demand when advertising raises/builds brand value

impact of advertising is reflected here in the increased willingness to pay of each of the N consumers.

14.4.2   Advertising and Extending the Reach

In contrast to the building value case, advertising may alternatively expand the potential number of consumers interested in buying the product. Suppose that, as in Grossman and Shapiro (1984), no consumer would know about the firm's product if it were not advertised. Hence, the firm must send out advertising messages if it is to make any sales at all. Suppose further that when a firm sends out an ad, not every potential customer will actually receive it. Some will miss it altogether. Others may see it but not really pay attention to its content. Consequently, advertising messages are received (in the sense of being understood) only randomly by consumers.

Specifically, let the initial set of uninformed consumers be of size N. Each consumer, once fully informed about the product, has demand for the product given by $q(p)$, which we assume is decreasing in price p. Hence, if all N consumers were in fact perfectly informed about the product, the firm's demand curve would be $Q(p) = Nq(p)$.

To become informed, a consumer must receive (i.e., see and understand) an advertisement. As just noted, however, when an advertising message is sent out, it is not necessarily received by all potential consumers. We model this "hit or miss" aspect of advertising by assuming that if the monopolist sends out only *one* ad to the group of N potential customers, then each such consumer has a probability $\frac{1}{N}$ of receiving it. Alternatively, each consumer has a probability of $\left(1 - \frac{1}{N}\right)$ of not receiving the one ad. Of course, the firm can send out more than just one ad. Suppose that the firm sends out α messages. Then the probability that a consumer does *not* receive any one of these α advertisements is $\left(1 - \frac{1}{N}\right)^{\alpha}$. When N is a large number, the probability that any one consumer *does not receive* an ad can be approximated by the function $e^{-\frac{\alpha}{N}}$ since as N grows large the probability $\left(1 - \frac{1}{N}\right)^{\alpha}$ converges to $e^{-\frac{\alpha}{N}}$ in the limit. Since the probabilities of all possible events must sum to 1, this in turn means that the probability that any one consumer *does receive* an ad from the monopolist is $1 - e^{-\frac{\alpha}{N}}$.[15]

Therefore, of the N potential consumers, the number of consumers the monopolist can actually expect to hear about the product when α ads are sent out is $\left(1 - e^{-\frac{\alpha}{N}}\right) N$. Since each of these consumers will, when informed, exhibit a demand for the product equal to $q(p)$, the monopolist's expected demand is

$$Q(p, \alpha) = \left(1 - e^{-\frac{\alpha}{N}}\right) Nq(p) \tag{14.30}$$

Assuming that the individual consumer demand function $q(p)$ is linear in price, then the market demand function is also linear in price and can be more simply represented by

$$Q(P, \alpha) = g(\alpha)(a - bP), \text{ where } g(\alpha) = \left(1 - e^{-\frac{\alpha}{N}}\right) \tag{14.31}$$

As in the previous case, increases in advertising or α will raise the expected demand at a given price. However, in this case, the effect is to rotate the demand curve out in the way

---

[15]   Our analysis essentially adopts the specification of advertising in Butters (1977).

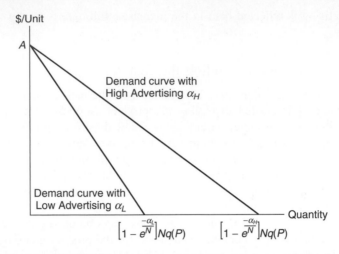

$$\left[1 - e^{\frac{-\alpha_L}{N}}\right] Nq(P) \qquad \left[1 - e^{\frac{-\alpha_H}{N}}\right] Nq(P)$$

Figure 14.3   Effect of advertising services α on firm's demand when advertising extends reach

that we have shown in Figure 14.3. When the firm increases the amount of advertising, the demand curve for the product again shifts out; but now the willingness to pay of the consumer who is on the margin of buying or not buying increases proportionately more than that of the inframarginal consumer. Advertising rotates the demand curve along the quantity axis, raising the number of consumers who would buy the product. Hence, we refer to this as the *extending reach* case.[16]

14.4.3   The Nature of Advertising, Product Prices, and Welfare

The distinction between the *building brand value* and *extending reach* cases just described are important for a number of reasons. For example, Norman, Pepall, and Richards (2008) show that the relationship between industry structure and the advertising-to-sales ratio will depend on which case applies. In a related piece, Zheng, Bar, and Kaiser (2010) show that the benefits of group advertising—such as the dairy industry's "Got Milk?" campaign—will disproportionately favor the larger firms if the extending reach case applies. The source of these differences stems from the way in which advertising affects the equilibrium price.

Consider first the building brand value case. As we showed above, this case implies a general linear demand function of the form $Q(p, \alpha) = A - \frac{B}{v(\alpha)}p$, or, equivalently, an inverse demand function $P(Q, \alpha) = v(\alpha)[A' - B'Q]$ where $A' = A/B$ and $B' = 1/B$. If production cost is c per unit and advertising cost is m per unit, the profit function is

$$\pi = v(\alpha)[A' - B'Q] - cQ - m\alpha \tag{14.32}$$

Let α^* be the profit-maximizing level of advertising. The necessary first-order condition with respect to output then implies the following price and output outcomes:

$$Q^* = \frac{Av(\alpha^*) - c}{2Bv(\alpha^*)} \quad \text{and} \quad p^* = \frac{Av(\alpha^*) + c}{2} \tag{14.33}$$

---

[16]   See Clark and Horstmann (2005) for a discussion of advertising in the presence of network effects.

Now, consider the extending reach case. The inverse demand function for this case can be written as $P(Q, \alpha) = A - \left[\frac{B}{g(\alpha)}\right] Q$. As illustrated in Figure 14.3, increases in advertising make the slope of the inverse demand function less negative. Therefore, the profit function is now

$$\pi = AQ - \left[\frac{B}{g(\alpha)}\right] Q^2 - cQ - m\alpha \tag{14.34}$$

In this case, the profit-maximizing price and output, conditional on the optimal choice of α, are

$$Q^* = \frac{(A - c)g(\alpha)}{2B} \text{ and } p^* = \frac{A + c}{2} \tag{14.35}$$

Comparison of the two cases shows that the impact of advertising on prices and output differs according to how advertising rotates the demand curve. In the building value case, advertising raises the optimal price but leaves the output level largely unaffected. The profit-maximizing output in this case will be completely unaffected if, as is often the case, we normalize the production cost c to 0. This is, in fact, a major reason that we refer to this as the building value case. In equilibrium, advertising mainly raises the price or value of the advertised product.

In contrast, in the extending reach case, advertising has no impact at all on the profit-maximizing price. Instead, advertising works here to raise the number of units sold at that price. Here, advertising expands the reach of the firm to sell to more customers without lowering its price.

Without explicit functional forms for $v(\alpha)$ and $g(\alpha)$, we cannot solve for either the profit-maximizing or socially optimal level of advertising in either of the two cases above. We might suspect that because the firm does not charge consumers for the advertising and efficiency requires price equal to marginal cost, the profit-maximizing level of advertising would be socially excessive. Yet, a complementary view of advertising implies that it is considered to be *one* of two goods that consumers wish to consume together.[17]

Because advertising does raise the product's price in the building value case but not in the extending reach case, this complementarity argument suggests that any possibility of excessive advertising is most likely relevant to the latter. The deeper logic of this intuition, however, comes from our work in Chapter 6 on product quality. Close inspection of the analysis above reveals that it is qualitatively identical to our modeling of the impact of quality in that earlier chapter. Hence, by analogy, there is likely to be too little advertising in the building value case, while there is some possibility of excessive advertising in the extending reach case.

Our discussion so far has focused on a single firm. As we have already seen, competition changes matters. When the products are differentiated, as in the Grossman and Shapiro (1984) model, the complementary impact of advertising is likely to be positive for the firm doing the advertising—but negative for its rival. In this case, each firm's choice of advertising can lead to wasteful advertising competition, as pointed out above. However, when firms market a more or less a homogenous product, then advertising by any one of

---

[17]   This result is shown formally in Becker and Murphy (1993, p. 957–958), which also offers a more general model of advertising as a complementary good. In effect, the market for advertisement is not cleared by price but, instead, rationed by the monopolist. Hence, the true marginal benefit to consumers may be either above or below the "price" for advertising that we actually observe.

them increases overall market demand for the product to the benefit of all firms. Thus, in this case, there may be a "free-rider" effect that results in suboptimally low advertising as each firm tries to free ride on the advertising of its rival.[18]

Because the free-rider effect diminishes as the number of firms in the market declines, there is a prediction that advertising and concentration will be positively associated in a homogenous goods market. Sutton (1991) makes a similar prediction regarding advertising and concentration in differentiated product markets. As explained briefly in Chapter 3, his work builds on the stylized fact that the greater the extent of sunk costs in the industry, the higher the equilibrium concentration tends to be.[19] Advertising may be viewed as such a sunk cost. Once the ad campaign is mounted and waged, the associated expenses can never be recovered. Hence, Sutton argues that in industries in which product differentiation is especially enhanced (or complemented) by advertising, then advertising expenditures will be high. These industries will be characterized by both considerable sunk cost and a high degree of concentration.

In both the homogenous and differentiated goods case, it is important to identify the link between concentration and advertising. In the first case, it is the greater concentration that induces more advertising—not the reverse. In differentiated goods industries, where advertising is a sunk cost and a complement to the product, both high concentration and high advertising are observed. In neither case does rising advertising intensity by itself lead to higher concentration.[20]

There are numerous empirical studies linking advertising intensity to either profitability or concentration, and the evidence on the relationship between advertising and concentration is quite mixed. Telser (1964) did one of the first studies to look for evidence of an advertising-concentration link. He found that, if anything, higher advertising was associated with *lower* industry concentration. Many other such studies soon followed. The findings of all these studies may be closely approximated by the summary statement that about half of them support Telser's original finding and half support the opposite view—that advertising is positively associated with concentration. To this summary statement we must again add that any observed link between concentration and advertising intensity reflects correlation and not necessarily causation.

14.5   EMPIRICAL APPLICATION: ADVERTISING, INFORMATION, AND PRESTIGE

There has been considerable debate over the role that advertising plays in influencing consumer demand. Advertising could offer basic information, signal quality, or provide a complementary aspect of social status or perhaps prestige to the advertised product.

---

[18]   However, Norman, Pepall, and Richards (2008) provide an offsetting argument based on the idea that when the impact of an advertising campaign is random, the payoff to advertising may rise with the number of firms seeking an effective advertising campaign.

[19]   More precisely, the greater the advertising sunk cost, the higher the *minimum* concentration ratio tends to be. This relationship is developed in Section 4.2, Chapter 4.

[20]   Schmalensee (1978) foreshadows this point. He considers a circular spatial model of a product differentiation with a few incumbent firms. The firms suppress price competition, but compete heavily on advertising. In turn, the heavy advertising makes it impossible for new firms to enter, because the consumer demand at a potential entry point is not sufficient to cover advertising or sunk entry costs. In other words, the price coordination leads to heavy advertising by incumbents such that there is no "room" left for a potential entrant.

While important insights come from exploring each of these approaches, the question of advertising's actual role may ultimately be an empirical one. It is difficult, however, to come up with good, clean empirical evidence that identifies the nature of advertising's role. A relatively recent paper by Daniel Ackerberg (2001) does offer though some interesting and promising results.

Ackerberg's paper studies the introduction of a new yogurt product by Yoplait, the second-largest yogurt firm in the United States. In April 1987, the company introduced Yoplait 150 as its first entry into the low-calorie and low-fat yogurt product line. This period falls within the time frame of data collected by the A. C. Nielsen Co. for just under 2,000 households split roughly evenly between Sioux Falls, South Dakota, and Springfield, Missouri. Scanner data was used to monitor the shopping trips and purchases of these households. They also had TV meters installed in their homes that allowed Nielsen to monitor their television viewing and, hence, their exposure to Yoplait 150 advertising over 12 months, starting three months after the Yoplait 150 introduction (i.e., from July of 1987 to July of 1988). Thus, the data are a panel of observations covering consumers in two cities at weekly intervals over a one-year period.

Ackerberg considers two broad effects that advertising could have. The first of these is an information effect. Advertising may either inform consumers of the good's existence, as in Grossman and Shapiro (1984), or signal quality or other information about the product's attributes, as in Nelson (1970) and Kihlstrom and Riordan (1984). In contrast, the Becker and Murphy (1993) model of complementary advertising and the advertising as persuasion models suggest that the role of advertising is not informative, but rather one that confers a separate recognition or prestige effect of its own. Ackerberg (2001) argues that if advertising plays an informational role, then it should have little effect on experienced consumers. This is particularly the case if the relevant information is, as in Grossman and Shapiro, simply about the existence and availability of the good. Once a consumer has bought it, they presumably know these facts, so further advertising exposure will have no impact on them—if, of course, this is the way advertising works.

This is also true, but to a lesser extent, if the information is about the quality of the product. Yoplait 150, for example, came out in many different flavors. It may take consumers a few tries to determine whether there is a flavor that they really like or not. In this case, advertising about alternative flavors will still have some effect on consumers over time, but one that should definitely diminish as they become more experienced with the product. However, if advertising confers a recognition effect, then there should be little distinction between its impact on experienced and inexperienced consumers. The complementary gains in consuming a well-recognized product should basically be the same whether a consumer is enjoying them for the first time or the tenth.

Ackerberg hopes to identify the role of advertising by distinguishing between its effects on experienced and inexperienced buyers. Two preliminary ordinary least squares (OLS) regressions suggest that this strategy may work. In these regressions, he looks at the total Yoplait 150 purchases over specific days in his sample and then divides these into two types. In one group are the sales that reflect first-time purchases. In the other group are the sales that reflect repeat purchases, each measured as a fraction of the number of shopping trips that day. Ackerberg creates separate time series of first-time sales and repeat sales on specific market days over the 12-month period. For each of those making either a first-time or a repeat purchase, Ackerberg (2001) also has data on the average Yoplait 150 price for each market day (PRICE), and, for each purchase, the number of Yoplait 150 TV ads the buyer was exposed to in the last four days (ADS). Since Yoplait 150 generally

Table 14.3 Preliminary results

Dependent Variable	Initial Purchases		Repeat Purchases	
Independent Variables	Coefficient	Std. Error	Coefficient	Std. Error
PRICE	−0.038	(0.013)*	−0.029	(0.014)*
ADS	0.030	(0.015)*	0.014	(0.017)
MARKET	0.002	(0.001)*	0.006	(0.001)*

*Indicates significant at the 5 percent level.

sold much better in Springfield, he also includes a dummy variable (MARKET) equal to 1 if the data are from Springfield, but 0 if they are from Sioux Falls. These preliminary results are shown in Table 14.3 above.

Observe first that the price effects are negative and statistically significant. Likewise, there is clearly a stronger preference for Yoplait 150 in Springfield than there is in Sioux Falls. Of most importance, however, is the differential effect of advertising on the two types of expenditures. Recent advertising exposure has a far greater positive effect on first-time buyers of Yoplait 150. In fact, the effect on repeat purchases is not statistically significant from 0. Thus, this evidence gives rough support to the idea that advertising provides information in that it has little effect on experienced consumers, who presumably already know of the existence and quality (taste) of Yoplait 150.

To get a deeper understanding of the role that advertising plays, Ackerberg exploits more fully the panel nature of his data and the variation among consumers that this implies. His approach, with some simplification, is to hypothesize that the propensity of consumer i in period t to purchase Yoplait 150 (y_{it}^*) is a linear function of k different exogenous variables X_{it} and a random factor ε_{it}. That is

$$y_{it}^* = \sum_{j=1}^{k} \beta_j x_{jjit} + \varepsilon_{it} \tag{14.36}$$

However, one does not observe y_{it}^* directly. All one actually observes is whether consumer i at time t bought Yoplait 150 ($Y_{it} = 1$) or does not ($Y_{it} = 0$). The standard assumption in this case, then, is that we observe $Y_{it} = 1$ when $y_{it}^* \geq 0$, and $Y_{it} = 0$ when $y_{it}^* < 0$. This implies that the probability of observing a purchase $Y_{it} = 1$ is given by

$$\text{Prob}(Y_{it} = 1) = \text{Prob}\left[\sum_{j=1}^{k} \beta_j x_{jit} + \varepsilon_{it} \geq 0\right] = \text{Prob}\left[\varepsilon_{it} > -\left(\sum_{j=1}^{k} \beta_j x_{jit}\right)\right] \tag{14.37}$$

$$= 1 - F\left[-\left(\sum_{j=1}^{k} \beta_j x_{jit}\right)\right]$$

where F () is the cumulative distribution of ε_{it}. It is convenient if F () has a symmetric distribution so that $1 - F(-Z_{it}) = F(Z_{it})$. Then we have

$$\text{Prob}(Y_{it} = 1) = F\left(\sum_{j=1}^{k} \beta_j x_{jit}\right) \tag{14.38}$$

Clearly, much depends on the choice of the distribution of the random term ε_{it}. If ε_{it} is assumed to be distributed normally,[21] one gets the Probit estimation procedure. A popular alternative is to assume instead that ε_{it} has a logistic cumulative distribution, in which case

$$F(Z_{it}) = \frac{e^{Z_{it}}}{1 + e^{Z_{it}}} \tag{14.39}$$

The reason for the popularity of this distribution is that this transformation implies that $\ln\left[\frac{F(Z_{it})}{1-F(Z_{it})}\right] = Z_{it}$. In other words:

$$\ln\left[\frac{F\left(\sum_{j=1}^{k} \beta_j x_{jit}\right)}{1 - F\left(\sum_{j=1}^{k} \beta_j x_{jit}\right)}\right] = \ln\frac{\text{Prob}(Y_{it} = 1)}{\text{Prob}(Y_{it} = 0)} = \sum_{j=1}^{k} \beta_j x_{jit} \tag{14.40}$$

The ratio of the probability $Y_{it} = 1$ to the probability that $Y_{it} = 0$ is known as the *odds ratio*. By assuming a logistic distribution for ε_{it}, the logit estimation procedure assumes that the log of the odds ratio is a linear function of the key exogenous variables. This is a very convenient feature for estimation purposes.

Ackerberg (2001) presents a number of regressions based on the above logit procedure. The independent variables X_{it} include (1) the amount (in time) of Yoplait 150 advertising the household has seen up to that time divided by the total time spent watching television, ADS; (2) the price of Yoplait 150 in the relevant market at that time, OWN PRICE; (3) a comparable measure of the average competitor's price, RIVAL PRICE; (4) the number of times (possibly 0) the household had purchased Yoplait 150 previous to that time, NUMBER PREV; and (5) the key (1,0) variable indicating whether the household had any previous purchases of Yoplait 150, EXPERIENCED or INEXPERIENCED.[22] Some of his main results are summarized in Table 14.4 (next page).

Consider the first regression results. Advertising has an important impact, but only for those who have not yet tried the new product. Again, this implies that advertising mostly plays an informative role. Specifically, the coefficient on the interactive term, ADS*EXPERIENCED, captures the impact of advertising on consumers who know the quality of Yoplait 150—and therefore should reflect only complementary prestige or recognition effects. This coefficient is not statistically different from 0. In contrast, the coefficient on ADS*INEXPERIENCED reflects both prestige and information effects. It *is* statistically different from 0, and this suggests that the information effect is behind this, since our estimate of prestige effects is not distinct from 0.[23]

The second regression tries to discriminate more between the two types of information that advertising provides. In the first regression, the assumption is that a household becomes fully informed after just one purchase of Yoplait 150. This would likely be the case if the important information provided by advertising were simply knowledge of the good's existence and availability. Once a household has bought the product, it

---

[21]   This assumption was made in the empirical applications in Chapters 13 and 19.
[22]   Household size and income and, as before, a market dummy for Springfield households were also included. Ackerberg (2001) also includes a random, household-specific intercept to control for household heterogeneity in time-persistent preferences for the product.
[23]   To be precise, the difference between the two coefficients, ADS*INEXPERIENCED and ADS*EXPERIENCED, is a direct estimate of the pure information effects. Standard techniques yield a t-statistic for this difference of about 1.5.

Table 14.4   Effect of advertising in the low-fat yogurt market

	Dependent Variable: Purchase (or Not) of Yoplait 150 by Household i at Time t			
Independent Variable	Coefficient	Std. Error	Coefficient	Std. Error
ADS*INEXPERIENCED	2.306	(0.776)*	—	—
ADS*EXPERIENCED	0.433	(1.212)	—	—
ADS	—	—	2.014	(0.790)*
ADS*(NUMBER PREV)	—	—	−0.356	(0.108)*
NUMBER PREV	−0.267	(0.093)*	−0.270	(0.092)*
(NUMBER PREV)^2	0.009	(0.001)*	−0.001	(0.001)
OWN PRICE	−5.584	(0.350)*	−5.616	(0.356)*
RIVAL PRICE	0.761	(0.217)*	0.768	(0.219)*

*Indicates significant at the 5 percent level.

presumably has this information. Learning brand characteristics such as taste, calories, and so on may however take a little longer and may be facilitated by continuing advertisements. For this reason, the regression includes ADS alone as an independent regressor, but then also includes this variable in an interaction term with NUMBER PREV, the number of prior purchase of the Yoplait 150. The idea is that the pure effect of advertising measured by ADS will decline as the consumer's experience grows. The more rapidly this decline occurs, the more likely it is that the primary information obtained from advertising is existence and availability. The more slowly it declines, the more likely that the information provided concerns product attributes that take time to learn. Sure enough, the coefficient on ADS*(NUMBER PREV) is negative, but a relatively small −0.36. This implies that it takes six or seven purchases of Yoplait 150 before the advertising information is no longer useful. As noted, this implies that part of the information provided concerns product attributes.

Are these coefficient estimates sensible? It is difficult to say immediately since the coefficients in the logit model relate to the effect of advertising on the *probability* of purchase and not directly to demand. However, there are some aspects of the results that give us confidence in the findings. First, in each case, the price of Yoplait 150 had a strong negative impact (and the rival's price a strong positive effect) on a household's purchase decision. Second, one can simulate the model to see what overall demand features the price and advertising coefficients imply. When Ackerberg (2001) conducts such simulations with the full model, he finds that, taken at the mean, the own-price elasticity of demand is 2.8—a fairly elastic response. He also finds that the elasticity of demand with respect to advertising is 0.15. Taken together, the advertising and price elasticities would imply, by virtue of the Dorfman-Steiner condition, an advertising-to-sales ratio of 0.15/2.8 = 0.054 or 5.4 percent. This is a quite reasonable result, given that Yoplait's overall advertising-to-sales ratio was reported at the time to be about 7 percent. Overall then, Ackerberg's findings seem to be quite plausible.

In short, the evidence from Ackerberg is that the primary role of advertising is to provide consumers with information. Some of this information is simply making consumers aware of the product's availability, but some of it concerns educating consumers about the product's key features. There is little evidence that in this particular market advertising provides complementary effects due say to prestige or similar factors. The data are based, however, on a perishable consumer food product purchased with some frequency. Whether it applies to other more durable consumer goods, or to goods such as medications that consumers buy less frequently, must await further investigation.

Summary

Advertising plays a role in informing consumers of the availability of a product, its brand image, and sometimes product attributes. This role can be played even when the actual information content of the advertising message is low. When consumers are uncertain about product quality, the very fact that a product is advertised heavily may signal that its quality is high. Moreover, the suppression of some information in advertising messages may enhance social welfare in a setting in which consumer transactions have significant costs.

   The observation that advertising appears to increase with market power may be valid but, by itself, it does not justify a conclusion that advertising is causal in obtaining and sustaining such power. Economic theory makes clear that the causality likely runs in the opposite direction in which the forces that underlie a firm's market power also raise its optimal advertising level.

   Indeed, when advertising informs consumers of the availability of substitute products, it actually tends to increase price competition. To be sure, such competition may sometimes exceed the welfare-maximizing level. However, one cannot infer such socially excessive advertising merely from the fact that consumers receive commercial messages without charge. Advertising may be viewed as a complement to the product advertised. As with any complement, an increas in the supply of advertising raises the demand for the promoted product. In this view, what really matters is the total price that consumers pay for the product and the advertising together. In any event, to the extent that advertising does provide information the fact that information is a public good also suggests that at the margin its cost is zero. Recent detailed microeconometric evidence suggests that advertising does play such an informational role.

Problems

1. Suppose that the demand for a new wrinkle cream is described by a nonlinear demand function $Q(P, A) = P^{-1/2}A^{1/4}$. Show that the price elasticity of demand is $\eta_P = 1/2$ and that the advertising elasticity of demand is $\eta_A = 1/4$. What do you predict the advertising-to-sales ratio would be in this industry? Does it depend on how costly it is to advertise for this product?

2. A firm has developed a new product for which it has a registered trademark. The firm's market research department has estimated that the demand for this product is $Q(P, A) = 11,600 - 1,000P + 20A^{1/2}$ where Q is annual output, P is the price, and A is the annual expenditure for advertising. The total cost of producing the new good is $C(Q) = .001Q^2 + 4Q$. The unit cost of advertising is constant at $m = 1$.
   a. Calculate the optimal output level Q^*, price P^*, and advertising level A^* for the firm.
   b. What is the firm's profit if it follows this optimal strategy?
   c. What is the consumer surplus if the firm adopts this strategy?

3. Imagine that there are 1,000 consumers. For each consumer, the willingness to pay for a widget is distributed uniformly over the interval (0, 1) depending on the style of the widget. A retailer with a particular style of the good knows this distribution. Her costs are 0. Consumers do not know the style that the retailer has stocked, and each incurs a transport or search cost of $T = 0.125$. Once this cost is incurred, it is sunk. At that point, a consumer in the retailer's store will purchase the product so long as her valuation is greater than or equal to the price charged by the retailer.
   a. Show that facing a random selection of customers, the retailer's profit-maximizing price is $p = 0.5$.

b.   Show that with $T = 0.125$, all consumers will come to shop expecting a price of 0.5. What would happen if $T = 0.15$?

4.   Suppose that the retailer in question 3 could communicate in some way to those customers with valuations less than 0.5 of the style that she has in stock and tell them that it is not worthwhile coming. If the retailer keeps the price at 0.5, how large can the transport cost T now be before the market collapses? Will the retailer keep the price at $p = 0.5$?

5.   Let there be two firms, 1 and 2. Each firm sells a product of with material quality $Z = 1$ and each chooses its price, p_1 and p_2, respectively. However, Firm 1 also gets to choose an advertising level a_1. Consumers perceive the overall product quality to be the product's advertising level times its material quality. In other words, consumers perceive product 1 to be of quality a_1 and product 2 to be of quality 1. Consumers are indexed by v distributed continuously from 0 to 1, where v_i is consumer i's willingness to pay for quality. Consumer i's net gain from consuming product 1 is $v_i a_1 - p_1$, while consuming product 2 generates a net gain of $v_i - p_2$. There is no production cost. However, Firm 1 incurs advertising cost of $(a_1/2)^2$.

a.   Assume all N consumers always buy the product of either Firm 1 or Firm 2, that is, the market is always covered. Derive the condition for the marginal consumer v^m and derive the demand facing each firm.

b.   Derive the equilibrium values of p_1, p_2, and a_1.

c.   Suppose Firm 2 is permitted now to advertise at any positive level a_2 between 0 and 0.5. What level of advertising will it choose if it takes Firm 1's choice a_1 as given?

References

Anderson, S. and R. Renault. 2006. "Advertising Content." *American Economic Review,* 96 (March): 93–113.

Ackerberg, D. 2001. "Empirically Distinguishing Informative and Prestige Effects of Advertising." *Rand Journal of Economics,* 32 (Summer): 316–333.

Archibald, R., C. A. Haulman, and C. E. Moody. 1983. "Quality, Price, Advertising, Published Quality Ratings." *Journal of Consumer Research,* 9 (March): 347–353.

Bagwell, K., and M. Riordan. 1991. "High and Declining Prices Signal Product Quality." *American Economic Review,* 81 (March): 224–239.

Bagwell, K., M. Riordan, and G. Ramey. 1994. "Coordination Economies, Advertising, and Search Behavior in Retail Markets." *American Economic Review,* 84 (June): 498–517.

Becker, G., and K. Murphy. 1993. "A Simple Theory of Advertising as a Good or Bad." *Quarterly Journal of Economics,* 108 (August): 941–964.

Butters, G. 1977. "Equilibrium Distribution of Sales and Advertising Prices." *Review of Economic Studies,* 44 (June): 465–491.

Caves, R. E., and D. P. Green. 1996. "Brands' Quality Levels, Prices, and Advertising Outlays: Empirical Evidence on Signals and Information Costs." *International Journal of Industrial Organization,* 14 (February): 29–52.

Clark, C., and I. Horstmann. 2005. "Advertising and Coordination in Markets with Consumption Scale Effects." *Journal of Economics and Management Strategy,* 14 (June): 377–401.

Comanor, W. S., and T. A. Wilson. 1967. "Advertising Market Structure and Performance." *Review of Economics and Statistics,* 49 (November): 423–440.

————. 1974. *Advertising and Market Power.* Cambridge: Harvard University Press.

Dixit, A., and V. Norman. 1978. "Advertising and Welfare." *Bell Journal of Economics,* 9 (Spring): 1–17.

Dorfman, R., and P. O. Steiner. 1954. "Optimal Advertising and Optimal Quality." *American Economic Review,* 44 (December): 826–836.

Ellison, G., and S. Fisher Ellison. 2005. "Search, Obfuscation, and Price Elasticities on the Internet." Working Paper, MIT Department of Economics.

Fluet, C., and P. Garella. 2001. "Advertising and Prices as Signals of Quality in a Regime of Price Rivalry." *International Journal of Industrial Organization,* 20 (September): 907–930.

Galbraith, J. K. 1958. *The Affluent Society.* Boston: Houghton-Mifflin.

Grossman, G. M., and C. Shapiro. 1984. "Informative Advertising with Differentiated Products." *Review of Economic Studies,* 51 (February): 63–81.

Kaldor, N. V. 1950. "The Economic Aspects of Advertising." *Review of Economic Studies,* 18 (February): 1–27.

Kihlstrom, R., and M. Riordan. 1984. "Advertising as a Signal." *Journal of Political Economy,* 92 (June): 427–450.

Kotowitz, Y., and G. F. Mathewson. 1986. "Advertising and Consumer Learning." In P. M. Ippolito and D. T. Schefman, eds., *Empirical Approaches to Consumer Protection Economics.* Federal Trade Commission. Washington, DC: U.S. Government Printing Office.

Milgrom, P., and J. Roberts. 1986. "Price and Advertising Signals of Product Quality." *Journal of Political Economy,* 94 (August): 796–821.

Nelson, P. 1970. "Information and Consumer Behavior." *Journal of Political Economy,* 78 (May): 311–329.

———. 1974. "Advertising as Information." *Journal of Political Economy,* 82 (August): 729–754.

Nichols, W. H. 1951. *Price Policy in the Cigarette Industry.* Nashville: Vanderbilt University Press.

Norman, G., L. Pepall, and D. Richards. 2008. "Generic Product Advertising, Spillovers, and Market Concentration". *American Journal of Agricultural Economics,* 90 (August): 719–732.

Schmalensee, R. 1978. "A Model of Advertising and Product Quality." *Journal of Political Economy,* 86 (June): 485–503.

Schwartz, A., and L. L Wilde. 1985. "Product Quality and Imperfect Information." *Review of Economics Studies,* 52: 251–262.

Solow, R. M. 1967. "The New Industrial State or Son of Affluence." *Public Interest,* 9 (Fall): 100–108.

Stigler, G. 1968. "Price and Non-Price Competition." *Journal of Political Economy,* 76 (February): 149–154.

Sutton, J. 1991. *Sunk Costs and Market Structure.* Cambridge, MA: The MIT Press.

Telser, L. 1964. "Advertising and Competition." *Journal of Political Economy,* 72 (December): 537–562.

Tirole, J. 1988. *The Theory of Industrial Organization.* Cambridge, MA: MIT Press.

15

Research and Development

When the human genome project was completed, the world learned that we homo sapiens have only 30,000 separate genes—much fewer than the approximately 100,000 genes that were initially predicted—and less than twice the 19,098 genes of the very humble roundworm.[1] This was bad news for the pharmaceutical companies, since the rough equation they had been quoting prior to the project was "one gene, one patent, one drug."[2] The discovery that the number of human genes was far fewer than originally thought implied that decoding the genome was not going to lead to anywhere near as many new successful (and profitable) treatments for disease as had been anticipated.

However, the bad news was quickly followed by some good. Subsequent research has found that much of human biology is determined at the protein level rather than at the DNA level, and we have well over 1,000,000 different proteins in our bodies. This has led to the emergence of a whole new science, proteomics (the study of how genes control proteins), with a view to using this research to create tailored, disease-specific drugs. Proteomics is being pursued by an increasingly wide number of companies and institutions. Harvard University, for example, has created a new Institute of Proteomics.

The race to understand the proteomic causes of diseases and to develop new drugs targeted at those diseases will not come as a surprise to anyone familiar with the popular business literature of the past 20 years. That literature is characterized by the dominant theme that the most successful firms find new ways of doing things, or develop new products and new markets.[3] A now-prevalent view is that firms become industry leaders by conducting research and development (R&D) leading to innovations in their production technologies or the products they provide. In his 1990 work *The Competitive Advantage of Nations*, Michael Porter writes that any theory of competitive success

> must start from the premise that competition is dynamic and evolving... Competition is a constantly changing landscape in which new products, new ways of marketing, new production processes, and whole new market segments emerge.... [Economic] theory must make improvement and innovation in methods and technology a central element. (p. 20)

---

[1] If you are interested, the complete human genome is available as a free download from http://gdbwww.gdb.org/.

[2] "Scientists, Companies Look to the Next Step After Genes." *The New York Times* (13 February 2001).

[3] This is virtually the mantra in the best-selling book by Peters and Waterman, *In Search of Excellence: Lessons from America's Best-Run Companies* (1982). The argument is repeated frequently in other business books, including, as noted below, Porter's (1990) encyclopedic volume.

Porter's quote could almost have been taken verbatim from Joseph Schumpeter's classic work written almost 50 years earlier. Schumpeter was both an economist and a historian. He brought a historical perspective to his study of competition and the rise and fall of corporate empires. The following dramatic passage appears in his book *Capitalism, Socialism, and Democracy*, first published in 1942.

> (I)t is not... [price].. competition which counts but competition from the new commodity, the new technology, the new source of supply, the new type of organization... competition which commands a decisive cost or quality advantage and which strikes not at the margins of the profits and outputs of existing firms but at their foundations and very lives. (p. 84)

An important issue, raised by Schumpeter, concerns the market environment most conducive to R&D activity. Schumpeter conjectured that R&D efforts are more likely to be undertaken by large firms than by small ones. He speculated also that monopolistic or oligopolistic firms would more aggressively pursue innovative activity than would firms with little or no market power. Accordingly, Schumpeter argued that the benefits of competitive markets reflected the rather modest gains of allocating resources efficiently among a *given set of goods and services produced with given technologies*. In contrast, the benefits of markets dominated by a few large firms stem from the much larger dynamic efficiency gains of developing new products and new technologies. He wrote "[A] shocking suspicion dawns upon us that big business may have had more to do with creating (our) standard of life than with keeping it down" (p. 88).

The validity of Schumpeter's ideas—often referred to as the Schumpeterian hypothesis—is the key issue addressed in this chapter. Do larger firms do more R&D? Does a concentrated market structure provide a better environment for the development of new innovations than a competitive structure does?

Table 15.1 lists the 10 companies awarded the most patents by the U.S. Patents and Trademark Office (USPTO) in 2006 as well as their ranks in 2005 and 2004. Each of these is a large company. Most operate in oligopolistic markets with only a few large competitors. Moreover, there is considerable stability in the rank ordering, at least over these three years. It is tempting to conclude on the basis of such data that Schumpeter was right and that large firms in concentrated markets are more innovative. However, great

Table 15.1   Top ten US patent-receiving firms in 2006 and their rank in 2005 and 2004

Company	# of Patents in 2006	Rank in 2005	Rank in 2004
International Business Machines	3,621	1	1
Samsung Electronics	2,451	5	3
Canon Kabushiki Kaisha	2,366	2	4
Matsushita Electric Industrial	2,229	4	2
Hewlett-Packard	2,099	3	6
Intel Corporation	1,959	7	5
Sony Corporation	1,771	12	7
Hitachi	1,732	8	8
Toshiba Corporation	1,672	9	9
Micron Technology	1,610	6	11

Source: U.S. Patents and Trademarks Office

Table 15.2   Top ten patent-receiving industries in 2006 and cumulative patents to that year

Industry Class	Patents Granted in 2006	Cumulative Patents Granted
Semiconductor device manufacturing: process	4,467	50,224
Active solid-state devices (e.g., transistors, solid-state diodes)	4,287	42,436
Drug, bio-affecting and body treating compositions	2,784	73,234
Multiplex communications	2,754	25,157
Chemistry: molecular biology and microbiology	2,423	46,466
Telecommunications	2,271	20,624
Stock material or miscellaneous articles	2,263	54,326
Static information storage and retrieval	2,019	24,710
Optical: systems and elements	2,013	28,024
Computer graphics processing and selective visual display systems	2,004	22,507

Source: U.S. Patents and Trademarks Office

care is needed before reaching that conclusion. Rather than implying that large firms do more R&D, these results could imply that firms that do more R&D become large.

The most active areas for research activity are likely to vary over time. Table 15.2 (above) lists the top patent-receiving industries or research areas in 2006 and the cumulative patents in that area up to that year. While there is some consistency across the two columns, there is also considerable variation. Thus, while semiconductor and solid-state devices have led the patent parade in more recent years, bioscience drugs and molecular chemistry have accounted for many more patents in total over time.

Introducing a new product often undermines the marketability of existing products, and development of a new production process reduces the value of existing productive capacity. Because new products or processes inevitably replace old ones, Schumpeter dubbed such competition by innovation "creative destruction." Since some of the products and processes that are made obsolete may well be those of the innovating firm itself, we can ask our central question in a somewhat different way. Why do firms undermine existing activities (including their own) in this way? More generally, what are the incentives to engage in innovative activity, and how do these vary with firm size and market structure?

15.1   A TAXONOMY OF INNOVATIONS

Research and development takes three broad forms. *Basic research* is research that will not necessarily lead to specific applications but, instead, aims to improve our fundamental knowledge in ways that may subsequently be helpful in a range of activities. The derivation and validation of the theory of laser technology is a good example. *Applied research* generally involves substantial engineering input and is aimed at a more practical and specific usage than basic research. The creation of the first laser drill for dentistry would be an example of applied research. The *development* component of R&D aims to move from the creation of a prototype to a product that can be used by end-users and that is capable (to some extent at least) of mass production. The transformation of the first

Reality Checkpoint

Creative Destruction in the Pharmaceutical Industry: Will Prozac Work if Viagra Fails?

Perhaps no market offers better examples of Schumpeter's "creative destruction" than that for pharmaceuticals. Consider the market for antidepressants. For several years after its introduction in 1987 by Eli Lilly & Co., Prozac dominated this market. Originally envisioned as a treatment for high blood pressure and, when that failed, an antiobesity drug, Lilly was pleasantly surprised when hospital tests on mildly depressed patients showed a marked and widespread positive effect. Lilly took its fluoxetine drug, as it was then called, and asked Interbrand, one of the major branding companies in the world, to develop a new name and sales campaign. Prozac was born, and soon it dominated the antidepressant market. By the early 1990s, Prozac accounted for nearly a quarter of Lilly's $10 billion revenue.

However, rivals were soon at work inventing around Lilly's patent. In 1992, Pfizer Inc. introduced a rival (Zoloft), which quickly jumped to a third of the market. This was shortly followed by SmikthKline Beecham's Paxil, which soon had 20 percent of the market. All three drugs increased the levels of the neurotransmitter, serotonin, in the brain. But all three had slightly different chemical bases and different side effects. Finally, in 2001, the Prozac patent expired. Within two weeks, prescriptions for generic fluoxetine exceeded those for brand-name Prozac. Within a year, Lilly had lost 90 percent of its Prozac prescriptions. Lilly countered with a new drug—duloxetine, with the brand name of *Cymbalta*—that works on two neurotransmitters, serotonin and norepinephrine.

This brings us to the story of Viagra, the original drug to combat male impotence patented by Pfizer in 1996. Like Prozac, the drug originally known as sildenafil citrate was originally envisioned as a treatment for high blood pressure and angina. Even though it failed in that regard, its many male users reported a dramatic increase in sexual function. Pfizer received approval from the Food and Drug Administration (FDA) to market the drug as a treatment for erectile dysfunction and relaunched the drug under the name *Viagra* in 1998. Sales topped $1 billion within a year.

Once again, success brings competition. By 2003, two new drugs were approved by the FDA as treatments for male impotence. These were Levitra (made by Bayer and GlaxoSmithKline) and Cialis (developed by a small startup firm, ICOS, and marketed by Lilly). Both work in much the same way as Viagra but, again, there are important differences and side effects. Levitra penetrates cell walls in as little as 16 minutes rather than the 30 minutes minimum required for Viagra. Cialis works about as fast as Viagra, but has a serum half life of nearly 18 hours. Hence, it can be effective for up to 36 hours, or nine times longer than the typical duration of Viagra. The relative efficacy of these two products has made them fierce competitors to Viagra. Within the United States, the two drugs combined quickly for as much as 40 percent of the market. In countries such as Australia and France, Cialis alone claimed 40 percent of the market within its first year. Of course, the real competition will start in 2011 when the Viagra patent expires. If the Prozac experience is any guide, competition from generics will very quickly become fierce, and Viagra sales will decline even as the general market rises. Drug firms like Lilly and Pfizer could take a double hit as the change in lifestyles that may then occur may lead to a decline in the demand for antidepressants among both men and women.

Sources: R. Langreth. "High Anxiety: Rivals Threaten Prozac's Reign." *The Wall Street Journal* (9 May 1996), p. A4; A. Pollack. "Lilly Pays Bid Fee Up Front To Share in Rival of Viagra." *The New York Times* (2 October 1998), p. C1; S. Carey. "Lilly Reports 22% Decline In Net Income As Generics Hurt Sales of Prozac." *The Wall Street Journal* (16 April 2002), p. C2; and "Viagra Rival Cialis Wins Up To 40 Percent Market Share." *Reuters News Wire* (23 March 2004).

laser drill into a small handheld product that is affordable and usable by a large number of dentists would be an example of the development stage. We will focus on applied research rather than development, but we shall touch upon some of the important issues that characterize the decision to move from research to development.

It is common to distinguish two types of R&D. *Process innovation* is the discovery of a new (typically cheaper) method for producing existing goods. *Product innovation* is the creation of a new good. For the most part, we shall concentrate on process innovations, but we shall also present examples showing how the analysis can be extended to product innovations.

Finally, we can divide innovations into *drastic*, or major innovations, and *nondrastic*, or minor innovations. Roughly speaking, a drastic innovation creates a monopolist unconstrained by any fear of entry or price competition—at least for some time. By contrast, a nondrastic innovation gives a firm some advantage over its rivals, but not one so large that the firm can act like a monopolist without fear of competition.

The formal distinction between a drastic and nondrastic process innovation can be easily illustrated. Suppose that aggregate demand for a particular product is $Q = D(p)$ and that currently the market is supplied by a set of Bertrand competitors, each with constant marginal cost c_h. Now, suppose that one firm gains access to a process innovation that reduces its marginal costs to c_l. Furthermore, suppose that this firm (perhaps because of a patent) is the only one able to use the new low-cost technology. If this innovator acts as an unconstrained monopolist, it will set the monopoly price $p^m(c_l)$. The innovation is a drastic one if $p^m(c_l) < c_h$, because the reduction in cost is so great that the innovating firm can charge the full monopoly price associated with its new low cost and still be able to undercut the marginal costs of all other firms. The innovation is nondrastic otherwise.

As a more specific example, suppose that demand is linear, of the form $Q = a - bp$, and that preinnovation marginal costs are c_h. If the innovation reduces marginal cost to c_l, then the innovating firm, acting as an unconstrained monopolist, would set the monopoly price $p^m(c_l) = (a + bc_l)/2b$. The innovation is drastic, therefore, if $c_l < 2c_h - a/b$. It follows that with linear demand, there can be no drastic innovation if $c_h < a/2b$.

15.2   MARKET STRUCTURE AND THE INCENTIVE TO INNOVATE

We now turn to some of the basic questions economists have asked regarding how the incentives to spend on R&D are affected by market structure. Recent analysis has framed these questions in terms of the *replacement effect* and the *efficiency effect*. The replacement effect, discussed in Nobel Prize winner Kenneth Arrow's seminal work (1962), suggests that an incumbent monopolist has less incentive to innovate than a potential entrant because the incumbent is reluctant to replace its existing technology, whereas the entrant has no such technology to replace. The efficiency effect, by contrast, suggests that since competition undermines profit, an incumbent monopolist has a stronger incentive to innovate to protect its monopoly position than does an entrant to become, at best, a duopolist; the classic work on this is Gilbert and Newbery (1982). We will consider both analyses and then present an approach that brings them together.

15.2.1   Competition and the Replacement Effect

Consider a market in which aggregate demand is $Q = D(p)$, and suppose that each incumbent firm has marginal cost c_h. Now, suppose that one of these firms can lower its marginal cost from c_h to c_l by undertaking research at some cost K.[4] The innovation is protected by a patent of unlimited duration that cannot be "invented around" by other potential or actual firms. What value will be placed on this innovation? In our analysis we assume that the innovation is nondrastic, but it is simple to confirm that the results extend to drastic innovations. For convenience, we assume that marginal cost, whether c_h or c_l, is constant.

First, consider how society as a whole values the innovation. Social optimality requires that price be set to marginal cost. With marginal cost pricing, the per-period social value of the innovation is the increase in consumer surplus it generates:

$$v^s = \int_{c_l}^{c_h} D(c)\, dc \qquad (15.1)$$

This is illustrated as the shaded area in Figure 15.1(a) for the case of a linear demand curve.

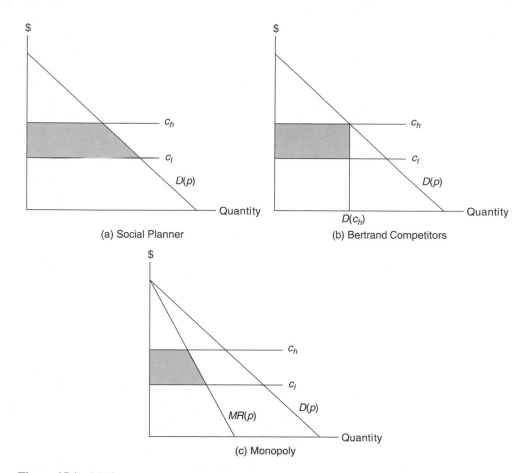

Figure 15.1 Market structure and the incentive to innovate

---

[4] We ignore for the moment the important question of which firm will undertake the innovation. This is an issue that we return to in the next two sections.

Now, consider the value that a firm places on the innovation. Suppose that the industry is populated by Bertrand competitors. Prior to the innovation, competition between these firms drives price to marginal cost c_h. The value that an innovating firm places on the innovation is the additional profits that the innovation generates. Since we have assumed a nondrastic innovation, the best strategy for this firm is to undercut its competitors just slightly, driving them out of the market and giving it an effective monopoly. The per-period profit that it makes from doing so, and so the per-period value it places on the innovation, is

$$v^b = (c_h - c_l)D(c_h) \tag{15.2}$$

This is illustrated by the shaded area in Figure 15.1(b).

Now, consider the value placed on the innovation by a monopolist who faces no threat of entry. The gain from introducing the innovation is the additional profit it makes as a result of being able to produce at a lower marginal cost. Denote the firm's marginal revenue function by $Q = MR(p)$. The additional per-period profit that the monopolist reaps from the innovation and, hence, the per-period value that it places on the innovation is

$$v^m = \int_{c_l}^{c_h} MR(c)\, dc \tag{15.3}$$

This is illustrated in Figure 15.1(c).

It follows immediately that that $v^p > v^c > v^m$. The social planner places the highest value on the innovation and the incumbent monopolist the lowest. The first inequality follows, since from (15.1) and $c_h > c_l$ we have $v^s = \int_{c_l}^{c_h} D(c)dc > \int_{c_l}^{c_h} D(c_h)dc = v^c$. The reason is simple: the Bertrand firm considers only the profit it can earn as a result of the innovation. It ignores the increased consumer surplus that the innovation generates.

The second inequality follows, since $MR(p) = D(p) + p.D'(p) < D(p)$ provided only that $D'(p) < 0$ (i.e., that demand is decreasing in price). The reason that the monopolist places a lower valuation on the innovation than a Bertrand firm is again easily explained. A Bertrand firm just breaks even prior to adopting the innovation and so values the innovation at the full additional profits it generates. By contrast, the monopolist is already earning a monopoly profit with its existing technology. Introducing the new process replaces and therefore undermines that investment. (Note also that the monopolist ignores the increase in consumer surplus.)

It is (relatively) simple to show that the same qualitative result applies to a comparison of a monopoly firm with firms engaged in Cournot competition. While a Cournot firm enjoys some preinnovation profits, these are much smaller than those of a monopolist. Therefore, a Cournot competitor has much less to lose than does the monopolist from pursuing the innovation.

One final point should be made in closing this section. We have followed convention in referring to this analysis as illustrating the *replacement effect*, but the term is misleading. After all, society also values the innovation by comparing it to the technology that it is replacing. The important reason the monopolist undervalues the innovation is because the monopolist restricts output to less than the socially optimal level. To see why, suppose that the monopolist could employ first-degree price discrimination. Then, as you are asked to show in the end-of-chapter problems, the monopolist's valuation of the innovation would exactly equal society's valuation.

15.2.2   Persistence of Monopoly and the Efficiency Effect

The analysis in the previous section assumes that there is only one innovator. If that firm does not innovate, no one does. As a result, this analysis does not truly capture the spirit of Schumpeter's contention, since his point is that firms compete by means of innovation. In other words, to examine Schumpeter's hypothesis fairly requires that we use a model in which some competition is present. As we will see, this can reverse the previous results.[5]

Consider the following simplified model. An incumbent monopolist and a potential entrant play a three-stage game. In stage 1, the incumbent decides whether or not to undertake process R&D. In stage 2, a potential entrant decides whether or not to enter.

We assume that innovative effort is successful and that the innovation is protected by a patent of unlimited duration that cannot be "invented around" by other potential or actual firms. As a result, if the incumbent has not undertaken R&D, the entrant can choose whether or not to undertake R&D; whereas if the incumbent has innovated, then the entrant chooses not to innovate. Denote the per-period postentry duopoly profit of the incumbent as $\pi_i^d(c_i, c_e)$ and that of the entrant as $\pi_e^d(c_i, c_e)$, where c_i is the marginal cost of the incumbent and c_e is marginal cost of the entrant. Without R&D, both firms' marginal costs are c_h, while with innovation each firm's marginal costs are reduced to c_l. The extensive form of this game is illustrated in Figure 15.2.

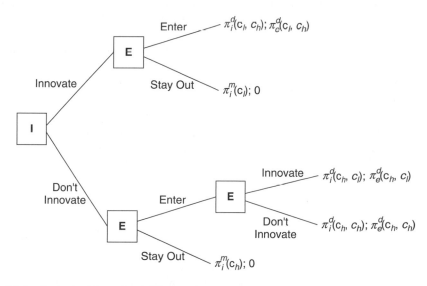

Figure 15.2   Extensive form for the innovation and entry game

---

[5]   The underlying analysis can be found in Gilbert and Newbery (1982). Reinganum (1983) shows, however, that this conclusion might not hold when the timing of the successful breakthrough is uncertain. The incumbent monopolist might delay innovation in order to enjoy its current profits. A potential entrant has no such incentive to delay its innovative activity.

Assume first that innovation by the incumbent does not deter entry. In other words, $\pi_e^d(c_l, c_h) > 0$. Consider the entrant. Suppose that the incumbent does not innovate. If the entrant innovates, it earns $\pi_e^d(c_h, c_l)$; if it does not innovate, it earns $\pi_e^d(c_h, c_h)$. The per-period value of the innovation to the entrant is, therefore

$$v^e = \pi_e^d(c_h, c_l) - \pi_e^d(c_h, c_h) \tag{15.4}$$

To keep the analysis interesting, we assume that the discounted value of the innovation by the entrant exceeds the costs of innovation, so that the entrant always innovates if the incumbent does not.

Now consider the incumbent. If it does not innovate, then from (15.4) it faces innovative entry and earns $\pi_i^d(c_h, c_l)$. By contrast, if it innovates, it faces noninnovative entry and earns $\pi_i^d(c_l, c_h)$. The per-period value of innovation to the incumbent is, therefore

$$v^m = \pi_i^d(c_l, c_h) - \pi_i^d(c_h, c_l) \tag{15.5}$$

Symmetry tells us that $\pi_i^d(c_l, c_h) = \pi_e^d(c_h, c_l)$; $\pi_i^d(c_h, c_h) = \pi_e^d(c_h, c_h)$. As a result,

$$\begin{aligned}
v^m - v^e &= \pi_i^d(c_l, c_h) - \pi_i^d(c_h, c_l) - \pi_e^d(c_h, c_l) + \pi_e^d(c_h, c_h) \\
&= \pi_e^d(c_h, c_h) - \pi_i^d(c_h, c_l) = \pi_i^d(c_h, c_h) - \pi_i^d(c_h, c_l) > 0
\end{aligned} \tag{15.6}$$

The final inequality holds, since the incumbent always prefers to compete against a high-cost rather than a low-cost entrant. Even if innovation does not deter entry, the incumbent values the innovation more than does the entrant.

Now, suppose that innovation by the incumbent deters entry. The per-period value of the innovation to the entrant is unchanged. By contrast, the per-period value of the innovation to the monopolist is $\pi^m(c_l) - \pi_i^d(c_h, c_l)$. This is clearly greater than the value of the innovation with entry, since $\pi^m(c_l) > \pi_i^d(c_l, c_h)$. A low-cost incumbent always prefers monopoly to sharing the market, even when the sharing is with a high-cost rival.

To summarize, no matter whether innovation by an incumbent monopolist maintains its monopoly or not, the incumbent firm values the innovation more highly than a potential entrant, because replacing oneself is better than being replaced by a newcomer. This is referred to in the literature as the *efficiency effect*.

15.2.3 A Possible Synthesis[6]

The approaches to innovation discussed above are reasonable, but suffer from an important limitation. It seems reasonable to assume that the results of innovative effort are uncertain both for the incumbent and for the potential entrant. There are two kinds of uncertainty: whether (and when) the innovation will be discovered, and who will discover it. Introducing such uncertainty means that the incumbent's innovative efforts

---

[6] This section draws on the Working Paper by Phillip Weinschenk (2009), "Persistence of Monopoly and Research Specialization," Max Planck Institute for Research on Collective Goods, Bonn 2009/11.

provide only partial protection against entry; this gives rise to the possibility that the two approaches can be synthesized. To see why, note that if the probability of successful innovation is high, we might expect the incumbent to innovate in order to deter entry—the efficiency effect. By contrast, when the probability of successful innovation is low, innovation by the incumbent is unlikely to deter entry; and the replacement effect is likely to dominate.

We formalize these ideas in the following simplified model. There are two firms—an incumbent monopolist and a potential entrant—who play a four-stage game. In stage 1, the incumbent (Firm i) decides whether to expend resources on an uncertain process innovation. In stage 2, a potential entrant (Firm e) makes the same decision. For both firms, the innovative effort costs k and is successful with probability $p \in (0, 1)$. In stage 3, nature determines whether or not each firm's innovative effort has been successful. The firms are Bertrand competitors in stage 4.

If a firm's innovative effort is successful, it can produce at low marginal cost c_l. If Firm i does not invest (or its investment fails), it can produce at high marginal cost c_h, provided that Firm e does not innovate (or its innovation is unsuccessful). Should Firm e not invest, or should its investment fail, it cannot produce at all. It might be, for example, that Firm e incurs some setup costs of entry that can be recouped only if it successfully develops the low-cost technology. By contrast, if Firm e's innovative effort is successful while Firm i's is not, Firm e replaces Firm i as a monopolist.

As in the previous section, we denote the two firms' profits as, respectively, $\pi_i^d(c_i, c_e)$, $\pi_e^d(c_i, c_e)$ if they are duopolists and $\pi_i^m(c_i)$, $\pi_e^m(c_e)$ if they are monopolists. Given that we assume Bertrand competition, the following conditions characterize the profits of the two firms:

$$\pi_i^d(c_l, c_l) = \pi_i^d(c_h, c_h) = \pi_i^d(c_h, c_l) = \pi_e^d(c_l, c_l) - \pi_e^d(c_h, c_h) = \pi_e^d(c_l, c_h) = 0 \quad \text{(C.1)}$$

$$\pi_i^m(c_l) > \pi_i^m(c_h) > 0 \quad \text{(C.2)}$$

$$\pi_i^m(c_l) \geq \pi_e^m(c_l) > \pi_i^m(c_l) - \pi_i^m(c_h) \quad \text{(C.3)}$$

The properties (C.1) and (C.2) are straightforward, but (C.3) needs some explanation. Consider the first inequality in (C.3). If the innovation is drastic, then (C.3) holds with strict equality. By contrast, it holds with strict inequality if the innovation is nondrastic. In the latter case we can think of the entrant as being constrained by possible reentry of the incumbent or by entry of another firm if the incumbent's preinnovation technology is common knowledge. This is an example of the *efficiency effect* discussed in the previous section. The incumbent places greater value on maintaining its monopoly than the entrant does on replacing the incumbent. The right-hand side inequality repeats our analysis of the *replacement effect* in section 15.2.1. Here, the entrant has a greater incentive to become a monopolist than the incumbent has to innovate when innovation involves replacing its existing technology.

Denote the incumbent's investment decision as $a_i \in \{0, 1\}$ and the entrant's best response to a_i as $b_e(a_i) \in \{0, 1\}$, where 0 denotes no investment and 1 denotes investment.

The Potential Entrant's Investment Decision

(i) $a_i = 0$: the incumbent has not invested in innovation.

The entrant's profit if it does not invest is 0. Its expected profit from investing in innovation is

$$p.\pi_e^m(c_l) + (1 - p)\pi_e^d(c_h, c_h) - k = p.\pi_e^m(c_l) - k$$

The first term is profit if the entrant's innovative effort is successful, while the second is profit if the innovative effort is unsuccessful. We then have

$$b_e(0) = 1 \Leftrightarrow k < p.\pi_e^m(c_l) = k_1(p) \tag{15.7}$$

The entrant will invest in R&D if and only if the cost of doing so, k, is less than $k_1(p)$.

(ii) $a_i = 1$: the incumbent has invested in innovation.

Again, the profit of the entrant if it does not invest is zero. Its expected profit if it invests is

$$p^2\pi_e^d(c_l, c_l) + (1 - p)p\pi_e^m(c_l) + (1 - p)^2\pi_e^d(c_h, c_h) - k = (1 - p)p\pi_e^m(c_l) - k$$

The first term on the left-hand side is the entrant's expected profit if both firms successfully innovate; the second is expected profit if only the entrant's investment in innovation is successful; and the third term is expected profit if neither firm's investment is successful. We then have

$$b_e(1) = 1 \Leftrightarrow k < p(1 - p)\pi_e^m(c_l) = k_2(p) \tag{15.8}$$

Once again, the entrant invests only if the research cost k is sufficiently low.

Clearly, $k_1(p) > k_2(p)$. From (15.7) and (15.8), therefore, the dominant strategy for the entrant is not to invest ($b_e = 0$) if $k > k_1(p)$, while its dominant strategy is to invest ($b_e = 1$) if $k < k_2(p)$. For $k \in [k_2(p), k_1(p)]$, we have $b_e(0) = 1$ and $b_e(1) = 0$. The entrant invests (does not invest) if the incumbent has not invested (invested).

The Incumbent's Investment Decision

Given the nature of the stage game, the incumbent makes its investment decision, correctly anticipating the response of the entrant. We need to consider three possibilities for the incumbent.

(i) $k > k_1(p)$, so that $b_e = 0$. The entrant does not invest and so does not enter the market.

If the incumbent invests, it has expected profit $p\pi_i^m(c_l) + (1 - p)\pi_i^m(c_h) - k$; while if it does not invest, it has profit $\pi_i^m(c_h)$. We then have

$$\text{If } k > k_1(p) \text{ then } a_i = 1 \Leftrightarrow$$
$$k < p\pi_i^m(c_l) + (1 - p)\pi_i^m(c_h) - \pi_i^m(c_h) \tag{15.9}$$
$$= p(\pi_i^m(c_l) - \pi_i^m(c_h)) = k_3(p)$$

It follows immediately from (C.3), equation (15.7), and equation (15.9) that the constraints $k > k_1(p)$ and $k < k_3(p)$ are mutually contradictory. In other words, if $k > k_1(p)$, neither firm invests; and the incumbent maintains its monopoly as a result of the structural barrier to entry provided by the high cost of pursuing the process innovation.

(ii) $k < k_2(p)$ so that $b_e = 1$. The entrant invests and enters the market. If the incumbent invests, it has expected profit

$$p^2\pi_i^d(c_l, c_l) + p(1-p)\pi_i^m(c_l) + (1-p)p\pi_i^d(c_h, c_l) + (1-p)^2\pi_i^m(c_h) - k.$$

This simplifies to $p(1-p)\pi_i^m(c_l) + (1-p)^2\pi_i^m(c_h) - k$. By contrast, if the incumbent does not invest, it has expected profit $(1-p)\pi_i^m(c_h)$; it maintains its high-cost monopoly provided that the entrant's innovation efforts fail. We then have

If $k < k_2(p)$ then $a_i = 1 \Leftrightarrow$

$$k < p(1-p)\pi_i^m(c_l) + (1-p)^2\pi_i^m(c_h) - (1-p)\pi_i^m(c_h) \qquad (15.10)$$
$$= p(1-p)(\pi_i^m(c_l) - \pi_i^m(c_h)) = k_4(p)$$

From (C.3), we know that $k_2(p) > k_4(p)$. As a result, if $k < k_4(p)$, both firms invest in innovation; while if $k \in [k_4(p), k_2(p)]$, the incumbent, anticipating correctly that the entrant has a dominant strategy to invest, does not invest.

(iii) $k_2(p) \le k \le k_1(p)$ so that $b_e(1) = 0, b_e(0) = 1$.
If the incumbent invests, the entrant does not enter; but if the incumbent does not invest, the entrant invests and—if successful—enters and replaces the incumbent.

If the incumbent invests, it knows that the potential entrant will not enter. The incumbent therefore has expected profit

$$p\pi_i^m(c_l) + (1-p)\pi_i^m(c_h) - k$$

If the incumbent does not invest, it knows that the potential entrant will invest and enter. Expected profit to the incumbent is then

$$p\pi_i^d(c_h, c_l) + (1-p)\pi_i^m(c_h) = (1-p)\pi_i^m(c_h)$$

We then have

If $k \in [k_2(p), k_1(p)]$ then $a_i = 1 \Leftrightarrow k < p\pi_i^m(c_l) = k_5(p)$ \qquad (15.11)

From (B.3), we know that $k_5(p) \ge k_1(p)$. As a result, if $k_2(p) \le k \le k_1(p)$, the incumbent invests in innovation and the potential entrant is deterred from innovation and entry. In this region, the incumbent uses innovation as a strategic barrier to entry that maintains its monopoly in the market.

Summary and Perfect Equilibrium

Equations (15.7)–(15.11) fully characterize the equilibria for this model. Denote the equilibrium research decisions as $\left(a_i^*, b_e^*\left(a_i^*\right)\right)$. Then

$$(a_i, b_e\,(a_i)) = (1, 1) \text{ for } k \in \left[0, k_4(p)\right)$$
$$(a_i, b_e\,(a_i)) = (0, 1) \text{ for } k \in \left[k_4(p), k_2(p)\right)$$
$$(a_i, b_e\,(a_i)) = (1, 0) \text{ for } k \in \left[k_2(p), k_1(p)\right)$$
$$(a_i, b_e\,(a_i)) = (0, 0) \text{ for } k \geq k_1(p)$$

(15.12)

We illustrate this equilibrium in Figure 15.3 below.

For parameter combinations (p, k) in the region $(k_2(p), k_1(p))$, the efficiency effect dominates. In this region, the incumbent knows that if it does not invest, then the potential entrant will invest. The incumbent also knows, however, that by investing it can preempt the potential entrant and so protect its monopoly position, even if its investment is unsuccessful. Moreover, in this parameter region, preemption is profitable as a result of which the incumbent does, indeed, use its innovative effort strategically to deter entry and maintain its monopoly.

By contrast, for parameter combinations in the region $(k_4(p), k_2(p))$, the replacement effect dominates. In this region, the incumbent knows that the costs of innovation are sufficiently low that the potential entrant has a dominant strategy—to invest. At the same time, the costs of innovation are sufficiently high that it is not profitable for the incumbent also to invest, given that successful innovation replaces its existing assets. All the incumbent can hope for in this region is that the innovative effort by the potential entrant fails.

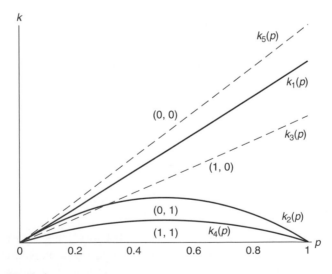

Figure 15.3   R&D choice

Finally, in the parameter region $(0, k_4(p))$, the cost of innovation is sufficiently low that both firms choose to invest. They are then effectively involved in a race to be the first to invent and patent, a subject to which we return in the next chapter.

In order to make the relative incentives to innovate by incumbent and entrant more explicit, we need to impose some additional structure on the model. We make the following assumption:

Assumption A.1: The conditional density of k given a probability of successful innovation p, $h(k|p)$ is uniformly distributed on $[0, k_1(p)]$.

Intuitively, $A.1$ assumes that innovation with a high (low) probability of success has a high (low) expected cost.[7]

From $A.1$ and equations (15.7)–(15.12), the probability $\rho_i(p)$ that the incumbent will undertake research is the probability that k lies in the regions $(0, k_4(p))$ or $[k_2(p), k_1(p))$, which is

$$\rho_i(p) = \frac{k_1(p) - k_2(p) + k_4(p)}{k_1(p)} = \frac{p\pi_e^m(c_l) + (1-p)\left(\pi_i^m(c_l) - \pi_i^m(c_h)\right)}{\pi_e^m(c_l)} \qquad (15.13)$$

The probability $\rho_e(p)$ that the entrant will undertake research is the probability that k lies in the region $(0, k_2(p))$, which is

$$\rho_e(p) = \frac{k_2(p)}{k_1(p)} = 1 - p \qquad (15.14)$$

It follows that the incumbent is more likely than the potential entrant to undertake research if the following condition is satisfied:

$$\rho_i(p) > \rho_e(p) \Rightarrow p > \underline{p} = \frac{\pi_e^m(c_l) - \left(\pi_i^m(c_l) - \pi_i^m(c_h)\right)}{2\pi_e^m(c_l) - \left(\pi_i^m(c_l) - \pi_i^m(c_h)\right)} \qquad (15.15)$$

Intuitively, given our assumption $A.1$ regarding the relationship between the probability of successful innovation and the expected cost of innovation, the efficiency effect is more likely to dominate when innovation has a high probability of success (and high expected cost); whereas the replacement effect is more likely to dominate when innovation has a low probability of success (and a low expected cost). Indeed, Figure 15.3 indicates that when $p = 1$ (the implicit assumption in sections 15.2.1 and 15.2.2), the replacement effect disappears, and only the efficiency effect is operative.

Another way of looking at this is that, given $A.1$, potential entrants are more likely to undertake risky innovation—innovation with a low probability of success—whereas incumbents are more likely to undertake safe innovation—innovation with a high probability of success.

---

[7] Assumption $A.1$ has the advantage of allowing us to generate some clean results. Weinschenk (2009) indicates that the same qualitative conclusions hold with weaker assumptions on the conditional distribution of k.

15.3   A MORE COMPLETE MODEL OF COMPETITION AND INNOVATION

The efficiency effect we have discussed in the previous section derives from the recognition by the incumbent monopolist that its noninnovation may encourage innovation by a rival, with the result that the incumbent is replaced. Clearly, the strategic interaction from potential entry through innovation seems closer to the view Schumpeter (1942) presents. Yet, while the analysis usefully reveals some important considerations that may influence a firm's decision to innovate, it does not fully address the Schumpeterian hypothesis. Yes, there are settings in which a monopolist is more likely to innovate than a potential entrant, which seems to support the hypothesized link between market power and innovation. However, the motivation for innovating by either the incumbent or potential entrant is the competition from the rival. In this sense, the analysis leaves unresolved the issue of whether market power or competition provides the greater inventive spark. Moreover, because the analysis is set in a specific two-player game, it is not capable of addressing how variations in market structure and power will be associated with variations in inventive activity.

We can get closer to testing the Schumpeterian argument by making the decision to spend on R&D an explicit part of a firm's strategy. The simplest model in this spirit is one due to Dasgupta and Stiglitz (1980), who assume an industry comprised of n identical Cournot firms, each of which has to determine the level of output q_i it will produce and the amount x_i that it will spend on process R&D. Each firm's unit cost is a decreasing function of the amount it spends on R&D, $c_i = c(x_i)$, with $dc(x_i)/dx_i < 0$ and $d^2 c(x_i)/dx_i^2 > 0$. In other words, there are diminishing returns to additional R&D expenditures.[8]

Profit for Firm i, π_i, is

$$\pi_i = P(Q)q_i - c(x_i)q_i - x_i \tag{15.16}$$

Symmetry implies that in equilibrium each firm spends the same amount x on research, giving each firm a unit cost of $c(x)$. Our analysis in Chapter 7 then tells us that in this symmetric, n-firm Cournot model, the equilibrium price-cost margin (or Lerner Index) is given by

$$\frac{(P - c(x))}{P} = \frac{s_i}{\eta} \tag{15.17}$$

Here, P is the industry price, s_i is the ith firm's share of industry output, η is the elasticity of market demand, and x is the amount that each firm spends on R&D in equilibrium. Since all firms are identical, s_i is just $1/n$. Therefore, equation (15.17) can be written as

$$P\left(1 - \frac{1}{n\eta}\right) = c(x) \tag{15.18}$$

---

[8]   Note that, in contrast to earlier models in this chapter, we assume that one firm's innovation cannot preempt innovation by its rivals. We also assume that there is no spillover from one firm's innovative efforts to those of other firms, an issue to which we shall return next.

What about x? We need a second equilibrium condition, obtained by differentiating the profit equation (15.16) with respect to the R&D expenditures, x_i, to give the condition

$$\frac{\partial \pi_i}{\partial x_i} = -\frac{dc(x_i)}{dx_i}q_i - 1 = 0 \Rightarrow -\frac{dc(x_i)}{dx_i}q_i = 1 \tag{15.19}$$

What does this mean? Recall that an increase in R&D expenditures reduces marginal cost, so that $dc(x_i)/dx_i$ is negative. The left-hand side of equation (15.19) is, therefore, positive and equal to the marginal benefit of an extra dollar of R&D spending. The marginal cost of an extra dollar spent on R&D is simply $1. At the equilibrium level of R&D expenditures x, the marginal benefit of an extra dollar spent on R&D just equals its marginal cost.

What are the implications of the equilibrium conditions of equations (15.18) and (15.19)? The most obvious conclusion is that an increase in the number of firms in the industry decreases the amount that each firm is willing to spend on R&D. This is because such an increase decreases the amount that each firm chooses to produce. From equation (15.19), this reduces the marginal benefit that R&D spending yields to an individual firm. It follows that the equilibrium level of such spending per firm x falls as the number of firms rises.

This does not necessarily imply, however, that the total industry spending on R&D, which is nx, also falls. Dasgupta and Stiglitz show that aggregate spending on R&D may actually either increase or decrease as the number of firms in the industry increases. The key point is that for aggregate R&D spending to increase, the elasticity of market demand η must be fairly large. When demand is relatively elastic, the expansion of industry output resulting from a greater number of firms does not decrease the price too much and, as a result, does not decrease the marginal revenue of equation (15.18) very much either. Since this difference between price and cost is what finances a firm's R&D expenditure, such expenditure can be expected to rise in total with the number of industry firms, so long as η is relatively large. If, however, the elasticity of market demand declines as output expands (as is the case with linear demand curves), then increasing the number of firms will, beyond some point, lead to a reduction in total R&D efforts. Even for a relatively small number of firms in the market, adding one more firm induces a decline in total R&D spending. Therefore, the Dasgupta and Stiglitz model may be taken as partial support for the Schumpeterian hypothesis that concentration fosters innovation.

This analysis leaves undetermined the number of firms in an industry. Dasgupta and Stiglitz invoke a third equilibrium condition that, in the long run, free entry results in each firm earning zero profit. In other words, industry structure is determined endogenously by the firms' output and R&D expenditure decisions. The zero profit condition, when applied to equation (15.16) tells us that

$$P(Q)q - c(x)q - x = 0 \tag{15.20}$$

Aggregating this over the equilibrium number of firms in the industry n gives us

$$P(Q)Q - c(x)Q - nx = 0 \tag{15.21}$$

which implies that $(P(Q) - c(x))Q = nx$. Now, since each of the n firms is of the same size, each has a market share equal to $1/n$. By equation (15.17) we know that

$P - c(x) = P/n\eta$. Using this substitution, the equilibrium R&D outcome derived by Dasgupta and Stiglitz is

$$\frac{nx}{P(Q)Q} = \text{industry R\&D spending as a share of industry sales} = \frac{1}{n\eta} \qquad (15.22)$$

Equation (15.22) suggests that the share of an industry's total sales revenue that is devoted to R&D is likely to be smaller in less concentrated industries. In other words, all else equal, real-world data should show a positive correlation between industrial concentration and research intensity. In turn, this may be taken as evidence in support of Schumpeter's basic claim that imperfect competition is good for technical progress. However, it needs to be recognized that the relationship implied by equation (15.22) is not a causal one. That is, it does not say that increased concentration itself leads to more research and development. Both industrial structure and R&D are endogenous variables. In this light, what equation (15.22) really implies is that the factors that tend to lead to more concentration will also likely lead to greater research intensity.

15.4   EVIDENCE ON THE SCHUMPETERIAN HYPOTHESIS

The debate over the Schumpeterian hypothesis cannot be resolved by an appeal to economic theory alone. We must also consider the empirical evidence. The studies that have been conducted vary in the results that they report, but one general finding does emerge. R&D intensity appears to increase with industrial concentration, but only up to a rather modest value, after which R&D efforts appear to level off or even decline as a fraction of firm revenue.

Some of the earliest studies exploring the link between industry structure and R&D were those of Scherer (1965, 1967). His basic finding was that while firm size and concentration are each positively associated with the intensity of R&D spending, these correlations diminish beyond a relatively low threshold. That is, once firms reach a relatively small size or markets reach a relatively low level of concentration, any positive effects of firm size or market concentration on innovative activity tend to vanish. Subsequent studies, including those of Levin and Reiss (1984); Levin et al. (1985a and 1985b); Levin, Klevorick, Nelson, and Winter (1987); Lunn (1986); Scott (1990); Geroski (1990); and Blundell, Griffith, and Van Reem (1995) have tended to confirm Scherer's (1965) basic finding.[9]

In examining the influence of firm size and market structure on innovative activity, a number of important issues must be addressed. The first of these is that in comparing R&D efforts across markets, we should control for the "science-based" character of each industry: recall the very different patent activity by industry category in Table 15.2. Markets in which the member firms produce goods such as chemical products or computer hardware, have a strong technical base and general advances in scientific understanding can rapidly translate into either product or process innovations. Other markets, however, such as those for haircuts or hairstyling, have more difficulty making use of scientific breakthroughs and have less direct contact with universities and research laboratories. It turns out that measures of technological opportunities tend to be highly correlated with the degree of industry concentration. In other words, while the simple correlation between

---

[9]   See Cohen and Levin (1989) for an early summary.

concentration and innovation may be positive, this correlation reflects the positive effects on innovation that come with increases in an industry's opportunity for technical advances. The more recent studies cited above demonstrate that controlling for this factor is very important.

A second factor is the distinction between R&D expenditures and true innovations. While innovative effort can be measured by the ratio of R&D spending to sales, this approach actually measures the *inputs* to the innovative process. Presumably, what we are really interested in are the *outputs* of that process—the true number of innovations as perhaps measured by the number of patents a firm acquires. Even though different firms do the same amount of R&D spending, the Schumpeterian hypothesis might be validated if size or concentration leads that spending to be more productive. The studies cited above look at the patent output of firms. Here again, however, little evidence is found in support of the Schumpeterian claims. Cohen and Klepper (1996) conclude that large firms do proportionately more R&D than smaller firms but get fewer innovations from these efforts. A notable exception in this regard is Gayle (2002), who finds that firms in concentrated industries do generate many more patents when patents are not simply counted but, instead, are measured on a citation-weighted basis.[10]

Finally, a third issue is the endogeneity of market structure. Some firms, for example Alcoa or Microsoft, came to dominate their industry on the basis of a dramatic innovation. In the case of Alcoa, it was its unique process for refining aluminum. In the case of Microsoft, it was its unique Windows operating systems for personal computers. In these and other cases, the key technology that led to the firm's dominant position was associated with a number of patents. If this experience is pervasive, a naïve researcher may find that large, dominant firms are also firms with many patents and wrongly conclude that the Schumpeterian hypothesis is validated. In these cases, it is the innovative activity that leads to market power, and not the other way around. If the firms that come to dominate their markets start out as small operations and then grow on the basis of entrepreneurial skill and technical breakthroughs, the implication would be somewhat contrary to Schumpeter's prediction.[11]

15.5   PRODUCT AND PROCESS INNOVATION: COURNOT VERSUS BERTRAND

In our discussion thus far, we have focused only on process innovations and have confined our attention to cases in which innovation has the potential to maintain an incumbent monopoly. Even the most cursory look at "real life" markets, however, indicates that there is considerable product innovation—for example, improvements in cell phone technology as firms find ways to add more and more features; the steady advance in storage and

[10]   When a patent application is filed, the applicant must cite all the prior patents related to the new process or product. It is plausible that the most important patents are those that are cited most frequently. Hence, in evaluating a firm's true innovative output, one may want control of how often the firm's patents are cited.

[11]   Generally, market structure and innovative activity evolve together. For example, if experience raises R&D productivity, then older firms will tend to do more innovation (because it has a higher return for them); so early entrants will tend to dominate an industry over time. See Klepper (2002) for an analysis along these lines.

processing capacity of laptop and desktop computers; ever-larger and higher-definition television sets; and so on. Moreover, the great majority of both product and process innovation occurs in markets that are best described as being oligopolistic rather than monopolized.

In this section, therefore, we consider the incentive to undertake process or product innovation by oligopolists—more formally, duopolists—engaged in either Bertrand or Cournot competition.[12] For this to make sense, we need to work with a demand system in which the duopolists' products are differentiated; otherwise the Bertrand case would collapse to marginal cost pricing. Assume, therefore, that Firm 1 offers product 1, Firm 2 offers product 2, and that the inverse demand system for the two firms' products are

$$
\begin{aligned}
p_1 &= a - q_1 - sq_2 \\
p_2 &= a - sq_1 - q_2
\end{aligned}
\tag{15.23}
$$

In this system, the parameter s is an inverse measure of product differentiation: the products are identical if $s = 1$ and totally differentiated if $s = 0$.

Inverting this demand system gives the direct demand system

$$
\begin{aligned}
q_1 &= \frac{a(1-s) - p_1 + sp_2}{1 - s^2} \\
q_2 &= \frac{a(1-s) + sp_1 - p_2}{1 - s^2}
\end{aligned}
\tag{15.24}
$$

In the absence of product innovation, the degree of product differentiation is assumed to be $\bar{s}$. Firm i's investment in product R&D is denoted d_i, and this R&D increases the degree of product differentiation to $s = \bar{s} - (d_1 + d_2)$ (recall that a *lower* value of s is equivalent to a greater degree of product differentiation), with $0 \leq d_i \leq \bar{s}/2$. Note that we assume perfect spillover in product R&D: if Firm 1's investment increases the degree to which its product is differentiated from that of Firm 2, then it also increases the extent to which Firm 2's product is differentiated from that of Firm 1. Product R&D incurs a cost $F(d_i)$, where we assume $F(0) = 0$; $F'(d_i) > 0$; $F''(d_i) > 0$. In other words, product R&D is costly and exhibits decreasing returns. It is further assumed that $F'(0) = 0$ and $F'(\bar{s}/2)$ is "very large" (these are technical assumptions that ensure an interior solution).

In the absence of process innovation, each firm's marginal production cost is constant at c per unit. Process innovation by firm i at intensity x_i reduces firm i's marginal cost to $c - x_i$ and incurs cost $\gamma (x_i)^2/2$, where $\gamma > 0$. Again, R&D is costly and exhibits decreasing returns; but, in contrast with product R&D, we assume that there is no spillover from either firm's R&D efforts to the other firm's costs. In other words, process R&D can be kept completely secret from the firm's rival.

No matter the form that R&D takes, the duopolists are assumed to play a two-stage game: first they choose their R&D expenditures, and then they compete in the final product market.

---

[12]   A more extensive discussion can be found in Lin and Saggi (2002).

15.5.1   Product R&D

Assume first that the two firms undertake only product R&D. It is simple (but tedious) to show that the firms' profits as Cournot and Bertrand competitors in the second-stage game are respectively (ignoring the R&D costs)

$$\pi_i^C(s) = \frac{(a-c)^2}{(2+s)^2}; \quad \pi_i^B(s) = \frac{(a-c)^2(1-s)}{(2-s)^2(1+s)}(i=1,2) \tag{15.25}$$

In the first-stage game, each firm chooses its product R&D expenditure d_i to maximize $\pi_i^K(s) - F(d_i)$, where $K = C, B$. Note that since $s = \bar{s} - (d_1 + d_2)$, we have $ds/dd_i = -1$, so that $\partial\pi_i^C(s)/\partial d_i = -\partial\pi_i^C(s)/\partial s$ and $\partial\pi_i^B(s)/\partial d_i = -\partial\pi_i^B(s)/\partial s$. As a result, the first-order conditions for product R&D under Cournot and Bertrand competition are respectively

$$\text{Cournot: } \frac{2(a-c)^2}{(2+s)^3} = F'(d)$$

$$\text{Bertrand: } \frac{2(s^2-s+1)(a-c)^2}{(1+s)^2(2-s)^3} = F'(d) \tag{15.26}$$

These first-order conditions are illustrated in Figure 15.4 below.[13] It is easy to see that *Bertrand firms invest more in product R&D than do Cournot firms*. The intuition is relatively straightforward, determined by the very different strategic effects that characterize Cournot and Bertrand competition. With Cournot competition, product innovation by Firm 1, for example, induces Firm 2 to increase its output, potentially harming Firm 1. By contrast, with Bertrand competition, product innovation by Firm 1 induces Firm 2 to increase its price, potentially benefiting Firm 1. This can be put another way. Product innovation softens competition. This is likely to be more beneficial under Bertrand competition, which is relatively tough, than under Cournot competition, which is relatively soft.

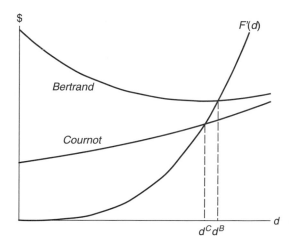

Figure 15.4   Product innovation

13   We have assumed in drawing this figure, without loss of generality, that $(a-c)^2 = 1$.

15.5.2   Process R&D

As we noted above, process R&D at intensity x_i decreases Firm i's marginal cost to $c - x_i$. The profit of Firm i in the second-stage quantity game, ignoring the process R&D costs, is

$$\pi_i^C = q_i(a - c + x_i - q_i - sq_j) - \gamma x_i^2/2$$

$$i = 1, 2 \qquad\qquad (15.27)$$

$$\pi_i^B = \frac{(a(1 - s) - p_i + sp_j)}{1 - s^2}(p_i - c + x_i) - \gamma x_i^2/2$$

We proceed as follows. First, we derive the best response functions for each firm from equation (15.27). Solving these gives each firm's equilibrium quantity or price as a function of the process R&D expenditures by both firms. Substituting these into (15.27) gives the profit of each firm in the first-stage R&D game as a function of the R&D expenditures x_1 and x_2. We then identify the R&D best-response functions and solve these to give the equilibrium R&D expenditures:

$$x^C(s) = \frac{4(a - c)}{\gamma(2 + s)^2(2 - s) - 4}$$

$$\qquad\qquad (15.28)$$

$$x^B(s) = \frac{2(a - c)}{\gamma(2 - s)^2(2 + s)(1 + s)/(2 - s^2) - 2}$$

These are illustrated in Figure 15.5. As can be seen, *Cournot firms invest more in process R&D than do Bertrand firms*. As with product R&D, the intuition is relatively straightforward. With Cournot competition, process innovation by Firm 1 induces Firm 2 to decrease its output, potentially benefiting Firm 1. By contrast, with Bertrand competition, process innovation by Firm 1 induces Firm 2 to reduce its price, potentially harming Firm 1. Again, this can be put another way. Process innovation toughens competition. This is likely to be less beneficial under Bertrand competition, which is already tough, than under Cournot competition, which is relatively soft.

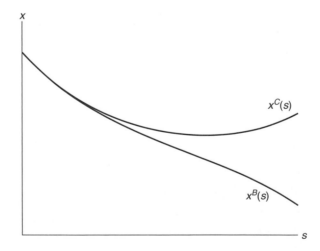

Figure 15.5   Process innovation

15.5.3   Product and Process R&D

We can, in principle, extend the analysis to allow for both types of R&D. In doing so, it seems reasonable to assume that the firms are involved in a three-stage game: first, choose their product R&D expenditures; next, choose the process R&D expenditures; and, finally, compete in the final product markets. The justification for this ordering is that it is difficult to optimize the production process until the firm knows the products that it actually wants to produce.

Solving this game analytically is far too complex, but we can give some flavor to what the solution will "look like". Recall the first-order conditions (equation (15.26)). Incorporating the second-stage process R&D equilibria, these become

$$\text{Cournot: } \frac{2\left(a - c + x^C(s)\right)^2}{(2+s)^3} = F'(d)$$

$$\text{Bertrand: } \frac{2\left(s^2 - s + 1\right)\left(a - c + x^B(s)\right)^2}{(1+s)^2(2-s)^3} = F'(d) \tag{15.29}$$

The left-hand side in both cases is greater than in equation (15.26), so we can certainly conclude that *the ability to undertake process innovation encourages product innovation*. In other words, the two types of innovation are complementary. What we cannot determine is which form of competition gives rise to the greater aggregate R&D expenditures.

15.6   R&D COOPERATION BETWEEN FIRMS

Thus far we have assumed that firms compete in their R&D choices. However, at least two features of the innovative process make cooperation in R&D attractive—not just for the firms, but also from the viewpoint of economic efficiency. First, modern technology is very complicated and often draws on different areas of expertise and experience. Because it is doubtful that the scientists and engineers in one firm possess all this know-how, it is desirable that firms share their experiences, experimental results, and design solutions with each other so as to realize fully the benefits from scientific study. Second, there is a potential for wasteful R&D spending as firms duplicate each other's efforts in a noncooperative R&D race.

There is some evidence on this score. One of the most dynamic and creative groups of firms in the U.S. economy in the 1980s and 1990s was the American steel minimills. These firms rely on small-scale plants using electric arc furnaces to recycle scrap steel. They are widely regarded as world leaders and have outperformed even the Japanese steel firms once thought to be invincible. Through a series of interviews, von Hippel (1988) found that these firms routinely exchanged technical information with each other. Indeed, sometimes workers of competing firms were trained (at no charge) by a rival company in the use of specific equipment. Such exchanges of information and expertise were made with the knowledge and approval of management, even though they had the effect of strengthening a competitor.

We develop the analysis using the linear, homogeneous good Cournot duopoly model. A new feature that we introduce is that we allow for research spillovers: a firm's research benefits its rivals to at least some degree.[14] We address two issues. First, how do research spillovers affect the incentives firms have to undertake R&D? Second, what are the benefits to be gained from allowing firms to cooperate in their research? Are these benefits worth the risk that cooperation in R&D might facilitate collusion between the same firms in the final product markets?

Suppose that inverse demand for a homogeneous good is linear and given by $P = A - BQ$. Two firms manufacture the good, each at constant marginal costs of c per unit. Marginal cost can be reduced by research and development activity, but it is possible that the knowledge developed by one firm spills over to its rival. This can happen, for example, because the firms fund common sources of basic research such as universities or research laboratories; or because the research direction that one firm is taking becomes known to its rival; or because some of the preliminary results of research effort leak out; or, of course, because of industrial espionage.

Specifically, we assume that if Firm 1 undertakes R&D at intensity x_1 and Firm 2 undertakes R&D at intensity x_2, the marginal production costs of the two firms become

$$
\begin{aligned}
c_1 &= c - x_1 - \beta x_2 \\
c_2 &= c - x_2 - \beta x_1
\end{aligned}
\tag{15.30}
$$

Here, $0 \le \beta \le 1$ measures the degree to which the R&D activities of one firm spill over to the other firm.[15] If $\beta = 0$, there are no spillovers; while if $\beta = 1$, spillovers are perfect. In the intermediate case $0 < \beta < 1$, spillovers are positive but imperfect.

We assume that R&D activity exhibits diseconomies of scale, becoming more costly the more research the firm does. To keep the analysis (reasonably) simple, we assume that research costs are the same for both firms and given by the research cost function

$$
r(x_i) = \frac{x_i^2}{2}, i = 1, 2.
\tag{15.31}
$$

The important properties of this function are, first, that it is increasing in x_i—research is costly—and second, it exhibits decreasing returns—marginal research cost $dr(x_i)/dx_i = x_i > 0$.

Throughout our analysis, we assume that the firms are engaged in a two-stage game: in the first stage they choose their research intensity x_i and in the second stage they compete in outputs. We look for a subgame-perfect equilibrium and, as usual, solve the game "backward."

---

[14]   The model is developed in d'Aspremont and Jacquemin (1988). A more general version of this type of investigation can be found in Kamien et al. (1992).

[15]   We confine our attention to the case in which the spillovers are positive. It is, however, possible that there might be negative spillovers. For example, firms might spread misinformation about their research or claim that they have made a breakthrough to discourage rivals from continuing with a particular line of research.

15.6.1   Noncooperative R&D

Consider first what happens when firms do not cooperate on research. Standard analysis gives the Cournot equilibrium outputs for given values of c_1 and c_2:

$$q_1^C = \frac{(A - 2c_1 + c_2)}{3B}$$
$$q_2^C = \frac{(A - 2c_2 + c_1)}{3B} \tag{15.32}$$

We also know that the firms' profits after paying the research costs are

$$\pi_1^C = \frac{(A - 2c_1 + c_2)^2}{9B} - \frac{x_1^2}{2}$$
$$\pi_2^C = \frac{(A - 2c_2 + c_1)^2}{9B} - \frac{x_2^2}{2} \tag{15.33}$$

Substituting from equation (15.30) allows us to express the equilibrium outputs in the second stage of the game as a function of each firm's first-stage choice of R&D effort and the degree of spillover from one firm's findings to the other firm's costs. The resultant equilibrium outputs for each firm are

$$q_1^C = \frac{(A - c + x_1(2 - \beta) + x_2(2\beta - 1))}{3B}$$
$$q_2^C = \frac{(A - c + x_2(2 - \beta) + x_1(2\beta - 1))}{3B} \tag{15.34}$$

and their profits are

$$\pi_1^C = \frac{(A - c + x_1(2 - \beta) + x_2(2\beta - 1))^2}{9B} - \frac{x_1^2}{2}$$
$$\pi_2^C = \frac{(A - c + x_2(2 - \beta) + x_1(2\beta - 1))^2}{9B} - \frac{x_2^2}{2} \tag{15.35}$$

Equation (15.34) indicates that the output of each firm is an increasing function of its own R&D expenditures x_i. Such expenditures reduce a firm's costs and thereby make higher output more profitable. By contrast, the effect of the *rival's* R&D effort on a firm's production can go either way. On the one hand, there is what we might call a *spillover effect*. The R&D activity of Firm 2 lowers Firm 1's costs, which has a positive effect on Firm 1's output. On the other hand, there is a *competition effect*. Firm 2's R&D reduces Firm 2's costs, making Firm 2 more competitive with respect to Firm 1, which has a negative effect on Firm 1's output. The net result of these two countervailing forces is reflected in the coefficient on x_2 in the q_1 equation and the coefficient on x_1 in the q_2 equation. This coefficient, $2\beta - 1$, is positive when spillovers are large—that is, when $\beta > 0.5$—and negative when spillovers are small (when $\beta < 0.5$). The same ambiguity appears in the profit equations (15.35). In other words, the spillover effect dominates when spillovers are large and the competition effect dominates when they are small.

In the first stage of the game, each firm chooses the level of research activity that maximizes its profit, given the research effort of its rival and correctly anticipating the outcome of the second stage of the game. In other words, we can identify the best-response or *research intensity reaction function* for each firm from the second-stage profit functions of equation (15.35). Differentiating these equations with respect to the research effort x_i of Firm i and setting the derivative equal to 0 yields

$$\frac{\partial \pi_i^C}{\partial x_i} = \frac{2(2 - \beta)[A - c + x_i(2 - \beta) + x_j(2\beta - 1)]}{9B} - x_i = 0 \tag{15.36}$$

Solving this for x_i gives the following best-response curves R_1 and R_2 for Firm 1 and Firm 2:

$$R_1: x_1 = \frac{2(2 - \beta)[A - c + x_2(2\beta - 1)]}{[9B - 2(2 - \beta)^2]}$$

$$R_2: x_2 = \frac{2(2 - \beta)[A - c + x_1(2\beta - 1)]}{[9B - 2(2 - \beta)^2]} \tag{15.37}$$

When research spillovers are low ($\beta < 0.5$), the research intensity reaction functions are downward sloping, indicating that the research expenditures of the two firms are *strategic substitutes*—more research by one firm reduces the amount done by the other. The intuition is that in this case the competition effect dominates the spillover effect. Increased research effort by one firm primarily reduces that firm's costs and so gives it a competitive advantage with respect to the other rival firm. This results in a reduction in the profitability of the rival firm, which can be offset only by the rival reducing its expenditure on research.

By contrast, when spillovers are high ($\beta < 0.5$), the research intensity reaction functions are upward sloping, meaning that the research expenditures of the two firms are *strategic complements*. When spillovers are this high, the spillover effect dominates. An increase in research intensity by one of the firms induces an increase in research intensity by the other. In this case, the intuition is that if one firm opts for a high level of R&D effort, the benefits of that activity spill over to the other firm to such an extent that the other firm's profit increases, providing that firm with the funds and the incentive to increase its own R&D spending.

However, determining whether the two firms' R&D efforts are strategic substitutes or complements does not tell us what the equilibrium level of R&D spending is. There can be no presumption that the presence of large R&D spillovers will result in a higher equilibrium level of R&D spending than the case in which spillovers are low. The Nash equilibrium occurs at the intersection of the two best-response functions, and how this intersection is affected by β is far from obvious.

The equilibrium must be symmetric, since the two firms have identical costs in the absence of R&D and face the same demand function. Thus, in equilibrium $x_1 = x_2$. Substituting this into R_1, for example, and solving for x_1 gives the Nash equilibrium research intensity

$$x_1^C = x_2^C = \frac{2(A - c)(2 - \beta)}{9B - 2(2 - \beta)(1 + \beta)} \tag{15.38}$$

This is decreasing in β, implying that increased research spillovers cause the two firms to reduce their research intensities. Why? The intuition is straightforward. When there are research spillovers, each firm has an incentive to free ride on the research activities of its rivals rather than spend resources on its own research. The greater the spillovers, the greater the temptation to free ride, and so the lower are equilibrium research expenditures.

This does not mean, however, that the overall impact of research is reduced as spillovers increase. From equations (15.30) and (15.38), the reduction in a firm's marginal costs from its own *and its rival's* research efforts is

$$\Delta c = x_i^C + \beta x_i^C = \frac{2(a - c)(2 - \beta)(1 + \beta)}{9B - 2(2 - \beta)(1 + \beta)} \tag{15.39}$$

Differentiating with respect to β gives $\partial \Delta c / \partial \beta = 18B(A - c)(1 - 2\beta) / (9B - 2(2 - \beta)$ $(1 + \beta))^2$. The reduction in a firm's costs as a result of the direct and spillover effects of research increases as β increases from 0 to 0.5 and decreases thereafter.

This is reflected in the relationship between research spillovers and each firm's output. Substituting from equation (15.38) into (15.34), the equilibrium output for each firm is

$$q_1^C = q_2^C = \frac{3(A - c)}{9B - 2(2 - \beta)(1 + \beta)} \tag{15.40}$$

It is easy to see that $\partial q_i^C / \partial \beta > 0$ if $\beta < 0.5$ and $\partial q_i^C / \partial \beta < 0$ if $\beta > 0.5$. Each firm's output increases, price falls, and consumers benefit with increased research spillovers—so long as the degree of spillover is less than 0.5. By contrast, output falls, price rises, and consumers lose from increased spillovers when the degree of spillover is greater than 0.5. In other words, some degree of research spillover benefits consumers, but perfect spillovers do not.

What about the firms? Substituting from equations (15.38) and (15.40) and simplifying gives the equilibrium profits of each firm:

$$\pi_1^C = \pi_2^C = \frac{(A - c)^2 \left[9B - 2(2 - \beta)^2 \right]}{[9B - 2(2 - \beta)(1 + \beta)]^2} \tag{15.41}$$

We cannot sign $\partial \pi_i^C / \partial \beta$ unambiguously,[16] but numerical analysis indicates that it is increasing in β if $\beta < 0.88$ and is decreasing in β as $\beta \to 1$. The firms benefit from increased research spillovers so long as these are not "very large." Intuitively, as spillovers increase, firms can cut back on increasingly costly research efforts by free riding on the research efforts of their rival. But when spillovers are nearly perfect, the temptation to free ride becomes so great that it actually undermines profitability.

15.6.2 Technology Cooperation

We now consider two alternative arrangements between the duopolists that can alter the outcome from that described above. The first possibility is that the two firms agree that while each will continue to do its own R&D, they will coordinate their research efforts

---

[16] The sign of the derivative is determined by a cubic function in B and β.

by choosing x_1 and x_2 to maximize their joint profit. However, they continue to compete as Cournot firms in the product market.

The other alternative we consider is that the firms explicitly share their R&D activities by setting up a Research Joint Venture (RJV). One way this scenario might work in practice would be for the two firms to jointly set up a laboratory for experimentation and analysis, with all the discoveries made at that laboratory to be made fully available to both firms. We introduce this RJV arrangement by letting the two firms pick x_1 and x_2 cooperatively, but by assuming that the degree of spillover is complete, that is, $\beta = 1$. Whatever is learned in the research lab—whether discovered by a Firm 1 scientist or a Firm 2 scientist—reduces the cost of both firms by the same amount.

We start with the simple coordination case. What we want to do is to pick the values of x_1 and x_2 that maximize the sum of the individual profit expressions shown in equation (15.35). Differentiating this sum with respect to x_1, taking advantage of the symmetry condition that in equilibrium $x_1 = x_2 = x^{RC}$ gives the equilibrium research intensity

$$x_1^{RC} = x_2^{RC} = \frac{2(A - c)(1 + \beta)}{9B - 2(1 + \beta)^2} \tag{15.42}$$

By contrast with the noncooperative case, this is increasing in β. The agreement between the two firms to set their R&D efforts jointly forces each firm to internalize the external benefits that such spending has upon its rival. In turn, this eliminates the free-riding problem that characterizes R&D competition when there are high spillovers.

This does not mean, however, that cooperation increases research spending. Comparing equations (15.42) and (15.38) indicates that $x_i^{RC} < x_i^C$ if $\beta < 0.5$ and $x_i^{RC} > x_i^C$ if $\beta > 0.5$. Intuitively, when spillovers are low the competition effect dominates. Noncooperation drives the two firms to overspend on R&D. Research cooperation "corrects" this overspending. By contrast, when spillovers are high the spillover effect dominates and research cooperation corrects the temptation to free ride.

The same ambiguity is found when we look at the impact that research cooperation has on the firms' outputs. Substituting equation (15.42) into (15.34) gives the equilibrium outputs with research cooperation:

$$q_1^{RC} = q_2^{RC} = \frac{3(A - c)}{9B - 2(1 + \beta)^2} \tag{15.43}$$

With research cooperation, equilibrium output increases with β. However, consumers do not necessarily benefit from the cooperation. Comparison with equation (15.40) indicates that $q_i^{RC} < q_i^C$ if $\beta < 0.5$ and $q_i^{RC} > q_i^C$ if $\beta > 0.5$. Consumers gain from research cooperation when spillovers are high, but lose when they are low. The reason is straightforward. When β is small, then without cooperation each firm tends to do a fair bit of research. This is great for consumers, since there a considerable cost reduction and therefore a sharp decline in the price they pay. Introducing a cooperative R&D agreement reduces R&D intensity. Unfortunately, the lower rate of innovation also implies a higher price to consumers.

By contrast, when the degree of R&D spillover is high ($\beta > 0.5$), consumers benefit from a cooperative R&D agreement because now the primary effect of the cooperation is to correct a market failure. R&D cooperation internalizes the effects of free riding because it forces the cooperating firms to look at the impact their R&D expenditures have on aggregate profit, rather than merely on their individual profit.

For the firms there is, as we might have expected, no such ambiguity. Substituting equation (15.42) into (15.35) gives the equilibrium profit to each firm:

$$\pi_1^{RC} = \pi_2^{RC} = \frac{(A - c)^2}{9B - 2(1 + \beta)^2} \tag{15.44}$$

Profit is increasing in β. Comparison with equation (15.41) indicates that research cooperation increases profit for the duopolists.

What about a research joint venture? As noted, an RJV can be best thought of as a case in which the firms take action not only to coordinate their research expenditures, but also to ensure that the spillover from one firm's research to the other's is complete, that is, so that $\beta = 1$. A little thought should convince you that an RJV will likely yield the maximum benefits to both firms and consumers. As we just saw, coordination of R&D results in an equilibrium in which an increase in the spillover parameter β increases the research intensity and the profits of each firm *and* increases the output that each firm brings to the market. In other words, *both firms and consumers benefit* from an increase in β. The RJV takes this to its logical conclusion by ensuring that $\beta = 1$, its highest possible value.

We can make this explicit. Substituting $\beta = 1$ into equations (15.42), (15.43), and (15.44) gives

$$x_1^{JV} = x_2^{JV} = \frac{4(A - c)}{9B - 8}$$

$$q_1^{JV} = q_2^{JV} = \frac{3(A - c)}{9B - 8} \tag{15.45}$$

$$\pi_1^{JV} = \pi_2^{JV} = \frac{(A - c)^2}{9B - 8}$$

The intuition behind the foregoing analysis is as follows. First, by maximizing the extent of spillovers, the RJV also maximizes the benefits of R&D. Every discovery is spread instantly to all firms in the industry. Second, despite this extensive spillover, the free-riding problem is now avoided. Because the two firms have agreed to coordinate their research efforts, they fully internalize the otherwise external effects of research. Thus, firms will aggressively pursue research, which—partly because of the extensive spillover effect of sharing—will lead to a sizable reduction in costs for every firm. This substantial cost reduction translates into an equally impressive reduction in the price to consumers.[17] The policy implication of this is obvious and important. Research joint ventures should be encouraged, because they benefit both consumers and producers—so long as the antitrust authorities can ensure that such cooperation on research effort does not also extend to cooperation in production and prices, that is, to a price-fixing cartel.

The potentially large benefit from technology cooperation is undoubtedly the reason that research joint ventures—unlike price-fixing agreements—are not treated as per se violations by the antitrust authorities. Instead, they are evaluated on a rule of reason basis. Indeed, the U.S. Congress passed legislation in 1984 to require explicitly the application of a reasonability standard in the specific case of RJVs.

---

[17]   While we have derived this result for a duopoly, Kamien et al. (1992) show that it extends to an n-firm oligopoly.

Reality Checkpoint
Spillovers, Pioneers, and Fast Seconds

While the jury is still out on the Schumpeterian hypothesis that larger firms or concentrated markets spur technological progress, there is certainly a good bit of anecdotal evidence regarding the prowess of individual inventors and small firms to come up with the big breakthrough. The personal computer, for instance, was mainly introduced by a then-small firm called *Apple*. The phonograph and wireless telegraphy were developed by individuals, Edison in the first case and Marconi in the second. George Westinghouse was a young man of 22, working alone, when he patented his model for a compressed air breaking system that was soon adopted by every train on both the Southern Pacific and Central Pacific railroads—and virtually all other U.S. trains within a few years. Xerox was a small firm called *Haloid* when it developed the Xerographic copying method. Intel, which controls two-thirds or more of the microprocessor market, started out as a small firm packaging transistors on a sliver of silicon. Google started as a small search service run by two Stanford graduates calling their engine BackRub. Amazon and eBay were both the creation of small independent entrepreneurs, and Genentech was just a tiny venture capitalist experiment when it launched the field of recombinant DNA.

As noted at the outset of this chapter, large, established firms often find it more profitable to let pioneering firms make the initial discoveries about a new product and its market rather than risk a product failure that may taint their established product line. Indeed, Markides and Geroski (2005) argue that this "fast second" strategy is typically the superior approach for large dominant firms and offer a quote from a Coca-Cola executive to illustrate that these firms recognize this fact. "We let others come out, stand back and watch, and then see what it takes to take the category over."

Norman, Pepall, and Richards (2008, 2009), explore this phenomenon in a model in which early entrepreneurs develop a new product market, all the while anticipating the possible later entry of a fast second. The model explicitly recognizes that the fast second can learn from the early entrants and use that information to develop a product for which consumers are willing to pay more. The result is that when it does enter, the fast second usually drives a large fraction of the pioneering firms out of business. Of course, the anticipation of this outcome acts as a disincentive for these upstarts to enter in the first place. This reduces the extent of competition and also limits the amount of learning the fast second can do, since the information it acquires from the initial entrants is positively related to the number of such entrants. In turn, this second effect means that the product enhancement that the fast second provides (and from which consumers gain) is reduced. Norman, Pepall, and Richards (2008) show that the result is that there will likely be too few pioneering firms relative to the efficient outcome. They also show that initial entry will be particularly low in markets in which price competition is fiercest. In a rough way, this may be taken as some support for the Schumpeterian Hypothesis. In a later paper, these authors show how patent policy can sometimes—but not always—restore the market to an efficient level.

Sources: Markides, C., and P. Geroski (2005), *Fast Seconds: How Smart Companies Bypass Radical Innovations To Enter and Dominate New Markets*. San Francisco: Jossey-Bass; Norman, G., L. Pepall, and D. Richards (2008), "Entrepreneurial First Movers, Brand-Name Fast Seconds, and the Evolution of Market Structure." *The B.E. Journal of Economic Analysis and Policy (Contributions)*, 8 (August), http://works.bepress.come/lynne_pepall/2; and Norman, G., L. Pepall, and D. Richards (2009), "Innovation, Fast Seconds, and Patent Policy." TILEC Working Paper, Tillburg University, Innovation and Intellectual Property Competition.

15.7   EMPIRICAL APPLICATION: R&D SPILLOVERS IN PRACTICE

R&D spillovers suggest a diffusion-like process. The greater is the spillover, the more rapid or the more complete is the diffusion of technological advances in one firm to the productivity of other firms. We might also suspect that a similar process is at work at a national and even international level. In particular, it seems likely that the R&D efforts of one country could spill over to enhance the productivity of its neighbors. Here again, the extent of such spillover is of interest. If technical advances in one country spread quickly to others, β will be high. In a world in which the international transfer of technical knowledge is weak, β will be low.

Wolfgang Keller (2002) explores the extent of international technical spillover by looking at data covering 12 broadly defined manufacturing industries from 14 countries over the years, 1970–95. To understand his basic approach, consider a simple Cobb-Douglas production function (see Section 4.5) for industry i in country c:

$$Q_{ci} = K_{ci}^{1-\sigma} L_{ci}^{\sigma} \tag{15.46}$$

Here Q_{ci} is output (value added) and K_{ci} and L_{ci} are capital and labor inputs, respectively, in industry i in country c, and σ is the share of costs accounted for by labor. Taking logarithms then yields

$$\ln Q_{ci} = (1 - \sigma) \ln K_{ci} + \sigma \ln L_{ci} \tag{15.47}$$

For industry i, we define $\ln \overline{Q}_{ci}$ to be the average log of output across all countries. Similarly, for industry i, let $\ln \overline{K}_{ci}$ and $\ln \overline{L}_{ci}$ be the average amount of capital and labor inputs (again in logs), respectively, across all countries. Defining total factor productivity, TFP_{ci} in industry i and country c as the difference between the log of output and the weighted average level of inputs, that is, $TFP_{ci} = \ln Q_{ci} - (1 - \sigma) \ln K_{ci} - \sigma \ln L_{ci}$, the *relative* (to the mean) factor productivity F_{ci} of industry i in country c at a point in time is

$$F_{ci} = (\ln Q_{ci} - \ln \overline{Q}_{ci}) - (1 - \sigma_{ci})(\ln K_{ci} - \ln \overline{K}_{ci}) - \sigma_{ci}(\ln L_{ci} - \ln \overline{L}_{ci}) \tag{15.48}$$

where we now let the cost share of labor σ_{ci} vary across countries and industries. Equation (15.48) is a measure of the extent to which output in industry i in country c remains above average even after correcting for any above average use of inputs. It is thus a measure of the productivity advantage (or disadvantage) in industry i in country c at any point in time. This is why it is called *relative* productivity. Of course, this will probably change over time due to R&D and other factors. For this reason, Keller (2002) measures relative productivity for each year from 1970–95. This means that for each of the 12 industries in each of the 14 countries, Keller (2002) has a measure of relative productivity in each year, 1970–95. Because we are now measuring this term over time as well as over industries and across countries, relative factor productivity now has an additional time subscript (i.e., F_{cit}). It is this series of relative productivity measures that Keller seeks to explain.

Because, by construction, variations in relative productivity F_{cit} reflect variations in factors other than capital and labor inputs, it is natural to infer that any remaining differences are due to differences in technology. In turn, these technical differences ought to reflect differences in R&D. Keller's (2002) approach in this respect is to distinguish a difference between R&D done domestically in industry i and that done abroad. The first research question is whether foreign R&D spills over to domestic productivity. The second is whether these spillovers are greater for countries that are closer to each other.

The 14 countries in Keller's (2002) sample are Australia, Canada, Denmark, Finland, France, Germany, Italy, Japan, the Netherlands, Norway, Spain, Sweden, the United Kingdom, and the United States. Five of these countries—France, Germany, Japan, the United Kingdom, and the United States—account for over 92 percent of all the R&D in the sample. Hence, Keller (2002) treats these G5 countries as the potential engines of technical change and examines how their R&D affects productivity in the remaining nine. Specifically, he estimates the parameters of the following equation:

$$F_{cit} = \alpha_{ci} + \alpha_t + \lambda \ln \left[S_{cit} + \gamma \left(\sum_{g \in G5} S_{git} e^{-\delta D_{cg}} \right) \right] + \varepsilon_{cit} \qquad (15.49)$$

Here, F_{cit} is the relative productivity measure derived above for industry i in country c in year t, measured for each of the nine countries examined. The first term is a country- and industry-specific constant that permits for a time-independent productivity advantage (or disadvantage) for that sector in that country. The second is meant to pick up productivity increases over time that affect all firms in all countries in common. The key parameters are embedded in the next term. S_{cit} is a measure of the R&D done in industry i in country c up to time t. In contrast, S_{git} is a measure of R&D in that same industry—but in one of the G5 countries—and D_{cg} is the distance of that country from the domestic country in question. ($D = 1$ implies a distance of 235 kilometers.) Together, S_{cit} and the summation term for the G5 countries are meant to capture the R&D relevant to productivity in the domestic industry i at time t.

The effect of that combined industry-based R&D on productivity in that same industry in the domestic country is captured by the parameter λ. However, two adjustments are included to distinguish the impact of foreign from that of domestic R&D. To understand the first of these adjustments, suppose that all G5 countries were right next to the domestic country in question ($D_{cg} = 0$). Then the contribution of their R&D on domestic productivity in industry i to total industry-relevant R&D, is adjusted by the parameter γ (taken to be same for all G5 countries). That is, if $\gamma < 1$, foreign R&D contributes less than the full effect of domestic R&D in adding to the knowledge relevant to a particular domestic industry's productivity. In many ways, then γ is comparable to the β of our industry analysis above. However, Keller (2002) also introduces a second source of distinction between domestic and foreign research by introducing the distance term, D_{cg}. As this distance grows, the contribution of that G5 country's R&D to domestic productivity diminishes if the parameter δ is positive. In short, the specification permits both for the possibility that simply because it was done in a foreign country R&D may contribute less to domestic technology than home-grown research, and also for the more complicated fact that spillovers from foreign R&D grow smaller as the foreign source of that R&D is farther away. Of course, the error term ε_{cit} picks up any remaining random factors that affect productivity.

The specification in equation (15.49) assumes that the decay parameter δ is the same throughout the time period. Keller (2002) recognizes, though, that increased globalization over the 25 years of his sample suggests that δ will decline over this period. He therefore estimates an alternative specification given by

$$F_{cit} = \alpha_{ci} + \alpha_t + \lambda \ln \left[S_{cit} + \sum_{g \in G5} \gamma_G (1 + \psi_F I_t) S_{git} e^{-\delta(1 + \psi_D I_t) D_{cg}} \right] + \varepsilon_{cit} \qquad (15.50)$$

In this equation, I_t is a $(1, 0)$ dummy variable equal to 0 over the first half of the sample to 1982, and then 1 in the 13 years thereafter. The coefficient ψ_F permits the effect of G5 R&D to have a different effect on domestic productivity in the second half of the sample than it does in the first, holding the distance between the domestic and G5 countries constant. Similarly, the coefficient ψ_D permits the extent to which spillovers decline with distance to change from the first half of the sample to the second half. Note, too, that this specification allows the effect of G5 R&D to differ across each G5 country by permitting a different coefficient γ_G for each one. This is reasonable, as the different languages in these countries may affect the ease with which a technology can be transferred.

Because the contribution of foreign R&D to the total relevant R&D depends on the parameters γ (or γ_G) and δ that are also to be determined, equations (15.49) and (15.50) cannot be estimated by ordinary least squares. Instead, a nonlinear least squares estimation is required. We begin with a starting value for the nonlinear parameters and estimate the regression with OLS. We then use these estimates to reiterate the process until the coefficient estimates stop changing and converge to stable values. Table 15.3 below shows the key parameter estimates and their standard errors that Keller (2002) obtains from this maximum likelihood process for both specifications.

The estimates in Specification 1 suggest that technical spillovers are strongly localized. The cumulative productivity effect of overall R&D is to raise productivity by 7.8 percent. However, foreign (G5) R&D contributes only 84 percent to the technical base that domestic research does, and that is only if the domestic country is right next to the G5 source nation so that $D = 0$. The estimate of $\delta = 1.05$ indicates that this contribution dies out rapidly. Half of it is gone when $D = 0.69$, or at a distance of 162 kilometers

Table 15.3   Regression estimates of international R&D spillovers

Parameter	Specification 1		Specification 2	
	Parameter Estimate	Standard Error	Parameter Estimate	Standard Error
λ	0.078	(0.013)	0.096	(0.008)
δ	1.005	(0.239)	0.384	(0.047)
γ	0.843	(0.059)	—	—
γ_J	—	—	1.000 (set)	set
γ_{US}	—	—	1.031	(0.059)
γ_{UK}	—	—	0.863	(0.060)
γ_{GER}	—	—	1.157	(0.060)
γ_F	—	—	1.011	(0.060)
ψ_D	—	—	−0.784	(0.068)
ψ_F	—	—	−0.061	(0.108)

(100 miles), and the rest is virtually eliminated once the source country of the foreign R&D is more than 400 miles away.

However, the results from Specification 2 qualify the foregoing findings. It is useful first to note that the estimate of ψ_F is insignificantly different from 0. Hence, correcting for distance and country of origin, the contribution of a G5 country's R&D on domestic technical know-how is pretty much the same throughout the sample years and, on average, not too different from the 84 percent found in Specification 1 when the distance to the G5 country is $D = 0$. The real change comes in the extent to which the impact of G5 R&D declines with distance. Now the estimate of δ is a much smaller 0.384, indicating that the effect declines much more slowly, even in the first half of the sample when $I_t = 0$. Over the latter half when I_t is 1, the estimate of $\psi_D = -0.784$ indicates that this small rate of decline is even smaller from 1983 to 1995 than it was previously. Together, these estimates indicate that at least half of the effect that a G5 nation's R&D would have had if the domestic country had been right next to it ($D = 0$) is still there as far out as 424 kilometers (263 miles) from 1970 to 1982, and is felt as far out as 1,963 kilometers (1,217 miles) after 1983. The degree of technical spillovers between industries in different nations has been growing.

Because Keller's spillover estimates apply to whole sectors separated by national boundaries, they may well be a lower bound for the extent of such spillovers between firms within the same domestic industry. If this is so, then these empirical estimates, when taken together with our analysis of the noncooperative outcome with high spillovers, suggest that the market will likely be characterized by inefficiently low R&D. If that is the case, then the argument for permitting R&D cooperation or joint ventures becomes noticeably more compelling.

Summary

Research and development is the wellspring of technical advancement. Such advancement is the true source of the rise in living standards that has characterized the developed economies for most of the last two centuries. It should be clear, however, that firms will only be willing to incur the heavy expenses and considerable risks associated with R&D if they can be reasonably assured that their efforts will be rewarded. Imitation by rivals has the social benefit of intensifying price competition after innovation occurs. However, this makes it less likely that the innovation will occur in the first place.

The tension between the gains from competition and the gains from innovation (i.e., the tension between the replacement effect and the efficiency effect) is unavoidable. It has led economists to consider which market environment—competitive or monopolistic—will foster greater research and development. The Schumpeterian hypothesis is, broadly speaking, that oligopolistic market structures are best in this regard.

Both theory and empirical data give ambiguous evidence as to the market structure most conducive to R&D effort. Competitive markets can sometimes fail to be as innovative as their less-competitive counterparts, but a surprising number of key inventions have come from small firms. Policy has a role to play here, too. One role for policy is to encourage cooperation in research efforts. Empirical evidence suggests that we live in an increasingly interconnected world in which the benefits from one firm's R&D spill over to other firms, including its rivals. In such a world, the noncooperative outcome is likely to be one with too little R&D effort. Policy that fosters research cooperation among firms can be helpful in this setting. Yet, caution is also necessary. The trick is somehow to foster cooperation on R&D without simultaneously inducing collaboration on prices and product design.

A similar tension arises in the role of patent policy. Patents can enhance the incentives for firms to pursue technological innovations. Yet, by temporarily granting monopoly power, patents can also weaken competitive forces and reduce consumers' access to those breakthroughs. We consider patents and related policy issues in the next chapter.

Problems

1. Consider a market with demand $Q = D(P)$ and served by a single monopoly firm with no threat of entry. Assume that the monopolist has a constant marginal cost c_H. Suppose that the firm makes a discovery that lowers its marginal cost to c_L.
   a. Show that if the monopolist can perfectly discriminate, she will place the same value on the innovation as would a social planner trying to maximize the sum of consumer and producer surplus.
   b. Suppose instead that the market is initially populated by n competitive firms, each with a constant marginal cost again equal to c_H. Now let one such firm make the same innovation that again lowers its marginal cost to c_L. Suppose that the innovation is non-drastic. What value will this firm place on the innovation if it can perfectly discriminate in price up to the maximum it can charge c_H?

2. Let the inverse demand for a particular product be given by $P = 250 - Q$. The product is offered by two Cournot firms each of which has a current marginal cost of $100. Both firms can invest a sum K to establish a research facility to develop a new process with lower marginal costs. The probability of success is ρ.
   a. Assume that the new process is expected to have marginal costs of $70. Derive a relation ship between K and ρ under which
      i. neither firm establishes a research facility
      ii. only one firm establishes a research facility
      iii. both firms establish a research facility
   b. Under what circumstances is there "too much" R&D in that both firms spend on R&D whereas aggregate profit is greater if only one firm does so?
   c. Under what circumstances is there "too little" R&D in that neither firms spend on R&D whereas total surplus is greater if at least one firm does so?

3. Let inverse demand be described by: $P = 100 - 2Q$, and let each firm have a marginal production cost of $c = \$60$. Assume now that each firm can choose its level of research intensity x_i and that the degree to which this research spills over to its rival is β. In other words, research intensities x_i and x_j result in marginal cost $60 - x_i - \beta x_j$. Suppose that if research intensity is x research costs are $x^2/2$.
   a. What are the Nash equilibrium research intensities, outputs, profits and price if the degree of spillover is $\beta = 0.25$?
   b. What are the Nash equilibrium research intensities, outputs, profits and price if the degree of spillover is $\beta = 0.75$?

4. Let inverse demand be given by: $P = 240 - Q$, and marginal cost be initially $c = \$120$. In addition, let the discount factor be $R = 0.9$.
   a. A research institute develops a process innovation that lowers marginal cost to $60 and offers to sell this new technology to at most one firm. Determine the value of the innovation to: (i) a monopolist; (ii) one of two Cournot competitors; and (iii) one of two Bertrand competitors.
   b. Now instead assume an initial monopoly but one in which the monopolist faces a rival entrant. If the institute can sell to just one firm, will it prefer to sell its technology to the monopolist or to the rival entrant?

5. Return to the two duopoly cases of Problem 4. Now let the research institute consider the option of selling the innovation to both firms. Will it find this profitable:
    a. In the Cournot case?
    b. In the Bertrand case?

References

Arrow, Kenneth. 1962. "Economic Welfare and the Allocation of Resources for Inventions." In R. Nelson, ed., *The Rate and Direction of Inventive Activity: Economic and Social Factors*. National Bureau of Economic Research. Princeton: Princeton University Press.

Blundell R., R. Griffith, J. Van Reenen. 1995. "Dynamic Count Data Models of Technological Innovation." *The Economic Journal,* 105: 333–44.

Cohen, W., and R. Levin. 1989. "Empirical Studies of Innovation and Market Structure." In R. Schmalensee and R. Willig, eds., *Handbook of Industrial Organization*, *Vol.2*.Amsterdam: North-Holland: 1059–1098.

Cohen, W., R. Levin, and S. Klepper. 1996. "A Reprise of Size and R&D." *Economic Journal,* 106: 925–951.

Dasgupta, P., and J. Stiglitz. 1980. "Industrial Structure and the Nature of Innovative Activity". *Economic Journal,* 90 (January): 266–293.

D'Aspremont, C., and A. Jacquemin. 1988. "Cooperative and Noncooperative R&D in Duopoly with Spillovers". *American Economic Review,* 78 (September): 1133–1137.

Gayle, P. 2002. "Market Structure and Product Innovation." Working Paper, Department of Economics, Kansas State University.

Geroski P. 1990. "Innovation, Technology Opportunity and Market Structure." *Oxford Economic Papers,* 42: 586–602.

Gilbert, R. J. 2006. "Competition and Innovation," *Journal of Industrial Organization Education* Vol. 1, Issue 1, Article 8. Available at: http://www.bepress.com/jioe/vol1/iss1/8.

Gilbert, R. J., and D. M. G. Newbery. 1982. "Preemptive Patenting and the Persistence of Monopoly". *American Economic Review,* 72 (June): 514–527.

Kamien, M. I., E. Muller, and I. Zang. 1992. "Research Joint Ventures and R&D Cartels". *American Economic Review,* 82 (December): 1293–1306.

Keller, W. 2002. "Geographic Localization of International Technology Transfer". *American Economic Review,* 92 (March): 120–142.

Klepper, S. 2002. "Firm Survival and the Evolution of Oligopoly". *Rand Journal of Economics,* 33 (Spring): 37–61.

Levin, R., and P. Reiss. 1984. "Tests of a Schumpeterian Model of R and D and Market Structure." In Z. Griliches, ed., *R&D, Patents and Productivity*. Chicago: NBER University of Chicago Press.

Levin, R., W. Cohen, and D. C. Mowery. 1985a. "R&D Appropriability, Opportunity, and Market Structure: New Evidence on Some Schumpeterian Hypotheses." *American Economic Review, Papers and Proceedings,* 75 (May): 20–24.

———. 1985b. "Firm Size and R&D Intensity: A Reexamination." *American Economic Review,* 75 (June): 543–565.

Levin, R., A. Klevorick, R. Nelson, and S. Winter. 1987. "Appropriating the Returns from Industrial Research and Development." *Brookings Papers on Economic Activity: Microeconomics,* 2: 783–822.

Lin, P., and K. Saggi. 2002. "Product Differentiation, Process R&D, and the Nature of Market Equilibrium". *European Economic Review,* 46 (January): 201–211.

Lunn, J. 1986. "An Empirical Analysis of Process and Product Patenting: A Simultaneous Equation Framework." *Journal of Industrial Economics,* 34 (February): 319–330.

Markides, C., and P. Geroski. 2005. *Fast Second: How Smart Companies Bypass Radical Innovations To Enter and Dominate New Markets*. San Francisco: Jossey-Bass.

Norman, G., L. Pepall, and D. Richards. 2008. "Entrepreneurial First Movers, Brand-Name Fast Seconds, and the Evolution of Market Structure." *B.E. Journal of Economic Analysis & Policy (Contributions)*, 8.1 (October).

Porter, M. 1990. *The Competitive Advantage of Nations*. New York: The Free Press.

Scherer, F. M. 1965. "Firm Size, Market Structure, Opportunity and the Output of Patented Innovations". *American Economic Review,* 55 (September): 1097–1125.

———. 1967. "Market Structure and the Employment of Scientists and Engineers". *American Economic Review,* 57 (June): 524–531.

Schumpeter, J. A. 1942. *Capitalism, Socialism, and Democracy*. New York: Harper.

Scott, J. T. 1990. "Purposeful Diversification of R&D and Technological Advancement." In A. Link, ed., *Advances in Applied Micro-economics,, Vol. 5*. Greenwich, CT, and London: JAI Press.

Von Hippel, E. 1988. *The Sources of Innovation*. New York: Oxford University Press.

16

Patents and Patent Policy

In 1769, an English inventor, Richard Arkwright, patented a spinning frame that would revolutionize the production of cotton cloth. Two years later, in 1771, Englishman James Hargreaves introduced another invention, the spinning jenny. With these inventions, Britain entered the Industrial Revolution. Equally important, the inventions allowed Arkwright and Hargreaves to establish a commanding position in the production of textile products. This allowed the inventors to reap large profits and to sell at a high price in the American colonies, even after these became independent states.

The British energetically protected their monopoly position. Westbound ships out of London were searched thoroughly to make sure that no passenger was a former Arkwright or Hargeaves employee or had a copy of the design plans for the Arkwright-Hargreaves machines that firms outside of Britain might copy. Such restrictions, along with the high textile price for British textiles, vexed many Americans. Consumers did not like paying the monopoly prices, and firms were eager to get some version of the machines that would permit them to compete with the British producers. Some firms offered "bounties" for English apprentices who would be able to obtain the necessary information. Finally, in 1789, an enterprising young Englishman and former Arkwright partner, Samuel Slater, responded to just such a bounty offer. After completely memorizing the engineering details of the Arkwright-Hargreaves machines, he disguised himself as a common laborer and set sail for America. Slater arrived in Pawtucket, Massachusetts, and established the first of many New England textile mills, consolidating the region's manufacturing base and finally breaking the British monopoly.

The issues raised by Slater's entrepreneurship (what some might call theft) lie at the heart of this chapter. The central question is how strongly a firm's innovation should be protected from imitative competition. On the one hand, information about an innovation is a public good for which the marginal cost of passing it on to one more person is essentially zero. Hence, once the information is produced, efficiency requires that access to this information (i.e., new production techniques and new products) should be unrestricted and available to all at a price equal to marginal cost to avoid any monopoly distortion. On the other hand, if the government does not protect innovators against imitation, there may be little incentive to innovate in the first place.

The patent system creates incentives for innovative activity. To quote the United States Patent and Trademark Office:

> A patent is an intellectual property right granted by the Government of the United States of America to an inventor to exclude others from making, using, offering for sale, or selling the invention throughout the United States or importing the invention into the United States for a limited time in exchange for public disclosure of the invention when the patent is granted. http://www.uspto.gov/patents/index.jsp

To be patentable, "an invention must meet four basic requirements: patentable subject matter, utility, novelty and non-obviousness" (Scotchmer, 2004, p. 66).

Given these conditions, the patent holder can act as a monopolist and earn a monopoly profit while the patent is in effect. This creates a tradeoff. The monopoly profit creates an incentive to undertake R&D, but also imposes a deadweight loss on society (and consumers) while the patent is in effect.

Getting this balance right is not easy. We can imagine just how much less productive the economy would be if the science behind electric lighting, the aerodynamics of airplanes, and semiconductors had never been developed. However, production would also suffer were those same technologies not widely available to all firms. At some point, policy must shift from a stance of protecting innovators from imitation to one of permitting the use of the innovation on as wide a basis as possible. The really challenging question is exactly where that point lies.

Part of the debate on the patent system relates to what can and should be patentable. For example, there has been controversy about U.S. patent number 5,960,411, awarded to Amazon's one-click purchasing system, or U.S. patent number 6,874,409, awarded to the J. M. Smucker Company governing the method for making a crustless sandwich. Business method patents are particularly controversial, with many patents that have been granted being criticized for being either trivial or relating to well-known methods. For example, U.S. patent number 5,794,207 covers a method for conducting a Dutch auction, an auction method that has been in use in the Netherlands for centuries.

These are important questions, but are beyond the scope of this chapter. The interested reader is recommended to consult Bessen and Meurer (2008) or Boldrine and Levine (2008).[1] Our major concern in this chapter concentrates on how far patent rights should extend. This has two dimensions. First, what is the length of time for which any patent rights ought to last? Second, to what range of products should the patent apply? Should the developer of a new AIDS treatment based on a special combination of protease inhibitors be protected against a rival's later development of an alternative AIDS treatment based on a different combination of protease inhibitors? What about a new AIDS treatment that is not based on protease inhibitors? Or what if a protease inhibitor treatment originally created as a treatment for AIDS is now applied as a treatment for multiple sclerosis? These issues—typically referred to as patent length and patent breadth—are the central questions in patent policy.

---

[1] Details of patents awarded in the United States can be found at http://www.uspto.gov/.

16.1   OPTIMAL PATENT LENGTH

Current patent law establishes a patent duration that varies from country to country. In the United Kingdom and the United States, patent law grants protection for 20 years from the date of filing the application. In both countries, it is up to the patent holder to ensure that the patent is renewed during its life and to ensure that the patent is not infringed.

Economic theory can provide some insights as to whether such a choice of duration makes sense. The key is to find a balance between the innovator's ability to earn a return on its R&D investment and the benefits that will accrue to consumers once the patent expires and competition emerges. Nordhaus (1969) presented the first formal analysis of this decision. The model that we present here is due to La Manna (1992).

Assume a market with linear demand $P = \alpha - Q$ and constant marginal cost $C(Q) = \gamma$. Furthermore, assume that—prior to any innovation—this market is "marginally unprofitable," by which we mean that $\alpha = \gamma$. Denote the extent of innovative effort by x. There are two types of innovation that can make this market potentially profitable. On the one hand, we might consider a product innovation that enhances the desirability of the product in the eyes of consumers and so increases α to $\alpha + x$ as in Figure 16.1(a). Alternatively, we might consider a process innovation that reduces marginal cost to $\gamma - x$ as in Figure 16.1(b). No matter which type of innovation we are considering, suppose that both types of innovation are protected by a patent of duration T. When the patent expires, new entrants come in and drive the price down to marginal cost.

With either type of innovation, it is easy to see from Figure 16.1 that in any period dt consumer surplus, profit, and deadweight loss while the patent is in effect are respectively

$$cs(x) = \frac{x^2}{8}; \ \pi(x) = \frac{x^2}{4}; \ d(x) = \frac{x^2}{8} \tag{16.1}$$

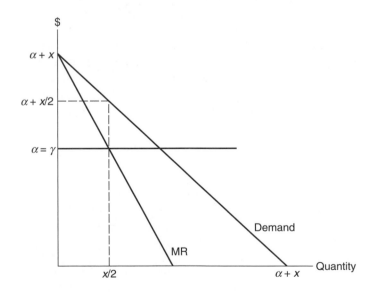

Figure 16.1(a)   Product innovation

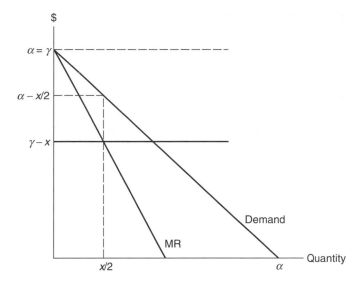

Figure 16.1(b)   Process innovation

In what follows, we shall refer to values such as $cs(x)$ as the "flow-rate", in this case of consumer surplus. This is necessary, since much of our analysis is going to be conducted in what is termed "continuous time" rather than in "discrete time." so that we may use continuous discounting (see Chapter 2).

We assume that innovative effort x costs

$$R(x) = \theta x^\beta \quad (2 < \beta < \infty) \tag{16.2}$$

In this equation, θ and β are direct measures of the cost of innovative effort. Note that $dR(x)/dx > 0$ and $d^2R(x)/dx^2 > 0$. Innovation is costly and exhibits diminishing returns.[2]

Now, imagine the following two-stage game between the Patent Office and the innovating firm. In the first stage the Patent Office sets the patent duration T. In the second stage, the firm chooses the amount of innovative effort x. Of course, as is usual with such stage games, the Patent Office can correctly anticipate the impact that its choice of T has on the firm's choice of x. Also, as usual, we solve this game "backward."

For any choice of T by the Patent Office, the firm chooses x to maximize profit:

$$\pi(x, \tau) = \int_0^T \pi(x)e^{-rt} - R(x) = (1 - e^{-rT})\frac{x^2}{4r} - \theta x^\beta = \frac{\tau x^2}{4r} - \theta x^\beta \tag{16.3}$$

In equation (16.3), r is the discount rate that the firm and society applies, and we have made the simplifying substitution that $\tau = (1 - e^{-rT})$. Here, τ is very similar to what Scotchmer (2004) refers to as "discounted time." As T increases from 0 to infinity, τ increases from 0 to 1.

---

[2]   The restriction that $\beta > 2$ is necessary to ensure that the second-order condition on profit maximization is met.

Differentiating equation (16.3) with respect to x and solving gives us the innovating firm's optimal choice of innovative effort, which we can also call the firm's patent life reaction function:

$$x(\tau) = \left(\frac{\tau}{2\theta\beta r} \right)^{\beta/(\beta-2)} \tag{16.4}$$

As we might have expected, expenditure by the firm on innovation increases as patent duration increases, decreases as the discount rate increases, and decreases as innovation becomes more costly.

When the patent expires, the flow rate of social surplus in any period dt is $cs(x) + \pi(x) + d(x)$. This gives the welfare function for the Patent Office:

$$W(x, \tau) = \int_0^\infty (c(x) + \pi(x) + d(x))e^{-rt}dt - \int_0^T d(x)e^{-rt}dt - R(x)$$

$$= \frac{x^2}{2r} - (1 - e^{-rT})\frac{x^2}{8r} - \theta x^\beta = \frac{4 - \tau}{8r}x^2 - \theta x^\beta \tag{16.5}$$

The first term is aggregate social surplus if there were no patent, the second term is the deadweight loss of the patent during the period of patent protection, and the third term is the cost of research at intensity x. The Patent Office can correctly anticipate the innovating firm's reaction function (16.3), and so substitutes equation (16.4) into (16.5) and maximizes the resulting welfare function with respect to patent life τ. After some reasonably complex manipulation, this gives us

$$\text{for } \beta < 4 \quad \tau^* = 1 \quad x^* = \left(\frac{1}{2\theta\beta r} \right)^{\beta/(\beta-2)}$$

$$\text{for } \beta > 4 \quad \tau^* = \frac{8}{4 + \beta} \quad x^* = \left(\frac{4}{(4 + \beta)\theta\beta r} \right)^{\beta/(\beta-2)} \tag{16.6}$$

What equation (16.6) tells us is that when innovation is "easy" or not subject to very strong decreasing returns (equivalent to $\beta < 4$), the optimal patent life is infinite; but if innovation is "hard" or subject to strong decreasing returns (equivalent to $\beta > 4$), the optimal patent life is finite. To see why, note that as the Patent Office increases patent duration, it induces greater R&D effort and so generates net surplus to producers and consumers. If patent duration is 0, the returns to an innovator are also 0, since the results of the innovation will be imitated immediately. Accordingly, there will be no R&D and no change in the social surplus. An increase in the patent length to $\tau > 0$ induces some innovation and, thereby, an increase in total surplus. Two forces work potentially to limit the optimal value of τ. The first is our assumption of diminishing returns to R&D activity. Because increased innovation is increasingly expensive, it takes progressively greater increases in τ to achieve a given increase in innovative effort Δx. The second force limiting optimal patent duration is the fact of discounting. Some of the consumer benefits (converting the deadweight loss into consumer surplus) will not be realized until after the patent expires. If the Patent Office chooses a very long patent duration τ, the present value of those benefits will be very small indeed. When the decreasing returns to innovation are strong, the result is an optimal duration that is finite. By contrast, when decreasing returns are relatively weak, the benefits of increased innovation outweigh the deadweight loss; and optimal duration is infinite.

This result is particularly important since it has been argued that innovation should be granted patent protection forever. Such a long patent duration puts a heavy value on the benefits that patent protection generates and gives little consideration to the additional consumer surplus that will emerge only after the patent protection has expired. Our analysis indicates that this proposal has merit only if innovation is "easy."[3]

16.2   OPTIMAL PATENT BREADTH

The question of optimal patent breadth is trickier than that of optimal patent length—mainly because there is no universally accepted measure of breadth, whereas time is an obvious measure of length. Conceptually, the idea is to define a minimum degree to which a new innovation must differ from an existing process (or product) in order for the new innovation to avoid infringing on an existing patent and to be patentable itself. The larger this required minimal degree of difference, the more difficult it is for other firms to "invent around" the patent and cut into the inventor's profit. We could, in principle, work out the optimal patent breadth just as we worked out the optimal patent length. But the lack of a clear method for measuring breadth makes doing so very difficult without some stylized assumptions.

This lack of precision is reflected in the language of the Patent Office. Each application for a patent is required to specify all the "related" existing patents and to indicate not only how the patent being applied for is a discovery distinct from those already patented, but also to show that the discovery is "novel, non-obvious, useful." Such language leaves the Patent Office a lot of discretion!

The question of the optimal patent breadth is made even more difficult because it cannot be divorced from the question of optimal duration. Patent policy must set both dimensions of patent protection. Effectively, this comes down to choosing between a system in which patents have a short duration but a broad coverage (the "short and fat" approach) or a long duration combined with a very narrow coverage (the "long and thin" solution). These choices involve balancing the need to maintain the incentive to innovate against the need to distribute the benefits of innovation as widely as possible.

Unfortunately, introducing breadth into the design of patent policy does not necessarily lead to settled conclusions. To see why, we contrast two approaches to patent length and breadth.[4]

16.2.1   Gilbert and Shapiro

We begin with the analysis of Gilbert and Shapiro (1990). Rather than define patent breadth directly, they assume that broader patents confer greater monopoly power and

---

[3]   Author Mark Helprin has argued for an infinite copyright for creative works ("A Great Idea Lives Forever, Shouldn't Its Copyright?" *New York Times*, May 20, 2007). It might be argued—although the authors of this text would not necessarily agree—that producing copyrightable work is "easier" than producing a patentable invention, in which case our analysis could be used to support this suggestion. Note that the argument for an infinite patent life is moot if there is continual innovation that effectively limits the economic life of any one patent.

[4]   Both papers were actually published in the same 1990 issue of the *RAND Journal of Economics*.

so generate a greater flow rate of profits π during the time that the patent is in force. The tradeoff that the Patent Office must make is one that we have already met: the benefits from the innovation against the deadweight loss from the monopoly power that the patent creates. Two key assumptions are made. First, Gilbert and Shapiro assume that the flow rate of social welfare $w(\pi)$ is decreasing in $\pi: w'(\pi) < 0$. This simply states that greater monopoly power reduces social welfare by increasing the deadweight loss of monopoly. Second, they assume that $w''(\pi) < 0$: increased patent breadth is increasingly costly because of its increased deadweight loss.

To keep the analysis reasonably simple, we assume that once the patent expires profits are driven to zero, so the flow rate of social welfare is maximized at $w(0)$.[5] We further assume that the innovating firm must receive a present value of profits from the patent of at least F if it is going to be willing to undertake the innovative effort. (F can be thought of as the fixed cost of innovation that leads to a successful patent application.) The present value of social welfare is

$$W(T, \pi) = \int_0^T w(\pi)e^{-rt}dt + \int_T^\infty w(0)e^{-rt}dt = \frac{w(\pi)}{r}\left(1 - e^{-rT}\right) + \frac{w(0)}{r}e^{-rT}$$

(16.7)

The first term of equation (16.7) is the present value of social welfare during the period of patent protection, and the second is the present value of social welfare once the patent expires. The Patent Office sets patent breadth as measured by π and patent length T to maximize $W(T, \pi)$ subject to the constraint that the present value of patentee's profits are exactly F:

$$F = \int_0^T \pi e^{-rt}dt = \frac{\pi}{r}(1 - e^{-rT})$$

(16.8)

Define $\phi(T)$ as the flow rate of profits that just satisfies the constraint (16.8). In other words

$$F = \frac{\phi(T)}{r}(1 - e^{-rT})$$

(16.9)

Differentiating (16.9) with respect to T gives

$$0 = \phi(T)e^{-rT} + \phi'(T)\frac{(1 - e^{-rT})}{r}$$

(16.10)

Now, suppose that patent length is set at T and patent breadth is set at $\phi(T)$. Then from equation (16.7), social welfare is

$$W(T, \phi(T)) = \frac{w(\phi(T))}{r}(1 - e^{-rT}) + \frac{w(0)}{r}e^{-rT}$$

(16.11)

Differentiate this with respect to T to give

$$\frac{dW(T, \phi(T))}{dT} = w(\phi(T))e^{-rT} + w'(\phi(T))\phi'(T)\frac{(1 - e^{-rT})}{r} - w(0)e^{-rT}$$

---

[5]   Gilbert and Shapiro do not make this assumption, but it loses no generality.

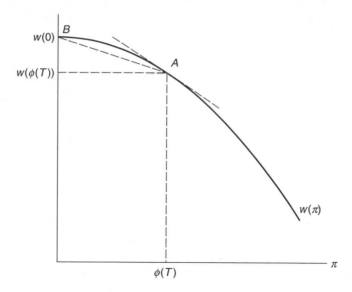

Figure 16.2   Patent length

This looks complicated, but can be simplified by substituting in the second term using equation (16.10) to give

$$\frac{dW(T, \phi(T))}{dT} = w(\phi(T))e^{-rT} - w'(\phi(T))\phi(T)e^{-rT} - w(0)e^{-rT}$$

$$= e^{-rT}(w(\phi(T)) - w'(\phi(T))\phi(T) - w(0)) \tag{16.12}$$

Consider the term in brackets. This is greater than zero if the following condition holds:

$$-w'(\phi(T)) > (w(0) - w(\phi(T)))/\phi(T) \tag{16.13}$$

Since we have assumed that $w(\pi)$ is concave, this must be true—as can be seen from figure 16.2 above. The left-hand side of equation (16.13) is the absolute value of the slope of the tangent to $w(\pi)$ at point A, whereas the right-hand side is the absolute value of the slope of the line AB. The former is clearly greater than the latter. As a result, $dW(T, \phi(T))/dT > 0$. What this tells us is that, no matter what patent duration the Patent Office chooses, a further increase in patent duration always raises social welfare. This leads directly to the conclusion that *optimal patent length is infinite*.

The intuition is quite straightforward. Patent breadth, as measured by the flow rate of profits $\phi(T)$, is increasingly costly in social welfare terms, so the Patent Office wants to set the patent length to minimize the detrimental impact of patent breadth. From (16.10), $d\phi(T)/dT < 0$. What this tells us is that the flow rate of profits necessary to ensure that the patent holder just recovers the cost of innovation decreases with patent length. As a result, the optimal policy is an infinite patent length. In turn, this implies a very narrow patent breadth. From equation (16.9), an infinite patent length implies that the breadth will be $\phi(T) = rF$, that is, just enough to permit a profit that covers the annual interest on the required fixed cost of innovation.

16.2.2   Klemperer

It is important to note, however, that the Gilbert and Shapiro (1990) approach is not the only way to model patent breadth. Klemperer (1990) offers an alternative that relates patent breadth more directly to product differentiation. If we think of a Hotelling line segment of finite length, Klemperer's view is that a useful definition of patent breadth is the fraction of the line segment that is covered by the patent.

We illustrate Klemperer's analysis by means of a specific example. Assume that there are N consumers located at 0 on a line market. Further assume that there is a firm located at 0 that has incurred innovative costs F, as a result of which it holds a patent of breadth β. While competing firms can offer the same product as the patent holder, they cannot locate closer than β to the patent holder—or to the consumers. Assume that there is a set of such competing firms who copy the innovative firm's product[6] (subject to the constraint on their location) and that (Bertrand) competition between them results in a product price equal to marginal cost, which we assume to be constant and can normalize to 0 without loss of generality.

A consumer at 0 can either buy from the patent holder at the price P that the patent holder sets, or travel the distance β, incurring transport cost, in order to purchase from the competing firms (at a purchase price of 0), or buy nothing. Each consumer is assumed to purchase exactly one unit of the product provided that the price (or the transport cost) is no greater than the consumer's reservation price.

The Patent Office is charged with the task of choosing patent breadth and length to maximize social welfare, subject to the constraint that the patent holder at least breaks even.

We consider two special examples of Klemperer's full analysis.

Example 1: Identical Reservation Prices, Different Transport Costs

Assume that all consumers have the same reservation price V for the product, but that they differ in their transport costs. Transport costs per unit distance are assumed to be uniformly distributed on the interval $[t_1, t_2]$, with $t_1 > 0$.

Ignore the reservation price for the moment. Suppose that the patent holder sets the price $P_1 = t_1\beta$. All N consumers buy from the patent holder, since price is no greater than the transport cost each consumer incurs in order to purchase from the Bertrand firms. Now, suppose that the firm sets a price $P_2 \geq t_2\beta$. All N consumers prefer to travel to purchase from the Bertrand firms. The patent-holder sells nothing. Next, assume that the patent holder sets a price P such that $P_1 < P < P_2$. Every consumer with transport cost parameter t less than P/β prefers to buy from the Bertrand firms, while the remaining consumers buy from the patent-holder, as illustrated in Figure 16.3. The fraction of consumers who purchase from the patent holder is $(t_2 - P/\beta)/(t_2 - t_1)$, and demand to the patent-holder is

$$Q_1(P, \beta) = (t_2 - P/\beta)N/(t_2 - t_1) = N(t_2/(t_2 - t_1) - P/\beta(t_2 - t_1)) \qquad (16.14)$$

Note that this is just a linear demand function.

---

[6]   After all, they can study the patent holder's patent application.

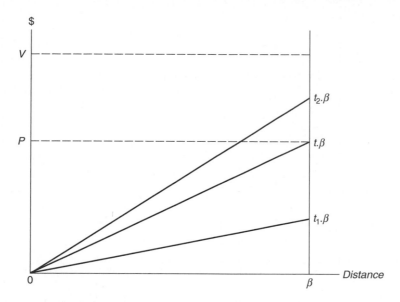

Figure 16.3   Patent breadth

This allows us to specify the demand $Q(P, \beta)$ to the patent holder, taking into account the reservation price and the unit nature of individual demand:

$$Q(P, \beta) = \begin{cases} 0 \text{ if } & P > V \\ \min \quad (N, Q_1(P, \beta)) & \text{if } P \leq V \end{cases} \tag{16.15}$$

It is useful to rewrite $Q_1(P, \beta)$ or equation (16.14) as an inverse demand function:

$$P = t_2\beta - \frac{(t_2 - t_1)\beta}{N} Q \tag{16.16}$$

Equating marginal revenue with marginal cost of 0 requires that the solution or output Q_0 be such that

$$Q_0 = t_2 N / 2(t_2 - t_1) \tag{16.17}$$

We have that $Q_0 < N$ if $t_2 > 2t_1$ and $Q_0 \geq N$ if $t_2 \leq 2t_1$. As it turns out, which of these two distributions of transport costs is actually the case is critically important. We analyze the two cases in turn:

Case 1: Wide Distribution of Transport Costs, or $t_2 > 2t_1$

Suppose first that the Patent Office sets a wide patent breadth $\beta_1 = V/t_1$. It is easy to check from equation (16.14) and (16.15) that $Q_1(P, \beta_1) = Q(P, \beta_1) = N$ when $P = V$, as illustrated in Figure 16.4. With this patent breadth, the patent holder sets his price to the consumer reservation price V. All consumers purchase the patent holder's product, so no consumer incurs transport costs, and we have the socially efficient outcome.[7]

---

[7]   You can easily confirm that we get the same outcome for any patent breadth greater than β_1.

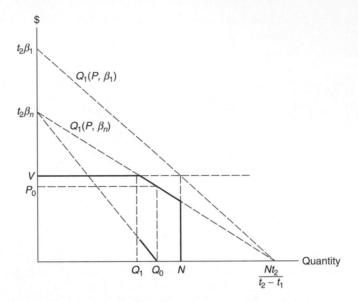

Figure 16.4   Identical reservation prices—optimal patent breadth—$t_2 > 2t_1$

Suppose, by contrast, that the patent holder sets a narrower patent breadth $\beta_n < V/t_1$, again as illustrated in Figure 16.4 above. The patent holder, in maximizing profit now has to choose between two options.

Option (i): Set price $P = V$ and sell $Q_1 < N$ units. Q_1 is determined by the fact that with this option, all consumers with transport costs less than $t_n = V/\beta_n > t_1$ prefer to travel to purchase from the Bertrand firms.[8] With $P = V$ and (16.14) we have

$$Q_1 = (t_2\beta_n - V)N/(t_2 - t_1)\beta_n \tag{16.18}$$

Option (ii): Choose output Q_0 where marginal revenue associated with $Q(P, \beta_n)$ equals marginal cost (zero). With this option, Q_0 is given by equation (16.17). Substituting in (16.16) gives the corresponding price $P_0 = \beta_n t_2/2$. In this case, all consumers with transport costs less than $t_0 = P_0/\beta_n = t_2/2 > t_1$ prefer to travel to purchase from the Bertrand firms.

No matter which of these options the patent holder chooses, some consumers prefer to travel to buy from the Bertrand firms, incurring transport costs and so reducing social welfare as compared with the wide patent breadth β_1. This leads to the following result:[9] Suppose that consumers have unit demands with identical reservation prices V and with transport costs uniformly distributed on the interval $[t_1, t_2]$. Suppose further that $t_2 > 2t_1$. Social welfare is maximized by setting patent breadth no less than $\beta_1 = V/t_1$.

What about the patent length? With patent breadth β_1, price is V; and the patent holder's flow rate of revenue is VN. With patent length T, the patent holder's profit is

$$\pi = \int_0^T VNe^{-rt}dt - F = \frac{VN}{r}(1 - e^{-rT}) - F = \frac{\tau VN}{r} - F \tag{16.19}$$

---

[8]   We have illustrated this case on the further assumption that $\beta_n > V/t_2$.
[9]   This is a variant on Proposition 2 in Klemperer (1990).

where, as in Section 16.1, we make the simplifying substitution $\tau = (1 - e^{-rT})$. The Patent Office should set a patent length of $\tau_1 = Fr/VN$. This patent length is finite $(\tau_1 < 1)$, since the maximum profit the patent holder can make is VN/r; and for the firm to be willing to innovate at all it must be that $VN/r > F$ or $Fr/VN < 1$. This is what we have referred to as the "short and fat" choice of patent length and breadth.

Case 2: Narrow Distribution of Transport Costs, or $t_2 \leq 2t_1$

This case is illustrated in Figure 16.5 below. As with Case 1, setting a patent breadth of at least $\beta_1 = V/t_1$ is socially efficient. Suppose, by contrast, that the patent holder sets a narrower patent breadth $\beta_n < V/t_1$. As in Case 1, the patent holder has two options.

Option (i): Set price $P = V$ and sell $Q_1 = (t_2\beta_n - V)N/(t_2 - t_1)\beta_n$ units. As we have seen, this is socially inefficient.

Option (ii): Set output Q_0, where marginal revenue associated with $Q(P, \beta_n)$ equals marginal cost (0). Since in this case $t_2 < 2t_1$, we have $Q_0 = N$ and price $P_0 = t_1\beta_n$. This is very different from option (ii) in Case 1. All consumers purchase from the patent holder, so the outcome is socially efficient.

So far as the Patent Office is concerned, it now matters which of these options the patent holder adopts. From the patent holder's perspective, the choice is simple. Choose the option with the higher flow rate of profits. For the patent holder to choose the socially efficient option (ii) requires that the patent breadth be such that option (i) is less profitable than option (ii), or

$$t_1\beta_n > V(t_2\beta_n - V)/(t_2 - t_1)\beta_n \tag{16.20}$$

This condition can be rewritten:

$$(V - t_1\beta_n)(V - (t_2 - t_1)\beta_n) > 0 \tag{16.21}$$

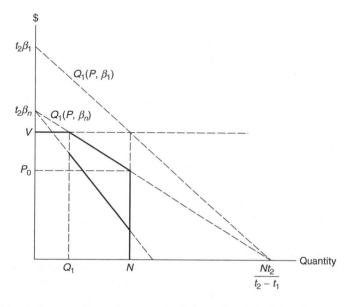

Figure 16.5   Identical reservation prices—optimal patent breadth—$t_2 < 2t_1$

Since $t_1\beta_n < V$ and $t_2 < 2t_1$, this condition always holds. In other words, *the patent holder will choose the socially optimal option for any patent breadth*. This implies the following:[10] Suppose that consumers have unit demands with identical reservation prices V and with transport costs uniformly distributed on the interval $[t_1, t_2]$. Suppose further that $t_2 < 2t_1$. No matter the patent breadth chosen by the Patent Office, the outcome is socially efficient.

In this case, can the Patent Office set a "very narrow" patent? To answer this question, we need to introduce the constraint that the patent holder must at least break even. With patent breadth β_n we have seen that price is $t_1\beta_n$, and so the flow rate of profit to the patent holder is $Nt_1\beta_n$. With a patent of duration T and breadth β_n the profit to the patent holder is

$$\pi = Nt_1\beta_n \int_0^T e^{-rt}dt - F = \frac{\tau Nt_1\beta_n}{r} - F \tag{16.22}$$

This allows us to refine our conclusion. Suppose that consumers have unit demands with identical reservation prices V and with transport costs uniformly distributed on the interval $[t_1, t_2]$. Suppose further that $t_2 < 2t_1$. The Patent Office can maximize social welfare and meet the patent-holder's nonzero profit constraint by offering a patent of infinite length and finite breadth $\beta_n = Fr/Nt_1$.

Since $F < NV/r$, it is certainly the case that $\beta_n < \beta_1$. In other words, when consumer transport costs are such that $t_2 < 2t_1$, the Patent Office has a choice. It can maximize social welfare by adopting the "short and fat" length/breadth policy (τ_1, β_1) or the "long and thin" policy $(1, \beta_n)$. Which should it choose? This question cannot be answered by looking at total surplus, since this is the same with both. There is, however, a very different temporal distribution of producer and consumer surplus with the two policies, and this may matter if we choose to apply differential weights to consumer and producer surplus.

With the "short and fat" policy, there is no consumer surplus until the patent expires. By contrast, with the "long and thin" policy, there is a positive flow rate of consumer surplus $N(V - t_1\beta_n)$ during the life of the patent. So, the question is whether the benefit to consumers in the early years of the "long and thin" policy is greater than the benefit to consumers in the later years of the "short and fat" policy. This question cannot be resolved without more knowledge of the precise parameter values. However, as a practical matter, many patents are invented around long before their formal expiry date. This favors the "long and thin" policy, since it does actually generate some consumer surplus in the early years of the patent.

We now turn to our second example.

Example 2: Variable Reservation Prices, Identical Transport Costs

In this example, we assume that all consumers incur the same unit transport costs t in traveling to purchase from the Bertrand firms. We further assume that consumers differ in their reservations prices for the product, with these reservation prices uniformly distributed on the interval $[0, V_N]$.

These assumptions allow us to identify the market demand function for the patent holder, assuming for the moment that there are no Bertrand firms. Suppose that the patent holder sets a price $P \le V_N$. All consumers with reservation prices of at least P purchase

---

[10]   This result contrasts with Klemperer's Proposition 2.

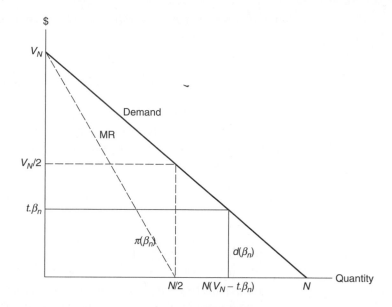

Figure 16.6   Identical transport costs—optimal patent breadth

the product, so that the fraction of consumers who purchase is $(V_N - P)/V_N$ and total demand is $Q(P) = N(V_N - P)/V_N$. This yields the inverse demand function

$$P = V_N(1 - Q/N) \qquad (16.23)$$

as illustrated in Figure 16.6 above. In the absence of the Bertrand competitors, the patent holder sets the monopoly price $P_m = V_N/2$. Only $N/2$ consumers purchase the product, leading to the familiar deadweight loss of monopoly.

Now introduce the Patent Office and the Bertrand competitors. Suppose that the Patent Office sets a patent breadth of $\beta_m \geq P_m/t$. Nothing happens. The patent holder can still set the monopoly price and lose no sales, since the cost of traveling to the Bertrand firms $t\beta_m$ is greater than the patent holder's monopoly price.

Suppose by contrast that the Patent Office sets a patent breadth of $\beta_n < P_m/t$. If the patent holder tries to set the monopoly price it will sell nothing: all of its existing consumers find that it is cheaper to buy from the Bertrand firms. The best that the patent holder can do is to set price $P = t.\beta_n$ and sell $Q_n = N(V_N - t.\beta_n)/V_N$ units, as illustrated in Figure 16.6. This still results in a deadweight loss. All consumers with reservation prices less than $t\beta_n$ are excluded from the market—their reservation prices are so low that they cannot purchase from either the patent holder or the Bertrand firms. The question is whether this narrowing of the patent breadth is a social improvement on the patent breadth β_m.

Consider the problem confronting the Patent Office. One way to view its task is that it aims to set the patent breadth to minimize the present value of the deadweight loss, subject to the constraint that the patent holder breaks even on its research expenditures. The present value of the deadweight loss with a patent of breadth β and length T is

$$D(\beta) = \int_0^T d(\beta)e^{-rt}dt = \left(1 - e^{-rT}\right)\frac{d(\beta)}{r} = \frac{\tau d(\beta)}{r} \qquad (16.24)$$

Given a flow rate of profit (ignoring research costs) of $\pi(\beta)$ and the research cost F, the profit constraint is

$$\int_0^T \pi(\beta)e^{-rt}dt - F = (1 - e^{-rT})\frac{\pi(\beta)}{r} - F = \frac{\tau\pi(\beta)}{r} - F = 0 \Rightarrow \tau = \frac{Fr}{\pi(\beta)} \tag{16.25}$$

Substituting equation (16.25) into (16.24) indicates that for any patent length T, the Patent Office should set patent breadth to minimize $d(\beta)/\pi(\beta)$. In other words, the Patent Office should set the patent breadth to minimize the ratio of the flow rate of deadweight loss to the flow rate of profit.

Returning to Figure 16.6, we can calculate the flow rates of profit and deadweight loss directly.

$$\pi(\beta) = \frac{N(V_N - t\beta)t\beta}{V_N}; d(\beta) = N\left(1 - \frac{(V_N - t\beta)}{V_N}\right)\frac{t\beta}{2} \tag{16.26}$$

The deadweight loss to profit ratio $d(\beta)/\pi(\beta) = V_N/2(V_N - t\beta) - 1/2$ is increasing in patent breadth β. As a result, the policy prescription for this example is straightforward. "Long and thin" is best. More formally, suppose that consumers have unit demands with reservation prices uniformly distributed on the interval $[0, V_N]$ and each with transport cost parameter t. The Patent Office should set an infinite patent duration and a patent breadth that is the narrowest consistent with the 0 profit constraint.

16.2.3   Some Conclusions

With patent policy, there is no one size that fits all. We have seen that there are cases in which "short and fat" is preferred and others in which "long and thin" is better. Gallini (1992) provides an additional reason why short-lived broad patents may be best. Imitators can often get around patent protection if they spend enough money to imitate the product without infringement. They will be particularly encouraged to do so when patents are long; because otherwise, entry into the market will be greatly delayed. When patents are short, imitation is less attractive, because firms now find it cheaper simply to wait for the patent to expire than to engage in costly efforts to imitate legally now. In other words, Gallini (1992, 2002) makes the important point that costly imitation efforts need also to be accounted for in considering the welfare effects of patent design. If these imitation costs are sizeable, then broad but short-lived patents are preferable.

Denicolò (1996) synthesizes many of these features in a framework that also incorporates the extent of market competition. He says: "Loosely speaking, the less efficient is the type of competition prevailing in the product market, the more likely it is that broad and short patents are socially optimal" (p. 264). By "efficient," Denicolò means roughly the extent to which competition drives firms close to the competitive ideal. Denicolò's statement implies that markets in which firms have a greater degree of monopoly power will do best with the "short and fat" approach to patent design, whereas markets characterized by greater competition will do best with patent design that is "long and thin."

As a policy recommendation, a major difficulty with optimal patent design is that it suggests different patent designs for different innovators depending on the structure of the innovator's basic industry. In reality, the rule of law cannot be applied so selectively without risking serious inconsistency. In addition, there is a further difficulty that it is not always easy to make the concept of breadth operational. We have no easy way to translate real markets into a spatial representation and no obvious measure of distance. Indeed, as Scotchmer (2004) has noted, Klemperer's (1990) horizontal concept of breadth can itself be limiting. There is also a vertical dimension reflecting how much better (or how much worse) a rival's product has to be before it infringes on the patented good. Recognizing this second dimension of patent breadth makes its measurement all the more difficult from a practical perspective. A one-size-fits-all policy of granting patents with "reasonable" breadth but "constrained" length may well be the best compromise outcome.

16.3   PATENT RACES

Schumpeter's vision of innovation is one in which firms race against each other to develop new technologies or new goods. He notes that this sort of rivalry is potentially deadly for those who come up short. This is particularly true when innovations are eligible for patent protection. Patents create a "winner takes all" environment. Finishing second is of no benefit. The loser of a patent race may see years of investment and hard work wiped out overnight when the rival patents its breakthrough. The question that we consider is whether patent races can lead to inefficient investment in R&D.

Consider a patent race between two firms, denoted 1 and 2, that can choose to invest in research to develop a new product. We assume that successful innovation generates a flow rate of profit π that is protected by a patent of duration T. When the patent expires, imitation drives the flow rate of profit to zero. We further assume that both firms (and society) apply a discount rate of r. As a result, using the same notation as in previous sections, the expected profit from successful innovation is $\pi = \tau\pi/r$.

To undertake the R&D, each firm has to establish a research division at a fixed cost of F. This covers the costs of research and of development if the research is successful and, once sunk, can never be recovered. Given that such a division is established, the probability of a successful innovation is ρ.[11] If only one firm is successful in its R&D efforts, that firm expects to earn $\tau\pi/r$ over the life of the patent. If both are successful simultaneously, both firms file a patent application and we assume that each firm has a 50 percent probability of its application being successful, so that expected profit is $\tau\pi/2r$ in this case. If neither firm attempts to develop the new product, neither firm will enter this new market.

We can now calculate the expected profit for each firm depending on whether or not it establishes a research division. If neither chooses to innovate, each earns 0 profit in this new market. If only Firm 1 establishes an R&D division, its expected profit is profit if the R&D division is unsuccessful, which is 0 and occurs with probability $(1 - \rho)$; plus profit if the R&D division is successful, which is $\tau\pi/r$ and occurs with probability ρ. As a result, the expected profit of Firm 1 if it is the only firm to establish an R&D division is

$$\pi_1 = \frac{\tau\pi}{r}\rho - F \tag{16.27}$$

The expected profit of its rival is, of course, 0.

---

[11]   For some of the earliest research on patent races with stochastic innovation, see Loury (1979) and Lee and Wilde (1980).

If both firms establish R&D divisions, the expected profit to either firm is profit if the firm's R&D division is successful and the rival's is not, which is $\tau\pi/r$ and occurs with probability $\rho(1-\rho)$; profit if both R&D divisions are successful, which is $\tau\pi/2r$ and occurs with probability ρ^2; or profit if neither firm is successful in R&D, which is 0 and occurs with probability $(1-\rho)^2$.

This means that the expected profit of each firm, given that they both operate R&D divisions, is

$$\rho(1-\rho)\frac{\tau\pi}{r} + \rho^2\frac{\tau\pi}{2r} - F = \frac{\tau\pi}{r}\rho\left(1-\frac{\rho}{2}\right) - F \qquad (16.28)$$

Note that the profit expressions (16.27) and (16.28) share the common term $\tau\pi/r = \pi$, which is the monopoly profit in this market. We can then define the parameter $S = F/\pi$, which is the share of the monopoly profit that is needed to establish the R&D division. With the substitution of S and π, the expected profits are summarized in the payoff matrix of Table 16.1. This matrix allows us to identify the possible Nash equilibria for the R&D game. As we shall see, these are dependent upon the relative magnitudes of S and ρ.

There are three possibilities:

1. *Neither Firm Wishes to Establish an R&D Division.* For this to be a Nash equilibrium requires that the strategy combination (No R&D, No R&D) is more profitable than the combination (No R&D, R&D). This requires that $\pi(\rho - S) < 0$, which implies that $S > \rho$, the probability of success is less than the fraction of monopoly profit required to fund the R&D. This expression is illustrated by the line 0A in Figure 16.7. All parameter combinations above 0A give the Nash equilibrium (No R&D, No R&D).

2. *Only One Firm Wishes to Establish an R&D Division.* For the strategy (R&D, No R&D) to be a Nash equilibrium, two conditions must be satisfied:

   a. Firm 1 expects to make more profit from the strategy combination (R&D, No R&D) than from the strategy combination (No R&D, No R&D). This is just the opposite of the expression derived above. It requires that $S < \rho$.

   b. Firm 2 prefers the strategy combination (R&D, No R&D) to (R&D, R&D). For this to be the case requires $\pi\left(\rho\left(1-\frac{\rho}{2}\right) - S\right) < 0$, which requires $S > \rho(1 - \rho/2)$. This is illustrated by the curve 0B in Figure 16.7. All parameter combinations between 0A and 0B are such that only one of the firms will establish an R&D division.

3. *Both Firms Wish to Establish an R&D Division.* For this to be a Nash equilibrium, Firm 1 expects to make more profit from the strategy combination (R&D, R&D) than from the strategy combination (No R&D, R&D). For this to be the case we

Table 16.1 Payoff matrix for the duopoly patent race

		Firm 2	
		No R&D Division	R&D Division
Firm 1	No R&D Division	0, 0	0, $\pi(\rho - S)$
	R&D Division	$\pi(\rho - S)$, 0	$\pi\left(\rho\left(1-\frac{\rho}{2}\right) - S\right)$; $\pi\left(\rho\left(1-\frac{\rho}{2}\right) - S\right)$

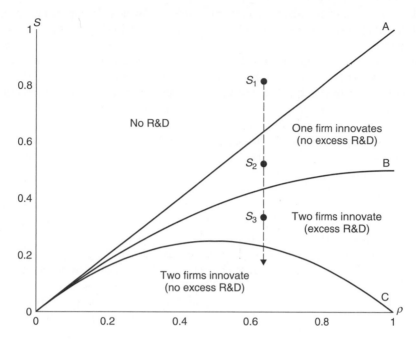

Figure 16.7   A duopoly patent race

must have that $\pi\left(\rho\left(1 - \frac{\rho}{2}\right) - S\right) > 0$, which requires $S < \rho(1 - \rho/2)$. All parameter combinations below OB are such that both firms will establish an R&D division.

We can now turn to the question of whether the potential profit from successful innovation can lead the two firms to overinvest in R&D. Neither of the firms will establish an R&D division unless this division is expected to be profitable. For the strategies (R&D, No R&D), (No R&D, R&D), and (R&D, R&D) to be equilibria, they must each give positive expected profits to the two firms. This tells us that no equilibrium in which only one firm invests in R&D is characterized by "excessive" R&D in the sense that the firms would be better off without the R&D. The question that is left is whether there is "too much" R&D when both firms establish R&D divisions. This occurs when the strategy combination (R&D, R&D) is a Nash equilibrium but generates less aggregate profit than the strategy combinations (R&D, No R&D) or (No R&D, R&D). For this to be the case it must be that $2\pi\left(\rho\left(1 - \frac{\rho}{2}\right) - S\right) < \pi(\rho - S)$ which requires that $S > \rho(1 - \rho)$.

This is illustrated by the curve OC in Figure 16.7. All parameter combinations between OC and OB lead to excessive R&D as the two firms race to be first to discover and introduce the new product.

Our simple model identifies three possibilities. First, neither firm will invest in R&D unless it is expected to be profitable. Hence, R&D must have a reasonably low cost relative to the monopoly profits that it might generate (low S), or a reasonably high probability of success. Second, for any given probability of success, a larger number of firms will establish R&D facilities when there is a lower cost of R&D relative to the profit the innovation is expected to generate. Third, there is an intermediate range of values for the cost of R&D in which there is excessive R&D in that both firms establish

R&D divisions, although this reduces their aggregate profits. In this range, the lure of profit from innovation involves the firms in a competitive R&D race that they would be better to avoid.

So far, we have only considered the gain that research brings in terms of the expected profit of the two firms. From a public policy perspective, however, increased profit is not the only benefit of innovation. We should also consider the gain in consumer surplus that development of this new product will generate. While we have just shown that the level of R&D activity can be excessive from the viewpoint of the firms' combined profits, we have not demonstrated that this is the case when judged by the objective of maximizing total surplus. R&D that seems excessive to the firms may be worthwhile to society, if the additional consumer surplus more than offsets the reduction in aggregate profit. However, R&D can be excessive even when evaluated with this broader criterion (you are asked to show this for a specific example in an end of chapter problem). The patent race can lead both firms to establish research divisions even when the total cost of such divisions is not justified by the sum of expected producer and consumer surplus.

Perhaps even more interesting is that we can easily show that the possibility of too little R&D—as judged from a social welfare perspective—is quite real. Suppose that $S > \rho$, in which case neither firm undertakes R&D. Suppose further that S is so close to ρ that one firm could almost expect to break even if it pursued the innovation and its rival did not. If the new product generates any significant consumer surplus at all, then it is socially desirable that the research takes place. The value of the expected consumer surplus more than provides the extra funds needed to ensure that the innovator breaks even. However, in the absence of government intervention, the fact that $S > \rho$ means that no such R&D efforts will occur.[12]

This brings us back to the role of patent length in influencing innovative activity. Recall that $S = F/\pi = Fr/\tau\pi$. The obvious parameter that the Patent Office can influence in S is patent length as measured by τ. Suppose first that $\tau = \tau_1$ is "short," giving $S = S_1$ in Figure 16.7. Then there is no innovation to develop the new product. If, however, patent length is increased to $\tau = \tau_2$, giving $S = S_2$ in Figure 16.7, one firm will be induced to undertake the innovation. Since this is profitable for the firm *and* is likely to generate consumer surplus even during the period of patent protection, this can be expected to be socially desirable.

So far, so good. Note, however, that if patent length is increased to $\tau = \tau_3$, giving $S = S_3$ in Figure 16.7, both firms will be induced to undertake the innovation; and we have socially wasteful innovation. In other words, we have yet another reason for being cautious in the design of patent policy. Very lengthy patents are attractive to firms and so may induce socially wasteful patent races.

We have focused on the potential for patent races to yield either too much or too little investment in R&D. Another issue to consider is the possibility that patent races will lead firms to pursue more risky innovations. The intuition behind this argument can be illustrated fairly simply. Suppose that firms can choose to invest either in a relatively safe R&D route that has an expected discovery time uniformly distributed between one and three years, or a more risky route that has an expected time of discovery uniformly distributed between zero and four years. Both discoveries are equally costly, and both are expected to become redundant or worthless in five years' time. We will also assume that

12   See Reinganum (1989) for a masterful survey of patent races and the timing of innovation, including the consequences for social welfare.

each discovery generates the same profit of $1 million per period during the time that it is utilized and is protected from imitation by a patent.

Since the expected date of discovery is the same (namely, two years for both routes), then assuming neither firm had any competition, a risk-neutral firm considering them would be indifferent between the two options and a risk-averse firm would go for the less risky route. However, when firms are involved in a patent race, competition between the firms may lead them to choose the more variable or risky route in which success can come anytime between zero and four years.[13] The reason is one with which you should now be familiar. When innovation is protected from imitation, all that matters is winning the race. The second-place firm loses the same amount no matter how close it is behind the winner. In our example, if my rival chooses the less risky R&D route, I have an incentive to choose the more risky route, since this offers the possibility of success and a quick victory right away. Similarly, if my rival adopts the risky strategy, I can see that, unless I do the same, there is a real possibility that I will be left behind in the race. Of course, my rival can work out all this too. The result is that both of us choose the more risky route.

16.4   MONOPOLY POWER AND "SLEEPING PATENTS"

Another way in which the patent system and innovative competition can interact to affect market structure is through "sleeping patents." Many students at first find it puzzling that a firm will hold a large number of patents all related to the same process or product, a large proportion of which are never acted upon. (Return to Table 16.1 for some evidence on this point.) What possible reason can a firm have to apply (and pay) for patent rights to products and processes that it never uses? That is, what could be the rationale for a firm to create and hold what is called a "sleeping patent"?

The motivation behind a sleeping patent is to create a buffer of protection for the monopoly profits generated by the truly valuable patent. Legal history and economic analysis have both documented that the protection granted by a single patent is often very limited. Edwin Mansfield and his associates (1981) found, in a study of 48 patented new products, that 60 percent were imitated within four years of their introduction. Firms often can and do "invent around" patent protection. Frequently, there are several technical solutions to a particular problem. Each such solution is a threat to the firm holding a patent on a particular process or product. Hence, by patenting as many of these solutions as it can, a firm increases the protection it has in developing and introducing the process or product it actually decides upon.

Suppose, for example, that an incumbent firm has a proprietary technology with a constant marginal cost of c_l. The firm has a patent that protects its technology. Let us also suppose that this technology is so efficient that entry is not possible. Thus, the incumbent is free to set the monopoly price $p_m(c_l)$ and earn a monopoly profit each period of $\pi^m(c_l)$.

Assume that there is also an alternative technology that the monopolist has discovered, which permits production at the higher constant marginal cost of c_h, which we assume is less than $p_m(c_l)$. Clearly, the monopolist has no incentive to switch to this technology. However, if c_h is low enough that another firm could acquire this technology and enter the industry, then the incumbent's current monopoly would be eroded.

---

[13]   This type of case is discussed in Klette and de Meza (1986).

Table 16.2   Patent use by inventor's employer

	Internal Use	Licensing	Cross-Licensing	Licensing & Use	Blocking Competitors	Sleeping Patents
Large companies	50.0%	3.0%	3.0%	3.2%	21.7%	19.1%
Medium-sized companies	65.6%	5.4%	1.2%	3.6%	13.9%	10.3%
Small companies	55.8%	15.0%	3.9%	6.9%	9.6%	8.8%

Source: Giuri, P., et al. (2005), p. 20.

It is easy to see that the incumbent has an incentive to patent the higher-cost technology as well as the lower-cost one, even though it will never use the alternative, higher-cost technology. By acquiring this patent and letting it lie dormant or sleep, the incumbent strengthens his hold on his monopoly position. The question that we need to ask is whether the incumbent's incentive to acquire the higher-cost technology is so strong that it actually exceeds the incentive of the entrant to acquire the technology and enter.

The simple answer is yes. If the incumbent does not patent the high cost technology, then it can expect to earn the duopoly profit $\pi_i^d(c_l, c_h)$. As a result, the value of the sleeping patent to the incumbent is $\pi^m(c_l) - \pi_i^d(c_l, c_h)$. The value of the patent to the potential entrant is $\pi_e^d(c_h, c_l)$. Since we can expect that $\pi^m(c_l) > \pi_i^d(c_l, c_h) + \pi_e^d(c_h, c_l)$—the profit of a low-cost monopolist is greater than the aggregate profit of a high-cost and low-cost duopolist[14]—the incumbent has a strong incentive to patent the high-cost technology and leave it undeveloped.

The data in Table 16.2 (above) provide some empirical support for this proposition. These data are drawn from a PatVal-EU survey of 9,017 patents issued by the European Patent Office between 1993 and 1997 to individuals located in France, Germany, Italy, the Netherlands, Spain, and the United Kingdom.[15] The survey asked the inventors to rate the importance that they put on different motives for patenting.

In this table, "blocking competitors" refers to sleeping patents that are used specifically for the strategic reasons we have been discussing in this section (what the researchers term *sleeping patents* are patents that, according to the respondents, were not used for any of the other six purposes identified in the table). As can be seen, large companies used fewer of their patents and used a higher proportion of patents for blocking purposes than did medium-sized or small companies, consistent with our "protecting monopoly power" analysis.

There are numerous instances of an incumbent attempting to inhibit rival expansion. Alcoa achieved its dominant market position largely on the strength of Charles Martin Hall's electrolytic process for the reduction of aluminum bauxite ore. Fifteen years after it was formed, the company bought up the competing Bradley patents on an alternative reduction process—one that Alcoa never used. Similarly, Du Pont's patent of the synthetic fiber nylon was accompanied by the company's filing of literally hundreds of other patents all based on variants of the same molecule. Perhaps the best example of the use of sleeping patents comes from Hollywood. Film companies regularly buy the film rights to

---

14   This is just a repeat of some of the analysis in the previous chapter.
15   For a detailed description and analysis of these data, see Giuri and Mariani (2005). "Everything you always wanted to know about inventors (but never asked): evidence from the PatVal-EU survey," available at http://www.lem.sssup.it/WPLem/files/2005-20.pdf.

books, staged plays, and submitted screenplays, knowing that many of these script ideas will never be turned into a final product. In part, each film company simply wants to make sure that a rival producer does not get the chance to make a film based on this material.

16.5   PATENT LICENSING

Efficiency requires that the existing stock of information should be available to all buyers at the marginal cost involved in sharing such knowledge. However, since this implies a "price for information" of near 0, it leaves little incentive for anyone to produce new information in the form of new goods or new technologies. Patent protection is an effort to cut a middle path between these two pressures. The firm receiving the patent is protected (to some extent) from sharing its discovery with others for free. In fact, it does not have to share it at all.

One interesting possibility is that an innovating firm might be willing to share its technical advance with other firms for a price. When this happens, it results in a licensing agreement between the patent owner and the patent user. Not sharing the patent at all can be interpreted as charging a very high (perhaps infinite) licensing fee. Actual licensing implies a price for information that is closer to the efficient price of near 0. In this sense, the licensing of a patent is unambiguously a good thing. The question is, does an innovating firm have a profit incentive to license its discovery?

The most obvious case in which a firm would prefer to license an innovation is if the licensee operates in a totally different market from the licensor. For example, a U.S. firm that has a patent on a particular product or process innovation may prefer to license a foreign firm to use this patent (for a fee, of course) rather than setting up a foreign subsidiary or exporting. The main reasons for not licensing are the following. First, the licensor may not be able to secure a satisfactory payment for the license except after extensive and expensive bargaining that either or both parties may decide it is simply not worthwhile. Second, the licensor may fear that, ultimately, the foreign licensee will expand into markets where it will compete directly with the licensor. Finally, there is the fear that the licensee may—by acquiring rights to use the new process or product—improve its ability to develop the next generation of this technology by itself and thereby enhance its future ability to compete.

While these fears are undoubtedly real, there are considerable offsetting benefits to licensing agreements. Licensing gains revenue for the innovator today. Because the cost of sharing the information is low, any such revenue translates into profit.

But what about cases where the licensor and licensee are not separated by large geographic distance, but instead are competitors in the same market? Will an innovating firm license its patented discovery for use by some or all of its rivals? Typically, the answer depends on the strength of competition in the market, which is the subject matter we turn to now.

16.5.1   The Incentive to License a Nondrastic Innovation

In this section we confine our attention to innovations that are nondrastic. These are innovations with which the innovator cannot monopolize the market at the postinnovation monopoly price. Let's first consider whether the licensing of technology is able to achieve

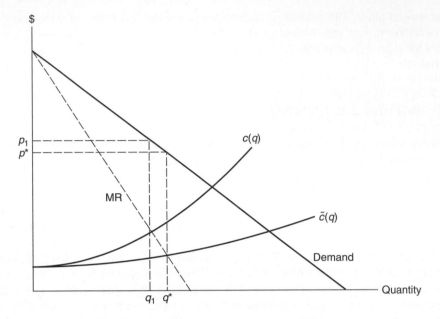

Figure 16.8   Optimal allocation of production—increasing marginal costs

efficiency in production.[16] Suppose that an innovator has a patent for a new product whose inverse demand for is $p = 1 - q$. This product can be produced at marginal cost $c(q)$, and we assume that $dc(q)/dq > 0$. In other words, there are long-run decreasing returns to scale. If the product is produced by a monopolist operating a single production facility, then—as can be seen from Figure 16.8 (above)—output is q_1 and price is p_1. If, by contrast, output is produced by a monopolist operating two plants, each at the same output level,[17] the marginal cost of the qth unit is $c(q/2)$. In other words, the aggregate marginal cost curve is now $\tilde{c}(q)$, such that twice as much output can be produced at each marginal cost. The profit maximizing aggregate output is q^* at price $p^*(q^*) = 1 - q^*$. Splitting output production over two plants benefits consumers.

Identifying q^* is reasonably straightforward. Aggregate profit with two plants, each operating at output $q/2$, is

$$\pi(q) = (1 - q)q - 2\int_0^{q/2} c(\hat{q})d\hat{q} - K_1 - K_2 \tag{16.29}$$

where K_i are sunk costs. Maximizing with respect to q gives the first-order condition:

$$d\pi(q)/dq = 1 - 2q - c(q/2) = 0 \Rightarrow c(q^*/2) = 1 - 2q^* \tag{16.30}$$

The profit maximizing price is $p^* = 1 - q^* = (1 + c(q^*/2))/2$.

We could repeat this process by adding yet more plants, potentially without limit. Suppose, however, that plant setup costs are sufficiently high that the efficient number of

---

[16]   This case is developed in Scotchmer (2004), p. 162 ff.
[17]   On the marginal principle, this is the efficient allocation of output.

plants is 2. The question we want to investigate is whether the innovator can use licensing to generate the two-plant monopoly price and output.

Assume that the innovating firm does not produce anything itself, but rather licenses two independent firms at a royalty rate of r per unit. Alternatively, we could assume that the innovator sets up its own manufacturing division as a profit center and licenses the technology to its independent manufacturing division and to an independent outside firm on the same terms—a royalty rate of r per unit.[18]

Under either scenario, assume that the firms are Cournot competitors with Firm 1 producing output q_1 and Firm 2 producing output q_2. The profit function for Firm 1 is

$$\pi_1(q_1, q_2) = (1 - (q_1 + q_2) - r)q_1 - \int_0^{q_1} c(\hat{q})d\hat{q} - K_1 \tag{16.31}$$

The first term is total revenue minus the royalty payment, the second is aggregate variable cost, and the third is fixed cost. The first-order condition on q_1 is

$$\frac{\partial \pi_1(q_1, q_2)}{\partial q_1} = 1 - q_2 - 2q_1 - r - c(q_1) = 0 \tag{16.32}$$

The first-order condition for Firm 2 is symmetric.

What the licensor would like to do is set a royalty rate such that each firm chooses to produce the aggregate profit-maximizing output $q^*/2$, where q^* is given by equation (16.30). We proceed in two steps. First, we identify the royalty rate that satisfies (16.30), assuming that each firm produces $q^*/2$. Second, we confirm that with this royalty rate, the output levels $q_1 = q_2 = q^*/2$ actually constitute a Cournot-Nash equilibrium.

So assume that $q_1 = q_2 = q^*/2$, substitute in equation (16.32), and use (16.30) to give

$$1 - 3q^*/2 - c(q^*/2) - r = q^*/2 - r = 0 \Rightarrow r^* = q^*/2 \tag{16.33}$$

Now, assume that r^* is indeed the royalty rate and assume that Firm 2 chooses $q_2 = q^*/2$. Is $q_1 = q^*/2$ a best response for Firm 1? Consider the first-order condition for Firm 1:

$$\left. \frac{\partial \pi_1(q_1, q_2)}{\partial q_1} \right|_{q_1 = q_2 = \frac{q^*}{2}} = 1 - \frac{3q^*}{2} - \frac{q^*}{2} - c\left(\frac{q*}{2}\right) = 1 - 2q^* - c\left(\frac{q^*}{2}\right) = 0 \tag{16.34}$$

where we have used equation (16.30) to solve (16.34). Since the profit functions for the two firms are well behaved, the Cournot-Nash equilibrium is unique, and so we have confirmed that a royalty rate of $r^* = q^*/2$ does, indeed, generate the two-plant profit-maximizing monopoly output and price.

We leave you to confirm that $p^* > c(q^*/2) + r^*$ so that the licensees earn positive rents on each unit sold. However, the licensor can extract any excess profit by charging a fixed fee in addition to the royalty. In other words, licensing can, indeed, replicate the profit-maximizing monopoly outcome.

This outcome depends on there being decreasing returns to scale in production. We now turn to the simpler case in which there are constant returns to scale. In doing so,

---

[18]   Scotchmer shows that if the licensor operates its production facility without a royalty fee, the efficient output allocation cannot be achieved.

we also consider the nature of the licensing contract more explicitly. The contract may consist of a royalty per unit produced by the licensee, a fixed fee paid by the licensee, or some mixture of the two. We continue to consider market outcomes in which the firms are Cournot competitors. To simplify the analysis, we investigate a duopoly market in which Firm 1 is the patent holder and Firm 2 the potential licensee.

Suppose first that the licensing contract requires that Firm 2 pays Firm 1 a royalty fee of r per unit.[19] Assume that Firm 2 currently operates a technology with constant marginal cost c_h and that Firm 1 can offer a licensing contract that gives Firm 2 access to its technology with constant marginal cost $c_l < c_h$. If the patent holder sets the license fee at $r^* = c_h - c_l$, the costs of the two firms are unaffected by the licensing contract, and so their equilibrium choices of outputs (q_1^C and q_2^C) are unaffected. However, production costs are reduced by $(c_h - c_l)q_2^C$, which is the aggregate royalty payment from Firm 2 to Firm 1 and constitutes an increase in industry profit. In other words, the licensing contract increases aggregate profit and so is potentially better for both firms than no licensing.

Is the proposed royalty of $r^* = c_h - c_l$ optimal for Firm 1? Assume that inverse demand is linear and given by $p = 1 - q$.[20] Further assume that Firm 1 sets a royalty rate of r per unit. Using the standard Cournot equilibrium equations, profit of Firm 1 (the patent holder) is

$$\pi_1 = \frac{(1 - 2c_l + (c_l + r))^2}{9} + r\frac{(1 - 2(c_l + r) + c_l)}{3}$$
$$= \frac{(1 - c_l + r)^2}{9} + r\frac{(1 - c_l - 2r)}{3} \tag{16.35}$$

The first term is Firm 1's profit from its own production, and the second is the royalty payment from Firm 2. Differentiating with respect to the royalty rate gives us

$$\frac{d\pi_1}{dr} = \frac{2}{9}(1 - c_l + r) + \frac{1}{3}(1 - c_l - 4r) = \frac{5}{9}(1 - c_l - 2r) \tag{16.36}$$

Suppose that $c_h = c_l + d$, so that Firm 2's prelicense Cournot output is $q_2 = (1 - c_l - 2d)/3 > 0$. Then we have that $d\pi_1/dr > 0$ for all $r \le d$. In other words, the royalty rate of $r^* = c_h - c_l = d$ is, indeed, optimal for the patent holder. Of course, such a high royalty rate leaves Firm 2 indifferent between accepting the license or not. However, since $d\pi_1/dr > 0$ for all $r \le d$, the two firms can bargain to a royalty rate somewhere between 0 and $r^* = d$ so that they both profit from the licensing agreement. (You are asked in the end-of-chapter problems to show that this result generalizes to the situation in which there are $N - 1$ rivals to the patent holder.)

A potential problem with royalty agreements based on per unit output sold is that "it is often not possible to monitor a rival's output as is necessary to enforce a royalty provision in a patent licensing agreement" (Katz and Shapiro, 1985, p. 508). Suppose, instead, that the licensing agreement requires that the licensee pays a fixed fee of A to the patent holder, in return for which the licensee obtains the patent holder's technology and operates at marginal cost c_l.[21] Consider the impact of the license agreement on the two

---

[19]   This case is based on Gallini and Winter (1985).
[20]   You should by now have noticed that with Cournot competition, this loses no generality as compared to the seemingly more general inverse demand $p = A - Bq$.
[21]   This analysis draws on Katz and Shapiro (1985).

firms, ignoring the fixed fee. Firm 2 now has a lower-cost technology and so enjoys an increase in profit. Firm 1, by contrast, faces a tougher competitor and so suffers a loss of profit. For the fixed fee to at least compensate Firm 1's loss of profit, it is necessary that $\pi_1(c_l, c_l) + A > \pi_1(c_l, c_h)$; while for the fee to leave Firm 2 no worse off than before the licensing agreement, it is necessary that $\pi_2(c_l, c_l) - A > \pi_2(c_l, c_h)$. What this tells us is that for the patent holder to be willing to offer the license, it is necessary that it increases aggregate profit.[22] The fixed fee can then redistribute the resulting profits while leaving both firms better off than without the license.

Return to our linear example, again with the substitution that $c_h = c_l + d$. Aggregate profit without the license agreement is

$$\pi_a^{nl} = \frac{1}{9}(1 - c_l + d)^2 + \frac{1}{9}(1 - c_l - 2d)^2 \tag{16.37}$$

Aggregate profit with the licensing agreement is

$$\pi_a^l = \frac{2}{9}(1 - c_l)^2 \tag{16.38}$$

The change in aggregate profit as a result of the licensing agreement is

$$\Delta\pi = \frac{d}{9}(2(1 - c_l) - 5d) \tag{16.39}$$

Aggregate profit is increased by the licensing agreement if and only if $d < d_0 = 2(1 - c_l)/5$.

The upper limit on d consistent with Firm 2 being able to produce a positive output $q_2 > 0$ prelicense is $d_u = (1 - c_l)/2 > d_0$; so there is certainly a range of costs $(c_l + d_0, c_l + d_u)$ for Firm 2 such that the patent holder will choose not to license its technology to Firm 2. More generally, we can show that *the patent holder will choose to license a "small" innovation for a fixed fee, but will choose to exclude the potential licensee if the innovation is "large."*

16.5.2 Licensing, Drastic Innovations, and Monopoly Power

Now, consider the feasibility of licensing when the innovation is drastic. These are innovations with which the innovator can monopolize the market at the postinnovation monopoly price. Let's suppose first that the innovation is made and patented by a Cournot firm in an oligopoly. In this case the innovating firm will not want to license its discovery.

To see this, take the simple case of a duopoly. Aggregate profit with licensing is $2\pi^C(c_l, c_l)$, the combined Cournot duopoly profits. Profit without a license is $\pi^m(c_l)$, the monopoly profit. Provided only that the firms cannot collude to secure the monopoly profit, licensing is less profitable than not licensing. Accordingly, a Cournot firm that makes a drastic innovation will not share its discovery with its rivals even for a fee. *Nothing can be gained by licensing.* This is also true for firms engaged in Bertrand competition. In all such cases, the oligopolist that makes a drastic innovation is better off being a monopolist and driving former competitors from the market.

---

[22] It should be noted that this condition holds regardless of the nature of the competition between licensor and licensee.

Now, assume that the innovation is made by a firm "specializing in R&D."[23] This is a firm that generates innovative ideas, but does not have the production facilities in place to exploit or commercialize these ideas. In order to do so, the innovating firm must license the ideas to a manufacturer.

Suppose that there is a monopoly manufacturer with current marginal cost c_h, and consider a licensing contract of the form $A + rq$ (i.e. a fixed fee and a royalty per unit) that gives the monopolist access to the new technology with marginal cost c_l. The first point to note is that the optimal royalty rate is $r^* = 0$. This royalty rate gives aggregate profit $\pi^m(c_l)$. Any higher royalty rate gives lower aggregate profit, since generally $d\pi^m(c)/dc < 0$.[24]

The fixed fee A will typically be settled by bilateral bargaining between the innovator and the monopoly manufacturer. In principle, the inventor can appropriate all the increased profit that the invention brings if the contract is written correctly, that is, with a fixed fee exactly equal to that additional profit. In practice, however, the patent holder's bargaining position will usually not be strong enough to achieve this outcome. When the manufacturer has a monopoly in the product market, the innovator needs the manufacturer just as much as the manufacturer needs the innovator. An obvious consequence is that the innovator does not derive the full additional profit that its innovation creates, weakening the incentive to innovate in the first place.

Now, suppose that the manufacturing sector contains n firms, each with marginal cost c_h. How many of these firms should the innovator license? Since the innovation is drastic, licensing one manufacturer results in the monopoly profit $\pi^m(c_l)$. Licensing more than one manufacturer results in duopoly or triopoly or...n-opoly profits, the aggregate of which is always less than the monopoly profit. So the optimal approach is to offer the license to at most one manufacturer.

How is this best achieved? Suppose that the innovator auctions its innovation, with a royalty rate of $r^* = 0$. Each manufacturer knows that if it loses the auction, its profit will be 0, because the innovation is drastic. As a result, each manufacturer is willing to pay up to $\pi^m(c_l)$ for the license, and competitive bidding between the manufacturers will secure this fee for the innovator.

Pulling this analysis together, we can conclude that *a drastic innovation will be exploited by a single firm* (Tirole 1989, p. 412). The license contract will specify a fixed fee and a 0 royalty rate.

16.5.3   Patent Licensing, Social Welfare, and Public Policy

That an innovator has an interest in licensing a discovery most of the time is a reassuring result, because our intuition is that licensing is a desirable outcome. Katz and Shapiro (1985) have provided a formal argument that licensing nearly always increases social welfare. Specifically, they show that licensing is socially desirable if total output increases as a result of the licensing activity. To see why, note that licensing will not take place unless the licensees see some benefit from it, and a license will not be offered unless the licensor also sees some benefit from it. If in addition to this mutual gain in profit, the license agreement increases total output, then the price will be lower and consumer surplus will

---

[23]   This is an approach used in Tirole (1989), p. 411.
[24]   One possible exception occurs when the patent holder needs to offer services or technical advice that increases with the frequency with which the technology is used.

be higher. In other words, if the license agreement increases total output, both consumers and producers gain from the agreement, and so the agreement is socially desirable. Yet, even if this fails to happen—even if the industry output is unchanged—licensing is still likely to be socially beneficial, since the licensing revenue at least increases producer surplus. Licensing allows more of that output to be produced at the lower marginal cost.

Moreover, licensing may have other beneficial effects. If a firm anticipates the gain in profits from licensing its research findings as well as (or instead of) exploiting the research itself, this should increase the incentive to undertake research. Furthermore, using licensing to access a particular innovation should reduce wasteful R&D that either duplicates existing research effort, or is intended merely to invent around an existing patent.

Consider, for example, a potential entrant whose profit (in present value terms) under duopoly is $5 million and who, in the absence of licensing, would incur an R&D expenditure of $3 million to break into the market. The entrant will pursue this investment, since it yields a net gain of $2 million. Yet if this is the case, then the monopolist incumbent knows that whether it licenses or not, it will soon be a duopolist. If instead the incumbent licenses its technology to the entrant for $3 million, the entrant is just as well off and the monopolist now gets the licensing revenue. In addition, society avoids the unnecessary expenditure of $3 million that the entrant would otherwise have made. The moral of this section therefore seems quite clear: public policy should actively encourage the licensing of innovations.

There is, however, need for a cautionary note. Licensing might involve some drawbacks. First, consider the risks associated with licensing based upon an output-related royalty. It is reasonable to assume that the licensing agreement holds for the outstanding duration of the patent that is being licensed since, after that, the information becomes publicly available. If the royalty rate extracts almost all of the additional profits that the licensee might expect to make, there is the risk that the licensee will take the license in order to gain experience with the technology, but then actually produce very little during the period of the license agreement; this means, of course, that very little is actually paid for the license. Alternatively, if output is difficult to monitor, the licensee has the incentive to lie about how much is actually being produced. What may be necessary is for the licensor to tie the license agreement to some agreed minimum level of output on the part of the licensee—but this is not always easy to negotiate or enforce.

A further drawback to licensing is that it can be difficult to write enforceable contracts that limit the ways in which licensees can use the license. Typically, the licensor will want to limit the markets into which the licensee can sell, for example, to avoid direct competition with the licensor or with other licensees. This may be possible within a particular jurisdiction such as the United States, although even here antitrust laws may prevent such market-limiting agreements. But it is almost impossible to write binding contracts that limit the international markets in which licensees can operate. In addition, access to a particular process or product technology may enhance the ability of a licensee to develop related technologies that are not covered by the patent being licensed. Once again, it is almost impossible to write enforceable contracts that protect the licensor from such imitation—or at least give the licensor some return from the new technologies that licensees develop.

Licensing raises public policy issues that suggest caution in favoring and promoting every licensing agreement. One danger is that licensing contracts include restrictions on price or create monopolies with exclusive territories—monopolies that would otherwise be illegal under the antitrust laws. Matters become particularly complicated when, as often happens, one patent leads to another (complementary) development. One firm creates, say, a new antibiotic that has some occasional and serious side effects. Then another firm develops a means to undo the side effects of the first firm's drug. The two firms may strike a deal licensing each to produce the other's product. Yet, it is easy to see that this agreement may often include terms that exclude other firms. Such dangers are recognized by U.S. policy, which tends to limit severely the ability of reciprocal licensing agreements to include exclusive provisions. Still, the example serves to make clear that the tension between promoting licensing and realizing its associated benefits, on the one hand, and the potential risk of collusion that licensing may foster, on the other, is real.

Indeed, the increasing complexity of technical advances and associated patents has resulted in what is referred to as a "patent thicket." As advance builds on advance, and technical progress increasingly draws from learning in different fields, the technology involved in bringing a new product to market may build a host of patented techniques, each of which is owned by a different entity. The innovator may then need to get the approval of each of the individual patent holders before proceeding. This introduces some of the coordination issues that we described in Chapter 8. Acting individually, each patent holder may set too high a license fee with the result that all are worse off. Cross-licensing agreements, by which firms agree to license their patents to each other, and patent pools, by which a group of firms agrees to pool a set of patents and license them as a package, have become increasingly popular ways to solve the coordination problems inherent in the "patent thicket." However, they run the risk of permitting cooperation beyond the technological sphere and giving the parties a chance to wield their technological power collectively against potential entrants. Yet without such efforts, it may be impossible for any new entrants to cut their way through the thicket and thereby provide any competitive pressure.[25]

16.6   RECENT PATENT POLICY DEVELOPMENTS

In the first half of the 1980s, a number of events occurred that greatly increased the legal protection of patent rights in the United States. The first and perhaps most crucial step was a legal reorganization that gave the Court of Appeals for the Federal Circuit (CAFC) in Washington, DC, exclusive jurisdiction over patent appeals in an effort to unify the legal treatment of patent rights. This court is widely considered to have a very "pro-patent" view and, until recently, its decisions were left unquestioned by the U.S. Supreme Court. The CAFC emerged as the final and sole arbiter of patent disputes, and its pro-patent views became widely reflected in lower court cases. Just how much stronger patent protection would get became apparent in the 1986 patent infringement suit filed by Polaroid against Kodak regarding Kodak's production and sale of an instant-film and instant-picture camera.

Prior to that decision, losers in a patent infringement case had typically paid small penalties and been permitted to continue to produce, so long as they paid appropriate royalties to the winner. When Polaroid won, though, Kodak was required to pay very large penalties and, most importantly, forced to stop producing its instant camera. Since shutting down a high-volume production line is very expensive—even if only for a few

---

[25]   See Lerner and Tirole (2004).

weeks—the fact that the courts were willing to impose such a penalty put all firms on notice that patent infringement cases were serious business.

Moreover, the Kodak-Polaroid case was quickly followed by very aggressive behavior on the part of one firm, Texas Instruments (TI), in filing infringement suits (mostly against foreign firms) and raising royalty fees that also served to put high-technology firms on notice. In the technology sector, where reverse engineering has always been important, TI was so aggressive that its royalty fees and court awards began to outstrip its production activities as a source of revenue.

In short, a new legal environment of much stronger protection for patent holders' rights emerged in the United States in the 1980s. It may not be surprising, then, to discover that there was an explosion of patent activity over the next several years. Between 1983 and 2000, the annual number of patent applications doubled, while the annual number of patents actually granted rose by an even greater 170 percent.

There has been increasing concern that the strengthened protection of patent rights has become too aggressive. Recent empirical evidence casts considerable doubt that stronger patent enforcement yields better innovation results. Drawing on a range of sources, Lerner (2000) identified 177 distinct patent policy changes in 60 countries over 150 years, such as those that lengthened or broadened patents, those that reduced the patent filing fee, those that required compulsory licensing, and so forth. He then examined the effect of these changes on the rate of patenting. He found that increased patent protection sharply increased patenting by foreign firms, but decreased patenting by domestic innovators. The overall effect was positive. However, the inference is that foreign companies used patents to protect themselves against domestic competitors. Hence, while patents may have enhanced international trade, their effect on innovation was negligible.

Moser (2005) constructed internationally comparable data using the catalogues of two 19th-century world fairs: the Crystal Palace Exhibition in London, 1851, and the Centennial Exhibition in Philadelphia, 1876. These included innovations that were not patented, as well as those that were, and innovations from countries both with and without patent laws. He found no evidence that patent laws increased levels of innovative activity. Instead, they simply affected the direction of innovation. Relative to countries with strong patent protection, inventors in countries without such protection simply concentrated their efforts in industries where secrecy was easily maintained, leaving the overall rate of innovative efforts unchanged. Similarly, Sakakibara and Branstetter (2001) found no evidence that a strengthening of Japanese patent laws in 1988 led to any increased R&D spending or innovative output.

Fears that patent protection had gone too far reached a dramatic high point in February 2007 when the 3 million customers of the BlackBerry wireless e-mail service were threatened with a shutdown due to a patent dispute. A small Virginia firm, NTP, had developed and patented the technology for a wireless e-mail device in 1990. However, NTP never produced a product, nor did it make any effort to license the technology to others. In 1998, the Canadian firm, Research In Motion (RIM), unveiled its first wireless e-mail device. Sales took off sharply. Although RIM claimed that it had developed the technology on its own, NTP filed suit against BlackBerry in 2001. In 2002, a U.S. jury found the Canadian firm guilty of 16 counts of patent infringement. On appeal, seven of these were dismissed in 2004; but that still left nine outstanding. In 2005, RIM offered $450 million to NTP to settle the case, but that settlement was rejected by the trial judge. In January 2006, the Supreme Court refused to hear any further appeal and a hearing to order a shutdown of the BlackBerry service was scheduled for Friday, February 24, 2006. The hearing did not

Reality Checkpoint

It Was Patently Obvious and, Therefore, Not Patent Worthy

On 30 April 2007, the U.S. Supreme Court issued an important ruling that substantially raised the bar for obtaining patents on new products that combine elements of preexisting inventions. The case involved a patent infringement lawsuit filed by Teleflex, Inc. against KSR International over the development of an adjustable gas pedal for use on cars and trucks equipped with electronic engine controls. The position of the accelerator pedal in many cars is not adjustable. Instead, the driver adjusts the position of the seat until the pedal is a comfortable distance away. However, in the 1970s, a number of inventors began to develop adjustable pedals that could slide forward or backward without changing the effect of depressing the pedal a specific amount. In older cars, that effect is transmitted by means of a cable that typically opens up valves in the fuel injection unit of the engine. In more modern cars, however, the cable has been dispensed with and the mechanical connection has been replaced with a computer sensor that electronically transmits the acceleration or deceleration signal to the engine. KSR is a company with a history of making adjustable mechanical pedals for the major automobile companies. In 1999, it won a contract with General Motors to provide an adjustable pedal with an electronic sensor mounted at the pedal's fixed pivot point to communicate the necessary information. Teleflex, which had a patent for one type of electronic sensor for gasoline pedals, claimed patent infringement and demanded royalties. KSR refused to pay on the ground that Teleflex had combined existing elements including those in other patented sensors in an obvious manner so that its patent was therefore invalid. KSR won in Federal District Court in Detroit, but that decision was overturned in 2005 by the CAFC, the court with exclusive jurisdiction over patent appeals.

For many years, the Supreme Court has let the CAFC judgments stand unreviewed. However, the court now seems to have taken interest in the CAFC decisions. In particular, the court took issue with the way the CAFC employed an approach referred to as the "teaching, suggestion, or motivation" test (TSM test). That approach holds that a patent claim is only proved obvious if "some motivation or suggestion to combine the prior art teachings" can be found in the prior art, the nature of the problem, or the knowledge of a person having ordinary skill in the art. The Supreme Court said that the CAFC was applying the TSM standard too rigidly. In particular, it ruled that when the innovation simply yields predictable results based on existing technology, then it is not entitled to patent protection regardless of whether that prediction has actually been tested in practice. The court found that the Teleflex patent on electric sensors was exactly this type of innovation, and so reversed the CAFC judgment and ruled in favor of KSR.

Because most inventions combine previously known elements, the decision in the *KSR v. Teleflex* case is widely recognized as a signal that two decades of aggressive patent enforcement were coming to an end. Indeed, it was accompanied by a second, very similar decision in which the court found for Microsoft against a charge of patent infringement by AT&T. The result of these decisions is almost surely that patents will be harder to obtain and harder to defend.

Sources: *KSR International Co. vs. Teleflex Inc.*, 550 U.S.____(2007); *Microsoft Corporation v. AT&T Corp.* 550 U.S.____(2007); and L. Greenhouse. "High Court Puts Limits on Patents." *The New York Times* (1 May 2007).

reach a final decision. However, after further negotiations, RIM and NTP reached a settlement in which RIM made a one-time payment of $615 million to the Virginian firm for unfettered use of the technology. The agreement came even as the U.S. Patent and Trademark Office (USPTO) was conducting a review of the legitimacy of NTP's patents. Many felt that the strong pro-patent laws had effectively allowed NTP to extort the payment from RIM and forced it to rush to a settlement before the USPTO completed its review.

In April 2007, the Supreme Court served notice that it too was concerned about excessive patent protection. In *KSR International vs. Teleflex, Inc* the court ruled that new products that combine elements of preexisting inventions and that result from nothing more than "ordinary innovation" with no more than "predictable results" were not entitled to patent protection. The decision was notable for its clear statement that the patent system could be used to undermine innovation and its unanimity. As a result, most experts believe that the decision raised the bar substantially for future patent applications. It also opened the door to a reexamination of existing patents and gave judges much more leeway to dismiss patent infringement suits.

16.7 EMPIRICAL APPLICATION: PATENT LAW AND PATENT PRACTICE IN THE SEMICONDUCTOR INDUSTRY

The semiconductor industry was not immune to the patent fever that spread through America in the last part of the 20th century. As Hall and Ziedonis (2001) document, patent awards per million dollars of R&D spending in this industry doubled in the 10 years following 1982. What makes this increase particularly striking is that semiconductor industry representatives have been surveyed repeatedly and have consistently reported that patents are not a very effective way to appropriate the returns on R&D investments. Because the semiconductor industry is one of rapid technological change where product life cycles are short, semiconductor firms have instead relied on lead time, secrecy, and product design tactics to reap the profits from their innovations. What, then, is the reason for the increased patent activity by semiconductor firms? How is it related to the changed legal environment?

Hall and Ziedonis (2001) examine the patent explosion in the semiconductor industry using data from 95 industry firms covering the years 1979–95. These firms were awarded over 17,000 patents in this period. Hall and Ziedonis (2001) model these successful patents as the outcome of a patent production process that relates the ith firm's production of patents in year t or p_{it} to a set of the firm's characteristics X_{it}. They recognize that p_{it} is what is called a count variable. That is, it counts the number of successes that take place during a time interval of given length. Thus, p_{it} can only take discrete integer values and often will be 0. If we consider p_{it} to have a random component, then we need to assume a probability distribution that recognizes these features. The natural choice for this purpose is the Poisson distribution, which gives the probability $f(\lambda, p)$ that there are p occurrences of a random variable in a fixed time interval as

$$f(\lambda, p) = \frac{e^{-\lambda}\lambda^p}{p!} \tag{16.40}$$

The Poisson distribution has a very nice feature in that it is fully characterized by the parameter λ, which is both its mean and its variance. Thus, Hall and Ziedonis (2001) model patent production as a Poisson process that has a conditional mean λ_{it} that is an exponential function of X_{it} as follows:

$$E(p_{it}|X_{it}) = \lambda_{it} = \exp(X_{it}\beta + \gamma_t) \tag{16.41}$$

where γ_t is a (1, 0) dummy variable for each year reflecting factors in that year that are common to the patenting activity of all semiconductor firms. We can linearize this relationship by taking logs to yield

$$\ln \lambda_{it} = X_{it}\beta + \gamma_t \tag{16.42}$$

Hall and Ziedonis (2001) measure p_{it} as the number of patents per employee. The characteristics for each firm i in X_{it} include (1) the log of firm R&D spending per employee; (2) a (1, 0) dummy variable equal to 1 if the firm reported no R&D spending that year and 0 otherwise; (3) the log of firm size measured as the number of employees in thousands; (4) the log of plant and equipment value per employee as a measure of the capital intensity of the firm's production; (5) a (1, 0) dummy variable equal to 1 if the firm entered the market after 1982 and 0 otherwise; (6) a (1, 0) dummy variable equal to 1 if the firm is a design firm doing no fabrication and 0 if it is a manufacturing firm; (7) a (1, 0) dummy variable equal to 1 if the firm is Texas Instruments and 0 otherwise; and (8) the log of the firm's age.

The first three variables reflect the standard view of patents as the output of a process in which R&D is the input and in which there may be scale economies. The fourth variable allows Hall and Ziedonis (2001) to test the hypothesis that part of the increased patenting following the change in the patent enforcement environment reflects the decision by firms with large sunk costs, who cannot afford to get "held up" in a patent dispute, to expand their patent portfolio rapidly to guard against such "holdups." The fifth and sixth variables allow them to test a second hypothesis, namely, that another reason for the rise in patent activity was that the new legal environment made it attractive for design firms who, unlike semiconductor manufacturers, rely heavily on patents to enter the market, and thereby they change the mix of firms in the semiconductor industry to one more likely to patent. The seventh variable captures the well-known super-aggressive patenting strategy adopted by TI, while the age variable allows for firm-specific learning.

Hall and Ziedonis observe the annual number of patents p_{it} by firm i in year t for 95 semiconductor firms from 1979–95. Because they are estimating a Poisson distribution, the assumptions of Ordinary Least Squares (OLS) do not hold. Instead, Hall and Ziedonis use Maximum Likelihood Estimation (MLE). Because λ is both the mean and the variance of the Poisson distribution, comparing the variance of the data with the mean is a natural test for the appropriateness of the underlying Poisson specification. The results of their two regressions that do best on this test are shown in Table 16.3 (next page).

The estimates in both regressions for the first four variables imply roughly constant returns to scale in patent production. As firm size (measured by the number of employees) grows semiconductor firms tend to increase their patent output proportionately. This is similar to the finding of other researchers, e.g., Hall, Griliches, and Hausmann (1986). It is also clear that TI has a markedly higher propensity to patent than do other semiconductor firms consistent with TI's well-known aggressive patenting policy during these years.

Most importantly, both of the key hypotheses are supported by these data. Firms with capital-intensive production as measured by the amount of plant and equipment

Table 16.3 Parameter estimates for expected patent output by semiconductor firms

Variable	Estimated Coefficient	Standard Error	Estimated Coefficient	Standard Error
Log R&D per employee	0.190	(0.084)	0.196	(0.117)
Dummy for no reported R&D	−1.690	(0.830)	−1.690	(0.840)
Log firm size	0.854	(0.032)	0.850	(0.034)
Log firm P&E per employee	0.601	(0.113)	0.603	(0.114)
Dummy for post-1982 entry	0.491	(0.169)	0.491	(0.199)
Dummy for design firm			−0.130	(0.185)
Dummy for Texas Instruments	0.799	(0.111)	0.798	(0.115)
Log of firm age			0.220	(0.146)

per employee do significantly more patenting than others do. In addition, it appears that the firms that entered the industry following the 1982 centralization of patent law cases at the CAFC were much more likely to patent than the firms that were already in the industry. The coefficient on the post-1982 entry variable is highly significant in both regressions. While the coefficient on the design firm variable is not significant in the second regression, it is if the post-1982 entry variable is omitted indicating that the entry variable reflects mostly entry by design firms.

In sum, Hall and Ziedonis interpret their results as indicating two major reasons for the jump in patenting efforts in the semiconductor industry after 1983. One is that the new pro-patent environment and the prospect of having production actually stopped by legal injunction were particularly threatening to capital-intensive firms with heavy sunk costs. The result was that they responded strategically by rapidly accumulating a portfolio of patents to protect their products and processes. The second was that the changed legal environment also induced entry of purely design firms that have an inherently greater propensity to patent their findings in any case.

The Hall and Ziedonis (2001) findings also reveal a third effect, namely, that the changed legal framework led all semiconductor firms to patent more. The evidence for this is in the time dummies (not shown). Figure 16.9 (next page) shows the pattern of these coefficients normalized, so that the 1979 effect is 0. The dotted line reflects the time dummy coefficients from the first of the two regressions above, while the dashed line reflects the same coefficients from the second regression.

What both sets of estimates clearly show is that after 1986, even after controlling the mix of semiconductor firm characteristics, there was a steady increase in the proclivity to patent with each successive year. The new pro-patent environment is the most obvious explanation for this rise that is common to all semiconductor firms.

Summary

By giving innovators a legally enforceable means of earning a return on their discoveries, patents and copyrights provide incentives for innovative activity that might otherwise not be undertaken. Yet, patents also confer monopoly power on the patent holder, with all the price distortions that such power entails. In addition, patent rules may enhance the ability of existing monopolies to maintain their current dominant position against would-be entrants. One mechanism by which this may occur is through the use of "sleeping patents" designed to buffer the invention against any and all attacks from rival innovations that might permit an entrant to "invent around" the original patent.

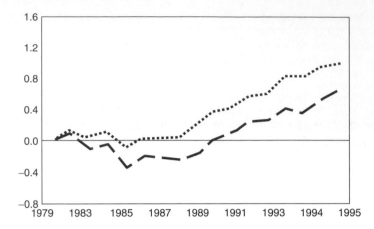

Figure 16.9   Pattern of regression time coefficients in semiconductor patent behavior

Licensing agreements by which firms permit the use of their patented knowledge for a fee can help ameliorate the patent tension. This is because such agreements both permit wider use of the innovation and also allow an innovator to earn a greater return on her R&D investments than she otherwise would receive. However, licensing contracts can be difficult to enforce except by imposing restrictions that can be harmful to competition.

Within the United States, the 1980s marked a sharp increase in the legal protection of patents against infringement. This was followed by an equally sharp increase in both patent applications and patent grants. Empirical evidence from the semiconductor industry suggests that this reflects in part the desire of firms with large sunk investments in products and processes to avoid disruption of their production by accumulating a large patent portfolio—and by the encouragement of entry by new firms that rely more heavily on patents to appropriate the gains of their innovations. That evidence also confirms that there was a general rise in patent proclivity across all semiconductor firms.

More recently, there has been concern that U.S. patent protection has been overly strong, especially since there is little evidence that it has led to faster innovation. Accordingly, recent court decisions have pared back these protections. Our discussions of licensing and of recent patent legal developments make clear that there is no way to eliminate the tension between allocative efficiency and innovative activity that a patent system raises, either in theory or in practice.

Problems

1. Take the Klemperer model in which consumers have identical reservation prices V but different transport costs t. Assume that $V = \$10$, $N = 100$, $F = \$20,000$ and $r = 10\%$.
    a. Derive a lower limit on patent breadth that will achieve the socially optimal outcome assuming that the consumers' transport cost parameters t are uniformly distributed on the interval $[1, 4]$. What is the optimal patent length τ?
    b. Derive a lower limit on patent breadth that will achieve the socially optimal outcome assuming that the consumers' transport cost parameters t are uniformly distributed on the interval $[2, 3]$ and that patent length $\tau = 1$.

2. Assume that inverse market demand is $p = 1 - q$ and that the market is currently supplied by N Cournot competitors each with marginal cost c_h. Now assume that one firm obtains a patent on a new technology with marginal cost $c_l < c_h.$.
    a. Derive a limit on c_h for this not to be a drastic innovation.

b. Assume that the patent holder decides to license its innovation to the other $N - 1$ firms at a royalty rate of r per unit. Show that the optimal royalty rate is $r^* = c_h - c_l$.

c. Assume instead that the firm chooses to license the technology at a two-part price $A + rq$. Show that the optimal royalty rate is $r^* = 0$. Hint: Show that aggregate profit is decreasing in the royalty rate r.

3. Assume that annual inverse demand for a particular product is $P = 150 - Q$. The product is offered by a pair of Bertrand competitors, each with marginal costs of \$75.

a. What is the current equilibrium price and total surplus?

b. The discount factor is 0.9. Assume now that if R&D is conducted at rate x, it incurs one-off costs of $r(x) = 10x^2$ and reduces marginal costs to $(75 - x)$. Suppose that one firm decides to conduct R&D at rate $x = 10$. This research will be protected by a patent of T years.

   i.   What is producer profit and consumer surplus during each year of patent protection?

   ii. What is producer profit and consumer surplus when the patent expires?

c. For a given patent length T what is the present value of current and future total surpluses?

4. Use your answers to 3(a) and 3(b) to write the total net surplus from the innovation as a function of the period of patent protection. Derive an approximation to the socially optimal period of patent protection.

5. Assume that there are 100 aspiring Olympic swimmers whose tastes for low-water-resistance colored swimming suits are evenly distributed over the color spectrum from black to yellow. The "length" of this spectrum is normalized to be one unit. Each of these swimmers values the loss of utility from being offered swimming suits in other than their favorite color at \$10 per unit of "distance." Each swimmer will buy exactly one swimming suit per period provided that the full price for the suit—the price charged by the firm plus the value of utility loss if there is a color difference between the suits on offer and the swimmer's favorite color—is less than \$100. Production of low-water-resistance swimming suits is currently feasible only in black and is controlled by a monopolist who has a patent on the production of the black material. The marginal cost of making a swimming suit is \$25.

a. What is the current profit-maximizing price per suit and what are the monopolist's per-period profits?

   Now assume that research can be conducted that will allow the swimming suits also to be manufactured in yellow at the same marginal cost of \$25.

b. If the monopolist undertakes the research and introduces the new color what will be the resulting equilibrium prices of black and yellow swimming suits? What is the impact on the monopolist's per-period profit, ignoring research costs?

c. If a new entrant undertakes the research and introduces the new color, what will be the resulting equilibrium prices of black and yellow swimming suits? What will the entrant's per-period profit be, again ignoring research costs? Confirm that the incumbent monopolist will be willing to spend more on researching the new color than the potential entrant.

d. Assume that the research costs can be split into some amount R, which is pure research cost, and another amount D, which is development cost—the cost of transforming a successful innovation into a viable product. Calculate limits on R and D such that the monopolist will be willing to undertake the research into manufacture of yellow swimming suits and patent it but then leave the patent sleeping.

References

Bessen, J., and M. J. Meurer. 2008. *Patent Failure: How Judges, Bureaucrats and Lawyers Put Innovators at Risk*. Princeton, NJ: Princeton University Press.

Boldrin, M., and D. K. Levine. 2008. *Against Intellectual Property*. New York: Cambridge University Press.

Denicolò, V. 1996. "Patent Races and Optimal Patent Breadth and Length". *Journal of Industrial Economics,* 44 (March): 249–265.

Gallini, N. 1992. "Patent Policy and Costly Imitation". *Rand Journal of Economics,* 23 (Spring): 52–63.

Gallini, N. 2002. "The Economics of Patents: Lessons from Recent U.S. Patent Reform". *Journal of Economic Perspectives,* 16 (Spring): 131–154.

Gallini, N., and R. Winter. 1985. "Licensing in the Theory of Innovation." *Rand Journal of Economics,* 16, 237–252.

Gilbert, R., and C. Shapiro. 1990. "Optimal Patent Length and Breadth". *Rand Journal of Economics,* 21 (Spring): 106–112.

Giuri, P., et al. 2005. "Everything You Always Wanted To Know About Inventors (But Never Asked): Evidence From the PatVal-EU Survey." Working Paper 2005/20, Laboratory of Economics and Management, Sant'Anna School of Advanced Studies, Pisa, Italy.

Hall, B. H., Z. Griliches, and J. Hausmann. 1986. "Patents And R and D: Is There A Lag?" *International Economic Review,* 27 (June): 265–283.

Hall, B., and R. H. Ziedonis. 2001. "The Patent Paradox Revisited: An Empirical Study of Patenting in the U.S. Semiconductor Industry, 1979–1995". *Rand Journal of Economics,* 32 (Spring): 101–128.

Katz, M., and C. Shapiro. 1985. "On the Licensing of Innovation". *Rand Journal of Economics,* 16 (Winter): 504–520.

Klemperer, P. 1990. "How Broad Should the Scope of Patent Protection Be?" *Rand Journal of Economics,* 21 (Spring): 113–130.

Klette, T., and D. de Meza. 1986. "Is the Market Biased against R&D?" *Rand Journal of Economics,* 17 (Spring): 133–139.

La Manna, M. 1992. "New Dimensions of the Patent System." In G. Norman and M. La Manna, eds., *The New Industrial Economics.* Aldershot: Edward Elgar.

Lee, T., and L. L. Wilde. 1980. "Market Structure and Innovation: A Reformulation." *Quarterly Journal of Economics,* 94: 429–436.

Lerner, J. 2000. "150 Years of Patent Protection." *National Bureau of Economic Research.* NBER Working Papers, 7478.

Lerner, J., and J. Tirole. 2004. "Efficient Patent Pools". *American Economic Review,* 94 (June): 691–711.

Loury, G. C. 1979. "Market Structure and Innovation." *Quarterly Journal of Economics,* 93: 395–410.

Mansfield, A., M. Schwartz, and S. Wagner. 1981. "Imitation Costs and Patents: An Empirical Study." *Economic Journal,* 91, 907–918.

Moser, P. 2005. "How Do Patent Laws Influence Innovation? Evidence from Nineteenth-Century World Fairs". *American Economic Review,* 95 (September): 1214–1236.

Nordhaus, W. 1969. *Invention, Growth and Welfare.* Cambridge, MA: MIT Press.

Reinganum, J. 1989. "The Timing of Innovation: Research, Development, and Diffusion." In R. Schmalensee and R. Willig, eds., *The Handbook of Industrial Organization.* Amsterdam: North-Holland, 849–908.

Sakakibara, M., and L. Branstetter. 2001. "Do Stronger Patents Induce More Innovation? Evidence from The 1998 Japanese Patent Law Reforms." *Rand Journal of Economics,* 32 (Spring): 77–100.

Scotchmer, S. 2004. *Innovation and Incentives.* Cambridge, MA: MIT Press.

Tirole, J. 1989. *The Theory of Industrial Organization.* Cambridge, MA: MIT Press.

Part VI
Special Topics: Networks and Strategic Trade Policy

The final two chapters address issues that do not fit easily within our earlier sections. The first topic is the increasingly important issue of network effects. We begin with a simple model of network effects based on Rohlf's (1974) work. We extend this model to show the potential for multiple equilibria in network markets, as well as to demonstrate that while competition will typically yield a more efficient outcome than monopoly, both will likely fall short of the optimal service. We then consider price competition and show that this will likely be quite fierce in a network setting, meaning that network markets will typically be served by only a few firms. The chapter then turns to systems and compatibility issues and the strategic concerns that arise when these choices are made. A final empirical application demonstrating hedonic pricing and estimation based on Gandal's (1994) study of spreadsheet competition concludes the chapter.

Chapter 18 then turns to a discussion of the strategic trade models rooted in the work of Brander and Spencer (1985) and Krugman (1986). Because the outcome of strategic trade policies depends so critically on that ability of firms and nations to commit, we precede this discussion with a formal analysis of the role of commitment in market analysis in general. For this purpose we draw heavily—but not exclusively—from the well-known Fudenberg and Tirole (1984) paper on commitments and strategic complements and substitutes. We then consider various strategic policies focused either on price or nonprice attributes. We conclude with a discussion of trade agreements that may serve to commit regions to *non*interventionist trade policies.

Students completing these chapters will understand that network effects and complementarities are critical features that raise difficult, if not altogether new, issues for firms and policymakers alike. They will also understand the notion of multiple equilibria and how to distinguish a stable equilibrium from an unstable one. In addition, they will understand that commitment is essential to any strategy that includes promises or threats of future actions contingent upon a rival's behavior, as well as the fact that such commitment has the downside of a loss of flexibility. They will also gain further appreciation for the tools of industrial economics as they may now be applied to international markets.

Special Topics: Networks and Strategic-Stance Policy

17

Network Markets

On Wednesday, January 27, 2010, Steve Jobs of Apple introduced the company's latest piece of iconoclastic hardware—the Apple *iPad*. With the ability to present online newspapers and books in an easy-to-read format as well as innumerable other applications, the new *iPad* may be a particular challenge to the current leading e-reader, the Amazon *Kindle*. For both devices, an important issue will likely be the number of books and media material available to download. This is likely to be a vicious circle. As more people buy the *Kindle*, for example, more material will likely be made available to it, which, in turn, will lead more consumers to want the *Kindle* and so on.

The sort of demand-side scale effect just described is a common feature of many products of the digital age. Microsoft's *Windows* benefited greatly from such positive feedback. As *Windows* became more popular, more and more applications such as spreadsheet and word processing programs were written to run on the *Windows* system—which made *Windows* more popular still. Similarly, as more people discovered the ability to buy and sell items on eBay, the online site became an even more valuable marketplace that enabled a buyer or seller to reach an increasingly broad market. When the value of a product to any one consumer increases as the number of other consumers using either that product itself or goods compatible with that product increases, we say that the market for that product exhibits network externalities or demand-side scale economies. When these effects are important, new strategic considerations come into play. In this chapter, we investigate these issues and the type of market outcomes that are likely when important network effects are present.[1]

17.1 MARKET PROVISION OF A NETWORK SERVICE

While the examples given above are modern ones, network effects have been recognized at least since the introduction of telephones. Think about it. A telephone has no value to a consumer if she is the only individual to have one; but value grows quickly as more consumers are hooked into the system. This is often referred to as a *direct network effect*. This is in contrast to the *Kindle* and *Windows* examples above, which exhibit *indirect*

---

[1] For a formal but very readable introduction to network externalities, see Economides (1996).

network effects in which the value of, say, the *Kindle*, to any one user rises with the number of books made compatible with the *Kindle* platform. We discuss first the direct network effects.

17.1.1 Monopoly Provision

An early but insightful analysis of direct network issues is that provided by Rohlfs (1974). Rohlfs's approach is quite straightforward and draws attention to the main issues that arise in network settings. It simplifies the supply side by assuming a monopoly, so that the analysis can focus on the central demand-side aspects that give rise to network effects. We present a simplified version of the Rohlfs model here.[2]

Assume that the monopolist (say, a telecommunications firm) faces a continuum of N potential consumers. The consumers are ranked in terms of the value that they ascribe to the service, which is given by fv_i. Here, f is the fraction of N consumers that have subscribed to the network, and v_i is a measure of consumer heterogeneity in willingness to pay for the service. We assume that v_i ranges continuously and uniformly from 0 to N. The network effect is captured by the fact that the willingness to pay of each consumer increases as the fraction f of consumers on the system increases. Consumer i will subscribe to the system at price p if her willingness to pay $fv_i \geq p$. That is:

$$q_i^D = \begin{cases} 0 & \text{if } fv_i < p \\ 1 & \text{if } fv_i \geq p \end{cases} \tag{17.1}$$

We use equation (17.1) to define the marginal consumer, denoted by the reservation valuation $\tilde{v}_i$. This is the consumer who is just indifferent between buying into the service network and not buying into it, so that $\tilde{v}_i = p/f$. The fraction f of consumers who subscribe to the service is

$$f = \int_{\tilde{v}_i}^{N} \frac{1}{N} dv_i = \frac{N - \tilde{v}_i}{N} = 1 - \frac{p}{Nf} \tag{17.2}$$

All consumers with a valuation less than $\tilde{v}_i$ will not subscribe to the service. The remainder will subscribe. Since v_i is distributed uniformly between 0 and N, the fraction of consumers with a valuation below $\tilde{v}_i$ is simply $\tilde{v}_i/N$. If we now solve for p, we obtain the inverse demand function confronting the monopolist, expressed in terms of the fraction f of the maximum potential number of customers who actually buy the service, as

$$p = Nf(1 - f) \tag{17.3}$$

This price or demand function is illustrated in Figure 17.1 (next page).

The price function shown in Figure 17.1 is interesting in a number of respects. Note first that the maximum of the function where $dp/df = 0$ occurs at $f = 0.5$. Hence, the maximum value of p is \$0.25N. At any price $p > \$0.25N$, no equilibrium with a positive value of f exists. If the monopolist has fixed costs such that it must charge a price greater than \$0.25N in order to break even, then the network will simply fail. This is true even though the network might be socially efficient.

---

[2] Economides and Himmelberg (1995) present a similar analysis in a competitive market.

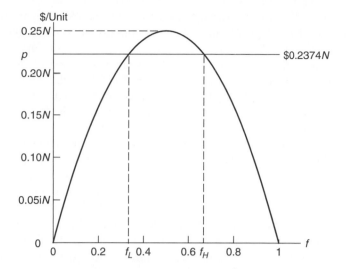

Figure 17.1   Demand to a monopoly provider of a network service
At price $p = \$0.2374N$, the fraction of consumers subscribing to the network could be either the low value
of $f_L = 0.388$ or the high value of $f_H = 0.612$.

For example, suppose that the monopolist incurs a cost per subscribed consumer of $\$0.26N$. When half the market (or $f = 0.5$) is served, consumer willingness to pay ranges from $\$0.25N$ to $\$0.5N$. The average willingness to pay when $f = 0.5$ is $\$0.375N > \$0.26N$. That is, the average willingness to pay at $f = 0.5$ is enough to cover the fixed cost per customer. Nevertheless, the market will fail. While the average consumer valuation is $\$0.375N$, the marginal consumer's valuation is equal to $\$0.25N$, which is less than the price the monopolist needs to charge to cover its cost. As a result, at a price of $p = \$0.26N$, some consumers will not subscribe. This will reduce f below 0.5 and, consequently, reduce the willingness to pay of all those remaining consumers as well. Absent discriminatory prices, it is not feasible to charge a price that will cover the firm's costs in this case.

What is the profit-maximizing price if the firm's cost per consumer c is such that $c = \alpha N < \$0.25N$? The profit function can be written

$$\pi(p) = (p - c)Nf = [Nf(1 - f) - \alpha N]Nf \tag{17.4}$$

Maximizing this with respect to f yields

$$f = \frac{1 \pm \sqrt{1 - 3\alpha}}{3} \tag{17.5}$$

Taking the larger root as the highest profit option then implies that the profit-maximizing price will be

$$p = N\left(\frac{1 + 3\alpha + \sqrt{1 - 3\alpha}}{9}\right) \tag{17.6}$$

For example, if $\alpha = 0$ (no cost), the optimal price is $p = \$0.222N$, at which price the firm would wish to serve $0.667N$ consumers. In contrast, if $\alpha = 0.1$, the optimal price is $p = \$0.2374N$, and the firm would wish to serve $0.612N$ consumers. At any price below the maximum value of $p = \$0.25N$, there are two levels of demand (i.e., two potential equilibria). When $\alpha = 0.1$ then with $p = \$0.2374N$, the demand curve shown in Figure 17.1 indicates that the fraction of all N consumers subscribing to the service could be the high value of $f_H(p) = 0.612$ just as the firm intends. However, it could also be the lower level of $f_L(p) = 0.388$.

Rohlfs refers to this lower fraction as a "critical mass" for the network because it is an unstable equilibrium. If the firm can reach this low level of demand, then any slight nudge beyond that point will raise the fraction f of consumers who are actually buying and so raise the value of the service to all and more consumers will buy. In turn, this will raise f still further—and with it, everyone's value of the service again. This process will continue until the higher level of demand equal to $0.612N$ is reached. Thus, so long as the firm can establish a number of subscribers just a bit greater than the critical mass $f_L(p)N$, the network will grow to contain the high fraction $f_H(p)$ of the population.

An important question is whether and how the monopolist can reach the critical mass. This is particularly important when subscribers join sequentially, since no one may want to join the network unless others have done so—in which case, the network may never get off the ground, let alone grow to its critical mass. One possibility is to provide the service free for a limited period of time, perhaps by bundling it for free with some other product. Another option is to lease the equipment to potential users with a guarantee that if the service does not achieve critical mass, the lease agreement can be canceled with no penalty. A further possibility, which was employed when fax machines were first being marketed, would be to target groups of large users first. In this regard, national and multinational companies or government agencies are the obvious examples of institutions that might want to operate their own internal networks. The idea is that once the network comes into common use for internal company communications, there will be a demand for it to be extended to those with whom the company does business. Before long, this may grow into a demand by company users of the service for it to be available in their homes.

17.1.2 Competitive and Optimal Provision of a Network Service

It is interesting to ask what would happen if the service were supplied by competitive firms. To consider this, we assume that f the parameter measuring the network effect on consumers applies to the total number of consumers without regard to which particular firm provides the service to any given consumer. We assume as well that each competitive firm has a constant marginal cost of c.

The competitive equilibrium follows immediately. Since price must equal marginal cost, we have $p = c$. Substituting this relation in equation (17.2) then yields

$$f = 1 - \frac{c}{Nf} \tag{17.7}$$

If, as before, we express the cost parameter proportionally to N so that $c = \alpha N$, we have that

$$f = \frac{1 \pm \sqrt{1 - 4\alpha}}{2} \tag{17.8}$$

A comparison of equation (17.8) with (17.5) then makes clear that, not surprisingly, the stable equilibrium outcome is larger under competition than it is under monopoly for all values of α in the permissible range $0 \leq \alpha \leq 0.25$. In other words, the competitively supplied network will be larger.

Considering the competitive outcome relative to the monopoly case naturally raises the question as to which outcome is closer to the optimal size of network. We can answer this question by first determining the network size that maximizes the total surplus. That total surplus is given by

$$TS(f) = \int_c^N \frac{(fv_i - c)}{N} dv_i = \frac{(N-c)}{N} \left[\frac{f(N+c) - c}{2} \right]$$

Or with $c = \alpha N$

$$TS(f) = (1-\alpha)N \left[\frac{f}{2}(1+\alpha) - \alpha \right] \tag{17.9}$$

Maximizing (17.9) with respect to f, it is easy to see that

$$\frac{dTS(f)}{df} \geq 0 \text{ for } 0 < \alpha < 1 \tag{17.10}$$

That is, the optimal network size rises continuously with α for all the permissible values of α. Hence, the optimal network size f must be

$$f = 1; \text{ and the entire market is served.} \tag{17.11}$$

Comparing (17.11) with (17.8) and (17.5) reveals that even a competitive market will tend to produce less than the optimal size of network (unless $c = 0$), but that the shortfall will be less than it is under monopoly. The intuition for this result is clear. In joining the network, each consumer considers only her own benefits fv_i, and not the benefits her joining brings to other members already in the network.

17.2   NETWORKS, COMPETITION, AND COMPLEMENTARY SERVICES

The model presented above makes clear many of the major difficulties that network externalities raise. The equilibrium market network will likely be too small. In some cases, the market could fail altogether. Alternatively, there could be more than one equilibrium outcome, and there is no guarantee that the market will choose the best one. These difficulties arise whether or not the market is competitive. However, we have so far considered only a very simple kind of competition in which everyone is part of the same network—regardless of what firm they purchase their service from. A more typical case is that the provider is network specific. It is typically the case that when a consumer hooks into the network for some service such as wireless telephoning or a banking ATM network, the consumer has direct access only to the services provided by that firm (e.g., Verizon or Bank of America). In other words, firms will likely compete in terms of network size and quality as well as in price. We now examine this sort of network competition.

17.2.1   Price Competition with Network Effects

Consider a model with two firms located at opposite ends of a Hotelling line one unit long and populated by a continuum of N consumers distributed uniformly along the line. Firm A is located at the West end of town ($x = 0$), and Firm B is located at the East end of town ($x = 1$). As usual, each consumer buys at most one unit of the good either from Firm A or Firm B. The net surplus earned by a consumer x is $V + ks_A^e - tx - p_A$ if she buys from Firm A, and $V + ks_B^e - t(1 - x) - p_B$, where s_A^e and s_B^e are, respectively, the market shares of consumers that the typical consumer *expects* to purchase good A and good B, respectively. V is large enough that consumers always buy from one of the two firms (i.e., the market is covered). Firms have zero costs and compete in prices, p_A and p_B, respectively. Note that the actual market shares for each good are, respectively, $s^A = x^m$ and $s^B = 1 - x^m$, where x^m is the location of the marginal consumer just indifferent between the two products of the two firms.

The standard Hotelling model serves as a benchmark case. In that model, there are no-network-effects so that $k = 0$. The marginal consumer x^m is defined by the condition $V - tx^m - p_A = V - t(1 - x^m) - p_B$. This implies that the demand and profit of each firm is

$$q_A^D = x^m N = \left(\frac{1}{2} + \frac{p_B - p_A}{2t}\right)N; \text{ and } \pi^A(p_A, p_B) = p_A\left(\frac{1}{2} + \frac{p_B - p_A}{2t}\right)N \quad (17.12)$$

$$q_B^D = (1 - x^m)N = \left(\frac{1}{2} + \frac{p_A - p_B}{2t}\right)N \text{ and } \pi^B(p_A, p_B) = p_B\left(\frac{1}{2} + \frac{p_A - p_B}{2t}\right)N \quad (17.13)$$

The best-response functions are

$$p_A = \frac{p_B + t}{2} \text{ and } p_B = \frac{p_A + t}{2} \quad (17.14)$$

from which it follows immediately that the equilibrium prices are

$$p_A = p_B = t \quad (17.15)$$

Now let us assume some network effects so that $t > k > 0$. In other words, the willingness to pay for a firm's product now increases as that firm has a larger market share. The marginal consumer is now defined by the condition that $V + ks_A^e - tx^m - p_A = V + ks_B^e - t(1 - x^m) - p_B$. This may be alternatively written as $2tx^m = t + k\left(s_A^e - s_B^e\right) + (p_B - p_A)$.

We assume that when the marginal consumer confronts a particular set of prices (p_A and p_B), and makes her purchase choice, she forms the rational expectation that $s_A^e = x^m$ and $s_B^e = 1 - x^m$. That is, as an equilibrium condition, the consumer's expected network size equal the actual network size. With this assumption, the demand and profit functions are:

$$q_A^D = x^m N = \left[\frac{1}{2} + \frac{(p_B - p_A)}{2(t - k)}\right]N; \text{ and } \pi^A(p_A, p_B) = p_A\left[\frac{1}{2} + \frac{(p_B - p_A)}{2(t - k)}\right]N \quad (17.16)$$

$$q_A^D = (1 - x^m)N = \left[\frac{1}{2} + \frac{(p_A - p_B)}{2(t - k)}\right] N; \quad \text{and } \pi^B(p_A, p_B)$$

$$= p_B \left[\frac{1}{2} + \frac{(p_A - p_B)}{2(t - k)}\right] N \tag{17.17}$$

The best-response functions now are

$$p_A = \frac{p_B + t - k}{2}; \quad \text{and } p_B = \frac{p_A + t - k}{2} \tag{17.18}$$

Hence, the equilibrium prices are

$$p_A = p_B = t - k \tag{17.19}$$

Comparing the price equilibrium in (17.19) with that in (17.15) makes clear that network effects intensify price competition. Each consumer is now valuable not just for the profit generated by her own purchase, but also because each additional consumer raises the willingness to pay of (and hence the profit earned from) all other patrons. As a result, the competition to win that marginal consumer is much greater than it was in the absence of network effects and the equilibrium prices are lower.

In the symmetric price equilibrium described by (17.19), the two firms spit the market evenly and each earns profit of $\frac{t-k}{2}N$. However, if each has a fixed cost $F > \frac{t-k}{2}N$, then that equilibrium is not sustainable. In that case, the market is really a natural monopoly. Yet which firm will emerge as the monopoly is unclear because the market is "tippy". Once a firm starts to lose customers, the value of its product to the remaining customers falls, causing it to lose more customers, its value to fall further, and so on. In such a setting, more than market share is at stake. Survival itself is on the line.

Moreover, while the "winner-takes-all" feature intensifies competition by itself, coupling it with an environment in which pricing below cost may be necessary just to get any network started makes the competition truly nasty. Some economists have argued that it was precisely this dynamic that was at work in the Microsoft versus Netscape case, and that what may look like predatory behavior in other markets is really just normal competition when applied in a setting of network goods.[3]

17.2.2   Network Competition and Complementary Services

Consider two firms, BNY1 and BNY2, operating passenger railroad lines from Boston to New York as in Figure 17.2(a). The firms have identical costs and compete in quantities with the result that each earns a duopoly profit π^D. After a while, a third firm called NYW begins to offer rail service from New York to Washington. As shown in Figure 17.2(b), this firm connects at BNY1's terminal, so the latter can now offer a connected service from Boston to Philadelphia. As a result, the original duopoly on the Boston–New York line is altered. Now, many of the customers currently using BNY2 will switch their demand to railroad BNY1.

[3]   See Schmalensee (2000) for a clear statement of the view that competition in network, or (what he calls) "winner take most" markets, is likely to be extremely fierce and easily mistaken for predatory conduct when practiced by a dominant incumbent.

Figure 17.2(a)   Initial configuration of Boston–New York rail market

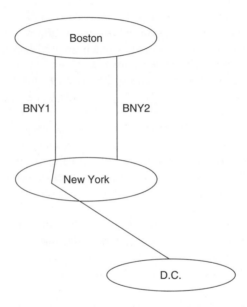

Figure 17.2(b)   Boston–New York rail market with connecting service to Washington

Afterwards, two other railroads connect to BNY1's New York terminal. The Second City Rail Road (SCRR) offers service to Chicago, and the Rockin' Land Line (RLL) offers service to Nashville. The availability of these new connections makes BNY1 even more popular relative to BNY2. Enough customers leave the disadvantaged BNY2 that it can no longer cover its costs; and it shuts down, giving BNY1 a monopoly on the original Boston–New York route. The set of connections and associated rail lines now available is shown in Figure 17.2(c), where the dashed line indicates that BNY2 is no longer in business.

The story just described illustrates two points. First, complementarities can play a critical role in generating network economies, in which case we call the network effects indirect. These complementarities are precisely what Amazon hopes to exploit with its *Kindle* and what Apple hopes to exploit with its *iPad*. Second, complementarities are particularly powerful when coupled with scale economies as may well characterize rail service.

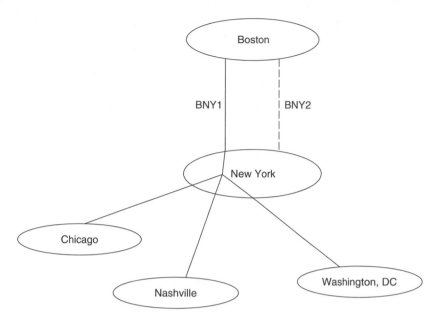

Figure 17.2(c)   Boston–New York rail market with connecting service to Chicago, Nashville, and Washington

Not only does the DC connection lead more customers to choose BNY1 but by making scale economies feasible, it both lowers BNY1's unit cost and encourages other firms to link to BNY1's network making BNY1 even more profitable and more preferred and so on.

The foregoing issues were at the heart of the recent Microsoft case. At the core of the charge that Microsoft had abused its market power was the claim that bundling its Web browser, *Internet Explorer*, with its Windows operating system was a deliberate predatory act aimed at driving the major alternative browser Netscape's *Navigator* from the market. Underlying this argument, though, was an even deeper one that rested on the fact that computer applications such as games, word processing programs, spreadsheets, and other programs are complements to the operating system. This relationship then makes possible a powerful positive demand feedback that allowed Microsoft to benefit from an important network effect sometimes referred to as the *applications barrier to entry*.

The basic idea is that the cost of producing computer applications comes largely upfront as a sunk design cost. Once the program is written and debugged, running off copies on CDs or making it available for Internet downloading is virtually costless. As a result of this high sunk but trivial variable cost structure, applications programs can potentially reap large-scale economies as these fixed costs are spread over a greater volume of users. In turn, this means that applications firms will want to design their products to interface with an operating system that has a large usage, such as Windows. This will intensify consumer preferences for Windows, making it virtually impossible for alternative operating systems to ever compete.

Indeed, in both our railroad case and the Microsoft case, we might see firms strategically subsidize the development of complementary services and offer them at a very low price to consumers as a means of driving rivals out of business or preventing their entry. This was, of course, precisely the charge leveled at Microsoft by Netscape. The argument was that because a browser might someday serve as an alternative platform for applications, Netscape's *Navigator* was a possible exception to the applications barrier. As the main browser of its time, it had a sufficient customer base that applications programmers could exploit the available scale economies. In terms of our railroad example, it was as if BNY2 had not existed initially but, instead, started out as the complementary New York–Washington service, raising the possibility that it might one day establish its own connecting New York–Boston line. In that case, it might well be BNY2 that survives the market competition. To prevent this, subsidizing its own complementary services makes sense for BNY1 or Microsoft—or any rational incumbent—even though it may be expensive. Once again, we see that with network effects, competition can be quite intense, especially when survival itself is in question.[4]

More generally, we note that indirect network externalities involve what might be called two-sided competition. On the one hand, the e-readers (Amazon's *Kindle* and Apple's *iPad*) compete for e-reader customers. On the other hand, they also compete for publishers to provide them with e-book content. Such two-sided competition can create some interesting dilemmas. On the one hand, Amazon and Apple want the price of e-books to be low to attract demand for their underlying platform (the *Kindle* and *iPad*, respectively). On the other hand, their competition for e-book content may lead them to bid up the prices that they offer publishers. In fact, the introduction of the *iPad* forced Amazon to do exactly that, with the result that it had to drop its previous practice of charging a low flat price of $9.99 for all its e-books.[5]

17.3   SYSTEMS COMPETITION AND THE BATTLE OVER INDUSTRY STANDARDS

In our hypothetical railroad case above, we assumed that BNY1's development of complementary rail services to other cities enabled it to put its rival BNY2 out of business. This need not be the case, however. Instead, we might observe BNY2 developing its own complementary connections to cities such as Chicago, Nashville, and Washington. In that case, we would have two rail systems that compete with each other, and both may survive. It is easy to find markets with a number of firms each operating its own network, including airlines, wireless phone companies, and credit card services. When we allow for the coexistence of two or more firms, each operating its own network, an additional issue that arises is the important issue of compatibility. In many ways, it makes sense for firms to establish a common industry standard and make their products compatible with each other. This increases each firm's volume—which, of course, enhances the network effect. However, compatibility may be expensive, especially when the agreed-upon format has been developed by a rival. Furthermore, compatibility may diminish the degree of product differentiation between firms and thereby intensify price competition. We address these questions in the next section.

---

[4]   On various interpretations of Microsoft's behavior, see Eisenach and Lenard (1999), Fisher (2000), and Schmalensee (2000).

[5]   See M. Rich and B. Stone. "Publisher Wins Fight with Amazon Over e-Books." *The New York Times* (31 January 2010), p. C1. For a thorough and insightful analysis of competition with two-sided platforms, see Evans and Schmalensee (2008). Pepall and Richards (2001) offer an analysis of two-sided competition in media markets.

17.3.1   A Simple Model of Compatibility and Competition[6]

Consider a market in which a continuum of N consumers either buy one good from one of two rivals, firms 1 and 2, or buy nothing at all. This decision is based in part on the expected size of the network with which a firm's product is compatible, y_i^e. When the two goods are compatible, the network size for either good is the sum of their total actual production, $x_1 + x_2$. That is, in this case, $y_1^e = y_2^e = x_1 + x_2$. When the two goods are not compatible, then Firm i's network size is just the level of its own production (i.e., $y_i^e = x_i$).

Given consumers' expectations about the size of each firm's network, firms compete in quantities; and consumer demand for each good then determines the actual network size. The $i$the consumer's willingness to pay for the good is $v_i + w(y_i^e)$. Here, v_i is the consumer's base valuation of the product and is assumed to be uniformly distributed between 0 and N. In contrast, the function $w()$ is common to all consumers and indicates the additional value a consumer enjoys as the good she purchases belongs to a larger network. We assume that $w' > 0$, so that the consumer is willing to pay more for a product with a larger network. However, there are diminishing returns to this effect, so $w'' < 0$. Thus, for any individual consumer i, the two products are vertically differentiated where the one belonging to a larger expected network is of higher quality and, hence, worth more.

Let p_i denote the price of Firm i's product. In any equilibrium in which both firms sell positive amounts, it must be the case that

$$p_1 - w\left(y_1^e\right) = p_2 - w\left(y_2^e\right) \tag{17.20}$$

In other words, although consumers differ in their basic value of the good v_i, each agrees that the product with a larger expected network is superior. Therefore, each will only buy a product with a smaller expected network if the price is correspondingly adjusted downward to compensate for this. Thus, the left-hand side of equation (17.20) may be taken as the quality-adjusted price of good 1 and the right-hand side as the quality-adjusted price of good 2. Let ρ denote the common value of this quality-adjusted price. For any given value of ρ, the only consumers who will be buying are those for whom $v_i \geq \rho$. That is, the total quantity bought at any value ρ is $N - \rho = x_1 + x_2$. Thus we have

$$x_1 + x_2 = N - \rho = N + w\left(y_1^e\right) - p_1 = N + w\left(y_2^e\right) - p_2 \tag{17.21}$$

Without loss of generality, we assume that each firm has unit cost $c = 0$. Equation (17.21) implies that each firm sells at a price $p_i = N + w\left(y_i^e\right) - (x_1 + x_2)$. Thus, each firm earns a profit π_i of

$$\pi_i = x_i\left[N + w\left(y_i^e\right) - (x_1 + x_2)\right] \tag{17.22}$$

Taking expectations as given, each firm will choose its output x_i to maximize equation (17.22). The necessary first-order condition, then, is

$$x_i = \frac{N + w\left(y_i^e\right)}{2} - \frac{x_j}{2}; i, j = 1, 2 \text{ and } i \neq j \tag{17.23}$$

---

[6]   The analysis of this section draws heavily from Katz and Shapiro (1985).

If we then invoke symmetry, we have

$$x_i = \frac{N + w\left(y_i^e\right)}{3}; i = 1, 2 \tag{17.24}$$

We now consider the expected network size. As we did in our earlier spatial model, we impose the equilibrium condition that the expected network size equals the actual network size, that is, $y_i^e = y_i$. With this requirement, a setting of no compatibility implies that $y_i^e = x_i^e = x_i$, while a setting of full compatibility implies that $y_i^e = x_1^e + x_2^e = x_i + x_2$. Thus, total output is

$$x_1 + x_2 = \frac{2[N + w(x_1)]}{3} \text{ if there is no compatibility} \tag{17.25a}$$

$$x_1 + x_2 = \frac{2[N + w(x_1 + x_2)]}{3} \text{ if there is compatibility} \tag{17.25b}$$

Let $X = x_1 + x_2$. Then equation (17.25) implies $3X/2 = N + w\left(\frac{X}{2}\right)$. If we graph each side of this equality, their intersection determines a unique equilibrium as shown in Figure 17.3(a). Similarly, equation (17.25b) implies that $3X/2 = N + w(X)$, and this also implies a unique equilibrium as shown in Figure 17.3(b) (next page).

By equations (17.20) and (17.21) only consumers with v_i values greater than or equal to $N - X$ will buy a product. Hence, the expected total consumer surplus is:

$$CS(X) = \int_{N-X}^{N} (v + X - N)\, dv = \frac{X^2}{2} \tag{17.26}$$

Similarly, the operating profit of each firm is $p_i x_i = (N + w(y_i^e) - X)x_i = x_i^2$ by equations (17.21) and (17.24). Since each firm produces more output under a full compatibility regime, and since consumer surplus increases with total output, it follows that total welfare is larger under a regime of full compatibility. However, this ignores any costs of converting to fully compatible products. Suppose that such a conversion requires that each firm incur a sunk conversion cost of F. If F exceeds the firm's profit

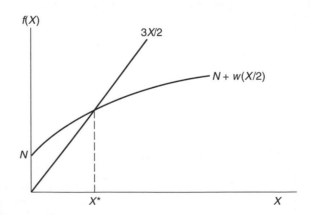

Figure 17.3(a)   Total output with no compatibility

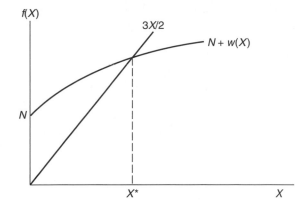

Figure 17.3(b)   Total output with compatibility

gain from having convertibility, then neither firm will sink this cost. Note that this raises the possibility of inefficiency, because even though a change to convertibility would impose losses on the firms, it would generate gains for consumers. Hence, the two firms may continue to offer incompatible products, even though it would be socially optimal if their products were compatible.

Matters may become particularly difficult if establishing compatibility means adopting one firm or the other's technology. In that case, the expenditure of F is no longer symmetric. If Firm 2 adopts Firm 1's format, only Firm 2 needs to incur the conversion cost F. If Firm 1 adopts Firm 2's format, then Firm 1 must pay the F expense. Even if side payments are possible, bargaining problems may make it difficult to reach an agreement on what format is to become the industry standard.

17.3.2   Compatibility, Standards, and Competition

Compatibility is clearly an important factor in technological choice. Apart from the cost incurred in achieving compatibility, however, the symmetric Cournot-type model just considered suggests that firms should welcome developments that facilitate compatibility, since these will enhance each firm's network size and consumer willingness to pay. However, there is a further drawback to compatibility that is more evident when firms compete in pricing. This is the fact that compatibility often means interchangeability; in turn, this implies that when each firm adopts the same technical standard, their products become very close substitutes. This is likely to intensify price competition. Hence, while technical differentiation by means of different technologies incurs the cost of foregoing possible network effects, it may have benefits and firms therefore have to make a judgment in this regard.

Of course the cost of establishing compatibility is likely to be less if a firm can establish its own technology as the industry standard. Viewed in this light, firms may choose to compete with different technologies with the precise aim of establishing their own format as the industry standard that all firms will adopt. Obviously, there is no a priori means of determining whether rewards will be greater under intratechnology competition "within the market," or under intertechnology competition "for the market." There are three main possibilities that we should consider. We illustrate these with three simple games: (1) Tweedledum and Tweedledee, (2) The Battle of the Sexes, and (3) Pesky Little Brother.[7]

1. Tweedledum and Tweedledee

Assume that the payoffs for the technology choice game are those given in Table 17.1 (below). There are two Nash equilibria in each of which the firms prefer to adopt incompatible technologies. This implies that the firms believe that network externalities are not particularly strong and that any gains from adopting a common technology will be more than offset by the particularly fierce intratechnology price competition that this will lead to. In some respects, this discrete choice game is similar to the continuous Cournot compatibility game above, with F large enough that nether firm wants full compatibility.

2. Battle of the Sexes[8]

Even if firms agree that the adoption of a common technology is desirable, they may well disagree over which standard is chosen. The payoff matrix in this case is shown in Table 17.2 (next page). Here, each firm would prefer a common standard; but Firm 1 prefers that the standard be Technology 1, while Firm 2 prefers that it be Technology 2. This is another instance in which commitment plays a crucial role. Firm 1, for example, may be able to persuade Firm 2 to accept Technology 1 as the standard by irrevocably committing itself to this technology. It could, for example, build an installed base rooted in Technology 1. Alternatively, it could invest in production capacity to build more units embodying this technology, or establish a large R&D program devoted to improving this format. The common intent here is to broadcast the clear message that Firm 1 will never give in on its demand that Technology 1 be the standard, because to do so would be to lose its costly investment.

Other possible commitments take the form of concessions rather than threats. Firm 1 could offer to license Technology 1 to Firm 2 for a low fee in return for Firm 2 agreeing that Technology 1 will be the standard. This is the practical meaning of the side payment described earlier.

Note too that if the two firms do converge on each using Technology 1, there will likely be some regret. Had both adopted Technology 2, the total surplus would have

Table 17.1   Tweedledum and Tweedledee (all payoffs in millions of dollars)

		Firm 2	
		Technology A	Technology B
Firm 1	Technology A	2, 2	4, 4
	Technology B	4, 4	2, 2

Two firms prefer to choose incompatible, rather than compatible technologies and will compete in distinct formats.

[7]   See Besen and Farrell (1994) for a more complete development of this framework. The language that follows is also borrowed from their discussion.

[8]   This title comes from a well-known game in which two individuals—perhaps man and wife—in choosing their entertainment for the night, agree that they would rather be together than apart, but put very different valuations on the entertainment they might share. These could be, for example, going to a ball game or to an opera.

Table 17.2   The Battle of the Sexes (all payoffs in millions of dollars)

		Firm 2	
		Technology 1	*Technology 2*
Firm 1	*Technology 1*	8, 5	3, 3
	Technology 2	3, 3	4, 10

The firms wish to be compatible, but cannot agree on the proper standard.

been larger. Once Technology 1 is chosen, however, it will be hard to dislodge it from its position as the industry standard. This is what some have referred to as the "lock-in" effect. As an example, this is what may have happened in the early days of home videos when two formats, VHS and Betamax, vied for dominance. For a variety of reasons, the balance swung in favor of VHS with the result that film studios began releasing the vast majority of video cassettes in this format—which, in turn, discouraged Sony from producing Betamax machines. Ultimately, all video cassettes were released in the VHS format, even though many feel that the Betamax technology was superior.[9]

3. Pesky Little Brother

In the "Tweedledum and Tweedledee" case, the two firms pursue intertechnology competition rather than adopt a common technology and confront each other in the market with technologically undifferentiated products. In the "Battle of the Sexes," each firm prefers competition between technically identical products, but the question of which technology is the appropriate standard remains an issue. What these two cases have in common is that there is some degree of consensus, if only on the terms on which competition between the firms will occur. If, however, there are asymmetries between the firms, it may be impossible for them to reach even this limited kind of consensus.

Assume, for example, that Firm 1 has established a dominant position with a large installed base and a powerful reputation. It will prefer incompatibility with a small rival in order to hold its customers. The smaller rival, Firm 2, will prefer compatibility in order to derive benefits from the network that the larger firm has established. As Besen and Farrell indicate: "The firms' problem is like the game between a big brother who wants to be left alone and a pesky little brother who wants to be with his big brother."

The payoff matrix now looks something like Table 17.3 (next page). There is no Nash equilibrium in pure strategies to this game when the firms make simultaneous choices—the two firms' strategic choices are inconsistent. Resolution of the game then comes down again to a question of timing and commitment.

Suppose that the dominant firm must commit to its technology choice first. This is perhaps the most plausible assumption, given that we have motivated the game by describing Firm 1 as a preexisting firm with a large installed base. In this case, the smaller

---

[9]   David (1985) has argued that the standardized QWERTY keyboard, used initially by typewriters and now by all PC keyboards, is an example of path-dependent lock-in to an inferior technology, with the superior one being the Dvorak keyboard. While Liebowitz and Margolis (1990) cast considerable doubt on this argument, the case nevertheless makes clear that such market failure is a real possibility. See also Arthur (1989).

Table 17.3   The Pesky Little Brother (all payoffs in millions of dollars)

		Firm 2	
		Technology 1	Technology 2
Firm 1	Technology 1	10, 6	12, 4
	Technology 2	13, 2	11, 5

There is no (pure strategy) Nash equilibrium in simultaneous play. Firm 1, the dominant firm (or big brother), prefers that the technologies be incompatible. Firm 2 (the little brother) prefers that they be compatible.

Firm 2 may actually enjoy a second-mover advantage. If Firm 1 is committed to its existing technology, either because it is costly to change or because such change would lose Firm 1 the guaranteed patronage it now enjoys from its customers, it may be unable to prevent Firm 2 from following. In this case, Firm 2's clear choice will be to follow with a compatible system, precisely the outcome that Firm 1 had hoped to avoid.

Two actions might be available to Firm 1 that would prevent Firm 2 from imitating its lead and offer Firm 1 relief from its "pesky little brother." These are (a) aggressive protection of its property rights and (b) changing its technology frequently. The first relates to the use of patents. If the technology the dominant firm has built up is protected by patents, then imitation may be preventable through strict enforcement of the protection such patents give and by building up a stock of sleeping patents that make it difficult for a smaller firm to invent around the current technology.

Alternatively, Firm 1 can try to hamper Firm 2's imitation efforts by changing its technology frequently. This can be expensive, of course, and runs the risk of alienating users of the existing installed base unless they can be protected; an example of such protection might be granting favorable access to the new generation of products. The advantage to this approach is that the target at which the bigger rival is aiming is constantly shifting in ways that are difficult for the small firm to predict. If you really want to avoid your pesky little brother, don't tell him where you are going!

In short, competition over technology has a variety of implications. Often, there may be large social gains from all firms adopting a common technical approach. However, the cost of converting to a mutually compatible framework and the incentive for firms to differentiate their products may well derail efforts to establish broad compatibility.

This raises the general question as to the proper role for the government in coordinating the technology choices of different firms with a view toward achieving standardization. Consider the market for mobile telephone service. As a result of legislation by the European Parliament, all mobile phones in Europe adhere to the same technical standard. Consequently, a British resident traveling on the continent can use her mobile phone to make calls in Italy just as easily as she can at home. This was much less feasible for U.S. residents, in part because there was no centralized authority coordinating the digital standard of American mobile phone companies. Instead, the mobile phone services in the United States initially adopted four different standards; and interservice communication was impossible. On the other hand, the presence of these different standards has led to increased competition and technical development. As mobile phone companies in the United States have expanded their coverage over wider and wider areas, the regional reach of an American consumer has become comparable to that of a European one, with the American consumer enjoying the added benefit of systems competition and technical advance.

Reality Checkpoint
Raise the Blu-Ray Standard

In the later 1970s, Sony introduced the Beta-Max technology for videocassette recorders (VCRs), thereby also initiating the war with the Video Home System (VHS), initially engineered by JVC Corporation, over the format standard for VCRs. Of course, Sony eventually lost that war. VHS won out as the standard, and a lot of consumers found themselves owning an increasingly obsolete BetaMax machine as more and more films were issued in VHS format. Then DVDs came along; and now, some 30 years after losing, Sony has found redemption. On Tuesday, February 19, 2008, Toshiba announced that it would cease production and marketing of DVD players using its favored HD DVD format. That ended a multiyear battle between the HD DVD and Blu-ray technologies. Toshiba and HD DVD surrendered. Sony and Blu-ray had won.

Prior to early 2008, however, the outcome of the conflict was anyone's guess. Both Sony's Blu-ray and Toshiba's HD DVD made use of a shorter-wavelength blue-violet laser technology, in contrast to the 650 nm-wavelength red laser technology that had been used in earlier DVD formats. As a result, the modern technologies used a finer beam that made DVDs capable of storing a much greater amount of information. Each side had a lot at stake and had fought hard to make its technology the industry standard. For its part, Sony had built the Blu-ray

technology into its PlayStation 3 game console. In addition, it had directed its film studios (including MGM) to issue high-density DVDs only in Blu Ray format, and persuaded both Fox and Disney to do the same with their films. Toshiba had countered by persuading Microsoft to incorporate its technology into its Xbox line, and also signed up studios including Paramount, Warner, and Dreamworks.

There was nothing retailers and consumers could do but wait uneasily. Storeowners could not be sure which format of film to stock. Customers were reluctant to buy a high-definition disc player, knowing that it might become the next BetaMax machine. Meanwhile, some firms like South Korea's LG Electronics began to market a machine that could play both formats. Unfortunately, the cost of making such a machine was close to the price one would pay to buy two separate machines.

Then came the decisive blow. In January 2008, Warner announced that it was switching from HD DVD to Blu-ray. That move tipped the industry irrevocably in the Blu-ray direction. Soon, others began to back off their HD DVD commitments. Given the network effects, Toshiba saw that the trickle would soon become a flood. It had lost.

Source: M. Fackler. "Toshiba Acknowledges Defeat AS Blu-ray Wins Format Battle." *The New York Times* (20 February 2008), p. C1.

17.4   APPLICATION: NETWORK EXTERNALITIES IN COMPUTER SOFTWARE—SPREADSHEETS

As noted earlier, computer software, operating systems, and web browsers are likely to exhibit important network effects. Users care about being able to run their programs on the computers of their friends or business associates. The more people use a specific software package, or the more compatible a software package is with add-on programs, the more valuable it should be. Gandal (1994) offers empirical evidence of this phenomenon from the early days of desktop computing.

A spreadsheet was initially a pencil-and-paper operation. Essentially, it was large sheet of paper with columns and rows organizing all the relevant data about a firm's transactions. Its name comes from the fact that costs or revenues connected to a specific operation were spread or displayed over the sheet in a manner allowing sums over a given row or column. In that way, management is able to focus on a specific factor—say, energy costs—in making an informed decision about company operations. The advantage of a spreadsheet format is that if a given cost factor or revenue assumption is changed, decision makers can trace through the implications of this change rather quickly. However, there is a natural limit to the speed of such adjustments when spreadsheets are "hard copy" and changes must be made by hand.

Beginning about 1980, electronic spreadsheets suitable for use on desktop computers began to make their commercial appearance. The first of these was VisiCalc (Visible Calculator). Computerization greatly enhanced the speed with which managers could assess the impact of cost or revenue changes. It thereby greatly increased the usefulness of spreadsheets in daily operations. Demand for such products grew, and so did the supply. Soon there were a number of spreadsheet programs including SuperCalc, VP Planner, PlanPerfec; Quatro Pro, Multiplan, Excel, and Lotus 1-2-3.

These early products differed both from each other and over time. The earliest versions had very limited, if any, graphing abilities. Some could link entries in one spreadsheet to others in another spreadsheet. Some could not. Only a few were able to link with external data and incorporate that data into the spreadsheet cells directly. The most flexible of all was the Lotus 1-2-3 program. Throughout the late 1980s and into the 1990s, this was the dominant product. Indeed, an important attribute of other spreadsheet programs was whether or not they were Lotus-compatible.

Gandal (1994) notes that spreadsheet demand will likely exhibit network effects because users like to be able to share their information and the results of their spreadsheet analyses with each other. Gandal then identifies three features of a spreadsheet program that should promote such networking. The first is whether or not the program was compatible with Lotus 1-2-3, the dominant product. This is measured by a variable $LOCOMP$, equal to 1 if the program is Lotus-compatible and 0 if it is not. The second network attribute is $EXTDAT$. This is a variable that takes on the value 1 if the program can import files from external data sources and 0 if it cannot. The final network feature is another $(1, 0)$ variable $LANCOM$ that indicates whether or not the program can link independent users through a local area network.

Gandal (1994) hypothesizes that if network externalities are present in the spreadsheet market, then a program's market price will be higher if it has any of the three features just describe (i.e., when for that product, any of the variables $LOCOMP$, $EXTDAT$, or $LANCOM$ is positive). A function that specifies how product price changes as the product's attributes change is known as a hedonic function. Estimating such functions is usually done by ordinary least squares (OLS) in a hedonic price regression. Gandal gathered data for 91 computerized spreadsheet products over the six years from 1986 to 1991. His basic regression equation is

$$\ln p_{it} = \alpha_0 + \alpha_1 TIME87_t + \alpha_2 TIME88_t + \alpha_3 TIME89_t + \alpha_4 TIME90_t$$
$$+ \alpha_5 TIME91_t + \beta_1 LMINRC_{it} + \beta_2 LOTUS_{it} + \beta_3 GRAPHS_{it}$$
$$+ \beta_4 WINDOW_{it} + \gamma_1 LOCOMP_{it} + \gamma_2 EXTDAT_{it} + \gamma_3 LANCOM_{it} + \varepsilon_{it}$$

The dependent variable is the natural log of the price of spreadsheet model i in year t. Not including the constant, the first five variables are time dummy variables equal to 1 if the year is that indicated by the dummy and zero otherwise. These variables pick up the pure effects of time on spreadsheet program prices while holding the quality attributes fixed. The next four variables pick up specific features that should add to the value of a spreadsheet program. *LMINRC* is the natural log of the minimum of the maximum number of rows or columns that the spreadsheet can handle. This is meant to capture the sheer computing power of the program. *LOTUS* is a (1, 0) dummy variable indicating whether the product is a Lotus spreadsheet. This term captures any brand premium that Lotus enjoyed during these years. *GRAPHS* is a (1, 0) dummy variable indicating whether or not the program can construct pie, bar, and line graphs. *WINDOW* indicates the number of windows a program can handle on a screen simultaneously. Of course, the last three variables are the networking effects described earlier. If there are network externalities, the coefficients on these variables should be significantly positive.

Gandal's (1994) results are presented Table 17.4 (next page). The first regression shown is the estimated hedonic equation described above. Note that all the attributes hypothesized to raise the value of a spreadsheet program do in fact exert a significantly positive effect on its price. There is a strong brand premium for Lotus. There is an almost as strong premium for programs that have graphing abilities. Most important of all however, the three networking variables are very strongly positive. *LOCOMP, EXTDAT*, and *LANCOM* all have a substantial positive effect on a program's price.

Regression 2 shows the effects of allowing the coefficients to change over time. Gandal splits the sample in half and adds, as regressors, values of the independent variables multiplied by 1 if the observation comes in the second half of the sample. Most of these interacted variables are not significant. However, the coefficients on both *MINRC* and *LINKING* do change over time, as indicated by the coefficients on *TMINRC* and *TLINKING*. These coefficients are interpreted as the difference between the marginal value of these features in the first half of the sample and that value in the second half of the sample. Note that this regression includes *TLANCOM* but not *LANCOM*. This is because connecting to local area networks was generally not possible for any program prior to the second half of the sample.

Gandal (1994) prefers Regression 2 as the better specification of the hedonic price equation. Note again that it implies strong network externalities. The coefficients on *LOCOMP, EXTDAT*, and *TLANCOM* are all very significantly positive. Consumers are willing to pay extra—a lot extra—for spreadsheets that others can use either because they are Lotus-compatible, easily able to import data from external programs, or able to exchange information over a local area network. These effects are powerful. Because the dependent variable is the log of the price, the coefficient is easily interpreted as the percentage increase in price a consumer would pay for that feature. Thus, being Lotus-compatible raised the price of a spreadsheet program by 66 percent according to Gandal's estimates. A program's ability to import data from an external source raised the price by 57 percent.

A frequent use of hedonic price regressions is to construct price indexes that trace the movement of a commodity's price over time. This is often difficult to do, because we do not have an easy way to adjust for quality. A television set today may cost much more than a television set from 10 years ago. However, it would be wrong to interpret all of that price increase as inflation, since today's television set has many more features than that of an earlier set such as high definition, DVD compatibility, and a flat screen, to

Table 17.4   Hedonic regression results for spreadsheet programs, 1986–91

Variable	Regression 1		Regression 2	
	Coefficient	t-statistic	Coefficient	t-statistic
CONSTANT	3.76	(12.31)	3.12	(9.50)
TIME87	−0.06	(−0.38)	−0.07	(−0.43)
TIME88	−0.44	(−2.67)	−0.45	(−3.03)
TIME89	−0.70	(−4.20)	0.92	(1.71)
TIME90	−0.79	(−4.90)	0.90	(1.67)
TIME91	−0.85	−5.30	0.85	(1.59)
LMINRC	0.11	(1.59)	0.26	(3.17)
LOTUS	0.56	(4.36)	0.46	(3.62)
GRAPHS	0.46	(3.51)	0.52	(4.18)
WINDOW	0.17	(2.14)	0.14	(1.92)
LINKING	0.21	(1.91)	0.26	(2.00)
LOCOMP	0.72	(5.28)	0.66	(5.17)
EXTDAT	0.55	(4.05)	0.57	(3.93)
LANCOM	0.21	(1.65)		
TLANCOM			0.61	(3.28)
TLMINRC			−0.34	(−3.07)
TLINKING			−0.31	(−1.49)

Source: Gandal (1994)

name just a few. Because the hedonic regression explicitly controls the value of quality features, it permits the easy construction of a quality-corrected price index by focusing on the changes that are due simply to the passage of time (i.e., holding quality constant). In Regression 1, these changes are fully captured by the year-specific dummies. Since the dependent variable is $\ln p_{it}$, the predicted price for a spreadsheet of constant quality in any year is $p_{it} = e^{\alpha_t YEAR_t}$, where the $YEAR_t$ variable is the dummy for that observation and α_t is the coefficient estimated for that dummy. If we normalize so that the price index P_t is 1 in the first year, 1986, then equation 1 says that the price index will be $e^{-0.06}$ in 1987, $e^{-0.44}$ in 1988, and so on. For Regression 2, constructing the quality-adjusted price index is slightly more complicated because the value of the some of the attributes also changes over time; but the basic idea is the same. We present Gandal's estimated spreadsheet price indices for both regressions in Table 17.5 below. It indicates that over the six-year period for which Gandal collected data, the quality-adjusted price of spreadsheet

Table 17.5   Quality-adjusted price indices for spreadsheet programs, 1986-91

	1986	1987	1988	1989	1990	1991
Price Index from Regression 1	1.00	0.94	0.64	0.49	0.45	0.42
Price Index from Regression 2	1.00	0.93	0.64	0.50	0.48	0.46

Source: Gandal (1994)

programs—like the price of much software and hardware in this time period—declined substantially. Here, the decline exceeded 50 percent.

Summary

In this chapter, we have focused on markets that exhibit important "network externalities." In such markets, the value of the good or service to any one consumer increases as the total number of consumers using the product increases. Services with important network effects, such as telecommunications and home electronics, play an increasingly large role in modern economies.

Markets with strong network effects present special issues. Multiple equilibria are common, and some clearly yield better welfare outcomes than others. Yet, there is no guarantee that the market will converge on the best equilibrium. Competition to establish a network service can be unusually fierce, leading to low prices that can be difficult to distinguish from predation. Often, such competition will result in only one firm surviving; so the market's ultimate structure is one of monopoly and therefore susceptible to the attendant problems that monopoly brings. There is also a nontrivial risk that the service will be underdeveloped or not developed at all. Similarly, the course of technical development exhibits a path dependency in which the market may eventually lock into an inferior technology.

There are no easy solutions to the problems raised by network goods. On the one hand, the possibilities for anticompetitive outcomes seem sufficiently clear that such markets necessarily invite examination by the antitrust authorities. However, it must also be acknowledged that it is not easy either to identify anticompetitive actions clearly or to devise workable remedies for the market failures to which network services are prone. Such tensions have dominated the debate over policies regarding the telecommunications industry and other "new economy" markets in the past. They will no doubt continue to be important in the future.

Problems

1. Two banks compete for the checking and savings deposit business of a small town. Each bank has its own ATM network that works only on its own bankcards, but Bank 1 has three times as many ATM machines as Bank 2. Depositors value a bank's services as an increasing function of the number of machines on the network. Bank 2 approaches Bank 1 and suggests that they merge their ATM networks so that all depositors can use either bank's machines.
    a. Is this merger in the interest of deposit consumers in general?
    b. Do you think that Bank 1 will agree with Bank 2's proposal?

2. Assume that consumers contemplating buying a network service have reservation prices uniformly distributed on the interval (0, 50) (measured in dollars). Demand by a consumer with reservation price w_i for this service is

$$q_i^D = \begin{cases} 0 & \text{if } fw_i < p \\ 1 & \text{if } fw_i \geq p \end{cases}$$

    a. Calculate the demand function for this service.
    b. What is the critical mass if price is set at $5?
    c. What is the profit-maximizing price for the service?

3. Many social customs exhibit network effects. To this end, consider a party given by a group of individuals at a small university. The group is called the *Outcasts* and has 20 members. It holds a big party on campus each year. These parties are good, but are especially good the more people are in attendance. As a result, the number of people who actually come to the Outcasts party depends on how many people are expected to attend. The more people that are expected

to attend, the more fun it will be for each attendee; hence, the more people who actually will come. These effects are captured by the equation $A = 20 + 0.95A^e$. Here, A is the number of people actually attending the party. This is equal to the 20 Outcast members plus 0.95 times the number of partygoers A^e that are expected to attend.

a. If potential party attendees are sophisticated and understand the equation describing actual party attendance, how many people are likely to attend the Outcasts party?

b. Suppose that each party attendee costs the Outcasts \$2 in refreshments, so the Outcasts need to charge a fee p for attending the party. Since going to the party requires paying a fee, the equation for attendance is $A = 20 + 0.95A^e - p$. What value of p should the Outcasts set if they want to maximize their profit from the party? How many will come to the party at that price?

4. Two firms play a technology choice game. The payoff matrix for the game between them is given by

		Firm 2	
		Technology 1	Technology 2
Firm 1	Technology 1	a, b	c, d
	Technology 2	e, f	g, h

a. Identify constraints on the payoffs a–h, such that the firms' choices reflect network externalities.

b. Assume that the constraints in (a) are satisfied. Identify further constraints that must be satisfied for the game between the two firms to be of the form
   i.   Tweedledum and Tweedledee.
   ii. The Battle of the Sexes.
   iii. The Pesky Little Brother.

5. Assume that a telecommunications market has three types of consumers, indexed by $i = 1; 2; 3$. There are 300 consumers of each type, or 900 potential subscribers in total. The number of people connecting to the service is q. The utility of each type i of consumer is given by

$U_1 = 2Q - P$ $if\ connected;\ 0\,otherwise$

$U_2 = 3Q - P$ $if\ connected;\ 0\,otherwise$

$U_3 = 4Q - P$ $if\ connected;\ 0\,otherwise$

a. Derive the demand curve for this industry.

b. Assume a monopolist with marginal production cost $c = 0$ operates the telecommunications service.
   i.   At price $P = \$600$, what is the industry critical mass level?
   ii. What is the monopolist's profit-maximizing price for the service?

References

Arthur, W. Brian. 1989. "Competing Technologies, Increasing Returns, and Lock-in by Historical Events". *The Economic Journal,* 99 (March): 116–131.

Besen, S. M., and J. Farrell. 1994. "Choosing How to Compete: Strategies and Tactics in Standardization". *Journal of Economic Perspectives,* 8 (Spring): 117–131.

David, P. A. 1985. "Clio and the Economics of QWERTY." *American Economic Review, Papers and Proceedings,* (May): 332–337.

Economides, N. 1996. "The Economics of Networks." *International Journal of Industrial Organization,* 14 (October): 673–699.

Eisenach, J. A., and T. M. Lenard. 1999. *Competition, Innovation and the Microsoft Monopoly: Antitrust in the Digital Marketplace.* Boston: Kluwer Academic Publishers.

Evans, D., and R. Schmalensee. 2008. "Markets with Two-Sided Platforms." In *Issues in Competition Law and Policy,* Volume 1 (Chapter 28): 667–693. Washington: American Bar Association (Section of Antitrust Law).

Farrell, J., and G. Saloner. 1985. "Standardization, Compatibility and Innovation". *Rand Journal of Economics,* 16 (Spring): 70–83.

Fisher, F. 2000. "The *IBM* and *Microsoft* Cases: What's the Difference?" *American Economic Review,* 90 (May): 180–183.

Gandal, N. 1994. "Hedonic Price Indexes for Spreadsheets and A Test for Network Externalities". *Rand Journal of Economics,* 25 (Spring): 160–170.

Katz, M., and C. Shapiro. 1985. "Network Externalities, Competition, and Compatibility". *American Economics Review,* 75 (June): 424–440.

Liebowitz, S., and S. Margolis. 1990. "The Fable of the Keys". *Journal of Law and Economics,* 33 (April): 1–26.

Pepall, L., and D. Richards. 2001. "Reach for the Stars: A Strategic Upstream-Downstream Game." *Economica,* 68 (November): 489–504.

Rohlfs, J. 1974. "A Theory of Interdependent Demand for a Communications Service". *Bell Journal of Economics,* 5 (Spring): 16–37.

Schmalensee, R. 2000. "Antitrust Issues in Schumpeterian Industries". *American Economic Review, Papers and Proceedings,* 90 (May): 192–196.

18

Strategic Commitments: Confronting Potential Entrants and International Rivalry

The first U.S. Secretary of the Treasury was the brilliant but prideful Alexander Hamilton, whose picture still adorns the U.S. $10 bill. Hamilton came to his position just as the new country was struggling with a pile of debt as the result of its long war for independence and the deficit financing that had thereafter characterized the eight years under the Articles of Confederation. Convinced that the young America had to establish its credibility in international financial markets, Hamilton argued forcefully that America had to raise sufficient taxes to pay off the debt and could not risk default. In Hamilton's view, such sovereign credibility was essential to the establishment of a sound national currency and to a sound domestic financial system in which businesses and households throughout the former colonies could conduct their affairs.

Hamilton also had a clear idea about the sort of taxes that would best serve the United States in pursuing its debt reduction strategy. In his *Report on Manufactures* (1791), he argued strongly for tariffs on manufacturing imports. This would help raise the necessary revenues and, by discouraging imports, encourage the development of U.S. domestic manufacturing, which Hamilton envisioned as central to the country's future economic success. In fact, he also recommended the establishment of a Society for Useful Manufactures to subsidize certain key industries that he saw as critical to that success.

The issues raised by Hamilton's analysis have carried forward to this day. Today we see the countries of the European zone finding themselves struggling to maintain credibility in the face of serious budget deficits and mounting debt among such member countries as Portugal, Ireland, Italy, Greece, and Spain. Likewise, in the wake of the global recession that began in 2007, many countries have grown increasingly critical of China and what they see as that country's currency manipulation and other tactics aimed at limiting imports into the country.

We will explore these topics in this chapter. While the work is closely related to much of what we have done in previous chapters, a general consideration of credibility and of international trade issues does not fit neatly within the models of the preceding chapters. The issues are sufficiently important, however, that we feel their explicit consideration is worthwhile.

18.1   THE STRATEGIC VALUE OF COMMITMENT

In one of the pivotal scenes in the popular 1964 film *Dr. Strangelove: Or How I Learned to Stop Worrying and Love the Bomb*, the top military and political leaders of the United States are gathered in the Pentagon War Room discussing the progress of a renegade jet on a mission to drop an atomic warhead on a Russian target. They are joined by the Russian ambassador and the U.S. director of weapons and research development, the brilliant but twisted Dr. Strangelove. It is the peak of the Cold War era and tensions are running high, since if the jet does drop its bomb, it could trigger a nuclear war. All assembled are at first hopeful that the American plane can be called back or, at worst, shot down. As the jet steadily evades Russian defenses, however, and moves ever closer to its target, talk begins to turn to the implications of a nuclear event.

Even this seems surmountable until the horror-stricken Russian ambassador reveals that his country has built a Doomsday Machine. When asked to explain, the ambassador informs the others that a Russian computer is programmed to respond to any nuclear strike by launching over 50 hydrogen bombs around the world. The bombs are coated with a substance called Cobalt Thorium G, which will result in a lethal radioactive cloud over the entire earth that will leave the planet's surface "as dead as the moon" for nearly a hundred years. The ambassador goes on to explain that the response of the Doomsday Machine is automatic and that it cannot be undone by any human command.

Amazed, the American President turns to his weapons director and asks, "But, how is it possible for this thing to be triggered automatically, and at the same time impossible to untrigger?" To which Strangelove then replies, "Mr. President, it is not only possible, it is essential. That is the whole idea of this machine, you know. Deterrence is the art of producing in the mind of the enemy... the fear to attack. And so, because of the automated and irrevocable decision-making process which rules out human meddling, the Doomsday Machine is terrifying. It's simple to understand. And completely credible, and convincing." Then Strangelove turns to the Russian ambassador, "But the whole point of the doomsday machine... is lost... if you keep it a secret! Why didn't you tell the world, eh?" To which the ambassador replies, "It was to be announced at the Party Congress on Monday. As you know, the Premier loves surprises."

Beneath the dark comedy of the film lie a number of important truths about strategic interaction. The ability of the Doomsday Machine to commit the former Soviet Union irrevocably to a specific action has value. If known and understood, it will prevent enemies from even contemplating a surprise attack. Indeed, it will lead countries like the United States to take extra precautions to prevent precisely the sort of accidental strike that lies at the heart of the film's plot.

Yet, as the movie also makes clear, the qualifiers "known and understood" are critical. To have strategic value, a commitment must be announced and understood; otherwise it serves no purpose. The announcement must make the nature of the commitment clear. It must also demonstrate that the commitment is irreversible and real. After all, anyone can claim to have built a Doomsday Machine. In fact, one character in the film, a U.S. general, felt the ambassador's statement to be "an obvious commie trick." Had there been more time, pursuing this discussion would have led to some interesting questions. How does one demonstrate the existence of a Doomsday Machine without triggering it? After all, the point of the machine is to deter attacks *without* being triggered. More generally, a central issue is how to make the announcement of a commitment credible. Talk is cheap; and unless credibility can be achieved, any announced commitment will have little effect.

Finally, note that while commitment has value, flexibility can also be important. It is often useful to avoid committing to a specific action and instead leave open the possibility of various actions as circumstances warrant.

18.2   STRATEGIC COMPLEMENTS AND SUBSTITUTES: CATS, DOGS, AND THE LEAN AND HUNGRY LOOK

As the Strangelove scene illustrates, commitment is particularly important in games where one player wishes to deter a possible action by a rival. A natural business analogy is a firm that wishes to deter a rival's entry. Considering deterrent strategies requires a two-stage game framework. The deterrent must be established and announced *before* the rival has a chance to make its decision if it is to influence that decision. So, in what follows, we assume a two-stage game. The second stage is where the rival makes its choice about entering the market and competing with the incumbent. Prior to that, however, the incumbent firm considers investments or other commitments in the first stage that will alter the second-stage game in its favor.

We have considered such two-stage games in the context of entry deterrence already—recall, for example, Dixit's (1980) model of entry deterrence in Chapter 9. A central point of the discussion here is that such commitment comes in different forms. In principle, a player could commit to peaceful coexistence rather than to mutually assured destruction or to aggressive action as in the Dixit case. In order to understand the possible nature of strategic commitment in a business setting, it is helpful to recall the distinction between strategic substitutes and strategic complements discussed in Chapters 7.

Suppose for example that two firms are engaged in Bertrand price competition and that demand for Firm i is

$$q_i = A - p_i + bp_j; \quad i, j = 1, 2 \text{ and } i \neq j; 0 < b < 1 \tag{18.1}$$

If each firm has a constant marginal cost of c, then the best-response function for Firm i is

$$p_i = \frac{A + c}{2} + \frac{bp_j}{2}; \quad i, j = 1, 2 \text{ and } i \neq j \tag{18.2}$$

In contrast, suppose that the two firms are engaged in Cournot quantity competition again with constant marginal cost c, and inverse demand is given by $P = A - Q$. In that case, the best response of Firm i to Firm j's output is

$$q_i = \frac{A - c}{2} - \frac{q_j}{2}; \quad i, j = 1, 2 \text{ and } i \neq j \tag{18.3}$$

In the first case, Firm i's price is positively related to Firm j's price; whereas in the second case, Firm i's output is negatively related to Firm j's output. As described in Chapter 7, a positive link between strategic choices implies a setting of strategic complements while a negative relation implied the case of strategic substitutes.

The framework of strategic substitutes and complements allows us to conceptualize two different types of commitments. Commitments are "tough" when they generally make matters less pleasant for one's rivals than they would have been. Conversely, commitments are "soft" when they make the outcomes for one's rivals better than they would have been absent the commitment. In the case of strategic substitutes, such as production levels in a Cournot quantity game, a firm may wish to commit to the tough or aggressive choice of high output. If successful, this forces the rival to choose a reduced production volume. In contrast, a commitment to a higher price softens competition in a Bertrand setting of strategic complements. Because prices are strategic substitutes, this commitment encourages the rival to set a higher price as well.

18.2.1   Strategic Complements and Competition: Fat Cats and Puppy Dogs

Consider again the Bertrand example in equation (18.2) and set the cost parameter $c = 0$. The Nash equilibrium for this game is easily found to be

$$p_i = \frac{A}{2 - b}; \quad i = 1, 2 \tag{18.4}$$

In this equilibrium, each firm earns profit of

$$\pi_i = \left(\frac{A}{2 - b}\right)^2; \quad i = 1, 2 \tag{18.5}$$

The game is illustrated in Figure 18.1. Both Firm 1's best-response function R_1 and Firm 2's best-response function R_2 are upward sloping, that is, prices are strategic complements. The intersection of the two best-response functions is, of course, the Nash equilibrium for this game.

Suppose the foregoing equilibrium characterizes the market outcome in the second of our two stages. In the first stage, however, the incumbent (Firm 1) is alone in the market, but aware of the potential threat of entry from Firm 2. In the event of entry, Firm 1 could of course contemplate a price war and selling below cost, but that would be expensive. Suppose, though, that that Firm 1 has an option to spend a fixed amount

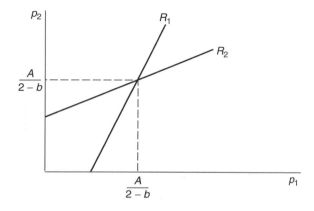

Figure 18.1   The price competition game

F on a promotional campaign and, as a result, shift its demand to

$$q_1 = A' - p_1 + bp_2 \qquad\qquad (18.6)$$

where $A' > A$. As a result, when Firm 1 competes with Firm 2, its best-response function becomes

$$p_1 = \frac{A'}{2} + \frac{bp_2}{2} \qquad\qquad (18.7)$$

Firm 1's equilibrium price and profit have now become

$$p_1 = \left(\frac{2A' + bA}{4 - b^2}\right) \qquad\qquad (18.8)$$

$$\pi_1 = \left(\frac{2A' + bA}{4 - b^2}\right)^2 \qquad\qquad (18.9)$$

It is easy to confirm that the price and profit in equations (18.8) and (18.9) exceed those in equations (18.4) and (18.5). If the profit increase exceeds F, then the expenditure is worthwhile.

The new game is illustrated in Figure 18.2. Because $A' > A$, Firm 1's best response function has shifted to the right, from R_1 to R_1'. As a result, in the second stage, it now sets a higher price for every price choice of Firm 2 than it did previously. That is, it prices less aggressively now, which is what we mean by saying that competition has been softened. In turn, because prices are strategic complements, this moves us along the upward-sloping best-response function of Firm 2 inducing that firm to set a higher price as well.

In this scenario, Firm 1 has responded to the threat of competition by accommodating it and taking action to soften competition in the postentry market. We can think of many types of investment that might have this effect. For example, suppose that Firm 1 is an incumbent hotel operator on a resort island and that Firm 2 is a potential entrant. Firm 1 might invest in luxury improvements and aim at the high end of the market to permit Firm 2 to enter as a discount motel. That is, Firm 1's investment serves to differentiate

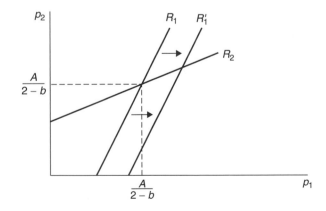

Figure 18.2   The "fat cat" strategy

Firm 1 may overinvest to shift its best-response function rightward to R_1' and soften competition.

the two products further. Fudenberg and Tirole (1984) call this the "fat cat" strategy—the analogy being that Firm 1 has invested in differentiating its product so as to commit to being a peace-loving "fat cat" rather than become entangled in fierce competition.

An alternative to the fat cat strategy is the "puppy dog" ploy. To understand this strategy, let us relax our assumption that $c = 0$, and assume instead that Firm 1's unit cost is $c > 0$, initially. Hence, its best-response function is

$$p_1 = \frac{A + c}{2} + \frac{b p_2}{2} \tag{18.10}$$

Note that this best-response function lies further to the right than the original best-response function of equation (18.2), since $c > 0$. Now, suppose that the firm can make a first-stage investment or contract that will in fact lower the unit cost to $c = 0$. For example, it could enter into a take-or-pay contract with its suppliers in which it invests in a large order of inputs for which it has to pay in any case. Clearly, this will result in shifting the best-response function leftward, as in Figure 18.3, from R_1 to R_1'. Thus, if it makes this investment, Firm 1 will commit to charging a lower price in response to any price set by Firm 2 than it would have previously. This investment would toughen price competition.

Note that when the investment in cost-reduction leads Firm 1 to price more aggressively, it moves the equilibrium down along the best-response function of Firm 2, inducing that firm to set a lower price as well. Hence, committing to the investment not only lowers Firm 1's best-response function directly, but also leads to a lower price via the indirect effect that induced by Firm 2. The cost-saving arrangement may actually result in lower prices and profit for both firms in stage 2.

On the other hand, Firm 1 may want to signal that it will *not* pursue the lower-cost technology or contract. This helps it avoid the commitment to price aggressively in stage 2. This would involve a decision not to adopt the process that shifts its response function leftward to R_1'. That is why we have drawn the latter as a dashed line. Fudenberg and Tirole (1984) call this underinvestment in cost-saving arrangements the puppy dog ploy because, effectively, Firm 1 is trying to signal to Firm 2 that it is a mild-mannered puppy dog, happy to take the profit that is left over when it has a high cost rather than compete by lowering its cost and cutting its price aggressively.

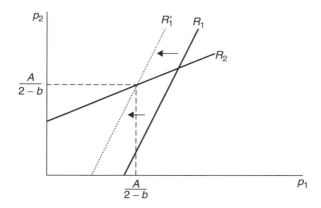

Figure 18.3   The "puppy dog" ploy
Firm 1 may underinvest and therefore not shift its best-response function inward to R_1' where it would be committed to fierce price competition.

To summarize briefly, when strategic choices are complements, firms may seek to soften price competition either by pursuing a fat cat strategy via overinvestment or a puppy dog ploy via underinvestment. Two insights follow immediately. First, the optimal response to potential entry need not be a large investment that commits the incumbent to an aggressive and costly war. Instead, a firm may decide it is better to accommodate entry. This may still require a large investment to be credible. Thus, a firm may invest heavily in advertising or other product-differentiating projects to further distance its product from the entrant's good and thereby soften price competition. This is the essence of the fat cat strategy.

Second, entry accommodation may not lead to overinvestment. In this case, the incumbent may find it profitable not to pursue a cost-reducing program that would, if followed, again intensify the second-stage competition. This is the essence of the puppy dog scenario. By underinvesting in programs that would shift its response function inward, the incumbent firm now avoids the commitment that goes with that shift to price aggressively afterwards.

18.2.2   Strategic Substitutes and Competition: Top Dogs and the Lean and Hungry Look

Consider the entry deterrence game in the case of strategic substitutes as in the Cournot model when the best-response function is equation (18.3). We know that with $c > 0$, the quantity equilibrium for this model is

$$q_1 = q_2 = \frac{A - c}{3} \qquad\qquad (18.11)$$

with the result that each firm earns the following profit:

$$\pi_i = \frac{(A - c)^2}{9} \qquad\qquad (18.12)$$

This equilibrium is shown in Figure 18.4. The equilibrium output for each firm $q_i = \frac{A-c}{3}$ is found at the intersection of the two best-response functions R_1 and R_2.

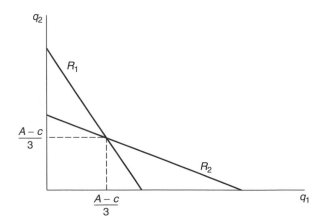

Figure 18.4   The quantity production game

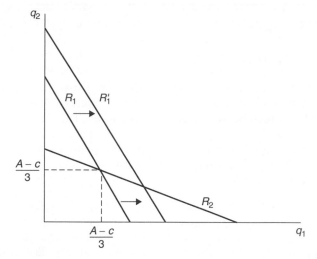

Figure 18.5   The Top Dog strategy
Firm 1 makes investments that lower its marginal cost and shift its best-response function outward, thereby reducing Firm 2's equilibrium output.

Now consider Firm 1's options in the first stage before the rival enters and the second-stage competition just described begins. Suppose once again that Firm 1 has a potential investment expense or contractual arrangement that, if made, will result in a lower unit cost of $c = 0$. Firm 1's best-response function in the second stage becomes

$$q_1 = \frac{A}{2} - \frac{q_2}{2} \tag{18.13}$$

Clearly, the best response function of equation (18.13) is further right than that of equation (18.3) as Figure 18.5 (above) illustrates. That is, the first-stage investment in cost reduction by Firm 1 now results in its producing more vigorously in stage 2. For any given level of production by Firm 2, Firm 1 now produces more than it previously did. In this case, Firm 1's choice has led to tougher competition with Firm 2. Firm 1 has adopted what Fudenberg and Tirole (1984) call the *Top Dog strategy* that enables it to take a dominant industry position. The outcome is that Firm 2 now produces a lower output level in stage 2 than it did when no investment to lower unit cost was available to Firm 1.[1]

This, of course, is exactly the situation analyzed in Dixit's (1980) model of entry deterrence discussed in Chapter 9. It is a classic case of overinvestment to establish a commitment to a large output and thereby make life difficult for the rival entrant. We saw in Chapter 9 that if the entrant needs a minimum scale of operations to break even, then the Top Dog strategy may prevent entry altogether.

Now, suppose that Firm 1 already has low unit cost and therefore its best-response function is equation (18.13). However, it has the opportunity also to enter into a second product market. On its own, that market is profitable; but there are *dis*economies of scope between the two goods. While the second market may be lucrative on its own, pursuing that strategy will raise the marginal cost in the current market and thereby shift Firm 1's

[1]   Cost reductions that shift the response function inward in a strategic complements case may also be a Top Dog choice.

Reality Checkpoint
Pump and Circumstance

A well-known story of strategic commitment is the Minnetonka Corporation's introduction of Softsoap in 1980. At the time, most households used the familiar bar soap. This was a perfectly serviceable product, but it did have the disadvantage of leaving an annoying pool of soapy water wherever it rested. In 1977, Minnetonka began marketing the Incredible Soap Machine, a liquid soap dispensed by a pump from ceramic containers and sold in a limited volume primarily by boutique retailers. That success, however, led Minnetonka's CEO to envision a much bigger future. The product was redesigned and renamed for the mass market. In 1980, accompanied by an expensive $7 million advertising campaign, Softsoap was launched and reached nearly $40 million in sales in the first year. The market for liquid soap was established, and analysts predicted that the market would quickly grow over the next several years. Now, however, that market and Minnetonka's product were on the radar screen of the major bar soap manufacturers, such as Procter & Gamble and Colgate-Palmolive. Minnetonka had to worry that they would soon follow as "fast seconds" and dominate the market that Softsoap had opened. Two factors helped Minnetonka prevail. First, prior to the launch of Softsoap, Taylor made a strategic commitment. Realizing that there were only two firms making the pumps required to dispense liquid soap, Minnetonka placed orders with both firms for 100 million pumps—the entire capacity of both pumpmakers for at least 18 months. Although very expensive, this made it impossible for rivals to duplicate Softsoap, even though it did not have (and could not get) a patent for nearly two years. During that time, Minnetonka was able both to establish its brand name and move down the learning curve to lower its production cost. Some special circumstances were the second factor that worked in Minnetonka's favor, including the fact that the major firms were reluctant to enter the market with their well-known brand names (such as P&G's *Ivory Soap*), partly for fear of the replacement effect (stealing business from their existing products) and partly out of concern that failure in the liquid soap market would taint the reputation of the established good. The result was that Softsoap was still the industry leader of a now much-enlarged liquid soap market in 1985 when the product line was bought by Colgate-Palmolive for $61 million. Four years later, after launching a successful pumped toothpaste product as well as the Calvin Klein fragrances *Obsession* and *Eternity*, Minnetonka itself was bought by Unilever for $376 million.

Sources: P. Dougherty. "Advertising: $6 Million to Back Minnetonka's Softsoap." *The New York Times* (5 February 1980), p. C9; M. Fedo. "Cleaning Up with Softsoap." *The New York Times* (29 June 1980), p. C2; and M. Freitag. "Unilever Unit to Acquire Minnetonka." *The New York Times* (3 July 1989), p. 125 (New York City edition).

marginal cost, as shown in Figure 18.6 (next page). In this case, Firm 1 may want to decline investing in production facilities for the second market. This allows it to maintain a tough competitive posture in the stage 2 game—or to keep what Fudenberg and Tirole (1984) refer to as a *Lean and Hungry look*.

18.2.3   Commitments and Strategies

This taxonomy of strategic commitment carries a number of insights. First, commitments typically require an investment or expense to be credible (i.e., to be subgame perfect). One way to pursue the Top Dog strategy, for instance, is to invest in capacity or otherwise

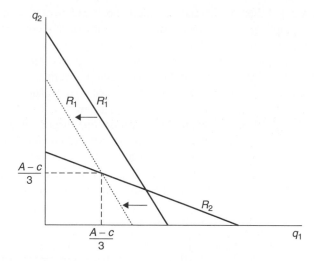

Figure 18.6   The Lean and Hungry Look strategy
Firm 1 avoids investments or contractual arrangements that raise its marginal cost so that its best-response function does not shift inward.

transform variable costs into fixed costs that must be paid regardless of sales volume. Absent such a commitment, the threat to produce aggressively in stage 2 would not be credible. It will therefore not have any entry-deterring effect.

Second, in determining whether or not to make such investments, firms need to understand the effect such investments will have on the stage 2 competition. Understanding whether the market competition is best described as strategic complements or strategic substitutes leads to further insight. Depending on the situation, a firm may wish to avoid making investments that commit it to a specific course of action. ADM's decision in the early 1990s to build a special lysine plant equal in size to half of the world's then-available lysine capacity committed it to an aggressive output level that led to a price war in the lysine market. Once that plant was in operation, ADM had few options but to produce at a level that pushed lysine prices down for all firms in the industry. The only possible release from this inexorable pressure to compete was to collude. Of course, ADM eventually did this—along with a number of other lysine producers—until the cartel was caught.[2]

18.3   STRATEGIC COMMITMENTS IN INTERNATIONAL MARKETS

We mentioned Alexander Hamilton at the start of this chapter. Hamilton's insistence on the importance of commitment in domestic fiscal policy places him in good company with contemporary economists. As it turns out, this is not the only economics topic in which Hamilton was prescient. Hamilton was among those who strongly advocated for a more strategic approach to trade policy, specifically arguing for tariffs and government intervention designed to aid particular firms and sectors of the domestic economy. While

---

[2]   See Connor (2001).

most economists since Adam Smith have lauded the benefits of free trade, some have questioned this presumption. Some models of trade policy now recognize the potential to use trade policy strategically just as Hamilton envisioned.

We begin with a simple numerical illustration. Assume that Boeing and Airbus are the only two international producers of large passenger aircraft. Assume that each is considering a major investment in the development of a new superjumbo jet capable of carrying over 500 passengers. Both recognize that the size of the jet may make it economical; but it also limits its market to routes connecting airports that have the demand for—and the facilities needed to—handle such a large passenger load. As a result, there is really only room for one firm to develop the aircraft successfully. If a firm sinks the development costs and is not the firm to survive, it will suffer a major loss. This is illustrated in Table 18.1 below, in which all payoffs are in millions of Euros.

Table 18.1   The strategic R&D game without subsidies

		Boeing	
		Don't Develop	Develop
Airbus	Don't Develop	0, 0	0, €6000
	Develop	€6000, 0	−€3000, −€3000

As can be seen, this simple game has two Nash equilibria. In one of these, Airbus develops the new superjumbo jet. In the other, Boeing does. Absent some explicit coordination or other device, there is no way to determine which of these two equilibria will prevail. Moreover, when the uncertainties of the passenger air travel market and fuel prices are included, it may turn out in actuality that neither firm develops the new plane.

Suppose, however, that the European Union makes a commitment to finance Airbus's R&D to the extent of €3.5 billion. With this change, the payoff matrix becomes that of Table 18.2.

Now Airbus has a dominant strategy, namely, to develop the new aircraft. The Nash equilibrium therefore becomes one in which Airbus develops the plane and Boeing stays out of the race. As a result, Airbus earns a surplus of €9,500 million. Assuming these funds accrue to Europeans, the Union as a whole has gained from its commitment to Airbus. The subsidy of €3,500 million has been worthwhile.[3]

Table 18.2   The strategic R&D game with a subsidy for Airbus

		Boeing	
		Don't Develop	Develop
Airbus	Don't Develop	0, 0	0, €6000
	Develop	€9500, 0	€500, −€3000

---

[3]   As it turns out, Airbus is the one that went ahead with the superjumbo project. The Airbus A380 made its first commercial flight as a Singapore Airlines plane in October 2007. However, production problems have slowed delivery and reduced demand for the plane. As of this writing, only about 25 A380s are in service. Whether Airbus won the race because of government subsidies and whether that race was worth winning are both points of debate among industry analysts. See N. Clark and C. Drew, "W.T.O. Says Aid to Airbus for A380 Was Illegal." *The New York Times* (4 September 2009), p. C1.

18.3.1 Strategic Subsidies in an International Cournot Model

To investigate the role of R&D subsidies more formally, suppose that there are two countries, A and B, in each of which there is a domestic monopoly firm, a and b, respectively. However, while Firms a and b do not compete with each other in their home markets, they do compete in other markets which we shall simply designate as the international market. Demand in this market is given by: $P = A - Q$, and each firm has a constant marginal cost $c > 0$. Hence, the equilibrium quantity and profit of each firm are $q_1 = q_2 = (A - c)/3$ and $\pi_a = \pi_b = (A - c)^2/9$, as given by equations (18.11) and (18.12) above.

Now, imagine that Firm a persuades its government to subsidize its costs to the extent of s per unit. As a result, Firm a now faces a reduced constant marginal cost of $c - s$. Its profit function will therefore be

$$\pi_a = (A - q_a - q_b - c + s)q_a \tag{18.14}$$

Maximizing this then yields Firm a's best-response function:

$$q_a = \frac{(A - c + s)}{2} - \frac{q_b}{2} \tag{18.15}$$

Combining this with Firm b's best-response function as given by equation (18.3), we have the new equilibrium outputs in the international market:

$$q_a = \frac{(A - c + 2s)}{3}; q_b = \frac{(A - c - s)}{3}; Q = \frac{2(A - c) + s}{3} \tag{18.16}$$

In turn, this implies that Firm a carns profit of

$$\pi_a = \frac{(A - c + 2s)^2}{9} \tag{18.17}$$

In the absence of any subsidy, $s = 0$, and Firm a earns profit $\pi_a = \frac{(A-c)^2}{9}$. Therefore, we can determine that the profit increase $\Delta\pi$ for Firm a that the subsidy generates is

$$\Delta\pi = \frac{(A - c + 2s)^2}{9} - \frac{(A - c)^2}{9} = \frac{4(A - c)s + 4s^2}{9} \tag{18.18}$$

The total cost $TC(s)$ of the subsidy is s times the number of units Firm a produces. Hence:

$$TC(s) = s\frac{(A - c + 2s)}{3} = \frac{3(A - c)s + 6s^2}{9} \tag{18.19}$$

Hence, the net benefit of the subsidy $NB(s)$ is

$$NB(s) = \Delta\pi - TC(s) = \frac{(A - c)s - 2s^2}{9} \tag{18.20}$$

Maximizing this with respect to s yields the optimum per-unit subsidy s^*:

$$s^* = \frac{A - c}{4} \tag{18.21}$$

Two key results may now be derived. First, substitution of the optimal subsidy value s^* from equation (18.21) into the net benefit $NB(s)$ function of equation (18.20) quickly reveals that, when done optimally, the net benefit is positive and equal to

$$NB(s^*) = \frac{(A - c)^2}{72} \tag{18.22}$$

Second, substitution of the optimal subsidy s^* into equation (18.16) shows that Firm a's output, when subsidized optimally $q_a(s^*)$, is

$$q_a(s^*) = \frac{A - c}{2} \tag{18.23}$$

This last expression should look familiar to you. It is the output that would be chosen by a monopolist. It is also the output that would be chosen by a Stackelberg leader (see Chapter 8) when both firms have identical unit costs. In Chapter 8, we emphasized how achieving the Stackelberg leader first-mover advantage required some sort of explicit commitment to that higher output level. The subsidy from Country A's government in effect serves as that commitment. Given that subsidy, Firm a can now credibly commit to the production level of a Stackelberg leader, and Country A enjoys net gains as a result.

18.3.2   Strategic Tariffs and Scale/Scope Economies

The foregoing analysis of a strategic subsidy captures much in the spirit of Alexander Hamilton's goal of assisting the domestic industry. However, because he was interested in raising tax revenue and paying off the debt, Hamilton focused more on protective tariffs to encourage the expansion of domestic manufacturing. As it turns out, the use of tariffs as the strategic weapon actually adds a further dimension to the analysis that is worth exploring.

We again assume a Cournot model with two firms, Firm a and Firm b (from Country A and Country B, respectively), and assume that each country is a separate market, perhaps because the goods produced for A and B are not identical. That is, the firms are competing for the Country A widget market, in which demand is described by $Q = A - P$, and the Country B gadget market, in which demand is again described by $Q = A - P$. We also assume that each firm currently has a constant unit cost equal to $c - s$ for producing either good.

From our earlier work, it is easy to work out the equilibrium in each case. Within each country, Firms a and b produce and earn profit as shown in Table 18.3 (next page).

Firm a sells $(A - c + s)/3$ in Country A and also sells $(A - c + s)/3$ in Country B. The same is true for Firm b. Now, suppose that Country A puts a tariff that is equal to s per unit on imports. Effectively, this translates into a cost increase of s for Firm b on all units sold in Country A. In other words, Firm b now has a cost of c per unit within Country A. From the previous section, we know that this results in a reduction in Firm b's output and profit in Country A, and a corresponding rise in these values for Firm a.

Table 18.3   Production and profit in the two-country Cournot game

	Country A		Country B	
	Production	Profit	Production	Profit
Firm a	$\dfrac{(A-c+s)}{3}$	$\dfrac{(A-c+s)^2}{9}$	$\dfrac{(A-c+s)}{3}$	$\dfrac{(A-c+s)^2}{9}$
Firm b	$\dfrac{(A-c+s)}{3}$	$\dfrac{(A-c+s)^2}{9}$	$\dfrac{(A-c+s)}{3}$	$\dfrac{(A-c+s)^2}{9}$

If this were the end of the story, the new output and profit configuration would be as described in Table 18.4 below.

The outcome described in the table above implies that the tariff does not have any impact on the rivalry between the two firms in Country B. In that country, the two firms produce and earn profit just as before. The tariff so far affects only the market outcomes in Country A.

As Krugman (1986) shows, however, the foregoing results change if there are scale or scope economies. The reduction in Firm b's output in Country A is also a reduction in its total output globally. If there are scale or scope effects such that a firm's unit cost rises as its output across the two markets declines, the production decline for Firm b will mean that its unit cost is no longer $c - s$, but something higher. Likewise, the expansion in Firm a's output may allow it to achieve even lower costs.

To work out the complete equilibrium would require that we fully specify the nature of the scale or scope effects and determine the Cournot equilibrium as those effects grow or diminish. Instead, we adopt a convenient shortcut here and simply assume that scale effects are exhausted for Firm a so that its unit cost remains $c - s$, but that as the result of its output reduction Firm b does experience a cost rise to c per unit. The consequent output and profit levels are shown in Table 18.5 (next page).

A comparison of Tables 18.5 and 18.3 shows that Firm a's total profit has increased by $6s(A-c)+11s^2$, while total output in Country A has fallen by $2s/3$. Given that aggregate demand in Country A is $Q = A - P$, this means that $2s/3$ measures the rise in price in Country A. Hence, Country A suffers a welfare loss of $2s^2/9$. However, Firm a now earns $(2s(A-c)+3s^2)/9$ more in profit in Country B than it did previously. This is more than enough to compensate for the domestic welfare loss. Moreover, there is the additional profit Firm a now earns in its home country that previously went to Firm b. The tariff does more than protect domestic production. It acts as a commitment that Firm

Table 18.4   Production and profit in the two-country Cournot game with a tariff on Firm b in Country A

	Country A		Country B	
	Production	Profit	Production	Profit
Firm a	$\dfrac{(A-c+2s)}{3}$	$\dfrac{(A-c+2s)^2}{9}$	$\dfrac{(A-c+s)}{3}$	$\dfrac{(A-c+s)^2}{9}$
Firm b	$\dfrac{(A-c-s)}{3}$	$\dfrac{(A-c-s)^2}{9}$	$\dfrac{(A-c+s)}{3}$	$\dfrac{(A-c+s)^2}{9}$

Table 18.5 Production and profit in the two-country Cournot game with a tariff on Firm b in Country A and scale economies

	Country A		Country B	
	Production	*Profit*	*Production*	*Profit*
Firm a	$\dfrac{(A - c + 3s)}{3}$	$\dfrac{(A - c + 3s)^2}{9}$	$\dfrac{(A - c + 2s)}{3}$	$\dfrac{(A - c + 2s)^2}{9}$
Firm b	$\dfrac{(A - c - 3s)}{3}$	$\dfrac{(A - c - 3s)^2}{9}$	$\dfrac{(A - c - s)}{3}$	$\dfrac{(A - c - s)^2}{9}$

a will be advantaged in Country A and therefore larger globally than its rival Firm b. It is therefore a commitment to insure that Firm a will have a lower unit cost than Firm b. This leads Firm b to lose additional market share and profit to Firm a in *both* Countries A and B.

18.3.3   Strategic R&D Subsidies

One problem with either the direct subsidy or the tariff policy just described is that they typically violate the international trade laws negotiated by the World Trade Organization (WTO) to promote free, unfettered trading arrangements. As a result, they are likely to lead to punishments and trade sanctions that will undermine their net benefits. We return to consider the WTO and trading policies later. At this point, we wish to explore an alternative and slightly less direct route to assist the domestic firm, namely, to subsidize its R&D.

There are many ways to subsidize R&D. Large grants to universities and hospitals, the provision of information to farmers about crop rotation and other techniques, and the award of production grants that permit firms to work their way down the learning curve may all be viewed as government support for the creation and dissemination of technical information. While each of these may be justified for other reasons, there can be little doubt that each may also provide advantages to domestic firms. American pharmaceutical and bioengineering firms likely benefited from the research support provided to university medical schools and faculty. American farmers clearly benefited from the Agriculture Department's Extension Service, and Boeing's strong position in aircraft may well reflect the head start it received from developing aircraft for the U.S. military. The same assertions could be made regarding firms in most other countries as well. In general, R&D subsidization of some sort is common. Indeed, this is what makes R&D subsidization so difficult to monitor as an unfair method of trade competition. It is difficult to distinguish policies meant purely to give a domestic firm an advantage over foreign rivals from policies to promote economic growth. Yet as we will see, R&D subsidization can be very similar to the direct subsidization of production itself.

We begin again with the Cournot duopoly model used above in which there is now just one international market with inverse demand $P = A - Q$. The output and profit of Firm a and Firm b are

$$q_a = \frac{(A - 2c_a + c_b)}{3}; \quad q_b = \frac{(A + c_a - 2c_b)}{3} \tag{18.24}$$

$$\pi_a = \frac{(A - 2c_a + c_b)^2}{9}; \quad \pi_b = \frac{(A + c_a - 2c_b)^2}{9} \tag{18.25}$$

Recall the Dasgupta-Stiglitz (1980) model of costly R&D. Each firm's unit cost c is a function of its R&D spending x, that is, $c = c(x)$. We assume that $c'(x) < 0$ and $c''(x) > 0$. Suppose that Firm a's government pays for $1 - f$ of Firm a's research expenditure x_a where $0 < f < 1$. That is, Firm a pays only a fraction f of its total research cost. Then we may rewrite equations (18.24) and (18.25) to reflect this subsidy as follows:

$$q_a = \frac{[A - 2c(x_a) + c(x_b)]}{3}; q_b = \frac{[A + c(x_a) - 2c(x_b)]}{3} \qquad (18.26)$$

$$\pi_a = \frac{[A - 2c(x_a) + c(x_b)]^2}{9} - fx_a; \pi_b = \frac{[A + c(x_a) - 2c(x_b)]^2}{9} - x_b \qquad (18.27)$$

These equations make clear that because each firm's unit cost depends on its R&D spending; ultimately, so does each firm's output and profit. The output game is really a game in R&D spending. Now, consider Firm a's profit-maximizing choice. Differentiating equation (18.27) with respect to x_a yields the first-order condition

$$[A - 2c(x_a) + c(x_b)]c'(x_a) = -\frac{9f}{4} \qquad (18.28)$$

Implicitly, equation (18.27) defines the best-response function for Firm a. We can derive the slope of this function dx_a/dx_b by totaling differentiating (18.28) to obtain

$$\frac{dx_a}{dx_b} = \frac{-c'(x_a)c'(x_b)}{[A - 2c(x_a) + c(x_b)]c''(x_a) - 2[c'(x_a)]^2} \qquad (18.29)$$

The numerator of equation (18.29) is definitely negative. The denominator will be positive so long as $c''(x_a)$ is relatively large, that is, if the marginal cost-reducing effect of R&D declines relatively rapidly. We make this assumption here. As a result, the best-response function for Firm a (and of course for Firm b as well) slope downward. In other words, the firms' R&D spending choices are strategic substitutes.

We already knew, of course, that for the given levels of x_a and x_b, firm outputs were strategic substitutes. As Firm a expands its output, Firm b's output shrinks. However, the position of these output best-response functions depends on the unit cost of each firm and therefore on its R&D spending. Consequently, the fact that R&D levels are also strategic substitutes once again opens up a possibility for government intervention to have a double-barreled impact. This is illustrated in Figures 18.7(a) and 18.7(b) on the next page. By subsidizing Firm a's R&D expenditure, Country A shifts out Firm a's best-response function in R&D and commits the firm to a level of R&D that it could not credibly threaten on its own. Since R&D levels are strategic substitutes, this leads Firm b to spend less. Both of these results have implications in the output market. The increase in x_a lowers c_a and therefore shifts the output best response of Firm a outwards. Simultaneously, the decrease in x_b raises c_b and shifts that firm's best output response inward. As Spencer and Brander (1983) show, the optimal R&D subsidy is always positive.

18.4   TRADE AGREEMENTS AS COMMITMENT DEVICES

We have now worked through three separate cases in which a country may enjoy net gains by intervening in international markets so as to advantage the domestic firm relative to foreign rivals. A natural question that arises in this context is why Country B should not

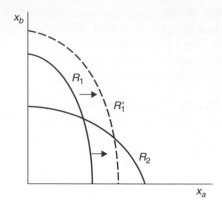

Figure 18.7(a)   Competition in R&D spending levels
By subsidizing Firm a's R&D spending, Country A shifts its response function out leading to more R&D by Firm a and less by Firm b in the new equilibrium.

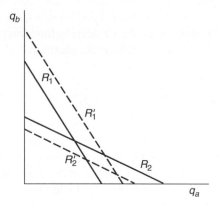

Figure 18.7(b)   Competition in output levels
Greater R&D spending by Firm a and less by Firm b implies a lower unit cost for Firm a and a higher one for Firm b. In output space, Firm a's response function shifts out and Firm b's response function shifts in.

react to Country A's intervention by doing the same thing. What happens if both impose tariffs or subsidized domestic firms?

Essentially, these questions point to a deeper-level game than the ones we have so far considered. This is the game between the governments of each country in which the variable of strategic choice is either a tariff or a subsidy of the cost of production (or of R&D). In general, the Nash equilibrium of this game has a prisoners' dilemma, in which both countries subsidize or impose tariffs to a greater extent than they would if they played cooperatively. Absent any formal agreement mechanism, however, cooperative play is not feasible.

This is where international trade agreements and organizations such as the WTO have become important. By joining such institutions, the member countries pledge themselves not to give in to the short-run temptation of intervening on behalf of domestic firms. Two features make this commitment more credible. First, such organizations act to police and punish members who violate their free trade promises. In this view, organizations such as the WTO may be analyzed using the same logic that we used to discuss the ability of firms to cooperate in Chapter 10. The necessary elements are an ability to detect violations and then to punish them. In this respect, one feature that is helpful in the case of the WTO is that, although violations are typically directed by one country at another, punishment is meted out by all members. Thus, if the United States imposes tariffs or intervenes to aid domestic producers of LCD screens against the Korean giant, Samsung, and if this action is deemed a violation of the WTO agreement, the penalty may include restrictions on U.S. exports to all member nations—not just South Korea.

A second source of credibility is that to some extent, joining the international agreement insulates domestic politicians from political pressure. When pressured by domestic industry representatives for unfair assistance, the domestic authorities can respond by saying that while they would like to help, the rules of membership are clear and "their hands are tied." The strengths of such commitment devices should not be minimized. A central feature of the U.S. Constitution was that it reserved jurisdiction over interstate commerce to the federal government. Prior to the Constitution's adoption, when the U.S. government was organized under the Articles of Confederation, the states had had considerable power to levy taxes and otherwise hinder the products of other states in an effort to protect their own. The result was a nightmare web of barriers to trade and inefficiencies as each state tried to protect its industry and raise revenue to pay its debts by taxing the products of out-of-state producers. In this light, the interstate commerce clause may be seen as a conscious effort to bind the states more fully to their commitment to trade freely with each other. Perhaps it is no wonder, then, that it was that student of commitment, Alexander Hamilton, who was one of the leading advocates for the Constitution's adoption.

Summary

Threats or promises can only be effective if the threats are credible (i.e., part of a subgame-perfect strategy). In many cases, this credibility can only be obtained by making some commitment that binds the player to carrying out that threat or promise in the event that a rival takes the action that the threat or promise was designed to prevent. Commitment is the key to credibility.

The precise nature of the commitment will, however, depend on whether the strategies are strategic complements or strategic substitutes. Strategic complements are defined by response functions that slope upward. Strategic substitutes are defined by response functions that slope downward. In either case, a firm's commitment—or lack of it—is a means of positioning the response function either to make things worse for a rival (tougher competition) or better (softer competition). In this connection, it is worthwhile recognizing that not making a commitment—committing not to commit—also can be valuable. Locking into a particular technology, production volume, or military response may make sense in light of current conditions; but if those conditions change, that commitment can become an unwelcome chain that prevents the firm from responding optimally to the new environment. In other words, there is value to flexibility, too. The tradeoff is that greater flexibility calls into question the credibility of any commitment.

International trade relations is one area in which the value of commitment can be most clear. In imperfectly competitive markets, a domestic firm may wish to commit to a particular output level or R&D expenditure as a means to achieve a dominant position in the international market. However, the only way this may be credibly done is often by means of government intervention. Domestic authorities can adopt policies that effectively make it easier for the domestic firm to commit to a high level of production or research spending. Such policies can raise the welfare of the domestic country that adopts such policies if others do not do the same. Unfortunately, other countries will likely pursue the same policies, and the noncooperative outcome of this game between nations will typically exhibit a prisoners' dilemma feature in which both countries are worse off than if neither had intervened. In this light, trade institutions like the WTO can be seen as a mechanism by which countries truly commit to their free trade promises.

Problems

1. Assume a market with two upstream manufacturers and two downstream retailers. Total demand downstream is (in inverse form) $P = 100 - Q$. The unit cost of manufacturing is $c_M = 23$. Similarly, the unit cost of retailing is $c_R = 23$. Assume that both upstream and the downstream firms compete in Cournot fashion.
    a. Determine the equilibrium wholesale and retail price and the profit for each firm.
    b. Show that if one upstream firm integrates with a downstream retailer, its profit will increase.
    c. Show that if one upstream firm integrates with a downstream retailer, the remaining upstream and downstream pair will merge as well.
    d. Show that if each upstream firm integrates with a downstream retailer, total profit to the combined manufacturer/retailer firm falls from what it was in the initial configuration before integration. Comment on the firms' ability to commit not to integrate.

2. The large unfunded liabilities of many public pension and health care systems raise the possibility for a number of countries that the government will meet these financial pressures by printing money rapidly, thereby generating inflation. Investors and other members of the public prefer low inflation to high, but care most about correctly anticipating the inflation rate so that the contracts that they write (which must be written in advance) are efficient. The government also generally prefers low inflation, but recognizes that if people expect inflation to be high and therefore sign contracts calling for high wages, there will be unemployment and recession if the government actually makes inflation low. Conversely, if it sets inflation high when people had anticipated it being low, the bad news of high inflation will be partly offset by the good news of a temporary economic boom as labor demand and employment rise. These sentiments are reflected in the payoff matrix below.

		Government Sets *Actual Inflation*	
		Low	High
*Public **Expects** Inflation To Be*	Low	2, 2	−2, 3
	High	−1.5, 1	1, 1.5

    a. Assume that the order of play is as follows: (1) the government announces its inflation target; (2) hearing the announcement, the public sets its inflationary expectation; (3) the government then sets actual inflation.
        i.   How credible is an initial announcement by the government that it will ultimately set actual inflation at a low level?
        ii. What is the Nash equilibrium for this game?
    b. What steps might the government take to make an initial announcement of low inflation more credible?

3. Suppose that there are "learning by doing" economies so that a firm's unit cost declines the more it has produced over time. Assume that an incumbent (Firm 1) that is alone in the market this period knows that an entrant (Firm 2) will arrive next period with whom it will then engage

in Cournot competition. The incumbent can either set a high monopoly price in the current period, or price low and sell many units. Explain why the latter approach may be considered a Top Dog strategy.

4. Consider the "Battle of the Sexes" technology game, where each of two firms agree that compatibility is best but differ over which technology should be the standard as shown below. What sort of strategies might a firm choose in order to show its rival that it is committed to one particular technology?

		Firm 2	
		Technology 1	Technology 2
Firm 1	Technology 1	8, 5	3, 3
	Technology 2	3, 3	4, 10

5. Comment on the most-favored-customer and meet-or-beat-the-competition clauses discussed in Chapter 10. How would you classify such tactics in terms of the Fudenberg and Tirole (1984) taxonomy described in Section 18.2?

References

Brander, J., and B. Spencer. 1985. "Export Subsidies and International Market Share Rivalry". *Journal of International Economics,* 18 (February): 83–100.

Connor, J. 2001. *Global Price Fixing: Our Customers Are The Enemy*. Boston: Kluwer Academic Publishers.

Dasgupta, P., and J. Stiglitz. 1980. "Industrial Structure and the Nature of Innovative Activity". *Economic Journal,* 90 (January): 266–293.

Dixit, A. 1980. "The Role of Investment in Entry Deterrence". *Economic Journal,* 90 (January): 95–106.

Eaton, J., and G. M. Grossman. 1986. "Optimal Trade and Industrial Policy under Oligopoly". *Quarterly Journal of Economics,* 100 (May): 383–406.

Fudenberg, D., and J. Tirole. 1984. "The Fat Cat Effect, the Puppy Dog Ploy, and the Lean and Hungry Look." *American Economic Review (Papers and Proceedings),* 74 (May): 361–366.

Hamilton, A. 1791. "Report on Manufactures." In W. Lowric and M. St. Clair Clarke, eds., *American State Papers,* volume 9. Washington, DC: T. B. Wait & Sons.

Krugman, P. 1986. *Strategic Trade Policy and the New International Economics*. Cambridge, MA: MIT Press.

Spencer, B., and J. Brander. 1983. "International R&D Rivalry and Industrial Strategy". *Review of Economic Studies,* 50 (October): 707–722.

Answers to Selected Problems

Chapter 1

2. In perfect competition, each firm is so small that one firm's actions have no impact on any other. There is no reason for any firm to react to the actions of a rival. Without reaction there is no interaction.

4. A finding that labor productivity rises as concentration increases has at least two explanations. One is that those industries that are more concentrated are characterized by scale economies. Such economies limit the number of efficient-sized firms in the market so that they are more concentrated. However, such economies also imply rising productivity when firms operate on a larger scale. A second, possibly related explanation is that more concentrated-industries are also more capital intensive. For example, for a constant returns Cobb-Douglas production function of the form: $Y = K^\alpha L^{1-\alpha}$, the cost-minimizing capital-to-labor ratio is: $\dfrac{K}{L} = \dfrac{w}{r}\dfrac{\alpha}{(1-\alpha)}$; while output-per-worker is: $\dfrac{Y}{L} = \left(\dfrac{K}{L}\right)^\alpha$. Both expressions increase in α. So, forces that increase the equilibrium capital-to-labor ratio also raise output-per-worker. If these forces are present in industries that are more concentrated, then concentration will be associated with increased worker productivity.

Chapter 2

2. Let the market demand for widgets be described by $Q = 1000 - 50P$. Suppose further that widgets can be produced at a constant average and marginal cost of $10 per unit.

    a. Perfect Competition: $Q = 500$; $P = \$10$. Monopoly: $Q = 250$; $P = \$15$.
    b. Perfect Competition: $\varepsilon_D = \dfrac{10}{500}(50) = 1$; Monopoly: $\varepsilon_D = \dfrac{15}{250}(50) = 3$
    c. $\text{Profit} = [P - c]Q(P) \cdot \dfrac{d(\text{Profit})}{dP} = Q + (P - c)\dfrac{dQ}{dP} = 0$ at max $\Rightarrow \dfrac{(P - c)}{P} = \dfrac{Q}{P}\dfrac{dP}{dQ}$

    $$= -\dfrac{(dP/P)}{(dQ/Q)}$$

    $$= \dfrac{1}{\varepsilon_D}$$

4. a. $Q = 32{,}000$; $P = \$1$.
    b. $Q = 16{,}000$; $P = \$2$.
    c. $WL = (P - MC)(Q^C - Q^M)/2 = (\$2 - \$1) = \$1(16{,}000)/2 = \$8{,}000$.

Chapter 3

2. The consultant has not distinguished between fixed and variable costs. Since the fixed costs will be incurred regardless of whether the train runs or not, there is no increase in fixed cost from making a trip during off-peak hours. What matters are the variable costs of making an off-peak hour trip. As long as they are less than the revenue from the sales of 10 tickets, the train should make the trip.

4. With a Leontief production technology: $q = \min(K/a, L/b)$, the input ratio is fixed at: $K/L = a/b$ and independent of the input prices. Let w be the price of labor and r be the cost of capital. Then for any output level q: $C(q) = rK(q) + wL(q) = raq + wbq = (ra + wb)q$. Average cost is constant and equal to marginal cost at $AC(q) = C(q)/q = (ra + wb)$. Hence, the scale economy measure is constant at 1, i.e. there are no scale economies or diseconomies with this production technology.

Chapter 4

2. In equilibrium, $\dfrac{[P - c(H)]}{P} = \dfrac{H}{\varepsilon_D} \Rightarrow P\varepsilon_D - \varepsilon_D c(H) = HP$. If P does not change when H changes we must have $-\varepsilon_D c' = P$ or $c' = -\dfrac{P}{\varepsilon_D}$.

4. a. $CR_4^{FT} = 0.48 + 0.30 + 0.07 + 0.06 = 0.91 = 91\%$

   $CR_4^{TP} = 0.30 + 0.20 + 0.16 + 0.12 = 0.78 = 78\%$

   $CR_4^{PT} = 0.37 + 0.18 + 0.12 + 0.11 = 0.78 = 78\%$

   b. $H^{FT} = .48^2 + .30^2 + .07^2 + .06^2 + .09^2$

   $= .2304 + .0900 + .0049 + .0036 + .0081 = .3370$

   $H^{TP} = .30^2 + .20^2 + .16^2 + .12^2 + .05^2 + .16^2$

   $= .0900 + .0400 + .0256 + .0144 + .0025 + .0256 = .1981$

   $H^{PT} = .37^2 + .18^2 + .12^2 + .11^2 + .04^2 + .18^2$

   $= .1369 + .0324 + .0144 + .0121 + .0016 + .0324 = .2298$

   c. Given the highest four-firm concentration ratio and a very high Herfindahl index, facial tissue is the most concentrated with two firms controlling 78% of the market.

Chapter 5

2. A monopolist with marginal cost of production of 40 sells to two distinct regions. In Region 1, demand is given by: $Q_1 = 300 - p_1$. In Region 2, it is given by: $Q_2 = 180 - p_2$.
   a. Uniform price: $p_1 = p_2 = \$140$; $q_1 = 160$; $q_2 = 40$.
   b. Separate Markets: $p_1 = \$170$; $q_1 = 130$; $p_2 = \$110$; $q_2 = 70$.
   c. At any given price, market 2 demand is more elastic. This is also true at the equilibrium discriminatory prices ($\varepsilon_1 = 17/14$; $\varepsilon_2 = 110/70$). Hence, the monopolist sets a lower market 2 price.

4. We have $T_1 = V(\theta_1, q_1)$ and $T_2 = V(\theta_1, q_1) + V(\theta_2, q_2) - V(\theta_2, q_1)$. Substituting in the specific functions we have: $\dfrac{T_1}{q_1} = \theta_1 - \dfrac{q_1}{2}$ and $\dfrac{T_2}{q_2} = \theta_1 \dfrac{q_1}{q_2} + \theta_2 - \dfrac{q_2}{2} - \theta_2 \dfrac{q_1}{q_2}$. Subsequent substitution from equations (5.45a) and (5.45b) reveals $\dfrac{T_1}{q_1} > \dfrac{T_2}{q_2}$ so long as $\theta_1 < \dfrac{\theta_2 + c}{2}$. In other words, θ_1 should not be "too large" relative to θ_2.

Chapter 6

2. a. By convention $\theta_H > \theta_L$. Offering both goods and pricing them appropriately earns profit of $N_H(\theta_H - c_H) + N_L\theta_L\sigma$. This dominates selling only the high-quality good to just the high θ consumers at price θ_H. However, three other single-product strategies exist. These are:

i) selling just the high-quality good to all consumers which yields profit $= (N_H + N_L)(\theta_L - c_H)$; ii) selling just the low-quality good to everyone and earning $(N_H + N_L)\theta_L\sigma$; or iii) selling just the low-quality good to high θ types for which profit $= N_H\theta_H\sigma$. Selling both goods will dominate strategy i if $\dfrac{N_H}{N_L} > \dfrac{\theta_{L(1-\sigma)} - c_H}{\theta_H - \theta_L}$. Selling both will dominate strategy ii if $\theta_H - \theta_L\sigma > c_H$. Selling both products will dominate strategy iii if $\dfrac{N_H}{N_L} > \dfrac{\theta_L\sigma}{\theta_H(1 - \sigma) - c_H}$. Thus, for the firm to prefer to sell both goods, we must have $\theta_H - \theta_L\sigma > c_H$ and $\dfrac{N_H}{N_L}$ greater than either $\dfrac{\theta_{L(1-\sigma)} - c_H}{\theta_H - \theta_L}$ or $\dfrac{\theta_L\sigma}{\theta_H(1 - \sigma) - c_H}$ whichever is larger.

4. a. Let positions on the line be designated by values ranging from zero to 1, e.g., $b = 0.5$ indicates Mr. Clean is at the center of the line. For convenience, we initially assume that $b \leq 0.5$. Since Mr. Clean can sell a unique dry cleaning plus delivery service to each customer, the price to any served customer will be V. The marginal consumer to his right satisfies: $X_R^M = \dfrac{(V - c)}{r} + b$ unless $V > c + r(1 - b)$ in which case he will serve the entire market. Assuming this is not the case, the marginal consumer to the left is either located at $x_i = 0$ if the firm is constrained in which case $V - c - rb > 0$, or satisfies $X_L^M = b - \dfrac{(V - c)}{c}$. In the first or constrained case, the fraction of consumers served will just be X_R^M. In the second case, he will serve the range of consumers from X_L^M to X_R^M. This is equal to $X_R^M - X_L^M = 2\dfrac{(V - c)}{r}$.

    b. Profit from any served consumer is: $V - c - r(\text{distance})$. Total profit is therefore obtained by integration over the relevant range of locations. In the unconstrained case, profit $= M\dfrac{(V - c)^2}{r}$, and is independent of b. A small change in location to the left or right would gain on one side what it loses on the other. In the constrained case, profit $= M\left[\dfrac{(V - c)^2}{2r} + (V - c)b - \dfrac{rb^2}{2}\right]$. The derivative with respect to b is $M[V - c - rb] > 0$ by virtue of the fact that the firm is constrained. Recall that $b < 0.5$ by assumption. An increase in b therefore represents a move toward the center. This would permit profitably serving more consumers on the firm's left without losing any on the right. By analogy, the same argument applies when $b > 0.5$.

Chapter 7

2. a. The intercept is 20 because all 20 Outcast members will attend the party regardless of how many others attend. For the remaining students, however, the attraction of the party increases as they expect more of their fellow students to attend. This is why the relation between actual attendance A and expected attendance X is positive.

    b. A rational expectations equilibrium is one in which the expectations are consistent with the underlying model. Thus, a value of $X = 100$ is *not* rational in that the model implies that this value of X will result in the actual attendance being $A = 80$. To find the rational expectations equilibrium we impose $A = X$ and solve to obtain: $A = X = 50$ in equilibrium.

4. a. Assume marginal costs of c_1 for Firm 1 and c_2 for Firm 2. The best response functions are: $p_1 = \dfrac{15 + c_1}{2} + 0.25p_2$ (Firm 1); and $p_2 = \dfrac{15 + c_2}{2} + 0.25p_1$ (Firm 2). Since $\dfrac{\partial p_i}{\partial p_j} > 0$ in each case, these functions are upward-sloping. The price variables are strategic complements.

b.   The Nash equilibrium prices are: $p_1 = 10 + 0.533c_1 + 0.133c_2$; and $p_2 = 10 + 0.133c_1 + 0.533c_2$. Outputs are: $q_1 = 10 - 0.4c_1 + 0.4c_2$ and $q_2 = 10 + 0.4c_1 - 0.4c_2$. Profits are given by: $\pi_1 = (10 - 0.4667c_1 + 0.133c_2)(10 - 0.4c_1 + 0.4c_2)$; $\pi_2 = (10 - 0.4667c_2 + 0.133c_1)(10 - 0.4c_2 + 0.4c_1)$.

Chapter 8

2.   Denoting firm 2 as the follower, Firm 2's best-response function is: $q_2 = \dfrac{1000 - c}{8} - \dfrac{q_1}{2}$. The profit-maximizing output for the Stackelberg leader (Firm 1) is: $q_1 = 120 + \dfrac{c}{8}$. Hence,

equality of q_1 and q_2 requires: $\dfrac{1000 - c}{8} - \dfrac{\left(120 + \dfrac{c}{8}\right)}{2} = 120 + \dfrac{c}{8}$. This would require an unrealistically negative value for c, namely, $c = -176$.

4.   Take All is a dominant strategy for Player 2. The promise to wait is not credible. Anticipating this, Player 1 will Grab the Dollar at the first opportunity.

6.

		Player 2	
		0	C
	0	0,0	0,10
	A	20,0	8,8
Player 1	B	11,0	−3,−3
	A,B	18,0	2,−2

a.   The Nash equilibrium with simultaneous play is A,C. Both players enjoy a payoff of 8.
b.   With sequential play, the Nash equilibrium becomes A,B for Player 1 and 0 for Player 2. The ability to commit stops Player 1 from switching to play A in response to Player 2's choice of 0.

Chapter 9

2.   a.   Denote the incumbent as firm 1, and the incumbent's marginal cost as Z. For $q_1 \le K_1$, the incumbent's marginal cost is $Z = w = 20$. The incumbent's best-response function therefore is: $q_1 = \dfrac{100 - 20}{4} - \dfrac{q_2}{2} = 20 - \dfrac{q_2}{2}$ for $q_1 \le K_1$ and $q_1 = 15 - \dfrac{q_2}{2}$ for $q_1 > K_1$. The entrant's best-response function is always: $q_2 = 15 - \dfrac{q_2}{2}$.

b.   The incumbent will produce at capacity $K_1 = 15$. As a result, the entrant will produce 7.5 units according to its best-response function. Total output will be 22.5. Hence, price will be $55. Operating profit per unit is $15 for the entrant implying an operating income of $112.5. Subtracting the fixed cost of $112.5 yields an entrant profit of $12.50. The incumbent's operating profit reflecting only variable costs will be ($35 × 15) = $525. From this must be subtracted the capacity cost of $300 plus the additional fixed cost of $100 leaving a net income of $225.

c.   If instead the incumbent commits to capacity and output $K_1 = q_1 = 16$, the entrant's best response calls for it to produce 7 units. Total output is now 23 units so that the equilibrium price is $54. The incumbent's operating profit is now $98, which is not enough to cover the fixed cost. Hence, the entrant will not enter the market. The incumbent's output of 16 then implies a price of $68, giving it a revenue of $1,088. It's total cost is: $320 + $320 + $100 = $740. Hence, the incumbent now earns net income of $348.

4.   a.   Since inverse demand is: $P = 100 - Q$, meeting all demand at price $P = \$74$ implies committing to an output of $q_I = 26$ units. At this output level, the incumbent's marginal cost is $dC/dq_i = 3q_I = \$78$. So, yes, price is below marginal cost.

b.   However, total variable cost $= 1.5q_I^2$. So, average variable cost is $1.5q_I = \$39$. This is well below the price. Average variable cost is often a poor proxy for marginal cost. Note that if the entrant were to produce 26 units, it would incur a total cost of $100 + 71 \times 26 = \$1946$, greater than its revenue of $\$1,924$. The entrant cannot steal the market from the incumbent.

Chapter 10

2.   The monopoly price is $\$140$ at which price an even division of the market results in each firm producing 30 units and earning profit $\pi_m = (\$140 - \$20)30 = \$3600$. The non-cooperative Nash equilibrium profit is of course $\pi_n = 0$ (with each firm producing 60 units). The one-period gain from deviating by cutting price just a tiny bit below $\$140$ is approximately $\pi_d = (\$140 - \$20)60 = \$7200$, as this results in the cheating firm acquiring the entire market. By equation (10.15), sustainability of the cartel requires that the probability-adjusted discount factor ρ satisfy: $\rho > \dfrac{(\pi_d - \pi_m)}{(\pi_d - \pi_n)} = \dfrac{(\$7200 - \$3600)}{\$7200} = 0.5$. Thus, the probability-adjusted discount factor must exceed 0.5 in order for the cartel to be sustainable.

4.   As before, the total monopoly output is $Q = 60$, and the monopoly price is $P = \$140$. With four symmetric firms, the cooperative collusive agreement that replicates the monopoly outcome is $q_i = 15$. Each firm earns a collusive profit of $\pi_m = (\$140 - \$20)15 = \$1800$. Each firm's non-cooperative best-response function is: $q_i = 60 - Q_{-i}/2$. Hence, the optimal deviation output for one firm is: $q_d = 60 - 45/2 = 37.5$. The resultant price will be: $P = 260 - 2(45 + 37.5) = \$95$. Hence, the deviation profit $\pi_d = (\$95 - \$20)37.5 = \$2812.5$ The noncooperative Nash equilibrium is $q_i = 24$ units, resulting in total output of $Q = 96$ and a price of $P = \$68$. The non-cooperative profit is $(\$68 - \$20)24 = \$1152$. By equation (10.15), sustainability of the cartel requires that the probability-adjusted discount factor ρ satisfy: $\rho > \dfrac{(\pi_d - \pi_m)}{\pi_d - \pi_n)} = \dfrac{(\$2812.5 - \$1800)}{(\$2812.5 - \$1152)} = 0.61$. Thus, the probability-adjusted discount factor must exceed 0.61 in order for the cartel to be sustainable.

6.   Sealed bids by themselves tend to make collusion more difficult as they limit the amount of communication firms can do and make detection of any cheating more difficult. The practice of announcing the winning bid as well as the winning bidder undercuts this effect and makes collusion more likely.

8.   Excess capacity makes it easier for the firms to "punish" a "cheater" severely. Also, in case the cartel breaks down, any excess capacity makes the post-cartel profits lower. Therefore, any excess capacity reduces the incentives to cheat on a cartel agreement, facilitating the maintenance of the cartel.

Chapter 11

2.   No, one cannot conclude that authorities should have permitted more mergers simply because the ones they did permit resulted in lower prices. There is a strong selection bias here in that, presumably, the mergers permitted were allowed precisely because the authorities foresaw that they were pro-competitive and would result in lower prices. This does not mean though that the ones not permitted were also of this nature.

4.   a. $dQ = dQ_{-I} + dq_i = -\lambda(N-1)dq_i + dq_i \Rightarrow \dfrac{dQ}{dq_i} = \dfrac{1}{1 + \lambda(N-1)}$

     b.   This follows immediately from the result in 4a. Since $\lambda > 0$, and $\dfrac{dQ}{dq_i} = \dfrac{1}{1 + (N-1)\lambda}$.

          Then $0 < \dfrac{dQ}{dq_j} < 1$ for any $N \geq 2$.

Chapter 12

2. a.   Each upstream and downstream firm produces $q_1^U = q_2^U = q_1^D = q_2^D = \dfrac{2A}{9}$. The wholesale price $r = A/3$. Upstream profit is $\pi_1^U = \pi_2^U = \dfrac{2A^2}{27}$. Downstream price is $P = 5A/9$. Downstream profit is $\pi_1^D = \pi_2^D = \dfrac{4A^2}{81}$.

   b.   The retail price is $P = 5A/12$. The independent(non-integrated) wholesale price is $r = A/4$. The integrated firm earns profit of $\pi_1^I = \dfrac{25A^2}{144}$ (integration is profitable for the two firms that merge). The independent upstream firm and the independent downstream firm each produce: $q = A/6$. Independent upstream profit is $A^2/24$. Independent downstream profit is $A^2/36$ (total profit for the firms that do not merge falls in response to the rivals' merger).

   c.   If both firms merge, each produces $q_1 = q_2 = A/3$. The retail price is $P = A/3$ and profit for each firm is $A^2/9$. Note: With complete vertical integration, total industry profit is less than without vertical integration.

4. a.   Since NorSyr and BenRup produce identical goods Ginvir and Sipep buy from the producer who charges the lowest price. (If NorSyr and BenRup charge the same price, we assume they split the market evenly). Since at any common price greater than $5, either firm can raise profit by cutting its price a small amount, the only Nash equilibrium is for each to charge $5.

   b.   The inverse demand functions may be jointly solved to yield $q_G = 16.67 - 1.33 p_G + 0.67 p_s$ and $q_s = 16.67 - 1.33 p_s + 0.67 p_G$. Profit for Ginvir is $\pi_G = (p_G - 5)(16.67 - 1.33 p_G + 0.67 p_s)$; and profit for Sipep is: $\pi_s = (p_s - 5)(16.67 - 1.33 p_s + 0.67 p_G)$. Differentiation then yields the best response functions: $p_G = 8.75 + 0.25 p_s$ and $p_s = 8.75 + 0.25 p_G$. The Bertrand-Nash equilibrium is therefore $p_G = p_S = \$11.67$. By substitution, profit for each firm is $\pi_G = \pi_S = \$59.82$.

Chapter 13

2. a.   With an RPM agreement, the monopolist can choose the price as if it were a fully integrated seller. Equate marginal revenue with marginal cost to obtain $Q = 40$, $p = 50$

   b. $CS = (\$90 - \$40) \times (40/2) = 800$

4. a.   Since the two upstream firms compete in prices and sell identical products, Bertrand competition will eliminate any downstream markup. Retail demand and wholesale demand are the same. In equilibrium, each upstream firm produces $q_i = A/3$. Total upstream output and retail sales are $Q = 2A/3$. The wholesale price and the retail price are both equal to $A/3$. Each upstream firm earns $A^2/9$ in profit while each downstream firm earns zero profit.

   b.   If the downstream market is monopolized, the demand curve in the upstream market becomes: $W = A - 2Q$ where W is the wholesale price. Profit maximization then leads each upstream firm to produce $A/6$ units. The wholesale price is $W = A/3$. Each upstream firm earns profit of $A^2/18$. The dealer now sets a retail price of $2A/3$. Since she pays $W = A/3$ per unit input, the dealer's profit is $A^2/9$.

   c.   By itself, this contractual arrangement would just replicate the monopoly outcome of 4b. As a result, it leaves both upstream suppliers worse off. Accordingly, they will not agree to the contract. In order for the exclusive dealing arrangement to be attractive, a different contractual arrangement, e.g., a two-part pricing contract, is needed. With such an alternative contract, it is possible for all three parties to gain from the exclusive dealing arrangement.

6. Suppose that competition between franchisees is Bertrand. Then if McDonald's has cost c, it can earn the monopoly profit associated with that cost, since downstream competition eliminates any double marginalization. However, if a rival supplier with lower cost undersells McDonald's, then McDonald's will earn no profit from sales of supplies. Nor will it earn any profit from franchise fees, since the Bertrand competition also eliminates any downstream profit. In addition, standardization of the product may be appealing to McDonald's consumers. Hence, having all franchisees buy from it may enhance total demand across the network of franchisees.

Chapter 14

2. a. Straightforward maximization yields: $A = 400$; $Q = 2,000$; and $P = \$10$.
   b. Profit $= \$20,000 - \$12,000$ (production cost) $-\$400$ (advertising cost) $= \$7,600$.
   c. Consumer surplus $= 1,600$.

4. If the store owner can identify potential patrons with a valuation of her style that is less than \$0.50 then, conditional on this fact, she knows that in any group of randomly selected customers now coming to the store, the conditional distribution is uniform between \$0.50 and \$1. Profit maximization again requires that $1 - F(p) - pF'(p) = 0$. Here, $F(p) = (p - 0.50)/0.50$; and $F'(p) = f(p) = 1/0.5 = 2$. Hence, profit maximization requires:

$$1 - \frac{p - 0.50}{0.50} - \frac{p}{0.5} = 0 \Rightarrow 0.50 - p + 0.50 - p = 0 \Rightarrow 1 = 2p \Rightarrow p = \$0.50$$

The profit-maximizing price remains the same at $p = \$0.50$. However, the average valuation in the group of store visitors is \$0.75. That is, those who now visit the store in response to an advertisement now know with certainty that they have an average value of the style in stock equal to \$0.75 Hence, the transport cost can now be as high as \$0.25 without deterring these consumers from visiting the store.

Chapter 15

2. a. We first find expected profits and surpluses as a function of K and ρ for each different situation.
      i. If neither firm has the innovation, competition is Cournot with symmetric costs of 100 each. So, we find quantities, price and profits are as follows: $q_1 = 50, q_2 = 50, \pi_1 = 2,500, \pi_2 = 2,500$; $P = \$150$, $CS = \$5,000$; $TS = \$10,000$.
      ii. If only one firm does the R&D and is successful, say it is Firm 1, then Firm 2's response function is unchanged, and the innovator's response function reflects its lower costs. The new quantities, prices and profits are as follows: $q_1 = 70, q_2 = 40, \pi_1 = 4,900, \pi_2 = 1,600$; $P = \$140$; $CS = \$6,050$; $TS = \$12,550$.
      iii. If both firms set up labs and if each succeeds at innovating, we again have Cournot with symmetric costs. With both firms' costs reduced to \$70, the new quantities, prices and profits are as follows: $q_1 = 60, q_2 = 60, \pi_1 = 3,600, \pi_2 = 3,600$; $P = \$130$; $CS = \$8,450$; $TS = \$15,650$.
      Now we consider *expected* profits and total surplus. If neither firm establishes a facility, the expected and actual total profit, as well as the consumer surplus are known with certainty as \$5,000 and \$5,000, respectively. If however, only one firm establishes a research facility, expected profit to that firm is: $E(\pi_{owner}|1\_firm\_establishes) = \rho(4900) + (1 - \rho)(2500) - K = 2500 + 2400\rho - K$. The rival's expected profit is: $E(\pi_{non\_owner}|1\_firm\_establishes) = \rho(1600) + (1 - \rho)(2500) = 2500 - 900\rho$. With probability ρ, the total surplus is \$12,550. With probability $1 - \rho$, the total surplus is \$10,000. So, if one firm does establish a facility, the expected total surplus is $\$10,000 + \rho\$2,550 - K$.

If both firms establish research facilities, expected profit to each firm is

$E(\pi_i|2\_firm\_establishes)$

$= \rho^2(3600) + \rho(1-\rho)(4900) + \rho(1-\rho)(1600) + (1-\rho)^2(2500) - K$

$= 2500 - 400\rho^2 + 1500\rho - K$

In this case, the expected total surplus is $\$10,000 + \rho\$5,100 + \rho^2\$13,100 - 2K$.

Neither firm will establish a research facility if No Facility is the best response to No Facility for both firms. This will be true for the following conditions: $K > 2400\rho$

Only one firm will establish a research facility if No Facility is the best response to Establish Facility and Establish Facility is the best response to No Facility. This is true for the following conditions: $2400\rho - 400\rho^2 < K < 2400\rho$.

Both firms establish a facility if Establish Facility is a best response to Establish Facility for both firms: $2400\rho - 400\rho^2 > K$.

b. "Too much" R&D in the sense that both firms establish research facilities, but the expected total surplus would be higher is only firm did require $2400\rho - 400\rho^2 > K > 2550\rho + \rho^2 13,100$

c. "Too little" R&D in the sense of no firm is doing it when the expected total surplus would be higher if at least one firm did requires $2400\rho < K < 2550\rho$.

4. a. i.   Monopoly: the pre-innovation profit is $\$3,600$. If marginal cost falls to $\$60$, this profit rises to $\$8,100$. This is a profit gain of $\$4,500$. The present value of this gain is $V^M = \dfrac{\$4500}{1-R} = \$45,000$. This is the amount the monopolist would be willing to pay.

    ii. Cournot: the initial profit of each firm is $\$1,600$. If only one firm has access to the technology, its output is 80 units and its profit is $\$6,400$. This is a profit increase of $\$4,800$. The present value and therefore willingness to pay for this higher profit stream is $V^{\text{Cournot}} = \$48,000$.

    iii. Bertrand: each firm initially earns zero profit. With one firm alone having access to the innovation, its profit becomes $(\$120 - \$60)120 = \$7,200$. Hence, the willingness-to-pay for a Bertrand competitor is $\$7,200/(1-R) = \$72,000$.

    b. If it sells to the entrant, the entrant can enter as a low-cost Cournot firm and earn a discounted profit of $\$64,000$ as in 4aii, above. If this is the only way the entrant can successfully enter, it gives extra incentive to the monopolist to buy the innovation. If it does not, it becomes the high-cost firm in a Cournot duopoly and earns only $\$400$ profit per period. If it does, it stays a monopolist and earns profit of $\$8,100$ per period as in 4ai, above. The periodic gain from buying the innovation is thus the present value of an annual increased flow of $\$8,100 - \$400 = \$7,700$, which has a present value of $\$77,000$. The monopolist is willing to pay more for the innovation.

Chapter 16

2. a. For the innovation not to be drastic requires that the monopoly price associated with cost c_L exceed rivals' marginal cost c_H. That monopoly price is $p^M(c_L) = \dfrac{1 + c_L}{2}$. Hence, we must have $c_L > 2c_H - 1$.

    b. Without loss of generality, denote the innovating firm as Firm 1. With a per unit royalty r, marginal cost of each rival is $c_L + r$. Hence, the maximum royalty any rival will pay is $r = c_H - c_L$. For any output q_1 of Firm 1, the combined output Q_{-1} of the $N-1$ rivals satisfies the best-response condition: $Q_{-1} = \left(\dfrac{N-1}{N}\right)[1 - q_1 - (c_L + r)]$. Hence, Firm 1's profit is: $\pi_1 = (P - c_L)q_1 + rQ_{-1} = (1 - q_1 - Q_{-1} - c_L)q_1 + rQ_{-1}$.

Likewise, Firm 1's best response function satisfies $q_1 = \frac{1}{2}(1 - c_L) - \frac{Q_{-1}}{2}$. Solving we then have $Q_{-1} = \dfrac{(N-1)(1-c_L) - 2(N-1)r}{N+1}$; $q_1 = \dfrac{1-c_L}{N+1} + \left(\dfrac{N-1}{N+1}\right)r$; and $P = \dfrac{1 + c_L + (N-1)r}{N+1}$. Firm 1's profit π_1 is then $\pi_1 = \left(\dfrac{1 + c_L + (N-1)r}{N+1}\right)^2 +$ $r\left[\dfrac{(N-1)(1-c_L) - 2(N-1)r}{N+1}\right]$. Taking the derivative of this function it is straight forward to show that profit is increasing in r. Hence, Firm 1 will maximize its profit by increasing in r up to the maximum value $r = c_H - c_L$. This yields the same equilibrium as occurs without licensing but earns r in profit for every unit of rivals' production.

c. For any r up to the maximum, the leasing rivals earn total profit $\pi_{-1} = \left[(N-1)\dfrac{[(1-c_L) - 2r]}{N+1}\right]^2$. Denote as D the amount of this that the rivals can negotiate as the profit they still retain after paying the fixed fee A (presumably, this will equal the amount earned without licensing). Then Firm 1's total profit becomes: $\pi_1 = \left(\dfrac{1 + c_L + (N-1)r}{N+1}\right)^2 + r\left[\dfrac{(N-1)(1-c_L) - 2(N-1)r}{N+1}\right] +$ $\left[(N-1)\dfrac{[(1-c_L) - 2r]}{N+1}\right]^2 - (N-1)D$. Differentiation then reveals that Firm 1's profit is now decreasing in r.

4. The innovation reduces marginal cost to $75 - x$. During each year in which the innovator has a patent, the price remains at \$75. Consumer surplus each year remains at \$2,812.5. However, with P at \$75, the innovator earns \$$x$ on each of the 75 units sold. So, producer surplus during each period of effective patent is \$75x, and total surplus during each such period is \$2812.5 + 75x. When the patent expires, the price falls to $75 - x$. Producer surplus falls to zero. Consumer surplus rises to: $0.5(75 + x)^2$. Thus, the net private gain NPV from reducing marginal cost by x, allowing for discounting and including the up $=$ front sunk cost is: $NPV^{\text{Profit}}(x, T) = -10x^2 + \$75x\left(\dfrac{1 - 0.9^T}{0.1}\right)$. Maximizing this with respect to x yields: $x = 37.5\left(1 - 0.9^T\right)$.

The present value of the total surplus from the innovation is the discounted value of the increase total surplus during and after the period of patent protection. As there is no change in consumer surplus when the patent is effective, the only gain during these T years is the gain in producer profit. Subsequently, there is a gain of $0.5(75 + x)^2 - \$2812.5 = 75x + 0.5x^2$. in consumer surplus when the patent expires and price falls to $75 - x$. The total value is:

$$NPV^{\text{Total}}(x, T) = -10x^2 + 75x\left(\dfrac{1 - 0.9^T}{0.1}\right) + 0.9^{T+1}\left(\dfrac{75x + 0.5x^2}{0.1}\right)$$

We may now substitute in our earlier result thet $x = (1 - 0.9^T)$. Subsequently, using the relation that $d(y^T)/dT = (lny)y^T$, differentiation implies that the optimal $T \approx 25$

Chapter 17

2. Assume that consumers contemplating buying a network service have reservation prices uniformly distributed on the interval $[0, 50]$ (measured in dollars). Demand by a consumer with reservation price w_i for this service is

$$q_i^D = \begin{cases} 0 & \text{if } fw_i < p \\ 1 & \text{if } fw_i \geq p \end{cases}$$

    a.   Inverse demand: $p = 50f(1 - f)$

    b.   If $p = \$5$, the critical mass is $f = 0.11702$.

    c.   Analogous to the text assume that that marginal cost is $\alpha 50$. If the service is a monopoly, the profit-maximizing price is $p = 5.56(1 + 3\alpha + \sqrt{1 - 3\alpha})$.

4. a.   Firm 1's payoffs are given first. From firm 1's perspective, positive externalities require that $a > e$ and $g > c$. From firm 2's perspective, positive externalities require that $b > d$ and $h > f$. For each firm, the opposite conditions imply negative externalities.

    b.   i.   Tweedledum and Tweedledee: Each firm will prefer to be incompatible so, we must have $a < e, g < c, b < d$ and $h < f$.

          ii. The Battle of the Sexes: Each firm will prefer to be compatible but there is disagreement over the technology to make standard. We must have $a > e$ and $g > c$; and $b > d$ and $h > f$. For Firm 1 to prefer coordination on Technology 1, we must also have $a > g$, while for Firm 2 to prefer coordination on Technology 2, we must also have $h > b$.

         iii. The Pesky Little Brother. We assume Firm 2 is the "pesky" one. Firm 1 prefers incompatibility while Firm 2 prefers compatibility. We must have: $a < e, c > g, b > d$, and $f < h$.

Chapter 18

2. a.   i.   Setting inflation "High" is a dominant strategy for the government. Regardless of the public's expectations, the government does best if it sets inflation "High". So, a mere statement that it will behave and keep inflation low is not very credible.

          ii. A rational public will recognize the government's dominant strategy of setting inflation "High". Therefore, the Nash equilibrium is for the public to expect "High" inflation and the government to set inflation "High". This is unfortunate as both parties would be better off with an outcome of "Low, Low".

    b.   To make its commitment to low inflation more credible, the government might set very strict limits on its discretion, i.e., enact legislation that constrains its ability either to print money or to take other actions that lead to inflation. Alternatively, it could set up an incentive system whereby policy-makers lose (gain) salary when inflation is high (low).

4.   As noted in the text, one way for either firm to commit more effectively to its own particular technology is to work with the producers of complementary products either to bundle the technology or otherwise tie the use of those products to the use of the firm's technology in an effort to establish a large installed base. This typically will require setting a quite low price for the bundled goods. Alternatively or, in addition, each firm may announce that it is incurring a large sunk cost in developing and improving its technology. In general, a number of commitment strategies are available.

Index